Praise for

KENNEDY *AND* KING

"Comparing and contrasting disparate historical figures can easily be artificial, misleading, even gimmicky. Steven Levingston, however, has walked this tightrope magnificently. In his important new book, *Kennedy and King*, the rest of us get an unusual chance to study each leader in part through the other over a tumultuous, pivotal eight-year period. As is always the case with major contributions to our understanding, Levingston's is grounded in diligent research and detail."

—Thomas Oliphant, *The Washington Post*

"Levingston's writing on King is unfailingly perceptive and eloquent.... Thanks to Levingston's impressive narrative skills, the spectacle of this president confronting the most divisive issue of his day is consistently fascinating." —*The Christian Science Monitor*

"Dual biographies are hard to pull off, but Levingston does it splendidly in his portrait of two divergent personalities finally coming together, if only briefly, over matters of gravest consequence."

—*The Dallas Morning News*

"Insightful and well-crafted.... At a time when cynicism about our political system abounds, [*Kennedy and King*] reminds us that outsiders can prod those in power toward progress and reform."

—*The Wall Street Journal*

"Levingston is a captivating storyteller and his account is both simple and profoundly moving." —*The Post and Courier* (Charleston, SC)

"A riveting episode in American history." —*Booklist* (starred review)

"Anyone who wants to understand America, the Civil Rights Movement, and the nature of leadership should read this book."

—Walter Isaacson, #1 *New York Times* bestselling author of
Steve Jobs and *Leonardo da Vinci*

"In this illuminating account Levingston charts the racial education of an ambitious Kennedy as he navigated the minefield of white Southern bigotry and King's uncompromising moral vision and how, together, they transformed a nation."

—Pamela Newkirk, author of *Spectacle*

"Steven Levingston's fascinating *Kennedy and King* reveals one of the most crucial American political relationships of the twentieth century, demonstrating the vital importance of great leadership during the time when the American civil rights movement was in the balance."

—Michael Beschloss, *New York Times* bestselling author of *Presidential Courage*

KENNEDY *AND* KING

ALSO BY STEVEN LEVINGSTON

Little Demon in the City of Light

The Kennedy Baby

KENNEDY
AND KING

THE PRESIDENT, THE PASTOR,
and the BATTLE OVER CIVIL RIGHTS

STEVEN
LEVINGSTON

hachette
BOOKS

NEW YORK BOSTON

For Suzanne, Katie, and Ben

Hachette Books

Hachette Book Group

1290 Avenue of the Americas, New York, NY 10104

hachettebooks.com

twitter.com/hachettebooks

First Trade Paperback Edition: March 2018

Hachette Books is a division of Hachette Book Group, Inc. The Hachette Books name
and logo are trademarks of Hachette Book Group, Inc.

The publisher is not responsible for websites (or their content) that are not owned by the
publisher.

The Hachette Speakers Bureau provides a wide range of authors for speaking events. To
find out more, go to www.hachettespeakersbureau.com or call (866) 376-6591.

ISBNs: 978-0-316-26738-0 (trade paperback), 978-0-316-26740-3 (ebook),
978-0-316-55245-5 (large print)

Printed in the United States of America

LSC-C

10 9 8 7 6 5 4 3 2 1

CONTENTS

FOREWORD FOR THE PAPERBACK EDITION

BY MICHAEL ERIC DYSON

Two titanic personalities, one white, one black, one a politician, the other a prophet, backlit the epic seizures of race in the sixties. John F. Kennedy and Martin Luther King have become saints in a political hagiography engulfed by nostalgia. In the end, each man earned his elevated position, as much by the vagaries and vicissitudes of destiny as by political calculation and moral imagination. While each met an assassin's bullet on the road to secular canonization, it was the blood shed in the streets that framed and fueled their fateful struggles, their fleeting encounters, their frustrating yet, finally, fulfilling partnership forged in the chasm of color. If each figure's initials have become monograms emblazoned on the loosely worn zeitgeist of a bygone era, JFK and MLK continue to imprint our consciousness with remarkable verve.

The tentative, then elaborate, dance between Kennedy and King is choreographed in vivid historical detail in Steven Levingston's masterly book. Levingston brilliantly sets the stage for Kennedy and King's parallel social gestures and competing political actions, showing us how each figure negotiated the challenges that hugged his path. Kennedy was a tactical politician who had to balance a consideration for civil rights—a priority he was forced to embrace in the rage of bitter national debates he could no longer avoid—against the sullying priorities of white Southern bigots. King was a prophet who, in elegiac cadences, called down fire to light the path to change. Kennedy's reticence, and King's resistance, defined their relationship in the early 1960s from their first tentative meeting, through an iconic phone call from the surging presidential candidate to the jailed freedom fighter's wife, to the Freedom Rides throughout the South, Governor George Wallace's segregationist siege at the University of Alabama, and the seismic shifts sent out from the march on Washington.

Kennedy and King dueled each other as they sought to shatter the lattice of hate and redesign the racial pattern of our democracy. As Levingston lucidly shows, Kennedy's feints against injustice, his dispiriting truces with bigotry, finally gave way to a demand from black folk and others to see civil rights as a moral issue, making a speech from the Oval Office declaring it so that brought King to tears. King agitated as a witness for the defense of black humanity and the reinvigoration of American democracy, and as Levingston eloquently argues, they were, as the enlightened understood, one in the same.

If Levingston offers us a King who took flight on the golden wings of black oratory, while managing to plumb the paradoxical depths of national identity, his subtitle offers a clue to King's identity, his cultural authority, that is too rarely probed: his pastor's heart. Levingston might have titled his book "The President, *the Prophet*, and the Battle Over Civil Rights," but he chose instead to underscore the religious provenance of King's power. Prophets rage against the ruin of social pathology, against the lethargy of insufficient good action. Pastors crave the currency of reconciliation and hope, speak in the language of forgiveness and love. The prophet seeks to shatter the status quo and remake the nation in light of its best destiny. The pastor offers a homily that can resonate throughout the land as the divine voice of compassion. King knew both were needed; his prophetic voice is often rightly feted, even feared, while his pastoral voice is ignored or presumed to drip in sentimentality. Levingston shows King in both modes, fully at home in both voices, rendering a dimension of the leader not often embraced: that it was not Billy Graham who was the nation's genuinely pastoral voice, its most authentic spiritual genius, but the black preacher from Georgia who rose to lift a nation on his soaring beliefs and his revolutionary rhetoric—and his saving and loving deeds.

Levingston's book is needed now more than ever, especially in the Age of Trump when human decency has been sacrificed on the altar of weaponized narcissism, and when true presidential leadership has gone the way of all flash, with little substance. It is always apparent that we need King's voice—lucid, melodious, rich, a baritone breathing in benevolence and blessing. But Levingston makes us pine for Kennedy's voice too—yes, halting at first, manipulative at its worst, compromising and opportunistic, too, but, then, finally, rising to echo the most sacred truths we have generated in a nation committed to finding the right register of freedom and equality in the national conversation. This book is an aching, poetic reminder of what once was, what might have been, and now, in our day, what should be.

"TO TEACH A PRESIDENT"

ON TUESDAY EVENING, June 11, 1963, President John F. Kennedy settled in behind his Oval Office desk, a pillow supporting his ailing back. Floodlights blazed, thick cables snaked across the floor, a bulky television camera stared at him. In minutes he was going live. Just three hours earlier, he had decided to speak to the nation. His speech had been hurriedly cobbled together, and was somewhat incomplete. But he knew what he wanted to say and, if necessary, he'd ad lib it. Looking down at his text, the president scratched out a few words and wrote in his own. Setting down his pen, he was ready. Although he was not fully conscious of it, President Kennedy had been building up to this moment for two and a half years. A technician called out a thirty-second warning.

America was at a crossroads on civil rights. Protesters opposed to segregation—some as young as six—had lately poured into the streets of Birmingham, Alabama, and were bullied by snarling police dogs and blasted off their feet by fire department water cannons. Demonstrations sprang up across the nation in solidarity. Earlier in the day, in Tuscaloosa, Governor George Wallace stood theatrically in the schoolhouse door to block the admission of two black students to the University of Alabama.

Just before 8 p.m., as the president put the finishing touches on his speech, Martin Luther King Jr. took a seat in front of his television in Atlanta, Georgia, joining millions of Americans coast to coast. Since Kennedy's razor-thin victory in 1960, King had implored the president to commit fully to the cause of racial equality. In telegrams and phone calls to the White House, in television interviews and newspaper articles, in face-to-face meetings, and in fiery rhetoric from the pulpit, the pastor pressed the president to confront racist Southern politicians and end the indignity of segregation. But King's pleas had been largely ignored.

In the Oval Office, the television camera's red light blinked on and President Kennedy went live. He began by chiding Governor Wallace for his puffed-up defiance in the schoolhouse door that afternoon; he expressed his regret that the Alabama National Guard had to be called out to enforce a court order to desegregate the state's classrooms. But he was pleased by the outcome: that two qualified black students were now going to attend the University of Alabama.

The president reminded the nation that while Abraham Lincoln had freed the slaves a hundred years earlier, "their heirs, their grandsons, are not fully free." He said America faced a moral crisis over race, and he called on all citizens to change the way they treated each other. It was time, he said, for action in Congress. Having refused to challenge lawmakers on this explosive issue, he now promised legislation to ensure equal treatment for black Americans. At last President Kennedy had found his voice—and his courage—on the most pressing domestic matter of the day: civil rights.

Watching in Atlanta, King leapt out of his chair. On the phone with friends, he wept. Hurriedly he shot off a telegram to the White House, calling the speech the clearest cry for black justice ever uttered by a president. It was a triumph not only for black Americans but for King himself. Although never claiming credit, King had played an instrumental role in Kennedy's transformation. He had directed his civil rights campaigns at the White House, knowing no real change was possible without the moral leadership of the president. His oratory, his pitched street battles, and his repeated jailings forced a distant president to pay attention. As John Lewis, the veteran civil rights activist and long-serving U.S. congressman, put it: "The very being, the very presence, of Martin Luther King Jr. pricked the conscience of John F. Kennedy."

In thirteen minutes on that June evening, Kennedy became the nation's first civil rights president. Looking back, King marveled at his evolution. "We saw two Kennedys," he explained, "a Kennedy the first two years and another Kennedy emerging in 1963." The second Kennedy, in King's view, was a man who not only saw the moral issues "but who was now willing to stand up in a courageous manner for them."

* * *

The civil rights story of the early 1960s is a tale of sit-ins, street protests, massive arrests, police brutality, church bombings, and unsolved murders. It is also a tale of two men—John F. Kennedy and Martin Luther King Jr.—and their complicated relationship. Kennedy and King towered over the national landscape, and their interactions defined the early years of the civil rights era. While broad, forceful trends propel the trajectory of history, prominent personalities like Kennedy and King ultimately guide the course of human life. The nineteenth-century thinker Thomas Carlyle believed that great individuals, or heroes, shaped the world's destiny. Historian Margaret MacMillan explains: "Leaders have choices and the capacity to take history down one path rather than another."

Although Kennedy and King shared the historical stage, the two men inhabited vastly different worlds. One was a wealthy New England Irish Catholic, the other a black Southern Baptist preacher. Kennedy was leader of the free world, King spoke for America's twenty million blacks. The men had little natural rapport. When they met face-to-face, their social styles clashed: Kennedy was cool and witty, King taut and high-minded. But they had much in common, too: Both men benefited from their oratorical brilliance and from the profound love of domineering fathers; and both knew the pangs of discrimination—the Kennedys as Irish Catholic immigrants in Protestant Boston, the King family as descendants of slaves.

Often clashing but always respectful, Kennedy and King established a model for protest that is relevant today. By his persistence, King discovered a successful strategy for speaking truth to power. President Kennedy, although ambivalent at first, proved that progress is possible when power listens and learns. But historic change is never easy. King had to overcome White House mistrust, disregard, and stonewalling before his message sank in. As he observed: "It's a difficult thing to teach a president."

PART ONE

TWO MEN, TWO WORLDS

JOHN F. KENNEDY had a problem with black voters. Running hard for the 1960 presidential nomination, the Democratic senator was sailing through the primaries, notching win after win, but a majority of blacks were not turning out for him. To beat the likely Republican nominee, Vice President Richard Nixon, in the fall, Kennedy had to reel in the black vote. But doing so, his campaign staffers realized, would take a near miracle. His young aide, Ted Sorensen, was blunt about black feelings toward the candidate. "Many are distrustful," he warned in a memo. "Some are suspicious, some are bitterly opposed, few are enthusiastic."

Blacks had reason for wariness. Early in his political career, when he was a young congressman from Massachusetts, Kennedy had championed the black cause, but as he set his sights on the White House he tempered his positions. In the 1950s, the suave, wealthy senator sought to ingratiate himself with a crucial constituency: segregationist Southern whites. In 1959, as he neared the launch of his presidential campaign, he invited Alabama governor John Patterson, a virulent racist, to breakfast at his Georgetown home. When the governor emerged from the private parley he endorsed Senator Kennedy for president, calling him "a friend of the South." Blacks wondered if a secret deal had been struck: What promises had Kennedy made to gain Southern support?

Kennedy's compromises on civil rights infuriated Jackie Robinson, the former Brooklyn Dodger who broke the color barrier in major league baseball in 1947. In retirement Robinson had become a blunt voice for racial justice, rousing the community through a column he wrote for the *New York Post*, and Jack Kennedy was a frequent target. Worse perhaps, Robinson had developed an affection for Richard Nixon. When the two men met for the first time during the 1952 Republican National Convention, Nixon congratulated the ballplayer on a home run he'd hit that day against the Chicago Cubs, and the pair formed an instant bond. Robinson's affection for Nixon was in keeping with a tradition among blacks:

Ever since Republican Abraham Lincoln had emancipated the slaves, blacks had largely favored the Republican Party. Franklin Roosevelt's New Deal during the Depression started to peel away some of that support, but many blacks still identified with the party of Lincoln. Nixon and Robinson quickly found grounds for their friendship. Both men had grown up in southern California and Nixon, astonishingly, recalled during that first chat together a football move Robinson had executed in a game in 1939 when he played for UCLA. A Republican accompanying Nixon recalled the scene: "I said to Nixon as we walked away that, while Robinson had undoubtedly met a lot of notables during his career, nevertheless I was sure there was one person he would never forget." Indeed, he had not. In 1957, Robinson wrote to Vice President Nixon, praising him for speaking out on behalf of civil rights during a trip to Africa. In his speech in Ethiopia, Nixon had declared: "We shall never be satisfied... until...equal opportunity becomes a reality for all Americans," prompting Robinson to offer: "In this endeavor you have my best wishes and steadfast cooperation."

In 1956, Robinson had been a strong advocate of the Eisenhower-Nixon ticket, but he became disillusioned with President Eisenhower's weak commitment to civil rights. As the 1960 presidential campaign neared, he leaned toward the Democrats—but only on the condition that their nominee was committed on civil rights. In a December 1959 column, he laid down his challenge: "If it should come to a choice between a weak and indecisive Democratic nominee and Vice President Nixon, I, for one, would enthusiastically support Nixon."

The following month, days after Kennedy announced his candidacy, Robinson condemned the Massachusetts senator for his meeting with Governor Patterson. Writing to a magazine editor, Robinson said he was "strongly in favor of Nixon's principles, ethics and intellectual honesty," adding, "Would you have me support a Kennedy who met with one of the worst segregationists in private, and then this man, the Governor of Alabama, comes out with strong support of Senator Kennedy?"

In the presidential primaries, Robinson still leaned Democratic, backing Minnesota senator Hubert Humphrey, who had a long-demonstrated, unwavering support for civil rights. To Robinson's chagrin, Kennedy thumped Humphrey in Wisconsin, Illinois, Pennsylvania, and West Virginia. But Kennedy's weakness among blacks was apparent. In Wisconsin, he lost by 3–2 margins in the predominantly black wards of

Milwaukee. Analyzing the Wisconsin vote, *Jet* magazine pointed out, "Sen. Kennedy won the war, but lost the racial battle." For Humphrey, the news was worse: His campaign was all but over; even Nixon declared Kennedy a "shoo-in" for the Democratic nomination. Recognizing the Kennedy momentum, Robinson vowed in his column: "I must repeat my own determination to look elsewhere for a candidate should Kennedy capture the Democratic nomination."

Robinson's stubborn opposition confirmed the campaign's worst fears: Blacks were not sold on John F. Kennedy. The senator's brother and campaign manager, Robert Kennedy, flew into full crisis mode. He invited Notre Dame law professor Harris Wofford to the Kennedy campaign headquarters at the edge of Capitol Hill. Since the mid-1950s, Wofford had immersed himself in the civil rights movement and had befriended its leaders; at ease in interracial situations, he was one of very few white students ever to attend the storied black institution Howard University. Under intense pressure, the younger Kennedy begged Wofford to help. Turning his piercing blue eyes on the earnest, young law professor, Bobby agonized: "We're in trouble with Negroes."

2

JOHN KENNEDY KNEW about discrimination not from the experiences of blacks but from his own family's immigrant history. From the moment they stepped ashore in Boston in the late nineteenth century, his Irish Catholic ancestors struggled against exclusion by the established, ruling Protestants. "He felt that as an Irishman somewhere along the line he had been discriminated against," recalled his friend George Smathers. Unlike many Irish immigrants, the Kennedys climbed out of the slums and prospered through politics and business.

Kennedy's maternal grandfather, John F. Fitzgerald, was a born politician, rosy cheeked and outgoing; known as Honey Fitz, he was so garrulous his banter became known as Fitzblarney. His bright-eyed amiability won him three terms in the U.S. Congress before he captured the job he most coveted: mayor of Boston, serving as the first city boss whose parents were born in Ireland. Kennedy's paternal grandfather, Patrick Joseph Kennedy, showed early promise as a businessman. In his twenties he bought a run-down saloon, using loans from his family and his earnings from work as a stevedore on the Boston docks, and swiftly turned it into a thriving watering hole. P.J., as he was known, was an imposing figure with a handlebar mustache and a barman's willing ear; he had sharp blue eyes, a thick mane of red hair, and was a rare Irish teetotaler. Soon he bought himself another saloon, then a partnership in a Boston hotel, and finally established a profitable whiskey-importing business. Eventually he became a leading state legislator and was invited to the Democratic National Convention in 1888, where he gave a seconding speech for the presidential nomination of Grover Cleveland.

Kennedy's father, Joseph P. Kennedy, sought to further elevate the family's social status by amassing a fortune. As a youth he felt the sting of second-class citizenship in help-wanted ads that asked for "Protestants only" and warned: "No Irish need apply." By the 1920s Joe was a millionaire, thanks to some crafty stock market speculation, and he tooled around Boston in his chauffeured Rolls-Royce. But he never overcame feelings of social inferiority. His enormous wealth wasn't enough to break down barriers to membership at the Cohasset Golf Club. Decades later he was still aggrieved, as he told a newspaper reporter: "Those narrow-minded bigoted sons of bitches barred me because I was an Irish Catholic and son of a barkeep."

Joseph Kennedy married the devout and iron-willed Rose Elizabeth Fitzgerald in 1914 and, after watching two games of the World Series in Philadelphia on their honeymoon, the couple began turning out a brood of nine children: Joseph Jr. arrived in 1915, and John in 1917, followed by five girls and two more boys, including Robert Kennedy in 1925. Joseph Kennedy nursed dreams of grand political success for his firstborn son as a path to social acceptance, and he was prepared to use his wealth and wits to choreograph Joe Jr.'s political ascent. Ever defiant, the patriarch enrolled young Joe Jr. and John in the elite private school Noble and Greenough in the 1920s, where bullies attacked them because of their Irish Catholic heritage. Of the two boys, Jack, at age seven, was the more frail; he was gaunt, with protruding ears, and because he had been frequently ill and had to convalesce for long periods, he had become a voracious reader. Joe, aged nine, was bigger, stronger, and healthier; he proudly wore the mantle of eldest, anointed son. Like his father, he was hot-tempered and resolved matters with his fists.

One day at recess, cocky Joe turned on his tormentors and a brawl ensued. Jack put up a tough front but he was not a fighter; instead he laid stakes on his brother. A classmate, Augustus Soule, recalled Jack Kennedy, already a cool-headed politician, circulating in the crowd betting on Joe Jr.'s grit. Wagers were made using the youthful currency of the day: marbles, which kids carried in a little bag in their pockets. By the end of the contest, Joe Jr. was battered but victorious and Jack was considerably wealthier in marbles. Later Soule admitted to his father that he lost all his marbles in a bet with Jack Kennedy. "It's an indelible memory," Soule recalled, "Joe fighting and getting all bloody, and Jack going around, betting marbles very quietly."

If the Kennedys suffered bias, their wealth and white skin cushioned the blow. What Jack and his family confronted was nowhere near as harsh as the day-to-day institutional degradation that blacks endured. Jack was intellectually opposed to discrimination, believing it was unfair and irrational. But his emotional grasp of black hardship did not go deep. Around the family dinner table, Jack and his siblings learned compassion for the disadvantaged, but blacks weren't singled out for special attention. "We did grow up with the idea that there were a lot of people that were less fortunate," Bobby Kennedy recalled. "And white people and Negroes were all put in the same category.... We had a social responsibility to try to do something about it. But as far as separating the Negroes for having a more difficult time than the white people, that was not a particular issue in our house."

Little evidence exists that Jack Kennedy harbored a racial bias. Seldom, if ever, was he heard to utter a slur. Once, as a teenager in 1936, he resorted to vulgar language during an extended illness, telling a friend that the Boston hospital where he was confined was a "nigger place." His usage of the epithet seemed an anomaly, occasioned more by naïveté and youth than a habit of bigoted slander. Insatiably curious about people, Kennedy did not seem to possess instinctive prejudice; nor was he given to the anti-Semitism that came easily to his father and his older brother. Jack did not isolate blacks on the basis of skin color; but if this attitude freed him of bigotry, it also prevented him from fully understanding racial discrimination.

Kennedy was as removed from the black community as most any

white American coming of age in the first half of the twentieth century. Black churches were foreign to him; he rarely ventured into black neighborhoods; his interaction with black professionals was minimal; and he had almost no exposure to the racial hardship experienced in the segregated South. Any black seen in the Kennedy household was almost invariably a servant. For the Kennedys, interracial friendships were almost nonexistent, and if one took root, it was not a relationship of equals. "I never saw a Negro on level social terms with the Kennedys in all my years of acquaintance with them, and I never heard the subject mentioned," observed journalist Arthur Krock, who was a longtime family friend and promoter of the Kennedy image until the relationship later ruptured. Young Jack Kennedy didn't brood over the condition of blacks in America; the bitter reality of their existence scarcely entered his consciousness. As his brother Bobby once explained, "We didn't lie awake nights worrying about it."

3

AT HARVARD IN the late 1930s, Jack had a black valet courtesy of his father. George Taylor looked after Jack's clothes and shoes and served as his chauffeur. Jack and George developed a casual, jocular relationship. Snubbing the social hierarchy of the elite institution, Jack treated Taylor almost as one of the boys, seeking his advice, smoking cigars together, and chatting with him about their mutual passion for girls. Jack was a fun-loving gadabout during his student days; buddying around with his valet was in part the antics of an irreverent, open-minded kid. "We were good friends," Taylor recalled in an interview in 1964.

In college Jack had not yet decided to enter politics, perhaps preferring to teach or write. But at about age twenty the lanky, handsome boy tested his oratorical skills by giving his first speech at the Boston YMCA, focusing on the Soviet threat. Afterward, he was eager to hear his valet's opinion of his performance. "Taylor, how'd I do?" Jack asked him. And the valet let him know: "Jack, terrific!" Often dashing off to see local movies, and Broadway shows, and the opera in New York, Kennedy sometimes took his valet along. "He'd say, 'Come on, Taylor,' And we'd go to an opera," Taylor remembered, where he would gamely sit through the show.

Despite his friendliness toward his valet, college-age Jack had little interest in racial advocacy. Even as a young man, Jack was adept at compartmentalizing his world, and blacks resided in a distant, unexplored corner. His interests lay elsewhere: in women, good times, and foreign affairs. Jack's father, Joseph P. Kennedy, was United States ambassador to Great Britain, and Jack spent considerable time in London and traveling through Europe, which fired a passion for international relations. He wrote his undergraduate thesis on why Britain was slow to rearm before the Second World War and, with the help of family friends, got it published as a book, *Why England Slept*, in 1940 at age twenty-three.

During the war, the Kennedy family was shattered when favorite son Joe Jr. died on a risky bombing mission in Europe. Jack survived his own wartime calamity: the sinking of the PT boat he commanded in the Pacific. For his courage and for saving the life of a crewman he earned national praise as a war hero. Once when he was asked by a high school student how he became a hero, he replied with his self-effacing wit: "It was easy—they sank my boat." With the loss of Joe Jr., Jack returned from the war and accepted the mantle of the Kennedys' oldest son and began seeking to fulfill his father's dream of political greatness for the family.

Jack threw himself into campaigning for a congressional seat in Massachusetts, ignoring constant, sometimes debilitating, pain from lifelong back troubles that had been aggravated by the PT boat incident. In his father's eyes, tough, robust Joe Jr. had been destined for the White House; now all that had changed. In 1946, gangly Jack at age twenty-nine took to the hustings, ill informed about his district and lacking a polished speaking style. Jack was swept along by the Kennedy name, which had been established by his father's wealth and his stint as an ambassador. Joe Sr. funded the campaign, coached the young candidate, and was masterful in drumming up publicity. Night after night, father and son reviewed Jack's performances onstage, the patriarch teaching the candidate how to improve his delivery, and over time Jack gained confidence. Demanding as Joe Sr. was, he loved his children with an all-consuming passion. He urged Jack on with a combination of flattery and sharp criticism. "If I walked out on the stage," Jack recalled, "and fell flat on my face, Father would say I fell better than anyone else."

Jack's valet, George Taylor, stayed with him after college, but now the relationship became strained. In a 1977 interview, Taylor claimed that Jack had given him the job of appointments secretary in this first campaign but then shoved him aside in favor of a family friend. When Taylor complained, he said Kennedy told him: "As of now, you will just have to do with the cooking, the shoes, and my clothes." To which Taylor replied, "Jack, to hell with you." Taylor quit as valet but remained loyal to the candidate and helped rustle up black voters. One night when Jack bought sandwiches for his volunteers at a Cambridge restaurant, he directed the races to sit in separate dining areas. Taylor was outraged. "They're all giving their time," he told Jack. "They're all human beings. Why segregate in this way?" Jack replied: "George, you're thin-skinned. That's one of the things of the time." Taylor responded, "They don't have a color line here in Harvard Square."

Jack handily won the election and arrived in Washington in 1947 as Massachusetts representative for the Eleventh Congressional District, the same seat his grandfather Honey Fitz had held fifty years earlier. In a series titled "New Faces in the House," the *Washington Post* featured the new congressman under the headline: YOUNG KENNEDY HARD WORKER. This image of the industrious young legislator was planted no doubt by his father, master media manipulator, to counter perceptions of Jack Kennedy as a rich-boy, do-nothing ladies' man. The paper alluded to the reputation: "One of Massachusetts' most eligible bachelors—handsome, 6-foot John F. (Jack) Kennedy—will be one of the youngest members of the new Congress." But then the *Post* hewed to the Kennedy line: "The social lions of the Washington 'Cocktail Circuit' may be in for a disappointment, for the serious-minded 29-year-old son of the former Ambassador has little time for anything but work."

* * *

During his freshman term, Jack Kennedy espoused bedrock liberal policies that included calls to eliminate racial prejudice. But he stopped short of challenging the Southern culture of segregation, partly out of respect for regional customs and partly because of his ignorance of actual conditions in the South. Although he had traveled much of the world he had still rarely, if at all, stepped foot in the American Deep South.

To avoid the sticky national debate over equal rights, Kennedy approached the question largely as a local issue. "We weren't thinking of the Negroes of Mississippi or Alabama—what should be done for them," recalled Bobby Kennedy, who managed his brother's winning congressional campaign. "We were thinking of what needed to be done in Massachusetts." By keeping the focus local, Jack was free to accord his constituent blacks the respect any human deserved without having to perform a political dance to justify it. As a World War II veteran, he appreciated the sacrifices of all soldiers, regardless of race. He spoke at a 1948 ceremony honoring two black war heroes, and strolled through black communities with the same ease and charm he brought to the white neighborhoods. "Northern pols were normally stand-offish," recalled Harold Vaughan, a black aide in Boston. "But Kennedy would just walk into a beauty salon in a black neighborhood, go right up to the woman below the hairdryer and say: 'Hi, I'm Jack Kennedy.' "

Early in his term, the young congressman was staggered by two personal crises. During the 1947 recess, he traveled to Europe on congressional business and became so ill with vomiting and fever—his skin turned a brownish yellow—that he was rushed to a hospital in London. Doctors diagnosed Addison's disease, an adrenal gland disorder that often shortened lives. (That Jack had such a condition was long rumored throughout his political career, but he never publicly acknowledged it.) A British doctor told an acquaintance of Jack's: "That young American friend of yours, he hasn't got a year to live." His condition was so perilous that while sailing home aboard the *Queen Mary* he was given last rites before being carried off the ship on a stretcher. Less than a year later, his favorite sister, Kathleen, known as Kick, was aboard an eight-seat plane in May 1948 heading to the French Riviera when it was thrown off course by a treacherous storm and slammed into a mountain, killing her at age twenty-eight.

* * *

Living in Washington, Congressman Kennedy gradually recognized the deplorable circumstances of segregation. The races had their own public parks, hotels, theaters, and restaurants. Congress, that bastion of democracy, kept black workers out of its swimming pool, barbershop, and dining areas. Kennedy spoke out, calling for fairness in employment opportunities and abolition of a poll tax that often kept blacks from voting. He also rejected a new D.C. sales tax that, he argued, added to the economic

hardship of blacks, who made up the majority of the district's population. He fought to give D.C. residents their own government, a move
aimed at ending Congress's power over the district. "When we talk about
civil rights," Kennedy declared, "we should remember that the people of
Washington have been denied the important right of self-government for
many, many years."

But Kennedy hesitated to throw himself fully into the cause. He was
most comfortable viewing equal rights through the lens of international
politics. The black plight, by his reckoning, was a foreign-affairs issue;
the United States could not reasonably promote democracy abroad if it
did not ensure freedom for all its citizens at home. How could America,
he asked, make the case that its political system was superior to the Soviet
Union's when its own citizens were oppressed and their rights trampled?

He resisted teaming up with liberal legislators in what he saw as excessive
moralizing on the black issue. He kept his distance from racial ideologues—
men he described as "attitudinizing liberals." On racial questions, as on most
every other issue, he maintained an invariably cool demeanor; he was a new
kind of Irish politician. He had broken with the old ways of the backslapping,
cigar-smoking, storytelling of the old-world pols, portraying himself during
his congressional campaign under the slogan "The New Generation Offers
a New Leader." The emotions-on-the-sleeve attitude of the old-guard Irish
bosses did not ring true to Jack Kennedy.

* * *

His smooth, unruffled style also played well in his private life. Women
adored him, and he had an obsessive need for their affections. Much has
been made of Jack Kennedy and the ladies: his amorality, his insensitivity in notching up conquests, the riskiness of some of his female pursuits.
From early childhood, he had battled one health scare after another, and
sex, it seemed, chased away pain and loneliness. At three, he had scarlet
fever; from his teens into adulthood, he suffered colitis, malaria, respiratory infections, ulcers, and bladder ailments. Severe back pain had hob-
bled him even before his PT boat was blasted by the Japanese.

His close aides marveled at how he hid his discomfort. When he was
on the campaign trail, his back was so bad he traveled with crutches,
leaving them in the car and walking with gritted teeth to greet voters
in an assembly hall. "When he came into the room where the crowd
was gathered, he was erect and smiling, looking as fit and healthy as the

light-heavyweight champion of the world," recalled his aide Kenneth O'Donnell. Afterward, back in the car, "he would lean back on the seat and close his eyes in pain," another close aide, Dave Powers, remembered. At the hotel, he would go upstairs on crutches and soak his back for an hour in the tub before going to bed. He was in pain "at least one-half of the days that he spent on this earth," his brother Bobby estimated. But Jack put forward a face of *vigah*, as he pronounced it, and constant activity. "Those who knew him well would know he was suffering only because his face was a little whiter, the lines around his eyes were a little deeper, his words a little sharper," explained his brother. "Those who did not know him well detected nothing." His mother was aware of Jack's superb acting ability. "He went along for many years," Rose recalled, "thinking to himself—or at least trying to make others think—that he was a strong, robust, quite healthy person who just happened to be sick a good deal of the time."

A keen sense of his own mortality infused Kennedy to live life hard and fast and pursue his goals quickly. To his friend George Smathers, Jack once said: "The point is that you've got to live every day like it's your last day on earth. That's what I'm doing." According to another friend, Chuck Spalding, Kennedy suspected that death was always hovering nearby: "It had taken Joe and Kick and it was waiting for him. So, whenever he was in a situation, he tried to burn bright; he tried to wring as much out of things as he could." To his admirers, Jack never ran from anything but rather projected a manliness that betrayed no suffering; it was an art he perfected by years of braving pain with equanimity.

4

AFTER FIVE YEARS in the House, Jack Kennedy, a young man in a hurry, set his sights in 1952 on the Senate seat of the formidable Republican Henry Cabot Lodge Jr. A challenge from Kennedy was a long shot. Lodge had won every election he'd entered since 1932, and he at first paid little heed to the young congressman.

But Jack's considerable energy and sharp campaign, led by his brother Bobby, turned the contest into a real race. Discovering that Lodge was vulnerable among the fifty thousand to seventy thousand blacks in Massachusetts—he had polled poorly among them in the past—Kennedy was soon speaking out across the state and in the House in favor of civil rights. He championed better employment policies, elimination of slums, and fair rental prices. He voiced his belief that racial discrimination harmed America's global prestige and enhanced Communism. He offered measured promises, if not a passion, for change. On the House floor he deplored the segregationist bombing of a home in Florida that killed two black schoolteachers, and he won favorable treatment in the Boston press.

Jack added blacks to his campaign staff and, unlike previous white candidates, took his campaign directly to the black community. He spent an entire day in the black wards of Jamaica Plain and Roxbury, pushing voter registration and walking into beauty salons and barbershops and pool halls. Later, with the race in a near dead heat, he sent his sister Eunice to a woman's tea in the home of a black campaign worker in a Roxbury housing project. Eunice showed up in a "billowing felt skirt that had 'Kennedy' emblazoned across it." Black women in their Sunday finest turned out for a similar event at the Copley Plaza hotel, where they chatted with Jack and heard him deliver a speech on civil rights.

* * *

On Election Day, November 4, 1952, Kennedy defeated Lodge by just over seventy thousand votes, lifted to victory in part by large majorities in the black wards. He also drew strength from a range of ethnic groups including the Irish, Italians, and Jews, as well as women. Among Catholic voters Lodge had lost as much as half the support he had won in previous elections. Kennedy's acceptance by blacks placed a new burden on the freshman senator: He now stood as a friend of the black community and had to answer to its rising expectations.

But as a senator with an eye on the presidency, Jack found himself in the grip of a new political reality. Both maneuvering within the Senate, and an eventual run for the White House, required bowing to a band of powerful Southern politicians; these Democratic senators and governors defended segregation with the fervor of Confederate soldiers. In place of Sharps rifles, the senators relied on invective and political maneuvering to derail any change to their way of life. This tight-knit cabal of white supremacists wielded immense power; in the Senate, they were repeatedly reelected and were in control of important committees. Among their ranks was Georgia senator Richard Russell Jr., who expressed his segregationist views subtly and used Senate procedures masterfully to obstruct efforts at reform. Mississippi senator James Eastland, chairman of the Judiciary Committee, made no secret of his racist views. After the Supreme Court declared public school segregation unconstitutional in 1954, he championed the White Citizen's Councils that sprang up across the South to deny blacks their constitutional rights. "Generations of Southerners yet unborn," he asserted, "will cherish our memory because they will realize that the fight we now wage will have preserved for them their untainted racial heritage, their culture, and the institutions of the Anglo-Saxon race." In all, the Southern caucus had twenty-two members in 1953 lined up in implacable opposition to black equality.

What Northern liberals failed to appreciate fully was that these senators were defending a way of life anchored by myth and imagination. Southerners still nurtured fantasies of a past in which demure ladies and cavalier gentlemen paraded through an agrarian landscape, a portrait that bore little resemblance to historical reality or the current-day experience. Essential to the continuation of the fantasy was that blacks had to remain in their place as an inferior race. Southern romantics clung to this bigoted dream world and were convinced their lifestyle was moral and inviolable.

But pressure for change was building. Near the end of World War II, a Swedish economist named Gunnar Myrdal awakened American sensibilities by publishing a massive study on the "Negro problem." Based on six years of travel in the South, his 1944 book, *An American Dilemma: The Negro Problem and Modern Democracy*, exposed the depth of Southern prejudice. Not only were blacks subjected to everyday discrimination, only a minuscule percentage were eligible to vote in the South because of poll taxes and unfair literacy tests. To escape Southern oppression, blacks migrated in massive numbers to the North. While 90 percent of the population lived in the South in 1900, almost half had moved north by 1950, becoming a new political force. Blacks also were incrementally improving their economic condition, even creating a nascent middle class. During the war, many moved from the countryside to jobs in new Southern defense plants; worker shortages provided opportunities they might not otherwise have had and gave rise to a new population of skilled black laborers. During the war, black membership in labor unions doubled. Membership in the National Association for the Advancement of Colored People also soared between 1940 and 1946, from fifty thousand to five hundred thousand, filled mostly by the black middle class, and the NAACP Legal Defense and Educational Fund achieved a series of successes in the courts in the fight against segregation.

Individuals began to take action in defiance of long-standing restrictions. In 1955, Rosa Parks refused to give up her bus seat to a white man in Montgomery, Alabama, igniting a black boycott of the city's buses and bestowing stardom on a young preacher named Martin Luther King Jr. Soon afterward, blacks in Tallahassee, Florida, rebelled against bus segregation. One boycotter sensed the historical moment: "It isn't the matter of buses any longer. It's much deeper than that. It is a matter of the spirit. You just get tired of being pushed around." Yet many white Southerners dug in fiercely to preserve their glorious way of life.

"So far from being modernized, in many ways [the Southern mind] has actually always marched away...from the present toward the past," observed W. J. Cash in his masterpiece, *The Mind of the South*. Published in 1941, Cash's book captured the persistent backwardness in Southern thinking that endured into the 1960s.

5

JOHN F. KENNEDY created a media stir when he took up his duties in the Senate in 1953. Adoring reporters ticked off his accomplishments and his allure: war hero, son of an ambassador, Harvard graduate. "A youthful 34," wrote Elizabeth Maguire of the *Washington Post*, "he himself is personable, brainy and brave." A year later, the *Boston Globe* was still asking if Jack wasn't the "capital's most eligible bachelor." The *Globe* reported that when Kennedy first set up his Senate office "his staff was swamped with requests from Washington girls who wanted to work for the tall, tanned and handsome lawmaker." Whispers were soon heard that Kennedy was a potential candidate for vice president in 1956. The senator knew he would need a groundswell of support from the Democratic Party at the national convention, including members of the Southern caucus, for a run at the vice presidential slot, and certainly for any later campaign for the presidency.

And so began a career-long high-wire act: For his political future, Kennedy had to balance the support of racist politicians against a civic obligation to fight for racial justice. In the years ahead, the tension between the two drove the politician to cozy up to Southern bigots, equivocate on civil rights, and then scramble to justify, or deny, his actions to the black community. Guided by his unrestrained ambition rather than a fixed moral viewpoint, Kennedy saw no inconsistency in navigating the two opposing worlds. He was determined to chart his own path and resisted being pigeonholed into prescribed political positions. When liberal critics complained that he wasn't liberal enough, he commented to a reporter: "I'd be very happy to tell them that I am not liberal at all. I'm a realist."

If that assertion pleased conservative Southerners, it also reflected an ideological agnosticism that troubled blacks. Kennedy could not be relied on to protect their interests with any consistency. He favored a political relativism that kept him from overcommitting to any cause or group. His ambivalence—his unwillingness to throw himself with passion into any liberal or conservative issue—left him suspect in both camps.

Ted Sorensen, one of Kennedy's most brilliant and faithful aides, took a job in his Senate office in January 1953, becoming the wordsmith of the Kennedy vision, and stayed with him for the next decade. Working intimately with him, Sorensen identified a crucial feature of the senator's mind and personality. Although Kennedy revealed little of his inner life—he was a public man who kept his thoughts private—he was in perpetual intellectual evolution. He has been described as protean, an elusive figure who regularly assumed new shapes and who was ultimately unknowable. Yet his character was anchored by certain observable traits. Deeply curious, Kennedy absorbed new information, circumstances, and attitudes, and sifted them for their significance, adjusting his perceptions accordingly. A voracious reader and patient listener, he was in a permanent state of becoming. As his observant young aide described Kennedy, "No attribute he possessed in 1953 was more pronounced or more important than his capacity for growth, his willingness to learn, his determination to explore and to inquire and to profit by experience."

* * *

If Kennedy had a White House campaign in his future, he needed to start looking presidential. In his father's eyes, that meant toning down his playboy antics and settling into marriage. Out of the multitude of eager women, only one suitable political spouse emerged: the poised and stunningly attractive Jacqueline Bouvier. "Joe Kennedy not only condoned the marriage, he ordained it," observed Jack's friend Lem Billings.

It was an exquisite match: Jack and Jackie both moved in elite circles, attended prep schools, had lived in Europe—Jack in London working for a summer at the U.S. Embassy when his father was ambassador, Jackie studying during her junior year at the Sorbonne in Paris; they shared an interest in reading, intellectual pursuits, and the achievements of artists; and both were very private, even lonely, souls. Jack's style of courtship favored books over flowers. As they got to know each other he gave Jackie copies of some of his favorite works: Edgar Allan Poe's *The Raven*, John Buchan's *Pilgrim's Way*, and a biography of Sam Houston.

Like Jack, Jackie had known personal trauma. Her stockbroker father, the movie-star handsome Black Jack Bouvier, as he was known, had suffered badly in the stock market crash of 1929, and was a heavy drinker and womanizer. Whatever her father's faults, he remained for her a figure of love and fascination. Her mother divorced him when Jackie was nine and married a much wealthier man, lawyer and stockbroker Hugh D. Auchincloss, just before Jackie's thirteenth birthday.

The tumult of her youth sharpened Jackie's innate reserve. She withdrew, put her trust in animals and nature, enjoying solitary time on horseback or strolling along the beach. Both she and Jack masked their emotions with some fine stagecraft. For all their good looks and charm, they moved through the world somewhat detached and alone. Jack was sociable and easygoing, but few of those close to him were given access to the man within. "Getting to know [Kennedy] intimately was not easy," observed his aide Ken O'Donnell, who for months hadn't been aware that Jackie had entered Jack's life. "There were many parts to him, many of his private opinions, emotional feelings and intellectual convictions, that he never revealed to anybody." With her attentive eye, Jackie peered past his exuberant exterior. Knowing his history of ill health, she was moved by the strength of imagination she sensed in him: "this little boy, sick so much of the time, reading in bed, reading history, reading the Knights of the Round Table." With no other woman had Jack found such unspoken communion. "He saw her as a kindred spirit," his friend Lem Billings recalled. "They both had taken circumstances that weren't the best in the world when they were young and learned to *make themselves up* as they went along.... They were both actors and I think they appreciated each other's performances."

6

ON SEPTEMBER 12, 1953, John F. Kennedy and Jacqueline Bouvier were married before six hundred guests in Saint Mary's Church in Newport, Rhode Island, amid a profusion of pink gladioli and white chrysanthemums. Boston archbishop Richard Cushing presided, reading a telegram from the Pope. Outside the church three thousand uninvited well-wishers swarmed the grounds hoping for a peek inside. The reception for twelve hundred guests at Hammersmith Farm, the Auchincloss estate overlooking Narragansett Bay, was, in the words of Jack's aide Ken O'Donnell, "one of those dream-perfect parties that you seldom see in real life."

Becoming a Kennedy was no easy matter. Jack's sisters, who had lavished their affections on him after the death of their oldest brother, Joe, were wary of the newcomer and feared she would draw Jack away from them; they teased her and made fun of her whispery voice. Jackie was challenged to take part in the highly competitive activities at the family compound in Hyannis Port, including intense touch football games and tennis matches, but she held back. In a conversation with historian Doris Kearns Goodwin years later, Jackie revealed just how different she was from the clan. "It was enough to enjoy the sport," she said of her tennis playing. "It wasn't necessary for me to be the best." While the others were off frantically competing with each other on the lawn or the courts, Jackie sat on the porch chatting with Joseph Kennedy; she nurtured a close relationship with him that was built on love and honesty. "I used to tell him he had no nuances," Jackie recalled in conversation with Goodwin, "that everything with him was either black or white, while life was so much more complicated than that. But he never got angry with me for talking straight to him; on the contrary, he seemed to enjoy it."

Jackie also had to adjust to life with her unreformed playboy husband; while she served her public purpose as a smiling political wife, Jackie endured Jack's continued womanizing and long absences. His health also shaped their life together. Barely a year into their marriage, she was tending to Jack's latest life-threatening infirmity. His weak back had been worsening for some time, and by 1954 doctors recommended surgery to repair his collapsed vertebrae. But patients with Addison's disease had a heightened chance of infection from even the smallest medical procedure: A dental visit could prove fatal. Assessing the danger of the operation, doctors gave Jack a 50 percent chance of survival. Earlier in the year, an Addison's patient had an appendectomy in the same hospital where Jack was to undergo his surgery, and three weeks later the forty-seven-year-old man died from a massive postoperative infection. Jack was in such unbearable agony that he decided to take the risk. Now reliant on his crutches, he told an aide: "I'd rather be dead than spend the rest of my life on these things."

His surgery was postponed twice as doctors worked to strengthen his body to withstand the trauma of the procedure. Finally, on October 21, 1954, surgeons inserted a steel plate into his spine to stabilize it in an operation lasting more than three hours. The medical team tried to ward off the expected complications, but after three days Jack succumbed to infection and fell into a coma. Jackie sat at his bedside holding his hand and reading poetry to him. His prognosis was so dire that a priest was summoned to give him last rites. While his son fought for life, Joe Kennedy wept freely in front of family and friends. But, as Jack had done in earlier crises, he gradually crept back from the edge and began a slow, painful recovery. Jackie spoon-fed him and sneaked the candy he loved into the hospital. His survival came with a new fear: that he would never walk again.

* * *

While Jack lay in the hospital, Wisconsin senator Joseph McCarthy was facing a showdown over his anticommunist demagoguery. McCarthy had been an obscure Republican senator until he discovered a potent issue to galvanize support for his reelection in 1952. Testing his sales pitch in a speech before the Women's Republican Club in Wheeling, West Virginia, in February 1950, he declared: "I have here in my hand a list of 205" names of Communist Party members working for the State Department and shaping U.S. policy. His charge of communist subversion detonated across America's Cold War terrain, and soon McCarthy had established himself as a crusading anticommunist intent on protecting America from the Soviet threat.

As his crusade gathered momentum, it became apparent that anyone, even the most reputable individuals, could fall under McCarthy's suspicion for an innocent remark or for not being as strongly anticommunist as he was. His allegations destroyed careers, families, and lives. He played to America's fear and uncertainty over Communism with such dramatic mastery that for a time he seemed invincible. McCarthy was a friend of Jack's, a fellow Irishman and womanizer in the capital whose company Kennedy enjoyed long before the anticommunist crusade. Jack's father also liked McCarthy and had invited him to the family estates in Hyannis Port and Palm Beach; McCarthy had even dated two of Jack's sisters, Patricia and Eunice.

By the time Jack entered the Senate in 1953, the Wisconsin senator was at the peak of his power. But his shaky edifice soon began crumbling. The harsher his attacks, the less convincing they became. He had few, if any, names of actual communists, and he could not substantiate his charges. By late 1954, as Kennedy recovered at New York's Hospital for Special Surgery, McCarthy was fending off Senate colleagues outraged at the way he had run roughshod over America's civil liberties. The Senate scheduled a vote of condemnation of Senator McCarthy for December 2, a turning point that pitted Kennedy's loyalty to his friend against his devotion to American principles.

Almost from the beginning Jack had straddled the controversy. He had judged, or hoped, that the Wisconsin senator's red-baiting campaign would quickly run its course and then fade away. In an appearance on *Meet the Press* in December 1951, Jack sounded optimistic: "I think that the stories of communism within the executive branch of the government have more or less died out." But when McCarthy's accusations continued, Kennedy privately acknowledged the strain on the country, the Senate, and the Constitution. "He referred to the McCarthy Committee with articulate dislike but showed no interest in saying so publicly," an aide said. Whenever Jack referred to the excesses of the committee, he refrained from attacking McCarthy personally.

Kennedy had won his Senate race in part on the strength of the Irish Catholic vote. Maintaining that support was crucial to his reelection hopes in 1958 and his quest for higher office. McCarthy was adored by Irish Catholics in Jack's home state, and a vote in favor of condemnation could antagonize that important constituency. "Hell," Kennedy told an aide, "half my voters in Massachusetts look on McCarthy as a hero." Jack was aware that in the 1952 elections McCarthy had campaigned against four Democratic senators, and they all went down to defeat.

Jack's view of McCarthy was complicated by the sentiments of his father, who appreciated the Wisconsin senator's conservative values and anticommunism. The elder Kennedy helped fund McCarthy's 1952 reelection campaign and afterward arranged a job for his lawyer son Bobby on McCarthy's investigations subcommittee. Although Jack disapproved of his younger brother becoming counsel to the committee, he resigned himself to it, saying: "Oh, hell, you can't fight the old man." After several months Bobby quit his position in disgust over the committee's tactics. His father, however, never lost his fondness for McCarthy.

Torn by the controversy, Jack tried to ignore it. As a close aide later put it, "McCarthyism simply did not strike him as one of 'his' issues." Jack failed to empathize with the people whose lives McCarthy ruined. "I agree that many of them were seriously manhandled," he admitted, but he acknowledged he didn't "get as worked up as other liberals did."

Before he left Washington for his surgery Jack had prepared a speech that he had intended to deliver on the Senate floor during early debate on McCarthy; but he never got the chance because a wrinkle in the proceedings ended the debate before he appeared. The speech, known at the time only to his aides, would have put Kennedy on the public record favoring condemnation, though his narrow reasoning turned the blame away from McCarthy. His argument focused on threats to the honor and dignity of the Senate posed by certain actions of McCarthy's associates on the committee.

When it came time to vote, Jack could have indicated his preference from his hospital bed. But he lost his nerve and remained silent. The condemnation passed by a large margin, and Kennedy was the only Democratic senator not to vote in favor of it. Later, he sloughed off his inaction by saying, "I was just darned sick." But some time after that, he recognized his lapse and acknowledged, "I never said I was perfect. I've made the usual quota of mistakes."

Three weeks after the Senate action when he was well enough to leave the hospital, Jack dreaded a possible confrontation with the press. Still too weak to walk, he was rolled out on a stretcher to a waiting ambulance, bundled in a plaid blanket against the December chill. Beforehand he fretted to a friend: "You know, when I get downstairs I know exactly what's going to happen. Those reporters are going to lean over my stretcher. There's going to be about ninety-five faces bent over me with great concern, and every one of those guys is going to say, 'Now, Senator, what about McCarthy?' Do you know what I'm going to do? I'm going to reach for my back and I'm just going to yell, Oow, and then I'm going to pull the sheet over my head."

To critics, particularly many Democrats and liberals, Kennedy's silence on the McCarthy vote was an act of cowardice; he had shown himself unwilling to stand up to vicious, false attacks on American citizens. During Kennedy's bid for the White House, liberal lawyer Joseph Rauh put the candidate's response to McCarthy in the context of the nation's debate over race: "A man who does not believe in the civil liberties of white citizens," Rauh warned, "cannot be trusted to stand up for the civil rights of Negro citizens."

7

FLYING DOWN TO the family's compound in Palm Beach to convalesce, Jack sought to resume work on a magazine article he had conceived before his surgery. The piece was to focus on political courage, a subject of interest to him before the McCarthy vote and one that had assumed particular relevance now. His nonvote on McCarthy was a blunder; he had failed to take the right moral and political stand, and it weighed heavily on him. Courage was integral to the self-perceptions of the Kennedy men. Joseph Kennedy Sr. insisted on a culture of manliness: Kennedys were men of action, risk, and domination. Jack's brother Joe Jr. took on a dangerous World War II bombing mission that killed him. Lieutenant Jack Kennedy received plaudits for his courage after his PT boat was rammed and cut in half by a Japanese destroyer. Throughout his life, Jack also exhibited quiet courage in response to his many painful ailments. Historian Arthur Schlesinger Jr. noted in his book on the Kennedy administration, *A Thousand Days*: "Robert Kennedy tells us that courage was the virtue his brother most admired. In the first instance, this meant physical courage—the courage of men under enemy fire, of men silently suffering pain, the courage of the sailor and the mountain climber and of men who stared down mobs or soared into outer space. And, when he entered politics, it came to mean moral courage."

Jack aspired to moral courage in the political arena, envisioning it as essential to a strong democratic leader. His magazine article was to highlight this quality in men of American history. But his recovery from his surgery was slow and painful, and he struggled to write. About a month into his convalescence, Jack was in such poor condition that he was flown back to the Hospital for Special Surgery in New York for another operation. Now surgeons removed the steel plate they had implanted and performed a bone graft. No serious complications ensued, and on February 25, 1955, Jack walked out of the hospital on crutches, silencing naysayers who were circulating rumors that he would never get up on his feet again and that his political career was over.

Back in Palm Beach Jack returned to his writing project, throwing himself into it with intensity. He became so captivated by the subject that now, instead of a magazine article, he wanted to write a book on political and moral courage. With the assistance of his aide Ted Sorensen and a few professors, Jack identified eight senators who risked their political careers to stand up for their principles. His rooms at the compound soon filled with books, and articles, and memorandums that Sorensen sent from Washington. Though fatigued and in pain, Jack persevered. "Unable to sleep for more than an hour or two at a stretch," remembered Ken O'Donnell, "Jack worked on the book day and night, reading and writing notes and then drafts of the chapters on long yellow legal pads."

At long last, Jack finally had a manuscript for his book, *Profiles in Courage*. Later, questions arose over who actually wrote it: Kennedy, Sorensen, or others; the controversy sparked acrimony, charges and countercharges, and threats of lawsuits. The book, by most appearances, was a collaborative effort inspired and directed by Kennedy, though Sorensen's literary hand was clearly evident.

Some historians and Kennedy aides have made light of the timing of Jack's work on the book. Sorensen discounted the role the McCarthy vote played in motivating Jack to tackle the project. "Many assumed that the book was intended as a 'personal catharsis,' a justification or substitute for his role in the McCarthy censure," Sorensen wrote. "In truth this was never mentioned, and the theme of the book predated the censure controversy."

Nothing compelled Jack to pursue the project; he could have dropped it, given his weakened state and his need to convalesce. Or he could have chosen another subject. But he was passionate about this issue. "In choosing to write about the moral courage of others," historian Doris Kearns Goodwin observed, "Jack Kennedy may well have been trying to sort out his thoughts about his own courage."

If Kennedy manliness demanded courage—physical, political, and moral—Jack may have needed to write *Profiles in Courage* as part of his personal journey. The book portrayed several American senators, independent-minded men who defied their constituencies and acted on their conscience for the good of the nation; the tales highlighted the significance of the action of a single man. Jack favored the great-man theory of history—the notion that larger-than-life personalities guided the course of human destiny; history was not a passive unfolding of events beyond the control of individual actors. The British historian Isaiah Berlin noted after a dinner with Kennedy that Jack's "eyes shone with a particular glitter" when he discussed men who shaped history. Jack wished to join the ranks of these trailblazers; he longed to mold himself into a figure who, by assertion of his political and moral courage, left his mark on history.

But for now his contribution was purely literary. He knew what it took to attain moral courage, but he was not among men of such rank. At the end of *Profiles in Courage*, Kennedy sounded as though he were urging himself to greater heights: "The stories of past courage can...teach, they can offer hope, they can provide inspiration. But they cannot supply courage itself. For this each man must look into his own soul."

The book received excellent reviews—the *New York Times* called it "splendidly readable"—and it became a smash best seller. Through the influence of Joseph Kennedy and his friends, it won a Pulitzer Prize. The young senator-author reeled in the plaudits, raising his profile and fashioning himself as a distinctive, thoughtful politician, even while he still privately wrestled with questions about his own political and moral courage.

8

HIS AMBITION WAS insatiable. In August 1956, still in pain but recovered from his back surgery, Jack was at the Democratic National Convention vying for the vice presidential slot. His radiant style stirred the nation. "He was the one new face that actually shone," the *Boston Herald* declared, playing up his charisma, dignity, and brains. "Senator Kennedy came before the convention . . . as a movie star," the *New York Times* gushed. Despite his Hollywood appeal, Jack failed to nudge aside the delegates' choice for vice president, Estes Kefauver, a defeat that hit him hard. He immediately set off for the Mediterranean to salve his wounds aboard a yacht filled with male friends and beautiful women. He left his wife, eight months pregnant, at home. The previous year Jackie had suffered a miscarriage after three months "and learned that carrying and delivering a child would always be difficult for her," Kennedy aide Kenneth O'Donnell recalled.

On August 23, 1956, less than a week after the convention, Jack was somewhere on the Mediterranean when Jackie awoke at her family's estate in Rhode Island and began hemorrhaging. Rushed to the hospital, she had an emergency Cesarean a month before term and delivered a stillborn girl. Jackie herself slid into critical condition—having lost a lot of blood she needed several transfusions—and a priest was called in case she needed last rites. The *Washington Post* highlighted Jack's absence in a front-page headline: SEN. KENNEDY ON MEDITERRANEAN TRIP UNAWARE HIS WIFE HAS LOST BABY. Sailing into port at Genoa three days later, Jack learned of the baby's death when he phoned home. He saw little point in rushing to Jackie's side, reasoning that the tragedy had already struck and his presence would do nothing to change the circumstances. Sailing mate George Smathers enlightened his friend to the political implications of such a decision, if not the personal insensitivity. "You better haul your ass back to your wife," he warned bluntly, "if you ever want to run for president."

His political career and his marriage survived. The following year, on November 27, 1957, Jackie delivered a healthy girl with no complications. Baby Caroline touched Jack's heart in ways he had never anticipated. Before she came into his life, he had a naïve curiosity about the joys of fatherhood, as his Navy buddy Paul Fay recalled: "When I'd tell him with great enthusiasm of an experience with my children, he'd say, 'I don't understand how you can get such a big kick out of your children.'" The magic of a child's natural affection—and the emotional response of a parent—seemed foreign to Jack. But he wanted to make sense of it, Fay remembered.

Now, filled with pride, he hauled his prep school friend Lem Billings into the hospital nursery. "Now, Lem, tell me, which one of the babies in the window is the prettiest?" Pointing to the wrong baby, Billings failed the test, and Jack refused to speak to him for two days. As Billings remembered later, "Jack was more emotional about Caroline's birth than he was about anything else." Caroline changed her father: She innocently initiated in him a slow, and sometimes invisible, process of maturity.

Over the next few years, the ambitious senator crisscrossed the country on a fervid speaking schedule, laying the groundwork for his presidential run, all the while battling his fragile health. Newly available injections of cortisone allowed him to manage his undisclosed case of Addison's disease. But, according to historian Robert Dallek, "Between May 1955 and October 1957, while he was launching his vice presidential and presidential bids, he was secretly hospitalized nine times for a total of forty-four days, including two weeklong stays and one nineteen-day stretch." Nonetheless, by sheer will, Jack displayed startling vigor. His easy smile landed him repeatedly on the covers of national magazines—*Time, Look, Life,* the *Saturday Evening Post.* Jack's savvy father, summoning a pitchman's hyperbole, explained the lure of his photogenic son. "Jack is the greatest attraction in the country today," he told an interviewer in the late 1950s. "I'll tell you how to sell more copies of a book. Put his picture on the cover.

Why is it that when his picture is on the cover of *Life* or *Redbook* they sell a record number of copies? You advertise the fact that he will be at a dinner and you will break all records for attendance. He can draw more people to a fundraising dinner than Cary Grant or Jimmy Stewart. Why is that? He has more universal appeal."

* * *

By mid-1960, deep into his presidential campaign, Jack needed more than movie-star looks to win the black vote. Within the Kennedy camp it was believed that blacks were swayed by the views of their own celebrities, and that Jackie Robinson's diatribes had damaged the candidate. To combat the baseball hero, Kennedy began pursuing one of America's most beloved black entertainers. His father had instructed him in the benefits of linking politics and Hollywood celebrity. The elder Kennedy—who had owned movie studios, scandalously squired the glamorous actress Gloria Swanson, and nurtured celebrity friendships—recognized that politics and film had much in common.

And Jack, as Lem Billings observed, had stepped into his political role "like a method actor." His Hollywood glamour only enhanced his allure as a politician. From Jack's perspective, it made perfect sense that praise from a black star would influence black voters. Working on that assumption, Kennedy placed his hopes on singing sensation Harry Belafonte. Luring Belafonte to his side would give Kennedy something even more valuable than celebrity approval; it would burnish his civil rights image. Not only was Belafonte a beloved entertainer, he was also a highly regarded activist.

Kennedy gave the task of corralling Belafonte to a black campaign worker named Frank Montero. But it was quickly apparent that Belafonte wanted nothing to do with Kennedy. The King of Calypso, as he was known, was a suave, light-skinned man of Jamaican descent, often pictured in an open shirt that revealed his smooth chest. His 1956 album *Calypso* had climbed to number one on the *Billboard* charts; and his presence on the street threw his fans into their own free-form rendition of his signature tune, "Day-O (The Banana Boat Song)." Montero's pitch was simple enough. The senator just wanted to meet with Belafonte so he could let him know that he was a strong advocate of racial justice, even if at times it looked otherwise. Belafonte ignored Montero: The singer was unimpressed by Kennedy's civil rights record—he believed some of his actions were appalling. Besides, Belafonte was already committed to former Illinois governor Adlai Stevenson who, despite heading the Democratic ticket in 1952 and 1956—and losing both elections—was looking for a lucky third time; and Belafonte trusted Stevenson for his strong advocacy of civil rights. "I didn't know why I was being approached," the singer said of Kennedy's interest. "But I figured out why soon enough: Jackie Robinson."

When Kennedy went after something—a meeting, a nomination, a woman—he refused to be denied. "Once you say you're going to settle for second," he observed, "that's what happens to you in life." On Kennedy's behalf, Montero was relentless. He was "very persistent and very insistent," Belafonte remembered. Montero hounded the singer. "He kept calling," Belafonte later said. "I tell you," Montero pleaded on the phone, "it costs you nothing to hear what he's got to say." Montero's persistence finally wore Belafonte down, and the activist-singer agreed to a meeting.

9

———

ONE LATE AFTERNOON in May, after a campaign swing through New Jersey, John Kennedy pulled up in front of 300 West End Avenue at Seventy-Fourth Street. It was here in Harry Belafonte's fifth-floor, twenty-one-room Manhattan apartment that civil rights leaders gathered from time to time to ponder strategy. Belafonte was proud that Martin Luther King Jr. regarded the Manhattan apartment as "his home away from home," and that he often put his feet up there on business trips to New York. The singer kept a bottle of Harveys Bristol Cream on hand designated specially for King, who humorously marked the liqueur's level on the bottle to scare off pilferers. It was here one evening that Belafonte first noticed King's facial tic, a pulling of his cheek to one side occasionally when he was under intense pressure.

Belafonte had risen spectacularly from his impoverished birth in Harlem. His mother was the daughter of a black sharecropper father and a Scottish woman. His father was the son of a Dutch Jew and a Jamaican woman. Throughout his life Belafonte felt a kinship with Jews; his second wife, Julie Robinson, was the daughter of Russian Jewish immigrants. In 1960 the singer performed the Shabbat song "Hine Ma Tov" on national television; in 1966 he and Danny Kaye sang the Jewish folk song "Hava Nagila."

A mixed-race child, young Belafonte grew up angry, plagued by a sense of fear and vulnerability. He tackled his anger through years of Freudian analysis but was never able to fully conquer it. "In the end, where your anger comes from," he discovered, "is less important than what you do with it." He channeled it into the fight for racial justice and was attracted by King's philosophy of nonviolence. "I wasn't nonviolent by nature," Belafonte recalled. But as he observed King's doctrine in practice, he savored its higher principle. "I would come to appreciate its spiritual and emotional value," he said. "I'd find I wanted to live by those values myself, both to help the movement and to wash away my personal anger."

If Kennedy knew any of this history, he didn't let on. Nor did it seem to have crossed his mind how Belafonte took up residence in the heart of a white neighborhood of the Upper West Side. The singer's seven-thousand-square-foot spread, appointed with the trappings of wealth and respectability, was a symbol in the fight against segregation in New York. To live where he did, Belafonte had waged his own civil rights battle a couple years earlier, deploying the tactics of savvy nonviolence.

In the fall of 1958, Belafonte and his white wife, Julie, went apartment hunting on the Upper East Side, where rental brokers sent a clear message: The couple would probably prefer another neighborhood. Outraged, the singer called a press conference to announce a formal complaint against the city. His predicament captured the attention of former First Lady Eleanor Roosevelt. "I am sure that every New Yorker was shocked the other day to read that Harry Belafonte and his charming wife and baby were finding it practically impossible to get an apartment in New York City except in what might be considered segregated areas or in a hotel," she wrote in her syndicated newspaper column "My Day." "I can think of nothing I would enjoy more than having Mr. and Mrs. Belafonte as my neighbors." Mrs. Roosevelt then phoned Belafonte to invite the family to move in with her. Although honored, Belafonte politely declined.

Soon afterward, the couple came upon an apartment at 300 West End Avenue, a drafty four-bedroom rental with a library and pantry, and they fell in love with it. "When we tried to rent it," Belafonte remembered, "the apartment was somehow suddenly unavailable." Belafonte sent a white friend to pick up the lease and then he signed it under his own name. The building manager, happy to have the apartment rented, paid little attention to the famous name on the document.

But the manager was not so oblivious when the Belafonte family showed up to move in; alarmed, he notified the building's owner, Ramfis Trujillo, who was the playboy son of Rafael Trujillo, the dictator of the Dominican Republic. The younger Trujillo feared that black renters would scare away white tenants and crush the value of his investment. He tried to toss the Belafontes out, but the building manager had countersigned the lease, so the entertainer was protected for the one-year term.

Belafonte embarked on a bold strategy not only to keep himself in the apartment long term but fully integrate the building. Through a series of deft financial maneuvers in conjunction with other tenants—and by risking more than $2 million of his own money—the singer acquired the building from Trujillo, who was willing to sell to raise cash as he grappled with the collapse of his father's brutal regime in the Dominican Republic. Belafonte then bought the apartment next to his own rental, knocked out walls, and expanded the space to create his enormous home. As other tenants chose to buy their rentals, Belafonte recouped most of his investment in the copurchase of the building. When white renters moved out he found newcomers to integrate this small slice of the Upper West Side. The revered jazz bassist Ron Carter, who would join the Miles Davis Quintet in 1963, moved in, and the singer Lena Horne, who was then a regular on television variety shows, took the penthouse.

* * *

By the time Jack Kennedy visited in May 1960, the Belafontes were comfortably settled into their mixed-race apartment house. The home décor was a mélange of cultures; there was an Afro-Caribbean accent in the Haitian wood carvings and a Jewish motif in the paintings of Marc Chagall and a Mexican flair in the works of Diego Rivera.

For all his eclecticism Belafonte wore some cultural blinders of his own. Years later he admitted that before he had met Kennedy he had formed a biased opinion of the Massachusetts senator. "He was kind of like this Irish Catholic guy," the singer said in a 2005 interview, "that was the classic stereotype for us of what Irish Catholics were, which were always drunk racists." The perception was inaccurate: Jack was neither a drunk—he drank sparingly—nor a racist; but he still had much to learn about racial matters. Although Belafonte and Kennedy both moved among the rich and famous, their crowds were strikingly different. Seeking a diverse community, Belafonte mixed with both blacks and whites in the entertainment world, while Kennedy, cloistered within his Irish and political clans, had few black acquaintances. Jack relied on several black advisors, but some of them complained they weren't accepted into the inner circle. In a telling encounter on the campaign trail, Jack was challenged by a black dentist to tell him exactly how many blacks he knew. Candidly Kennedy admitted: "Doctor, I don't know five Negroes of your caliber well enough to call them by their first names. But I promise to do better."

When the singer and politician sat down for their conversation, Kennedy came to the point: "I understand that you and others have reservations about me," he told Belafonte. By "others," Belafonte assumed, Kennedy meant other blacks. The senator then launched into a lengthy discourse on his aspirations for the presidency—what he could bring to the White House and the nation—and expressed optimism about his chances of getting there. Unspoken, however, was the uncertainty of the Democratic National Convention two months away in July. Although Kennedy was winning the state primaries, the delegates he gained from those contests were too few to assure him the nomination before the party gathering. There was always the possibility of a late convention surge for other candidates. Adlai Stevenson's emergence was still a distinct concern; and waiting in the wings was the ruthless Senate majority leader Lyndon Johnson, whose lust for the White House was as deep and wide as his home state of Texas.

While Kennedy's youth was exciting to many delegates—a taste of freshness and vibrancy in a staid political world—it was also a hindrance. In early May it became an issue when the Soviet Union shot down an American spy plane in Soviet airspace and captured its pilot, Francis Gary Powers, initiating a perilous period of Cold War tensions. Stevenson, far more seasoned in foreign affairs than Kennedy, suddenly seemed an attractive choice.

In a tight race for the nomination, every delegate, black and white, was vital to the Kennedy campaign. A rising delegate count could forestall any last-minute backroom deals to rob the Massachusetts senator of the nomination. And if Kennedy were nominated, black support could prove decisive in his battle against Richard Nixon in the fall. In this political environment Belafonte's backing was crucial. During their conversation Kennedy worked hard to peel the singer from the Stevenson camp. He highlighted his civil-rights-friendly stand on various issues and pointed to his high ranking in the polls, but to no avail. As Belafonte recalled: "I was quite forthright in telling him of my commitment to Stevenson."

The singer admitted to being charmed by Kennedy's style and intellect and even by his Boston accent; but throughout his long pitch the candidate said nothing to suggest that he empathized with the hopes of blacks. "Not once in his disquisition did I hear the phrase 'civil rights,'" Belafonte remembered.

The singer also set the candidate straight on how to attract black voters. The Kennedy strategy, he pointed out, had a serious flaw. "I am somewhat fascinated that you have sought celebrity to be the answer to celebrity," he told Kennedy. "And although Jackie Robinson may have some influence, and I may carry some as well, I think that all of you are really quite minuscule in your thinking." It was true that blacks were joined in a common struggle, Belafonte explained, but the community espoused a diversity of opinion and did not vote in sheep-like fashion. Celebrity did not guide sentiment in the black world. If Kennedy wanted to connect with that community he needed to find the pulse of black America. "You're making a big mistake if you think I can deliver the Negro vote for you," the singer told the senator. "If you want the Negro vote, pay attention to what Martin Luther King is saying and doing. You get him, you don't need me—or Jackie Robinson."

Kennedy seemed puzzled. "Why, he asked...was King so important?" Belafonte recalled.

The naïveté staggered Belafonte. That Kennedy asked such a question suggested that he had ignored the civil rights movement of the 1950s. More important, his question demonstrated that he was so out of touch with blacks that Martin Luther King Jr., now almost deified in the community, failed to resonate with him. Here was the leading Democratic presidential candidate—the man who might occupy the White House in eight months—and he was largely unaware of America's leading civil rights figure and of the issues driving the movement for equal justice. Belafonte gave the candidate some valuable advice about King: "The time you've spent with me would be better spent talking to him and listening to what he has to say, because he is the future of our people."

After more than an hour, the conversation wound down. Kennedy left the apartment displeased that Belafonte withheld his endorsement. For his part, Belafonte worried that his advice hadn't resonated with Kennedy. Soon he was on the phone with King, describing the senator's manner and his failings. But, Belafonte realized, this was a candidate to be reckoned with, and King needed to pay attention to him. "Kennedy, I told him, was cold, calculated, and unschooled in the now-sacred cause of civil rights. At the same time, I acknowledged, he was whip-smart and knew how to listen. I said if the candidate called him for a meeting, Martin should find the time."

10

ON A JUNE morning in 1960, Martin Luther King Jr. approached the entrance of an apartment building at 24 Central Park South in Manhattan. Down the block was the Plaza Hotel, the stylish home of Eloise, the precocious six-year-old in the 1955 children's book, who lived on the tippy-top floor and annoyed the adults who crossed her path. In this neighborhood of white privilege, a black man on the street, even one well attired in a dark suit, was either invisible or cause for alarm. As Harry Belafonte had discovered just a mile and a half north, New York City obeyed its own quiet rules of segregation.

The fact was, if you were black you belonged elsewhere in Manhattan, far north of Belafonte's apartment, in Harlem. It was a lesson every black New Yorker learned early. On his way from Harlem to the midtown library, thirteen-year-old James Baldwin recalled crossing Fifth Avenue: "The cop in the middle of the street muttered as I passed him, 'Why don't you niggers stay uptown where you belong?'"

Harlem was another world. To get there from where King stood that morning, he would have had to go up nearby Fifth Avenue, past the Metropolitan Museum of Art at Eighty-Second Street, past the northern tip of Central Park at 110th Street. Up there the East River turned into the Harlem River and apartment buildings gave way to housing projects, each one, as Baldwin described them in 1960, "as cheerless as a prison...

colorless, bleak, high, and revolting." Manhattan's black population was herded into this inhospitable pen known as Harlem, living in poverty and under constant threat by white policemen. "The only way to police a ghetto is to be oppressive," Baldwin observed. "None of the Police Commissioner's men...have any way of understanding the lives led by the people they swagger about in twos and threes controlling...They represent the force of the white world, and that world's real intentions are, simply...to keep the black man corralled up here, in his place."

Far from the world of the ghetto, Martin Luther King Jr. had come to the apartment on Central Park South, owned and maintained by Senator Kennedy's father. Despite his distrust of Kennedy's commitment to the cause, King agreed to meet him for breakfast on the recommendation of his friends Harry Belafonte and Harris Wofford, the white professor who had joined the campaign's Civil Rights Section.

Over several weeks Wofford had scrambled to find a date that worked for the two busy men, and now, finally, on June 23 there was a confluence of their schedules. King had had speaking engagements the previous week in Cincinnati, Buffalo, and Pittsburgh, and was scheduled to fly from New York to Rio de Janeiro, Brazil, on June 24 for a Baptist convention. Kennedy, who had been barnstorming the nation for votes and delegates, had left Durango, Colorado, on June 18, swept through North and South Dakota on June 19, and spent the evening of June 22 rallying Democrats in a dinner speech in Spring Lake, New Jersey.

Their meeting was unpublicized; they sacrificed the spotlight in the interests of having a substantive private chat. The two men had to size each other up. Martin Luther King Jr. needed to hear what John F. Kennedy knew about civil rights and how he intended to tackle the big questions. And Kennedy needed to learn about King and understand why this young leader was adored by the black masses, reviled by Southern politicians, trailed by journalists, and envied by some of his black associates. King's rise to stardom had seemed meteoric, but his path through the racial thicket of America, like that of many blacks, had been one of fear and anguish—navigated by courage.

* * *

Martin Luther King Jr. lost his racial innocence early. At age six, he was a happy, robust child in love with language, telling his mother: "You just wait and see. I'm going to get me some *big* words." Born in 1929, he enjoyed a sheltered, privileged young life growing up in Atlanta, Georgia, as the son of a prominent Baptist preacher. But he sensed something uncomfortable about black life; a menace hovered at the edges of his world: He knew he couldn't do certain things, he couldn't go to certain places, some playgrounds and water faucets were off-limits to him. But as a small boy Martin pushed these troubled thoughts aside. He was just happy to spend his time playing with his two best friends, two white boys. His friends' father owned a grocery store across the road from Martin's house, and every day Martin and the boys were inseparable. It was a time of youthful innocence, as King remembered years later: "None of us seriously thought anything about those white boys being different."

But when they grew up, the three boys were sent to different schools. Martin went to the one for blacks, his friends to the one for whites. One day after school, Martin sprinted across the road to play with his friends. But the boys' mother had something to tell Martin: Their father would no longer allow his boys to play with a black child. Martin recalled listening to their mother explain the circumstances, telling him that her boys "were white and I was colored." In that instant—without cause—their friendship was over.

The shock stayed with him. "Here for the first time I was made aware of the existence of a race problem," he wrote in a brief autobiography at age twenty-one during his theology studies. "I had never been conscious of it before." His outrage was born at a young age, and he carried it out into the world, admitting later: "I was determined to hate every white person."

Whites and their system of segregation tormented King. One afternoon when he was a teenager he went to an Atlanta movie theater where he was admitted not with the whites through the front door but with the blacks through the rear, and he was forced to sit in a filthy blacks-only section. Feeling demeaned, he found it impossible to enjoy the film. This was his first visit to the movie house, and his last. The shadow he sensed as a child was darkening his life.

Once while buying shoes downtown, he and his father were told to move to the back of the store if they wanted service. Daddy King, as his father was called, refused to budge, but no matter how long and how stubbornly they stood there the white clerk refused to serve them. Finally Daddy King declared that he would buy shoes at the front of the store, or he would not buy them at all; then he grabbed his son by the hand and led him out. "I don't care how long I have to live with this system," the father vowed to the son as they walked down the street, "I will never accept it."

Daddy King often erupted in the face of humiliating treatment from whites, even at the hands of police. Once, after he accidentally drove through a stop sign, an officer rolled up next to his car and demanded: "All right, boy, pull over and let me see your license." Unfazed by the possible repercussions, Daddy King retorted: "I'm no boy." Then pointing at his son, he lectured the officer: "This is a boy. I'm a man, and until you call me one, I will not listen to you." His tirade risked severe consequences, but Daddy King got lucky: The surprised officer became flustered, wrote up a ticket as fast as he could, and went on his way.

* * *

The King family, like most blacks, bore a painful legacy of racial injustice. Daddy King's grandfather, Jim Long, was a hardy slave put to use like a studhorse to breed more slaves; later, as a free man, Jim Long defied threats from the Ku Klux Klan and registered to vote in 1867. One of his sons, Daddy King's father, was a poor sharecropper who struggled with economic and racial hardships; Daddy King's mother was a tough, religious woman who worked the fields part of the season and washed and ironed for whites the rest of the year.

As a boy, Daddy King once was bringing a bucket of milk home to his mother when a white sawmill owner demanded that he carry water to his workmen. Wishing to get home, the boy politely declined. But apparently, he didn't have a choice. The man beat him and kicked over his milk bucket. His mother, later learning of the attack, tracked down the sawmill owner and went into a rage, knocking him over. Her sharecropper husband followed her toting his rifle and threatened to kill the man. Their small rebellion shattered the King family. Fearing for his life, Daddy King's father fled into the woods hearing that a white posse was coming for him; he was away for months before returning a drunken wreck. Daddy King remembered once as a youngster restraining his father as the miserable man drunkenly beat his mother.

For a few months every year, Daddy King attended a black school that had no books, no materials, not even a blackboard; the lessons given by the local pastor's wife excited him nonetheless. But his education sorely lagged, and by age fifteen he was barely literate: He had learned to read but was unable to write. His mother, meanwhile, carted him with her to church where he came to admire the preachers for their rich voices and command of scripture. By age twenty, Daddy King had set himself the goal of becoming a minister and, although young for the honor, he was soon ordained and named pastor of a small rural church in Georgia. Exceptionally ambitious, he left the following year and sought his destiny in Atlanta, where he met and courted the daughter of one of the city's most prominent ministers, A. D. Williams, pastor of Ebenezer Baptist Church.

Daddy King was struck by sixteen-year-old Alberta Williams's "gracious manners, captivating smile and scholarly manner," as he later put it. She was far ahead of him educationally and he worked diligently to catch up. "I had no natural talent for study," Daddy King acknowledged, "and my learning came after long, long hours of going over and over and over the work until I was falling asleep saying my lessons to myself." The Williams family was moved by his ambition and embraced him as a son. A. D. Williams had struggled with his own education and encouraged the young man to repair his deficiencies. Williams paved the way for Daddy King to attend Morehouse College, where he himself had earned his minister's degree. In 1926, Daddy King married Alberta in a celebrated ceremony at Ebenezer Baptist, six years after first laying eyes on her.

Soon after Williams's death in 1931, Daddy King succeeded him in the Ebenezer pulpit. By then, his own family had expanded: He now had three children, including the future civil rights leader Martin Luther King Jr. From his earliest days, under the strict authority of his father, young Martin absorbed a strong mix of religion and defiance. As Daddy King put it: "To prepare a child for a world where death and violence are always near drains a lot of energy from the soul. Inside you, there is always a fist balled up to protect them."

11

MARTIN LUTHER KING Jr. showed an early aptitude for expressing the reality of black life in powerful, vivid language. Blessed with a sharp mind, he skipped ninth grade and was placed in tenth at age thirteen. In 1944, as World War II raged far from home, King triumphed at a local public speaking contest, and he went on to a state competition. There, he delivered a speech he'd written titled "The Negro and the Constitution," describing the dissonance the teenager perceived in the ideals of American democracy and the plight of the black community. "We cannot have an enlightened democracy with one great group living in ignorance," he declared at the state contest in Dublin, Georgia. "We cannot have a healthy nation with one tenth of the people ill-nourished, sick, harboring germs of disease which recognize no color lines." He spoke of blacks being beaten down by Jim Crow laws and forced into bad—even criminal—behavior. He called on Americans to "give fair play and free opportunity for all people."

King captured first place, then boarded a bus with his teacher for the ride back to Atlanta only to confront the racism he had just lamented onstage. At a stop in a small town, the bus driver ordered him and his teacher to surrender their seats to boarding white passengers. Martin resisted but his teacher prevailed upon him, to avert a confrontation. For the next ninety miles, the teenager stood in the aisle, seething over the unjust comfort of the whites. "It was the angriest I have ever been in my life," he recalled.

As he grew older and delved into theology, he learned to manage his hate and transform it through faith. "Religion for me is life," he declared in the autobiography he wrote during his studies at the Crozer Theological Seminary. Of the white man, he said, "It was my duty as a Christian to love him."

* * *

In 1952, while working on his doctorate in theology at Boston University, King met a woman enrolled at the New England Conservatory of Music who dreamed of becoming a classical singer. Coretta Scott had grown up in rural Alabama picking cotton and suffering the typical indignities inflicted on a black child. She remembered having to enter the white-owned drugstore in town through a side door and having to wait while all the white kids were served their ice cream before her. When she was allowed to place her order, she was not free to choose her flavor. "No matter what flavor I asked for," she recalled, "the man would give me whatever he had too much of."

Her parents sacrificed so Coretta and her sister could have an education—her mother's schooling had ended in the fourth grade. After graduating from Antioch College in Ohio, as her sister had done before her, Coretta went off to the conservatory. In Boston, she was taken by the well-dressed PhD student from Atlanta two years her junior, despite his short stature. Standing just under five feet seven, King bantered like a philosopher-intellectual but was playful, too, teasing, joking, and dancing with her. He also conveyed to Coretta his passion for civil rights, his desire to fight for black freedom, and his hope to do so in Christ's spirit by loving one's enemies. He did not know what role he might play, but he was committed. His sincerity, firm conscience, and charm led Coretta Scott to marry Martin Luther King Jr. a year later, in 1953.

* * *

Then came a fateful decision: Just twenty-five years old, King was offered the pastorate at the Dexter Avenue Baptist Church in Montgomery, Alabama, the cradle of the Confederacy, the onetime capital of the warring South. He was torn over two dreams: to teach in a college or to lead a church congregation. He already had a teaching post waiting at Morehouse College in Atlanta, his alma mater. And his father, Daddy King, the pastor at Atlanta's Ebenezer Baptist Church, wanted nothing more than for his son to join him in the pulpit. Daddy King's scenario had Martin becoming copastor at Ebenezer on his way one day to assuming leadership of the four-thousand-member congregation.

Whenever he contemplated a major decision, Martin sought God's guidance. As he prayed, one question kept forcing its way into his thoughts: What was the moral decision? In what way, and in what place, King wondered, could he do the most good? In Coretta's words, "His conscience was a formidable thing that kept him on the path he thought was right."

Whatever the decision, it was to have life-changing consequences for Coretta. Her music career was blossoming in Boston. The conservatory had chosen her as a soloist in the premiere of a modern piece, *Motivos de Son*, by Cuban composer Amadeo Roldán. She was also teaching music to white schoolchildren. In the South, she was likely to be denied these kinds of diverse opportunities; her dream of a singing career had to be postponed. King felt the tug of a "moral obligation," as he put it: "Finally we agreed that, in spite of the disadvantages and inevitable sacrifices, our greatest service could be rendered in our native South." Coretta reconciled herself to Martin's passion, accepting that they had to pursue the mystery that God laid before them. "Even in 1954," she recalled, "I felt that my husband was being prepared—and I too—for a special role about which we would learn more later." It was unclear whether promise or tragedy lay ahead. "Martin and I . . . were like actors in a play, the end of which we had not yet read," Coretta later said. "We had the feeling that we were allowing ourselves to be the instruments of God's creative will." The young couple packed their belongings and headed off for Montgomery, Alabama.

12

WITH A BOLD—some cautioned ill-advised—decision, Martin Luther King Jr. set his destiny in motion and shaped the course of what was to become the American civil rights movement of the 1950s and 1960s. By the time he arrived in Montgomery, King had a perspective of the Southern black as hunched in fear, cringing and passive, broken by the white man. Even his assertive father had shown the symptoms. Daddy King railed against the Jim Crow laws that kept the races separate and oppressed millions of blacks. He had used his position as head of a large and influential church to push for change. In 1942, he led a campaign to encourage President Franklin Roosevelt to address discrimination on trains. He'd worked for equal pay for Atlanta's teachers, and he was a force in ridding the courthouse of separate elevators for whites and blacks. But for all his father's courage, the younger King detected in him—as in the majority of blacks—a palpable fear of the white man. It was not an unreasonable anxiety. The South's legacy of violence had left the black community watchful and wary: Who among them had not heard tales of friends, neighbors, and relatives kicked, whipped, or hanged from a tree for no sin other than having black skin? Before Martin was born his father had witnessed whites brutalizing blacks on a city bus, and ever since, the elder King had not stepped foot on public transport. While he spoke out within his own community, boldly condemning injustice, the elder King mostly avoided white society to lessen the chance of a run-in turning ugly.

In Montgomery many blacks were so beaten down that they had simply given up. "Acquiescence—while often the easier way—is not the moral
way," King believed. "It is the way of the coward." His predecessor at
Dexter, Vernon Johns, once tried to stir a small insurrection on a city bus.
Kicked off for planting himself in a front seat reserved for whites, he called
out to the other blacks to join him in his protest, but no one followed. Days
later a woman passenger on that bus scolded Johns for defying the consensus among the black passengers: "You ought to knowed better."

To King, black timidity reflected deep bruises that the Southern way
of life had inflicted upon his race. Simply boarding a bus was an exercise
in subservience: Blacks dropped their dime in the box at the front then
had to step out and walk to the back to board, and often as they made their
way to the rear entrance the driver sped off while spewing common slurs:
"niggers," "black cows," "black apes." Such abuse plunged black Southerners into a malaise of apathy. "Many unconsciously wondered whether
they actually deserved any better conditions," King observed. "This is
the ultimate tragedy of segregation. It not only harms one physically but
injures one spiritually. It scars the soul and degrades the personality."

Then one December afternoon in 1955, just over a year after King
had moved to Montgomery, a black seamstress in rimless spectacles riding on a crowded bus refused to give up her seat to a white passenger.
Rosa Parks was a hard worker and a regular churchgoer; she was an
efficient volunteer secretary of the NAACP's local chapter, and in her
heart lay a well of quiet activism. "I had had problems with the bus drivers over the years, because I didn't see fit to pay my money into the front
and then go around to the back," she recalled. "Sometimes bus drivers
wouldn't permit me to get on the bus, and I had been evicted from the
bus." That late afternoon on December 1, she was a little tired; she preferred not to stand up, so she kept her spot. Mostly, she was fed up with
the indignity of second-class citizenship. What separated this run-in
with the driver from her others was that the police were called, and Rosa
Parks was hauled away.

Her arrest brought together several prominent black leaders and
Montgomery's Women's Political Council to work out her legal defense,
and from those consultations there emerged a call for a one-day boycott
of local buses on December 5, to be followed by a mass meeting at a
local church. Word of a woman's arrest spread through the community

by hand-to-hand distribution of leaflets. "Don't ride the bus to work, to town, to school, or any place Monday, December 5," the leaflet said. E. D. Nixon, the former NAACP local chapter president and a prime motivator of the boycott, leaked the plans to an editor at the *Montgomery Advertiser*, promising "the hottest story you've ever written." That story in Sunday's paper—NEGRO GROUPS READY BOYCOTT OF CITY LINES—ensured that the news reached virtually every resident of Montgomery.

The evening before the boycott, Martin Luther King was overcome by a sudden ethical crisis: Was the use of a boycott a moral strategy for blacks? The racist White Citizen's Councils had relied on boycotts to enforce segregation—so were blacks now stooping to the tactics of the racists? The Councils boycotted black businesses and meted out economic punishment to whites who worked for racial progress. Previewing the bus boycott, the *Montgomery Advertiser* suggested that blacks were simply adopting the strategy of the White Citizen's Councils. King was appalled by any possible parallel; he wondered what separated the bus boycott morally from the actions of the White Citizen's Councils. That evening, he retreated to his study to struggle with an answer. "That awesome conscience of his began to gnaw at him," Coretta remembered, "and he wondered if he were doing the right thing."

In his contemplation, King thought back to his reading in college of Henry David Thoreau's *Essay on Civil Disobedience*, and he determined that, as Thoreau argued, people had an obligation to refuse to acknowledge unjust laws. What was segregation but an oppressive practice enforced by a series of unjust laws and customs? Blacks, King concluded, had a moral duty to disobey it. "We were simply saying to the white community, 'We can no longer lend our cooperation to an evil system,'" he explained. "Our concern would not be to put the bus company out of business, but to put justice in business." The White Citizen's Council wanted to bankrupt black businesses and the companies of sympathetic whites; the bus boycott was in fact the opposite of any action undertaken by the Council.

Before turning in for the night, Martin and Coretta debated what the next day would bring. Bus boycotts had been tried in Montgomery and other cities, and quickly fizzled out. Black timidity did not augur well for this one. "I still had doubts," King admitted. "I still wondered whether the people had enough courage to follow through." His expectations low,

King predicted that if 60 percent of blacks boycotted the buses, then the protest could be called a success.

* * *

The next morning Martin and Coretta were up at five thirty to keep an eye on the bus stop just outside their front window: The first bus was to roll by at 6 a.m. While getting coffee in the kitchen, he heard his wife call, "Martin, Martin, come quickly!" He raced to the window to see the first bus passing the house; usually it was packed with black domestics riding to their jobs in the white neighborhoods. "Darling," Coretta cried, "it's empty!" Two other buses rolled by at fifteen-minute intervals, also carrying no blacks. King jumped in his car and rode around town studying the city buses. "A miracle had taken place," he declared. "The once dormant and quiescent Negro community was now fully awake." On the first day, Negro compliance with the boycott was nearly 100 percent.

In the afternoon, black leaders met at the Mount Zion AME Church to consider their next step. The one-day action was such a startling success that the men resolved to continue the boycott indefinitely. They formed a new organization, the Montgomery Improvement Association, to coordinate the protest. Next came the sticky question of who should lead the group. Names were tossed out and discussed and then someone nominated Martin Luther King Jr., to his complete surprise. The new Dexter pastor was still learning his way after a year in the job, and he and his wife had had a baby girl just two weeks earlier. A few weeks before that, King had declined the presidency of the local NAACP chapter; he just didn't have the time. But now on an impulse, he accepted the presidency of the Montgomery Improvement Association. "Well, if you think I can render some service, I will," King told the gathered men.

And with that, his destiny was set in motion. Historian Taylor Branch explained the vagaries of fate behind this simple, momentous decision. "Idealists would say afterward that King's gifts made him the obvious choice," Branch wrote in his Pulitzer Prize–winning work, *Parting the Waters: America in the King Years, 1954–63*. "Realists would scoff at this, saying that King was not very well known, and that his chief asset was his lack of debts or enemies. Cynics would say that the established preachers stepped back for King only because they saw more blame and danger ahead than glory."

Thus began an intense period that repeatedly tested King's wits, stamina, and courage. Under his leadership, the boycott pushed on through crises, intimidation, and tortured negotiations with representatives from the city and the bus company, and despite the inconvenience, the blacks stayed off of public transport; they took to their feet or to car pools. As one seventy-year-old woman famously sighed, "My feets is tired, but my soul is rested."

As word of the boycott spread around the country, the press discovered Martin Luther King Jr., this "soft-spoken man with a learning and maturity far beyond his twenty-seven years," as the *New York Times* described him in a profile three months into the boycott. "His clothes are in conservative good taste and he has small trim mustache," the paper observed, noting his oratorical gifts in front of a congregation: "He can build to his climax with a crescendo of impassioned pulpit-pounding that overwhelms the listener with the depth of his convictions." As King's profile rose, the press pursued him on pulpits and stages in Hot Springs, Arkansas, Chicago, Nashville, Brooklyn, and Columbus, Ohio. In March, the black paper *Chicago Defender* reported sympathetically that King had lost eighteen pounds working nonstop on the boycott.

Inevitably, the emerging civil rights leader incited racist enemies. At a rally of the White Citizen's Council, the powerful Mississippi senator James Eastland whipped up a crowd of twelve thousand members. Vulgar handbills distributed at the gathering revealed the panic sweeping the white supremacist community. "We hold these truths to be self-evident," read one of the handouts, "that all whites are created equal with certain rights, among these are life, liberty, and the pursuit of dead niggers. In every stage of the bus boycott, we have been oppressed and degraded because of the juicy, unbearably stinking niggers." The attack concluded: "My friends, it is time we woke up to these black devils. . . . If we don't stop them African flesh eaters, we will soon wake up and find Rev. King in the White House." At home, when he answered his phone, King often heard the growl of bigots. If Coretta happened to pick up the receiver, she too was insulted, in sexually graphic terms.

Late one night just a month into the boycott, King heard a snarling voice on the other end of the line: "Nigger, we are tired of you and your mess now. And if you aren't out of this town in three days, we're going to blow your brains out, and blow up your house." Exhausted, King had suddenly landed on the hard edge of despair. He thought of his wife and baby daughter: "They can be taken away from me at any moment. I can be taken away from them at any moment." His courage was faltering. He brewed a pot of coffee, and paced, and contemplated the burden his fight for equal rights placed on his family. Fear consumed him, and he considered running away from the danger. "I was ready to give up," he admitted. "I tried to think of a way to move out of the picture without appearing a coward."

In his troubled state, he turned to God, bowing and praying out loud asking for direction; he told God of his desire to stand up for what was right and to lead his people. "But now I am afraid," he conceded. "If I stand before them without strength and courage, they too will falter. I am at the end of my powers. . . . I've come to the point where I can't face it alone." Struggling with his uncertainty, King had a revelation; he heard an inner voice, a voice he ascribed to the presence of the Divine. The voice ordered him to take on the fight for justice, and reassured him that God would stand by his side. And something came over him. "Almost at once my fears began to go," he recalled. His doubts vanished, and he felt a surge of courage. "I was ready to face anything."

* * *

Only three days later, he faced the unthinkable. He was at church in the evening, conferring with associates and collecting funds for the boycott, when a bomb ripped through the front porch and windows of his house. His wife had just put their infant daughter down to sleep and was watching television in the living room with a member of the Dexter church congregation. Racing to the scene, King found a group of angry blacks outside his house, waving guns and knives and broken bottles ready to take their revenge on white Montgomery. The police struggled to keep the peace: Officers were threatening the crowd and the crowd threatened them right back. King rushed inside to find everyone safe in a back room. He then went out to confront the throng. Speaking from his damaged porch, he said his wife and daughter were unharmed; he begged the crowd not to give in to hostility. As King spoke, the mob fell silent. "We cannot solve this problem through retaliatory violence. We must meet violence with nonviolence," he urged. "We must love our white brothers, no matter what they do to us." He ended on a portentous note. "If I am stopped," he told the crowd, "this movement will not stop, because God is with the movement. Go home with this glowing faith and this radiant assurance."

The bombing horrified King's parents. His mother became physically ill and took to her bed. When King went to Atlanta shortly afterward, his father convened a meeting of community leaders to discuss whether his son should give up the battle in Montgomery. Martin saw the worry on their faces but insisted: "I have reached the point of no return." He knew that if he fought on, it would be painful for everyone who loved him, but if he ran away he'd have to face his own conscience. As he had told himself, he'd have to live with the knowledge that he "lacked the moral courage to stand by a cause to the end."

13

THE MONTGOMERY BUS boycott lasted more than a year. The city's black residents adhered to King's plea for nonviolent resistance, even when whites threatened them and bombed their houses. The buses remained empty despite cold and rain and escalating tensions with the mayor, the city commissioners, and the police. One evening, King was arrested for driving thirty miles an hour in a twenty-five-mile-an-hour zone. He was then taken on a harrowing ride in a police car and feared that he was going to be dumped before an angry mob in a desolate location. When he finally arrived at the city jail he was oddly relieved. "For the first time in my life," King recalled, "I had been thrown behind bars." He was soon released on bond.

To crack down on the protest, officials dredged up an old state law prohibiting boycotts and drew up a list of more than a hundred people for indictment, including King. Those targeted eagerly presented themselves to authorities, causing King to muse: "A once fear-ridden people had been transformed." Indictments were handed down but the chief culprit, in the eyes of the authorities, was Martin Luther King Jr. He was convicted, required to pay a fine of $500, plus court costs, or serve 386 days in jail, and released on bond, pending an appeal.

Along with the boycott, the activists filed suit in federal court arguing that bus segregation violated the Fourteenth Amendment to the Constitution guaranteeing equal protection for all citizens under the law. When the court agreed, the city appealed to the United States Supreme Court, led by Chief Justice Earl Warren, and lost: The high court ruled that bus segregation laws in Montgomery and throughout the state were unconstitutional. A federal order requiring integration of the buses arrived December 20, 1956. That evening a hopeful King spoke from the pulpit to an overflow crowd. "God struggles with us," he told the congregation, "and...the arc of the moral universe, although long, is bending toward justice." He instructed the congregants to return to the buses with calm dignity. A widely distributed flyer offered suggestions on how to integrate the buses smoothly, warning: "Do not deliberately sit by a white person, unless there is no other seat."

Blacks rode the buses again, taking their new, integrated seats in a respectful manner. But many in the white community were livid. Just hours after the Supreme Court's ruling, ten cars filled with white-robed members of the Ku Klux Klan rolled in a convoy through the black business district, followed by militant whites in other cars. "The Negroes along the busy thoroughfare ignored them completely and refused to be intimidated," reported the *Chicago Defender*.

By the end of December, desegregation had spurred several ugly moments. A black woman had been slapped by a young white as she left a bus; several white men had attacked a teenage black girl at a bus stop; snipers had fired at three buses; a pregnant black woman had been shot aboard a bus; and King's house had been hit by a shotgun blast.

The victory in Montgomery inspired the Reverend Fred Shuttlesworth of the Bethel Baptist Church in Birmingham to challenge segregation laws in his city, prompting a white backlash. On Christmas day, his parsonage was bombed, destroying his living room and slightly injuring his children. That same day, before the blast, Shuttlesworth preached at his Bethel Baptist Church, telling congregants: "Any time now, I'm lookin' for somebody to throw a stick of dynamite against my house." Afterward, a policeman, who was a member of the Ku Klux Klan, warned Shuttlesworth that the Klan was after him and he had better get out of town quickly. Strong-willed to the point of arrogance, Shuttlesworth was famous for his defiance and reckless bravery. "Well, you tell them that I'm not going out of town," he snapped right back at the officer. "I wasn't saved to run." The next month, in Montgomery, twelve sticks of dynamite landed on Martin Luther King Jr.'s front porch but failed to explode.

* * *

The eruption of violence revealed just how deeply bus integration had rattled the bigoted culture of Alabama. In the Northern white press and in the black newspapers, Martin Luther King Jr. was hailed as the hero of change in the South. He graced the cover of *Time* magazine on February 18, 1957, an honor that had been given successively a few weeks earlier to British prime minister Harold Macmillan and to conductor Leonard Bernstein. (Senator John F. Kennedy made his first appearance on a *Time* cover ten months later in December, when he began to look like a young prospect for the presidency.) The *Time* writer who came from the Atlanta bureau was himself abused by angry whites. "We know why you're in town and what you're planning to do, and you'd better not do it," a snarling voice warned him over the phone. In the February cover story, *Time* said of King: "In little more than a year [he] has risen from nowhere to become one of the Nation's remarkable leaders of men."

In an elegant analysis of the boycott, a prominent black journalist, Ethel Payne, suggested that King was at the forefront of a new type of political leadership in the South: the black pastor. In earlier days, pastors gave spiritual comfort and helped their flock endure the heavy burdens of daily life, leaving the pursuit of social progress to politicians, intellectuals, and NAACP lawyers. But in these early days of the civil rights movement, the churchmen had taken on a new role. "Today," Payne wrote in February 1956, "the Negro preacher is praying but he is also fighting for the democratic way of life for this people." The new era was being shaped by the rise of the political pastor. Calls for justice emanated from the church, and it was in the pews that protesters gathered their collective strength and then flowed out into the streets. In a piece a few months later, Payne noted that the NAACP's chief counsel, Thurgood Marshall, described King as "a natural born leader," and she enumerated King's rare combination of qualities. Not only was he "genuinely modest and self-effacing," but he was also a gifted orator. "He has the ability to translate into dramatic but simple terms the struggle of the people," she wrote. "The result is to inspire passionate fellowship from a people who were thirsty for leadership."

After his success in Montgomery, King fielded a flurry of accolades: citations from foundations, societies, and institutions, and honorary degrees. The organizers of the 1956 Democratic National Convention asked the civil rights leader to appear before its platform committee, where King declared that "segregation is evil [and] morally scandalous." He urged the federal government "to guarantee to all of its citizens the rights and privileges of full citizenship." His star rising, King landed a book contract to write his own story of the bus boycott. While writing *Stride Toward Freedom*, King consulted with Harris Wofford, whom he had met during the boycott. "From our first meeting I wanted to help King in any way I could," the white lawyer recalled. Wofford had studied in India and was an advocate of Gandhi's approach to politics and protest, and he recognized that King, too, appreciated Gandhi's techniques. He and King spent time discussing ways to adapt Gandhi's tactics to civil rights demonstrations. "Nonviolent direct action as a powerful new form of political persuasion was the Gandhian beam King was following," Wofford observed. "More and more King was coming to believe, with Gandhi, that the art of politics involved the skillful dramatic use of symbolic acts." After the boycott, Wofford helped King visit India so the civil rights leader could meet with people who had worked with Gandhi.

In May 1957, King and other leaders sought to awaken President Dwight Eisenhower to the urgency of civil rights by organizing a Prayer Pilgrimage for Freedom in Washington, D.C. The pilgrimage, planned for the third anniversary of the Supreme Court's *Brown v. Board of Education* ruling that desegregated public schools, aimed to attract fifty thousand people to the Lincoln Memorial for prayers, songs, and speeches. It drew roughly half that number but nonetheless was a stirring, peaceful demonstration for equal rights. In the closing address, King roused the audience by demanding: "Give us the ballot." And the pilgrims chanted back: "Give us the ballot." Many in the crowd had never witnessed King onstage, and his appearance served as a national milestone for him. The *New York Amsterdam News*, a black paper, declared that the boycott pastor had emerged as "the number one leader of sixteen million Negroes in the United States.... At this point in his career, the people will follow him anywhere."

President Eisenhower apparently also was listening. After long hesitation, he finally invited King and other civil rights leaders to the White House before the 1958 midterm elections largely to raise the Republican Party's profile among blacks. King was now on a whirlwind travel schedule. Over the past twelve months, according to *Jet* magazine, which called him the "Man on the Go," the much-in-demand pastor logged 780,000 miles in airplanes and gave 208 speeches, most of them for no pay; usually he accepted money only to cover his expenses.

But the attention heaped on King irritated other boycott leaders. "King's colleagues felt that he was taking too many bows and enjoying them," wrote L. D. Reddick, a friend and admirer. "He was forgetting that victory in Montgomery had been the result of collective thought and collective action." Some major black figures, however, found King's style and steadiness attractive. The writer James Baldwin, who was wary of preachers and their all-too-typical self-importance, discovered after meeting King in 1957 that he was something different. Baldwin was surprised by the pastor's apparent lack of "the hideous piety which is so prevalent in his profession." The writer was genuinely surprised: King was "not like any preacher I have ever met before."

Harry Belafonte, also skeptical of preachers, agreed to meet with King in Harlem in the spring of 1956 when the bus boycott was in full swing. After King delivered a sermon at the Abyssinian Baptist Church, the two men sat down together at a small table in a basement classroom. Belafonte, who had two number one albums on the *Billboard* charts that year—*Calypso* and *Belafonte*—was drawn to King's self-doubt. The young pastor sounded both inspired and daunted by the task that lay before him, and he sought Belafonte's advice. "I am called upon to do things I cannot do and yet I cannot dismiss the calling," he told the singer. "I need your help. I have no idea where this movement is going." Belafonte was so impressed he signed on to help, giving freely of his time, money, and celebrity.

* * *

Fame and good friends could not, however, shield King from a string of personal crises after the boycott's success. In early September 1958, he arrived at a Montgomery, Alabama, courtroom with his wife, Coretta, in support of a fellow pastor's case. But he was prohibited from entering by a police sergeant who told him to "get the hell away from here."

When King hesitated, two policemen rushed him. "Boy, you done done it," said one of the cops. "Let's go." One of them grabbed King's arm, twisting it hard behind his back as he led him through the shocked crowd that had gathered for the hearing. Coretta watched as her husband was whisked away; one of the cops glanced over his shoulder. "Gal, you want to go, too?" he warned. "Just nod your head." With his usual composure, King caught her eye and whispered, "Don't say anything, darling." A photographer captured the scene: the lanky, nasty-eyed cop shoving along Martin Luther King Jr. in his suit and fedora with his arm behind his back. The image quickly became a public relations disaster for the city. As King was hustled into a cell, news stories ricocheted around the country accompanied by the photo that suggested if not police brutality at least wanton injustice. King was convicted of loitering and ordered to pay a fine of $14 or serve fourteen days in jail. Opting for the jail time, he was quickly released after a mysterious benefactor paid his fine; the funds, it was soon discovered, came out of the pocket of Montgomery police commissioner Clyde Sellers who, as he put it, saw King's choice of jail time as "just another publicity stunt."

King faced danger simply because of his new status as a high-profile public figure. In late September, he was in Harlem to promote his book *Stride Toward Freedom* when he nearly lost his life to an assassin. While signing copies of his book at a table in a department store, King was attacked by a mentally unstable black woman. He was unable to react before she drove a knifelike letter opener into his chest just below his collar. The blade lodged between his heart and a lung, just at the edge of the aorta, and remained there during the journey to the hospital. Had he sneezed, King learned later, he could have driven the blade into the aorta, puncturing it and causing his death.

If physical threats weren't enough, the young protest leader had already fallen under the suspicion of the federal government. An FBI office memorandum to Director J. Edgar Hoover, dated January 4, 1956, about a month after Rosa Parks refused to give up her seat, indicated that an agent was assigned "to find out all he could about Reverend MARTIN KING, colored minister in Montgomery and leader in the bus boycott...to uncover all the derogatory information he could about KING." A scrawled note at the top of the memo suggested the FBI's concern: "Agitation among Negroes."

14

IN EARLY 1960, Martin Luther King Jr. gave in to his father's insistence that he join him as copastor at the enormous Ebenezer Baptist Church in Atlanta. King was struggling with his conflicting loyalties: He was simultaneously leading the congregation at Dexter Baptist in Montgomery and speaking extensively around the country and expanding the Southern Christian Leadership Conference, the organization he'd established in Atlanta soon after the end of the bus boycott. The SCLC aimed to build on the work of the boycott and coordinate with black activists nationally to defeat segregation and discrimination.

The move made sense, but leaving Dexter and Montgomery was an emotional passage for King and his congregants; for it was here that the modern civil rights movement had taken root in the historic bus boycott; and it was here that King had been anointed as spiritual guide to the black revolution. But it was time for a change. In his resignation remarks before the congregation, King said: "Little did I know when I came to Dexter that in a few months a movement would commence in Montgomery that would change the course of my life forever.... Unknowingly and unexpectedly I was catapulted into the leadership...[and] at points I was unprepared for the symbolic role that history had thrust upon me." Now he intended to dedicate himself fully to the black struggle, and as the 1960 presidential race began to take shape, he warned the candidates that the nation was headed for years of confrontation. "The time has come for a broad, bold advance of the southern campaign for equality," he told reporters in announcing his departure from Dexter. "After prayerful consideration I am convinced that the psychological moment has come when a concentrated drive against injustice can bring great tangible gains." He spoke of launching aggressive campaigns for black voter registration and for the dismantling of every shred of segregation. He vowed to train young and old in the strategies of nonviolent social change.

If Montgomery's white community was overjoyed to see King go,

Atlanta's establishment was reluctant to have him back in the city of his birth. "Wherever M. L. King, Jr., has been there has followed in his wake a wave of crimes including stabbing, bombings, and inciting of riots," Georgia governor Ernest Vandiver complained. "For these reasons, he is not welcome to Georgia. Until now, we have had good relations between the races." King's father hurried to his son's defense, telling reporters Martin was "not coming to cause trouble. Instead of that, he had chosen the pulpit."

Nonetheless, King's white detractors tried to destroy him. In early May 1960, King and his wife were driving a white novelist to Emory University Hospital in Atlanta for her cancer treatments when a police officer pulled them over. The officer, no doubt, was inspired to act when he caught sight of blacks and whites mixing in the same car. Discovering the car had expired plates, the officer issued a citation. Georgia law required residents to get a new license within three months of moving to the state, but the civil rights leader was still driving with his old one from Alabama. Six months later his tiny infraction would play a public—some argued decisive—role in the 1960 presidential election.

In late May, a few weeks before his meeting with Kennedy, King confronted another legal hurdle. He was back in Montgomery, defending himself in court against trumped-up allegations of tax fraud. Prosecutors charged King with perjury on his tax returns, contending his income was higher than he swore it was on his Alabama state returns in 1956 and 1958. Of all his tribulations, these charges profoundly disturbed King, for they challenged his most prized qualities: his honesty and integrity. Even if he prevailed in court, he feared that public opinion would forever label him a financial fraud. "My enemies have previously done everything against me but attack my character and integrity," he said. "Though I am not perfect, if I have any virtues, the one of which I am most proud is my honesty where money is concerned." Indeed, King lived far more modestly than he might have, despite rumors that he had installed his family in a mansion, drove an expensive car, and had misappropriated funds from the black organizations he headed to buy luxuries. "I don't even wish it were true," he said. "I own just one piece of property, a 1954 Pontiac." And he pointed out to anyone who asked that he was renting his house.

Although the charges were false, King still felt the burden of guilt, believing that the ordeal was harming the movement and that people were losing faith in him. "I had never seen Martin affected so deeply," his wife, Coretta, recalled. "To see him in this frame of mind troubled me very much." It was small comfort to King that the black press was fully behind him. The *Chicago Defender* opined that Montgomery was engaging in age-old techniques to suppress "those who dare raise their voices against oppressive social prescriptions." The paper explained that King represented a danger to traditional Southern society. "What Alabama has been looking for was some kind of a ground on which to discredit the Rev. King and check his ever widening influence," the *Defender* noted. "For King today poses the greatest threat to the South's medieval ways of social life."

King's lawyer revealed the flaw in the prosecution's case through his cross-examination of the state's tax agent. The state's witness admitted that King's income looked higher than what he reported to tax officials when reimbursement for travel and other expenses were factored in; but for tax purposes these add-ons were not measures of his total income. Although King's innocence was clear, his chances of winning the case seemed remote, given he was a notorious black man facing judgment from an all-white jury in a Southern town. With King facing five years in prison, the twelve men on the jury deliberated for three hours and forty-five minutes on Saturday, May 28, before returning its verdict. King braced for the worst as the foreman announced that the jury found the defendant not guilty. A chorus of hallelujahs arose in the packed courtroom. King, stoic as usual, was emotionless, while his father and mother and wife all burst into tears. Speaking to reporters afterward, King stressed the lesson he took from the case. "The verdict represents a ray of hope for justice and understanding in the South," he declared. "This was Alabama's opportunity to say to the nation and the world that a Negro can get a just trial in the state and the jury demonstrated this in a noteworthy manner."

The following day, Sunday, King preached at Ebenezer Baptist Church in Atlanta. In the audience was the astute James Baldwin, who noticed a maturity in the young leader. "He did not look any older," Baldwin wrote of the preacher, "and yet there was a new note of anguish in his voice. He was speaking of his trial," and those who brought the false charges against him, "the torment, the spiritual state of people who are committed to a wrong, knowing it is wrong." With an abundance of generosity, King insisted these people "were not ruled by hatred, but by terror," and he told his parishioners that "these people, the potential destroyers of the person, must not be hated." Watching from his pew, Baldwin perceived that Martin Luther King Jr. "had looked on evil a long, hard, lonely time." Searching for the mainspring of King's anguish, the writer suggested: "Perhaps young Martin was finding a new and more somber meaning in the command: 'Overcome evil with good.' The command," Baldwin explained, "does not suggest that to overcome evil is to eradicate it."

In his postboycott years, King wore his disciplined public face far more often now than he ever had done in the past. Only some very close friends still saw the teasing mimic King could be in private. Baldwin recalled speaking with him in his office the day after his sermon at Ebenezer; it was only the second time the writer had met the preacher, and he found him "kind and attentive, but far away." Historian David Garrow quotes King telling an acquaintance: "I'm sure I've become more serious. I don't think I've lost my sense of humor, but I know I've let many opportunities go by without using it. I seldom joke in my speeches anymore. I forget to."

15

LESS THAN A month after his tax-fraud acquittal, Martin Luther King Jr. arrived at the Kennedy apartment on Central Park South for his breakfast meeting with John Kennedy. Both men were rising stars, but at the moment King held the advantage: Kennedy was a politician on the make and he needed King. Although Kennedy was the front-runner, he was not assured the Democratic presidential nomination; and if he led the ticket, the White House was far from guaranteed. Questions about his fitness for the highest office still dogged him: His Catholic religion bothered many voters; his youth and inexperience were liabilities in a tense, Cold War environment; and his image as a playboy and rich dilettante troubled some Americans. Leaders of his party were working behind the scenes on behalf of other potential nominees. Former First Lady Eleanor Roosevelt was pushing hard for Adlai Stevenson, and she still disdained Kennedy for his failure to act against Senator Joseph McCarthy.

She was unimpressed by his book on political courage, preferring instead evidence of real grit on the political battlefield. As she put it, witheringly: "I would hesitate to place the difficult decisions that the next President will have to make with someone who understands what courage is and admires it but has not quite the independence to have it."

As a bona fide hero, King had much to offer Kennedy. An endorsement, or even positive words, could cloak the senator in the vestments of the civil rights movement and possibly even bestow on him the courage that King had demonstrated in the struggle. As one of several contenders for the White House, Kennedy had little to offer King other than promises, and given the senator's track record, the civil rights leader had reason to be wary.

The relationship between the senator and the pastor was in some ways defined by the way Northern whites interacted with blacks throughout history. James Baldwin, writing in the July 1960 issue of *Esquire* magazine, described the difference between Southern and Northern whites, ascribing to Southerners a passion about the Negro, albeit often a tormented, brutal one. Baldwin proposed that there was a time before the Civil War when the white Southerner imagined he loved the Negro and the Negro loved him. By contrast, the Northerner did not have these intense, often extreme reactions to black people. "None of this is true for the Northerner," Baldwin observed. Without referencing Kennedy, Baldwin had identified the elite senator's relationship to blacks at this point in his life, his casual indifference to them, except where political expediency was concerned. Writing of the Northern white, Baldwin continued: "Negroes represent nothing to him personally, except, perhaps, the dangers of carnality. He never sees Negroes. Southerners see them all the time. Northerners never think about them whereas Southerners are never really thinking of anything else. Negroes are, therefore, ignored in the North and are under surveillance in the South, and suffer hideously in both places."

Baldwin understood that the route to real change had to run through the North; he faulted the North for not tackling its own detachment. His *Esquire* piece was a pointed, perhaps unintended, critique of the obligations that lay ahead for the next president; indeed, it was a warning to an aspirant such as John F. Kennedy. "Neither the Southerner nor the Northerner is able to look on the Negro simply as a man," Baldwin regretted. "They are two sides of the same coin, and the South will not change— *cannot* change—until the North changes."

Upstairs, in the Central Park South apartment, Kennedy and King sat in solitary conference over breakfast. Both were willing listeners, but on this occasion it was Kennedy who did most of the talking. From his briefing by Harris Wofford, Kennedy knew that King had deep reservations about him and that he had to convey a sincere commitment to black justice to win the pastor's trust. King had not forgotten that Kennedy ignored black interests when voting on civil rights legislation in 1957 nor that the senator had cozied up to Southern segregationists to broaden his national appeal. It troubled King that Kennedy was so ambitious that "he would compromise basic principles to become President."

To combat King's wariness, Senator Kennedy said all the right things. When King expressed disappointment in President Eisenhower's civil rights commitment, Kennedy vowed to throw the weight of the White House behind black equality. "He agreed that there was a need for strong executive leadership and that this had not existed," King later remembered. Under the current administration, King pointed out, the pursuit of justice had languished; without a determined push by a new president, black rights were certain to suffer further setbacks. Kennedy assured King that he was ready to change the course of the civil rights movement. "If he received the nomination and was elected," he told King, "he could give this kind of leadership."

King outlined the top items on his agenda: an executive order ending discrimination in federally funded housing, a broad voting rights drive, and the introduction of strong civil rights legislation. Kennedy was in agreement with all these aims. "He felt that the whole question of assuring the right to vote was a key and basic question," King later recalled, "and that this would be one of the immediate things that he would look into."

King didn't hesitate to express his skepticism. "I was very frank about what I felt," he said. He challenged the senator on his 1957 vote on civil rights legislation. Kennedy had sided with segregationists on a complicated procedural motion that aimed to water down the bill. In response to King's objection Kennedy at first leaned on his previous explanation for his vote. "He gave me some legal answer," King recalled. But failing to sway King, the senator then sought to persuade him that his views had changed, that he was a more enlightened man now because of recent developments in the civil rights movement. "If he had to face the issue again," King later said about Kennedy, "he would reverse his position." Explaining this transformation, Kennedy said that blacks' persistence in trying to desegregate lunch counters had a powerful effect on him. "The sit-in movement had caused him to reevaluate his thinking," King recalled. "This movement had pointed up the injustices and the indignities that Negroes were facing all over the South and that, for this reason, he had reevaluated many of these things."

While King was impressed by Kennedy's "willingness to learn more about civil rights," as the pastor put it, he detected wide gaps in the senator's knowledge. "He did not have the grasp and the comprehension of the depths and dimensions of the problem," King concluded. Something else troubled him: Although Kennedy acknowledged the issues and spoke persuasively of his desire to tackle them, he did not convince King that he possessed any passion for the black cause. When Kennedy spoke of civil rights, he addressed the issue as a politician might discuss any domestic issue. In King's eyes, racial injustice transcended concerns about the economy or tax rates. Conditions in the South and in the slums were a profound legacy of America's history and required something beyond routine national discourse. King had a strict criterion for a leader of civil rights. In the black churches and in the White House, a leader had to embrace the moral imperative for change, or no real progress was possible. In this first meeting, King witnessed the cool detachment with which Kennedy addressed civil rights. "He had a long intellectual commitment," King acknowledged, "but...he didn't quite have the emotional commitment." Kennedy, King noted, was too isolated from the black community. "He didn't know too many Negroes personally," King said. "He had never really had the personal experience of knowing the deep groans and passionate yearnings of the Negroes for freedom."

For the most part, the secrecy of the meeting was maintained. The *New York Times* mentioned the breakfast only in passing three days later while reporting on other civil rights issues. King left the apartment pleased by the candor of the conversation. But he told Harris Wofford that Senator Kennedy lacked a "depthed understanding" of civil rights. For his part, Kennedy told Wofford that he believed he had "made some progress" in bringing King over to his side. The following day King wrote to Chester Bowles, a liberal Democrat and Kennedy foreign policy advisor, that he was "impressed by the forthright and honest manner in which [Kennedy] discussed the civil rights question. I have no doubt that he would do the right thing on the issue if he were elected president."

King also reported back to his friend Harry Belafonte. His appraisal was somewhat more honest than what he might have felt comfortable telling white political figures like Wofford or Bowles. According to Belafonte, King said there were "no sparks on either side. In fact, the two were fairly nonplussed by each other." Belafonte said that Kennedy asked King for an endorsement, a gesture the civil rights leader refused to make; as head of the Southern Christian Leadership Conference, King had a standing policy of remaining nonpartisan.

Writing years later, Belafonte portrayed the breakfast meeting as a moment when the two savvy politicians then moving into the national consciousness realized that their lives might become intertwined. "The stage had been set for a curious, long-running drama," he explained, "in which Kennedy and King would test each other warily, again and again, wondering how much each could trust the other, seeking common ground in private even as they staked out their differences in public."

16

AFTER HIS BREAKFAST with King, Senator Kennedy met behind closed doors with members of the New York State Liberal Party, and when he emerged for a press conference, his public comments were directed at King and black Americans as much as his hosts. He told reporters that black justice was far more than a law-and-order issue. Addressing a point of crucial importance to King, Kennedy vowed to bring "strong moral leadership" to the presidency. "That leadership," he declared, "will be exercised until every American, of every color and faith, has achieved equal access to all of American life—and that means equal access to the voting booth, to the schoolroom, to jobs, to housing and to the lunch counters." The *New York Times* coverage stressed another issue raised in the press conference. In a story headlined KENNEDY ASSURES LIBERALS HE SEEKS NO HELP IN SOUTH, the *Times* reported that the senator hoped to win the Democratic nomination "without a single Southern vote in the convention."

Kennedy unveiled his new tone in Washington, too. Soon after the *Times* story hit the streets, the senator attended a luncheon for African diplomats where he called equal rights "essentially a moral issue," and again he underscored the need for moral leadership in the White House. He voiced strong support of black protests, zeroing in on the peaceful sit-in movement, saying that "some unrest and turmoil and tension [were] part of the price of change." The sit-ins, he asserted, posed no reason for concern. "It is a good sign—a sign of increased popular responsibility, of good citizenship, of the American spirit coming alive again," Kennedy told the diplomats. "It is in the American tradition to stand up for one's rights—even if the new way to stand up for one's rights is to sit down."

With a new spirit, Kennedy addressed important black issues one by one as though ticking them off a checklist. Yet, blacks were not falling in line. To some, his focus on the morality of civil rights sounded hollow; his words seemed calculated for winning the nomination and did not reflect his actions over the years. The *Chicago Defender* expressed the mood in an editorial a few days into the Kennedy blitz. "After a long, unwise silence on the Negro question," the paper cautioned, "Mr. Kennedy at long last has been coaxed into grappling with an issue he would rather have avoided." Conceding that he had begun to hit the right issues, the paper nonetheless charged that his long silence and his welcome among Southern politicians have "given rise to an aura of suspicion." His latest remarks were "fine words expressed in their proper context," the paper allowed. "But they are uttered too late, we fear, to change the anti-Kennedy climate of opinion which has been in the process of development for quite a while among a substantial segment of the Negro population."

Jackie Robinson was still immune to the Kennedy charm, despite the senator's crusade to change the baseball hero's opinion. A few weeks before the Democratic National Convention, Robinson agreed to meet with Kennedy. At the outset, the conversation was courteous and candid. But Robinson was offended when the senator admitted that he knew few blacks and still had more to learn about the community's suffering. "Although I appreciated his truthfulness in the matter," Robinson said, "I was appalled that he could be so ignorant of our situation and be bidding for the highest office in the land." From there the meeting deteriorated: Robinson condemned Kennedy for his apparent friendship with John Patterson, the white supremacist governor of Alabama, whom the senator had entertained for breakfast in his Georgetown home in 1959. Robinson rejected Kennedy's attempt to explain away the breakfast as a courtesy extended to a state leader. During the Montgomery bus boycott, Patterson served as Alabama's attorney general and had tried to quash the protest by seeking several court injunctions. He was such a virulent enemy of the civil rights movement that when he ran for governor in 1958, he was supported by the Ku Klux Klan.

Eager to make amends, Kennedy asked Robinson what it would take to win his support. But the baseball hero misinterpreted him and became incensed, believing the wealthy candidate wanted to buy him off. "Look, Senator," he told Kennedy, "I don't want any of your money. I'm just interested in helping the candidate who I think will be best for black America." To make matters worse, Robinson was sure that during the meeting Kennedy refused to look him in the eye—further evidence of the senator's insincerity.

Afterward Kennedy wrote a long letter to Robinson, praising him for his civil rights efforts, stressing his own desire "for an end to all discrimination," and reiterating the innocence of his meeting with Patterson. In a reply five days later, Robinson said he still needed "more evidence regarding your sincerity in these matters" but he was "willing to wait and see what develops at the convention and what you do if nominated." Robinson, apparently, was still ticked off about one aspect of their encounter. "Please don't consider me presumptuous but I would like to make one suggestion," he wrote. "While trying to impress anyone with your sincerity you must be able to look them squarely in the eye."

Although still offended, Robinson toned down his public criticism. In his *New York Post* column of July 6 he described Kennedy as an "impressive man" who had a "willingness to learn," then added grudgingly: "Sen. Kennedy is a little late in seeking to make himself clear, after 14 years in Congress. But if he is sincere, there is still time to catch up."

17

As BOTH PARTIES prepared for their national conventions in the summer, Martin Luther King Jr. and other black leaders warned that they had to earn the black vote. King joined A. Philip Randolph, the revered labor leader and founder of the Brotherhood of Sleeping Car Porters, to complain publicly about the scant attention given to equal rights. Several weeks before the parties convened, King and Randolph stepped before CBS News cameras in New York to announce plans for massive demonstrations at both the Democratic and Republican national conventions. Black demands, they said, had been met by "the condescending smile of inert government, by incredible political deception and double-dealing, by an ingrained indifference to the democratic ideals of equality and freedom." Randolph might very well have been speaking directly to Jack Kennedy when he said that neither political party had made civil rights a significant issue in the election, adding that no "single candidate for the presidency has completely earned the right to expect the support of Negro voters in this campaign."

On Sunday, July 10, the day before the start of the Democratic National Convention, blacks marched two miles through the Los Angeles streets waving banners and chanting. Some seven thousand marchers then filled the Shrine Auditorium to hear from the candidates. Lyndon Johnson, who had announced a late bid, sent a representative to speak on his behalf. Johnson was largely reviled by the black community: He was not only a Southern senator from Texas but also the Senate majority leader who was instrumental in watering down the civil rights legislation in 1957. Kennedy was also scheduled to speak, and as he rode in a car toward the auditorium he learned that Johnson's stand-in was booed off the stage. Kennedy, nervous about his own reception, turned to Vel Phillips, an NAACP state leader from Wisconsin who was accompanying him, and fretted: "I'm still not sure that it is wise to go." Phillips, a thirty-six-year-old, light-skinned activist, had developed a "small crush" on Kennedy when she saw him on television nominating Adlai Stevenson at the 1956 Democratic National Convention in Chicago; she had fallen out with Kennedy over his vote on the Civil Rights Act of 1957 but was later brought back into the fold after the candidate spoke to her privately and acknowledged his mistakes. In the car heading to the rally, Phillips encouraged the candidate, but he was still worried: "Vel, it would be a very bad thing at this point if...they booed me right out."

Inside the auditorium, Kennedy approached the rostrum amid light applause, which the *Washington Post* described as "perfunctory." There was also some booing, which prompted an NAACP official to lecture the crowd briefly on its manners. At the rostrum, Kennedy smiled, exuding the charm that had delighted Vel Phillips and so many others. Looking unruffled, he launched into his speech. "We meet on the eve of a great national convention," he began and moved quickly into his promises. "I want no compromise of basic principles," he told the crowd, "no evasion of basic controversies—and no second-class citizenship for any American anywhere in this country." Addressing sensitivities over any deals he had struck with Southern politicians, he added: "And I have not made nor will I make any commitments inconsistent with these objectives." When he vowed to use the "immense moral authority of the White House" in the battle for civil rights, the audience applauded. Journalists offered varying critiques of Kennedy's performance, one asserting that the senator had turned the crowd to his favor and another characterizing the applause as a mere courtesy. Afterward, Kennedy was characteristically upbeat. Before departing, he had a few light moments with Martin Luther King Jr., meeting just long enough to renew their acquaintance.

When King addressed the crowd, he was combative, criticizing the South for closing schools as a way to defy the Supreme Court's six-year-old order to desegregate the classrooms. He called on the government to federalize schools that refused to act in accordance with the law and persisted in depriving black students of equal education. He warned both parties, Democratic and Republican—whichever one occupied the White House in 1961—that protests against segregation would go on as long as necessary. "The cause of justice and freedom has been betrayed by both political parties," King told the crowd. "We have looked patiently to Washington for our Constitutional rights, and then we have found a conspiracy of apathy and hypocrisy. Now we are tired. We are compelled to take the struggle into our own limited hands."

Although King talked tough, lobbing insults like a political outsider, he and other black leaders had been consulted on the contents of the Democrats' civil rights plank. The plank, which Chester Bowles and Harris Wofford ushered through six drafts, contained some zealous proposals. It promised action on voting rights; proposed that every school district under the Supreme Court's desegregation ruling submit a plan for compliance by 1963; backed empowerment of the attorney general to work through the courts to ensure civil rights; asserted the executive powers of the president to demand equal employment opportunities and integration within the federal government. Several of the proposals mirrored demands put forward by King and the other civil rights leaders.

The Kennedy camp vigorously supported the platform, though it's uncertain how closely either John or Bobby had read it; neither Kennedy was much interested in the drafting stages. Yet both brothers wanted it known at the convention that they were fully in favor of the proposals. When Joseph Rauh, a leading civil rights lawyer, saw Jack Kennedy on the first morning of the convention, the candidate assured him that he was going "all out" on civil rights and that he wanted the platform committee to have a "blank check" on writing its prescriptions. On that same morning, Kennedy aide Arthur Schlesinger remembered, Bobby Kennedy climbed up onto a chair in room 8314 of the Hotel Biltmore to speak to the campaign staff before they set off to drum up delegate support for the senator. Bobby was in shirtsleeves, his tie loosened. "I want to say a few words about civil rights," he began. "We have the best civil rights plank the Democratic Party has ever had. I want you fellows to make it clear to your delegations that the Kennedy forces are unequivocally in favor of this plank and that we want it passed in the convention. Those of you who are with southern delegations make it absolutely clear how we stand on civil rights. Don't fuzz it up." When the plank came before the full platform committee, it passed by a vote of sixty-six to twenty-four.

Martin Luther King Jr. was as effusive about the civil rights plank as Robert Kennedy. In an interview with the *Montgomery Advertiser*, he lauded the work of the platform committee. "I think it's the most positive, dynamic and meaningful civil rights plank that has ever been adopted by either party," he said.

On the third day of the convention, Kennedy won the Democratic nomination, beating back a strong challenge from Lyndon Johnson. But he immediately squandered any goodwill he might have built with blacks when he chose Johnson as his running mate. Kennedy had several other strong choices, including Hubert Humphrey and Missouri senator Stuart Symington. Johnson, in his own bid for the presidential nomination, had played especially rough, pounding away at rumors of Kennedy's poor health and alienating the candidate's brother Bobby. From a political perspective, Johnson brought several attributes to the ticket. As a Texan he could help round up Southern Democrats, and as a Protestant he could help blunt opposition to Kennedy's Catholicism. Blacks, however, doubted his commitment to civil rights. In a radio interview, King said: "I was certainly disappointed when Senator Johnson was nominated to run for vice president. I think at times he has compromised basic principles.

There is no doubt about the fact that he has not been a strong civil rights man." But King, ever hopeful, joked that as a pastor he believed in the possibility of a man's conversion. "I think he took the nomination in order to become an American rather than a Texan with the sectional yoke of the South," he observed. "And I believe more and more he will move toward liberal positions on the Negro question."

Following the convention, Kennedy kept up his courtship of blacks, particularly King and Robinson, although both men were elusive. After the Republicans nominated Richard Nixon as their candidate, Kennedy suffered a blow: The prickly and popular Robinson announced that he believed Nixon was "better qualified" and "more aggressive on civil rights" than Kennedy. Robinson even signed on to campaign for Nixon, taking a leave of absence from his executive position at the Chock Full o'Nuts Corporation and suspending his *New York Post* column.

In an expected tight election, the black vote was seen as an important weight on the scale. By one estimate, black voters could deliver victories in six key states: New York, Pennsylvania, California, Ohio, Illinois, and Michigan, which together accounted for 181 electoral votes out of the 267 votes needed to win the presidency. "Just how important is the Negro voter?" asked the *Chicago Defender*. "All you have to do is study the statistical data to understand the frenzy now being shown in both parties as they seek to curry his favor." The paper described efforts across the nation to bolster voter registration, revealing that of the 9.5 million black Americans of voting age in the previous presidential election in 1956 only 3.5 million voted, or 37 percent, compared with 58 percent of eligible white voters. The paper stressed the importance of black voters in the South and noted the obstacles they faced in exercising their right; if voting registration drives succeeded only marginally, the results in the South could be significant. Capturing the support of Martin Luther King Jr. now became critical for possibly bringing a key constituency to the Kennedy side.

Soon after Robinson went over to Nixon, Kennedy sought another private meeting with King. Juggling their schedules, Harris Wofford finally arranged a second get-together at Kennedy's Georgetown home in mid-September. Again the candidate asked for King's endorsement and again heard King explain that he could not publicly support either candidate. By now King had come to believe in Kennedy's commitment to civil rights; indeed, he had concluded that "he was the best man" for the presidency. But an endorsement was impossible. As the two men chatted, it became clear that Kennedy had to find a way to earn the trust not just of King but of the entire black population. King recalled telling him: "Something dramatic must be done to convince the Negroes that you are committed on civil rights."

That opportunity would come in sensational fashion just days before voters went to the polls—it would be the October surprise of the 1960 election.

PART TWO

A CALL TO CORETTA

18

BEFORE DAWN, ON Wednesday, October 26, 1960, Martin Luther King Jr. was sleeping in a prison cell in DeKalb County, Georgia, when sheriff deputies aimed their flashlight beams into his face and barked at him to get up. They handcuffed him, shackled his legs, and hustled him out of the cell. It was 4 a.m. Hurried along, he asked repeatedly for an explanation, but the men said nothing. With a terrible foreboding, King soon found himself seated in the back of a police car rolling into the night; the only light came from the headlamps piercing the darkness.

Like all black men, King feared the chilling portent of a late-night drive into the countryside; it had happened to others, the stories he'd heard were horrific, the final scenes were unbearable: a small crowd milling about on a lonely road staring in silence at a body hanging from a tree or bunched on the ground with a fatal bullet wound.

At home in Atlanta, Coretta King knew nothing of her husband's ominous ride. She was six months pregnant with their third child, and she had already had an emotional week.

* * *

King hadn't wanted to join the student-led sit-in. But the band of youths, members of the Student Nonviolent Coordinating Committee, insisted. The SNCC, which had been launched in April in response to the sit-ins in Southern cities, was well-organized and impatient. Its target was one of Atlanta's venerable institutions, Rich's department store; its goal: to desegregate the store's snack bars and restaurants. The young activists urged King to come along—and go to jail with them—to draw attention to their campaign. King advised the students to hold off until after the presidential election now just weeks away; but the students saw an opportunity to force the candidates to address the issue of segregation. If King were arrested with dozens of young protesters, then both contenders would have no choice but to speak out. "The plan was we would send telegrams to Nixon and to Kennedy and ask them to take a position on the civil rights movement here," said student leader Lonnie C. King, a muscular ex-boxer and Navy veteran. "We thought that with Dr. King being involved in it... we would really see where these guys stand."

To allow for his absence, King had scheduled an out-of-town event for October 19, the day of the sit-in, but that event had fallen through. Now King had another excuse. Less than a month earlier, he had appeared in a DeKalb County court before Judge J. Oscar Mitchell to face the charges from May over his out-of-date driver's license and expired car plates. Judge Mitchell dismissed the plates charge and imposed a $25 fine and twelve months probation on the second charge. If King violated any federal, state, or municipal laws during the year, he'd be in violation of his probation. An arrest during a sit-in would put him in legal jeopardy.

His father, the Reverend Martin Luther King Sr., pastor of Ebenezer Baptist, opposed the students' confrontational style. Daddy King preferred a slower approach that sought integration through the courts rather than through protest. He and "bullheaded" Lonnie King, as he described him, argued over whether King should participate and "ended up heatedly denouncing each other." The students were not intimidated by Daddy King, and they hounded his son to take part in the action.

Martin found himself in a delicate spot. Since his success with the Montgomery bus boycott four years earlier he had led few, if any, protests and had taken little direct action himself on behalf of black justice. For the most part, he had been on an extended speaking tour, accepting accolades, spreading his vision of nonviolent protest, promoting his book about the boycott, expanding the Southern Christian Leadership Conference, and building up his national and international profile. His many victory laps had raised the ire of some black leaders. The black newspaper *Pittsburgh Courier* didn't mince words, saying: "Jealousy among Negro leaders is so thick it can be cut with a knife."

The young protesters had grown dissatisfied with the pace of progress; they acknowledged the significance of the 1954 Supreme Court ruling *Brown v. Board of Education* as a turning point in racial justice. But after six years what real change had it brought? The students were infused with hope and youthful energy, and the sit-in movement was its expression. King had offered oratorical support but was in many ways an onlooker; if he remained aloof, he risked eroding his stature. To validate his leadership he needed to sit down in a segregated dining room with the students and get marched off to prison with them. These activists had gotten under his skin. Here was a man who had stared down racist threats and bombings to desegregate Montgomery's buses; his reward was unimaginable fame and distinction. But now his moral authority was dimming. Had Da Lawd, as he was mockingly called by some, become soft? These young, strong-willed protesters demanded that King reclaim his courage.

Their plan was to walk into Rich's snack bar on the Crystal Bridge over Forsyth Street and demand service. The sight of blacks swarming the whites-only counter would ensure a call to the police and a trip to the station for the participants. By hitting Rich's, the students were sending a message to all of Atlanta. Rich's was the city's largest department store and a cornerstone of the community; its credo was customer service, low prices, and easy credit. Atlanta residents turned out for the annual Christmas tree lighting, raved over the store's coconut cake, and kids rode the famed Pink Pig monorail in ecstasy. At Rich's, blacks were welcome to shop; they were free to spend their money but not free to rest their feet in the dining areas. Many blacks had a Rich's charge card. "They viewed that Rich's charge account as a necessity, easy credit, pretty good terms," Lonnie King explained.

The students were determined to raise the consciousness not only of white Atlanta but also of black shoppers: It was time to underscore the incompatibility of patronizing a store that heeded the city's segregationist customs. A black shopper needing a restroom had to leave Rich's and find a colored one somewhere else; a black wanting a sip of water had to go outside and find a colored drinking fountain. Lonnie King and his student comrades wanted black shoppers to boycott the store. "All we're asking you to do," he told blacks on the street, "is just don't buy, just stay at home." And they drew up a slogan: "Close out your charge account with segregation, open up your account with freedom."

The students' passion—and conscience—were impossible for Martin Luther King Jr. to ignore. Despite his father's reservations—and his own—King gave in. But his decision was largely forced upon him. As Andrew Young, a leader of the Southern Christian Leadership Conference, explained: The students "literally shamed him into gettin' involved in the Atlanta movement."

The day before the sit-in, student leader Lonnie King laid out the stakes. "Well, Martin, you've got to go to jail," he told King. "You are the spiritual leader of the Movement, and you were born in Atlanta, Georgia, and I think it would add tremendous impetus if you would go."

"Well, where you going to go tomorrow?" King asked.

"I'm going to be on the bridge down at Rich's."

"Well, I'll meet you on the bridge tomorrow at ten o'clock," King agreed.

On Wednesday, October 19, word of the sit-in was buzzing throughout the city. No one was surprised when King and the students arrived at the snack bar. The police were waiting, but the managers declined to have the protesters arrested, spoiling their plan for a well-publicized night in jail. Undeterred, the demonstrators marched off to an elegant tea room on the sixth floor called the Magnolia Room. Stepping past the tall white columns framing the entrance, the students found themselves in a dining spot steeped in Southern charm. The tables were covered in mimosa-yellow linen and the walls were painted dark green and creamy white to evoke the magnolia blossom. Women dined here in chic hats and white gloves. The menu offered, among other Southern dishes, a New Orleans shrimp cocktail followed by a Plantation Salad—served by black waitresses dressed like mammies. Black patrons were not welcome. Defying hallowed customs, King and the student protesters refused to leave, and this time, store officials ordered police to arrest them. King and thirty-five others were carted off to prison for violating an antitrespass law.

When King was brought before a judge later in the day he refused bond, saying he and the other protesters did nothing wrong by seeking service like any diner. "I cannot in all good conscience accept bail," he told the judge. "I will stay in jail a year, if necessary." He agreed to leave prison only if the charges were dropped. In notes King prepared before his court appearance he said it was his "moral obligation" to remain in jail. According to a newspaper report, he told the court: "It is our sincere hope that the acceptance of suffering on our part will serve to awaken the dozing consciousness of our community."

After King and the thirty-five students were arrested, waves of other young activists hit eating establishments across the city, including subsequent runs at Rich's; the sit-ins at other dining locations passed without incident. Only Rich's had protesters arrested. By Thursday night, King and more than sixty other demonstrators were behind bars in city and county jails while Atlanta's leaders scrambled for a resolution.

19

THE ARRESTS POSED a dilemma for both presidential candidates. Neither Kennedy nor Nixon wanted to risk alienating white Southern voters just weeks before the election by speaking out on behalf of King and the protesters; but to do nothing was to miss a chance to galvanize black voters North and South. In the Kennedy camp, zealous civil rights aide Harris Wofford had watched from afar as the sit-in unfolded and King and his fellow protesters sat in jail for two nights. By Saturday he was scolding himself for his inaction. He recalled thinking, "What an incompetent civil rights man I am for Kennedy when my friend, King, was in jail in Atlanta and I hadn't done a thing about it or thought about it or imagined what ought to be done about it."

Unable to stand idly by, Wofford phoned a powerful Atlanta attorney named Morris Abram and urged him to use his influence to free King. Morris was a longtime civil rights advocate, a Jew who grew up in rural south Georgia where he gained a perspective on life as an outsider. He became the first Jewish Rhodes scholar and used his brains and his gift of oratory to champion the causes of the oppressed. Among his passions, he led the campaign to prohibit the Ku Klux Klan from burning crosses and wearing hoods to hide their faces.

Wofford caught Abram on Saturday morning just as the lawyer was going out with his nine-year-old daughter for "her promised day with Daddy." Wofford insisted that his phoning was a private, back-channel effort, not instigated by the campaign. He stressed that "Senator Kennedy did not know of my call." Nonetheless, Wofford conveyed—possibly speaking out of line—that Kennedy "would appreciate a satisfactory resolution, with King's release from jail as soon as possible." He implored

Abram to immediately press the case with Atlanta mayor William Hartsfield. When Abram pointed out that he was on his way out the door with
his daughter, Wofford had a solution: "Take her with you." He then
coached Abram, advising him to tell Hartsfield that after King's release
the mayor could claim he had acted "because of Senator Kennedy's interest and concern."

When Abram phoned Hartsfield offering Wofford's strategy, the
mayor felt he had been handed a gift. He was already engaged in intri-
cate negotiations for the protesters' release. That Saturday morning, he
had met in his office with a group of black leaders. Getting King and the
protesters out of jail required Hartsfield to perform a delicate dance with
an array of partners: the police, the prosecutor, black leaders, Richard
Rich—the department store owner who had pressed the charges—and
King and the protesters, who insisted on leaving jail only on their own
terms.

Now, the crafty mayor was able to bring pressure to bear on all the
parties by invoking the Kennedy name. "Yeah, come down at once,"
Hartsfield told Abram. With his daughter in tow, Abram rushed to City
Hall.

While Mayor Hartsfield had been ridiculed as bombastic and glory
seeking, he was also a perceptive politician who was in some ways an ally
of the protesters. Abram recognized a "rugged decency" in the mayor
and believed he was an example of a "distinct and marvelous southern
prototype, the rough-hewn, even comical character who knows the difference between right and wrong and has the guts to act accordingly and the
wits to survive." From the 1920s, when he was elected to the Atlanta city
council, through his years in the Georgia state legislature in the 1930s,
and finally as Atlanta mayor off and on beginning in 1936, Hartsfield
demonstrated an uncommon sensitivity to historical trends and an appreciation for the evolving role of the city's blacks.

In Daddy King's eyes, Hartsfield stood virtually alone among local
politicians in acting to improve social and business conditions for black
residents in the 1940s. In describing him, Daddy King said: "Only one
white politician made what I still consider the most sincere effort of that
time. And if he hadn't been alone so much of the time, his name might
be even better known outside the South." Daddy King remembered that
Hartsfield accorded blacks dignity and respect, which was rare from

whites, and particularly from community leaders. "He addressed black men and women as Mr., Miss, or Mrs., in defiance of an old southern custom that called for whites to speak to Negroes the way they spoke to children," Daddy King recalled. "Hartsfield was even photographed *shaking hands* with Negroes."

By 1960 the mayor was sympathetic to desegregation and certainly didn't want the protesters, particularly Martin Luther King Jr., in prison in his city for actions that put its whites-only rules in the spotlight. By seeking a swift resolution, he also was hoping to preserve the peace. Since the arrests, the Ku Klux Klan had marched through the streets in protest of the student activism and blacks who were picketing. Telegrams from across the country were piling up in city offices both praising the students and excoriating them.

After several hours of negotiation, an agreement was hammered out. "Sit down and hold on to your seat," Abram told Wofford on the phone. He explained that Hartsfield had just announced to the press that a settlement in the sit-in conflict had been reached thanks to the personal intervention of Senator John Kennedy. Wofford was suddenly in a panic. The mayor's statement went much further than he ever intended. Declaring that Kennedy had personally intervened posed serious repercussions not only for the campaign but for Wofford himself.

Before Wofford could speak, the mayor grabbed the phone. "This is Bill Hartsfield," he began. "Now I know that I ran with the ball farther than you expected, Harris, my boy, but I needed a peg to swing on and you gave it to me, and I've swung on it. You tell your senator that he and I are out on the limb together, so don't saw it off. I'm giving him the election on a silver platter, so don't pull the rug out from under me."

Hartsfield's announcement took the Kennedy campaign by surprise. "Hartsfield said *what*?" irate political aides howled at Wofford. "You did *what*?" Far from delivering the election to Kennedy, in the political strategists' view the mayor's action had the potential of handing the election to Nixon. An expression of sympathy for blacks at this late stage endangered Kennedy's support in Georgia and the rest of the South. Disgruntled whites were now likely to flock to Nixon. The political aides recognized that Kennedy needed the black vote, but this was no way to go about getting it. The campaign flew into damage control.

Press secretary Pierre Salinger rushed out a bland statement that straddled the controversy, neither a total denial of Kennedy's role nor a full commitment to King and the protesters. "As a result of having many calls from all over the country regarding the incident in Atlanta," the statement began, "Senator Kennedy directed that an inquiry be made to give him all the facts on that situation and a report on what properly should be done. The Senator is hopeful that a satisfactory outcome can be worked out."

While Hartsfield had kicked up a political storm, he had succeeded in his goal. Under his terms, black leaders and the business community agreed that the charges would be dropped, King and the students would be released, and talks would begin on desegregating downtown businesses. But on Sunday evening, October 23, four days after the sit-in, there was a hitch. All the protesters were set free except one: Martin Luther King Jr.

That night, the students celebrated their release at a black-owned, integrated restaurant called Paschal's. Coretta King, unaware her husband was still behind bars, showed up to greet him. But she couldn't find him. "I somehow did not want to ask about him, having a premonition of evil," she recalled. "It was so strange to sit there, amid the celebration, afraid of what I would hear." Then she heard it: "Someone told me, 'They kept Dr. King in jail.'"

* * *

The dark hand behind King's prolonged detention was the judge who had ruled on his driver's license misdemeanor in May. A foul-mouthed racist, Judge Oscar Mitchell refused to let King insult the Southern tradition of segregation as he had at Rich's and then simply go free. King's arrest at the Magnolia Room, the judge asserted, violated the terms of his probation, and he ordered King held in prison pending a hearing.

With the jail emptied of student protesters, King spent Monday night alone in his cell. On Tuesday morning two DeKalb County detectives in fedoras, a cigarette dangling from the lips of one and a cigar bobbing from the mouth of the other, shackled King in handcuffs and leg irons and took him by the arm toward a squad car. King, dressed in a suit and tie, was shoved into the backseat beside a German shepherd police dog for the ride to Judge Mitchell's courtroom.

Coretta, Daddy King, Martin's brother A.D. and sister Christine were all in the courtroom when the judge handed down his ruling. On the question of whether King had violated the probation terms of his suspended sentence on a misdemeanor, Judge Mitchell decreed: "I find the defendant guilty and sentence him to six months' hard labor in the State Penitentiary at Reidsville." Christine began crying, and Coretta, realizing that Martin would be in prison when their baby arrived in three months, also burst into tears. Transferring his own outrage, Daddy King turned on Coretta and reprimanded her for losing her self-composure. Martin was escorted back to his cell.

Later, when Coretta and Daddy King visited the prisoner, Martin implored his pregnant wife: "Corrie, dear, you have to be strong. I've never seen you like this. You have to be strong for me." Peering into the future, Coretta burst into tears again. Sensibly, Martin told his two visitors: "I think we must prepare ourselves for the fact that I am going to have to serve this time."

King was to be transferred to a maximum security prison in rural Georgia, housing some of the state's toughest criminals. The dangers were incalculable for a black man, especially one as controversial as King. A battery of lawyers and other supporters flew into action on his behalf. His chief lawyer, Donald Hollowell, worked on King's release, while preparing an appeal. King was willing to accept bail in this case, because his imprisonment had been set in motion by a traffic violation—not an issue of black justice such as a sit-in or other equal rights protest. But now, Judge Mitchell had turned the case into a matter of racial oppression and transformed King's jailing into a cause célèbre.

20

EARLY WEDNESDAY MORNING, October 26, having been suddenly roused from his sleep, Martin Luther King Jr. was in handcuffs and leg shackles riding into the Georgia countryside in the back of a squad car under the cover of darkness, drawing on reservoirs of courage and faith to steel his nerves. He had no idea where the two deputies were taking him. An hour passed, and he realized he was deep into "cracker" country where no one protested a lynching. By dawn, King discovered he had been granted a less evil fate as the squad car turned into the maximum security state prison in Reidsville.

But his danger was far from over. If he were put to hard labor, as the judge ordered, he would work side by side in a road gang with ruthless white criminals, many of them killers who had nothing to lose and every-thing to gain—national notoriety and prison respect—by murdering a black celebrity.

"Through contacts around the state," Daddy King said, "I was able to learn that the authorities were hoping to create a situation that would result in M.L.'s being killed in a fight with another inmate at Reidsville. Later, according to this plan, much regret would be expressed over the incident, and it would be looked upon as one of those unfortunate things that sometimes happen."

Inside the prison, the deputies handed over their charge. King was freed of his restraints and permitted a brief phone call to Coretta. She was stunned—she had no idea Martin had been transferred, and hearing his voice from the state prison hours away in rural Georgia devastated her. "This seemed more than I could bear," she wrote years later. She wanted to go to visit him immediately, but the distance to Reidsville and her physical condition prevented her. "I knew that it was...more than a day's journey there and back, and I was so pregnant, I did not know if I could make it," she recalled.

After his phone call, King was dressed in an inmate's white-striped uniform and locked alone in a cell.

That same morning, his attorney Donald Hollowell was angered to learn that King had been whisked away in the night. He had intended to submit a writ of habeas corpus arguing for King's release on grounds he was being unlawfully imprisoned in DeKalb County, but this legality was useless now because his client sat in the state prison miles away.

* * *

On that same Wednesday morning, Senator John Kennedy phoned the governor of Georgia, Ernest Vandiver. To Kennedy, Judge Mitchell's jailing of King for four months on a minor traffic violation was a judi-cial abomination. Some quiet, back-channel way had to be found to free the civil rights leader. Kennedy was motivated by his outrage, by his sympathy for the King family, and by bald political calculation. In their meeting just weeks earlier, King had urged the senator to take some dramatic action to prove to blacks that his commitment to their cause was genuine. His moment had arrived. If Kennedy were able to play a decisive role in King's release, the black community was likely to reward him with an outpouring of support. But if he acted on King's behalf, he risked a vicious backlash from Southern whites. The senator had to walk a fine line: show decency to a black man without alienating the white community.

The political machinations around King's arrest were so delicate that Kennedy told few, if any, of his advisors about his efforts, and for years afterward his quiet petitioning remained unknown, or underplayed, by Kennedy chroniclers and historians. That Kennedy sought out Governor Vandiver was itself politically dangerous. Being seen as too cozy with the racist Vandiver could stain Kennedy in the eyes of civil rights advocates. Vandiver had already gone on record condemning King's return to Georgia. The governor had a long, public record of bigotry. When running for office in 1958, he declared to his white supporters: "Neither my child nor yours will ever attend an integrated school during my administration, no not one."

Kennedy already had raised suspicions in the black community by his blatant courtship of Southern white support. After the Democratic National Convention in July, he began shoring up his reputation among Southern leaders, meeting privately with them to allay fears that he would be an aggressive civil rights president. The governor of Virginia, J. Lindsey Almond, endorsed the senator after a private parley, hinting that Kennedy had special respect for Southern values. "Kennedy is deeply concerned for our way of thinking," Almond told reporters. "And the world knows just what the South's way of thinking is." Around that time, Kennedy also met with Vandiver in Lyndon Johnson's Senate office. Kennedy promised Vandiver that as president he would never use federal troops to force Georgia to desegregate its schools. In return, Vandiver declared his support for the senator and vowed to lead Georgia into the Kennedy column on Election Day.

Some three months later, early in the morning at the governor's mansion in Atlanta, the telephone jangled on the bedside table, waking Vandiver and his wife. On the line was Senator John Kennedy speaking in his New England accent. "Governor," he said, according to Vandiver's recollection of the conversation, "is there any way that you think you could get Martin Luther King out of jail? It would be of tremendous benefit to me."

"Senator, I don't know whether we can get him released or not," Vandiver replied.

"Would you try and see what you can do and call me back?" Kennedy said. In case the governor had trouble reaching him, Jack gave Vandiver Bobby Kennedy's phone number.

Working in secrecy, Vandiver swung into action for the senator. He instructed an aide to get in touch with George Stewart, who was secretary of the Georgia Democratic Party and a close friend of Judge Mitchell, the man at the center of the King kerfuffle. Stewart had considerable sway with Mitchell not only because of their friendship but also because he had prevailed upon one of Vandiver's predecessors to appoint Mitchell to the bench. Stewart informed the judge that the Kennedys were interested in King's release, and he advised Mitchell to follow the letter of the law, which required bail pending appeals on misdemeanors. Mitchell agreed to let King go, but he wanted proof that Senator Kennedy had in fact spoken with Governor Vandiver. So the governor used the telephone number that Senator Kennedy had given him and got Bobby Kennedy on the phone, informing him that he had spoken to the judge. Politically savvy as he was, Vandiver no doubt expected that Bobby would phone Judge Mitchell himself now, proving the Kennedy connection.

In addition to calling Vandiver, Jack Kennedy expressed his concern over King in a letter to the governor dated the same day as the call. He wrote that he was "surprised and disturbed" to learn of King's imprisonment and sentence for an auto registration violation. "I feel sure that under Georgia justice punishment in a prison work camp is meted out only to those whose offenses are major and largely involve crimes of moral turpitude," Kennedy observed. "It seems hard to argue that violation of an automobile registration statute involves moral turpitude." In a letter that might somehow go public, the senator was careful not to make demands on the governor. "I neither desire nor seek to interfere in the administration of Georgia justice," he asserted, "but as a friend of the people of Georgia and as an American citizen I do wish to inform you of my interest."

21

As NEWS OF King's jailing spread, telegrams and phone calls poured into Georgia. The Jewish Labor Committee called on Vandiver to issue an immediate pardon to King, saying his "arrest and imprisonment...will be played up in the Soviet and stooge press in order to buttress Khrushchev's contentions" that the United States was a land of bigotry and discrimination. Eleanor Roosevelt publicly lashed out at Atlanta's mayor, William Hartsfield: "I wish to protest the imprisonment of Dr. Martin Luther King and hope you will use your good office to correct this injustice." Hartsfield rushed to correct any misperceptions, announcing that he and the city of Atlanta were not responsible for King's jailing at Reidsville; he rightly laid blame on county and state officials.

Both presidential candidates received a petition from the Southern Christian Leadership Conference and nearly twenty other civil rights organizations demanding that they "speak out against the imprisonment." The groups declared that King's jailing harmed "the prestige of our nation and our moral integrity as a people." When the students had launched their protest against Rich's, they hoped their action would force the candidates to reveal exactly where they stood on racial justice. Now there was a chance Kennedy and Nixon would do so as the tight campaign wound down toward Election Day a little more than a week away.

In the Nixon camp, strategists calculated the political consequences and concluded the best course of action was silence. Nixon, hoping to steal a portion of Southern white Democrats from Kennedy, chose not to act, or speak, on King's predicament. Even though Daddy King had endorsed the vice president and his son had praised him over the years for his views on civil rights, the candidate nonetheless issued a terse "no comment" through his press secretary, Herb Klein.

Nixon held fast to his decision even after a visit from his staunch supporter Jackie Robinson. As William Safire, then Nixon campaign aide and future *New York Times* columnist, told the story, Robinson came out of his ten-minute meeting with "tears of frustration in his eyes."

Complaining bitterly, he told Safire: "He thinks calling Martin would be 'grandstanding.'" Robinson was so distraught he declared: "Nixon doesn't deserve to win." Yet, the baseball star continued to support the Republican and later said the outcome of the election had left him "terribly disappointed."

In the Kennedy camp, the imprisoned preacher had two passionate proponents: Harris Wofford, longtime friend of the Kings, and Sargent Shriver, the senator's brother-in-law and head of the campaign's Civil Rights Section. But they had only limited influence. Because of their fervor for black rights, Wofford and Shriver were regarded as overly sentimental activists with impaired political judgment and were relegated to the periphery of the campaign. Shriver ran the Chicago Merchandise Mart, which was owned by the patriarch, Joseph Kennedy, and his opinions were largely dismissed from serious political discussions. But as the husband of Jack's sister Eunice, he had standing within the family. The two men, Shriver and Wofford, exerted a subtle yet powerful influence on the campaign: They forced a sense of conscience upon the political realists.

22

WHILE THE CAMPAIGNS strategized, Martin Luther King Jr. braced himself for four months in prison away from his wife and two children. After his phone conversation with Coretta, he scrawled a letter to her; his tone was stoic, revealing few details of his harrowing morning other than he'd been roused at 4 a.m. for the 230-mile ride to the prison. Sensitive to her distress, he tried to calm her by appealing to the virtue of the black struggle. "I know this whole experience is very difficult for you to adjust to, especially in your condition of pregnancy," he wrote, "but as I said to you yesterday this is the cross that we must bear for the freedom of our people." He impressed upon her that if she were strong in her faith it would strengthen him and confessed how hard it was for him to be away from her and the children for four months. "I am asking God hourly to give me the power of endurance."

Settling in for the long haul, King told his wife he was allowed visitors twice a month and he hoped that despite her condition she would be able to come. He was not going to sit idly behind bars—he intended to work. He asked Coretta to bring him some reading material, including *The Parables of Jesus*, a volume on Gandhi, a Bible, a dictionary, and a book called *Increasing Your Word Power*. He also wanted a stack of his own sermons, and a radio.

* * *

After her too-brief phone conversation with her husband that morning, Coretta had hung up and called Harris Wofford. Martin's incarceration in such dangerous circumstances had thrown her into a panic. Ever since her husband had emerged as the leader of the Montgomery bus boycott, Coretta had lived with an abiding sense of dread. Wofford recalled that one night in the 1950s, she acknowledged her foreboding. "She told my wife how her recurring dream was that her husband was going to be killed in this movement, lynched or shot," Wofford said. Now, with him at Reidsville, imprisoned among violent criminals, Coretta foresaw doom. She beseeched Wofford to find some way to save her husband. "They are going to kill him," she cried into the phone. "I know they are going to kill him."

Wofford quickly contacted Kennedy's campaign aides, but they ignored his calls. Next he phoned Louis Martin, a successful black businessman and newspaper publisher who had deep political roots and was helping the campaign reach out to the black community. Martin was concerned about King, and after commiserating, the two men batted around some ideas. "What Kennedy ought to do is something direct and personal," Wofford told Martin, "like picking up the telephone and calling Coretta." It would be enough, Wofford observed, for the candidate to show his sympathy for her.

"That's it, that's it!" Louis agreed. "That would be perfect."

Now came the hard part: getting this idea to Kennedy, who was campaigning in Chicago, and persuading him to act on it. After his private call to Governor Vandiver in the morning, the candidate had attended a breakfast with fifty businessmen. Now he was in a hotel suite at O'Hare Airport waiting to leave town.

After several tries Wofford finally tracked down Sargent Shriver, who was also in Chicago but not with the Kennedy entourage out at the airport. Understanding the urgency, Shriver listened to Wofford then said, "All right, all right," and asked for some telephone numbers. When Wofford rattled off the numbers for the power brokers in Atlanta—Mayor Hartsfield and attorney Morris Abram—Shriver stopped him: "No, no. Where is *she*? Give me *her* number." Shriver jotted down Coretta King's telephone number and stuffed it into his pocket. "I'll go right straight out to the airport," Shriver said. "I'll put it to Jack right now. It's not too late."

As Shriver raced out to the airport hotel, Wofford was exhilarated but also overwhelmed by doubt. "I wasn't sure whether anything was really happening," he recalled.

* * *

When Shriver got to the hotel suite he found Kennedy surrounded by aides, all rigidly opposed to the idea. Although the senator had already expressed his concerns privately to Governor Vandiver, he worried that a public telephone call to Coretta King could be perceived as a "gimmick" to reel in black votes. His key advisor, Ken O'Donnell, saw little political upside. "I felt my job was to always focus on the political factors and implications," O'Donnell recalled. "The moral issues would be raised by Bobby, Sarge [Shriver], Harris Wofford, or others." When Kennedy pulled O'Donnell aside to confer privately, Ken told him: "While I am sympathetic to what Mrs. King and her family must be going through, from a political point of view, all I can see is that it could backfire." How could Kennedy, a candidate who was criticized for his lukewarm support of black issues, justify this unusual bighearted action? "There are a million ways politically it could be a mess," he warned Kennedy.

Shriver hovered, waiting to make his case alone. Finally the aides began to disperse: Wordsmith Ted Sorensen left to work on a speech, and press secretary Pierre Salinger went out to speak with reporters. But O'Donnell stuck around—besides advising Kennedy, he was the man who controlled access to the candidate and later to the president, and he now stood between Jack and his brother-in-law. Ready to pull rank, Shriver approached O'Donnell. "I never use my family connection or ask for a favor, but you are wrong, Kenny," he said. "This is too important. I want time alone with him."

In O'Donnell's view, the issue was decided and he didn't want it reopened. But he also knew Shriver didn't use his family position to advantage. "Unlike others," O'Donnell said of Shriver, "he never asked or abused that [family] relationship, and, at some level, morally I suspected he might be right, though politically I still was against it." Shriver, a Yale College and Yale Law School graduate, had married Kennedy's sister Eunice in 1953 and along with his wife showed an early interest in the underprivileged. The Shrivers devoted themselves to a Kennedy family foundation for mentally handicapped children (Rosemary Kennedy, Jack's sister, suffered from the condition), and Sargent became the foundation's first executive director. Out of respect, or courtesy, or simply because he was hungry, O'Donnell stepped aside, allowing Shriver a private moment with Jack.

In parting, O'Donnell said softly he hadn't eaten, he was going to get a hamburger, and the two men shook hands.

"You know I am right," Shriver said as O'Donnell started off.

"Maybe," O'Donnell replied. Then reminding him of how things often went in the rough and tumble of politics, he observed: "If it works, you'll get no credit for it; if it does not, you'll get all the blame."

The two aides shared a laugh.

* * *

Shriver went into Kennedy's room and found his brother-in-law alone, folding his clothes into his suitcase. As Shriver built his case, describing King's terrifying drive through rural Georgia and Coretta's anguish, Kennedy didn't seem to be listening. His mind was elsewhere. "Jack," Shriver pressed, "you just need to convey to Mrs. King that you believe what happened to her husband was wrong and that you will do what you can to see the situation rectified and that in general you stand behind him."

Kennedy was not paying attention. To engage him, Shriver appealed to his conscience. "Negroes don't expect everything will change tomorrow, no matter who's elected," he told Jack. "But they do want to know whether you care. If you telephone Mrs. King, they will know you understand and will help. You will reach their hearts and give support to a pregnant woman who is afraid her husband will be killed."

Although cool and detached, Kennedy was in a quiet way sympathetic to the suffering of others and had a reflexive dislike of unfairness. All at once, Shriver noticed a change of heart in his brother-in-law. As he remembered it, Jack zipped up his suitcase then turned to him and said: "That's a pretty good idea. How do I get to her?"

When Shriver handed over Coretta's telephone number to him, Kennedy said: "Dial it for me, will you? I've got to pack up my papers." As Jack filled his briefcase, Shriver sat down on the edge of the bed and put his finger into the rotary dial.

When the phone rang that morning, Coretta was getting dressed to go see the lawyer Morris Abram about her husband's plight. She listened as Sargent Shriver introduced himself and told her he was with Jack Kennedy in Chicago. Senator Kennedy "wanted to speak with her for a moment," Shriver informed her. "Would that be okay?"

After several seconds, she heard a voice familiar to her; she had just recently watched Kennedy give a smooth performance in the televised debates. "Good morning, Mrs. King," the voice said. "This is Senator Kennedy." After a brief exchange of pleasantries, Kennedy offered his sympathy: "I want to express to you my concern about your husband. I know this must be very hard for you." He mentioned that he was aware she was expecting a baby. "I just wanted you to know that I was thinking about you and Dr. King," he said cordially. "If there is anything I can do to help, please feel free to call on me."

Coretta thanked him, saying: "I would appreciate anything you could do to help."

And that was it: The call lasted no more than ninety seconds.

When Shriver informed Kenny O'Donnell, the campaign's political master groused: "You just lost us the election."

23

HEARTENED BY KENNEDY's call, Coretta phoned a surprised Harris Wofford, who had heard nothing from Shriver. As she had planned, Coretta then went with Daddy King to see Morris Abram in his law office. For Daddy King, Kennedy's call changed everything. He couldn't contain his appreciation. Long wary of the Irish Catholic candidate, the Southern Baptist preacher proclaimed: "If Kennedy has the courage to wipe the tears from Coretta's eyes," he would vote for him "whatever his religion."

Pressure now mounted from several directions for King's release. Inevitably, word of Kennedy's gesture trickled out to the press, and Anthony Lewis of the *New York Times* called Wofford wondering why Coretta refused to speak to reporters. Wofford then got Coretta on the phone and asked if Senator Kennedy had instructed her not to say anything publicly. "When she said he had made no such request," Wofford recalled, "I said I was sure Kennedy wouldn't be issuing any statement but she should feel free to say anything she considered appropriate."

By that afternoon, Coretta had spoken to a reporter from the *Atlanta Constitution*, telling him that it had made her "feel good that [Senator Kennedy] called me personally and let me know how he felt." The paper reported that she believed the senator "would do what he could to see that Mr. King is let out of jail."

* * *

Just as he protected his Vandiver conversation, Jack Kennedy was in no hurry to reveal that he had chatted with Coretta. He didn't tell his press secretary Pierre Salinger until his campaign plane lifted off that afternoon from Chicago's O'Hare Airport on its way to Detroit. In the air, he nonchalantly mentioned it to Salinger who, recognizing a potential media firestorm, immediately relayed the news via the onboard radiophone to campaign manager Bobby Kennedy in Washington. Bobby was apoplectic when he learned that Shriver, Wofford, and Louis Martin had conspired and put Jack up to the call. Now the campaign had to prepare to control the damage.

For Sargent Shriver, it was impossible to forget Bobby's irate phone call. "Bobby landed on me like a ton of bricks....He scorched my ass," Shriver recalled. "Jack Kennedy was going to get defeated because of the stupid call," Bobby fumed. He then turned his wrath on Wofford and Louis Martin, summoning the men to the campaign headquarters and berating them "with fists tight, his blue eyes cold," as Wofford remembered it. Bobby had made the political calculations and didn't like what it all added up to. "Do you know," he fumed, "that three Southern governors told us that if Jack supported Jimmy Hoffa, Nikita Khrushchev, or Martin Luther King, they would throw their states to Nixon? Do you know that this election may be razor close and you have probably lost it for us?"

After dressing down Wofford and Martin, Bobby Kennedy headed out to the airport for a speaking engagement in New York. In the car, Bobby told his aide John Seigenthaler: "I think I should call that judge and give him a piece of my mind, tell him exactly what I have in mind, tell him why I think he's wrong." Seigenthaler tried to dissuade his boss from contacting Judge Mitchell. "If I were you, I wouldn't do it. I would forget it," he told Bobby. "When I put him on the plane," Seigenthaler later recalled, "I was certain that I had talked him out of it."

That same evening, John Kennedy also landed in New York on a campaign stop. Reporters were waiting for him. When he was asked if he had phoned Coretta King, Kennedy said only: "She is a friend of mine and I was concerned about the situation." He implied that as her friend it was not extraordinary for him to give her a call at a difficult time like this. But he was being somewhat disingenuous: Although he had spent a little time with her husband, he'd never met Coretta.

24

THE NEXT MORNING, Thursday, October 27, Judge Oscar Mitchell announced the release of his prisoner on a $2,000 bond, saying his action was mandatory under Georgia law. That afternoon, after about thirty hours of confinement at Reidsville, Martin Luther King Jr. walked out of his cell for his flight home to Atlanta. About two hours later he stepped off a chartered plane at Peachtree-DeKalb Airport into the arms of his relieved wife and other supporters. Altogether, he had spent eight nights in three different jails.

Speaking to reporters at the airport, King said he was indebted to Kennedy for his role. "I understand from very reliable sources that Senator Kennedy served as a great force in making the release possible," he said. "For him to be that courageous shows that he is really acting upon principle and not expediency." Kennedy's participation, he said, was "morally wise." Leaving no doubt about his appreciation, King nonetheless stopped short of endorsing the candidate. "I hold Senator Kennedy in very high esteem," he said. "I am convinced he will seek to exercise the power of his office to fully implement the civil rights plank of his party's platform."

King also took the opportunity to say that he had not heard from Vice President Richard Nixon and knew of no Republican efforts on his behalf. Years later, in an interview four months after President Kennedy's assassination, King reiterated his disappointment. He explained that at the time of Reidsville he had a closer relationship with Nixon than he had with Kennedy; they'd known each other longer, and Nixon had frequently called on him for advice. "And yet, when this moment came, it was like he had never heard of me," King said. "So this is why I really considered him a moral coward and one who was really unwilling to take a courageous step and take a risk."

After speaking to the press, King climbed into a huge black Cadillac limousine for the ride to Ebenezer Church, where he was to speak to the faithful welcoming him home. Along the route King crossed out of DeKalb County and into Fulton County, where about a hundred black students waited, refusing to step over the line into hated DeKalb. The big black car pulled to a stop and King emerged and waved. The young students' spirits soared at the sight of their leader, his presence prompting a spontaneous chorus of "We Shall Overcome."

Pat Watters, a white Southern journalist at the scene, had never heard the song before. "I stood listening there in the moonlight, a soft wind breathing," he recalled. "Their voices were so young, clear—and so unafraid." He watched from the side of the road, thinking about the long, troubled acceptance on both sides—white and black—of the indignities that had become commonplace, "our mutual acquiescence making the evil seem immutable and the South hopeless."

Separated by culture and color, Watters listened as the students raised their voices in song: "Deep in my heart, I do believe, we shall overcome someday." To Watters, the students seemed emboldened by King's presence. "I listened and heard them saying in the song that the way things used to be was no more, was forever ended," Watters observed. "And knowing all that that meant for them, and for me," he recalled, "I cried. I cried for the first time in many years, cried unabashedly, cried for joy—and hope."

25

THAT EVENING, JUST before the network news programs aired, Harris Wofford picked up his phone to hear the voice of anchor David Brinkley, one half of *The Huntley-Brinkley Report*. What Brinkley told Wofford seemed utterly impossible: A story breaking over the news wire claimed that a brother of the senator had called the judge in the case directly to get King released, Brinkley said.

Wofford's mind whirled. That brother could not have been Ted Kennedy, who was out in California and knew little of what was going on. Perhaps the wire service had gotten it wrong and it was no brother at all but rather a brother-in-law, Sargent Shriver. But that didn't seem reasonable, either. The final possibility was the least likely: Bobby Kennedy would never have done something like that, Wofford thought, especially given how he had blown up over Jack's call to Coretta. "It just can't be true, David," Wofford told the TV anchor.

"We're going on the air in about ten minutes," Brinkley replied. "Should I disregard the story?"

"I just can't believe it," Wofford honestly answered him.

That night, NBC didn't report the story.

* * *

Bobby's aide John Seigenthaler also got wind of a Kennedy brother's call to the judge, and this time that brother was identified as Bobby. When Bobby phoned Seigenthaler that evening, the aide said: "Guess what that crazy judge in Georgia's done?"

"What's that?" Bobby wondered.

"He put out a statement saying you had called him and criticized him for arbitrary use of judicial power." Seigenthaler said the judge had called

Bobby "a young whippersnapper" who had stuck his "nose into the judicial process of the State of Georgia." To ensure Bobby that nothing would come of these rumors, Seigenthaler told Bobby he had issued a denial; of course, Robert Kennedy would never have made any such call.

After a long silence, Bobby admitted: "Well, I did."

"After what you told Harris and Louis yesterday?" Seigenthaler wondered. "What do you mean?"

Bobby explained that on his flight to New York the previous day he couldn't stop thinking about what happened in Georgia. He was infuriated that the only reason King sat in jail without the legal right of bond was because he was black. "It just burned me all the way up here on the plane," he told Seigenthaler. "It grilled me. The more I thought about the injustice of it, the more I thought what a son of a bitch that judge was." Bobby was so upset he ignored the bundle of work he'd brought on board with him. "I was so sore at that cracker Georgia judge putting a decent American in jail and sentencing him to six months on a hard-labor gang for driving with an out-of-state driver's license, when it was actually because he was black and fighting for civil rights." By the time the plane landed on Long Island, Bobby was so worked up he went to a pay phone and called Judge Oscar Mitchell.

* * *

How that conversation went has been described in different ways over the years in the various recollections of Bobby and his aides. In one account, Seigenthaler said Bobby told him: "I just got so mad that I got that judge on the phone and said, 'Are you an American or not? If you're an American, you get that man out of jail.'" In another rendering, Seigenthaler recalled Bobby's telling him he kept the discussion strictly to legal matters. Bobby impressed upon the judge that there was no legal basis for keeping King in prison on a misdemeanor. In Harris Wofford's telling, Bobby expressed his fury at the judge for "screwing up my brother's campaign and making our country look ridiculous before the world." In an oral history interview about a year after his brother's assassination, Bobby described the conversation in his own words. "I called the judge, and said, 'Well, will he get out on bail?'" he recalled. "I don't know what he did, [but] he got him out." Bobby remembered their conversation as being civil. Judge Mitchell told him, "Bob, it's nice to talk to you. And I don't have any objection to doing that."

In his oral history, Bobby mentioned something he had left out from his previous recollections. Perhaps spurred by his brother, Bobby had made several phone calls to Georgia governor Ernest Vandiver seeking King's release. Vandiver, Bobby said, had encouraged him to phone Judge Mitchell. "I talked to the governor," Bobby explained. "And he said that if I called the judge, that he thought that the judge would let Martin Luther King off." Bobby kept his contact with Vandiver secret, even from his aides, and instead depicted his call to the judge as an initiative he had undertaken because of his own outrage over the injustice. No doubt Bobby was outraged; he saw the world through a lens of moral clarity: right and wrong with no shading. But he kept quiet about his Vandiver conversations until his 1964 oral history for the same reason his brother had remained silent about his phone call to the governor: extreme political sensitivities. Not only would it have been suspect for either Kennedy to be secretly cooperating with a racist Southern governor, but Vandiver would have been ruined among his constituency had these negotiations been revealed.

* * *

After coming clean to his aides, Bobby wanted to minimize any political repercussions from his call to the judge. He, Seigenthaler, and Wofford struggled to craft a careful explanation. The wording was tricky, because Bobby had also stepped into a legal minefield: The ethics of the American Bar Association held that no lawyer should ever intervene in a case to try to sway a judge.

"Can't you just say I was inquiring about Dr. King's constitutional right to bail?" Bobby asked.

In the end he acknowledged that he phoned the judge in response to a flood of support for King that had "swamped" the campaign headquarters. He then tried to make amends to Louis Martin, the civil rights aide he had scorched. Bobby had special respect for Martin; he regarded him as the finest campaign aide on civil rights, the one who had the broadest range of contacts in the black community and the best judgment. At around 3 a.m., in an eccentric act of decency, Bobby phoned Martin and woke him up. "Louis," he explained, "I wanted you especially to know that I called that judge in Georgia today, to try to get Dr. King out." Martin groggily asked Bobby to repeat what he had just said, and in the second telling Bobby sounded proud of his intervention. Now fully comprehending, Martin was also proud of Bobby and praised his passionate pursuit of black justice: "*You* are now an honorary Brother!"

In the morning, the *New York Times* carried the story of Martin Luther King's release, along with Judge Mitchell's cagey words about pressure from "a member of a Presidential nominee's family." When asked which member, he said only that it was a brother; and when asked which brother, Robert or Ted, he said: "Well, I will say that I have never heard Ted's name mentioned."

26

KING'S RELEASE HAD an immediate and profound impact on the black community, unleashing a wave of support for Kennedy. In a single day, the senator beat back years of skepticism about his commitment to racial justice. Debates raged over whether his call to Coretta was a calculated political act or a true expression of compassion. Whatever the truth was, the act inspired a flood of raw emotion. The front page of the *Chicago Defender* featured a photo of King holding his young son and rubbing cheeks with him while his wife, Coretta, kissed him on his other cheek and his daughter stood at his elbow peering up at him. Above the photo was a large headline: REV. KING FREE ON BOND—HAIL SEN. KENNEDY'S ROLE IN CLERIC'S RELEASE. The *New York Post* sent a reporter into Harlem to gauge the reaction. "Many Harlemites were indignant at Nixon's refusal even to comment on the case," the reporter wrote. The *Post* published the comments of John Patterson, publisher of the Harlem paper *Citizen-Call*. "Mr. Nixon, in his refusal to comment or take a stand on the civil rights issue that Rev. King's arrest symbolized, merely extends the say-nothing, do-nothing rule by golf-club philosophy of President Eisenhower regarding this moral issue." By contrast, Senator Kennedy was praised in newspapers across the country. A widely distributed Associated Press dispatch reported a version of the comforting words Kennedy said to Coretta on the phone: "This must be pretty hard on you, and I want to let you both know that I'm thinking about you, and will do all I can to help."

With his customary effusiveness, Daddy King went much further than his son in praising Kennedy. At Ebenezer Church on the evening of Martin's release, he announced to his congregation what he had told Morris Abram in private: that he was flipping his allegiance from Nixon to Kennedy. "I had expected to vote against Senator Kennedy because of his religion," he explained. "But now he can be my President, Catholic or whatever he is." Daddy King appreciated the boldness of Kennedy's action, his willingness to wade into an issue that posed a political risk. "It took courage to call my daughter-in-law at a time like this," Daddy King observed, adding: "I've got all my votes and I've got a suitcase and I'm going to take them up there and dump them in his lap."

Jack Kennedy was pleased to learn of the pastor's epiphany but couldn't help noting the irony of Daddy King's religious prejudice. "Imagine Martin Luther King having a bigot for a father," Jack quipped to an aide. "Well, we all have our fathers, don't we?"

* * *

Daddy King's kind words were welcome, and his son's expressions of gratitude were valuable. But the campaign expected more. It wanted Martin Luther King Jr. to endorse Kennedy, a move that would galvanize blacks less than two weeks before the election. Harris Wofford asked Atlanta lawyer Morris Abram if he could "get King to announce his support for Kennedy in view of 'all we had done for him.'" Abram was not hopeful.

King and his advisors were sharply divided on the question. Daddy King pressed his son to announce an endorsement: The candidate's kindness demanded repayment. But other aides to King urged him to remain neutral: His strength as a civil rights leader derived from not riding political tides but remaining strictly nonpartisan.

These discussions had begun even before King's arrest. After the Kennedy-King meeting in New York early in the campaign, King's aide Stanley Levison had strongly advised against favoring one candidate over another. Levison argued that candidates and campaigns burst onto the scene and faded away, while the movement for civil rights was enduring and outlived political fads. Attaching himself to a politician would diminish King's authority. Writing to King in mid-October 1960, Levison explained: "Sometimes I think these people see you too much as a personality of glamour not as a leader whose responsibilities will continue over decades and through changes of great magnitude." Levison advised taking the long view. If King were to speak for one party or another, Levison said, "what is lost is a rare leader whose selflessness has been long established and highly prized by the people."

A fresh debate, however, had erupted in light of Kennedy's action. Harry Belafonte was adamant that King had to maintain his independence; an endorsement meant being identified with a politician whose future actions were unpredictable and could skew from the movement's convictions. Belafonte said of Kennedy: "If you anoint him and become his black mouthpiece, you'll pay a huge political price if he lets us down."

Daddy King had no patience for such judgments. Amid the flurry of phone calls following King's release, Daddy King intercepted one from Belafonte and laid into him. "You just don't understand," he told the singer. "You can't have a man do what Kennedy did and not pay your debt."

No endorsement ever came, infuriating the Kennedys. After the election Belafonte visited Bobby Kennedy at his house in McLean, Virginia, and the men fell into conversation about King's hesitation. "It's true we were angry," Bobby told him with a wry smile. "But we could see it was politically shrewd, a clever move."

27

IF KING RESISTED an alliance, the Kennedy campaign intended to grab the political rewards of his release by its own means. Sargent Shriver, Louis Martin, and Harris Wofford developed a two-pronged strategy to generate coverage of Kennedy's call to Coretta King in black publications and to flood black communities with printed material highlighting the senator's compassion. The goal was to enthuse blacks about a Kennedy presidency while minimizing white defections in the South.

Longtime newspaperman Louis Martin contacted every black paper in the country, concentrating in particular on those in the North. Southern blacks were less important in Martin's publicity blitz because so few were able to vote, held back by registration hurdles, skullduggery, and other discriminatory practices. If blacks in Northern cities showed up at the polls in droves to vote for Kennedy, along with the smaller numbers in the South, the election could tilt his way. "The problem was to excite the community to action," Martin remembered. "The King call fired up Cleveland, Philadelphia, and Detroit, Chicago, New York—this is where I worked the hell out of it."

The black press responded. Rallying their readers, these newspapers across the country endorsed Jack Kennedy. Even two papers long known for their support of Republican candidates—the *Norfolk Journal and Guide* and the *New York Amsterdam News*—fell in line. Others jumping into the Kennedy camp included the *Chicago Defender, Baltimore Afro-American, Michigan Chronicle, Kansas City Call*, and *St. Louis Argus*. Martin Luther King Jr. told the *Baltimore Afro-American* he received "innumerable letters" from voters in Atlanta, Chicago, and Detroit who "told him that they planned to express their appreciation to Sen. Kennedy at the polls."

As the campaign hoped, the coverage of Kennedy's call in the white media was fairly muted. The *New York Times* reported King's release on its front page, noting that John and Bobby Kennedy had "sought to intervene in the case." But, the story added, Judge Mitchell made clear that "the release was mandatory under Georgia law and not the result of any pressure put on him." If there was a backlash in the South, it garnered little coverage. In a tiny, four-paragraph story buried on page twelve, the *Times* reported that four staffers of Georgia governor Ernest Vandiver resigned in protest over Bobby Kennedy's call to the judge. *US News and World Report* said nothing about Kennedy in its story about King's prison ordeal in an edition dated one day before the election, and *Time* magazine focused more on King's rough treatment than on Kennedy's role in his release, saying "the whole performance reeked of red-neck justice." The television networks' news programs mentioned Kennedy's call but didn't pursue the story with much vigor.

Kennedy suffered only minor fallout among Southern white voters. On the Sunday following King's release, Claude Sitton of the *New York Times* reported that Kennedy appeared "to be gaining strength in Southern states once considered safe for Vice President Nixon." In the concluding paragraphs, Sitton acknowledged that Kennedy's role in King's release from prison "may hurt the Democratic cause somewhat among white Southern voters" but that the repercussions "had been milder than expected." If there was a strong reaction, it was among Southern blacks who were now more favorably disposed toward Kennedy. Despite voting restrictions that prevented Southern blacks from casting ballots in numbers that their population justified, their impact could be substantial. As Sitton reported, blacks "cast the decisive vote in close elections in some Southern states."

Meanwhile, Shriver, Martin, and Wofford scrambled to produce a pamphlet lauding the senator's call to Coretta. It was to be distributed to blacks, mostly in the North where their voting numbers were large enough to sway outcomes in tight states. The aim was to contrast Kennedy's compassion toward blacks with Nixon's hard-heartedness and to ignite black outrage over the judicial treatment of King. The combination, the men believed, would fire up the community to turn out for Kennedy. Polls in some states indicated that blacks were already leaning toward Kennedy. But simple expressions of support were not enough. As Louis Martin observed, "However supportive people may be, it doesn't mean a darn thing unless they go to the polls."

Shriver and his men had one major antagonist: Bobby Kennedy. As his brother's campaign manager, Bobby was still obsessed by the possible loss of Southern support. As his aide John Seigenthaler recalled, "Suddenly, civil rights was a crucial part of that 1960 campaign and we were flooded in the campaign headquarters with calls from governors and state party leaders from all across the South." Panicking, Bobby prohibited Shriver's Civil Rights Section from issuing any new statements or taking any independent action. Additional publicity, he feared, would only drive away Southern white voters in numbers large enough to overwhelm the migration of black voters to Kennedy.

But the civil rights team pushed forward anyway, certain that the plan was in the best interests of the campaign. In the words of Louis Martin: "The motivation was moral and political" and defying Bobby was imperative. "We now had the ammunition and we were going to use it," recalled Harris Wofford. "That was precisely what we weren't supposed to do at all according to Bobby."

The men believed they were doing nothing that violated Bobby's rules. The pamphlet included statements that had already been issued, so it did not upset Bobby's ban on new editorializing; it contained previously published remarks from King, his father, and Coretta, and less publicized comments from other black leaders such as King's friend the Reverend Ralph Abernathy. "It was not just Dr. King on trial," Abernathy was quoted in the pamphlet, "America was on trial." As a result of Senator Kennedy's kindness, Abernathy declared, "I earnestly and sincerely feel that it is time for all of us to take off our Nixon buttons."

The leaflet reprinted part of a *New York Post* editorial noting that Kennedy knew his call to Coretta would inflame white Southern racists but he dialed her up anyway. "In this dramatic human episode Senator Kennedy has looked a lot larger and warmer—bolder—than his opponent," the *Post* said. In one original, unpublished statement, defying Bobby's edict, the pamphlet summed up the contrast between the two men vying for president: " 'No comment' Nixon versus A Candidate With a Heart, Senator Kennedy."

The pamphlet, printed on cheap blue paper, carried the title "The Case of Martin Luther King Jr." and was handed to blacks as they arrived at church in Saint Louis, Detroit, Chicago, Philadelphia, Atlanta, and elsewhere. "I stood outside the Ebenezer Baptist Church in Chicago...and handed those things out myself on the Sunday before election," Shriver said. "You could see people taking them and carrying them home. It was absolutely remarkable."

An initial print run of 50,000 copies was followed by another 250,000. Copies flew off the presses and rolled down the highways in postal trucks. As the election neared, bundles were loaded onto Greyhound buses and delivered to terminals where waiting civil rights workers snatched them up and drove them to the churches. In the end, some two million copies of the pamphlet made their way into black communities.

28

ON ELECTION DAY, John Kennedy voted in Boston then flew to Hyannis Port where the family and close aides assembled to wait for the returns. Bobby Kennedy ran a command center out of his house in the family compound. Voting was so close that the day dragged into the night without a decision. By 3:30 a.m., definitive outcomes still loomed in Pennsylvania, Missouri, Illinois, Minnesota, Michigan, and California. Confident yet uncertain of victory, the senator turned in for the night. The next morning at around 9 a.m., aide Ted Sorensen went upstairs to find Kennedy in white pajamas sitting on his bed. He brought good news: The senator was now president of the United States, having captured the White House by the slimmest of margins. If blacks hadn't turned out for him in large numbers, Kennedy might have had to deliver a concession speech. In Illinois, for instance, where he topped his rival by 9,000 votes, 250,000 blacks voted for Kennedy. In Michigan, he won the votes of another 250,000 blacks and carried the state by 67,000 votes. In South Carolina, he carried the state by 10,000 votes with 40,000 blacks casting ballots for him.

In his book *The Making of the President 1960*, campaign historian Theodore White assessed the impact of the millions of pamphlets that reached blacks across the country just before the election. "One cannot identify in the narrowness of American voting of 1960 any one particular episode or decision as being more important than any other in the final tallies," he wrote. But, he added, the "instinctive decision [to call Coretta and blanket black communities with pamphlets] must be ranked among the most crucial of the last few weeks." White observed that blacks were convinced that they had anointed Kennedy. "Some Negro political leaders claim," White wrote, "that in no less than eleven states (Illinois, New Jersey, Michigan, South Carolina, Texas, Delaware, Maryland, Missouri, North Carolina, Pennsylvania, Nevada), with 169 electoral votes, it was the Negro community that provided the Kennedy margin of victory."

Nationwide, Kennedy got only 118,574 more votes than Nixon did out of a total 68,370,000 ballots cast. Kennedy tallied 49.7 percent of the popular vote to Nixon's 49.6 percent. In the crucial electoral votes, Kennedy amassed 303 to Nixon's 219, enough to catapult him into the White House. Altogether, blacks turned out for Kennedy in staggering numbers. A Gallup poll put the figure at 70 percent, and an IBM poll came up with 68 percent. (In 1956, Adlai Stevenson got 60 percent.) From the black perspective, those numbers left no doubt of the community's role in sending Kennedy to the White House. Just as Martin Luther King Sr. believed blacks had a debt to Kennedy for his kindness to Coretta, his son and the black community now believed that Kennedy had to repay black voters with solid action on civil rights.

In the aftermath of the election King and his followers were emboldened by the vote tallies to assert that they had a claim on the president's ear and his policies. Despite black skepticism early in the campaign and ferocious attacks by baseball-star-turned-activist Jackie Robinson, Kennedy drew blacks to him at the polls in greater numbers than Adlai Stevenson had in the 1956 election, both in the North and in the South. Stevenson, whose support of black causes was unquestioned, tallied fewer votes in 1956 than Kennedy did in 1960 in black wards in Houston, Texas; Louisville, Kentucky; Nashville, Tennessee; and Richmond, Virginia; among others. In the previous election, Eisenhower captured some of those areas which this time went to Kennedy. Writing in the *New York Times*, Anthony Lewis explained that "Negroes in Northern cities have voted overwhelmingly Democratic in recent years," giving Kennedy less room for improvement in the North. "Nevertheless he did better in most of these areas than Mr. Stevenson had done." This was evident in black districts in Cleveland; East Saint Louis, Illinois; Pittsburgh; Buffalo; Philadelphia; Detroit; and Chicago. In some of these areas, Eisenhower prevailed in 1956, and in 1960 Kennedy grabbed them for the Democrats.

To explain the larger black migration to the Democrats, some analysts pointed out that blacks traditionally identified with New Deal policies for lower-income groups. "But," Lewis noted, "civil rights also played an important part, most observers agree. The feeling is that Vice President Nixon did very little to identify himself with the black cause in the campaign and that Senator Kennedy did a great deal." Lewis singled out the late-campaign call to Coretta followed by the flood of pamphlets in black communities.

Nixon was embittered by his narrow loss and the surprising black turnout for Kennedy. Later explaining his "no comment" at the height of the King uproar, he admitted "this was a fatal communication gap. I had meant Herb [Klein, his press secretary] to say that I had no comment *at this time*." This explanation doesn't quite conform to reality. Nixon in fact had heard a drumbeat of voices within his campaign begging him to speak out immediately, but he remained silent.

President Eisenhower had an opportunity to help Nixon but declined. During the King crisis, Attorney General William Rogers strongly urged Eisenhower to speak out. A statement was prepared, with plans for Eisenhower to read it on television. He was to say that King's arrest was "fundamentally unjust" and that he had "asked the Attorney General to take 'all proper steps' to join with Dr. Martin Luther King in an appropriate application for his release." But he never appeared on TV to read these words, and they were never released to the press. "Had this recommendation been adopted," Nixon wrote in his 1962 book *Six Crises*, "the whole incident might have resulted in a plus rather than a minus as far as I was concerned."

Nixon also lashed out at Robert Kennedy for inappropriately influencing the judge in the case. Even though he felt that King was "getting a bum rap," Nixon believed Bobby stepped over the line when he called Judge Mitchell. "It would be completely improper for me or any other lawyer to call the judge," Nixon explained in *Six Crises*. "And Robert Kennedy should have known better than to do so."

For all his grousing, Nixon emerged from the election wiser. He even laid some of the blame for his loss on himself. Speaking to *Ebony* magazine in 1962, he said, "I could have become president. I needed only 5 percent more votes in the Negro areas. I could have gotten them if I had campaigned harder."

For his part, Eisenhower delivered a rather churlish postmortem on the election. Speaking to a group of businessmen a month after the Republicans' loss of the White House, the president alluded to Jack Kennedy's call to Coretta and Bobby's call to Judge Mitchell. He touted his own administration's fine record on voting rights and integration over the previous eight years and yet, he said dismissively, blacks had flocked to the Democrats because of a "couple of phone calls."

29

JOHN KENNEDY NEVER explained his reason for placing the call to Coretta King. Was the candidate driven by politics or by goodwill? Cynics see only a man of callous manipulation, and torchbearers for Kennedy see only his grace and humanity. As Martin Luther King Jr. himself recognized, both impulses inspired Kennedy's call, and they did not necessarily contradict each other.

Before the idea of reaching out to Coretta even surfaced, Kennedy had secretly phoned the governor of Georgia to express his concern over King's imprisonment. He was aware that Coretta was six months pregnant while her husband sat in prison facing a four-month term and that she feared her child would be born without him. At the time, his wife Jackie was eight months pregnant with their second child. Since his daughter Caroline's birth, Jack had felt the tug of family in demonstrative and subtle ways. He was still a womanizing cad, but his love of Caroline matured him and stirred empathy for other parents. Arthur Schlesinger, a Kennedy champion, rightly believed Jack "had an instinctive tendency to put himself into the skin of others," something he demonstrated on the phone with Coretta. "The call to Mrs. King was only one of a number of personal gestures revealing the grace and force of feeling which lay beneath the supposedly cool façade," Schlesinger explained. "By mid-October one began to feel that the real Kennedy was coming over."

To ascribe a purely political motive to Kennedy's call overlooks a compelling fact: At the time, a positive political outcome from the gesture was far from certain. That Kennedy defied his political advisors underlines that he believed placing the call was the right thing to do.

Writing in his 1980 memoir, Daddy King took issue with those who argued that Jack's call sprang from base political motives and that the elder King was a fool to switch his vote from Nixon to Kennedy. "It was said the Kennedys put one over on us because we weren't really astute enough to see how we were being used," Daddy King wrote. "Oh, we were called blind and ignorant." Only a parent, Daddy King asserted, could understand how important the Kennedys' actions were. "I still feel in my heart," he wrote, "that anyone who would have hesitated to welcome the help the Kennedys offered has never had a son or daughter in the kind of danger M.L. faced at Reidsville."

His son, Martin Luther King Jr., speaking with the wisdom of hindsight after Kennedy's assassination, asserted there was both a political reason and a higher purpose for placing the call to Coretta. "There are those moments in history...that what is morally right is politically expedient, politically sound," he said in an oral history interview in 1964. "I would like to feel—I really feel this—that he made the call because he was concerned. He had come to know me as a person then. He had come to know more about...civil rights and what the Negro faces....So I think that he did something that expressed deep moral concern, but at the same time it was politically sound."

With that call, John F. Kennedy and Martin Luther King Jr. became inextricably linked. In black homes and churches and communities, King was deemed responsible for Kennedy's election, and now the president had a responsibility to King and the twenty million blacks seeking a just life in America. Black hopes and dreams were vested in the two men and their relationship. "King, by that time, had become a kind of epitome of black aspirations," said Sam Proctor, a friend of King's who later became associate director of the Peace Corps. And Kennedy was believed to be a new leader ready to acknowledge those aspirations. The call to Coretta sent a message of hope to blacks that after the indifference of the Eisenhower administration and nearly a hundred years after the end of slavery, a president truly had their best interests at heart. Proctor said the call "was a kind of an existential affirmation before black people that this candidate cared about our well-being, showed respect for us."

That ninety-second conversation with Coretta laid massive expectations on the Kennedy presidency. Before he even settled into the White House, Jack Kennedy was put on notice that blacks from Harlem to Montgomery expected him to listen to their leader Martin Luther King Jr. and hear their cries for equality.

PART THREE

"TOMORROW MAY BE TOO LATE"

30

THE DAY AFTER his victory, President-elect Kennedy rode in the front seat of a white Lincoln Continental toward the Hyannis Port Armory, waving to hordes of well-wishers along the wooded road. Television cameras followed the slow progress of the motorcade as correspondent John Chancellor narrated with excitement. "There's the white Lincoln just behind the tree," the newsman called out when he spotted the car. "There he is, there he is! The next president of the United States."

When Kennedy entered the packed armory and threaded his way toward the rostrum he received "one of the rarest of tributes," as a TV reporter noted on air, "a standing ovation from newsmen, a very very unusual thing indeed."

With his pregnant wife, Jackie, at his side and aides nearby, Kennedy addressed the crowd. Political advisor Ken O'Donnell, watching from the wings, was moved by the metamorphosis of his boss: In a matter of moments, the senator disappeared and the president emerged. "Everything was different," O'Donnell remembered. "He was no longer Jack Kennedy, the candidate....He was humble and grateful, yes, but now wearing 'the hat,' as we called it, the heavy burden of the presidency. Jack was not the same man."

Theodore White also witnessed the birth of President John Kennedy that day. His book *The Making of the President 1960*, published several months after the election, served as a real-time window on Kennedy as he set the course of his administration. His challenge, according to White, was to navigate America's complex politics on war and peace, employment, and, as the author put it, "the meeting of white and black." If the president wished to spotlight a particular need in American society, he was in the position to do it. "The President of the United States has power to educate the people of America, to draw new battle lines," White wrote. "He is the President. It is an entirely personal office. What the President of today decides becomes the issue of tomorrow. He calls the dance."

Watching the president-elect inside the armory, White had a chance to see firsthand what most Americans only caught on television. Before the cameras, Kennedy addressed the nation for the first time as president in waiting, reading out loud wires he'd received from Vice President Nixon and President Eisenhower on his election and his replies to them. Thanking his staff for their work and the voters for their support, Kennedy highlighted the closeness of the election and expressed his wish to have both parties work together in coming years. "I can assure you that every degree of mind and spirit that I possess will be devoted to the long-range interest of the United States and to the cause of freedom around the world," he said. "So now my wife and I prepare for a new administration and for a new baby."

As Kennedy spoke, the camera zoomed in for a tight shot of his face. Theodore White, watching from his spot inside the armory, noticed something that the viewing public did not see on the television screen. As Kennedy alluded to the many dangers and complexities that lay ahead, White wrote, he "spoke evenly, with no tremor in his voice—only his hands . . . shook and trembled, but they were below camera range."

31

ON THE SUNDAY after the election, Martin Luther King Jr. fulfilled a year-old promise to speak at Cornell University. Inside Sage Chapel, he delivered a sermon called "The Dimensions of a Complete Life," a pastoral he had given in various forms since 1954. Before an audience that included Cornell's president, students, and faculty, King distilled for his listeners what he considered the basis of a meaningful life in a speech peppered with Christian and Jewish allusions. "I should submit to you this morning," he offered, "that unless an individual can rise above the narrow confines of his individualistic concerns to the broader concerns of all humanity he hasn't even started living."

The preacher then pivoted from the religious to the political. As he often did, King framed the political through the ethics of religion. "Segregation is wrong because it relegates persons to the status of things," King told his chapel audience. "Segregation is wrong because it assumes that God made a mistake and stamped a badge of inferiority on certain people because of the color of their skin. Therefore," King said, as though challenging the new president, "all men of goodwill have a moral obligation to work assiduously to remove this cancerous disease from the body of our nation."

Many politicians, including Kennedy, had offered a menu of reasons segregation must die but, to King's sensibility, their arguments missed the crucial point. "It must be done," he told his listeners, "not merely to meet the Communist challenge, although it will be diplomatically expedient to do it. It must be done not merely to appeal to Asian and African people, although it would be expedient to do it." Rather, black justice must come for one overwhelming reason. "In the final analysis," King concluded, "segregation and discrimination must be removed from our nation because they are morally wrong."

During a question-and-answer session afterward, the civil rights leader expressed confidence that President Kennedy intended to give a high priority to racial equality in his new administration. "We have seen something very significant in this election," he said, referring to the fact that both political parties had put forth their strongest civil rights planks in history. Pressure at home and abroad, King believed, was expected to drive implementation of many of the proposed reforms.

Just two days before the election, King had praised Kennedy's stand on civil rights on the Atlanta radio station WAOK. "On the civil rights issue," he told Zenas Sears, a white program director and disk jockey known for broadcasting black music, "I think [Kennedy] has taken a much more forthright stand within recent weeks than he did before the nomination or right after it."

King was pleased that Kennedy promised to use the weight of the presidency to enforce Supreme Court–mandated desegregation. The civil rights leader was confident that Kennedy had the strength of character to follow through on his pledges. "Now, there were some people who had doubts about Senator Kennedy's courage from the beginning, including Mrs. Roosevelt, which was one thing that she strongly stated before the convention—that Senator Kennedy lacked courage," King told Sears.

"But I think more and more he has demonstrated a great deal of courage, and this has been impressive."

King had reason to believe that Kennedy would act boldly and even stand up to a recalcitrant Congress if necessary. As far back as January 1960, soon after he announced his candidacy, Senator Kennedy had declared that "in the coming months we will need a real fighting mood in the White House—a man who will not retreat in the face of pressure from his congressional leaders." Speaking at the National Press Club, he promised to throw himself into the "very thick of the fight" in pursuit of his legislative goals. "Roosevelt fulfilled the role of moral leadership. So did Wilson and Lincoln, Truman and Jackson and Teddy Roosevelt," the candidate said. "They fought for great ideals as well as bills. And the time has come to demand that kind of leadership again."

Kennedy concluded his speech with a nod to Abraham Lincoln, depicting the sixteenth president at the moment he acted with unwavering courage to sign the Emancipation Proclamation. "If my name goes down in history, it will be for this act," Kennedy quoted Lincoln as saying. "My whole soul is in it. If my hand trembles when I sign this proclamation, all who examine the document hereafter will say: 'He hesitated.' "

By referencing Lincoln, Kennedy set a high bar for his own courage. He envisioned himself, like Lincoln, as a man of grace and grit, able to act on issues of moral importance whatever the opposition. He longed for his own hand to be steady and firm in the face of formidable national challenges. Concluding this early campaign speech, he extolled the sixteenth president's toughness: "But Lincoln's hand did not tremble. He did not hesitate. He did not equivocate. For he was the President of the United States. It is in this spirit that we must go forth in the coming months and years."

Later in the campaign, imagining himself an intrepid leader, Kennedy declared that he would bring Lincolnesque boldness to the pursuit of civil rights. Addressing an NAACP rally in July 1960, just before the Democratic National Convention, he vowed to use "the immense moral authority of the White House ... to direct implementation of all Constitutional rights." He enumerated the issues his White House was prepared to act on: voting rights, school desegregation, discrimination in government employment, Federal housing, and contracts."

Now, just days after the election in front of the Cornell audience,

King surveyed the arc of Kennedy's progress and declared himself satisfied. The civil rights leader was prepared to assist the new president in early and swift action on racial justice. Referring to his meeting with the candidate during the campaign, King said during the Cornell question-and-answer session, "I have spoken to Senator Kennedy and I am very impressed with his grasp of the problem." In an ominous aside, King added: "I will be very disappointed if he does not take a forthright stand in this field."

32

SOON AFTER THE election, Martin Luther King Jr. telephoned John Kennedy to offer his congratulations and his unsolicited recommendations on White House staffing. Although their face-to-face contact had been minimal, King expected to have Kennedy's ear far more than he ever had President Eisenhower's. While Eisenhower had given tepid support to limited civil rights bills in 1957 and 1960 and had promoted desegregation of public facilities in the District of Columbia, he had never spoken out forcefully in favor of the Supreme Court's 1954 decision in *Brown v. Board of Education* declaring school segregation unconstitutional. Just before the election, King had chastised Eisenhower for his failure to use the power of his office to rally the nation around court-mandated desegregation. "He could have at least used moral persuasion to get people to see that this is the law of the land, it is morally right, and this is something that we as a nation must do in order to maintain our position in the world," he told disk jockey Zenas Sears in his WAOK radio interview.

It wasn't until five years into his presidency that Eisenhower had admitted a black delegation to the White House, and even then he was reluctant, and agreed to the meeting only at King's insistence. Nothing much came of the gathering attended by King, Roy Wilkins of the NAACP, A. Philip Randolph of the Brotherhood of Sleeping Car Porters, and Lester Granger of the National Urban League. As author Taylor

Branch explained: "Publicly, the Eisenhower meeting remained an empty still-life, framed but devoid of substance."

Eisenhower had been old-school, born and raised in an era that accepted segregation and black subservience, an era when even as president he circulated nigger jokes that came to him from his Southern friends. But the 1950s were over, and as Eisenhower was departing from the White House, so too was the world moving away from his sensibility. The 1960s dawned with new vigor and cultural creativity—Elvis was shaking his hips, Allen Ginsberg was defying literary constraints, the birth control pill was promising sexual liberation—and the youthful John Kennedy represented a generational shift in national leadership. His dynamic style offered hope to all Americans—black and white—that the nation was moving forward.

Embracing the new spirit, King proposed his choice for America's new solicitor general: Morris Abram, the white Atlanta attorney and civil rights advocate. The solicitor general was a crucial figure in constitutional battles for racial justice; as the lawyer representing the United States before the Supreme Court, the solicitor general was often known as the tenth justice.

King had telephone conversations with both the president-elect and the newly named attorney general, Robert Kennedy. But by the time King offered his recommendation, the administration had already decided on Harvard Law professor and Kennedy advisor Archibald Cox. King recalled Bobby Kennedy explaining the decision: "He was very honest with me about it, saying that they thought a great deal of Morris Abram... but that they had kind of committed themselves to Cox.... So that was that."

While King received a cordial response, he soon discovered, to his great chagrin, that the White House gates were closing to him. Although he had played a prominent, possibly even decisive, role in getting Kennedy elected, the new president showed no interest, as Daddy King might have put it, in repaying the debt. After his initial, unproductive phone call, King had virtually no contact with the president for months into the new administration.

33

THE PRESIDENT-ELECT EXPECTED a heating up of civil rights activity, but he hoped to keep it from interfering with his primary focus on the economy and foreign affairs. He named his brother Bobby attorney general partly to shift racial justice issues away from himself and onto someone he implicitly trusted. Explaining his decision to Tennessean newspaperman John Seigenthaler, who became an assistant to Bobby, John Kennedy said: "You're from the South. You know how difficult this is going to be....I don't want somebody who is going to be fainthearted." Kennedy wanted an attorney general who would give him the "unvarnished truth," someone who understood the political risks inherent in addressing civil rights issues and yet would deal with them honestly. "When these civil rights problems come up," Kennedy told Seigenthaler, "if my Administration takes the rap for it, I want to know why we took the rap....And with Bobby there I can count on him completely." Chiefly, however, while the president-elect heard the rising chorus of black grievances, he wanted Bobby and others in the administration to deal with them.

Inside the transition team, King's advocate Harris Wofford tried to arrange an early White House invitation for the civil rights leader but was repeatedly rebuffed. Kennedy was uninterested in face-to-face meetings with black leaders. Wofford's role, in his boss's view, was to serve as an intermediary; the president-elect directed his aide to hold meetings himself with prominent black figures such as King and Roy Wilkins, executive secretary of the NAACP, then brief him on their concerns. Playing the buffer intensely annoyed Wofford. "It was good neither for [Kennedy] nor for the civil rights leaders," Wofford explained. "What they conveyed to me lost its freshness and impact when passed on secondhand to the President." With little choice, King and other black leaders had to accept this less than satisfactory mode of communication with the new president.

Wilkins sensed soon after the election that Kennedy was turning away from his campaign promises. "My illusions faded very quickly,"

he recalled. He gleaned from "careful readings around Washington...
that Kennedy had no intention of beginning his Administration with a
full-scale legislative program for civil rights." Instead, Kennedy was
determined to secure a path for his extensive economic agenda focusing on taxes, unemployment, Social Security, wages, and housing; to
enhance the chances of his economic plan, he abandoned any notion of
civil rights legislation. The president-elect calculated that confronting
powerful Southern Democrats with proposals on black equality would
split the party and endanger his program. "This simply floored me,"
Wilkins said. "I felt that this was a tactical error....I thought he should
have kept riding his horse that he was riding in September and October
and charge the opposition." The president-elect was so afraid of the
Southern power brokers he "was giving away his game even before it
started," Wilkins complained. "The South couldn't be wangled into the
slightest crumb if Kennedy said from the start that legislation was out."

In place of civil rights legislation, the incoming administration promised small steps to improve employment diversity throughout the executive branch and the government. The president drove his cabinet to add
blacks to the foreign service staff, the Justice Department, Agriculture
Department, Treasury, and elsewhere. But while these measures were
meaningful, they were small compared to the comprehensive change that
black leaders and the community envisioned from civil rights legislation.
Kennedy's sincere but low-profile approach revealed the presence of his
conscience but also the weakness of his courage.

In late December, about three weeks before Inauguration Day, Roy
Wilkins publicly blasted Kennedy for shying away from his campaign
promises, becoming the first major black leader to voice his disenchantment with the president-elect. Speaking at a conference in Washington,
Wilkins complained that an "atmosphere of super-caution" pervaded the
new Kennedy team. "We don't see why we should be Mickey Mouses
or Minnie Mouses when it comes to civil rights," he told the assembled
crowd.

Wilkins's criticism was carried in the New York Times along with
attacks from other liberal leaders attending the conference. Russell Baker
of the Times quoted a twenty-six-page report from the National Urban
League titled "The Time Is Now," which declared that progress on racial
equality rested on "the power, the will, the talent of the President." The

report left no doubt that the black population was unwilling to wait for change. The Urban League insisted that Kennedy's pledge to move in the "right direction" on civil rights with "all deliberate speed" was not good enough. "There must be full speed ahead," the report demanded. "And the leadership must come from the top. Tomorrow may be too late—the time is now."

Wilkins touched a nerve. The president-elect, hoping to head off a possible cascade of criticism before he even stepped foot into the Oval Office, invited the NAACP head to a private meeting in New York. Wilkins had met Kennedy in 1957 when they had lunch together in the Senate dining room, smoking cigars and sipping coffee. At an NAACP banquet that year Kennedy charmed Wilkins's wife, Minnie, insisting she join in a photo when she started to scoot out of the way. Asking Wilkins, instead of King, to the White House was an easy decision for the president. Not only had Wilkins gone public with his charges but also he was more pleasing company than King. That Wilkins headed the NAACP, which was dedicated to legal redress of civil rights injustice, appealed to Kennedy more than preacher King's take-to-the-streets model. Moreover, Wilkins knew how to talk with Kennedy. The rapport between the two men was, in Wofford's words, "easy and sophisticated."

Wilkins's invitation inflamed a not-so-secret tension between the leaders of the two most important black organizations in America. The birth of King's Southern Christian Leadership Conference following the Montgomery bus boycott posed a challenge to the long-standing preeminence of the NAACP, and the leaders of those two groups, King and Wilkins, were said to be personally at odds. Younger blacks, more impatient for change than the leaders of either group, added another layer of complication. While King and Wilkins tried to minimize the conflict between their organizations, the *New York Times* reported "some of the more ambitious men in the SCLC have made no secret of their scorn for the [NAACP], calling it the 'black bourgeois club'—and worse."

On January 6, Kennedy met with Wilkins and Arnold Aaronson, a Jewish leader and secretary of a coalition of social justice groups called the Leadership Conference on Civil Rights. When the president-elect invited them into his suite at the Carlyle Hotel, Wilkins caught sight of an impressionist painting on the wall by black artist Romare Bearden, on loan from the Parke-Bernet Gallery across the street. "I wondered if this painting had any significance insofar as the Kennedy policies were concerned on the Negro," he recalled.

Any hope inspired by the work of art was short-lived. The new administration had no intention of altering its plans: The president-elect made clear he would rely on executive action to push the ball forward on civil rights. Turning on the charm, Kennedy managed to win Wilkins's acceptance of the strategy. If legislation was out, then Wilkins urged the president-elect to issue a sweeping executive order to address an array of racial injustices in housing, employment, education, and public accommodation. The president-elect took in the proposal with courteous skepticism. "He didn't assail it," Wilkins recalled, "but he did say that he didn't know whether he had the authority, or whether it would be wise even if he had the authority."

With apparent open-mindedness, Kennedy encouraged Wilkins and his associates to think through their proposal. "Why don't you get in touch with [Kennedy aide and speechwriter] Ted Sorensen and maybe prepare a memorandum on this," Kennedy suggested, "and let him talk it over with some of the staff members and we'll see what comes out of it."

It was impossible to know if the offer was an empty gesture or a sincere attempt by the new president to find a way to issue a comprehensive executive order, bypassing Congress to answer the call of his conscience. Indeed, Wilkins was among many who believed Kennedy was guided by laudable instincts on civil rights, even if he shrank from dramatic proof early in his administration. As he remembered: "Through all the years I knew and watched Kennedy, I did not for a moment doubt his moral fervor, and his sympathy for black Americans was real enough as well, but getting him to turn those emotions into tangible political action was a matter of an entirely different order."

After the meeting, Wilkins quieted his complaints and cheered approvingly as Kennedy brought blacks into top government jobs. Robert Weaver gained the highest executive post ever held by a black, the sub-cabinet position of chairman of the Housing and Home Finance Agency; later he became the first black cabinet member under President Lyndon Johnson. Kennedy also chose blacks as deputy assistant secretary of state, assistant White House press secretary, and U.S. attorney for Northern California. Several months later he named Thurgood Marshall to the U.S. Circuit Court of Appeals, beginning Marshall's journey toward the Supreme Court.

34

ON INAUGURATION DAY, January 20, 1961, the new president settled into the reviewing stand in front of the White House to watch the traditional post-swearing-in parade. The eight-mile-long procession moved along Pennsylvania Avenue in a twenty-degree chill; eight inches of snow had fallen in Washington and was swept away in a massive operation overnight. Despite the cold, Kennedy sat for three and a half hours watching forty-one floats and seventy-two marching bands. Amid the music and pageantry one jarring note jumped out at him. After the parade, in his first moments in the White House, President Kennedy caught his aide Richard Goodwin in a corridor near the Oval Office.

"Did you see the Coast Guard detachment?" Kennedy asked.

The president had closely studied the honor guard of the United States Coast Guard Academy as it marched past the reviewing stand. As Goodwin searched his mind to recall the unit, the president continued: "There wasn't a black face in the entire group. That's not acceptable. Something ought to be done about it."

Goodwin raced back to his office, wondering who was in charge of the Coast Guard. Some quick research turned up the answer: the Treasury Department under Secretary Douglas Dillon. When Goodwin got Secretary Dillon on the phone he informed him of the president's observation. Dillon, navigating his first day on the job, replied: "Tell him I'll get right on it."

Roy Wilkins was pleased to learn of Kennedy's action on the Coast Guard. The president might have ruled out a legislative push, believing he was hamstrung by an intransigent Congress, but he was not nearly as insensitive to racial inequities as President Eisenhower had been. The shabby treatment of blacks offended Kennedy both intellectually and morally, and on Inauguration Day Wilkins believed he got a glimpse inside the president. "This is the most important day in a man's life—the day he is inaugurated President of the United States," Wilkins recalled.

"Yet he took time out of that day to notice there were no Negroes in the Coast Guard unit."

Wilkins also was pleased by an initiative Kennedy undertook days after the inauguration. Concerned about the level of black participation throughout the federal government, the president directed his cabinet secretaries to boost the number of blacks in their departments. He called for a census of government employees to determine the number of blacks already on the job and their grade levels. When that study turned up the expected dismal results, he ordered the departments to draw up steps to correct the imbalance. For the most part, these efforts were conducted without much publicity, shielding the president from a political backlash among Southern whites. While Wilkins applauded the efforts on employment, he remained skeptical of Kennedy's larger commitment. "All these gestures could not make up for defaulting on a legislative program. It looked very much like a holding action," he complained. Quiet steps did not point to a bold civil rights policy, Wilkins concluded. "We were off to a very bad start with Kennedy."

35

THE EISENHOWER YEARS had intensified black resentment over presidential inaction, and strong White House leadership was now imperative, Harris Wofford advised Kennedy in a memo. If the president balked on an early legislative thrust, blacks would regard it as a "sellout." Raising a note of alarm, Wofford cautioned that "no one can predict when the Negro cup of bitterness and skepticism is going to overflow." Kennedy ran from a legislative showdown, Wofford believed, because he had never mastered the politics of the Senate during his term there. "The president feared the power of the senatorial club he knew well but in which he had always been something of a junior member," Wofford observed.

Kennedy perhaps need not have cowered before Congress. If he had shown some backbone right after the election and challenged seg-regationist senators, he might have been able to subdue them. In his book *The Bystander*, Nick Bryant showed that the stranglehold Ken-nedy believed Southern Democrats wielded over Congress had signifi-cant weaknesses. Even one of the great political masters, the staunch white supremacist senator Richard Russell of Georgia, sensed a chang-ing mood in Congress. In 1959, he declared that "the representatives from the states of the old confederacy no longer present a common front." Shortly before the presidential election Russell expressed con-cern over the Democratic platform, which contained several pledges on civil rights, telling a constituent it would be difficult to save "our South-land from the evil threat."

In a further sign of a potential opening on civil rights, the Republican Party was becoming more liberal and progressive. Nixon's loss suggested that Republicans in Congress needed to soften their conservatism and focus more on social justice to attract Northern blacks. "Of the thirty-six Senate Republicans who Kennedy identified as [conservative] coali-tion members, as many as a dozen were reform-minded liberals from the party's pro–civil rights wing," Bryant pointed out. Some Senate Republi-cans went so far as to say that their party would support Kennedy on civil rights.

Evidence came in other ways. In March Kennedy had to fill two slots on the six-member Civil Rights Commission, an independent panel cre-ated in 1957 to keep watch over civil rights across the nation, investigate concerns, and recommend actions for improvement. Kennedy replaced two departing conservatives with appointees who were opposed to seg-regation. The new members won Senate approval without obstruction by Southern power brokers.

Analyzing recent congressional voting results, Russell Baker of the *New York Times* concluded that the new Senate was "predominately lib-eral in complexion." *Newsweek* declared that if Kennedy "jumps right in with a broad new legislative program, he will find Congress so receptive that his record might well approach Franklin D. Roosevelt's famous 'One Hundred Days,'" when FDR pushed through fifteen major bills in 1933 to combat the dire circumstances of the Great Depression.

Yet Kennedy shrank from asserting his leadership. Although he had risen to the presidency, he was still intimidated by some Southern

legislators he had observed while serving in the Senate. He cringed before
the stunning political skills those racists deployed to obstruct legislative
proposals that they viewed as threats to their Southern way of life. Speaking of the extraordinary gifts of these senators, he told a newspaperman:
"The good [Southern] ones seem to have a grasp of government and how
to carry out the political maneuvers quite beyond that of the able men
of other regions." In Bryant's view, Kennedy was "overawed" by these
Southern goliaths. The new president believed the Southern power brokers "should be charmed, and on occasion, gently cajoled, but never confronted directly."

The president's fears of confronting Congress were confirmed inside
the administration's echo chamber; his advisors lined up one after the
other in support of his hesitation. As aide Ted Sorensen asserted: "No
amount of Presidential pressure could put through the Eighty-seventh
Congress a meaningful legislative package on civil rights. The votes were
lacking in the House to get it through or around the Rules Committee.
They were lacking in the Senate to outlast or shut off a filibuster."

Kennedy, backed by his advisors, constructed a scenario that pointed
to inevitable legislative defeat. As the president said, "There is no sense
in raising hell, and then not being successful."

36

To THE NEW president, Martin Luther King Jr. was an unwelcome
reminder of White House inaction. Although he was largely ignored by
the administration in these early days, he nonetheless lay on the president's conscience. If Roy Wilkins represented the legal ambitions of the
civil rights movement, Martin Luther King Jr. stood at its moral center. In
his writings, and preaching, and manner of life, King propounded ideas
and principles the president found uncomfortable.

Shut out by the administration, King nonetheless was determined to
make his voice heard inside the White House. Overshadowed at first by
Roy Wilkins, he stepped up his criticism and prodding of the president,

chastising him for his moral surrender and urging him to summon the strength of character to pursue a legislative battle. Unable to arrange a private meeting, King resorted to sending his messages through the media. In an article in the *Nation* on February 4, he challenged Kennedy to accelerate the "intolerably slow pace of civil rights." He called on the president to "take the offensive, despite Southern opposition, by fighting for a really far-reaching legislative program." Success required bold action.

Kennedy was in position to exploit the goodwill of the nation. Pollster Louis Harris put the president's approval rating in March at 92 percent, while Gallup had it at 72 percent. King urged Kennedy to use "moral persuasion" and the prestige of his office to lead the country toward the elimination of racial discrimination. He suggested that the president hold mixed-race conferences on segregation at the White House and even discuss equal rights in fireside chats. By embracing a leadership role on civil rights, the president could encourage a change in the culture of discrimination. "Even in the hard core South," King noted, "a small but growing number of whites are breaking with the old order. These people believe in the morality as well as the Constitutionality of integration." If the president became actively engaged, Americans north and south would recognize the necessity of equal rights.

His arguments were provocative but King knew that pleas in magazines and newspapers had limited impact. What got the president's attention was powerful collective protest. In a warning, he extolled the virtues of nonviolent direct action by the masses, calling the protest movement "a method of securing moral ends through moral means." Implying that blacks had to take determined action on their own— and not rely simply on the government to act—King pointed out that "thousands of courageous students, sitting peacefully at lunch counters, can do more to arouse the Administration to positive action than all of the verbal and written commentaries on governmental laxity put together."

On the television program *The Mike Wallace Interview* that same month, King reiterated his challenge to the president, saying: "I think he has a real opportunity. I think he understands the problem and I think he has a real concern and I'm very hopeful." But then he added: "I hope I'm not engaging in superficial optimism."

If King expected that he, like Wilkins, deserved a private meeting with the president, he was disappointed. King posed a particular political problem. As leader of the Montgomery bus boycott and an uncompromising, high-profile opponent of segregation, he was a controversial, even hated, figure in the South. If the president worked too closely with him, he could damage his relationship with the Southern Democrats he needed for his economic legislative agenda. The president was not drawn personally to King in any case; the civil rights leader was not the kind of man the president envisioned for a close, consultative relationship. From his youngest days, Kennedy had a weakness for lively personalities; an engaging demeanor sometimes was all it took to bust open the door to the Oval Office. This was nowhere more apparent than in the president's welcome to Bobby Troutman, a conservative patrician and long acquaintance from Georgia whose usefulness to the administration was rather minor. But Troutman nonetheless got himself into the Oval Office whenever he was in Washington largely because he amused the president. "A funny man, full of jokes, Troutman could bluff his way into almost any office," Wofford recalled.

By comparison, King was a serious, circumspect visitor not given to the witty banter that Kennedy delighted in. While King was a confident, fiery orator, he had a natural reserve when not on the pulpit. A white associate found that face-to-face he was "very thoughtful, quiet, and shy—very shy," adding, "The shyness was accented...with white people." James Baldwin said that as a civil rights advocate the preacher had a "winning" presence but, Baldwin acknowledged, "he does not give the impression of being particularly outgoing or warm." It didn't help his relationship with Kennedy that King carried on his shoulders the dreams of vast numbers of blacks; he bore his burden lightly but nonetheless with an unspoken messianic aura.

Kenneth O'Donnell, who scheduled the president's appointments, knew to keep King away from the Oval Office. As much as King and the president's civil rights aide Harris Wofford petitioned him for a meeting, Kennedy always had something more pressing to do than see Martin Luther King Jr.

37

THE NATION'S CIVIL rights leader had made himself unpopular to President Kennedy in another way. In his February article in the *Nation*, Martin Luther King Jr. had called for integrating all levels of the federal government, including the FBI. And he implied that white FBI agents did not investigate rigorously enough the crimes of Southern racists. "If, for instance," King wrote, "the law-enforcement personnel in the FBI were integrated, many persons who now defy federal law might come under restraints from which they are presently free." The remark erupted inside the corridors of the FBI, and particularly riled its director, J. Edgar Hoover.

After the *Nation* piece, Hoover again turned his wrath and his agency's considerable investigative resources on the civil rights leader. The director, whom Attorney General Robert Kennedy later characterized as "dangerous" and "a psycho," drove his men to fabricate allegations that King was under the sway of communists, bogus information that eventually made its way into the hands of the attorney general, who then passed it on to his brother the president. The damning reports, accepted as fact, could not help influencing the president's arm's-length approach to the preacher. The FBI agents developing the charges against King knew the reports were false but were forced into satisfying Hoover's racist mania. As William Sullivan, the assistant director in charge of the FBI Domestic Intelligence Division, later admitted: "We had to engage in a lot of nonsense which we ourselves really did not believe in. We either had to do that or we would be finished."

Keeping his distance from King, the president cultivated intermediaries such as Harry Belafonte. The well-loved singer posed little political threat to the White House, even though he was active in civil rights causes. As a celebrity, Belafonte polished the president's own star image and at the same time was able to serve as a hinge between the Kennedys and King. "I really was right in the middle between Martin Luther King, on the one hand, and the Kennedys, John and Bobby, on the other, as a new administration took office and hopes rose for change," Belafonte recalled. Shuttling between the two sides, Belafonte believed he had a role "both in counseling the Kennedys to help Martin and in counseling Martin on how much we could expect from the Kennedys." The president and the attorney general saw "Martin as the movement's leader, and me as a conduit to him, one they felt more at ease with than a goodly number of the southern Baptist preachers who made up most of Martin's circle." Belafonte was offered a role in Kennedy's new Peace Corps program as a cultural advisor on African nations and was asked to join the Corps' governing board. "Unofficially," Belafonte admitted, "I suspected my greater role was to talk Martin and the other civil rights leaders into doing what the administration hoped they would do."

Having established back-channel communication with King, the administration still shunned him. In early March, the civil rights leader was excluded from a meeting with Attorney General Kennedy to explore ways to pursue racial justice in the absence of major legislation. Among the proposals presented was a White House program to champion equal employment opportunities for blacks. The following day, the president issued an executive order aimed at ending job discrimination among federal contractors; a month later, as the program went into effect, the president described employment equality as "a high moral purpose." At the attorney general's meeting, Bobby Kennedy also announced plans for a Justice Department effort to increase the ranks of black voters. A push on voting rights was far less inflammatory to Southerners than a drive to desegregate schools across the region. As Bobby Kennedy remembered: "How could anybody, really, get very mad because you're making an effort to make sure that everybody votes? I mean, they can. But they can't come out as openly as they can on schools: 'We don't want our little blond daughter going to school with a Negro.'" King's absence from the meeting was a disappointment to the civil rights leader and a blow to his Southern Christian Leadership Conference, which had long advocated for black jobs and voter registration.

Several days later, King begged the president for a private meeting. "If it is at all possible," he asked on March 16, "I would like to have a conference with you within the next three or four weeks." He acknowledged the president's busy schedule but impressed upon him how important it was for the two of them to discuss the current state of civil rights in America. Harris Wofford and Frank Reeves, a black special assistant to the president, both became aware of King's request and encouraged appointments secretary O'Donnell to invite the civil rights leader to the White House. "Such a meeting with King is important now," Wofford advised O'Donnell, "to lay the groundwork for his understanding why there will be no substantial civil rights legislation his year."

Besides Kennedy's natural reluctance to see him, King had to compete with a world of troubles demanding the president's time. Just then Kennedy was spending hours in deep discussion with his military and foreign policy advisors over a civil war in a tiny, landlocked country on the other side of the earth that was unknown to most Americans. The impoverished Southeast Asian kingdom of Laos was battling Soviet-backed communist insurgents, and the administration was scrambling for ways to prevent a communist takeover. Soviet Premier Nikita Khrushchev had challenged the incoming president in a speech made public in January two days before the inauguration declaring that he intended to support "national liberation movements...fighting against colonial rulers or against capitalist governments." Laos was sinking into the Soviet-American morass in Southeast Asia.

At a press conference on March 23, President Kennedy told the American people of "this difficult and potentially dangerous problem." To give himself a wide hand, he framed Khrushchev's threat in the broadest possible terms. "The security of all Southeast Asia will be endangered if Laos loses its neutral independence," he told reporters. "Its own safety runs with the safety of us all."

The tensions overseas provided a convenient excuse to deny King's request for a few minutes in the Oval Office. On March 25, O'Donnell informed the civil rights leader that President Kennedy was unable to see him due to the "present international situation."

38

THREE MONTHS INTO his term, the president finally acknowledged that his administration needed to take the measure of Martin Luther King Jr. in person. But because King was a political hazard, Kennedy was still leery of inviting him to the White House for a public meeting. So a secret get-together was arranged away from Pennsylvania Avenue. On April 22, King joined Attorney General Robert Kennedy and several others for an off-the-record luncheon in a private dining room at the Mayflower Hotel a half mile from the White House. King, who was allowed just one advisor, arrived with Stanley Levison. On the administration's side Bobby was joined by Assistant Attorney General Burke Marshall, who headed the Civil Rights Division, black political consultant and deputy chairman of the National Democratic Committee Louis Martin, Harris Wofford, Kenneth O'Donnell, administrative assistant John Seigenthaler, and a couple other Justice Department staffers. King listened while Marshall laid out the Justice Department's approach to civil rights, highlighting the limits the Constitution imposed on its enforcement of desegregation. Marshall pointed out that the department was better able to intervene in protecting voting rights. The government, he said, was currently engaged in lawsuits to stop some counties from obstructing black registration.

During a break in the discussion, Wofford quietly informed Robert Kennedy about the aide accompanying King. Stanley Levison, he explained, had been mentioned ominously during Wofford's own vetting to gain FBI clearance for his job in the White House. In the 1950s, Levison had come under J. Edgar Hoover's scrutiny as a possible communist. A wealthy lawyer, he was known through FBI phone taps to have assisted King in some writing projects and in developing the Southern Christian Leadership Conference. When Wofford was getting to know King in the 1950s, he spoke several times by phone with Levison, and the conversations were picked up by the FBI. Under questioning for the White House job, Wofford had rejected the agency's suspicions about Levison. "Whoever had listened to the phone conversations could verify their substance," he said during his White House scrutiny. "They would indicate that Levison was devoted to King personally and to the idea of nonviolence." When Wofford pointed out King's associate to Bobby Kennedy at the Mayflower, the attorney general brushed off any concerns: Levison had a quiet, thoughtful manner, and hardly looked sinister. But that didn't keep the FBI director at bay; his campaign of vilification was only beginning. In Hoover's imagination, the unassuming lawyer was a communist who influenced Martin Luther King Jr. and cast the suspicion of communist infiltration over the entire civil rights movement.

When King spoke at the Mayflower luncheon he agreed with the administration's emphasis on voting rights and noted similar efforts of the Southern Christian Leadership Conference. He was low-key, despite displaying a hint of the orator, but he didn't strike the men at the table as preachy. Louis Martin of the Democratic National Committee came away from the meeting believing King was "the most self-effacing national leader I have ever known." The Kennedy men were impressed but weren't quite sure what to make of King: He was either "a saint or a pushover, or both," according to author Taylor Branch. "He was not the type they would think of asking out for a beer, but he was reasonable." Bobby Kennedy was so comfortable with King that he wanted "to culti-vate him politically rather than to disengage," according to Branch, who interviewed the participants in the meeting. When King informed Bobby that voter registration workers were often threatened and unable to reach the FBI for help, Kennedy jotted down Seigenthaler's and Marshall's tele-phone numbers and handed them to him. "Any hour of the day or night," Bobby told King, "you call."

After the meeting, Wofford took King to the White House, and word of his presence soon spread to the Oval Office. Just four days earlier, the new president suffered a humiliating defeat when a CIA plan to topple Fidel Castro turned to disaster. Castro's forces quickly subdued an inva-sion team of Cuban exiles, in what became known as the Bay of Pigs incident. Privately the president blamed the fiasco on the CIA, which he said had misled him with promises that an internal Cuban rebellion would erupt when the invasion force landed—a rebellion that never came. On April 18, with the failure weighing on him, Kennedy held a late-night meeting in the Oval Office with two close aides during which he suddenly stopped speaking. The disconsolate president went out into the Rose Garden and he paced for nearly an hour. When his press sec-retary Pierre Salinger went to see him the next morning in the family quarters, he found the president crying in his bedroom. That evening Kennedy attended a dinner at the Greek Embassy with Jackie and his parents. Describing her husband's condition to his mother, Rose, Jackie said that "he was so upset all day & had practically been in tears." Jackie comforted him until he went to bed, saying she "had never seen him so depressed" except for the dark days he grappled with his back surgeries. His anguish was still with him days later when he wandered out of the Oval Office to shake hands with Martin Luther King Jr.

"It's good to see you," he told King. "I've been keeping up with you and with your work."

The president introduced King to several White House staffers, and assured him that his brother kept him apprised of developments. Their conversation was cordial but the shadow of the Bay of Pigs hung darkly over the president. "He was obviously very worried. I could tell," King remembered. "He was attempting to be warm and friendly, but you could see that this thing was weighing on him very heavily. So we didn't even discuss civil rights then." In less than five minutes, the impromptu meeting was over, and Kennedy sent King on his way, saying: "If you ever need me, you know the door is always open to you."

The session had been unplanned, and was insubstantial. As the days passed, the president's open-door invitation rang increasingly hollow, both because of his hesitance to fully embrace civil rights and his determination to shield himself from King's disruptive political influence.

39

WHILE THE PRESIDENT had marred his image by the failed Cuban invasion, the pastor had his own troubles. Once an idealized civil rights leader, Martin Luther King Jr. was losing esteem among some activists. Since the bus boycott in Montgomery in 1956, King had led no new demonstrations. Other activists, meanwhile, were launching imaginative new campaigns, leading blacks into battle, while King had in some measure retreated to the sidelines. In an early sympathetic biography, published in 1964, Lerone Bennett Jr. noted that during this time other men were dominating the headlines. "King seemed somehow marginal," Bennett wrote. If the president was concerned about new forms of unrest and possible bloodshed in the streets, there were organizers who were greater threats than King.

Less than a week after King had his brief encounter with the president, a Howard University theology school graduate named James

Farmer, who was now national director of the Congress of Racial Equality (CORE), sent a letter to President Kennedy, beginning in mild enough fashion: "We expect you will be interested in our Freedom Ride, 1961." Farmer explained that he had organized CORE members, white and black, to travel as interstate passengers on Greyhound and Trailways buses across the South "to challenge, en route, every form of segregation met by the bus passenger." Farmer included a day-by-day itinerary of the journey, which was to begin on May 4 in Washington, D.C., and proceed through Virginia, North and South Carolina, Georgia, Alabama, and Mississippi, and end in New Orleans on May 17. Farmer assured the president that the group was "experienced in, and dedicated to, the Gandhian principles of non-violence." But the nature of the undertaking posed a distinct possibility of bloodshed unleashed by offended Southern whites. Whatever the personal risks, Farmer believed there was a greater threat at stake. "We feel that there is no way to overstate the danger that denial of democratic and constitutional rights brings to our beloved country," he wrote in the letter. "And so we feel it our duty to affirm our principles by asserting our rights." Farmer sent similar notices to Attorney General Robert Kennedy, to the FBI, and to the Greyhound and Trailways bus companies. The warning was sent to the officials in accordance with the Gandhian principle of openness about protest actions. Reminded of the letters years later, Farmer laughed: "We got no reply. We got no reply from Justice. Bobby Kennedy, no reply. We got no reply from the FBI. We got no reply from the White House, from President Kennedy. We got no reply from Greyhound or Trailways. *We got no replies.*"

The Kennedy administration was largely blind to the new creative ways of protest. Pushing protest in a new direction, Farmer believed it was time to expand beyond localized efforts; the sit-ins had been effective but limited because they challenged only local laws. Farmer sought federal action to prohibit segregation for all passengers using buses, terminals, restaurants, and waiting rooms when crossing state lines. The Supreme Court and the Interstate Commerce Commission had already declared segregation in interstate travel unconstitutional, but Southern states and the federal government had not enforced the orders.

By sending integrated buses through the South, Farmer hoped to provoke confrontations that would force the government to act with finality.

As he explained: "We planned the Freedom Ride with the specific intention of creating a crisis. We were counting on the bigots in the South to do our work for us." He expected that the government would respond only if headlines featuring white attacks on blacks ricocheted around the world, threatening America's image overseas. "An international crisis, that was our strategy," he said. It was a strategy that clashed head-on with the hopes of President Kennedy, whose aim was to keep a lid on civil rights disturbances; a crisis over racial equality would disrupt the pursuit of his other national and international goals.

NAACP head Roy Wilkins had no doubt that violence would erupt when biracial groups were sent into white-only facilities in the South. In Wilkins's view, Farmer knew exactly what to expect from this frontal assault on segregation in the heart of Dixie. "The real test he was setting was for the White House and Justice Department: How far would the Kennedys go to protect the riders when the inevitable violence occurred?" Wilkins observed. "It was a desperately brave, reckless strategy, one that made those touch-football games played by the Kennedys look like macho patty-cake."

Jet magazine reporter Simeon Booker, who was joining the rides to write a series of articles, stopped by the Justice Department beforehand. Hoping to ensure some protection for the riders, he poked his head into Bobby Kennedy's office to warn him of possible trouble. "Okay," Bobby said, "call me if there is." Then, in a gesture of solidarity, Bobby added: "I wish I could go with you." But Booker wasn't reassured; he left the Justice Department uncertain that the attorney general comprehended the explosive nature of the journey.

40

ON AN UNSEASONABLY cool Thursday, May 4, thirteen Freedom Riders rolled out of Washington, D.C., on two buses—a Greyhound and a Trailways—and traveled through Virginia and North Carolina. Although the bus companies didn't respond to Farmer's letter, they had taken note and removed the FOR COLORED and FOR WHITES signs at some terminals along the route.

If the Freedom Riders hoped to grab the public spotlight at the outset, they were disappointed. With no early confrontations, the newspapers looked elsewhere. On Friday, May 5, just one day after the riders hit the road, Americans turned their attention to the skies. Some fifty million viewers watched live on television as astronaut Alan B. Shepard Jr. climbed into a nine-by-six-foot Mercury capsule called *Freedom 7* at Florida's Cape Canaveral. At 10:34 a.m., viewers heard the final countdown: "Three...two...one...zero...ignition...*liftoff*!" Packed into his capsule that reporters described as "spacious as a telephone booth," Shepard shot into the sky atop a Redstone booster rocket and hurtled to an altitude of 115 miles during a flight lasting fifteen minutes. He was now a national hero, the first American to blast into space.

The launch was America's rebuttal to the Soviet Union's superior space program. In 1957, the communists sent the satellite Sputnik 1 into low orbit around the earth, and over the following years the Soviets continued to outdo the United States. A month before Shepard's flight, cosmonaut Yuri Gagarin rocketed the Soviets into the next phase by becoming the first man to orbit the earth.

Shepard's achievement was modest but the noncommunist world cheered: France called the brief flight "astonishing" and "sensational." In the wake of the Bay of Pigs disaster and setbacks in Laos, President Kennedy wanted to rebuild America's pride at home and its standing in the world. Shepard's accomplishment gave the president a chance to extol America's open society over the government secrecy that pervaded the Soviet Union. While the Soviet leadership kept the public in the dark about its space exploits until the ventures proved successful, the United States played out its own risky launches on live TV. "I want to pay cognizance to the fact that this flight was made out in the open with all the possibilities of failure which would have been damaging to our country's prestige," Kennedy told the nation. "Because great risks were taken in that regard, it seems to me that we have some right to claim that this open society of ours which risked much gained much."

The newspapers proclaimed Mercury a triumph of American values, and astronaut Alan Shepard was hailed as the quintessential American.

He was, in this telling, the common man who thrives in a free society by his ambition and skill. James Reston of the *New York Times* made much of the fact that Shepard was not in the top of his class at the United States Naval Academy in Annapolis: "He was well down in the middle, with over 400 ahead of him." Yet he was poised and gracious and honest as he stood before newsmen after his singular act of courage. "Shepard turned out to be that recognizable American character," Reston wrote, "the kid next door, the dream of the easy athletic all-American boy." In his climb to hero status, "he symbolized...the free and natural man."

Shepard's ascent was a journey possible only for a white man. No blacks were in training to become astronauts. At Cape Canaveral, very few blacks were employed other than as janitors. An exception was Julius Montgomery, who had studied at Tuskegee Institute and worked on the military side of the space program in missile technology apart from the astronauts. He was a member of the Range Rats, a team responsible for repairing ballistic missiles and their tracking systems. A group of exceptional black women mathematicians was employed at a NASA facility in Virginia to do calculations for rocket launches, including Shepard's. President Kennedy, sensitive to the racial gap at NASA, saw a chance to send a sharper message to the Soviets by bringing blacks into the astronaut corps. Two months after Mercury's success, the White House demanded that NASA find black recruits to become future astronauts. While the campaign was well-meaning, it also had clear propaganda value. In initiating the effort, the president's special assistant, Frederick Dutton, explained that black participants were important "for symbolic purposes" and that their role "would find great response throughout the world."

While America celebrated its newest hero, the Freedom Riders were rolling into the deep South to challenge an ignoble legacy of inequality. Like Shepard, the thirteen bus riders were venturing into the unknown in a quest to fulfill what astronaut and activist alike believed was America's unique promise. James Reston's depiction of Shepard could easily have applied to each Freedom Rider: "Danger he took as part of life and duty without question and even with a kind of quiet pride."

41

AS THE FREEDOM Riders pushed on, Robert Kennedy headed to the South for a long-planned visit to the University of Georgia in Athens to deliver his first major speech as attorney general. In January, the university admitted two black students, Charlayne Hunter and Hamilton Holmes, under a federal court order that predated the Kennedy administration. In her first class, Hunter had listened as her psychology professor discoursed on the nature of human behavior and then she exited the classroom to hear a student in the hall holler: "Back up and let the nigger through."

That night rioting had erupted on campus as a mob swarmed Hunter's dormitory howling and cursing and throwing rocks and firecrackers at the building; some students marched behind a bedsheet banner with a taunt written in red: NIGGER GO HOME. The rioters spilled onto nearby U.S. Highway 441, hurling bricks at cars and rolling logs into the street. The Ku Klux Klan, led by the grand dragon of Georgia, circulated in the mob handing out racist literature. After about an hour, the police finally moved in with tear gas and fire hoses. The university's answer to the violence was to suspend the two black students, as a dean of students explained, "in the interest of their personal safety and for the safety and welfare of more than 7,000 other students at the university."

Five days later, as the campus cooled down, Hunter and Holmes returned to class escorted by university officials and armed guards. Police cruisers and unmarked security vehicles snaked through the grounds. Thirteen students had been arrested for their role in the rioting, and several others had withdrawn from the university in protest over the admission of the black students. The mood now had lightened somewhat. Claude Sitton of the *New York Times* described the scene on campus: "Several students shouted mockingly, 'Hey gal, how y'all' at Miss Hunter as the 18-year-old coed walked from one building to another. Others, however, smiled and spoke pleasantly to the two."

Bobby Kennedy had spent weeks fussing over the language and tone of his speech. When he arrived at the university on May 6 the blacks' presence on campus, although grudgingly accepted, still caused unease. Georgia's leading politicians boycotted Kennedy's appearance. Georgia governor Ernest Vandiver again found himself squeezed by the complexities of his political alliances; although he had supported John Kennedy's presidential ambitions and secretly assisted in getting Martin Luther King Jr. out of jail before the election, the governor vanished from the state when the attorney general came to speak. He explained that Bobby's address fell on the same day as the Kentucky Derby, and he was planning to be in Louisville. The top officials on hand were the mayor of Athens and a state senator. While the attorney general had provided no hint of the topic of his speech, it was a foregone conclusion that civil rights was on the agenda. Angered by the attorney general's visit, a few students had painted a plea on the sidewalk: "Yankee go home"; but the words had been washed away before his arrival. Five fundamentalist ministers picketed with signs that read: THE BIBLE TEACHES SEPARATION, and they were carted off by police.

Kennedy mounted the stage and stood at a monstrous, tiered rostrum that seemed almost to swallow him as he addressed 1,600 white alumni and students and Charlayne Hunter and Hamilton Holmes, who were also in the crowd. The audience was comprised of Southerners whose beloved lifestyle was under assault, and the Northerner charged with enforcing the laws reshaping their world now stood before them. Whatever hostility awaited him, Bobby had decided to lay out clearly and forcefully the administration's intentions on civil rights. His hands shaking, he launched into his speech with a bit of light humor: "They have told me that when you speak in Georgia, you should try to tie yourself to Georgia and the South, and even better, claim some Georgia kinfolk." He noted that there were a lot of Kennedys in Georgia but as far as he knew none were relatives. But he did have one direct tie to Georgia. "This State," he said, "gave my brother the biggest percentage majority of any state in the union and in this last election that was even better than kinfolk."

Moving on to the meat of the speech, the attorney general noted that he had come to the university's law school to participate in Law Day, which gave him his opening to discuss the fundamental importance of laws to a free society. Man had struggled a long time, he said, to create a system of law and government that ensured basic freedoms. Alluding to court rulings on school desegregation, Kennedy said: "The decisions of the courts, however much we might disagree with them, in the final analysis must be followed and respected. If we disagree with a court decision and thereafter, irresponsibly, assail the court and defy its rulings, we challenge the foundations of our society."

As the Kennedys often did, the attorney general framed the respect-for-law argument in the context of the battle against the Soviet Union, where citizens were robbed of their freedoms by the rule of autocrats in place of the rule of law. "We must come forward," he declared, "with the answer of how a nation, devoted to freedom and individual rights and respect for the law, can stand effectively against an implacable enemy who plays by different rules and knows only the law of the jungle."

Finally Kennedy came to the specific topic on everyone's mind: civil rights. As he built his case, a dead silence fell over the crowd. The attorney general was firm in asserting the government's intent to enforce the law but he was also sympathetic to the travails of the modern Southerner. "You may ask: Will we enforce the civil rights statutes? The answer is: Yes, we will." But he added, "We will not threaten, we will try to help." The government, he promised, will play its role "without regional bias or political slant." He said that he understood that the Supreme Court ruling on school desegregation "required difficult local adjustments," noting that "the decision in 1954 required action of the most difficult, delicate and complex nature, going to the heart of Southern institutions." The attorney general had come to realize, he said, that "the hardest problems of all in law enforcement are those involving a conflict of law and local customs."

Speaking with candor and steering clear of the hypocrisy that he said Southerners abhorred, Kennedy admitted that he approved of the Supreme Court's ruling. "I happen to believe that the 1954 decision was right. But my belief does not matter—it is now the law. Some of you believe the decision was wrong. That does not matter. It is the law." He praised Georgia's acceptance of the ruling. "By facing this problem honorably, you have shown to all the world that we Americans are moving forward together—solving this problem—under the rule of law." Surprising many of his listeners, the attorney general had managed to convey not only his dedication to the law but also his moderation in dealing with the South. Americans had a larger purpose, he suggested, and that was to join together in a commitment to unity and to the eventual triumph of the United States over the Soviet Union.

As he stepped away from the podium, there was silence. For several seconds, it was unclear what was coming next: the hissing and jeering

Bobby had feared, or something more respectful. Then, rising to their feet, the white students, faculty, and alumni gave Robert Kennedy a sustained ovation, the applause lasting, in the view of several observers, about a half minute. One paper called the response "enthusiastic." Another said the audience "applauded warmly…the reception…seemed to be one of appreciation for his frankness."

Bobby's speech, which landed on the front page of the *New York Times* and the *Washington Post*, heartened civil rights advocates. Martin Luther King Jr. shot off a telegram to the attorney general welcoming his words. In a letter, Jackie Robinson told Bobby that the speech helped boost American prestige throughout the world. Noting his earlier disapproval of the Kennedys, Robinson said he was encouraged that Bobby had shown a "sincere desire to support the principles" of his office. "Because of an earlier misunderstanding, I had grave doubts about your sincerity," Robinson wrote. "In this case, I find it a pleasure to be proven wrong." The *Pittsburgh Courier* printed the text of the address, calling it "courageous, frank and all-embracing…one of the most forthright statements ever uttered on the status of contemporary race relations in the United States of America by a high-ranking federal official."

Bobby Kennedy's fair and forthright language on a subject of exceeding delicacy filtered out over the campus and across the state and the South. For Charlayne Hunter the impact was tangible. A month after the speech, she walked into the university dining room for her first time since arriving on campus in January: She entered with three white classmates just like any other student, and there was no jeering or taunting. As she walked from class, students nodded or smiled or greeted her in some other reasonable way. Later at her dorm, she recalled, "a tall, blonde, rather attractive girl came in with a bag of groceries in her arms. 'Hi,' she said smiling. 'Let's cook dinner. I'm starved.' " Looking out her window, Hunter remembered her first night when a brick and Coke bottle crashed through the glass into her room and mobs swarmed outside. Now there was no tear gas in the air, no patrol cars at the curb. "Only beautifully landscaped ground, green shrubbery and, across the street, a lovely modernistic church whose steps—once crowded with on-lookers, demonstrators and cameramen—were deserted in the shadows of the late afternoon." Writing in June 1961, Hunter felt optimistic. "Maybe I am poorly qualified to predict what tomorrow will be like," she mused, "a tomorrow made up of days which may be weeks, months and even years in coming...when Charlayne Hunter and Hamilton Holmes will be forgotten except by those who have come to know them as classmates or as friends."

For Holmes, such optimism proved elusive. Prejudice and threats haunted his campus experience. Throughout his term at the university, he went to class during the week in Athens then fled to his home in Atlanta on weekends. His unease among the white students at times escalated to dangerous levels. In one tense incident, Holmes had parked his car behind the Kappa Alpha Order fraternity house to study in a nearby language lab. That fraternity celebrated the Confederacy and its house flew the Confederate flag. When Holmes came back from the lab, he found his car blocked in by two fraternity cars. To clear a path for his car, he climbed into the fraternity vehicles one after the other and rolled them out of the way. As he was finishing with the second car, a group of about twenty fraternity brothers descended upon him. The conversation escalated, led by the smallest guy in the group. Casually, Holmes reached into his own car and secretly removed a flashlight from his glove box and tucked it into his belt beneath his jacket. "Okay, look, if you want trouble, that's what you're gonna get," he told the ringleader. And he rested his hand on his jacket, making a show of the bulge underneath that had all the appearances of a gun. The little bully retreated to the safety of his fraternity brothers, and they all vanished. "After that, I didn't have any other trouble," Holmes recalled. "The word sorta got around that I had a gun."

After he graduated, Holmes became the first black admitted to the Emory University Medical School in Atlanta and he eventually became an associate dean and a member of the medical school's faculty; he was an orthopedic surgeon and chairman of the orthopedic unit at Grady Memorial Hospital in Atlanta. Charlayne Hunter, later known as Charlayne Hunter-Gault, became a reporter for the *New York Times* and then a correspondent for the *MacNeil/Lehrer NewsHour*. Twenty-five years after her Georgia graduation, she returned to the campus to deliver a commencement speech. Speaking to the class of 1988, she recalled hearing Robert Kennedy declare that her and Holmes's admission to the university was a frontline attack in the Cold War against the Soviet Union. Kennedy said that their graduation "will without question, aid and assist in the fight against Communist political infiltration and even guerilla warfare."

In her 1988 talk, Hunter-Gault told graduates she was astonished to hear Kennedy elevate her and Holmes into warriors of the Cold War. "I almost fell over," she remembered. "I hadn't thought of it in quite those terms."

With his eloquent speech in Georgia, Robert Kennedy became the face of the administration on civil rights. That the attorney general—and not the president—took the lead underscored the approach of the Kennedy White House. As Bobby declared, the administration was determined to enforce civil rights laws vigorously, which placed the attorney general and the Justice Department at the forefront. But more significant, a strictly legal approach allowed President Kennedy to move into the shadows on civil rights. The administration's voice was to be the attorney general's, not the president's: The law of equal justice took precedence over its morality. In handing the nation's day-to-day racial struggles over to his brother, President Kennedy sidestepped his leadership role early in his tenure and denied himself the bully pulpit to rally the nation toward just treatment for blacks.

In several ways, Bobby was a better administration figurehead on civil rights than the president. He had not only a fierce commitment to the law but also a clarity on racial justice. Bobby had sided with blacks during the wave of sit-ins in the South, telling journalist Peter Maas that his sympathy was "with them morally." By contrast, the president early in his tenure was tormented by a Hamlet-like dithering on civil rights.

The positive reaction to Bobby in Atlanta suggested that the South was learning to accept change, or at least, to recognize its inevitability. In such a climate, President Kennedy had a chance to prevail upon the Southern powers to join him in pursuing swift progress. But he was still reeling from the debacle in Cuba, and he was wary of risking his political fortunes on a battle as unpredictable as civil rights. The president miscalculated the depth of black disenchantment; he hoped he could avoid a racial showdown simply by ignoring the combustible conditions, the fearless resolve of the black activists, and the stubborn opposition of white extremists. Had the president exploited the power of his office to push for early reconciliation on racial rights, he might have averted the violence that lay ahead.

can develop.

Your Employee Assistance Program (EAP) offers a wide rang
of support and resources, available at no extra cost, to help

- Develop an optimistic outlook.
- Practice self-compassion.
- Focus on your strengths.
- Build your confidence.

42

THE FIRST SIGN of trouble for the Freedom Riders came in South Carolina when John Lewis, a twenty-one-year-old farm boy from Alabama, was blocked from entering the white waiting room in the town of Rock Hill. Standing up to the hooligans barring his way, Lewis declared: "I have every right to enter this waiting room," and he cited the Supreme Court case *Boynton v. Virginia*, which had outlawed segregation at bus terminals. The racists replied, "Shit on that," and clubbed him to the ground. Lewis, who grew up without electric lights and indoor plumbing, had been inspired by the Montgomery bus boycott and its leader, Martin Luther King Jr. While in college at Fisk University he organized sit-ins in Nashville, Tennessee, then volunteered for the Freedom Rides. As Lewis fell to the ground, another Freedom Rider named Albert Bigelow, a white, burly Navy captain in World War II, stepped peaceably between the goons and the farm boy. The racists knocked Bigelow off his feet. The two Freedom Riders, adhering to their pledge of nonviolence, absorbed the blows without fighting back. Police finally rolled up and put an end to the assault but made no arrests.

So far, the national press had scarcely covered the Freedom Rides. United Press International sent out a brief dispatch on the Rock Hill incident, which showed up on page twenty-five of the *New York Times*. The tempered language of the wire service hinted at the explosiveness of the Freedom Rides. "Members of a biracial 'peace corps' touring the South by bus to test segregation statutes," the May 10 report said, "charged that they were beaten yesterday by white 'hoodlums' at a Greyhound bus terminal."

Three days later the Freedom Riders arrived safely in Atlanta for a meeting with Martin Luther King Jr. The civil rights leader had offered advice and support but so far was largely a bystander in this campaign. On the day of the Rock Hill attack, King was in Montgomery, Alabama, overseeing an SCLC board meeting. In Atlanta, King agreed to have a private dinner with the riders at Paschal's, followed by a larger, public meeting at Warren Memorial Methodist Church. For an undisclosed reason—rising tensions over the rides may have played a role—the public gathering was canceled. During the dinner at Paschal's, King took *Jet* reporter Simeon Booker aside and delivered some frightening news: "I've gotten word," King told him, "you won't reach Birmingham. They're going to waylay you."

Ignoring the threats, the Freedom Riders boarded their buses in Atlanta on May 14 and headed off for Birmingham. Organizer James Farmer wasn't on board for this leg of the trip. Two hours before the buses departed he learned that his father had died from cancer in a hospital in Washington, and he set off to be with his family. His mother said afterward that his father willed his own death at that time to prevent Farmer from joining the most dangerous part of the mission into Alabama and Mississippi. Well aware of the violence that befell blacks in the Deep South, his father had said to his son: "There, somebody will probably take a potshot at you, and I just hope they miss." Every day in the hospital, the elder Farmer studied the itinerary. When the group got to Atlanta, he spoke up about the dangers that lay just ahead, warning: "Oh, tomorrow he goes through 'Bama." And then he died. Farmer promised to meet up with the Freedom Riders again after taking care of his family obligations. "I must confess," he said some years later, "that while I felt guilty at leaving, there was also a sense of relief at missing this leg of the trip, because all of us were scared."

Martin Luther King Jr. also stayed behind. It was unclear whether his decision was based on a crisis of courage, common sense, or a philosophical difference with Farmer's strategy. King was searching for how best to push forward the cause of civil rights, but at this point he did not see it in the confrontational tactics of the Freedom Rides. Historian Adam Fairclough has observed that King regarded the Rides as "brave but also reckless and provocative." King had left the front lines of the civil rights battlefield, ceding some of his authority, Fairclough believed. He "seemed strangely ambivalent about embracing the new tactics by personal example," the historian wrote. His "leadership seemed less than inspiring and betrayed an impression of timidity and indecisiveness."

King was occupied with other pursuits. His Southern Christian Leadership Conference was in a period of transition, expanding its fund-raising activities, hiring organizers, and improving its administration—activities that took the leader's time and attention. His withdrawal from confrontational protest was aimed at improving his rapport with the president. He still hoped for an entrée to the White House and understood that what President Kennedy wanted most was peace on the streets. If King presented himself as sympathetic to this concern he had a better chance of gaining the president's ear. But building a relationship with Kennedy was a tricky undertaking. King couldn't reliably know what the president thought of him. Although his inside advocate Harris Wofford provided his perceptions, he was somewhat marginalized and not privy to the most sensitive conversations within the White House. Nor did King know the depth of the smear campaign that FBI director J. Edgar Hoover had launched to poison his reputation with the administration.

While a closer alliance between the president and the famous civil rights leader had the potential to help temper civil unrest, Kennedy wasn't inclined to befriend Martin Luther King Jr. or even to turn to him as an arm's-length advisor. Their personalities, the fragile politics, the FBI's insidious meddling, and an array of domestic and international distractions thwarted any workable cooperation between the two men. And so, as the Freedom Riders set off to shatter the foundations of Southern life, neither President Kennedy nor Martin Luther King Jr., together or apart, had the ability, or even perhaps the authority, to influence an increasingly combative movement.

On the day the Freedom Riders started toward Birmingham, the renowned civil rights reporter of the *New York Times* Claude Sitton published a front-page story headlined WAVE OF NEGRO MILITANCY SPREADING OVER THE SOUTH. It made no mention of the Freedom Rides but explored the broad ambitions motivating the black population. As Sitton observed, the community was impatient for "full equality—nothing less." Blacks were invigorated to fight for their rights in cities and suburbs and small towns and in sharecroppers' communities. "The lack of progress has fired the Negro's determination to a point where no sacrifice is too great," the newsman wrote. Sitton visited with Martin Luther King Jr., still regarded by the news media as the crowned head of the movement. Despite King's recent irresolution, the *Times* reporter hailed him as "the popular symbol of the new militancy" and sought his explanation for the changing mood. King told the journalist that he believed the new passion had been unleashed by improvements in the economic and cultural lives of blacks. He attributed the change to black migration from rural areas to urban industrial centers and to a population better informed by the press, radio, and television. "The new militancy grew out of the Negro's growing sense of dignity and destiny," King told Sitton. "Whenever people get a new sense of dignity they become more determined to do away with the barriers to freedom."

The black hope for freedom, however, clashed with Southern obstinacy to change. And now, in the absence of national leadership, two Greyhound and Trailways buses containing strong-willed desegregationists were flying down the highway toward the first racial cataclysm of the Kennedy presidency.

43

ON THAT MOTHER'S DAY, May 14, 1961, President Kennedy spent a leisurely Sunday at the oceanfront home of his father in Palm Beach, Florida. He attended Mass at Saint Edward's Church with Jackie and his mother, Rose, seated in a pew toward the rear near a red phone connected to the White House. The pastor, the Reverend Jeremiah P. O'Mahoney, delivered a special tribute to deeply religious Rose, honoring her for her piety. In the afternoon the president was on the golf course with friends.

Reminders of the failed Cuban invasion still dogged him. A group of grieving Cuban mothers whose refugee sons gave their lives in the U.S. attack had planned to take part in a large motorcade from Miami to Palm Beach; the goal was to bring attention to their tragedy and encourage the president to keep up pressure on the Castro regime. Wishing to quash the demonstration, the administration managed to talk them out of it in return for a presidential statement at an anti-Castro rally. Press secretary Pierre Salinger appeared at the rally in Miami's Bayfront Park and read the president's message declaring that "Freedom will come." Salinger and two American military leaders then met briefly with about fifty Cuban women and ten refugee men at the Palm Beach Town Hall.

As was often the case, foreign affairs were foremost in the president's mind. On Tuesday he was to head north for a two-day state visit to Canada, and at the end of the month he was off to Paris for discussions with French president Charles de Gaulle. As the Greyhound bus carrying the Freedom Riders flew down Highway 78 through Georgia then into Alabama and onto Highway 21 toward Anniston, the White House was leaking the biggest international news story of the day. Reporters were rushing around Palm Beach to get tight-lipped public comment from administration officials on a tip that President Kennedy hoped to meet with Soviet Premier Nikita Khrushchev in a European city after his talks with de Gaulle in Paris. In the aftermath of the debacle in Cuba and the troubles in Laos, Kennedy had decided that personal diplomacy at the highest level was the best hope for easing Cold War tensions. One goal high on the White House agenda was to restart stalled negotiations for a ban on nuclear weapons testing. The president and his entourage were so focused on the sun, the sea, and the Soviets that they paid no heed to the black and white Freedom Riders arriving in the racially explosive Deep South of Alabama.

As the Greyhound bus pulled into the terminal at Anniston—a Ku Klux Klan stronghold—it was swarmed by a throng of white men armed with iron bars. Before the bus door opened, Anniston police swooped in and cleared a path, allowing the driver to speed away. The mob was ferocious—and quick—scrambling to cars and chasing the bus, some two hundred men in fifty vehicles pursuing their prey. Just six miles out of town the bus pulled over, disabled, at the side of the road. Some riders reported the tires had been shot out, others said the tires had been slashed back in the Anniston terminal.

One of the Freedom Riders on board was Henry Thomas, a brawny Howard University student born poor in rural Florida. At Howard he felt out of place among the young, privileged blacks who comprised most of the student body; he'd come on the Freedom Ride in response to years of humiliation and to get away from the bourgeois confines of Howard. Now he watched through a window as a mob surrounded the bus and the driver ran out the door, taking off "like a rabbit," he recalled. "I couldn't very well blame him."

The passengers—seven Freedom Riders, two journalists, and five other travelers—had nowhere to run. Windows began shattering; bricks were flying, pipes and axes rained down on the vehicle. The large back window suddenly caved in, showering glass in all directions; then a firebomb was hurled through the opening. Thomas panicked as flames and black smoke rose from the aisle. As the smoke thickened, he realized that he would die if he stayed aboard. He and the other passengers pushed toward the front and found the mob outside pressing against the door, trapping them inside.

On the bus were two plainclothes Alabama Highway Patrolmen planted on board with hidden microphones to snoop on the Freedom Riders. One of the men, E. L. Cowling, sprang into action; he pulled his revolver and ordered the mob to back off, freeing the door. Alabama's racist governor, John Patterson, later claimed that his decision to put the troopers on board saved the lives of the Freedom Riders. The governor's motives of course had nothing to do with safety, and whether Cowling acted out of altruism or self-interest we'll never know. He and his fellow officer were trapped on the burning bus along with everyone else, and in such circumstances death would have chosen its victims without regard to skin color.

Tumbling out of the smoky vehicle, Thomas staggered into the fresh air racked by the dry heaves. And no sooner had he stepped outside than someone attacked him. "I got whacked over the head with a rock or I think some kind of a stick as I was coming off the bus," he recalled. In fact, the weapon was a baseball bat. The white thugs swarmed the Freedom Riders, pummeling them bloody, stopping only after Alabama state troopers rolled up.

* * *

The second group of Freedom Riders aboard a Trailways bus had left Atlanta for its journey to Birmingham an hour after the Greyhound bus. At the Anniston station, the racially mixed group of riders bought sandwiches at the whites-only restaurant and, as they were settling back into their seats at the front of the bus, several white men boarded. The driver then announced over the loudspeaker that the first bus had been burned and its passengers beaten and taken to the hospital; the same fate awaited this bus, the driver said, "unless we get these niggers off the front seats." When one of the riders declared that interstate laws gave people the right to sit wherever they liked, one of the white thugs answered by whacking him in the face, and a mini one-sided riot erupted. With fists flying the racists knocked the Freedom Riders to the floor and stomped on them, then dragged them to seats at the back of the bus. As trained, the Freedom Riders took the blows without fighting back. A white Freedom Rider, sixty-one-year-old former Michigan State University professor Walter Bergman, who was beaten badly, said several policemen stood outside the bus watching the violence inside. The white assailants stayed on board as the bus left the Anniston terminal for Birmingham, while the Freedom Riders lay bleeding in the back.

In Birmingham, an ugly welcoming committee awaited the Trailways bus through a collaboration between city police, the FBI, and the Ku Klux Klan. The mob had planned to greet the other bus at the Greyhound station. But an FBI informant named Gary Thomas Rowe received a call from police informing him that the Greyhound riders had been waylaid and that a Trailways bus was soon to arrive. Rowe swiftly got the news to the Klansmen waiting at the Greyhound station, and everyone hightailed it to the Trailways terminal. As Rowe remembered the scene: "We made an astounding sight...men running and walking down the streets of Birmingham on Sunday afternoon carrying chains, sticks, and clubs....We barged into the bus station and took it over like an army of occupation. There were Klansmen in the waiting room, in the restrooms, in the parking area."

At the Trailways station, a white, Harvard-educated Freedom Rider named James Peck and a quiet black student named Charles Person, both battered from their beatings at the Anniston terminal, climbed off the bus and walked together toward the whites-only waiting room. Expecting trouble, Peck warned Person, and the black student "responded by simply saying, 'Let's go,'" as Peck recounted in his 1962 memoir. When they entered the waiting room, heavyset Klansmen started throwing punches while others moved in with baseball bats, chains, and lead pipes. In the confusion, Person escaped, running out of the terminal and into the street. Left to the barbarity of the Klansmen, Peck eventually needed fifty stitches to close the wounds on his head. Other Freedom Riders who had stepped off the bus were hunted down and beaten. The rampage went on for fifteen minutes—blood flowing, bones cracking, bodies collapsing to the ground—without any sign of police. When officers finally showed up no Klansmen were arrested.

More than a dozen years later, a Klansman revealed that the city's public safety commissioner, Eugene "Bull" Connor, promised to give the mob fifteen minutes to do its damage before he would send any policemen to the scene. Soon after the attacks, when he was asked what took police so long to arrive, the public safety commissioner offered that the good men were off visiting their mothers on Mother's Day.

44
———————

WITH THE BLOODSHED in Alabama, the civil rights movement entered a new phase. The riders' strategy of direct confrontation threw a bright spotlight on desegregation and on the delicate line between federal power and states' rights. Federal law was definitive: In *Boynton v. Virginia*, the Supreme Court had held that it was illegal under the Interstate Commerce Act to maintain segregation at public transportation facilities. But local law and custom stood in stark defiance of what national law decreed—and so far local jurisdictions in the South were able to preserve segregation at bus terminals because the Interstate Commerce Commission had failed to enforce the desegregation provisions of the act.

The burden now lay on the federal government: Would the Kennedy White House intervene to enforce the law and protect blacks in what the South believed was a local matter, and if so, how? The administration confronted a twin crisis of states' adherence to federal law and a breakdown in public safety and order. Alabama clearly intended to follow its own customs. The absence of a police response to the assault on the Freedom Riders—and no arrests—suggested that Southern authorities were ill disposed toward maintaining order and eager to protect troublemakers in their midst. As reluctant as President Kennedy was to focus on civil rights, he was now forced to pay attention.

Soon after the violence, Freedom Riders tried to get a response from the president. Organizer James Farmer, who was still in Washington, fired off a telegram to the White House, decrying Alabama's defiance of the Supreme Court and the Interstate Commerce Commission. The attacks, Farmer wrote, "served notice that Negro interstate bus passengers may not travel with dignity in parts of our country except at risk

of life and limb." He condemned the failure of Alabama police to intervene, an outrage that "desecrated the fate of our nation before the world."
He called on the president to act. "Federal investigation and intervention
urgently required," he pleaded. "Equally imperative that moral force of
your office be exerted. The President must speak."

Witnessing the carnage in Birmingham, Simeon Booker of *Jet* magazine remembered Robert Kennedy's offer: Call if there was trouble. Even
though it was Sunday, Booker got a Justice Department operator and
insisted he had to get in touch with the attorney general. Soon Bobby's
special assistant, John Seigenthaler, phoned and promised to pass the
dire news immediately to Robert Kennedy. In minutes he called again to
assure Booker and the Freedom Riders that the Justice Department was
set to take action to protect them and their right to travel safely on interstate highways.

But Seigenthaler made an impossible demand. At Bobby Kennedy's
bidding—and possibly the president's—he told Booker that all journalists
and photographers had to withhold coverage of the grisliest aspects of the
story. "I couldn't believe my ears," Booker recalled. "There was no way
to put a lid on it." Along with Booker, there were two other journalists
on the buses: Moses Newson of the *Baltimore Afro-American* newspaper, who was writing and taking photos, and Theodore Gaffney, a free-
lance photographer working for *Jet*. Other newsmen had converged on
the scene, including Howard K. Smith, a CBS News correspondent who
was in Birmingham researching a television documentary on racism in
the city; he was tipped off by a white supremacist who told him he would
want to see what was about to go down at the bus terminal. Soon Smith's
vivid reporting was streaming nationally over the CBS radio network.
"One passenger was knocked down at my feet by twelve of the hoodlums
and his face was beaten and kicked until it was a bloody pulp," Smith
reported. He explained that the attacks were not spontaneous "but carefully planned and susceptible to having been easily prevented or stopped
had there been a wish to do so." Obviously disgusted, Smith concluded
that the "laws of the land and purposes of the nation badly need a basic
restatement, perhaps by the one American assured of an intent mass hearing at any time, the president."

That the administration sought to restrict the news underscored the
political complications posed by the violence. The president and the

attorney general were appalled by the white bigots and by the flouting of established law; but they were also infuriated with the Freedom Riders. "They were sickened by the hatred and brutality of the whites," John Lewis recalled, "but they were just as upset with *us*." In the Kennedys' eyes, the Freedom Riders were instigators, inciting unrest when the president was staking much of his credibility on a series of foreign initiatives. "Back then, still early in the game," Lewis said, "it was the problems of the Kennedys that were the Kennedys' major concern, not the problems of black America."

* * *

On Monday, the president returned from Palm Beach looking "refreshed from his four-day golfing holiday" and refusing to answer any questions about plans for a summit with Khrushchev in June. He also was silent about the other big story of the day: Splashed across the front pages were disturbing photos of the chaos in Alabama. In one shot, the Greyhound bus at Anniston was ablaze with thick black smoke billowing from its windows. Another image showed a black passenger from the Birmingham bus not associated with the Freedom Riders being beaten by a mob of Klansmen; a white man was pictured with his arm raised high brandishing a stick or an iron rod. Later in the day, the battered Freedom Riders went before television cameras. White activist James Peck, his face bandaged, described the beatings he endured first in Anniston and then again in Birmingham.

Staring at the press coverage, the president and his aides began to understand that this crisis was far more than a passing flare-up. Somewhat naïvely they were witnessing the acceleration of the quest for civil rights among an awakening black population. "None of them had had to deal with a racial situation of this magnitude before," John Lewis explained. "They had no map, no directions, not even a sure sense of the scope of what was unfolding in the South." Lewis recalled White House civil rights aide Burke Marshall admitting as much years later. "The Freedom Ride was an education to me, to the attorney general and to the White House," he told Lewis.

45

ON MONDAY, MAY 15, at around 10 a.m., Bobby Kennedy phoned the Birmingham home of the Reverend Fred Shuttlesworth looking for Simeon Booker. The *Jet* reporter had taken refuge at the parsonage after the bus attack the previous day. By now, the rest of the Freedom Riders, nursing broken teeth, battered ribs, and bloodied scalps, were safe at the pastor's home. Some made it there on their own by taxi; others had been swept up by Shuttlesworth and whisked away. As soon as the pastor learned that the Freedom Riders in Anniston were in danger he had sprinted into action; he organized a convoy of black drivers, armed with shotguns and rifles, to rescue the injured riders from Anniston Hospital sixty miles away; doctors had refused to treat them for fear of retaliation from the marauding mob. Henry Thomas remembered the chaos throughout the wing. "The people at the hospital would not do anything for us," he recalled. "And I was saying, 'You're *doctors*, you're medical personnel.' They wouldn't."

Booker was eating his breakfast in Shuttlesworth's kitchen when the call came from Washington. Someone on the line said, "The attorney general wants to speak to you," and in a moment Robert Kennedy's voice came through the receiver. Booker described the beatings in detail, the serious wounds, the lingering sense of menace. Kennedy then spoke with Shuttlesworth, who explained that in their battered, exhausted condition the riders wanted to carry on to Montgomery. Although displeased, Bobby promised to arrange safe passage with Alabama authorities. His call lifted everyone's spirits. "It was the first time during the modern civil rights movement that the leader of a Southern integration effort had the ear and undivided attention of the attorney general of the United States," Booker explained.

But Bobby Kennedy ran into immediate complications: Alabama governor John Patterson refused to guarantee the safety of the Freedom Riders whose "sole purpose," he insisted, "was to violate certain state laws to get them tested in court." Patterson had been a staunch supporter of Senator Kennedy, endorsing him early and braving attacks from local media for backing a Catholic for the presidency. "I liked the man personally," Patterson said. "I considered him a friend. I liked his views." But he loathed Jack's baby brother, especially when "he would ask me to do things which I conscientiously could not do and still be governor of Alabama." Like his fellow Alabamans, Patterson resented the Freedom Riders as outsiders meddling in the state's private affairs. Why, he asserted, did these troublemakers deserve protection?

In the early afternoon the frustrated riders, pushing on bravely, or recklessly, headed out to the Greyhound terminal to catch the 3 p.m. bus to Montgomery, despite no assurances of safe passage from the Justice Department. Klansmen and other racists awaited them; newspapermen and broadcasters were also there, a sight that emboldened the riders. "The whole world would be watching, unless the police allowed the Klan to take down the TV cameramen and bevy of reporters gathered there this time to record the encounter," Simeon Booker recalled. Local police managed to keep the troublemakers back as the riders filed into the white waiting room. Then news of Patterson's decision came over the radio. "The citizens of the state are so enraged," he asserted, "that I cannot guarantee protection for this bunch of rabble-rousers." With armed segregationists congregated all along the route to Montgomery ready to attack, the Greyhound driver refused to take his seat behind the wheel. His defiance forced George Cruit, the manager of the Greyhound station in Birmingham, to cancel the 3 p.m. bus.

Reverend Shuttlesworth, who escorted the eighteen riders to the station, called Robert Kennedy on a pay phone and put the station manager on the line. When Cruit explained to the attorney general that no drivers would get on the bus, Bobby shot back: "Do you know how to drive a bus?" To Cruit's admission that he did not, Bobby witheringly replied: "Well, surely somebody in the damn bus company can drive a bus, can't they?" He reminded Cruit that the law entitled the riders to transportation. "Somebody better get in the damn bus and get it going and get these people on their way."

The attorney general's bullying yielded nothing. At 5 p.m. the riders, still marooned in the station, decided to give up on the bus to Montgomery; instead they would fly to New Orleans. Many were in such bad shape that to risk further violence on the road was ill-advised anyway. The Freedom Rides had not failed, they told themselves, because they had amply proved that basic laws of the land were being ignored and that Americans could not travel freely in their own country. Flying would give the riders an opportunity to take part in a commemoration in New Orleans on May 17, marking the seventh anniversary of the *Brown* decision. As they headed out to the Birmingham airport, hoping to quickly board a flight out of the city, Klansmen and their cohorts scrambled after them in pursuit.

46

IN NASHVILLE, ACTIVISTS of the Student Nonviolent Coordinating Committee (SNCC) were alarmed that the Freedom Rides might wind down without achieving their goal of desegregating interstate travel. These students, including John Lewis, the Fisk University student who was knocked to the ground at Rock Hill, South Carolina, had been instrumental in desegregating department stores, theaters, and various Nashville locations through sit-ins, stand-ins, and other actions. With creativity and determination, the young Nashville activists stood at the forefront of the student movement. Lewis had left the Freedom Ride for several days to keep an appointment for an interview in Philadelphia; he was considering a two-year program after graduation to build homes in Africa or India. He had returned to Nashville ready to resume his participation just as the Anniston and Birmingham violence was erupting.

After long debate the Nashville students had decided to serve as reinforcements for the injured Birmingham riders. Fearing the Freedom Rides were disintegrating, the Nashville desegregationists took matters into their own hands. As Lewis explained, he and the others were driven by "the most basic tenets of nonviolent action—that is, that there can be no surrender in the face of brute force or any form of violent opposition." The students were adamant. "Backing away is not an option," Lewis said. "It is simply not a choice."

Since the rides were a project organized by the Congress of Racial Equality, the young activists had to coordinate with national director James Farmer. But the students, particularly Lewis, were unimpressed by Farmer, a big, burly man with a baritone voice and massive ambitions. His chief aim was to ensure maximum recognition for CORE, the organization he cofounded in 1942. "I understood that that ambition was in the name of CORE," Lewis said. "Everything he did and said seemed to be in the interest of CORE. He was completely committed to the organization, as if it had a life of its own." But now in the face of the violence, the students believed Farmer wanted to call off the rides.

Diane Nash, cofounder of the SNCC, was chosen to inform Farmer of the students' intention to launch another round of rides. Nash was the group's dynamic leader, a twenty-one-year-old Catholic from a black middle-class Chicago family, and one of the most clever and effective young black desegregationists. John Lewis saw something else in her: "The first thing you have to say about Diane—the first thing anyone who encountered her noticed, and there was no way *not* to notice—is that she was one of God's beautiful creatures, just about the most gorgeous woman any of us had ever seen."

Nash phoned Farmer in Washington before his father's funeral and asked him if he objected to the Nashville students taking up where the CORE riders had left off.

"You realize it may be suicide," Farmer replied.

"We fully realize that," Nash told him, "but we can't let them stop us with violence. If we do, the movement is dead."

Farmer's response irritated Nash and her fellow students. As Lewis put it, "It was a little insulting to assume that we hadn't already considered the brutal reality that lay ahead of us. Farmer wanted to back down from that brutality."

Privately fearing that he was about to lose control of the Freedom Rides, Farmer nonetheless gave the students his blessing, promising to rejoin them after his father's funeral.

47

In Washington, Robert Kennedy and his staff were preoccupied with getting the injured Freedom Riders safely on a plane out of Birmingham. Although hostile white supremacists infested the airport, the riders' departure still looked promising: They had seats aboard an early evening Eastern Airlines flight to New Orleans. But before they could get into the air, disappointment set in. "No sooner had we boarded [the plane] than an announcement came over the loudspeaker that a bomb threat had been received," James Peck recalled. Everyone filed off the plane for baggage inspection and after considerable delay the flight was canceled. As the hours wore on, the airport filled up with a menacing mob, mostly men in T-shirts; the riders clustered in a corner protected by a fairly sizable force of police. At a pay phone, *Jet* magazine's Simeon Booker informed the attorney general. "It's pretty bad down here," he explained. "We don't think we're going to get out." Sensing trouble, Bobby ordered John Seigenthaler, his special assistant and the only Southerner on his staff, to fly down to Birmingham immediately. "He thought that would give [the Freedom Riders] some umbrella of protection," Seigenthaler recalled, "and a sense of security, and very well might mean that, with a federal representative with them, they would not be harassed by local authorities." When night fell, the riders felt a sense of doom. "This is a trap," one whispered to Booker. "We'll all be killed." Booker's prediction that the riders would be stranded in Birmingham seemed bleakly accurate when another bomb scare canceled a second flight.

By the time Seigenthaler arrived at around 11 p.m., the terminal was on the edge of violence. A mob had swarmed around the small, frightened cluster of riders bunched into a corner. Making his way to the gate, Seigenthaler came upon what he described as a "sad befuddled group. They were literally shaking." He tracked down an airline official, telling him he'd flown down on instructions of the attorney general. "We want to get these people out of here and on their way. It's going to be better for you if you do that."

The official told Seigenthaler about the two bomb scares and two cancellations. He laid out little hope of the riders getting on a plane. "We have another flight coming up now," he said, "and I'm afraid we're going to have another bomb threat." Seigenthaler encouraged the airline rep to ignore any further bomb threats, impressing upon him that no one truly was going to blow up the airplane. "You don't want these people here forever," he reasoned. "Why don't you get them the hell out of here, and we'll all be better off."

Seeing the sense of it, the airline official devised a subterfuge to get the riders onto the incoming plane without anyone noticing. To prevent another bomb threat, there was no terminal announcement of the latest flight to New Orleans. When the aircraft pulled up to the gate, it continued to rev its engines as all passengers—except the riders—were loaded on; the activists sat quietly as if they were going nowhere. "When I give you the high sign, we'll go," the rep told Seigenthaler, informing him that the control tower was in on the plot. "You get them on quickly. We'll get the plane off the ground as quickly as possible." *Jet* reporter Simeon Booker, who was among the group hoping to sneak out of Birmingham, had had enough of the threats and violence. He just wanted to get safely off the runway. "The sweat in our armpits wasn't just from the heat," he recalled. With a signal from the rep, the riders hastily filed on board before anyone knew what was happening. No bomb threat came. "I got on with them," Seigenthaler recalled, "and we were in the air. It was the quickest takeoff of any plane I've ever flown."

On arrival in New Orleans, the exhausted Freedom Riders wept with joy and shared a moment of jubilation with comrades from the Congress of Racial Equality there to welcome them. In Washington, Robert Kennedy savored the news that the Freedom Riders were safely out of Alabama, confident the crisis in the South was fading.

But the relief was short-lived. At 3 a.m., civil rights aide Burke Marshall in Washington phoned Seigenthaler in his hotel room in New Orleans. "Do you know Diane Nash in Nashville, Tennessee?" Marshall asked him. Groggily Seigenthaler said he had heard of her but didn't know her personally. "Well," Marshall continued, "she's getting ready to lead a group to Birmingham to take up where the other group left off. Could you call her and ask her not to do that?"

When Seigenthaler got Nash on the phone he learned that she herself wasn't going on the ride but she confirmed that a group was heading to Birmingham. Seigenthaler was blunt. "You know, they're going to kill them," he told her.

"If they kill them," Nash replied, "we'll just have that many more down there, and sooner or later we'll get somebody through."

48

As President Kennedy flew off to Canada on Tuesday, May 16, for a two-day state visit, the new Freedom Riders were completing their plans for their journey from Nashville to New Orleans with stops in Birmingham, Montgomery, and Jackson. Around noon on Wednesday, ten riders—two whites and eight blacks, including John Lewis—rolled into Birmingham. "It was not until we reached the Birmingham city limits, two hundred miles south of Nashville, that the trouble began," Lewis recalled in his memoir, *Walking with the Wind*. At the terminal police climbed onto the bus, taped newspapers over the windows, and trapped the activists on board. One rider, posing as an ordinary traveler, managed to slip off and get away. Over the next several hours, the riders remained on the bus as a mob collected and newsmen took up position. Just before boarding time for the 5 p.m. bus to Montgomery, the riders were let off and allowed to wait inside the terminal, which had been cordoned off. Shortly before they boarded, a man in his sixties came striding toward them. "He was short, heavy, with big ears and a fleshy face," Lewis remembered. "He wore a suit, his white hair was slicked straight back above his forehead, and his eyes were framed by a pair of black, horn-rimmed glasses." Here was the notorious Eugene "Bull" Connor, the city's public safety commissioner. This was the man who cleared the police out of the Trailways bus station on Mother's Day so racist hooligans were free to savage the activists. Now Connor informed the Freedom Riders that he had come to arrest them for their own protection and then carted them off in paddy wagons. In jail that night, the riders sang hymns to keep their spirits up and to annoy Bull Connor and the guards. "He couldn't stand their singing," Burke Marshall explained. It "drove him crazy."

* * *

In Canada, the president met with Prime Minister John Diefenbaker, visited the U.S. Embassy, and spoke to Parliament. The First Lady stole the limelight, dazzling Canadians in her claret-red wool suit and a red beret. Back at the White House on Thursday morning, Kennedy held an urgent breakfast meeting with the attorney general and his two top aides, Byron White and Burke Marshall; at 8:30 a.m., the Justice Department trio joined the president, still dressed in his pajamas, in a sitting room next to his bedroom. Around the same time, the Freedom Riders were waking up after their first night in the Birmingham jail. Coming right to the point, Bobby told his brother: "As you know, the situation is getting worse in Alabama."

The team then outlined the issues: what the president's powers were if he had to launch federal action and what his options were for the use of force, short of deploying military troops. On a less cataclysmic scale, White had begun gathering a force of federal marshals, drawing on personnel from the U.S. Marshal Service, the Border Patrol, the Bureau of Prisons, and the Bureau of Alcohol, Tobacco, and Firearms. "It was explained to the president... that one of his choices was, if he had to take direct action, whether to use troops or to use marshals," Burke remembered. "Our recommendation to the president was that he should not use troops unless it was unavoidable."

The sight of helmeted troops with bayonets at Central High in Little Rock, Arkansas, in 1957, was still raw in the public consciousness. President Dwight Eisenhower had sent in the Army's 101st Airborne Division to maintain order after nine black students arrived to integrate the school. News reports and photos of the ensuing mob violence and the troops on the ground ricocheted around the world, stirring a wave of criticism. Eisenhower bore the brunt of the blame for the Little Rock crisis because of his lukewarm support for civil rights generally and his near silence on the importance of the 1954 *Brown* decision ruling against segregation in schools. He further encouraged segregationists when, as the 1957 school year was approaching, he declared that he could not "imagine any set of circumstances that would ever induce me to send Federal troops to enforce the orders of a Federal court."

If President Kennedy was privately comparing his situation with Eisenhower's, he didn't let on; he kept the focus on the current circumstances: what actions were needed to preserve law and order and ensure the safety of the travelers. "The President was a very good listener," Marshall said. "My first impression of him from that meeting was just of a tuned-in intelligence. I mean, a real intelligence at work on gathering all this data and understanding it, weighing it, and accepting it." The president was prepared to act, if he had to, although he preferred to try to persuade Alabama governor John Patterson to maintain order and public safety. Wasting no time, Kennedy put a call through to Patterson's office, to no avail. Unbelievably in the midst of the crisis, a secretary claimed the governor had gone fishing in the Gulf of Mexico.

After fifteen or twenty minutes the sitting room conference was over. Although the president sensed that racial discord was threatening the nation, he kept publicly silent about it: He initiated no political discussion about civil rights; he did not moralize about the injustice that drove blacks to risk their lives. "He realized there was going to be all sorts of consequences in the future," Marshall observed, but "he didn't make a speech about it." As Marshall filed out he noticed that the pajama-clad president "never ate his breakfast.... Left it sitting there."

49

BY THE SECOND night of their imprisonment, Bull Connor had had enough of the inmates' Freedom songs. Around midnight, he hustled several of the riders out of their cells, their bodies limp in defiance, and threw them into waiting cars for the journey back home to Nashville. "A midnight ride in the Deep South with a man like Bull Connor?" John Lewis wondered. "The fact that he had brought along a couple of newspaper reporters did not make it feel any safer." Connor rode with the activists, even attempting to make light chitchat, until the cars reached the small town of Ardmore at the Alabama border. "This is where you'll be gettin' out," he told them. He dumped the group into this known Klan territory in the dead of night, then he and the newsmen sped away.

The riders walked through the dark until they came upon the shack of an elderly black couple who, although frightened, allowed them inside to use their phone. The couple sheltered the group overnight, and at noon the following day, Leo Lillard, a volunteer, rolled up in a tan Studebaker. Boasting that he'd raced from Nashville ninety miles away to Ardmore in just over an hour, Lillard crammed the riders into the car and took off back to Birmingham, to the safety of the Shuttlesworth parsonage. Another group of eleven Freedom Riders from Nashville had already been recruited and was at the parsonage, expecting to take up the journey for the jailed activists.

Wasting no time, the expanded group of Freedom Riders headed to the Greyhound terminal to catch the 5 p.m. bus to Montgomery. Reverend Shuttlesworth accompanied them, his own ticket in hand. At the terminal, the riders found a hostile mob of several hundred whites, watched by a dozen police officers and a few newspaper and television reporters. They eased their way into the waiting room where several Klan members were pacing about in their robes. A long wait ensued. The 5 p.m. bus was canceled, as was the next one; no drivers were willing to risk the journey. As the evening dragged on, the mob thickened to at least three thousand, and the police brought in dogs to help keep the peace. With no buses running, the riders resigned themselves to spending the night on benches in the waiting room.

In Washington, President Kennedy tried again to get Alabama's governor on the phone only to be told again that Patterson had gone fishing. The president wanted to extract a promise from Patterson that he would ensure the riders' safety in the terminals and on the roads of Alabama. If the governor intended to snub the White House on the issue of public safety, the attorney general sent word to his aides that the president had no choice but to send in federal marshals. On hearing this, Patterson immediately dropped the "gone-fishing" charade. He phoned Bobby Kennedy, and the two enemies had a long shouting match. Patterson sharply defended the South's right to segregate the races. Refusing to believe the federal government's sole interest was order and safety, he accused Robert Kennedy of supporting the aims of the Freedom Riders who wanted to rob the South of its beloved local laws. Their conversation was so bitter that Patterson broke off phone contact and demanded to speak in person in Alabama to a personal representative of the administration. Without delay, Tennessean John Seigenthaler raced down the highway in a rented car to the state capital in Montgomery. Uncertain of Patterson's next ploy, Seigenthaler took a seat in a conference room in the capitol at a long table filled with the governor and his cronies. Glad to welcome a fellow

Southerner, Patterson shook Seigenthaler's hand and then "launched into a diatribe...really a fist-pounding diatribe," the Justice Department aide recalled. He ranted for about ten minutes. "The people of this country are so goddamned tired of this namby-pamby business in Washington where these Negroes are concerned," he bellyached, "and I'm sick of it. I'm sick of these spineless people that I supported not standing up. I'll tell you, I've got a stack of letters over there in my desk, and I am more popular today in the United States—not only with the people of Alabama, but with people all across the country—for the stand I've taken against these people than Jack Kennedy ever will be. And it just makes me sick to see this happen."

His next target was Bobby Kennedy, followed by the blasphemy of desegregation, and then he came to the matter at hand: "By God, I'm telling you if federal marshals come into Alabama, there'll be blood in the streets. You'd better not send federal marshals into Alabama." The Kennedy administration knew that Patterson was going to rebel at any federal presence in his state but Bobby had hoped, in vain, that the governor might have understood that the marshals represented a much softer action than the deployment of federal troops.

Listening to the governor spew his venom, Seigenthaler replied in a calm and reasonable manner, telling him that as a Southerner himself he respected his views because a lot of people down here felt the same way. But he cautioned that he did not agree with everything Patterson said, noting that personally he believed people had the right to travel the highways; but, more important, it was the law of the land. "The United States government was going to make sure, if necessary," Seigenthaler told Patterson, "that people had the right to safe travel and free access on public conveyances and on public highways; and that if he was not capable or willing to provide safety to travelers that we would provide it in any way that we could."

If the governor did not provide assurances, Seigenthaler warned, the U.S. government stood ready to send in federal marshals and take whatever other steps were necessary for safe passage.

Cornered, Governor Patterson caved: "The state of Alabama will provide safe travel for all who travel the highways," he promised, "including visitors, on the highways and elsewhere while they're in this state. You can tell the Attorney General I said that."

Just to be sure, Seigenthaler repeated the governor's pledge: "Well, that's a firm commitment from you, then, that these people can expect safe travel, that you'll protect them."

But then Patterson began to wriggle, no doubt suddenly worried how his accommodation of black desegregationists would play to his local constituents. "Yes," he said, "we have the means and the desire. Now I'm not going to say I'm going to protect a bunch of goddamn foreign trouble-makers who come in here to stir up trouble. I can't say that. But I am going to say this: that we have the means and the desire to protect on the highways and elsewhere citizens and visitors, and we will provide them safety."

At Seigenthaler's request, the two men agreed to get the attorney general on the phone; but before he placed the call Seigenthaler asked the governor how he intended to protect the travelers. "Well, now I'll tell you," Patterson snarled, "we ain't going to have no escorts. We ain't going to get a police car in back of them, but we'll take care of them."

"How will it be done?" Seigenthaler pressed.

Patterson turned toward the state's public safety director, Floyd Mann, and said he'd take care of it. Mann, who was in charge of the state highway patrol, was known as a professional who took seriously his job of protecting the public. Despite Patterson's waffling, Seigenthaler was reassured when Mann confirmed he would protect the Freedom Riders. "I'll make sure," he said, "that they'll never be out of sight of an Alabama highway patrol."

When Robert Kennedy came on the speakerphone, Seigenthaler repeated Patterson's promise to protect the riders.

"Will he issue a statement to that effect?" Bobby wanted to know, his voice filling the room.

Patterson refused. "I ain't going to say nothing," he insisted. He wanted the attorney general to handle any statements. "You can say that I have given you assurance that we will provide safe conduct on the highways and elsewhere for citizens and others."

"Well, that's fine," Bobby said. "Has he said this in front of other people down there?" When Bobby learned that Patterson's men around the table were listening, he was satisfied. "I don't believe we've got a problem," he said.

Seigenthaler then phoned Greyhound to assure the company that Patterson had agreed to protect not only the travelers but the buses, and arrangements were made to have the Freedom Riders leave Birmingham in the morning. His task completed, Seigenthaler had dinner with John Doar, a top staffer in the Civil Rights Division, who happened to be in Montgomery working on a separate Justice Department matter. When he turned in for the night, Seigenthaler felt satisfied that the Freedom Riders would arrive in Montgomery the following day on their way to New Orleans: "I thought I'd done a good day's work."

50

ON SATURDAY MORNING, the Freedom Riders roused themselves off the hard benches in the waiting room and boarded the 6 a.m. bus to Montgomery. Their driver, realizing who his passengers were, mutinied at the last minute and refused to get behind the wheel. But by 8:30 a.m., a willing driver was located and the riders were on the road under massive protection by Birmingham police; motorcycle units with sirens screaming escorted the bus to the city line, then the Alabama Highway Patrol took over all the way to Montgomery. Not eager to prolong his experience, the Greyhound driver flew down Highway 31; one journalist clocked his speed at eighty-seven miles an hour. Several highway patrol cars cushioned the bus in front and vehicles loaded with FBI agents, Alabama plainclothes detectives, and reporters filled in behind. A highway patrol plane overhead followed the convoy's progress.

In Montgomery, Seigenthaler and Doar heard on the radio that the bus was on its way. Confident that the ride would go smoothly, they had a leisurely breakfast then Seigenthaler dropped Doar off at the federal courthouse building across from the bus station and circled the block in his car. The speeding bus pulled in a little ahead of schedule to a mostly empty terminal. A few journalists were milling about and there was no sign of the police. Montgomery public safety commissioner L. B. Sullivan, a virulent racist, had taken a page out of Bull Connor's playbook and arranged to keep his officers out of sight for a half hour. He reportedly was parked a block away, sitting in his car, as Klansmen and other white thugs, armed with lead pipes, baseball bats, bricks, chains, rakes, and hoes, converged on the station.

When the Freedom Riders stepped off the bus, newspaper and television reporters approached them for interviews. Twenty-one-year-old John Lewis, who had been designated as spokesman, began to speak. "We just got out of Birmingham," he said. "We got to Montgomery—" and he paused. His eye drifted over a reporter's shoulder to see a mob coming from all directions. Just then a woman in a prim yellow dress shouted: "Get those niggers!"

Some of the riders ran and got away, clambering into taxis and hurrying to the safety of the Reverend Ralph Abernathy's First Baptist Church. Others were trapped in the snarling mob of big-bellied men clenching cigars between their teeth, women brandishing their purses like weapons, even children smacking and clawing the riders. Some blacks unaffiliated with the activists were pummeled—and whites, too: anyone deemed a nigger lover. The attackers snatched luggage. Suitcases flew into the air and crashed to the ground, snapping open, spilling out a bow tie, a purple nightgown, a Bible. Other bags were hurled like weapons at fleeing blacks, knocking them off their feet.

Unable to flee, John Lewis was surrounded by a wall of raging faces. "Someone grabbed my briefcase," he remembered. "I pulled back but it was ripped from my fingers. At that instant I felt a thud against my head. I could feel my knees collapse and then nothing. Everything turned white for an instant, then black." Lewis fell unconscious to the asphalt, dropped by a wooden Coca-Cola crate that was smashed against his skull.

From the Federal Building overlooking the terminal, John Doar spoke by phone with Burke Marshall in the attorney general's office in Washington. His voice was frantic. "Oh, there are fists, punching," he reported. "A bunch of men led by a guy with a bleeding face are beating them. There are no cops. It's terrible. It's terrible. There's not a cop in sight. People are yelling, 'Get 'em, get 'em.' It's awful."

Floyd Mann, the state's public safety director, hadn't trusted his local counterpart L. B. Sullivan to take proper measures to prevent mayhem. Although he had no jurisdiction inside the city, Mann felt an obligation to help bring order; with several highway patrolmen waiting in their cars nearby, Mann waded into the terminal. Making his way through the chaos he came upon Freedom Rider William Barbee lying on the asphalt as several Klansmen beat him savagely. Barbee, a student at the American Baptist Theological Seminary, was pinned down by one thug while another rammed a pipe into his ear and a third pounded his skull with a baseball bat. Barbee incurred injuries, according to historian Raymond Arsenault, that inflicted "permanent damage that shortened his life." During the assault, Mann was unable to yank the men off of Barbee so he drew his pistol and fired two warning shots. "I'll shoot the next man who hits him," he barked. "Stand back! There'll be no killing here today." Mann's warning stopped the beating, and the thugs within hearing of the pistol shots ambled away. One man, however, continued to blindly pound a Birmingham television reporter and held his punches only when Mann threatened to pull out his gun again.

James Zwerg, a twenty-one-year-old white Freedom Rider from Fisk University in Nashville, was barely conscious after his beating; he'd been hit in the face with his own suitcase, then pummeled viciously while he was on the ground. One of his attackers lifted his head and pinned it between his knees while others took turns savagely hitting him. Afterward his eyes were open but expressionless. John Lewis, fearing his friend was near death, tried to get him out of the terminal to a hospital. When a reporter asked a detective dressed in a natty brown suit and straw hat if he could help, the man replied: "We ain't arranging transportation for these people. We didn't arrange their transportation here and we ain't going to take them away." Zwerg's lips and eyes were so swollen they distorted his blood-soaked face. As he struggled to see and breathe, a teenager from the mob moved close to him and shouted: "You're a rotten son of a bitch. Your mother is a dog. You are a dog. You know what? You ride with the niggers." Before the bus had left Birmingham, Zwerg had stood on the platform and sung black spirituals with the other riders, soloing a few lines of "Oh Lord, keep your eyes on the prize."

When public safety commissioner Sullivan finally strolled into the terminal he was asked about the carnage. Feigning innocence, he said: "I really don't know what happened. When I got here all I saw were three men lying in the street. There was two niggers and a white man."

Outside the terminal John Seigenthaler rolled up looking for a parking space unaware of the chaos inside. As he came closer he saw an inexplicable sight: "suitcases and bags being hurled into the air." He drove on and realized all hell had broken out when he saw a black boy in a blue suit running down the street pursued by about ten white men. The man leading the charge wore overalls and had a lame leg; his slowness was hindering the other chasers, causing Seigenthaler to silently raise a cheer for the fleeing black boy: "That's a fellow they'll never catch."

He drove around the corner and saw the bus in its parking space and people swarming, shoving, and pushing to get at the Freedom Riders. In the road about twenty yards ahead, he spotted a young white woman getting whacked over the head by a woman with a pocketbook. Moving slowly forward he honked his horn in a futile effort to break it up. When he stopped the car, someone pushed the woman hard into the front fender; he hopped out, taking her by the arm and asking, "Are you hurt?" noticing she was bleeding a little from the mouth; he tried to pilot her to the car door but she resisted, saying: "Mister, get away. Leave me alone. You're going to get hurt. You're only going to get killed. This is not your fight."

Seigenthaler then realized another young woman had climbed into his car seeking safety. "I'm with her," she said, indicating the bleeding woman. Later he discovered the two women were white Freedom Riders, Susan Wilbur and Sue Harmann. As Seigenthaler tried to pry the resistant young woman's hand off the door and get her into the car, a man appeared and bellowed at him: "Who the hell are you?"

"Get back," Seigenthaler warned. "Get back. I'm a federal man."

At that moment, this Tennessean Justice Department representative, the personal assistant to Attorney General Robert Kennedy, felt a sharp blow above his left ear, and everything went dark.

51

NOBODY COULD LOCATE Robert Kennedy on Saturday morning, May 20. Confident that Alabama governor John Patterson would protect the Freedom Riders, Bobby went out horseback riding around the same time the bus was flying down the highway from Birmingham to Montgomery. Bobby often used sports as a form of catharsis. He was an avid horseback rider but also a reckless one. As a riding companion remembered, "if you got to a flat place where he could gallop, he just took off." After his ride that morning, he watched an intramural FBI baseball game where he threw out the first ball.

By the afternoon, Bobby was in his office at the Justice Department, still in his baseball cap, having learned of the attack on Seigenthaler. He was conducting an emergency meeting with Deputy Attorney General Byron White and Civil Rights Division head Burke Marshall. As livid as he was over Patterson's betrayal, nothing anguished Bobby more than his assistant's injury. Seigenthaler had suffered a savage blow to the head from a pipe and was knocked unconscious. When he fell to the ground, the mob pushed his inert body halfway under his car, where it lay for twenty minutes until he came to. Somehow he dragged himself back into the front seat of the car.

When a policeman poked his head in the window, a groggy Seigenthaler asked: "What happened?"

"You've been hurt. You better sit still."

Seigenthaler replied: "You better call Mr. Kennedy."

"What Mr. Kennedy?" the officer wanted to know.

"Robert Kennedy."

"Why?" the policeman asked. Then a light flashed in his eye: "Who are you?"

"I work for him. I'm with the Department of Justice."

Suddenly alarmed, the policeman knew he had to get medical care for the injured Justice Department officer. "Get out," he said, opening the car door.

As soon as Seigenthaler stood up, he passed out again. He woke up in the hospital.

52

WANTING AN EXPLANATION for the violence, Robert Kennedy called Governor John Patterson but the governor, ignoring his least favorite Kennedy, didn't take the call. In response, Bobby decided to mobilize the federal marshals. His next call went to the president at a four-hundred-acre estate called Glen Ora that he leased in the countryside near Middleburg, Virginia. The weekend White House in the heart of hunt country provided the president and his wife with the privacy they craved. In seclusion, Jackie enjoyed horseback riding, and Caroline, now nearly four years old, was learning to ride. The retreat also allowed the president to conceal his poor health from the public. In addition to his terrible back, Kennedy suffered a range of other ailments early in his presidency, including problems with his stomach, colon, and prostate, high fevers, dehydration, abscesses, sleeplessness, and high cholesterol. Isolated in the countryside, the president kept his distance from the civil rights crisis and its potential political backlash. As he had in his youth, John Kennedy was unwilling to step into the fight, preferring instead to operate in the background; in prep school he had assigned his battles to his older brother, Joe, and now in the White House he let his little brother, Bobby, become the face of courage.

In a brief conversation with Jack, Bobby gained authorization to send the marshals to Montgomery; he then dispatched Deputy Attorney General Byron White to the city to oversee the operations. Soon a motley force of four hundred men began assembling from points around the country and shipping out. These were not spit-and-polish uniformed soldiers, like the paratroopers of the Army's 101st Airborne Division that Eisenhower marched into Little Rock; the Kennedys were intent on keeping the military in the barracks and thereby avoid Southern cries of a federal takeover. The men, cobbled together from various federal agencies, were identified by their bright yellow armbands marked with the words U.S. MARSHAL; they carried sidearms, tear gas bombs, and nightsticks. Burke Marshall later described them as "middle-aged, fat, lethargic people with no law enforcement experience. Many of them came from the South and really thought they were being asked to protect black people whom they considered Communists, or worse." Byron White, observing that some were redneck agents from the Bureau of Alcohol, Tobacco, and Firearms, fretted: "I wonder which side they'll take on."

Next Bobby turned his attention to his wounded assistant. When he first heard of the attack, he had been visibly shaken. "I think Bob changed on the day...Seigenthaler got hit over the head in Montgomery," recalled Peter Maas, then a *Saturday Evening Post* reporter who had become a Kennedy family insider. "I was in his office right afterward. He was possessed by an enormous anger," feeling as if "he had been down in Montgomery himself and been hit." The horror of racist cruelty might never have jolted Bobby so forcefully had the attack not targeted one of his own. Seigenthaler lying on his back in a hospital bed with a concussion, a fractured skull, and broken ribs was a transformative figure for his boss.

Bobby placed his first of several calls to the hospital that day. "How are you? How do you feel?" he inquired.

"All right," Seigenthaler told him. "I've got a small headache."

Learning that the marshals were on their way, Seigenthaler apologized, feeling somehow responsible such a step had to be taken.

"Sooner or later something had to happen," Bobby said. "You did the right thing. You did what you had to do."

"It's going to create an awful stink," Seigenthaler said. He knew how hostile Alabamans already were toward Bobby. "Let me give you some advice."

"Yes?" the attorney general said.

"Never run for governor of Alabama. You couldn't get elected."

53

NOW THAT FEDERAL marshals were in motion, President Kennedy could no longer maintain his lofty detachment; he had to address the issue publicly. In a statement on Saturday, May 20, he said the absolute minimum, avoiding direct mention of the marshals, and indicating that his brother the attorney general was dealing with the unrest. Expressing his "deepest concern" over the situation in Alabama, the president said: "I have instructed the Justice Department to take all necessary steps." He neither took Alabama to task for its lapse in policing nor alluded to the Freedom Riders' right to travel safely. In a political straddle, he called on the governor and all Alabama officials "to prevent any further outbreaks of violence" while also urging locals and visitors, meaning Freedom Riders, to "refrain from any action which would in any way tend to provoke further outbreaks."

Privately the president was infuriated at the Freedom Riders for complicating his latest venture in international diplomacy. "As these events unfolded, the President was busy preparing for his forthcoming encounter with Khrushchev," wrote Harris Wofford. "He did not appreciate the crisis CORE had deliberately precipitated in Alabama." Kennedy would complain to his aides about "this Goddamned civil rights mess." One day Wofford picked up his phone to hear the president demand: "Stop them! Get your friends off those buses!" Kennedy assumed that his civil rights aide had some control over the Freedom Riders, because he was chummy with the nation's black leaders. But Wofford sensed that the Freedom Rides were part of a widening movement, warning the president: "I don't think anybody's going to stop them right now."

Having issued his statement, President Kennedy retreated from the crisis. For inquiries his press secretary, Pierre Salinger, directed reporters to the attorney general's spokesman, Edwin Guthman. Bobby, as faithful vassal to his brother—and, in the words of some close observers, as "assistant president"—willingly assumed management of the Southern showdown, which meant absorbing the personal and political fusillades. As Ramsey Clark, an assistant attorney general at the time, explained: "Bob became a lightning rod for the president, and drew away from him a lot of the antipathy that comes from doing your duty, particularly in the civil-rights area."

The attorney general led with toughness and clarity. In a telegram to Alabama governor Patterson, he outlined the series of events that had ultimately forced him to take federal action: the burning of the bus in Anniston, the governor's failed promises of safe passage for the Freedom Riders, the riots at the Montgomery terminal, the beatings of the riders and others, including "the president's personal representative," Seigenthaler, and the governor's unwillingness to take the phone calls of the president and attorney general to discuss these circumstances. "The federal government," Bobby concluded, had "no alternative" but to send in "United States officers to begin to assist state and local authorities in the protection of persons and property and vehicles in Alabama."

When the newspapers published the telegram the following day, the governor found a phone and placed a call to the attorney general. In a heated conversation, involving "four-letter words," Patterson complained that the presence of federal marshals was going to embarrass him politically. Years later he described how he felt pushed into a corner: On the one hand, if he guaranteed the safety of the Freedom Riders he faced scorn from his constituency for allowing activists to violate state segregation laws; on the other, if he refused to protect them and rioting broke out, the federal government would claim he couldn't maintain order in his own state. The demands from Washington, he insisted, were impossible to answer.

To protect himself politically, Patterson went public with his own tough statement. "We have the men, the equipment and the will to keep the public peace and we need no help—from the Federal Government, 'interested citizens' or anyone else," he declared. "We are fully able to enforce the laws of this state." However, he made clear that he had no patience for outside "rabble rousers" who come into the state "for the avowed purpose of disobeying our laws, flaunting [*sic*] our customs and traditions and creating racial incidents." Despite his swagger, the governor gave assurances that he was prepared to deploy appropriate force to head off further violence.

If Robert Kennedy had any hope the Freedom Rider disturbances might soon wane, he miscalculated the resolve of the riders. The activists had succeeded dramatically in one respect: They had highlighted the problem of segregation in the South. "We had a national stage now," John Lewis said. The press and the Justice Department were forced to pay attention. "Segregation was a *national* problem now." The rides had galvanized protesters across the country. "The outrage generated by the ugly resistance we met that May—precisely the resistance we had hoped to elicit—swelled the movement with new members, hundreds of young men and women eager to put their own bodies on the line."

Even riders already bloodied were determined to carry on. From their hospital beds on Saturday, May 20, two wounded Freedom Riders gave defiant interviews to the *Montgomery Advertiser.* White student James Zwerg, who had cracked teeth, bandages on his face and head, and bruises all over his body, told a reporter: "You may inform the people in Montgomery and the rest of the Deep South states that we intend to continue our 'freedom rides' until the last vestige of segregation disappears from bus stations." Zwerg countered President Kennedy's complaint that the rides put America in a bad light overseas and gave the Soviet Union and other nations fodder for anti-American propaganda. "We're not doing this just for ourselves, but for all Americans," he argued. "How can we meet the Communist threat, win the allegiance of African and Asian nations, as long as there is injustice against minority groups in this country?"

His fellow traveler William Barbee, a black student at the American Baptist Theological Seminary in Nashville, wore the evidence of his pummeling at the station on his massively swollen face. He echoed Zwerg's sense of purpose, vowing to "surrender my life for the cause of justice." His voice was so weak the reporter could barely hear his words. Barbee was unaware that during his beating Alabama public safety director Floyd Mann had intervened, brandishing his pistol and possibly saving his life. Now he thanked Mann and praised him for his courage. As a member of Alabama's public security force, Mann stood apart for his sense of duty and compassion. When John Seigenthaler landed in the hospital, his first visitor was Floyd Mann. During a bedside visit, this Southern lawman offered the battered Justice Department official a tearful apology.

54

_____

ON SATURDAY EVENING, Robert Kennedy and his staff gathered in the attorney general's office, hopeful that the federal marshals and Governor Patterson could keep the peace. By 8 p.m. Byron White was at Maxwell Air Force Base in Montgomery to oversee deployment of the four hundred marshals. But that meager force suddenly seemed inadequate when news came that Martin Luther King Jr., interrupting a speaking tour in the North, was headed to Montgomery to lead a mass meeting at the First Baptist Church the following day.

King's presence, Bobby knew, would magnify attention on Montgomery and vastly complicate security. The attorney general phoned King, catching him in Chicago, and begged him to reconsider. King refused. Spurred by the sit-ins and the Freedom Rides, he was awakening to the power of direct confrontation. He was evolving, moving toward reclaiming an active role in an increasingly impatient black movement. With the outlook for peace in Montgomery diminishing, the attorney general set up an open phone line between his office and the president's country retreat in Virginia for emergency communication.

* * *

King canceled an appearance at Dartmouth College and instead flew into Montgomery airport at noon on Sunday, May 21. Fearing a mob might converge, the attorney general took no chances. Fifty armed marshals were on hand to greet the civil rights leader. But the heavy security turned out to be overkill: The airport was quiet. Without incident King was whisked through the city, home of his first civil rights achievement—the bus boycott that catapulted him to fame. He stopped for a brief meeting with Nashville student leaders Diane Nash, who also rushed to town, and John Lewis, still bandaged and recovering from his beating. The students had mixed feelings about King's presence in Montgomery. On the one hand, King added luster and publicity to their cause but he also threatened to co-opt it; worse, the students feared he might negotiate away any gains they achieved or soften their militancy before the government. Just thirty-two, King was already an interloping adult to the students, an unwelcome voice of moderation. With his massive marshal escort, he then carried on to the parsonage of his longtime friend the Reverend Ralph Abernathy of the First Baptist Church. Already unhappy about the arrival of the marshals in his state, Governor Patterson was aghast at the massive contingent the federal government laid on for a rabble-rouser like King. "Fifty marshals...escorted him through town," the governor groused more than a decade later, "just like he was the president of the United States."

The governor had prevailed upon a local judge to issue an injunction making it illegal for the Freedom Riders to travel in Alabama, in essence, to be in Alabama at all; in the eyes of the local courts they were now outlaws and subject to arrest, and the governor wanted to get his hands on them and make a show of tossing them into prison. But he didn't know where the riders were. He called for a meeting with Deputy Attorney General Byron White and invited the press. Then, playing to reporters, he railed at the invasion of these troublemakers into the city.

"Will you make available all the information you have about the Freedom Riders who came in yesterday?" Patterson demanded.

"No," White answered.

"You know where some of these Freedom Riders are, don't you?"

"Yes," White replied drily, "in the hospital."

"Do you know where the others are?"

"No, I don't."

"If you knew where some of these people are, would you inform us?"

White silenced Patterson's interrogation by saying: "I will never know where these people are."

At that moment, the Freedom Riders were in the basement of Ralph Abernathy's First Baptist Church where they had fled for safety after the station melee; they met with Martin Luther King Jr., who was preparing to lead a mass rally at the church that evening.

Still speaking less to White than to his own Southern constituency, Patterson charged that the Justice Department had stomped on states' rights by sending in the federal marshals. "We don't need your marshals," he declared for the newsmen, "we don't want them, and we didn't ask for them. And still the federal government sends them here to help put down a disturbance which it helped create."

55

THE FIRST BAPTIST Church began filling up at 5 p.m., three hours before the rally. The church had been established soon after the Civil War as the first institution in Montgomery for free blacks. After fire destroyed its wood-frame building in the early twentieth century, a brick structure was constructed over five years. Parishioners were asked to contribute a brick a day to its construction, and after its completion in 1915 the place was known as the "Brick-A-Day Church." As blacks filed in on that Sunday evening, a mob of whites began to gather outside. Some in the crowd waved Confederate flags and hooted rebel yells. Governor Patterson had declared that if there was a need for order in Montgomery, state and local police were more than able to handle the task. In recognition of the governor's pledge, Byron White sent only a small force of a dozen marshals. By 8 p.m. at least a thousand parishioners had filled the brick fortress of First Baptist while the crowd outside had swelled to about three thousand fanning out in all directions. The mood was growing ugly: The whites were shouting and throwing rocks at the church. No local officers or squad cars were anywhere in sight.

In the pews sat nicely dressed parishioners: housekeepers and teachers and janitors and shopkeepers and students. There were men in white shirts and slacks, women in their churchgoing best clutching shiny purses, the elderly and the young, and middle-aged veterans of the bus boycott. The Freedom Riders, obvious only by their wounds, were scattered throughout the sanctuary to prevent their easy roundup and arrest. Almost everyone inside the church was black, except for several newsmen and a handful of white sympathizers; among the crowd was Jessica Mitford, who was to publish her groundbreaking exposé on the funeral home industry, *The American Way of Death*, in 1963, and was in Montgomery to write on civil rights for *Life* magazine.

The Alabama evening was warm, and the temperature climbed inside the packed church. In the pulpit, the Reverend S. S. Seay, a fearless proponent of the 1955–1956 bus boycott, praised the Freedom Riders and said a few words about Diane Nash, who had an honored seat on the dais. Although hostile noises filtered in from outside, the congregants remained calm and sang hymns. "It was not easy to intimidate them, not after what they had already gone through with the bus boycott," John Lewis observed. "They had been through fire. They knew what it felt like."

Downstairs in a basement study, Martin Luther King Jr. conferred with fellow black leaders. So far the handful of marshals had managed to keep order, setting up Ripley Street in front of the building as a buffer between the churchgoers in the pews and the mob outside. But to columnist Murray Kempton, the marshals on the front lines appeared frighteningly unseasoned, as he described them: "these gallant but unskilled conscripts." Kempton observed that "the average marshal was puffing after he had lumbered so much as ten feet. . . . No wise man would have bet on them to hold off a minority of dedicated hoods—nor more than fifty—who dared to aggress against them."

Alarmed by the rising antagonism of the mob, King said he wanted to gauge the mood outside for himself. It was a dangerous proposition, but King needed to prove his courage to the young activists who doubted his leadership. His colleagues strongly discouraged him, but King nonetheless opened the church door to confront the rabble. John Lewis knew what was behind the drama. "He wanted to show the mob he wasn't afraid—and to show the people who had come to hear him speak that he wasn't afraid as well."

King, accompanied by a few protectors, walked around the outside perimeter of the church, which was surrounded by angry Alabamans. No local police were in sight. Just two plainclothes detectives were on duty on orders from the conscientious Alabama public safety director, Floyd Mann. At first, no one seemed to recognize King. Then a cry went up: "Nigger King!" And rocks and other projectiles headed his way; a metal canister looking like a bomb landed nearby. After a moment of panic, the men realized it was an empty tear gas cylinder. But it was danger enough: The church door opened, and the group scurried back inside. Mounting the rostrum, King reassured the congregation, with little to support his assertion, that the marshals had the situation under control.

Other preachers took to the pulpit, while King went to a window and saw an overturned car blazing in the street; the vehicle, it turned out, had been loaned to Jessica Mitford. Its gas tank exploded, electrifying the mob. There were cries of "Let's clean the niggers out of here!" Several thugs dashing toward the church were repelled by the marshals brandishing their nightsticks; the two undercover detectives helped by shoving the hooligans away. Others surged forward, hurling rocks and bricks and Molotov cocktails, prompting the marshals to fire off tear gas. The noxious fumes lay heavy over the street and drifted inside the church through a brick-smashed window, sickening some parishioners. Other congregants tried to clear the air by waving hand fans that had been donated by a neighborhood funeral home.

Under siege, the marshals radioed to Byron White, and he called Bobby Kennedy who was appalled to hear of the deteriorating conditions. But Bobby was reluctant to add marshals, knowing the move would inflame Governor Patterson and renew his cries of a federal takeover. But the situation required action, and the attorney general gave the go-ahead to release another four hundred marshals who were on standby at Maxwell Air Force Base just outside the city. Unable to wrest vehicles from resistant state officials, the commanders loaded the men into mail trucks sent over by the city postmaster. At First Baptist, the marshals fired repeated rounds of tear gas to keep the mob at bay. Undeterred, some whites stormed toward the church and pounded on the doors. Inside, the children were sent downstairs to the crypt for their safety. On the pulpit Reverend Seay led the congregation in singing "Love Lifted Me," but the voices of the frightened parishioners were thin and dirgelike. "Nobody is singing as if he believes," Reverend Seay called out. "I want everybody to believe." Another preacher, the Reverend B. D. Lambert, took to the rostrum with a message for the thugs in the street: "Bless all those cowards standin' outside that can't fight unless they have a mob to come with them." And a message for the state's highest official: "Bless that stupid Governor of ours."

Robert Kennedy wanted least of all to expand the federal presence, but he knew he had to be prepared in the event of a full-blown riot. After launching the marshals, he asked the Pentagon to put federal troops on alert at Fort Benning in Georgia just across the Alabama state line. Since no deployment was possible without the president's approval, a proclamation was prepared and flown by helicopter to President Kennedy's retreat in Middleburg. Meanwhile, the troops at Fort Benning were placed aboard aircraft to await orders. Still hoping to avoid a troop deployment, Bobby Kennedy tried to warn Governor Patterson that he needed to send in state security forces to protect the church; but the governor didn't respond. Floyd Mann recognized the escalating emergency and the threat to lives and in defiance of the governor ordered some of his state troopers to assist the marshals. Bernard Lafayette, a young Freedom Rider and veteran of the sit-ins, explained the respect that Mann earned from activists. "He was Southern," Lafayette said of Mann, "but I don't think he had the same kind of passion for preserving segregation at any cost as some of his colleagues. I think he was...caught in a system where he had to perform certain duties, but he wanted to do it in the most humane way."

From his command center at the Justice Department, the attorney general monitored the scene in Montgomery. The reports were discouraging: a marshal bloodied by a brick, black homes nearby randomly fired upon, tear gas supplies dwindling, and the incensed mob pushing toward the church doors. "At one point," Burke Marshall recalled, "it really looked as if the mob might overcome the marshals and get in there."

56

AS THE NIGHT wore on and the danger escalated, King called Robert
Kennedy from the church basement and described the scene: the swarming mob, the burning car, the rock throwing, the Molotov cocktails,
and the thousand people inside the church trying to cope. Through the
receiver Bobby could hear the congregants singing. Burke Marshall, who
listened in on the conversation, described King as "panicky" and "very
upset." To Marshall, the situation sounded "very, very dangerous"; he
could hear "the fear in [King's] voice." The attorney general reassured the
civil rights leader that a large number of federal marshals were on their
way. Still uneasy, King instructed a colleague to rush the news upstairs
to the packed church while he grilled Robert Kennedy: When would the
marshals arrive? Where were they at that moment? The attorney general
didn't have those answers. Several years later, Bobby still remembered
the preacher's anxious tone. "Martin Luther King was concerned about
whether he was going to live and whether his people were going to live,"
Bobby said in an oral history. "He kept getting these reports that the
crowds were moving in and that they were going to burn the church down
and shoot the Negroes as they ran out."

Bobby, like Jack, found it difficult to talk to King, all the more so
under the circumstances. King was no easy conversationalist, especially
when his own life and many others were at stake. Even at the most perilous moments, however, the Kennedys found ways to lighten the mood.
With the tension high, the attorney general tried to loosen King up a little,
quipping that "as long as he was in church, he might say a prayer for us."
Unamused, King told the attorney general that the marshals needed to
arrive soon or there was likely to be bloodshed. "He rather berated me for
what was happening to him at the time," Bobby said. "And I said to him
that I didn't think that he'd be alive if it wasn't for us, and that we were
going to keep him alive, and the marshals would keep the church from
burning down." At that moment, several parishioners raced in to report

that red-white-and-blue mail trucks were pulling up in front of the church and marshals were leaping out and forming a barricade against the mob.

Relieved, King thanked the attorney general. As contentious as the conversation had been, King believed Bobby understood the need for black rights, even better than his brother, and had a fervor for the cause that exceeded the president's. If he showed restraint, or seemed unsympathetic, he was either responding to political considerations he or his brother perceived or was fulfilling the president's wishes. Although Bobby sometimes acted on his own, even overstepping, for the most part he was a weather vane of his brother. "I felt that he was doing exactly what the President wanted him to do and had instructed him to do," King said. "In fact, whenever I talked with the Attorney General, I always felt that I was talking with the President, in a sense, knowing that they were so close. And I felt that when he said something to me, he was speaking for the President."

In some ways, black hopes lay heavily on Bobby, who not only carried out his brother's commands but also had the power to influence Jack. Although the younger Kennedy could be uncompromising and even manipulative, King was confident that within Bobby lay a compassionate soul; he recognized this from early in the attorney general's term, despite the blemish on Bobby's character for his past work as legal counsel to the communist-hunting demagogue Joseph McCarthy. "Somewhere in this man sits good," King told Harry Belafonte soon after the Kennedys entered the White House. "Our task is to find his moral center and win him to our cause."

* * *

After his phone conversation, King went upstairs and mounted the rostrum. "I just talked to Attorney General Kennedy," he told the congregation. The civil rights leader offered words of comfort and encouragement. "We aren't going to become panicky," he said. "We're going to stand up for what we know is right." The churchgoers took it in calmly, many flapping their faces with their funeral home fans. Columnist Murray Kempton captured the feeling of strength in the pews that night: "A Montgomery cook takes it for granted that while she sits under siege, Martin King can call the Attorney General of the United States on a Princess phone in the basement downstairs."

Outside, marshals pushed back the surging mob, firing repeated volleys of tear gas. Since few marshals had gas masks, they had to run for cover from their own stinging attacks. As the air cleared, the marshals rushed back into place but by then the determined mob had pushed forward. The marshals were outnumbered and swamped by the rage in the streets. Rioters reached the church and pounded on the doors; a few bullied their way inside and the marshals drove them out. Inside the hot, sweaty church the gas sickened some parishioners; most remained calm, singing their way through the trying hours. While battles raged outside, voices rose inside singing hymns and freedom songs.

Word of the escalating pandemonium reached Byron White in the staging area at Maxwell Air Force Base; he relayed the development to Bobby Kennedy in Washington, and the two men discussed options. Lacking reinforcements for the marshals, the attorney general contemplated his dreaded next step: the release of federal troops from Georgia's Fort Benning. Before phoning the president for troop approval, Bobby tried to reach Governor Patterson to urge him to take action to bring peace to the streets. But Patterson still wouldn't take his calls.

At the governor's orders, a telephone operator was eavesdropping on the line at Maxwell Air Force Base and informing the governor of the conversations between Bobby Kennedy and Byron White. In 1967 the governor recalled: "We had information that the administration had moved a company of the Second Infantry from Fort Benning in here and put them in a hangar out here at Maxwell Field." It was unclear whether federal troops had already been moved into Alabama, or whether years later Patterson was engaging in hyperbole, but on that evening in 1961, the governor was eager to head off federal intervention. Just as the chaos outside the church was reaching a crisis point, Patterson acted: Squads of Montgomery police flooded into the area followed by more than a hundred helmeted Alabama National Guardsmen carrying arms with fixed bayonets. The governor had declared martial law.

When the news reached Washington, Robert Kennedy tried again to get Patterson on the line, and this time the governor picked up the phone. "Now you got what you wanted," Patterson griped. "You got yourself a fight, and you've got the National Guard called out and martial law, and that's what you wanted. We'll take charge of it now with the troops, and you can get on out and leave it alone."

57

WITH THE ARRIVAL of the state forces, Bobby Kennedy ordered the federal marshals to stand down. The safety of the parishioners was now in the hands of the Alabama National Guard under the command of Adjunct General Henry Graham, an ardent segregationist. At first the blacks in the church mistook the Alabama guard for federal troops and cried out in joy and offered thanks to President Kennedy. Disappointment quickly followed when the truth spread through the crowd; the guard, however, brought a measure of calm to the streets outside the church.

Appearing on the rostrum again, Martin Luther King Jr. this time delivered remarks he had prepared during his morning flight to Montgomery. He told the crowd that as he sat in a jet at thirty-eight thousand feet he thought of the marvels of technology that compressed time and distance. He thought of the scientific genius of Americans. Then his mind turned to Alabama: Anniston, Birmingham, Montgomery. "Through our scientific and technological developments we have lifted our heads to the skies," he said, "and yet our feet are still firmly planted in the muck of barbarism and racial hatred."

His language was raw, his eloquence poignant. King praised the fearlessness of the students who risked their lives to dramatize racial inequality. "These courageous freedom riders have faced ugly and howling mobs in order to arouse the dozing conscience of the nation." King challenged the president to take on "America's chief moral dilemma," reminding his listeners in Montgomery—and Washington—that the South would not change on its own. No clearer proof was needed than the violence of the past week. "The deep South will not impose limits upon itself," King explained. "The limits must be imposed from without." And he put the president on notice: "Unless the Federal Government acts forthrightly in the South to assure every citizen his constitutional rights, we will be plunged into a dark abyss of chaos. The federal government must not stand idly by while bloodthirsty mobs beat non-violent students with impunity."

He blamed Governor Patterson for provoking the terror and encouraging the mob. "His consistent preaching of defiance of the law, his vitriolic public pronouncements, and his irresponsible actions created the atmosphere in which violence could thrive," King declared, adding that the governor was "consciously and unconsciously aiding and abetting the forces of violence."

King finished speaking around midnight, and the congregants were ready to go home after seven anxious hours confined inside the church. Although the Guard apparently had quieted the scene, the mob still had not dispersed. Troops stood in the doorways, preventing anyone from entering the church but also blocking anyone from leaving. Unable to depart, the parishioners were essentially in the custody of the state. Exhausted parents and grandparents with sleeping children in their arms moved toward the exits but were blocked. "The troops, which had been facing the crowd across the street, now turned to face *us*," John Lewis recalled. "There was no way for us to get through that mob, we were told. No transportation had been arranged. It was too dangerous." Some of the churchgoers feared the soldiers. "Their rifles were pointed our way. They looked like the enemy."

Only Martin Luther King Jr. was permitted to step outside and confer with General Graham. The area still teemed with angry whites under the control of local security forces: the Alabama guard, the city police, and the highway patrol. King was disheartened to see that all the federal marshals were gone. General Graham adamantly rejected King's request to allow the weary congregants to go home. At King's insistence, the general agreed to come inside the church to deliver the message himself. With an absence of sympathy, Graham stood before the tired group and just read Governor Patterson's declaration of martial law, which laid blame for the disorder on the federal government and on "outside agitators" who came into Alabama "to violate our laws and customs." No one, the general ordered, was leaving the church until morning.

As the congregation settled in for a long, dismal night—children were carried back downstairs, the elderly were given the cushioned pews, and others found space on the floor to sleep—Martin Luther King went to the phone in the basement to complain to Robert Kennedy. When the attorney general came on the phone, King could barely contain his outrage: How could the federal government have turned the congregation over to the Alabama National Guard? Kennedy was in the middle of an interview with *Time* magazine reporter Harold Meyers. The attorney general's press secretary, Edwin Guthman, was also in the room and he recalled: "Bob held the phone away from his ear, and Meyers, sitting about fifteen feet away, could clearly hear Dr. King's deep, angry voice."

The attorney general tried to calm the anxious civil rights leader, assuring him that he had spoken to General Graham and Floyd Mann and had confidence in them; the congregants were to be escorted home once it was safe to leave the church. King accused the attorney general of betraying him. "Now, Reverend," Bobby interrupted, "you know just as well as I do that if it hadn't been for the United States marshals you'd be as dead as Kelsey's nuts right now!" Stumped by the phrase *Kelsey's nuts*, King fell silent. In the church basement, he turned to whoever was nearby and asked: "Who's Kelsey? Anyone know Kelsey?" *Kelsey's nuts* was an old Boston Irish expression—an odd one to throw at a black civil rights leader from Georgia. The phrase was obscure, even to Bobby Kennedy. Recalling the scene in a 1964 interview with journalist Anthony Lewis, Bobby asked Lewis: "Have you ever heard that expression?" Lewis replied: "Never have. Who's Kelsey?" To which Bobby answered, laughing: "I don't know who Kelsey was." But that didn't matter: Bobby was linked to the Irish lore in a way that King wasn't. If any further proof was needed of the cultural gulf between King and the Kennedys, the usage of the expression *Kelsey's nuts* served the purpose. With those two words, Bobby had—perhaps not unintentionally—underscored that Martin Luther King could never find a true welcome within the tight Kennedy clan.

58

AFTER SPEAKING TO King, Robert Kennedy got a call from an irate Governor Patterson, who shouted so loud that the attorney general again held the receiver away from his ear for the benefit of his visiting *Time* magazine reporter. The Alabama governor accused Bobby of unleashing the

Freedom Riders on his state and asserted that the attorney general had to take the blame for the violence. Behind the governor's rant was his need to shift political responsibility away from himself and onto an aggressive, interventionist federal government that ran roughshod over states' rights.

"Now, John," Bobby said, "you can say that on television. You can tell that to the people of Alabama, John, but don't tell me that."

Patterson informed Bobby that the Alabama National Guard had the situation well under control; the people inside the church were protected, and there was quiet on the streets. But, he threatened, he could not guarantee the safety of Martin Luther King Jr. Fearing utter mayhem should anything happen to King, Bobby shot back at Patterson: "I don't believe that, John. Have General Graham call me. I want to hear a general of the United States Army say he can't protect Martin Luther King."

Revealing the real cause of his agitation, Patterson hollered that he was in a "very serious political situation" because Bobby had let the federal marshals loose in the state. "You're destroying us politically."

"John," Bobby replied, "it's more important that these people in the church survive physically than for us to survive politically."

By dawn, the mob had mostly straggled away and the weary captives were escorted out of the church and loaded into National Guard trucks and jeeps. Bobby's all-night vigil, aided by his representatives on the ground, had prevented a melee. But the Kennedy administration had done little to promote civil rights; it had only demonstrated its will to maintain order. The issue at the heart of the crisis went unaddressed: Neither the attorney general nor, more important, the president said a word about the prevailing injustice that had inspired blacks to risk their lives.

On Monday, May 22, the newspapers shouted the news from Alabama, and still President Kennedy kept silent, carrying on publicly as though no racial unrest ruffled his America. A three-line headline was emblazoned on the front page of the *New York Times*: MONTGOMERY UNDER MARTIAL LAW; TROOPS CALLED AFTER NEW RIOT; MARSHALS AND POLICE FIGHT MOB. Photos showed the marshals on the scene and blacks inside the church with handkerchiefs smothering their faces to block the tear gas fumes.

59

THE ALARMING NIGHT at the First Baptist Church in Montgomery rang in a new era of racial conflict. Yet President Kennedy maintained a profile so low as to be almost invisible. Instead, he focused on his coming diplomatic challenges with de Gaulle in Paris and Khrushchev in Vienna. While he hoped the confrontation in Alabama would not sully his important summits, it was already playing large overseas. "The current toward racial integration has now acquired irresistible force," *Le Monde* said, "and it is because they know themselves beaten that advocates of white supremacy have turned to the worst violence. They can thus slow the evolution but not stem it."

On the Monday after the church siege, the president had a previously scheduled meeting with a group advising him on the development of the Peace Corps. The advisory council, comprised of blacks and whites, included singer-activist Harry Belafonte, Yale Law School dean Eugene Rostow, and Morehouse College president Benjamin Mays. During the Freedom Rides, these men urged civil rights aide Harris Wofford to press the president to speak out in moral terms about segregation and racial discrimination. Wofford was reluctant to push his boss too much on such a sensitive issue and encouraged the men to bring the matter up when they saw him. At the meeting, the president chatted casually then got down to a discussion of the Peace Corps. No one had the nerve to turn the conversation to equal rights. Finally, as Kennedy was departing, Wofford stepped in and asked if the president had a minute to hear the group's thoughts on the Freedom Rides. "Sure," Kennedy said and turned back. After an awkward moment, Harry Belafonte spoke up.

"Mr. President," he said softly. "I know how much you're doing in civil rights. I deeply respect your leadership." He said he trusted the president on the issue. "But perhaps you could say something a little more about the Freedom Riders." Before the president could respond, Eugene Rostow pointed out bluntly that the desegregation of public facilities needed the president's moral leadership.

With deft deflection, Kennedy asked if the men had seen his statement on the rides in the papers over the weekend. When they said—to Wofford's surprise—that they hadn't, the president said he believed they would find it sufficient. Once they tracked it down later, they saw that the statement only stressed the need to maintain order and urged both sides to refrain from violence; it contained no moral considerations, no appeal to the conscience of Americans for acceptance of equal rights.

Soon after the men left, a White House guard summoned Wofford to the Oval Office. "Who the hell was that man with Harry Belafonte?" the president wanted to know. The man, Wofford informed the president, was Gene Rostow, the brother of his foreign policy advisor Walt Rostow. "Well, what in the world does he think I should do? Doesn't he know I've done more for civil rights than any president in American history? How could any man have done more than I've done?"

Despite his outburst, the president was conscious that he had not done nearly enough on civil rights. As a man of intellect and compassion, Kennedy knew that four months into his term he had not given black justice the attention it deserved. His irritation with Rostow suggested that he wanted to do more to right the nation's historical wrongs but that he was failing to take the necessary courageous steps. Recalling the president's outburst, Wofford was struck by "how sensitive he was to criticism about his moral leadership."

60

MARTIN LUTHER KING Jr. emerged from the church siege still distrusted by some activists. Although he was clearly the man in charge, the one who could negotiate with the attorney general, he fell short in the eyes of the younger, more radical protesters—the bloodied Freedom Riders themselves. During one of King's intense phone conversations with Robert Kennedy, Nashville organizer Diane Nash was pushed out of the basement to keep her from interfering. Nash was a savvy leader; the Justice Department had consulted with her before King showed up in

Montgomery. Still she was elbowed aside. "There was a certain inevitability to the way King and his people had taken over the moment they arrived," author David Halberstam observed. "King was the leading figure of the Movement, by now the de facto leader of black political America, the person to whom the media and the white politicians turned in all moments of crisis. When he arrived during a crisis he became the central figure."

But to the early Freedom Ride organizers, King seemed at times too willing to listen to the government. At the height of the Montgomery crisis, Bobby Kennedy asked King to stop the Freedom Rides for a while to implement a "cooling-off period." Diane Nash feared that King was receptive to the idea, something she adamantly opposed. The rides had to carry on, she believed; otherwise, the forces of racism won. "The Nashville Student Movement wants to go on," she said. "We can't stop it now, right after we've been clobbered." James Farmer, the original organizer of the rides, also resisted Bobby's suggestion. "Please tell the attorney general that we have been cooling off for 350 years," Farmer told King. "If we cool off any more, we will be in a deep freeze."

* * *

And so the rides went on. The activists prepared to take to the road again on Wednesday, May 24, on a journey from Montgomery to Jackson, Mississippi. To ensure maximum attention, Diane Nash urged Martin Luther King Jr. to join a Freedom Ride. King was hesitant. To the young activists, it was unclear whether his qualms came from a lack of courage or a leadership flaw; his reluctance tarnished him in their eyes. At first, King's aides explained that he was too valuable to the movement to risk the dangers of a Freedom Ride, an excuse that rang hollow to those putting themselves on the line. At a meeting of the riders in the downtown Montgomery YMCA, King explained his quandary; he pointed out that he was still on probation for his traffic violation arrest in Georgia in 1960, the arrest that had landed him in jail just prior to the presidential election, and another arrest could mean six months in prison. His excuse did not impress anyone.

"I'm on probation, too," one rider shouted.

"Me, too," another called out.

"We're all on probation," a third person chimed in.

King's reply only diminished him further among the young. "I think," he said, "*I* should choose the time and place of my Golgotha."

By alluding to Golgotha, the spot where Jesus was crucified, King underscored his self-importance in the eyes of the other activists. Several got up, shook their heads, and walked out. As they left, one disillusioned youth mocked King, muttering in disgust: "De Lawd!" As John Lewis explained, "There couldn't have been a more concise way to capture the split that was widening between the generations in the movement than the simple phrase: *De Lawd*."

But Lewis was sympathetic to King's predicament. Several years earlier King might have jumped aboard the bus. "But now his position and his responsibilities had grown so incredibly large that his every step, his every word had to be measured for its impact," Lewis observed. "That's a great burden for any man." Lewis was sensitive to King's quandary and annoyed that the other students were forcing a moral decision on him; it was contrary to the wisdom of the protests' spiritual leader Mahatma Gandhi, who taught that each person must decide for himself how to act.

King had another reason to stay off the bus. As the designated voice of the movement, he served as the direct channel between blacks and the Kennedy administration; it was King who conveyed the movement's demands and fears to the highest offices of the land. The Freedom Ride tensions drew King and the Kennedy administration into a close, if contentious, working relationship. An opportunity had opened for King to build on this interaction; there was the chance that his voice might now reach more readily and more regularly into the Oval Office. To expand on that relationship King had to project an image of reason and responsibility; leaping aboard the next Freedom Bus just as Robert Kennedy was calling for a cooling-off period might send the wrong message to Washington. As much as he wanted to seize this opening with the White House, King nonetheless was tormented by his decision to stay on the platform while the next Freedom Ride left the station. He keenly felt the moral sting of sending others into harm's way without putting himself on the line.

61

WHEN TWELVE FREEDOM Riders boarded a Trailways bus on Wednesday, the Montgomery terminal was surrounded by three hundred troops of the Alabama National Guard. In a show of support, Martin Luther King came out to see the riders off. He went with them into the all-white waiting room where the group ordered coffee and snacks from the counter becoming, in the words of the bus terminal manager, the first blacks ever served there. Pulling out of the Montgomery station at around 7 a.m., the bus had an escort of motorcycle policemen through the city, then it headed out of town in a caravan of some forty vehicles filled with highway patrolmen, reporters, and FBI agents. In the skies overhead, two helicopters and three Border Patrol aircraft kept a vigil. Later in the morning, a second bus left the Montgomery Greyhound station carrying fourteen Freedom Riders. When the buses crossed the state line, the Alabama escort dropped off, and Mississippi police and guardsmen took over. Under such massive security, the buses, not surprisingly, made it to Jackson without incident. But as soon as the Freedom Riders arrived, they were arrested and charged with refusing to disperse. In prison, they rejected bail and threatened to go on a hunger strike.

At 9:15 p.m. Bobby Kennedy and King had a testy phone conversation. King noted sourly that the overwhelming show of police protection rendered the ride meaningless; blacks, apparently, were free to travel in desegregated buses only under heavy police escort. When Bobby pressed him on the riders' refusal to post bond, King explained: "It's a matter of conscience and morality.... Our conscience tells us that the law is wrong ... but we have a moral obligation to accept the penalty."

"The fact that they stay in jail," Bobby said with irritation, "is not going to have the slightest effect on me."

"Perhaps it would help," King pushed back, "if students came down here by the hundreds—by the hundreds of thousands."

"Don't make statements that sound like a threat," Bobby replied. "That's not the way to deal with us."

King fell silent for a moment then decided to take a softer approach. "It's difficult to understand the position of oppressed people," he said. "You must understand that we've made no gains without pressure, and I hope that pressure will always be moral, legal and peaceful."

The attorney general insisted that these actions were no way to achieve the movement's goals; the path to change was through strong actions by the federal government.

King accepted that the government's role was essential; but he pointed out the reality: The government, and the courts, tended to move slowly, and often not at all, if not forced to act. It was becoming clear that pressure applied by direct confrontation such as the sit-ins and the Freedom Rides accelerated the process and roused slumbering public officials. "I'm deeply appreciative of what the Administration is doing," King offered. "I see a ray of hope." But he was embracing the enthusiasm of the young protesters; he felt their urgency for change. Their courage emboldened him to reclaim the spirit of protest that he had once personified. As he told Bobby, "I am different than my father. I feel the need of being free now."

62

As THE PRESIDENT's overseas journey neared, the Kennedys intensified pressure on the activists to call off the protests. Bobby Kennedy went public with his call for a cooling-off period, noting that any further violence would mar the president's delicate foreign summits. "It would be wise for those traveling through [Alabama and Mississippi] to delay their trips until the present state of confusion and danger has passed and an atmosphere of reason and normalcy has been restored," the attorney general said in a statement. "I think we should all keep in mind that the President is about to embark on a mission of great importance. Whatever we do in the United States at this time which brings or causes discredit on our country can be harmful to his mission."

Bobby told the *Washington Post* that the Birmingham and Montgomery riots and the Jackson jail protest were "not the way either to advance civil rights or to maintain American prestige." He also warned that an invasion of Freedom Riders into the South was not "the most effective way of breaking segregation barriers." If King believed the attorney general leaned toward the blacks in disputes over their rights, he had reason to reconsider his optimism. Bobby told the newspaper that when violence broke out, his only job was to maintain law and order. "He does not feel that the Department of Justice can, at those times, side with one group or the other in disputes over constitutional rights," the newspaper reported.

A week before his departure for Europe, the president spoke to a joint session of Congress and left no doubt where civil rights stood in his hierarchy of national concerns. The speech, which came while the Freedom Riders sat in jail in Mississippi, was presented as a "Special Message to the Congress on Urgent National Needs." His civil rights aide Harris Wofford urged Kennedy to add a statement on desegregating interstate bus terminals, but the president rejected the idea; he made no mention of Alabama, Montgomery, black rights, or the Freedom Riders. It was as though the civil rights turmoil, which had played so prominently in the newspapers and on television, didn't exist. Speaking to Congress he declared: "These are extraordinary times," and described America's role as the "leader in freedom's cause.... We stand for freedom."

But the freedom the president had in mind was far from American shores. "The great battleground for the defense and expansion of freedom today is the whole southern half of the globe—Asia, Latin America, Africa and the Middle East—the lands of the rising peoples," he said. It was this battle pitting democracy against Communism that most interested him—not the struggle waged for equality in Alabama and Mississippi. Winning the overseas battle also meant beating the Soviets in the space race. In response to the Soviets' early lead, Kennedy offered this challenge: "I believe that this nation should commit itself to achieving the goal, before this decade is out, of landing a man on the moon and returning him safely to the earth."

Despite his lofty ambitions for America, the president in his speech revealed just how deaf he was to the cries for freedom at home. His apparent indifference to the violence erupting in the South was not lost on those committed to righting the wrongs of American society. Father Theodore Hesburgh, president of Notre Dame University and a member of the Civil Rights Commission, put it succinctly in a note he inserted into the commission's Second Report to the President and Congress. "Personally," he said, "I don't care if the United States gets the first man on the moon, if while this is happening on a crash basis, we dawdle along here on our corner of the earth, nursing our prejudices, flouting our magnificent Constitution, ignoring the central moral problem of our times, and appearing hypocrites to all the world."

63

ON MAY 31, President Kennedy landed in Paris to present himself to America's allies and enemies as protector of the free world. Over five days in Paris and Vienna his charm ran only a close second to his wife's. For weeks before the trip, French newspapers and magazines were filled with reports and photos about the presidential couple, noting with particular interest Jackie's skill with the French language. Anticipation over Jackie's imminent arrival soared after French television broadcast an interview with the First Lady speaking "very commendable" French. Paris also was eager to assess Jackie's outfits, which were promised to be creations of Oleg Cassini and Chez Ninon of New York.

The president, appreciative of Jackie's public relations value, was self-effacing and witty at a press luncheon in Paris. "I do not think it altogether inappropriate to introduce myself to this audience," he told the gathering of French and American journalists. "I am the man who accompanied Jacqueline Kennedy to Paris, and I have enjoyed it." In Vienna, Jackie caught the eye of Soviet premier Nikita Khrushchev. At an Austrian state dinner hosted in Schönbrunn Palace, a country residence of former Habsburg emperors, the premier was asked by a photographer to shake hands with President Kennedy. Nodding toward Jackie, who looked resplendent in a long white gown, Khrushchev said: "I'd like to shake her hand first."

In his meetings with Khrushchev, Kennedy was immediately on the defensive debating the relative virtues of democracy and Communism, deflecting the premier's assertion that the communist system would inevitably win out over the American way. Sixty-seven-year-old Khrushchev stood only as high as Kennedy's nose and was described by one journalist as "fat as a sausage." Here was the bullying world leader who a year earlier had taken off his shoe and banged it on the table during debate at the UN General Assembly. Wishing to ground their conversations in reality, Kennedy steered the men toward discussion of how to avoid miscalculations that could lead to military confrontation. After some resistance, Khrushchev finally agreed that the two nations needed to find ways to improve their relations. Later rounds, however, revived the antagonism between the two leaders, with Khrushchev competing fiercely to emerge as the more powerful global figure. Riding an amphetamine high, Kennedy held his own against the Soviet premier. The amphetamine injections were administered by Max Jacobson, a doctor who supplied a dubious drug concoction to ease Kennedy's back pain during the presidential campaign. Known as Dr. Feelgood, he had become a regular White House presence, even traveling with the president. In Vienna, as the latest dose wore off and the president wearied, Khrushchev gained the upper hand in the verbal sparring. During the two-day summit, Kennedy once retreated to the ambassador's residence in a gloomy mood. When his personal secretary, Evelyn Lincoln, asked how the talks were going, he admitted: "Not too well. He treated me like a little boy. Like a little boy."

Khrushchev's hostility only worsened when the talks resumed. The premier attacked Kennedy for his invasion of Cuba, arguing that the failure only strengthened Castro. When the men discussed the possible banning of nuclear weapons testing, Khrushchev dismissed the idea of allowing U.S. inspectors on Soviet soil. Discussions on Berlin prompted the premier to threaten that any U.S. opposition to the Soviet satellite of communist East Germany would be met with force. "It is up to the U.S. to decide whether there will be war or peace," he warned Kennedy. If there had been any miscalculations at the talks, it was Kennedy's failure to prepare for Khrushchev's wild mood swings and his unrelenting belligerence. By the end of the summit, the president described the talks as "somber." His aide Arthur Schlesinger Jr. captured the president's grim mood: "Kennedy had never encountered any leader with whom he could not exchange ideas—anyone so impervious to reasoned argument or so apparently indifferent to the prospective obliteration of mankind."

President Kennedy had come into office with a love of foreign affairs and a belief in his expertise. But now the world viewed him as young and inexperienced and not tough enough to go nose to nose with the top Soviet bulldog. After only six months in office Kennedy had flubbed the Cuba invasion and had been crushed diplomatically and personally in a face-off with Khrushchev. He had gone to Vienna hoping to diminish the chance of war, but after the summit he worried that the United States was now closer to a confrontation with an unpredictable opponent armed with an arsenal of nuclear weapons. If he gave scant attention to civil rights before his encounter with Khrushchev, he was even less likely to make it a priority in the aftermath of his Vienna trip. President Kennedy's foremost concern was reestablishing his international stature. Everything else had to wait.

64

THE FREEDOM RIDES carried on through the summer and into fall, with more than four hundred riders taking part. But a massive police presence and hundreds of arrests had quelled the crisis, giving the president a respite from headlines on civil rights disturbances. Now fully committed, Martin Luther King Jr. helped with the rides and with uniting often-competing interests. In late May he led the founding meeting of a new group, the Freedom Ride Coordinating Committee, which linked together his own Southern Christian Leadership Conference, James Farmer's Congress of Racial Equality, and the Student Nonviolent Coordinating Committee in the Freedom Ride cause. The new group established an action plan that included pressuring the president and attorney general to reaffirm the rights of interstate travelers. The Interstate Commerce Commission had issued an order in November 1955 directing bus companies to stop segregating passengers, but the order did not directly address segregation in the terminals. In 1956, the Supreme Court affirmed the ICC's ruling but confusion still reigned over enforcement, and in the South the rules were roundly ignored.

Breaking his long silence, President Kennedy finally spoke on bus-terminal segregation in July in response to a question at a press conference. Although he took no moral stand, he did express his support of the riders' right "to move freely in interstate commerce." In a subtle prod for change in Southern attitudes, he voiced the hope that the right of free travel across state borders "will become the generally accepted view." He stressed that America's constitutional protections gave everyone the right to move uninhibited about the country. "So the basic question is not the Freedom Riders," he told journalists. "The basic question is that anyone who moves in interstate commerce should be able to do so freely. That's a more substantive question, not the question merely of the Freedom Riders."

For the first time, the president acknowledged that the Freedom Rides were more than just a law-and-order issue. Between May and July, he had undergone a subtle but important evolution, spurred in part by the pressure exerted by the Freedom Rides and by his own subtle recognition of the principles behind the protests. His remarks at the press conference reflected actions his administration had already taken. At the end of May, attorney general Bobby Kennedy recognized the wisdom of the Freedom Ride Coordinating Committee's insistence that the ICC clarify its rules on interstate travel. Ignoring the supposed independence of the ICC, Bobby had the Justice Department staff draw up a petition calling on the commission to issue a ruling on segregation in interstate travel. The intent was not to lay down a new law—laws already existed—but rather to demand enforcement of those existing laws.

The Justice Department was clear about what it sought from the ICC. It wanted the commission to publicize and adhere to its own rules that prohibited discrimination against passengers traveling across state lines. Such action, the petition said, was "necessary to create order out of chaos, to lessen the possibility of mob action, to guarantee to all passengers their rights under the Interstate Commerce Act and vindicate those rights against inconsistent and unlawful action by state or local authorities." The attorney general pointed out that "flagrant violations" of the Interstate Commerce Act were apparent in the existence of segregation on buses and in terminals. The petition called for the removal of all signs in the terminals that separated people by race, color, creed, or national origin. It noted that just as the Constitution was "color-blind," so too was the Interstate Commerce Act.

Like his brother, Bobby was evolving—and with greater speed and passion than the president. Just days before he issued his petition to the ICC, the attorney general went on the Voice of America and said repeatedly how disturbed he was by the violence in Alabama. Broadcasting to some sixty countries, he stressed the progress America had made in tolerance, noting that when his Irish immigrant grandfather arrived in Boston, "the Irish were not wanted there. Now an Irish Catholic is president of the United States." Bobby then offered a prediction which, from the vantage point of 1961, might not have seemed realistic. "There is no question about it," he said. "In the next forty years, a Negro can achieve the same position that my brother has."

The attorney general drove his Justice Department staff to badger the notoriously slow-moving ICC, and their hounding delivered a ruling in September—just four months for a decision that normally took years. As historian Taylor Branch put it, "Experts considered the lobbying feat a bureaucratic miracle." The ruling ordered that all interstate transportation terminals, restaurants, waiting rooms, water faucets, restrooms—everything—had to be desegregated beginning November 1. By December, the signs designating "colored" facilities had come down.

The success of the Freedom Rides did not emanate merely from the softening of John Kennedy's and Robert Kennedy's hearts, although there was an element of that. Most significant was the precedent the Freedom Rides set for waging battle; the riders threw themselves into nonviolent, direct confrontation against injustice and the brutal response of white racists was splashed across newspapers and television screens across the country. One of the white Freedom Riders, Montgomery native and Wesleyan professor John Maguire, explained: "Here was a classic instance where the pressure of concerned people simply moved the government much faster—infinitely faster—than otherwise would have been the case."

The lesson was not lost on Martin Luther King Jr. Searching for ways to drive the movement forward under his leadership, King absorbed the example of the student-led Freedom Rides, pondered it, and understood its profound implications. What was needed was not just quiet resistance but sustained, publicized pressure on the government. In a letter to Harold Courlander, a writer who supported the movement, King hinted at his thinking about future civil rights campaigns. "Public relations is a very necessary part of any protest of civil disobedience," he wrote in October

1961. Without the publicity the Freedom Rides generated, King believed there would not have been enough pressure to force the administration and the ICC to act. King later came to believe that Robert Kennedy himself appreciated the power of pressure on the government. "After the Freedom Rides ended," King said, "the Attorney General had to admit that they had real value in bringing the issue so much out into the open."

But President Kennedy was still hesitant to quicken the pace of civil rights reform. While he took a small step forward with his statements at his press conference, he did not follow up in any determined way. The White House gave no sense of leadership on civil rights; the president introduced no grand moves, no legislation; he did not use his bully pulpit to encourage broad cultural change. Kennedy was still largely inattentive to the demands for black justice, and his indifference made the Freedom Rides' celebration in many respects a narrow victory. What the president failed to properly calculate was the message of the rides: that the momentum of the civil rights movement was outrunning his wish to contain the cries for equality. Although he hoped to deal with civil rights at his own pace, he soon was forced to confront the impatience of Martin Luther King Jr. and other blacks across the country. "The sit-ins and the Freedom Rides upset everybody's chart and tables," observed Thurgood Marshall, the director of the NAACP's legal team. Everybody had "to move faster than they had moved before."

PART FOUR

"PAWNS IN A WHITE MAN'S POLITICAL GAME"

65

AT LONG LAST, some ten months into the new administration, Martin Luther King Jr. was headed to the White House for a private meeting with the president. His first request had been made in March, two months after the inauguration, followed by repeated pleas from his friend Harris Wofford, the president's civil rights aide. But just as Kennedy felt no urgency to move on grand civil rights initiatives, he felt no pressing need to meet with the man who stood at the forefront of the movement. Despite the gravity of the Freedom Rides, the president still relegated civil rights to a distant corner of his mind and kept it there so he could devote himself to recovering his footing on the world stage and pursue his domestic agenda on the economy. In his political calculation, the time simply wasn't right for dramatic presidential action on discrimination, segregation, and racial injustice.

Whenever Wofford consulted with the president on a civil rights matter, the meetings were brief. "He'd ask for very quick answers," Wofford recalled. Kennedy relied on his trademark joking to avoid deep conversations on the subject, a casualness that wore on the earnest presidential aide. "I got tired of his accosting me with a grin and asking, 'Are your constituents happy?'" Even still, Wofford sensed a contradiction in the president. Kennedy, he perceived, had a strong, unexpressed desire to right racial wrongs but was biding his time to see how developments played out before taking meaningful action. In this sense, Wofford believed, "Kennedy had a touch of the Lincoln concept of letting a thing ripen before you move on it." He was awaiting a concrete, inescapable moment to apply himself fully to a solution. "You don't deal with things in the abstract," Wofford explained. "I think more or less that was his attitude about civil rights."

King had no illusions about the president's reluctance on civil rights, but he nonetheless rode up to the White House gates on October 16, 1961, intending to deliver a grand proposal. He had already introduced the idea several times, most pointedly in December 1960, just over a month after the election. Speaking at a rally honoring the ninety-eighth anniversary of President Lincoln's Emancipation Proclamation, he urged Kennedy to issue a second Emancipation Proclamation in the form of an executive order banning all forms of discrimination across American society. King revisited the matter in June 1961 in the wake of the bloody Freedom Rides in Alabama. In a press statement delivered at the Sheraton Atlantic Hotel in New York, he asserted: "Just as Abraham Lincoln had the vision to see almost one hundred years ago that this nation could not exist half slave and half free, the present administration must have the insight to see that today the nation cannot exist half segregated and half integrated." From inside the presidential cocoon, Kennedy had kept silent. Now, as King approached the White House, the civil rights leader was able to force the issue personally upon the president.

But King was at a distinct disadvantage: The power that rested with him before the election had shifted to Kennedy. When the men first met in New York during the presidential campaign, King was dominant: Kennedy had desperately courted King in hopes of drawing reluctant blacks into his camp. But Kennedy's victory had dramatically changed the power dynamic. Even though blacks claimed a decisive role in Kennedy's election, the president felt no pressing responsibility to honor the debt. King, after all, had refused to endorse Kennedy even after the candidate called Coretta during a period of deep anxiety for her. King's reluctance no doubt caused a wariness about his loyalty to Kennedy and deterred the president from risking a close relationship.

King had another obstacle in winning the president's confidence: The FBI had intensified its smear campaign against him. Scurrilous, inaccurate information about King and his purported communist associations was flowing into the White House. FBI chief J. Edgar Hoover had latched on to King's close aide, Stanley Levison, who was long suspected of Communist Party affiliations. According to the FBI, Levison had helped fund the Communist Party in the United States from the mid-1940s through the mid-1950s. Although some evidence existed to support these assertions, Levison's activities and associations with the party had ceased by 1955. Around this time he met King and devoted himself to the civil rights movement. By March 1957, the FBI had so little connecting him anymore to the Communist Party that Levison was deleted from its communist watch list. According to historian David Garrow, who deeply probed the FBI's interest in King, some former bureau officials had heard top communist leaders in the United States acknowledge that Levison had terminated his party activities.

Undeterred, Hoover sent agents after fresh allegations against King. He had established a nonstop, systematic investigation of the civil rights leader relying on wiretapping, physical surveillance, and stakeouts. With no solid evidence against King, Hoover delivered a continuous stream of spurious charges to the White House. His reports, brimming with fabrication and manufactured evidence, nonetheless stirred the president's suspicions and choked off any possibility of a trusting relationship with the civil rights leader. It hardly mattered that Kennedy himself distrusted Hoover. He had wanted to replace the FBI chief early in his administration, but was in a bind; Hoover had been collecting potentially explosive information on Kennedy's sex life, embarrassing and politically compromising material that ensured his continued employment and gave him leeway to pursue his many vendettas. As the FBI's chief of domestic intelligence, William Sullivan, recalled: "We never put any technical surveillance on JFK, but whatever came up was automatically funneled directly to Hoover. I was sure he was saving everything he had on Kennedy, and on Martin Luther King, Jr., too, until he could unload it all and destroy them both." President Lyndon Johnson later eloquently summed up Kennedy's predicament—and his own—when he also kept Hoover in his position: "I would rather have him inside the tent pissing out than outside the tent pissing in."

* * *

On his long-awaited first official visit to the White House, a moment of expected triumph, King arrived under a cloud of suspicion. He first stopped at the office of his advocate Harris Wofford, who escorted him through the corridors to meet the president. The two men climbed into the tiny elevator that serviced the private quarters, but instead of going up, as expected, the car sank down to the basement. When the door opened, there stood Jackie Kennedy in jeans, her face smudged with dirt. Wofford introduced her to King. Stepping in, she spoke in her whispery voice: "Dr. King, you would be so thrilled if you could just have been with me in the basement this morning. I found a chair right out of the Andrew Jackson period, a beautiful chair."

King was at a loss for words. "Yes—yes," he replied slowly. "Is that so?"

Jackie either was oblivious to King's anxiety at seeing the president, or was graciously avoiding difficult civil rights subjects, or had simply been caught off guard herself and was struggling to make polite small talk. As the elevator reached the family quarters, she concluded: "I've just got to tell Jack about that chair." Then perhaps noticing King's taut face, she said: "You probably have other things to talk to him about, don't you?"

In a frank, hour-long discussion, King laid out the harsh conditions blacks faced in the South, striking the moral tone of both minister and civil rights leader. Although he later said the president "listened very sympathetically," Wofford sensed a fundamental incompatibility between the two men: King's moral fervor was "not Kennedy's style and made him uncomfortable." Nonetheless, the president "gave every indication of having a lot of respect for King," Wofford observed. The president also conveyed that he was hemmed in by thorny politics that prevented him from taking action on civil rights in ways he wanted to do. In their wide-ranging discussion on legislation, executive orders, and voting rights, the president told King he could not act on many things at the moment. "But, believe me," he promised, "I am going to do them."

King already was disappointed by the president's failure on one major pledge, a campaign promise to issue an executive order on housing. During the televised debate with Richard Nixon in October 1960, with the election just a month away, Senator Kennedy raised the prospect of guaranteeing equal opportunity in federally assisted housing through "a stroke of the President's pen." He reiterated the promise on housing less than a week later before a crowd at the National Conference on Constitutional Rights and American Freedom in New York, declaring: "Many things can be done by the stroke of a Presidential pen." His words came back to haunt him. As he delayed action, blacks and civil rights advocates inundated the White House mailroom with thousands of pens marked "one stroke of the pen." Seeing no humor in the flood of pens, Kennedy growled at his staff: "Send them to Wofford!" Once again, as he had during the early days of the Freedom Rides, the president was blaming his ardent aide for his own shortcomings on civil rights. For his part, Wofford was growing disillusioned with the president, especially in light of his dawdling on the housing order. "What disappointed me most," Wofford recalled, "was not so much the President's recurring decision to wait, for

which he had reasons I understood, as the way he made the decision—
each time hurriedly, at the last minute, in response to Southern political pressures without careful consideration of an overall strategy." As the
president constantly hedged on civil rights, Wofford began to wonder if
he could continue to serve him in good conscience.

As part of King's visit, the president took him on a tour of the White
House, stopping to point out the table where Abraham Lincoln had signed
the Emancipation Proclamation in 1862. Standing beside the historic
treasure, King seized his opportunity, saying: "I would like you to sign
a Second Emancipation Proclamation on this very table." In one stroke
of his pen the president had the opportunity to wipe away a legacy of
institutional segregation in all walks of life. King wanted the president
to declare all segregated facilities unconstitutional and illegal in accordance with the Fourteenth Amendment. An executive order would save
the president from having to battle Congress over legislation to enact the
same protections.

At a news conference after his meeting, King was generous in his
appraisal of the visit, characterizing it as "fruitful and rewarding." He
told reporters that he raised the question of the executive order on housing then gave the president some cover, pointing out that the White House
had been studying the matter. But King also made it clear that ending discrimination in housing was a crucial step toward black equality. "As long
as there is housing segregation, as I said to the president, we will have
segregation in public schools; we will have segregation in recreational
facilities and all areas," he said. "So that this is a pressing need, and I
think it would solve a great problem if we could get such an order." King
also pointed out that the first Emancipation Proclamation was an executive order, so a second proclamation was not "too much to ask."

When newsmen pressed him on the president's reaction to a second
proclamation, King was cagey. He acknowledged that he got a sympathetic ear and that the president agreed to consider the proposal. "But,"
he added, "you would have to speak to [the president] concerning the
possibilities of this actually becoming a reality." What he failed to tell
reporters was that President Kennedy offered a shred of hope: He encouraged King to draw up a legal memorandum for such a proclamation and
to deliver it to the White House. Embracing the president's offer, King
embarked on what became a six-month project to prepare an executive

order that would eliminate with a single pen stroke all segregation laws from statute books across the country.

King came away from the White House troubled by the duality of President Kennedy. Listening to him explain why he had delayed the housing order, King heard a man who wanted to act but feared a political backlash. "My feeling is that the President was not sure that he had a consensus," King recalled. But if the president had a deeper appreciation of the moral injustice of segregation and discrimination, King believed, he would have found the courage to ignore detractors. But Kennedy caved to pockets of pressure. "He was afraid politically to go too far," King said.

That evening King dined with Wofford, and afterward the two men strolled the streets of Washington contemplating the impasse at the White House. Wofford discerned that King was disappointed by his encounter with the president. For nearly a year, he had hoped the White House would recognize the urgent needs of the black community and display genuine leadership. But so far Kennedy had chosen to do next to nothing; he defined civil rights as a law-and-order issue and hid behind his brother. King allowed, however, that the administration's engagement with the issue far surpassed that of President Eisenhower, indeed, that of any other president. But, he explained, "this didn't mean that [Kennedy] was giving the kind of leadership...that the enormity of the problem demanded." Wofford recalled King saying, "[Kennedy] has the understanding and political skills but so far I'm afraid that the moral passion is missing."

66

ALTHOUGH UNFAILINGLY GRACIOUS with each other, near the end of 1961 John F. Kennedy and Martin Luther King Jr. were heading into a period of sharp contention. King was moving toward a full embrace of militant protest as a way to pressure the White House and force the president to take decisive action. If legislation was out of the question, King wanted him to deliver on his promised executive order on housing and on a second Emancipation Proclamation. But the president, for his part, was largely disinterested in King's provocations. Again he had turned his gaze overseas. His preoccupation with the Soviet Union, Germany, Vietnam, and Cuba caused him to miss the fact that civil rights protest was taking new and creative forms of expression. Without the president's resolve on black equality or even so much as a guiding hand, the nation was hurtling in small explosive steps toward what King would later call "America's third revolution—the Negro Revolution." The long-suffering black community wanted an end to segregation immediately. King saw what the president missed: an inevitable march of incompatible cultures toward an unpredictable showdown. "How many people understood, during the first two years of the Kennedy administration," King observed, "that the Negroes' 'Now' was becoming as militant as the segregationists' 'Never'?"

Young activists wasted no time in trying to extend their successes in knocking down barriers to racial equality. Twenty-four-year-old Charles Sherrod, a hot-tempered veteran of the sit-ins and Freedom Rides, and nineteen-year-old Cordell Reagon rode into Albany, Georgia, on a Trailways bus on November 1, 1961, to test implementation of the Interstate Commerce Commission order banning segregation at terminals. The ICC ruling went into effect the same day. But Sherrod, Reagon, and their companions from the Student Nonviolent Coordinating Committee weren't welcome in the segregated waiting room. Tipped off, ten Albany police officers confronted them at the station and ordered them to leave or climb into squad cars for a trip to jail. The young protesters weren't seeking arrest; they were in search of information, and departing the station, they now had their evidence. The ICC mandate was clearly being ignored.

And not only in Albany. Throughout the South, activists tested implementation of the ruling. In Jackson, Mississippi, protesters were arrested for walking into a whites-only waiting room in a bus terminal. In Martin Luther King Jr.'s home town of Atlanta, four students were arrested at a private restaurant in a Trailways bus station. In response, King fired off a telegram to Atlanta's mayor, William Hartsfield. In the abbreviated language of a telegram, he said: "Distressed that our city after having moved forward so creatively in race relations has today taken a step backwards." He called on the mayor to address the arrests and to prevent future violations of the ICC ruling. King also sent a telegram to the chairman of the ICC, Everett Hutchinson, imploring him to ensure that the ruling was enforced.

In Albany, the business-as-usual segregation at the bus terminal encouraged the SNCC activists to team up with other organizations such as the Southern Christian Leadership Conference, the Congress of Racial Equality, and the NAACP to launch a wave of student protests that became known as the Albany Movement. Looking beyond the limited aim of ensuring compliance with the ICC ruling, the movement sought the broad goal of desegregating all institutions across the city, including rail and bus terminals, downtown businesses, libraries, hospitals, and parks. Not only that, the organizers hoped to gain an agreement with the city to expand job opportunities for blacks and to end police brutality.

Albany was a city of wealth and sophistication in southwestern Georgia. For a population of fifty-seven thousand there were eighty churches and a look-the-other-way attitude toward gambling and drinking. Bars at the city's hotels and motels sold mixed drinks, in violation of a state prohibition, and gambling, also illegal, was found at any number of night spots. The white people of Albany were proud of their city and its approach to drinking and gambling. "It's all done in a high-class way," one local told the *New York Times*. "You don't see any drunks roaming the streets or causing trouble. We wouldn't stand for that. Albany is a moral town." There was, however, strict enforcement of segregation. The police, the city commission, and the local newspaper, the *Albany Herald*, unflinchingly supported separation of the races. When blacks complained, the white community wondered why they weren't satisfied with their lot.

At the outset, the bus station protests in Albany failed to stir the larger community or the nation; there were no clashes or dramatic national headlines. The relative tranquility was the doing of one man: Laurie Pritchett. The city's wily police chief had done his homework; he'd read *Stride Toward Freedom*, Martin Luther King Jr.'s account of the Montgomery bus boycott, gaining valuable insight into the ways of nonviolent protest. He intended to conquer nonviolence with nonviolence, placing a large force of officers on the streets and training them in how to make arrests with firmness but without offense. He understood that the way to keep the federal government out of his state—and thereby preserve Georgia's segregated culture—was to ensure that the protests did not spiral into mayhem, as they had in Alabama. As historian Adam Fairclough described the police chief: "The fat, drawling Pritchett looked like the archetypal southern cop, but his calm, canny handling of the demonstrations defied the stereotype."

Chief Pritchett's tactics were soon apparent. On November 22, three high school students bought bus tickets and then tried to get served at the white lunch counter in the terminal. Police quickly moved in and swept the students off to prison. Their arrest brought hordes of other young protesters swarming into the terminal, and they too swiftly found themselves in jail. The demonstrations carried over into December in large numbers, with the same rapid response: The streets of Albany remained quiet while the jails filled up.

Unlike his counterpart in Montgomery, the vicious public safety commissioner L. B. Sullivan, Chief Pritchett was a cordial segregationist. He was soft-spoken, avoided abusive language, and forbade his officers from using their clubs or any other weapons. When a jailer roughed up a protester, Pritchett fired the man. "I don't want a man like that in my jail," he told a reporter. If there were such a thing as a polite arrest, the chief ensured that his officers were well-schooled in it. "Pritchett conducted arrests the way crossing guards helped school children," observed the Reverend Ralph Abernathy. "All of this 'tender loving care' beguiled many reporters and blinded them to the true nature of segregation in Albany."

By December 13, nearly five hundred protesters—mostly high school and college students—sat in Albany area prisons. One band of 267 students had marched three abreast to City Hall and circled back, chanting "We Want Freedom" and "We Are Not Afraid," until they were herded into a yard behind the police station and arrested.

From his reading of Martin Luther King Jr.'s work, Chief Pritchett was aware of Gandhi's tactic to overwhelm the jails and institutions to force concessions from authorities. In *Stride Toward Freedom*, King had noted the inspiration he gained from Gandhi's Salt March to the Sea, a massive nonviolent act of civil disobedience to protest British rule in India and its onerous salt taxes; the protest began with a few dozen people, and by the end some sixty thousand were in jails. The Albany jail did not have room for swarms of prisoners, so Chief Pritchett farmed them out to available cells miles away.

"I had made arrangements," Pritchett recalled. He'd gotten agreements with jails in surrounding counties as far as a hundred miles away to take prisoners. The protesters were booked, fingerprinted, and photographed in Albany, then "they'd come right out and enter the buses and be taken to some other jail."

Hoping to perpetuate Albany's segregated culture, Pritchett nonetheless was a realist; he acknowledged that the South's destiny was full integration. "It might not be in my lifetime, or in my children's, but it will come," he said. "As the laws change to meet the times, I will support the law." But in the meantime he did his best to keep the races separate.

As long as Albany was riot-free the Kennedy administration had no intention of intervening. Even though the jails were filling with young people exercising their right to protest an inimical system of segregation, the president kept silent. He argued long-term change could come only if law and order were preserved. A case in point was the 1962 Georgia gubernatorial race in which a moderate candidate, Carl Sanders, offered a hope of progress after the current segregationist governor Ernest Vandiver. Sanders aimed to knock down racial barriers as part of his plan to bolster the state's economy; he favored growth over segregation, which conformed to Kennedy's ambitions. The president believed that if the racist passions of white voters were held in check, the moderate candidate had the best chance of victory and of integrating Georgia society. By maintaining a hands-off approach in Albany, and thereby preventing the white population from flocking to more extremist candidates, the administration contended it promoted forward-looking, if painfully incremental, change in the South.

Under Chief Pritchett's firm authority, the Albany Movement had fallen into disarray. Friction among its leaders became as debilitating as Pritchett's roundups of protesters. Weak and directionless, the coalition found itself powerless to negotiate an end to segregation in the city. The Albany Movement was going nowhere and needed a strong new voice.

67

IN ATLANTA, MARTIN Luther King Jr. got a message from William G. Anderson, an Albany physician who was president of the protest coalition. Anderson, a friend of King's close associate Ralph Abernathy, begged the civil rights leader to come to Albany to help shine a national spotlight on the injustice playing out there. King was wary. Whenever he appeared at a locally organized protest, he opened himself up to accusations of usurpation. The Freedom Riders' mockery of him as "De Lawd" still rang bitterly in his ears. But Anderson, describing the dire circumstances in Albany, prevailed upon King, even though the movement's future looked grim. King agreed to travel to Albany if for no other purpose than to lift protesters' spirits.

On the evening of December 15, he and Abernathy drove in a winter chill more than 150 miles south to Albany. Immediately they discovered that the leaders of the protest coalition were in deep dissension. "By the time we arrived," Abernathy recalled, "any unity they may have achieved had already collapsed. Everyone had a different strategy. Everyone wanted to be in charge. Everyone was mad at everyone else. And as soon as we arrived in town, everyone was mad at us."

King and Abernathy listened to the woes of Dr. Anderson, who had been patiently herding the many egos and ambitions of the coalition members, all of whom were frustrated by the movement's failure to get a desegregation agreement from city officials. King zeroed in on how to stir consensus within the black community. "Which of the pastors are cooperating?" he asked Anderson and learned that the two most active were Reverend Grant of the Mount Zion Baptist Church and Reverend Boyd of Shiloh Baptist, who were both holding meetings that night.

Not long afterward, Martin Luther King Jr. stood before a packed sanctuary at Mount Zion (he also spoke at Shiloh across the street the same evening before a total crowd at both churches of about a thousand people). By now, more than seven hundred protesters were sitting in jails in and around Albany. In his speeches, King offered solace to the imprisoned protesters and to Albany's black community, and he goaded local officials reluctant to negotiate on segregation. But he also directed his rhetoric at the figure most important to the cause: President John Kennedy.

More often now, in his speeches, interviews, and published articles, King challenged the man in the White House, often without mentioning him. King flung verbal darts at the president to awaken him to America's racial crimes and to spur him to act.

Before the congregants at Mount Zion, King warned those "who are telling us to slow up, who are telling us that we are pushing things too fast. We must say to them that the hour is late"—from the crowd came a murmur: *That's right. That's right*—"that the clock of destiny is ticking

out"—from the crowd: *yes*—"and we must act now before it is too late."
King warned that in a Cold War world, democracy was under threat and
the country had to strengthen its commitment to the democratic ideal of
equality. "The price that America must pay for the continued oppression
of the Negro," he declared, "is a price of its own destruction."

Dr. Anderson stepped up to the dais to thank King and to announce a
new round of demonstrations: Those wishing to join Martin Luther King
Jr. on a march to City Hall were instructed to assemble back at the church
bright and early the following day. "Be here at seven o'clock in the morning," Anderson said. "Eat a good breakfast. Wear warm clothes and wear
your walking shoes."

Saturday was rainy and unusually cold. King, dressed in a suit, white
shirt, tie, and fedora, fell in with more than 260 marchers; as they reached
City Hall they were met by a large force of police in yellow slickers. The
arrests were peaceful, but the sight of Martin Luther King Jr.'s being
carted off to Sumter County jail in Americus suddenly gave this local
movement national significance; the press coverage of King sitting in a
prison brought the Albany protests to the doorstep of the White House.
Taunting Kennedy to react, King announced he would not accept bond,
and planned to be in prison through Christmas. The Southern Christian
Leadership Conference heightened emotions surrounding King's circumstances when its executive director, Wyatt Tee Walker, said the people of
Albany should forgo Christmas celebrations while the civil rights leader
was in jail. "Tell the children that we are postponing Christmas," he
declared. "We don't want a single Christmas tree lit. We want no Christmas toys bought downtown. We want to turn downtown Albany into a
ghost town."

President Kennedy was conveniently out of town, riding through the
streets of Caracas, Venezuela, in his limousine to cries of "Viva Kennedy" on a brief swing through Latin America where he encouraged "the
yearning of the common man...for a better life." Back in Washington,
King's arrest stirred a storm of reaction. Telegrams poured into the White
House and Justice Department urging the federal government to intervene; one called the absence of any action "shocking and deplorable." In
a telegram to Attorney General Robert Kennedy, the NAACP protested
the arrest of King and the others; King's close associate, Stanley Levison,
urged the attorney general to send federal marshals to Albany because

local officials had subverted the laws of the nation. Word spread of the dismal conditions in the prisons; the protesters were not only subjected to verbal abuse but one of the leaders was shoved into the bars of his cell, injuring his head. King complained about being called "boy" and later described the Sumter County sheriff as the "meanest man in the world." In a token gesture, Bobby instructed assistant attorney general for civil rights Burke Marshall to take whatever steps were necessary to ensure King's safety; if King were harmed, the repercussions within the black community were unpredictable. Bobby's real intention, however, was to stay out of the way; and as long as the crackdown caused no bloodshed, the attorney general was more than pleased to watch from a distance.

From prison, King sent a telegram to the president urging him to intervene on behalf of the hundreds of protesters in jail simply for exercising their constitutional right to march for freedom. King considered this a good opportunity to remind the president of the blanket action he had at his disposal to free blacks from second-class citizenship—a second Emancipation Proclamation that he could deliver by executive order. In the two months since King proposed the proclamation in his White House meeting, the president had expressed no further interest. Addressing the president's affinity for foreign affairs, King put his plea in a global context, imploring Kennedy to defend equal rights in his own democracy at home as vigorously as he did human rights overseas. "Then and only then," he said, "can we justify the claim to world leadership in the fight against communism and tyranny." The reply from the White House was silence.

Pressured by the media attention, the Albany government started to cave. For a moment it seemed that the bright glare focused on King had enlightened the city commission to its moral obligation. On December 18, an agreement was struck: If the demonstrations were called off for thirty days, the local government promised to comply with the ICC order, release the protesters on bail, and allow the Albany Movement to present its proposals to the commission.

King emerged from prison victorious just two days after his arrest, and a week before Christmas. Although he was dissatisfied with the breadth of the agreement he was willing to allow the process to continue. "I would not want to stand in the way of meaningful negotiations," he told the press. He then headed back to Atlanta.

The terms were indeed meager; while the city agreed to comply with desegregation rules at bus terminals, Chief Pritchett crowed in the press that "Negroes had been promised nothing that marked a departure from the city's established policies." No changes in segregation policies were implemented; the city had manipulated the movement, and tricked King into leaving Albany. Soon afterward, the local government reneged on its promises.

The press came down hard on King. The *New York Herald Tribune* called the outcome "one of the most stunning defeats of his career." A few years later, King told *Time* magazine: "Looking back over it, I'm sorry I was bailed out. I didn't understand at the time what was happening. We thought that the victory had been won. When we got out, we discovered it was all a hoax."

The president and the attorney general were pleased; the nation had skirted another potential uprising without incident. In gratitude, Bobby sent a telegram to Albany's mayor, Asa Kelley, congratulating him on the way the crisis was handled. In jubilation, Kelley and Pritchett hosted the press at a segregated country club for a celebration dinner; gloating over the defeat of the Albany Movement and his embrace by the Kennedy administration, Mayor Kelley read the telegram out loud to the assembled crowd.

68

ON HIS RETURN from South America, President Kennedy stopped over for a night at his father's estate in Palm Beach. On December 18, the day Martin Luther King Jr. walked out of the Sumter County jail, the president rode out to the airport with his father and four-year-old Caroline for his flight back to Washington. The patriarch, Joseph Kennedy, saw his son off then took in an early morning round of golf at the Palm Beach Country Club. While on the course, the seventy-three-year-old family patriarch lost his balance and felt faint. When he got home he went upstairs to nap, brushing off Jackie's concerns about his condition. After a short time he woke up, "coughing and unable to speak or move on the right side," according to a niece, Ann Gargan, who was with him. The president was still airborne but, as historian David Nasaw tells the story, when he got to the White House, the " 'hot line' was flashing amber."

By the time the president returned to Palm Beach, his father was in Saint Mary's Hospital, having suffered a massive stroke; and he had been given last rites. Miraculously he awoke from his coma the next day and four days later appeared to have weathered the immediate threat; but his life—and the dynamics of the Kennedy clan—was forever changed. "Now, suddenly, on day 322 of his son's presidential term, three months into his seventy-fourth year, he was in an instant transformed from the most vital, the smartest, the dominant one in the room to a gnarled, crippled, drooling, speechless, wheelchair-bound, utterly dependent shell of a man," Nasaw wrote. "Yet he appeared to understand everything that was said to him, everything he read or heard or saw."

Joseph Kennedy was a man who drove his sons to accept nothing less than victory, a man of unrelenting competitiveness, who found a way around every setback, who crafted his life to overcome discrimination, criticism, and resentment with such success that his family stood at the pinnacle of American society. Now his son, the leader of the free world, could do little to ameliorate his suffering other than kiss him on the top of the head and cheer him on for very small victories in rehabilitation.

In the past, Jack was noticeably tense around his father. In Joe's presence the son fidgeted, tapped his front teeth and stroked his jaw, signs of his anxiety that were familiar to friends and associates. Now the president was as tender with his father as he was with his children; if Caroline and John Jr. taught Jack to express affection in surprising new ways, his father's debility stirred unexpected depths of consideration and empathy. At the same time, the stroke freed Jack from the force of his father's personality; he lost Joe's consultation and advice but simultaneously could now become more his own man.

In the absence of his father's intelligent, often ruthless, calculations, the president leaned more heavily on his brother Bobby, who shared the elder Kennedy's tough, uncompromising nature. But Bobby had something else that rubbed off on the president. When newsman Ben Bradlee once asked the president what made Bobby valuable to him, John said: "First, his high moral standards, strict personal ethics. He's a puritan, absolutely incorruptible." But there was another quality of Bobby's that in the months ahead had a subtle influence on the president and guided his actions in unexpected ways. In his response to Bradlee, the president summed up this powerful quality of his little brother: "He's got compassion, a real sense of compassion."

69
———

WOUNDED BY ALBANY and disappointed in John Kennedy, Martin Luther King Jr. took to his pen to complain about the president's timidity on civil rights throughout his first year in office. Writing in the March 3, 1962, issue of the *Nation*, he laid out the moral failures of the administration. "As the year unfolded," he wrote, "executive initiative became increasingly feeble, and the chilling prospect emerged of a general administration retreat." But King acknowledged the president's successes: investigations of voter registration violations and appointments of blacks to jobs in the government. "While the president has not yet earned unqualified confidence and support," King offered, "neither has he earned rejection and withdrawal of support." Prodding and warning at the same time, King appealed to the president's better angels while threatening unrest: "Perhaps his earnestness of attitude, fed with the vitamins of mass action, may yet grow into passionate purpose." With firm leadership, King instructed, Kennedy could defeat bigoted Southern legislators. The president, he said, "can be confident that correct policy, sound issues and an aroused people are a fortress mightier than a hundred reactionary committee chairmen."

Most important, the time for action was now: Nothing was possible without a courageous fight by the president on behalf of the nation's twenty million blacks. "The President has proposed a ten-year plan to put a man on the moon," King said. "We do not yet have a plan to put a Negro in the State Legislature of Alabama."

The White House response to King's scolding was silence. Unbeknownst to King, FBI director J. Edgar Hoover was driving his agents hard for dirt on King. "He wanted it proved that King had a relationship with the Soviet bloc," recalled the FBI's head of intelligence, William Sullivan. Not only that, he wanted his agents to provide him with information showing that King was embezzling or misusing money. Writing in his memoir about his years in the FBI, Sullivan asserted that "no damning information on [King] had been unearthed." But that didn't stop the FBI director. "Hoover was monomaniacal about that case," Sullivan reported. "Many of us, myself included, sent Hoover memos that would echo his attitude toward King just to get him off our back."

In January, a classified FBI memorandum had landed on the desk of Robert Kennedy. It went further than raising an alarm about the communist influence of King's associate Stanley Levison; it suggested that since the communist-tainted King had been welcomed into the White House, the communist danger now reached into the corridors of power. By connecting King—a communist threat—with the Kennedys, the FBI director brought the danger posed by the civil rights leader uncomfortably close to the White House, ensuring the matter was addressed. Hoover had another way to force Kennedy's compliance with his wishes. Not only did the FBI director have compromising material on the president's sex life but he had supplemented it with reports on the Kennedy clan's supposed connections with the Mafia. Confident of his power, Hoover knew his reports on King and his cohorts would be taken seriously.

In February, he dropped another memo on the attorney general. It began: "On January 8, 1962, I advised you of the close association of Stanley David Levison, a secret member of the Communist Party (CP), and King."

Soon afterward, the bureau placed a wiretap on Levison's office phone in hopes of trapping King and his advisor in discussion of their communist activities; no talk of that sort ever surfaced. But the eavesdropping allowed Hoover to show that Levison, a purported communist, was in fact advising King in a variety of ways and even encouraging him to influence White House decisions. When the president was considering candidates to fill a vacant Supreme Court seat in late March, a wiretap picked up a conversation between Levison and Wyatt Tee Walker, the SCLC's executive director, on a possible nominee. Walker told Levison that King wanted to publicly pressure President Kennedy to name distinguished black appeals court judge William Henry Hastie to the position. Hastie's name had been mentioned in news reports speculating on possible nominees. On the phone, Levison voiced his support for Hastie and, offering his advice, said: "My tendency is for Martin to issue a statement on it and speak of it as a superb opportunity coming at this critical juncture in history." In language echoing Levison's, King immediately sent a telegram to the president urging him to consider not only Hastie but also Thurgood Marshall for the seat.

King's (and Levison's) influence on Kennedy's decision was negligible. The same day that King sent his telegram, the president announced he was naming deputy attorney general Byron White to the bench. A week later King received a note from Kennedy's special assistant and political aide Lawrence O'Brien thanking him for his recommendations of Hastie and Marshall and assuring him that the president chose White after "careful consideration."

Hoover used the wiretapped conversation behind the telegram to build his case that a communist was directing the thoughts, and even the language, of Martin Luther King Jr. Not only that, Hoover took the opportunity to besmirch Judge Hastie, even after White's announcement had been made. The bureau quickly dispatched a report to Attorney General Kennedy connecting Hastie to ten communist organizations. Author Taylor Branch aptly described the convolutions of Hoover's latest absurdity: "That Communist agent Levison had advised Negro leader King to urge upon the President a Negro judge of questionable loyalty." To great effect, Hoover marshaled fear, innuendo, and falsehood to manipulate the president into believing an alternate reality. Worried for their own reputations and unable to personally discount Hoover's charges, the Kennedys were backed into a corner over King. Neither the president nor the attorney general could reasonably ignore the FBI memos; and neither man believed Hoover's allegations were entirely spurious.

70

In April, Attorney General Robert Kennedy asked King to come to the Justice Department to discuss violations of voter registration rules in the South. King and his Southern Christian Leadership Conference had long focused on voting rights. Changing the political structure of the South meant getting blacks into the voting booth, but many obstacles lay in their path. Southern states had imposed poll taxes and literacy tests, in addition to the old standbys: intimidation and violence. The small numbers of black voters in the South proportionally to their population reflected the determination of white supremacists to maintain racist rule. Blacks had the Fifteenth Amendment on their side; passed in 1870, it guaranteed the right to vote to all citizens. But over the years, progress in turning that right into a reality had been slow and minimal: In 1940, about 5 percent of eligible Southern blacks were registered to vote; by 1947, that figure had risen to 12 percent, and by 1952 it had reached 20 percent. Whether those registered voters braved the threats and actually voted was another matter. In the 1960 election, in which blacks helped lift Kennedy to victory, that support was most pronounced in the North, where voting restrictions were not as onerous.

Improving access to the ballot was an early target for the president under the leadership of his brother the attorney general; if the constitutional right to vote was being subverted, that was a matter for the Justice Department. Aiding citizens in their quest to vote seemed a clear American virtue, but there were political stakes, too. Bobby explained: "You had almost 50 percent of the population in the state of Mississippi who were Negro, 40 percent of the state of Alabama, and a large percentage in Georgia.... If they registered and participated in elections—even if a half of them or even if a third of them...they could have a major influence." But many Southern whites saw the implications and rebelled against voter expansion efforts, sometimes violently.

By 1962, the administration had thrown its weight behind a campaign called the Voter Education Project, which analyzed voting conditions and helped register blacks. The attorney general ordered the FBI to study black voting patterns in the South and investigate any obstruction of workers trying to register blacks. But FBI compliance was lackluster. Many agents were Southerners on friendly terms with the racists who were intent on keeping blacks away from polling sites. Despite the frustrations and dangers, the Southern Christian Leadership Conference threw itself into the Voter Education Project, as did other civil rights groups, although some of the young activists balked at first, fearing the administration was trying to sidetrack them away from direct action protests. King saw the government-sponsored voter registration program as worthwhile and an opportunity to collect some funding for the SCLC and to foster good relations with the White House.

Summoned to the Justice Department, King, along with the Reverend Fred Shuttlesworth, the SCLC's Wyatt Tee Walker, and others, listened as the attorney general laid out evidence of violations of voting rights; he promised to step up protections and to put the Justice Department to work on any cases of racial discrimination in registering and voting. While King was encouraged by his welcome, he quickly had reason for concern: No sooner had the meeting concluded than he learned that invisible forces were poisoning his relationship with the administration.

After his meeting with Robert Kennedy, King was privately escorted downstairs by the attorney general's administrative assistant, John Seigenthaler. It had fallen to Seigenthaler to gently warn King about the possible dangerous affiliations of the people close to him. The two men walked along the sidewalk outside the Justice Department. "I went down with him to get his car," Seigenthaler recalled in a 1966 oral history. "I explained to him, without mentioning any names, that I thought one thing that could damage the influence of his organization was association with Communists."

Seigenthaler divulged that the department had information that several aides close to King had communist backgrounds and that the attorney general was worried that these people could be used by others against King to smear him. "I was sure," Seigenthaler told King, "it would be difficult for him to reject anybody who came with an open heart. But that I hoped for our sake, as well as for his own, he would examine the situation carefully and closely."

King listened quietly, according to historian David Garrow, who interviewed Seigenthaler for his 1981 book, *The FBI and Martin Luther King Jr.* King looked Seigenthaler "directly in the eye," Garrow wrote. "He gave no indication of familiarity with the subject."

According to his oral history, Seigenthaler told King that the Justice Department stood ready to assist him in any way with advice and support. If communists were working inside the movement, King seemed impervious to their pull, and informed Seigenthaler that he was not inclined to accuse anyone who was dedicated to the cause of civil rights. "I didn't have the feeling," Seigenthaler recalled, "that he was concerned, primarily because I didn't think he thought they could change his will or the course of action of the Movement."

During his brief stay in Washington, King looked in on his one genuine friend in the White House, Harris Wofford, the president's civil rights aide. But even Wofford had to follow the administration line. He had been pressured by Burke Marshall to speak with King about the suspected communists close to him, particularly Stanley Levison. "Marshall could not himself verify the charge that Levison was an active Communist agent, with Soviet connections, but insisted that if you believed the FBI at all, you would have to believe that there was a basis for serious concern."

Wofford himself had had a bad experience with the FBI when he was vetted for his White House position. As part of his background check, the FBI had delivered to the White House evidence of a dozen or more phone calls between Wofford and Levison in the late 1950s. These calls, captured through early wiretaps of Levison's phone, revealed nothing of a communist nature; the men discussed Martin Luther King Jr.'s planned trip to India and his book on the Montgomery bus boycott. Yet, in assessing Wofford for his White House position, the FBI cast a shadow over his integrity by suggesting he had a nefarious connection to the suspected communist Levison.

Not surprisingly, Wofford was skeptical of the FBI's information on King and his associates but, under pressure from Marshall, he reluctantly agreed to raise the agency's questions with the civil rights leader. King told Wofford the charges were absurd; whatever Levison's previous beliefs, he was now a selfless, valuable asset to the civil rights movement and King's trusted friend. He asked Wofford how the FBI had gathered its information and what specifically it had. But Wofford could only say what he had been told: The bureau had to keep the evidence secret—it was so damning. The manufactured charges Hoover sent to Attorney General Robert Kennedy were never separately investigated by the administration; nor did anyone see the actual FBI reports used for creating the summaries that reached the White House. "Unfortunately," historian David Garrow observed, "no one questioned the presumption on which this sort of reporting was based—the belief that Levison still represented, in his dealings with King, the same interests with which he had been associated in 1954. The lack of any direct confirming evidence of any present-day contacts of Levison's was ignored."

In the course of the conversation, Wofford recalled, King became "depressed and dumbfounded." King reacted as he had with everyone else who had repeated the charges, saying simply "he could not believe it." He told Wofford "he had far more reason to trust Levison than to trust Hoover."

* * *

King had no serious affinity for Communism. The accusations against Levison were distressing enough; but they also implied that King was part of a hidden plot to bring the civil rights movement under communist control, a charge he found particularly repugnant. King was an intellectual and had pondered the relative merits of the social systems vying for predominance during the Cold War. Although he recognized the appeal of a society that purported to put all people on an equal footing, he stopped far short of exalting, or even accepting, Communism as a way of life. King's thinking was evident in a letter he wrote to his future wife, Coretta Scott, in 1952. After first discussing his love for Coretta, he switched to "something more intellectual" and expounded on his feelings about Communism; he had just read Edward Bellamy's *Looking Backward*, an 1888 futuristic novel that conceives of a socialist utopia. "I imagine you already know that I am much more socialistic in my economic theory than capitalistic," he told Coretta. "And yet I am not so opposed to capitalism that I have failed to see its relative merits."

Six years later, in his book about the Montgomery bus boycott, King addressed another of his objections to Communism. He recounted having studied two works of Karl Marx, *Das Kapital* and *The Communist Manifesto*, over the Christmas holidays in 1949 when he was just twenty years old. Writing nearly a decade later in 1958, he explained that his views of Communism settled in at a young age. "In reading such Communist writings," he wrote, "I drew certain conclusions that have remained with me as convictions to this day....Communism, secularist and materialistic, has no place for God. This I could never accept." He also had no illusions about the political totalitarianism of Communism; he abhorred the fact that a person's rights were often swept away by the demands of the state. "His liberties of expression, his freedom to vote, his freedom to listen to what news he likes or to choose his books are all restricted," King observed. "Man becomes hardly more, in communism, than a depersonalized cog in the turning wheel of the state."

King's account of the Montgomery bus boycott, *Stride Toward Freedom*, was a repudiation of communist values; if J. Edgar Hoover needed any illumination on where King stood on Communism, he needed only open the book.

But Hoover created his world as he wished to see it. And King roused Hoover's fury by speaking his mind. As the Albany protests faltered, King asserted publicly that the FBI agents working in the South sided with white racists and therefore failed to carry out investigations into beatings and intimidation of blacks. "If an FBI man agrees with segregation," King told a reporter, "he can't honestly and objectively investigate." He urged the government to assign agents to the South "who are at least in agreement with the law of the land." King's criticism stung Hoover and kept him restlessly on the lookout for material he could twist to discredit the civil rights leader. He found a rich opportunity when W. E. B. DuBois defected to the U.S. Communist Party. In applying for membership at age ninety-three, DuBois, a famous black historian and sociologist, wrote in a public statement that he had been "long and slow" in deciding to join the party, "but at last my mind is settled." He also declared that "capitalism cannot reform itself; it is doomed to self-destruction." Although the statement had no pertinence to King's beliefs or intentions, Hoover placed it in King's file as if the words reflected King's own thoughts. In a letter written at the time, King revealed what in fact was in his mind: He lamented that DuBois, a cofounder of the NAACP, had taken such action; and he feared it was a sign of black disappointment with progress on justice in America. "There can be no doubt," King wrote in the letter, "that if the problem of racial discrimination is not solved in the not too distant future, some Negroes, out of frustration, discontent, and despair, will turn to some other ideology."

71

KING'S TENUOUS RELATIONSHIP with the White House got even flimsier during the spring of 1962 when his inside advocate made plans to depart. Harris Wofford had become frustrated by Kennedy's repeated delays on civil rights. Sensing that racial unrest was on the verge of intensifying, Wofford urged the president to fill the civil rights position he was vacating with a black appointee. Martin Luther King Jr. and other black leaders seconded that notion, endorsing newspaperman Louis Martin, who was deputy chairman of the Democratic National Committee and an advisor to the president. But on Wofford's departure, the president chose to abolish the position, placing the portfolio under his assistant Lee White in the office of speechwriter and special counsel Ted Sorensen. Without a sympathetic figure like Wofford or Louis Martin in place, the president widened the distance between his administration and the black community. "King was fairly low on John Kennedy when I left," Wofford recalled.

Ever the idealist, Wofford had assessed that he could still make a powerful contribution to the world by devoting himself to the creation of the Peace Corps, one of the signal achievements of the Kennedy administration. He had been asked by Peace Corps director Sargent Shriver to move to Addis Ababa, Ethiopia, to take up the role of special representative for the organization in Africa. Wofford embraced the chance to help foster educational, social, and economic development for the struggling nations there.

If Wofford's departure was hopeful for Africa, it was a blow to Martin Luther King Jr. and other black leaders. Wofford tried to reassure them, saying the president wanted to eliminate discrimination, even if he had been slow to take the necessary steps. From the moment he assumed office—and demanded that the Coast Guard begin integrating its ranks—Kennedy showed a subtle yet steadfast disgust with segregation. Although some have contended that his integration moves were ceremonial, or were for the sake of appearances, his actions sprang from an instinct to treat all humans equally. Unthinkable for any president before him, Kennedy danced with black women at his inaugural balls; indeed, some five thousand blacks attended the galas, prompting the *Pittsburgh Courier* to declare: "The inaugural festivities were completely integrated." Among his directives targeting equality, he named a black, Andrew Hatcher, as an associate press secretary; he brought the first black agent into the president's Secret Service detail; at his first cabinet meeting, he ordered the men around the table to begin the process of placing blacks in high-ranking positions in their departments. Soon blacks held jobs in government they had never attained before: there was an ambassador to Norway, a senior advisor in the Treasury Department, a special assistant to the secretary of labor, a director of public information at the Commerce Department. By July 1961, blacks held nearly fifty high-ranking positions in the administration.

One of those appointees, Carl Rowan, a newspaperman who became a deputy assistant secretary of state for public affairs, was nominated for membership in the Cosmos Club, an exclusive social and intellectual club in Washington that, since its founding in 1878, had welcomed presidents, Supreme Court justices, Nobel Prize winners, and prominent journalists, but no blacks. Rowan was surprised to discover that his application was pending at the same time as President Kennedy's; the president had been nominated by the esteemed economist John Kenneth Galbraith, who was serving as U.S. ambassador to India. But in January 1962, Rowan learned his nomination had been rejected. Both the *New York Times* and the *Washington Post* announced the news in front-page stories. "The general assumption among members of the club and in Government circles was that [Rowan] had been rejected because of his race," the *Times* reported. Galbraith immediately resigned from the club, taking with him his nomination of President Kennedy. The president sided with Rowan. As press secretary Pierre Salinger told reporters: "It is my judgment that the proposal of the President for membership in the Cosmos Club will not be resubmitted." A flurry of resignations from the club followed. As the controversy swirled, Rowan commented publicly: "It is my understanding that this is Washington's club of intellectuals. If it is the intellectual judgment of the membership committee that I do not merit membership, I can do no more than note this judgment and wish the club well." That night Rowan picked up his telephone and heard President Kennedy's voice on the line: "Your statement was perfect, Carl," he said. "You couldn't have hurt the bastards more with a cannon." Under fire, the Cosmos Club a week after Rowan's rejection announced it would no longer bar membership on the grounds of race, religion, or national origin—but the new rules did not reverse the decision on Rowan.

Kennedy's response to Rowan's rejection and his orders to add blacks to his administration pointed to a president who wished to live in an integrated world, even if Southern racists in the streets and in Congress sought to prevent it as long as possible. The black population sensed Kennedy's inner conviction. "What JFK managed to do," wrote *Jet* reporter Simeon Booker, "was keep the trust alive, in a way Eisenhower had failed to do. He did it, in large part, by the force of his words and his own powerful personality, emphasizing time and again that he had set a goal for himself, for which he expected to be held accountable." Blacks saluted the president for "appointing Negroes to high offices [and for] breaking down many racial barriers in informal ways," Booker observed. As a result, Kennedy "captured the heart of black America," the *Jet* newsman concluded. "As many blacks saw it, 'Lincoln freed us, FDR gave us jobs, and JFK gave us pride in ourselves.'"

Departing for Africa, Wofford was pleased by the black community's goodwill toward the president but also understood that Kennedy still had much further to go on his civil rights agenda. The president had not issued his executive order banning discrimination in federally funded housing, even though the document had been sitting fully prepared since November 1961 awaiting his signature; he held back fearing the loss of Southern congressional support for his other domestic programs. With similar reasoning, he had ignored King's calls for a second Emancipation Proclamation. In this timid climate, civil rights legislation was nowhere in sight. But Wofford intuited Kennedy's wish to achieve a range of goals on civil rights. Before leaving he produced a memo listing actions the president ought to take, including integration of the National Guard, issuing the executive order on housing, and another requiring that aid to higher education be based on nondiscriminatory policies. Looking over the list, the president told Wofford: "It will take some time, but I want you to know that we are going to do all these things. You will see, with time I'm going to do them all." Wofford set off for Africa believing Kennedy's pledge was sincere, even if his courage was lacking.

72

IN MAY 1962, Martin Luther King Jr., feeling impatient with Kennedy, took to the podium at a luncheon at the Sheraton Carlton Hotel in Washington. He had come to D.C. to announce the founding of the Gandhi Society for Human Rights, an organization dedicated to providing financial and legal support for the civil rights movement. In his speech, King noted that this new society began its life on the eighth anniversary of the *Brown v. Board of Education* Supreme Court decision declaring school segregation unconstitutional. He reminded his audience that the hundredth anniversary of the Emancipation Proclamation was only months away, and for that reason he had made sure to have delivered to the White House "a document we consider to be a landmark contribution in the struggle for civil rights." That document was the Second Emancipation Proclamation that King and his lawyers and associates had labored over for more than six months. In the morning, the Reverend Walter Fauntroy, the SCLC's representative in Washington, had handed the 115-page, leather-bound proclamation to Brooks Hays, a special assistant to the president, who assured the messenger that President Kennedy would take "a great deal of interest in the document and be sympathetic to the sentiments expressed within it."

In his speech, King challenged the president to rise to the occasion of the hundredth anniversary of the original Emancipation Proclamation. He laid out the many injustices that still held blacks down, condemning the "grotesque array of race problems" that still riddled the country and the "backward and brutal institutions of segregation and discrimination." In dismay he pointed out that "millions of qualified Negroes still...have no vote [and are] as totally excluded from the democratic electoral process as their slave forebears had been." He beseeched the president to sign the Second Emancipation Proclamation declaring all segregation laws in the South unconstitutional and then to enforce the declaration with the full powers of his office. "Just as Abraham Lincoln made the tragic sacrifices of the civil war worth enduring when he ended human chattel [*sic*] slavery with a stroke of the pen," King said, "President Kennedy can change the totality of life of the Negro in the South by the issuance of this executive order we have proposed."

* * *

If the president was listening—King gave a press conference after the luncheon and reiterated his plea—there was no sign from the White House. King received no acknowledgment that the document ever got into the president's hands.

Two days after the Gandhi Society event, President Kennedy traveled to New York to celebrate his forty-fifth birthday at a Democratic Party fund-raiser in Madison Square Garden. While in the city he visited his father at the Rusk Institute for Physical Rehabilitation, where Joe Kennedy periodically underwent treatment. Watching the strenuous workouts, the president encouraged the old man as he fought with his typical intensity for the smallest improvements in his feeble condition. The son couldn't help being moved by the suffering of his father and his battle against the constrictions of his life. Once when Joe Kennedy was rolled into the Oval Office for the first time in his debilitated state, still aware but unable to express himself in words, he wept uncontrollably. The president, pretending not to notice, pushed his father's wheelchair toward the window near the rocker he used to soothe his bad back. "This is my rocker, Dad," he said as he sat opposite his father. "It looks as though we both need special chairs, doesn't it?"

At Madison Square Garden, Kennedy was feted for his birthday by the biggest names in entertainment: Jack Benny, Ella Fitzgerald, Danny Kaye, Henry Fonda, Maria Callas, Jimmy Durante, Mike Nichols, and Elaine May. Many saluted the president with their own performances, but only one delivered a historic showstopper. When Marilyn Monroe was introduced she at first failed to appear. The spotlight shone but she was not in it, offering a comedic take on her well-known tardiness. Then when introduced a second time, she suddenly stepped into the light and skittered across the stage to the microphone. With the entire Garden now riveted, she removed her coat to reveal a dress so tight that Adlai Stevenson said it looked "like flesh with sequins sewed onto it." Monroe jauntily flicked a finger against the microphone, testing it, then looked out into the darkened arena with a hand raised like a visor shielding her eyes. At last she began to sing, in a soft, cooing voice, what became an unforgettable rendition of "Happy Birthday, Mr. President." She sang slowly, luxuriantly, flashing a smile now and then, and sliding her hands sensuously up her body along her hips stopping just shy of her breasts. She called on everyone ogling her to sing along as two porters dressed as chefs walked across the stage balancing between them a giant cake with candles flaming. Though it seemed to last an eternity, her song was brief, and when it was over, President Kennedy hopped up a small flight of stairs to the stage and made his way to the microphone to raucous applause and cheers. The president, a slim figure in a dark suit, unflappable and charming, tilted his head and quipped: "I can now retire from politics after having had 'Happy Birthday' sung to me in such a sweet, wholesome way."

73

ON JULY 10, 1962, Martin Luther King Jr. and his friend, fellow clergy-man, and protester Ralph Abernathy stood solemnly before Judge A. N. Durden in Recorder's Court in Albany, Georgia. The men had returned to Albany to hear the verdict in the case brought against them for their roles in the demonstrations in December. For violating an ordinance against parading without permit, King and Abernathy were each sentenced to forty-five days in jail; if they wished to avoid the prison term they were given the option to pay a $178 fine. Neither man put up the money, believing it was "better to go to jail with dignity and self respect than to pay an unjust fine and cooperate with evil and immorality."

Soon after the 10 a.m. ruling, King and Abernathy were led down into the basement to the Albany City jail, where they began their sentences with a twenty-four-hour fast. On a yellow notepad, King began keeping a diary of his mental state and of jailhouse conditions. "There is something inherently depressing about jail," he observed. "It is almost like being dead while one still lives." He consoled himself by remembering the "great cause and purpose" that put him behind bars. But looking around the cells he realized he was to have the "companionship of roaches and ants," and lacking mattresses inmates slept on the steel frames of the bunks. "The jail is by far the worst I've ever been in," he jotted onto his pad. "It is a dingy, dirty hole." Soon after his arrival, a work crew swept in armed with water, soap, and Lysol, and scrubbed the entire cell block. King suspected the sprucing up was ordered by Chief Laurie Pritchett, who was "conscious of the fact that he had some political prisoners on hand" who were able to make his prison's deplorable conditions "known around the nation."

Looking out over the next forty-five days, King feared a soul-crushing monotony. His only solace came in thinking about his wife and children. When Coretta visited at 1:30 p.m., along with Abernathy's wife, Juanita, she was "calm and sweet, encouraging," King noted. But on hearing that their six-year-old daughter, Yolanda, cried over her daddy going to jail,

King felt the tug of emotion. "Somehow I have never quite adjusted to bringing my children up under such inexplicable conditions," he confided to his diary. He wondered how you explain to a child why you're in prison, then noted the confident answer Coretta gave the kids: "She tells them that daddy has gone to jail to help the people."

While King languished behind bars battling the oppressive heat on that July afternoon, President Kennedy sat in a front-row box seat, padded with white leather cushions, at the thirty-second All-Star baseball game. The president threw out the first pitch at the new District of Columbia Stadium, completed the previous October (it was to be renamed RFK Stadium in 1969 after Robert Kennedy's assassination). The National League, backed by three hits by outfielder Roberto Clemente and fancy base running by shortstop Maury Wills, beat the American League 3 to 1. During the game, "President Kennedy seemed as happy as any of the yelling schoolboys in the stands behind him," observed a *Washington Post* columnist. "Several times he jumped out of his seat and turned expectantly to see where a ball batted into the stands high above his box landed."

In prison the following morning King awoke early. Breaking his fast, he was surprised by the tastiness of the eggs, grits, and sausage; the meal came not from the jail's kitchen but from a café across the street. Adding to the surprise of the breakfast was coffee with cream and sugar—two tiny pleasures he'd never been offered in any other jail. Later in the day he was heartened to hear protesters outside marching on City Hall singing freedom songs. Chief Pritchett swiftly shut down the demonstrators, arresting thirty-two. Signaling an escalation in black defiance, King's associates told the press that the protest was "the first wave" of a "now or never" battle to end discrimination.

The support on the streets emboldened King; he was further heartened to learn that the news coverage was stirring blacks throughout the South. From Birmingham came a note from the indomitable Fred Shuttlesworth, the pastor instrumental in the Freedom Rides, who cheered King on to "win this battle for our country." Pledging to help in any way, Shuttlesworth declared: "There can be no retreat." His courage rising, Martin Luther King Jr. was developing a fierce, new determination to turn the tide against segregation in America. If he endured forty-five days of prison, King saw it as an opportunity to underscore the outrage of racial injustice in Albany, demonstrate his own toughness to younger protesters who had ridiculed him, and attract widespread publicity to pressure the president to finally take dramatic action on racial justice.

74

AS KING SAT in jail in Albany, something extraordinary was unfolding in Washington: Reading the newspapers and conferring with his aides, President Kennedy grew impatient with the unacceptable hard line in Albany. Instead of turning away from civil rights strife, as he often had done, or delegating it to his brother the attorney general, the president took a personal interest in the predicament of Martin Luther King Jr. The intense press coverage may have motivated him; newsmen were comparing King's latest troubles to his imprisonment just before the presidential election. Or the president may have reacted to his usual fear: that the unrest in Albany might get out of hand. Whatever drove him, he was unusually engaged, speaking several times to Burke Marshall, assistant attorney general for civil rights, about King's predicament. "He was worried about it," Marshall said, "and he didn't know what to do about it.... He asked me often why we couldn't do anything." From a legal standpoint, the federal government had few options in this local matter. Yet the president wanted to give the King family some hope. He instructed Marshall to phone Coretta King to convey the administration's "interest in her husband's case [and to say] it would use whatever influence it could to obtain his release."

Although reluctant to show it in public, the president was increasingly aggravated by officials in Albany. "They were imposing very rigid restraints on free speech," Marshall recalled. "People were arrested as soon as they appeared on the streets." King and the other protesters in prison embodied the virtues that Kennedy had commended a half-dozen years earlier in *Profiles in Courage*: These were men of conscience who stood on principle in the face of sharp opposition. Unable to pursue a direct White House solution—and still lacking the courage himself to take dramatic, blanket action through an executive order or the introduction of legislation—President Kennedy set in motion a flurry of back-channel pressures on Albany officials. Mayor Asa Kelley and Police Chief Pritchett wanted nothing more than to keep the protests from escalating, resolve the crisis, and turn attention away from Albany. City authorities had a direct line to the president through a local prominent Democrat and newspaper publisher, James Gray. Chairman of the Georgia Democratic Party and owner of the city's leading newspaper, the *Albany Herald*, Gray had grown up in Massachusetts, attended Dartmouth, and befriended John Kennedy's older brother, Joe Jr., during his Harvard days; in their youth the two men spent time together at the Kennedy Palm Beach estate. After Joe Jr.'s death, Gray maintained a friendship with John, and aided his political fortunes in the South. His role at the *Herald* came to him through his marriage to the daughter of the paper's owner, and his views on race were in perfect step with his adopted home. During the Albany protests in December he had appeared on the town's only television channel, in which he held a majority stake, and described King and others as "a cell of professional agitators" who had more in common with "Lenin and Stalin [than with] George Washington, Thomas Jefferson, and Abraham Lincoln." On the same broadcast, he praised segregation as "a system that has proved over the years to be true and rewarding." Blacks in Albany regarded Gray as their "most implacable foe."

John Kennedy, long accustomed to a world of complicated politics, was soon talking with James Gray on the phone in the Oval Office. In Albany, the stakes had risen overnight when a small riot erupted after a group of blacks attending a mass meeting at Shiloh Baptist Church spilled out into the street and hurled rocks and bottles at policemen. Getting King out of prison—and out of the city—was now a priority. With Mayor Kelley listening in, Gray complained to the president about having King in the city jail. "The damn media is having a field day. We don't want him in jail, but what can we do? He violated our law." The conversation ended with an agreement that an emissary from Albany would fly immediately to Washington for discussions with Robert Kennedy; and within hours, B. C. Gardner, a partner in Kelley's law firm, had met with the attorney general and returned to Albany with a secret plan to spring King from jail. The scheme was so crafty that it ensured no loss of face or any political backlash for the men in the White House or the officials in Albany.

75

ON THE MORNING of July 12, after King and Abernathy had been in jail just two days, B. C. Gardner showed up early at the prison while a lone desk sergeant was on duty and handed over $356 in cash. The sergeant, who had been apprised of the scheme, accepted the cash as payment for the King and Abernathy fines and filled out a receipt for the jail's files in the names of the inmates. When Chief Pritchett came to release the men, King was suspicious: No one he knew would have posted his bond; the city obviously had pulled a fast one to get rid of him. In response to King's questions, the chief said he didn't know who paid the fines and claimed the benefactor was "an unidentified, well-dressed Negro man." Press coverage hinted at some shenanigans in the fee payments: "there were indications...that local whites, who would like to have Dr. King leave the city and thus avert further protests over his imprisonment, might have had some part in the action." Outraged but unable to interfere in their own release, King and Abernathy were driven by two detectives to the home of Albany Movement leader William Anderson. At a press conference later, King complained that this was one time he was unhappy to be out of jail.

Behind the scenes, the Kennedy administration had maneuvered the release of King. By doing so, President Kennedy believed he had furthered progress toward a settlement of black grievances. Chief Pritchett told King on his release that he would drop charges against more than seven hundred protesters arrested in December, and that the demands of the Albany Movement were "reasonable." Among those demands were that the city promise to end segregation in local terminals and to set up a biracial commission to work out desegregation of all public facilities in the city. Speaking for the administration, Robert Kennedy praised the outcome of the crisis. "Dr. King's release should make it possible for the citizens of Albany to resolve their differences in this situation in a less tense atmosphere," he told the *Albany Journal*. But no sooner had a resolution presented itself than it crumbled. Chief Pritchett immediately retracted the comments he'd made to King: The Albany Movement's demands had not been accepted, and only if the demonstrators agreed never to return to the streets would he drop the charges against them. Further muddying the situation, the Kennedy administration soon found itself having to fend off accusations it had paid the fines for King and Abernathy.

With King out of prison and Albany quiet, the White House kept its distance from the conflict. Manipulated and ineffectual, the Albany Movement floundered, and King came in for blame. The *New York Times,* assessing his role as a civil rights leader, observed that while his star rose after the Montgomery bus boycott, "lately...some of his difficulties have...become more visible." The paper went through a litany of problems that had bedeviled him, from infighting among black organizations to overzealous associates. The *Times* acknowledged that "few will dispute Dr. King's success as a spokesman for the Negro" but then it quoted an unnamed black leader as saying: "He's woefully inadequate in organizational ability." Facing criticism and possible failure, King only intensified his resolve. If the mayor and police chief had hoped to rid the city of him, King told newsmen he planned to stay until "officials met at least the minimum demands of local Negro leaders."

Over the next several days, King and the other movement leaders tried to negotiate with city officials to reach agreement on desegregation; but each time the blacks believed the city had accepted their demands, the agreement fell through. The black community was growing restless and frustrated, but the leaders refrained from calling for protests. King spoke at mass meetings at Shiloh Baptist Church, decrying the "subtle and conniving methods" used to get him out of jail and calling out Chief Pritchett for "saying one thing to us behind closed doors and then we open the newspapers and he's said something else to the press." Seeking peaceful means to counter the city's bad-faith negotiations, the movement drew up an Albany Manifesto charging that in its discussions on desegregation the city had a "long history of double-talk, unkept promises, subtle intimidation and lack of integrity." The document demanded speedy and fair trials for the more than seven hundred arrested protesters or summary dismissals of charges; it petitioned Attorney General Kennedy to restrain public officials from enforcing segregation at city bus terminals in compliance with the recent Interstate Commerce Commission ruling; and it resolved to remove segregation everywhere. Signaling its intent to ramp up its defiance, the movement concluded: "We band ourselves together to do whatever must be done to deliver the death-knell once and for all to the system of segregation in the city of Albany, Georgia with earnest hope that the example we set here shall spread across the South."

King and the Albany Movement leaders sent the manifesto to city officials along with a telegram seeking a meeting within two days. In a not-so-subtle threat, King told the press that if the city commission didn't meet with black leaders the movement had no choice but to resort to a new round of protests. Refusing to be intimidated, the city responded in a terse statement: "The City Commission is in receipt of a telegram from a purported Albany movement requesting a special meeting of the commission. It is the decision of the commission not to deal with law violators." Noting the movement's plan for renewed demonstrations, King told the *New York Times*: "The situation is much more serious now."

King took to the podium in front of more than a thousand people at a mass meeting inside Shiloh Baptist that evening, saying: "They tricked us out of jail, thinking"—and laughter spread though the crowd—"that this would stop the movement." The crowd erupted in applause. "And when they tricked us out, I guess they thought this would mean that we would get the first plane back to Atlanta and that the mass meetings would come to an immediate halt and that the Negro citizens of Albany would go back to their homes willing to accept their conditions as they existed." In a voice of disbelief the crowd cried: *Yeah*. "But your presence here tonight demonstrates that we are more determined now than ever before." The church erupted in another round of applause.

King then emboldened the congregants to march again, reminding them that no one broke any laws the last time they took to the streets. "This is what they call us: lawbreakers," he said. But he pointed out that protest was part of the "democratic creed" protected by the Constitution. Peaceful, nonviolent, orderly protest was part of the American heritage, he declared. Rallying the crowd, King peered into the future. "Now, since they refused to talk with us, since they refuse to meet us across the conference table, we must make it palpably clear that they will have to meet us in some other way." The crowd loved it, calling out *Yeah*, and applauding for a while. "If they will not listen to our words," King continued after the room quieted, "they will have to face our bodies." There were chants of: *Yes. Yes.* And in a final marshaling of the forces, King called on the people to mobilize. "I want you to be committed now to go with us all the way." Up went the cry: *Yeah.* "I want you to be committed now. I don't want you to wait until next week.... I want you to become committed this minute."

76

BEFORE MARCHING INTO the streets, the Albany Movement leaders tried one final time to bring the city to the negotiating table. In a telegram on July 17, they asked the city commission "in the interest of democracy and the brotherhood of man" to reconsider its refusal to meet. The city was unmoved. On that same day, black leaders tested the resistance to segregation among white supervisors and workers at public facilities. Billed as "the first step in an all-out campaign against segregation" in the city, the leaders sent four girls and one boy to an all-white library seeking to check out books. When they asked to apply for library cards, the librarian, identified as Mrs. Harold Todd, directed them to a new, smaller black branch. Later, twenty more students were turned away at the library door by the librarian's husband, Harold Todd, who was also employed there. Before departing, a teenage girl told him: "Don't worry, we'll be back."

* * *

Demonstrations were put off for another day when King went to Washington to speak to the National Press Club, a professional organization comprised only of white male journalists. No black man had ever addressed the members at one of the club's periodic newsmaker luncheons. King's invitation had nearly fallen through. He'd been asked to speak on June 25, but the offer was rescinded after Southern members objected; just a scheduling conflict, he was told. The opposition was smoothed over, and a new date was set. On July 19 King was on his way to Washington, unaware that his appearance had ignited passions in the capital just the way it did in backward Southern towns.

King's speeches often operated on several levels at once: They were intended for consumption by the immediate audience before him—whether white male journalists or black Southern Baptists—but also through subsequent press coverage his words often reached the eyes of the president, a voracious newspaper reader, while he ate his breakfast. Without mentioning Kennedy directly, King suggested in his speech that the president's perspective needed to evolve on the issue of equal rights, warning him that the fires of protest had been ignited and he had to choose how to extinguish them. King reminded the packed house of four hundred journalists: "Victor Hugo once said that there is nothing more powerful in all the world than an idea whose time has come."

King subtly took the president to task for not going far enough, criticizing him for token actions in place of significant moves on civil rights. He had addressed the administration's hesitance in a piece in the *Nation* in March, disparagingly titled "Fumbling on the Frontier." In the article, he had condemned Kennedy's slow, incremental approach, his backing away from legislation and instead promising executive orders that never came. What was needed, King declared, was a national, comprehensive strategy led by the White House, a "sweep of positive action." Activists had achieved integration of buses and lunch counters in isolated locations, but these partial steps were not enough; they did not wash away the racism and discrimination that lingered. Now, in front of the National Press Club, King on the one hand called for legislation but on the other astutely acknowledged that "you cannot legislate morals." But, he pointed out, court actions and the implementation of laws educate people and help them understand the importance of integration. "The habits, if not the hearts, of people have been and are being altered every day by federal action," King told the crowd. "These major social changes have accumulated force, conditioning other segments of life."

For his audience, which was largely unschooled in his tactics, King described the power of nonviolent protest. Black men and women who placed their lives on the line for a moral purpose and withstood verbal abuse and physical blows had a transformative impact on those who confronted them. They had an influence, King implied, not only on racists in the streets but on the president in the White House. "The method of nonviolent resistance is effective in that it has a way of disarming the opponent," King said. "It exposes his moral defenses, it weakens his morale, and at the same time it works on his conscience."

If the president were listening, King gave him reason to discount J. Edgar Hoover's persistent accusations against him, reiterating that his beliefs and tactics had nothing in common with communists. King asserted that he rejected outright the brutality and deceit implicit in Lenin's notion that the end justified the means. "This is where nonviolence breaks with Communism," he said.

Setting the stage for his return to Georgia, King sent a message to both Albany officials and the president. His warning was clear: Nonviolent resistance was coming to Albany. "We will take direct action against injustice without waiting for other agencies to act," King said. "We will not obey unjust laws or submit to unjust practices."

King rounded off his address with a rhetorical flourish that in modified form was to become an historic declaration that personified the man and his mission. He told the crowd that he yearned for the American dream of equal opportunity for all men, "a dream of a land where men no longer argue that the color of a man's skin determines the content of his character." A year later he was to raise his voice in front of thousands assembled on the National Mall for the March on Washington and echo those words in one of the most lucid pleas in the American oratory on race, when he dreamed aloud in similar terms for his own children. In his presentation at the Press Club, King was part pastor, part educator, and part civil rights activist, and in recognition of his historic appearance, the members rose from their seats and gave him a standing ovation.

Afterward, King took questions from the newsmen and spoke directly to the president on civil rights. "There is still a great deal to be done," King observed, "and I must honestly say that I do not think the president has yet given the kind of leadership in this area that the enormity of the problem demands."

77

ON HIS RETURN to Albany, King plunged back into the battle. When the city commission again refused to negotiate on the movement's demands, black leaders planned a large demonstration for Saturday, July 21. Ahead of the march, King got word that the city had asked a federal judge for an injunction to block further protests. His defiance escalating, King declared at a mass meeting: "Injunctions, various legal maneuvers, subtle delay tactics will not stop us—we've gone too far now to turn back."

The injunction was served early Saturday morning and specifically targeted King and other Albany Movement leaders, prohibiting them from participating in demonstrations. The U.S. District Court judge who handed down the order, J. Robert Elliott, was an ardent white supremacist President Kennedy had appointed to the bench in January. The president had named a host of segregationist federal judges in the South to satisfy powerful Southern political leaders. Elliott was a known bigot who had served in the Georgia House of Representatives and had declared during an election campaign in 1952: "I don't want those pinks, radicals and black voters to outvote those who are trying to preserve our own segregation laws and other traditions." His ruling on the Albany protests was just one of many ill-reasoned decisions, and it caused deep consternation for both King and Kennedy. "I was... strongly contemplating violating [the] injunction," King recalled, and the president was "very, very upset about this." The U.S. court injunction risked bringing the Kennedy administration into the Albany dispute in a way it never wanted: If King defied the order and marched, the federal government would have to arrest him for contempt of court and try him—publicity-stirring events the White House wanted to avoid at all costs. "I know it was a problem for them because it meant that the federal government would have the responsibility of prosecuting me," King recalled. "And they just didn't want that day to emerge."

In heated phone conversations with Robert Kennedy, King debated the consequences of ignoring Judge Elliott's injunction. The attorney general, making clear he spoke on behalf of the president, said King's defiance could imperil efforts of the federal government to enforce desegregation rulings across the South. If King disobeyed the federal court order, segregationist governors and school authorities might in response flout federal orders to desegregate. King acknowledged Kennedy's argument but insisted the situations were different: He and other blacks were exercising their First Amendment right, and were battling patently unjust laws, and were justified in their moral stance. Frustrated, King blamed the administration for the latest crisis. President Kennedy's efforts to placate the racist Southern power bloc had made this ruling possible: The president had appointed this bigoted federal judge. It was this man

Kennedy put on the bench who had subverted the intent of constitutional law by denying peaceful protest.

Judge Elliott's inverted reasoning argued that the black protests denied whites equal protection under the law which was guaranteed by the Fourteenth Amendment; the judge asserted that white neighborhoods would be unprotected when police officers were sent out of the area to work the protest sites. Commenting on the judge's ruling, the *New York Times* said, "Ironically, one of the chief Negro contentions has been that segregation denies them equal rights under the Fourteenth Amendment." King told the attorney general that the president and the administration were now having to face up to the consequences of its pandering to white Southern interests. "Some of these problems," he said, "you have created yourself by appointing these segregationist federal judges."

After careful reflection, King decided to abide by the court's ruling even though it was blatantly unjust. He acquiesced partly in deference to the federal courts, whose rulings had significantly helped progress of the civil rights movement: "I would go along with not violating the injunction in appreciation for the fact that the federal judiciary on the whole had been the one agency or the one branch of the government that had given the most forthright leadership."

While the injunction named King and the other leaders, it did not specifically enjoin the Albany community from demonstrating. On Saturday night, the movement had a temporary new leader, the Reverend Samuel B. Wells, pastor of the William Springs Baptist Church. He fired up a crowd of seven hundred blacks at a mass rally at Shiloh Baptist, intoning: "I've heard about an injunction but I haven't seen one. I've heard a few names but my name hasn't been called. But I do know where my name is being called. My name is being called on the road to freedom." He then sang out to the crowd: "When shall we go? Not tomorrow! Not at high noon! Now!" The place erupted in thunderous applause, shouting, and cheering.

Just after 9 p.m., the crowd marched out of the church, voices raised in song. The musical choice was a popular tune of the Freedom Rides, "Ain't Gonna Let Nobody Turn Me Round": "I'm gonna keep on a-walkin', keep on a-talkin' / Marchin' down to freedom land!" Reverend Wells, a short man in a black suit and white shirt, marched in front with a thirteen-year-old boy striding next to him and nearly the entire congregation—estimated at five hundred protesters—behind him.

Claude Sitton of the *New York Times* witnessed the scene. Before the throng reached City Hall, Sitton reported, Chief Laurie Pritchett intercepted Reverend Wells.

"Well, Rev, you got a permit?" he asked.

"I have no permit," Wells replied. "We're going to the City Hall to pray."

The chief spoke to the protesters through a bullhorn. "Does anybody in this group have a permit? I want to tell you you are in violation of the city ordinances."

Reverend Wells then sank down to his knees and prayed. In a wave, the other marchers dropped to their knees; some were teenage girls, sobbing, nearly fainting.

Chief Pritchett called out: "You're all under arrest."

Backed by some two hundred state, county, and local policemen, Pritchett rounded up the protesters, although many scattered before they could be arrested. The police grabbed 112 demonstrators and carted them to the city jail. When a second wave of protesters set out an hour later, forty-eight of them joined the others behind bars, bringing the total arrests for the night to 160. The charge was parading without a permit.

Although there was no violence, the protests and the arrests had sharply escalated tensions in the city. Local officials publicly voiced fears that rioting would erupt and black leaders echoed the concerns. Albany Movement leader William Anderson foresaw trouble: "The city of Albany has invited violence by seeking to enjoin the leaders who teach and practice nonviolent techniques." He warned that other leaders unschooled in nonviolence and preaching extremism could arise if the nonviolent leaders were hindered.

If King couldn't march he could speak out. Exasperated by the intransigence of Albany officials, he directly challenged the president to act. In a television interview broadcast in Washington, he attacked the president for taking only modest steps on civil rights. The only solution to the denial of basic rights by local municipalities was comprehensive action on the federal level. King criticized the president for failing to take "a vigorous stand" in the pushing for civil rights legislation. He conceded that the president "certainly had done a good job in some areas of civil rights," but he was dissatisfied that "on the other hand, there are things to be desired." Appearing on a program called *Opinion in the Capital*, King said of the president: "I think he could do a little more in the area of moral persuasion by occasionally speaking out against segregation and counseling the nation on the moral aspects of this problem." Now, more than a year and a half into his term, President Kennedy had yet to say much at all publicly about the denial of basic freedoms for twenty million Americans.

78

WHILE CALLING THE president to task, King himself came under fire from young protesters unhappy with the lack of progress in Albany. Acknowledging their concern, King agreed to meet with members of the Student Nonviolent Coordinating Committee. Slater King, a leader of the movement and the son of a well-to-do black lawyer, brought the civil rights leader and the students together at his house. For three hours, Martin Luther King Jr. sat in the backyard quietly taking verbal blows: The students berated him for abiding by Judge Elliott's injunction. How could he obey a ruling from a segregationist judge? And his praise of the federal courts? That was ill informed, they contended; the courts had only acted slowly and without enthusiasm on behalf of blacks. What was more, King's leadership was erratic and authoritarian; he failed to consult with them before making decisions. King listened patiently and explained his acceptance of the injunction: He had a wife and family and was therefore somewhat more conservative than the students who had fewer obligations. Slater King's father, C. B. King, who witnessed the encounter, was impressed by King's manner with the young activists. Summing up the acrimonious afternoon, C. B. King said: "Martin was about the most imperturbable person I have ever known." But King's conversation with the students changed nobody's mind. The bitter differences between Albany blacks made the battle for rights in the city all the more complicated.

King's credo of nonviolence was put to the test soon after the latest roundup of protesters. On Monday afternoon, July 23, Marion King, the wife of Slater King, set off to the Mitchell County Jail in Camilla, Georgia, a little more than twenty-five miles south of Albany, where some of

Chief Pritchett's many detainees were being held. Conditions in the prison were abysmal, and Marion King was bringing food to the inmates, one of whom was her maid's daughter, a young woman named Ella Mae. Martin Luther King Jr. had notified Attorney General Kennedy about the state of prisoner life at the Mitchell County Jail, decrying the "inhumane treatment and unhealthy conditions." Prisoners were refused visits from clergy, had poor diets, lacked bedding materials, and suffered from overcrowding.

When she arrived, Marion King joined a group of blacks outside who were waiting for visiting hours and were passing the time singing freedom songs. When she and the others were ordered to move away from the prison fence, she couldn't move as quickly as the others: Marion King was five months pregnant and carrying her three-year-old daughter in her arms. To get her going, the Mitchell County sheriff shoved her and, when she still didn't scoot fast enough for him, he slapped her across the face, as she told historian Taylor Branch in an interview. The blow knocked her daughter from her arms. The sheriff, making an example of her to the others, slapped her a second time as a deputy kicked her, knocking her to the ground; while she lay there, the deputy continued to kick her, causing her to black out. Four months later she delivered a stillborn child. As word of Marion King's beating spread through the black community, an urge for violent retribution took root.

*   *   *

The morning after the attack, as anger at the beating began to boil over, Martin Luther King Jr. was in Atlanta seated in the front row in the U.S. Court of Appeals for the Fifth Circuit when Judge Elbert Tuttle ruled that the injunction against the Albany Movement leaders was unconstitutional. Relieved, King returned to Albany and spoke in the evening at mass meetings at two churches, declaring that "this morning something happened...to transform the fatigue of despair into the buoyancy of hope." The Albany Movement sent a conciliatory note to Mayor Asa Kelley and the city commission, saying it did not consider the lifting of the injunction a victory but rather "a sober and sound decision...to preserve basic constitutional rights." Pleading again for a meeting, the movement said: "The real victory will come when we as brothers sit down and discuss ways and means to grant citizenship rights that can no longer be postponed." The mayor rebuffed the request, using the same language he had in the past: The commission did not talk to "lawbreakers."

At the mass meeting that evening, the community prepared for immediate protests. But as a conciliation to the city commission, King and the
Albany Movement leaders planned to sit out the demonstrations. Addressing the crowd, King spoke of his journeys in India and the struggles for its
independence. He reminded the audience that the prime minister, Jawa-
harlal Nehru, was imprisoned fourteen times, and the president, Rajendra
Prasad, spent three years in jail before achieving the goal of independence. He spoke of the seven arrests of Nehru's daughter, Indira Gandhi,
and of the jail time of men who were now governors of various Indian
provinces. King then drew the audience to his travels in Africa. While
in the newly independent nation of Ghana, King said he noticed that the
president and his cabinet members wore unusual caps. Inquiring, King
learned that the caps were prison garb, reminders that all the men running the country had spent time in jail. "I say all of this in a round-about
way," King told the crowd, "to try to tell you tonight that there's nothing wrong with going to jail because you can rise from prison to power."
He then implored anyone taking part in the demonstration to maintain
strict adherence to nonviolence. "The most potent weapon available to
oppressed people as they struggle for freedom and justice is the weapon
of nonviolence," he said to cries from the audience of *yes, yes.* "Let us
keep this weapon. Let's keep it in the forefront." To which the crowd
agreed: *Yes.*

About forty people marched through the black neighborhoods toward
City Hall, and when they reached the edge of the town's white section they
were met by police and arrested. Blacks from the area streamed in, and
soon two thousand spectators had gathered. Anger born of long-standing
injustice and inflamed by the beating of Marion King erupted into violence. Bricks and rocks and bottles flew at police: One officer was struck
in the face and lost two teeth. Blacks unschooled in nonviolence poured
out of the nearby pool halls and taverns of Albany's Harlem district. As the
streets veered toward all-out rioting, Chief Pritchett called in reinforcements; more than a hundred city policemen and state highway patrolmen
converged on the scene. Mocking King's pledge of nonviolence, Chief
Pritchett quipped to a reporter: "Did you see them nonviolent rocks?"

The disorderly blacks had tainted the nonviolent movement, leaving
King distraught. The white community, particularly the intransigent city
commission, was more than ready to use the melee against the activists.
At a press conference the following day, King was contrite: "We abhor

violence so much that when it occurs in the ranks of the Negro community we assume part of the responsibility for it." For that reason, he called for a day of penance. Over the next twenty-four hours there would be no protests. Speaking to newsmen, he mentioned the beating of Marion King and an earlier police killing of a forty-nine-year-old restaurant owner. In trying to explain the unrest but not excuse it, King said: "All of these things developed within the people a sense of discontent and at times a sense of bitterness.... If they continue it would be very difficult for those of us who believe in nonviolence and who give our lives to this method and philosophy to control violent outbreaks." King, speaking as pastor, educator, and community leader, then announced that he and several others "who are well-grounded in the philosophy" would spend the day visiting pool rooms and taverns in the black areas teaching the locals and "calling for absolute commitment to nonviolence."

In a rare show of unanimity, King was joined by young men from the Student Nonviolent Coordinating Committee on his tour through Albany's Harlem district. Television cameras and journalists and two city detectives tagged along. King, dressed in a short-sleeved shirt opened at the collar, strolled through the neighborhood stopping on street corners, at a shoe shop, a filling station, shaking hands and chatting with locals. His entourage stepped into a pool hall as a player was lining up a shot, oblivious to the visitors. The balls clicked against each other on the table as one of the student activists, Charles Jones, said to the shooter: "We want to talk to you about the situation out in front last night."

"Who wants to?" the man answered.

"Doctor King," the student said. "This is Doctor King."

"How're you, gents?" King said smiling shyly at a handful of men. "I hate to hold up your pool game. I used to be a pool shark myself."

King then gave a short speech, asking for everyone's support of the movement to end segregation in Albany. "One thing about the movement," he said, "is that it is nonviolent. As you know, there was some violence last night." He explained that violence was exactly what the opposition wanted to see, because it discredited the movement. King spoke earnestly with furrowed brow, turning from side to side, addressing each man individually. "I wanted to talk to you all and urge you to be nonviolent, not to throw bottles. I know if you do this, we are destined to win," he promised. "We don't need guns and ammunition—just the power of souls." Before heading out, King grabbed a cue stick and, leaning over the table, showed his pool-shark prowess. The men had listened but it was impossible to measure King's impact in the hard faces, some with cigars crunched between their teeth.

At his next stop, the South Grand Terrace, King drank water from a thin cocktail glass and spoke to patrons amid red-checkered tablecloths and a jukebox. In another, smaller place down an alley, he shook hands with a woman in a man's felt hat. Outside another joint, the Beehive, from which bottles had been launched the previous night, five large men sat on a bench. Inside another place called Dan's, King came upon a group of workmen, one wearing a construction helmet, others in cowboy hats, and a woman in a straw hat. Praising the young activists with him, King said: "Do you know what they have done? Do you know that all over this South there were segregated lunch counters, but that two years after the movement began lunch counters in more than a hundred and fifty cities are integrated—as a result of the work of young men like these. They didn't do it with violence. You have to be nonviolent in spirit and militant in action."

Pat Watters, a white Southern journalist covering the movement, tried to make sense of King's pilgrimage to the dives and joints of Harlem. He found the downtrodden blacks of the neighborhood mostly unresponsive: For them, King's message was abstract and intellectual. But Watters found that King communicated on another level simultaneously. "It was not the words but the emotional tone Dr. King expressed," Watters observed. "The meaning of the movement was [in] the people, the morality, the strengths, the poetry inside them." Somehow King managed to convey his message of peace. And, Watters pointed out, "there was no more violence from the people in the dives."

79

On the day after his neighborhood canvass, King and a group of nine other black leaders marched to City Hall with reporters in tow to ask in person for a meeting with the city commission. When they reached the steps of City Hall, Police Chief Laurie Pritchett intercepted them. "Folks,"

he said in a friendly tone, smiling, "the next meeting of the commissioners will be August 7. You can come back then."

Everyone, including Pritchett himself, knew his advice was a charade.

"But they won't let us into the meetings," King reminded the chief.

"Nevertheless, that is the time of the next meeting," Pritchett replied.
"Now you can't stay around here in such a large group."

A standoff ensued. The black leaders and the police chief stood in
silence, staring at each other. At last, Pritchett shook his head seeming
genuinely chagrined to have to take the next step.

"If you don't leave in three minutes, I'm afraid I'll have to place you
under arrest," he said. "Please don't force me to do that."

King asked fellow marcher the Reverend Ralph Abernathy to lead
them in prayer, and they all kneeled. Pritchett kept his eye on the second
hand of his watch and after three rotations, he sighed and had his officers
make the arrests.

For the third time in eight months King and Abernathy were back in
prison; their cell was familiar—the same one they had occupied on their
previous lockup.

"Look at this place," King said to his fellow inmate. "The floor's covered with grime again."

"Still, it's not as filthy as it was the last time we moved in," Abernathy
offered.

"No," King answered, "but it sure is hotter."

With the temperature outside in the nineties, the prisoners sweltered
in the cell. Their coats and ties came off, and their shirt collars were
opened. But it was little relief. They dreamed of an electric fan and tried
to settle in, their eyes stinging with sweat.

80

WHILE KING STARTED his weekend in prison, Kennedy was in Hyannis
Port celebrating Jackie's thirty-third birthday and boating on the spar-
kling sea. Yet the president was keenly aware of the differences in his and

King's circumstances. "Somehow, he just got it in his head that he was going to worry about Albany that weekend," recalled Assistant Attorney General Burke Marshall, who was on vacation fishing in the Pocono Mountains in Pennsylvania and fielded a series of phone calls from the president. "We talked constantly." The president was troubled by the intransigence of the segregationists. He instructed Marshall to work on the Albany officials. "We discussed it over the telephone," Marshall said, "and I would call down to the Mayor or the city police...and try to get something accomplished."

The legacy of bigotry and discrimination was pressing in upon the president, and with growing annoyance, he perceived that it was simply incompatible with the principles of American life. On the morning of King's arrest, the *New York Times* carried a front-page story of voter intimidation in the hamlet of Sasser, Georgia, about fifteen miles northwest of Albany. Reporter Claude Sitton had visited a voter registration rally at the Mount Olive Baptist Church. A crowd of whites had gathered outside the church, their threatening voices filtering inside, causing the blacks to stiffen and glance at the door from time to time. Far from protecting the thirty-eight blacks and two whites inside the church, Terrell County sheriff Z. T. Mathews and his nephew and chief deputy, M. E. Mathews, harassed them. As the deputy stood fingering his leather cartridge belt and .38-caliber revolver, the seventy-year-old sheriff told the *Times* reporter: "We want our colored people to go on living like they have for the last hundred years." In an unsubtle threat, the officers mentioned that there was no telling "what 'disturbed white citizens' might do if this and other rallies continued." Blacks in Terrell County outnumbered whites by nearly two to one; but of the 8,209 black residents only fifty-one were registered to vote, largely because of intimidation and other tactics. When the group left the church some found their car tires slashed or their gas tanks filled with sand. A policeman taunted a black man coming out of the church: "I know you. We're going to get some of you." President Kennedy read the article, as did his brother the attorney general, who was overseeing the government's voter registration efforts, and both were incensed.

Over the next several days as the nation became transfixed by King's imprisonment, the president was under mounting pressure to speak out. In Albany, the protests continued, as did the arrests. Roy Wilkins of the NAACP and James Farmer of the Congress of Racial Equality demanded a forceful statement from the president. On Saturday, King got a jail visit from Chief Pritchett, who revealed that the entire town was on edge. "You don't know how tense things are, do you?" Pritchett said. "Do you know what happened?" When King said he didn't, Pritchett told him that C. B. King, one of two black lawyers in Albany, tried to visit a white protester in jail; and when he left the courthouse, he had blood streaming from his head. "Somebody almost busted C. B. King's head wide open," Pritchett explained. The attacker was D. C. Campbell, the sheriff of Daugherty County, who whacked the lawyer with a walking cane. The seventy-six-year-old sheriff, dressed in a white Panama hat and white shirt, told a reporter: "Yeah, I knocked hell out of him, and I'll do it again. I let him know I'm a white man and he's a damn nigger."

On hearing this, King immediately arranged for a movement leader to send a telegram to the president telling him "that something had to be done." The next day, President Kennedy read the story of the beating on the front page of the Sunday *New York Times*. Also on Sunday, Albany Movement president William Anderson appeared in place of Martin Luther King Jr. on the television newsmaker show *Meet the Press*, broadcast across the nation. When asked during the show whether he thought the protesters had been "let down" by President Kennedy, Anderson replied that blacks in Albany felt the administration "had not done as much as it can do." He promised that demonstrations would continue "as long as segregation exists in the city of Albany."

Ministers in Washington circulated petitions at their Sunday services protesting King's arrest. On Monday, fifty clergymen walked in two columns to the White House to present about five thousand signatures. Walter Fauntroy, the local representative of King's Southern Christian Leadership Conference, was one of four ministers allowed inside to deliver the petitions to assistant special counsel Lee C. White. Picketers descended on the White House carrying signs reading: ALBANY, GA., A CAGE OR A CITY? and JUSTICE DELAYED IS JUSTICE DENIED and GEORGIA HOLD YOUR HEAD IN SHAME. A nineteen-year-old picketer, Ann Feingold, told a reporter: "Look, we don't expect miracles. We don't expect President Kennedy to stick his head out the window and say, 'Oh, oh, pickets, I'd better do something.' But even he needs a push." Across the country, from Fresno, California, to New York City, ministers held prayer vigils declaring they would not stop until the federal government acted.

By now President Kennedy was losing patience with Albany officials.

Back at the White House after his Hyannis weekend, he kept an eye on developments and pondered the continued incarceration of Martin Luther King Jr. At midweek, he was preparing for one of his regular press conferences when he called in Burke Marshall for consultation. Clearly annoyed, the president told Marshall he was still unable to fathom why praying in front of City Hall should land someone in jail; he also found it incomprehensible that city officials refused to sit down for discussions with black leaders. After venting to Marshall, the president went off to his news conference. Speaking to reporters, he expressed his views on many pressing subjects—from the dangers of the sedative thalidomide to hurdles in reaching a nuclear test ban treaty—but in his remarks on Albany the president showed something new. Cracks were appearing in his steely reserve on civil rights: He found the bullheadedness of Albany officials so unreasonable that he was ready to speak out.

In response to a question about conditions in Albany, the president revealed the high degree of his involvement in the standoff there. He said he was getting daily reports and was in constant contact with the attorney general who spoke regularly with Albany authorities. Then Kennedy pivoted from what sounded like a concerned, yet unbiased, observer to an exasperated president sending a grave warning to the segregationists in Albany. "Let me say," he said, a clip in his voice, "that I find it wholly inexplicable why the City Council of Albany will not sit down with the citizens of Albany, who may be Negroes, and attempt to secure them, in a peaceful way, their rights." The president then put the Albany conflict in a context meant to shame local officials: If he, as president, can negotiate with Khrushchev on the world stage, why was it so hard for authorities in a little town in Georgia to talk to its own people? "The United States Government is involved in sitting down at Geneva with the Soviet Union," the president scolded the city commission. "I can't understand why the government of Albany, City Council of Albany, cannot do the same for American citizens.... The situation today is completely unsatisfactory from that point of view."

After more than a year and a half in office, President Kennedy had finally expressed himself, and with vehemence, at a crucial moment in the civil rights battle. The president's remarks were by far his most direct, and harshest, rebuke yet of bigoted officials in the South. On the day Kennedy spoke, another five blacks were arrested in Albany for sitting down in a restaurant and asking to be served; their incarceration brought the total number of arrests to 305 since July 11, and more than 1,100 since the protests began in October. The arrests, the beatings and intimidation, the infringement of rights, the twisting of the law, the stubbornness of local authorities, and King's repeated imprisonment shattered the president's equanimity. His long silence had suddenly burst into public outrage. Recognizing the change in the president's temperament, the *New York Times* displayed his remarks prominently on the front page the following day.

When Martin Luther King Jr. was informed of Kennedy's comments, he asked that a telegram be sent off immediately to the White House. He thanked the president but also, aware of Kennedy's inclination to retreat, kept the pressure on him to go further. "Gratified by directness of your statement to Albany crisis," King said in the telegram. "Rev. Abernathy and I earnestly hope you will continue to use the great moral influence of your office to help this crucial situation." Telegrams of appreciation flowed into the White House from other civil rights leaders such as the NAACP's Roy Wilkins and A. Philip Randolph of the Brotherhood of Sleeping Car Porters. The power of the president was clear: His words stirred people to action. Liberal Republican senator Jacob Javits rounded up ten senators, Republicans and Democrats, for a meeting with Burke Marshall at the Justice Department; the senators called for a federal investigation into the Albany arrests and mistreatment of blacks. In Chicago, fifty people knelt and prayed on the sidewalk in front of City Hall on behalf of King and the others in Albany prisons.

If President Kennedy's support pleased the protesters, it riled Southern leaders. In Albany, Mayor Asa Kelley called the president's comments "inappropriate," adding: "This is purely a local problem which can be solved with local people." As for sitting down for discussions with blacks, he reiterated his oft-repeated vow: "We will certainly never negotiate with those who admittedly have no respect for local laws or state laws or federal injunctions," he told reporters. President Kennedy's one-time friend James Gray, the owner of the *Albany Herald*, launched a blistering attack in his own paper on the Kennedy brothers, calling them "two ambitious Bostonians, who have been as practically connected with the American Negro in their lifetimes as Eskimos are to the Congo Democrats."

The two Bostonians, however, had apparently become more sympathetic to black grievances. A week after President Kennedy spoke out

at his press conference, his brother sent an emissary into the court of
J. Robert Elliott, where the judge was hearing another petition by the
city for a permanent injunction against black demonstrations. Just before
the close of the proceedings, Jerry Heilbron, a Justice Department lawyer with the Civil Rights Division, filed a friend of the court brief sid-
ing with the movement. The brief said the city had not come into court
"with clean hands"; it asserted that the city first denied blacks their right
to integrate public facilities granted under federal court rulings and then
sought to stifle their right to protest against that infringement. The Kennedy administration action was in part a self-protective move: If Judge
Elliott imposed a permanent federal injunction, Robert Kennedy's Justice
Department would be required to enforce it, meaning federal marshals or
troops would be responsible for stopping black protests.

The Justice Department action tipped the balance and forced the city
to reevaluate its position. Compromise was now in the air, and Mayor
Kelley was beside himself, calling the Feds' move "an affront to those of
us in the South who are prepared to stand fast for law and order." Aware
of the far-reaching implications of a stronger Justice Department role,
Kelley said the government's "revolutionary policy may write off the
civilized efforts at racial solutions in courts of law in countless Southern
communities."

From his jail cell, Martin Luther King Jr. said that the Justice Department had "vindicated" the position of the Albany Movement. He praised
the Justice Department's friend of the court brief as the administration's
expression of its "legal and moral support." The backing of the White
House, King said, was "of inestimable value for the ultimate solution of
the problem."

* * *

Two days later, King and Abernathy went on trial in Recorder's Court
on charges of disorderly conduct two weeks earlier for praying at City
Hall and failing to obey Chief Pritchett's order to disperse. Judge A. N.
Durden Sr. found both men guilty but suspended their sentences. King's
lawyer was C. B. King, who appeared in court with his head still wrapped
in bandages from his beating by the county sheriff. After handing down
his ruling, the judge warned King and Abernathy not to violate the
law or their sentences would be reinstated. Since the law was a murky
thing in the South, C. B. King asked the judge to clarify: Were the city's

segregation ordinances counted among the laws blacks had to obey? Judge Durden, seeming to side with the protesters, explained that "these ordinances have been so expressly overruled by the Supreme Court that cases will not be made on that basis."

81

BY SOME APPEARANCES, the Albany Movement was hitting its stride. Its successes were multiplying: Martin Luther King Jr. had won his release from prison, the judge in the case had sided with the Supreme Court in rejecting local segregation laws, and the Kennedy administration had lent its considerable clout to the cause. And King was talking tough. "Segregation is on its deathbed in Albany," he declared in front of a thousand people at Mount Zion Baptist Church two days after leaving jail, "and the only thing uncertain about it is how costly the city commission will make the funeral."

But the reality was something quite different: The spirit and promise of the Albany Movement had been crushed. When King was set free he announced that he would leave Albany in hopes that city officials would sit down for negotiations with local black leaders. While his offer seemed conciliatory, it was a recognition that the city commission was never going to budge as long as outside agitators, as they called men like King, were still in town. But whether or not outside agitators were present, the city had no intention of sitting down in good faith with the protesters; nor did city officials waver at all in their determination to maintain segregation. In his wisdom, Chief Pritchett had not based his arrests of demonstrators on violations of local segregation laws but rather on disorderly conduct, or loitering, or some other subjective infraction that did not challenge any Supreme Court rulings.

After King's departure, protesters planned to test segregation laws that excluded blacks from city libraries and parks. But the city acted fast. To head off any disturbances, officials closed all parks and libraries, saying the action was taken "indefinitely, in the interest of public safety."

On hearing of the shutdowns, King spoke like a general at the head of an assembled army ready to attack. "The present action of the city commission can lead to the most explosive racial situation in the United States today," he told a reporter. Far from backing down, he threatened to "regroup our forces and renew mass nonviolent demonstrations in order to keep this issue before the conscience of Albany and the nation." But his words were more a wish than a promise. And his rhetoric fell short of the truth. Few soldiers could be enlisted for the fight.

Returning to Albany in protest of the city's latest actions, King spoke to a crowd at Mount Zion; there was fervor inside the church, but it did not translate into mass demonstrations on the streets. The city's brash tactics were exhausting the Albany Movement, and infighting among the leaders dissipated enthusiasm. Fewer men and women were willing to risk uncertain justice by participating in a protest. As Ralph Abernathy put it: "They saw no concrete results from the previous demonstrations and trips to jail." On the day of King's return to Albany, just two youths picketed the city's closed library in the afternoon, and two others followed them a short time later; when police told them to disperse they went away. As historian Diane McWhorter put it: "After ten months of discipline, courage, and self-sacrifice, the demoralized Albany Movement's rank and file hung up their marching shoes."

In recognition of the waning protests, Albany Movement president William Anderson shifted the focus to voter registration. But that campaign enraged local racists. Two days after King's return to Albany, the Shady Grove Baptist Church, a voter registration center ten miles away in Leesburg, burned to the ground in the dead of night. When King arrived at the scene the next day all that remained along this quiet stretch of State Highway 195 were parts of the church's concrete block walls. Local officials claimed they had found no evidence of a bombing or arson, and speculated the church's destruction was caused by a lightning strike during a fierce overnight storm. "The church is burned up," said Lee County sheriff R. A. Forrester. "That's all I can see." King told reporters it was obvious the cause was a bombing. "I think it is a most appalling incident and a tragic expression of the lengths some people will go to deny Negroes their constitutional rights," he said. "It strikes at two very basic liberties in the American tradition—freedom of worship and the right to vote." In Lee County, blacks outnumbered whites 3,889 to 2,314; but just twenty-nine blacks were registered to vote, compared with 1,210 whites.

In the evening King led a pray-and-song session amid the ruins as a carload of whites rode past hollering curses. In response to the fire, the FBI sent men to investigate; and from the White House there was not so much as a murmur.

That same night, the city commission finally made good on a lukewarm agreement to hear from representatives of the Albany Movement, excluding Martin Luther King Jr. Officials allowed a delegation of five blacks to sit at the back of the commission room during a regularly scheduled meeting. About fifty white businessmen crowded into the room, while 150 whites lined the street outside City Hall. Marion Page, the movement's executive secretary, read a three-page petition that included demands that the city abide by ICC rules desegregating bus terminal facilities and city buses, and stop interfering with the constitutional right of protest. Not surprisingly, Mayor Kelley dismissed all the demands, telling reporters afterward that he had no intention to act on any of them. Learning of the outcome, a dispirited King said the city "holds the Negro citizen of this community in utter contempt." At a mass gathering at Shiloh Baptist Church after the meeting, William Anderson, the movement's president and head of the delegation, tried to rouse the community in the face of another affront. "We'll continue to picket, sit-in, wade-in, pray-in, kneel-in, and if we have to, we'll march," he told a crowd of six hundred. Their cheerleading, however, rang hollow.

* * *

Mayor Kelley, Police Chief Pritchett, and the city commission had proved to be canny, implacable foes. As the NAACP's Roy Wilkins described their effect: "Direct action, for all the exhilaration it had produced in Montgomery, with the sit-ins and the Freedom Rides, had...come up against a hard unmoving rock." King's close associate Ralph Abernathy conceded that the Albany Movement was no closer to its goals now than it had been when he and King first went to jail in December 1961. "In fact," Abernathy observed, "the city government seemed stronger and more adamant about their position in late summer than they had been the previous fall."

King slipped out of Albany the day after the commission meeting and did not return again for eleven days; he began cutting back on his time in the city and spending longer periods at home in Atlanta. As the number of local protesters dwindled, King tried to import outsiders to Albany.

On August 27 he was back in town to greet seventy-five people, mostly clergymen, from the North and Midwest who had come at his request for a prayer vigil in front of City Hall. In one plea he had sent to New York clergy, he said: "We are asking you to come to Albany and make witness in behalf of your congregation against the segregated way of life. Your presence would be a great boost to the freedom-loving people of that community."

As the visitors' cars rolled along Pine Street in downtown Albany, a bystander murmured: "This looks like the Yankee preachers." The marchers descending on Albany included Jews, Catholics, and Protestants: fifty-four whites and twenty-one blacks. In twos, they marched on that muggy Monday toward City Hall where they were met by Chief Pritchett and twenty police officers. For a moment, no one spoke, prompting a policeman to wonder out loud: "Is everybody bashful? Ain't nobody gonna say nothing?" A couple of the clergy then read from the Scriptures. Afterward, Chief Pritchett ordered the protesters to disperse and when no one moved he turned to his officers and said: "All right, put them in jail." As the group was rounded up and herded through a side door of the building, some four hundred white spectators on the street cheered.

Most of the clergy posted bail within a day or two. But four days later, fifteen Protestant and Jewish leaders were still behind bars and on a fast, and their protest and arrests were capturing headlines in the national press. King, wishing to stir the president, sent a telegram to the White House. The clergymen, he said, were fasting to "arouse the conscience of this nation to the gross violations of human dignity and civil rights." He called on the president to "uphold the moral ideal and the democratic principles" that were under threat because of the denial of rights to millions of black citizens. He asked the president to act as a mediator in the dispute between the Albany Movement and the city commission. The jailed clergymen also sent a letter to the president asking him to intervene. "We are all agreed, Catholic, Jew and Protestant," they told him, "that God wills the end of all racial discrimination and segregation in His world." The attorney general responded on the president's behalf with a pro forma reminder that the administration was dedicated to protecting "the rights of all Americans" regardless of their "race color or creed." But if the president remained disturbed over the ugly conditions in Albany, no one outside the White House was aware of it. He had gone silent again.

82

INSIDE THE WHITE House, the president and his advisors were huddled over another crisis. In late July, it was discovered that the Soviet Union had begun unloading military supplies at Cuba's ports, and the administration was scrambling to understand why. In early September, after six days of talks with Cuban leaders, Premier Nikita Khrushchev announced he was sending a military training mission and weapons to Cuba. The *New York Times* sounded an alarm, declaring that the moves were "a callous exercise in brinkmanship by the Kremlin" and "the first acknowledged Soviet military penetration of this hemisphere."

Vacationing in Newport, Rhode Island, the president declined to comment on the Soviet-Cuban agreement. Playing down the media outcry, the State Department discounted the communiqué as nothing new. "We have been saying right along that the Soviet Union has been sending military equipment and technicians to Cuba," a State Department spokesman told the press. But concern within the administration ran much deeper than its public comments suggested. U.S. intelligence had secretly reported in August that the Soviet weaponry included antiaircraft missiles that could be fitted with nuclear warheads. Although the Soviet Union had never supplied nuclear warheads to another nation, the report concluded, "there is also little reason to suppose that the Soviets would refuse to introduce such weapons if the move could be controlled in the Soviet interest."

Clearly, tensions were rising, and there were fears that a misstep on either side could ignite dangerous consequences. Just days earlier, two Cuban gunboats opened machine-gun fire on a U.S. Navy attack bomber conducting a training mission over international waters near the island. The White House issued a sharp rebuke vowing that if U.S. aircraft or ships were fired upon in international waters, "the United States armed forces [would] employ all means necessary for their own protection and [would] assure their free use of such waters." Soon after the Soviet-Cuban pact, the president issued a statement acknowledging the arrival in Cuba of the antiaircraft missiles and the radar and electronic equipment to operate them, and the presence of Soviet-made torpedo boats outfitted with ship-to-ship guided missiles. Some 3,500 Soviet military technicians also were either on their way to Cuba or already on the island. The president dismissed any immediate threat and assured Americans that should any Cuban aggression arise, it would "be prevented by whatever means may be necessary."

Over the next several days, the political clamor over Cuba intensified as the president asked Congress for stand-by authority to call up 150,000 military reservists. The move, meant as a show of strength to the Soviets, provoked a blistering response from the Kremlin, which accused the president of preparing to attack Cuba. Striking an apocalyptic tone, the Soviet Union said it needed to draw the attention of all countries of the world to the U.S. "provocations which might plunge the world into the disaster of a universal world war with the use of thermonuclear weapons."

* * *

As hysteria over Cuba escalated—Republican senators cried out for a range of actions from Castro's overthrow to a blockade of the island—white supremacists in Georgia torched two wood-frame black churches near Albany in the middle of the night. Mount Olive Baptist Church in Sasser, where voter registration workers had been threatened by the county sheriff in July, went up in flames around 2 a.m. Mount Mary Church, about five miles away in Chickasawhatchee, was torched an hour later. Jackie Robinson had come to Albany several days earlier at the request of Martin Luther King Jr. to raise the withering spirits of the black community. He spoke to a large crowd and watched seven- and eight-year-olds sing "We Shall Overcome." Then he went to Sasser to see the smoldering ruins of Mount Olive Baptist. "Have you ever attended the funeral of a church?" he later wrote in his column in the *New York Amsterdam News.* "I watched a strong man, the Rev. F. S. Swaggott, the pastor of the church, weeping as though his heart would break as he looked out over the debris and wreckage."

Robinson pledged $100 to help rebuild the church, then spearheaded a national rebuilding fund that King had initiated. He asked readers of his column for funds: "We must not only rebuild these churches. We must also prepare to rebuild others," he wrote. "There will be more churches destroyed before this battle is over." Donations poured in: New York governor Nelson

Rockefeller gave $10,000, writing to Robinson "as a Baptist layman and as an American deeply concerned that all my fellow Americans shall be assured the right to worship and the right to vote." Heavyweight champion Floyd Patterson promised some of his earnings from his upcoming fight against Sonny Liston (a bout he lost, surrendering his title). Frank Schiffman, who owned Harlem's Apollo Theater, contributed $1,000 and between performances passed the collection plate. Over the next two years, Robinson collected $50,000 to rebuild the burned churches.

Immediately after the latest blazes, Charles McDew of the Student Nonviolent Coordinating Committee sent a telegram to President Kennedy demanding action to stop the "Nazi-like reign of terror" in the region. He told the president that not only were racists burning churches but they were shooting voter registration workers. In Mississippi, two students registering black voters were shot through the window of a home, one in the head, the other in the arm. In his telegram, McDew urged Kennedy not only to investigate but to come to the South "where the Ku Klux Klan and the segregationists make a mockery of democracy." King kept the pressure on the president. In a telegram to the White House, he raised the possibility of John Kennedy's worst fear in the civil rights battle: blacks erupting into violence. Noting the attacks in the South, King said: "If Negroes are tempted to turn to retaliatory violence, we shall see a dark night of rioting all over the South." King promised to discourage blacks from resorting to extreme measures but, he warned, "I fear my counsel will fall on deaf ears if the Federal Government does not take decisive action." The president announced publicly that the attorney general was already at work on a report of the church burnings and was to present it to him the following day.

* * *

The same week the churches burned, Georgia voters went to the polls in the Democratic primary for governor. To Kennedy's satisfaction, the moderate Democratic candidate, Carl Sanders, trounced his bigoted opponent, Marvin Griffin. Sanders's primary win virtually guaranteed his election, because Republicans were not expected to field a candidate for the November contest. With extremists intimidating, firebombing, and shooting blacks, even the outgoing governor, Ernest Vandiver, an old-school racist, rejected Griffin's rhetoric during the campaign and supported Sanders. Griffin, who was backed by the Ku Klux Klan and other white supremacist organizations, at one appearance offered his view on how to deal with black agitators: "There ain't but one thing to do and that is to cut you a blackjack sapling and brain them." In Vandiver's view, Griffin's "inflammatory and incendiary statements" during the campaign were "directly linked" to the church burnings.

The day after the election, President Kennedy strode into the State Department auditorium for his regular press conference. With Cuba still topmost in Americans' minds, the president began with a statement intended to calm nerves. Without mentioning the din from hawkish Republicans he said, "Rash talk is cheap," then reiterated that if the Soviets in Cuba endangered the United States, America would "do whatever must be done to protect its own security and that of its allies."

After a few follow-up questions, the president was asked about Martin Luther King Jr.'s telegram seeking federal intervention in Georgia. "Mr. President," a reporter asked, "could you tell us whether you have answered Dr. King, and...can you give us a comment on the problem?"

President Kennedy, who seemed to have lost his voice on civil rights over the past six weeks, said that he was in contact with King, then spoke with disgust about the terror that blacks confronted in the South. "I don't know any more outrageous action which I have seen occur in this country for a good many months or years," he began, "than the burning of a church—two churches—because of the effort made by Negroes to be registered to vote." He stressed that the Constitution provided the right to vote to every American and that no one should be denied the opportunity to exercise that freedom. The shootings of voter registration workers and the church burnings, he said, were "cowardly as well as outrageous." If Americans obstruct the right to vote, he continued, "then all of our talk about freedom is hollow." He encouraged everyone to vote and commended the men and women who worked to register citizens, and he promised to give them the protection of the United States government.

At the very end of his long sermon he raised the prospect of something he had long fended off and that King had long begged him to do. "We shall do everything we possibly can to make sure that that protection is assured," he told the newsmen, "and if it requires extra legislation and extra force, we shall do that." After dismissing any chance of civil rights legislation—so stymied was he by a perceived monolithic political wall—the president now hinted for the first time that seeking congressional action had found a spot in a corner of his mind.

83

ALTHOUGH MARTIN LUTHER King Jr. and the protesters in Albany had failed in their battle with the city commission, they had achieved something of potential greater significance: They had roused John F. Kennedy to righteous anger on the state of civil rights in America. For a man known for his coolness in public, the president had revealed a well of outrage inside him and shown an ability to express it. Earlier in 1962, he had exploded over a separate domestic issue: No one had ever seen him so furious. His close advisor Kenneth O'Donnell described him as "livid with rage—white with anger." Kennedy had stormed around the Oval Office, seething: "He fucked me. They fucked us and we've got to try to fuck them." The object of his ire was Roger Blough, chairman of U.S. Steel, who minutes earlier had left the Oval Office after dropping a bombshell. Instead of holding the line on steel prices in 1962, as agreed, his company was at that very moment announcing a price hike of 3.5 percent. Other steel companies were soon to follow. "You double-crossed me," Kennedy fumed at Blough. Rising steel prices risked igniting inflation and a recession, a two-punch economic reversal the White House wanted to avoid at all costs. What was more, the president's inability to jawbone executives into price compliance handed Soviet Premier Nikita Khrushchev an opportunity to ridicule him: Here was another example— after the Bay of Pigs debacle and the young president's stumbles at his summit with the canny Khrushchev in Vienna—of a weak and irresolute John F. Kennedy. His stunned aides watched as the president let loose: "Businessmen were all pricks," he frothed. "God, I hate the bastards.... They kicked us right in the balls."

Still indignant the following day, the president went public with his anger. At a press conference he opened with a long statement holding nothing back, calling the steel companies' actions "wholly unjustifiable and irresponsible." Newspapers across the country heralded the president's outrage. "Righteous indignation in spades," said the New York *Daily News*; a "bitter denunciation," chimed the *Atlanta Constitution*. Not content just to speak out, the president then personally managed a war against the steel companies to bring them to heel. He was shameless in his tactics; he weighed charges of collusion, shifted defense contracts to smaller, more obedient steel companies, considered legislation to roll back the price increases, and even investigated the executives' expense accounts and tax returns. In the end, the hounded executives bowed to the president's fury and overwhelming power: The price increases were rescinded.

Among the millions observing the president's rage was Jackie Robinson. Soon after the price rollback, he published an open letter to the president as one of his regular columns in the *New York Amsterdam News*. "One thing is sure," he wrote, praising the president's muscle. "You were definite. You were strong in your stand and you displayed a flash of anger and spunk which many people admired. To make a long story short—you got angry." Then Robinson pivoted to his real topic: civil rights. Why, he wanted to know, hadn't the president shown the same passion over the injustices heaped daily on blacks in America? Didn't the president believe, Robinson asked, that first-class citizenship for blacks was in the best interests of our democracy?

"Without meaning to be impertinent, Mr. President, we have a suggestion," Robinson said. He advised the president to go off somewhere alone and think about racial prejudice until he got as angry as he was about steel prices. Then the president could channel his fury into "the battle against the bigots in this country who are working harder to destroy it from within than any foreign power is working to destroy it from without." Robinson wanted the president to inject some passion into his fight for civil rights. "Why Mr. President," the baseball hero urged, "why don't you get angry again?"

Although far from asserting leadership on civil rights, the president had in fact begun a subtle process of transformation: He had stepped onto a path of very gradual evolution in his thinking on racial justice. Although he was prone to hesitate and even backtrack, a slow process of change was at work within him. As historian Nick Bryant put it, the president "had crossed an important psychological threshold" in the summer of 1962. "The Albany Movement—often cited as a low point of the civil rights era—did subtly transform the president's thinking about America's racial crisis. He had never used words like 'outrageous' or 'cowardly' in public to describe attacks on blacks.... The cool detachment with which he had responded to the Freedom Rides crisis seemed to be giving way to a more heartfelt involvement." The president was listening to the pleas from the black community. Stars like Jackie Robinson were elegant spokesmen—but it was Martin Luther King Jr., the celebrity leader most often in front of newsmen and television cameras, who captured the president's attention and sympathies. King's jail terms, his eloquent rhetoric, his impassioned telegrams, and his prodding for justice conveyed his own suffering and that of twenty million other Americans. His expression of the black experience educated the president and gradually touched his conscience.

But King knew that the president's outbursts were not nearly enough and that the snail-like pace of his evolution was inadequate. He wanted Kennedy to throw himself into the battle against white supremacy now—and with the same vigor he had attacked the steel industry. He wanted an end to segregation and discrimination, and the president, however impassioned his language, had taken no concrete steps to change conditions in Albany or anywhere else in the South. He still favored economic and foreign issues. *Jet* magazine chided him for failing to regard the "reign of terror against Negroes" with the same urgency as the mounting troubles in Cuba. "In the case of the Cuba crisis," the magazine wrote, "the President asked for and got Congress to give him the power to call up military reserves as he sees fit. In the case of the burning of Negro churches by night raiders and other terroristic tactics against Negroes, the President merely condemned such actions as 'cowardly as well as outrageous.'" To activist professor Howard Zinn, Kennedy's outrage over the church burnings merely reflected the White House's "antipathy to nationally publicized violence and its careful defense of voting rights (but not other rights) guaranteed by the Constitution." The president was focused on getting the two sides in Albany to sit down together for talks which, in Zinn's view, allowed him to skirt "the moral issue of racial equality" and stick to "procedural questions: the law, negotiation." Regretting the White House's narrow approach, Zinn wished the president showed "moral leadership" and provided "education and persuasion" on civil rights.

84

IN SEPTEMBER, PRESIDENT Kennedy faced a crucial test of his resolve to protect the constitutional rights of blacks in the South. On September 13, the same day that the president spoke to the press on the church burnings, Mississippi governor Ross Barnett defied a Supreme Court order to integrate the University of Mississippi. Barnett was a simple, amiable man reared in poverty in the clay hills of central Mississippi, the son of a Confederate veteran and the youngest of ten children. Through hard work he became a successful lawyer, generous to those seeking their own way up. But his kindnesses did not extend to blacks. His views on white supremacy and separation of the races were grounded in the Bible. "When God made the Universe," Barnett preached, "He put the races apart—the white man in Europe, the red in Asia, the black in Africa. They were meant to stay apart. Every time the races have mixed there's been nothing but trouble."

Barnett could not fathom that a black man would ever attend the hallowed all-white institution Ole Miss. But James Meredith, a black Air Force veteran, had his own perception of God's plan. Inspired by John Kennedy's election, he had filed his application for admission the day after the new president's election. As Meredith told a reporter in 1966: "Nobody handpicked me. I believed, and I believe now, that I have a Divine Responsibility to break White Supremacy in Mississippi."

Like Barnett, Meredith was one of ten children; his father, Moses, scrabbled out a decent living growing cotton and corn on an eighty-four-acre farm he owned outside of Kosciusko, Mississippi; he was considered a "good Negro" and therefore was allowed to vote (only thirty-four blacks in the county were accorded the privilege out of a total voting population of 5,179). Among his large brood, his son James was an independent boy, a loner who read a lot, and was not particularly close to his siblings; he was strangely fearless at night in the eerie landscape of the countryside. James straddled country and city life, staying with his family on the farm but going to school in town. At a young age, he took exception to the patronizing or unjust treatment he got as a black person in a white world. When an important local white man handed out pennies and nickels to black children he refused to take them. At age fifteen while traveling by rail from Detroit, he was forced to change to a black car when his train pulled into Memphis. It was his first exposure to Jim Crow laws on trains, and he cried the rest of the way home.

After applying to Ole Miss, Meredith waited for more than a year and a half as his request was batted back and forth in the courts: The state filed for repeated delays, which were answered in NAACP countersuits demanding his admission. On September 10, Supreme Court Justice Hugo Black handed down a ruling that set aside all lower-court stays and ordered the state to allow Meredith, a transfer student from all-black Jackson State College, to join white students at Ole Miss in the fall. Refusing to give in, Governor Barnett went on statewide radio and television to condemn the "evil and illegal forces of tyranny." Tapping into deep Southern wounds, he denied the federal government's power to assert its will in his state; he relied on a state doctrine drawn up before the Civil War that he insisted allowed him to interpose state sovereignty between the U.S. government and the people of Mississippi. Addressing Southerners, Barnett never imagined his words were incendiary: His tone was simply the local sensibility that got him elected. In campaigns it was common, even tribal, to hold forth on protecting the sacred honor of the South in colorful and hyperbolic language. What the governor hadn't reckoned was what might happen when his sentiments ricocheted beyond Mississippi's cloistered world. With naïve chest-thumping, he declared to his state radio and television audience: "No school will be integrated in Mississippi while I am your Governor."

85

AMERICA WAS HEADING into a period of centennial celebrations for Abraham Lincoln's freeing the slaves, when Mississippi's governor denied James Meredith's admission to Ole Miss. The *Chicago Defender* captured the civil rights tension gripping the nation. "On this 100th anniversary of the Emancipation Proclamation," the black paper observed, "James H. Meredith could well be used as a symbol of where the Negro stands after a century of 'freedom.'"

At a New York state commemoration dinner on September 12, Martin Luther King Jr. challenged President Kennedy to move swiftly and forcefully to break the South's resistance to racial equality. Speaking to a crowd of two hundred at New York's Park Sheraton Hotel, King accused the South of "ceaseless rebellion" against the laws and values of the United States. "It is an autonomous region whose posture toward the Central Government has elements as defiant as a hostile nation." By now, King had largely given up on his plea that President Kennedy enact a second Emancipation Proclamation abolishing all segregation laws in the South; the president had ignored it. In his speech, King derided the political caution that killed the second Emancipation Proclamation. "No president can be great, or even fit for office," he observed, "if he attempts to accommodate injustice to maintain his political balance."

Initially the White House expressed enthusiasm about a September 22 event at the Lincoln Memorial marking the day the original proclamation was issued in 1862, and it set the Civil Rights Commission to work on preparations. Confusion ensued when erroneous reports circulated that the president planned to deliver a major civil rights address at the Lincoln Memorial. *Jet* magazine promised readers that Kennedy was to headline the celebration filled with music, speeches, and spirituals by gospel singer Mahalia Jackson. The magazine reported: "Administration aides said Kennedy will use the opportunity to discuss civil rights issues and progress in that area." The White House rushed out a clarification: No speech was intended. Not wishing to offend Southern leaders, the president pulled out of the ceremony. It was announced that he had a prior out-of-town commitment; on the day of the commemoration, President Kennedy would be in Newport, Rhode Island, watching the America's Cup races.

Kennedy's latest retreat frustrated King and the black community. And it provided an opportunity for New York governor and liberal Republican Nelson Rockefeller to enhance his position with blacks before his expected run for the presidency in 1964. Rockefeller had been a key figure behind the proclamation tribute at the Park Sheraton; in his speech to the crowd, he took a stab at Kennedy, saying that enforcement of the

Supreme Court's ruling on school desegregation had been "painfully slow." Ten days later, at the Lincoln Memorial commemoration, Rockefeller shared the stage with Thurgood Marshall, newly confirmed judge on the U.S. Circuit Court of Appeals, and Mahalia Jackson. In an odd display of both privilege and affinity with blacks, Rockefeller showed up at the ceremony with an original copy of the Emancipation Proclamation, owned by his family.

The absent President Kennedy sent a brief recorded message that was broadcast over loudspeakers. In his remarks he unintentionally sounded as if he were excusing himself for having done little on civil rights to this point in his administration. "Like the Proclamation we celebrate, this observance must be regarded not as an end, but a beginning," Kennedy told the gathering, many of whom, like King, were impatient with the president's slow progress. Begging for more time, he added: "The best commemoration lies not in what we say today, but in what we do in the days and months ahead to complete the work begun by Abraham Lincoln." The president sent his brother the attorney general in his stead. But Bobby Kennedy resented Rockefeller's appearance at the event in what the attorney general believed was purely for political purposes. Bobby arrived late, had no speaking role, and "he didn't look happy about the whole affair," observed Berl Bernhard of the Civil Rights Commission.

The president, meanwhile, spent the day with his wife and daughter aboard the USS *Joseph P. Kennedy Jr.*, a destroyer named after his deceased brother, watching the Australian yacht *Gretel* challenge the American sloop *Weatherly* for the America's Cup. The First Family was dressed for boating: the president in a blue yachting blazer with brass buttons, the first lady in a black leather crew-neck windbreaker; daughter Caroline, who was nearly five years old, wore a pink sweater and pink slacks.

President Kennedy wasn't the day's only noticeable absence at the Emancipation Proclamation ceremony. Instead of showing up, and thereby tacitly accepting the White House's feeble embrace of the commemoration, Martin Luther King Jr. was preparing for the SCLC's annual convention in Birmingham, Alabama. Three weeks later, he described his discontent with the president in a commentary he wrote for the black newspaper *New York Amsterdam News*. Drawing on some of the same themes and language in his speech at the Park Sheraton Hotel, King expressed his bitter disappointment with the course of civil rights in America, implicitly rebuking the president for his cowardice and calling on him to "reaffirm democracy by deeds as bold and daring as the issuance of the Emancipation Proclamation." He extolled Lincoln's original proclamation for what it set in motion: the freeing of the slaves, the emboldening of blacks to play a role in their own advancement, the reaffirming of equality, and the empowering of a president to fundamentally reshape the nation. In another implied prod to the current president, King advised: "There is but one way to commemorate the Emancipation Proclamation. That is to make its declaration of freedom real."

86

ATTORNEY GENERAL ROBERT Kennedy was on the phone repeatedly with Governor Ross Barnett, cajoling, charming, negotiating to steer him away from a collision course with the federal government. The attorney general's goal was the swift, peaceful enrollment of James Meredith at Ole Miss. Any other outcome threw into question the authority of the Supreme Court and the entire judicial system. Bobby believed he could win this battle through the courts and by personal diplomacy.

President Kennedy laid the burden of the crisis on his brother, just as he had done during the Freedom Rides, consulting when necessary and receiving regular, detailed reports. Neither he nor Bobby wanted to force Barnett's hand by the use of federal troops. But Bobby was realistic enough to begin preparing for a possible limited step: deployment of U.S. marshals. After their successful performance during the Freedom Rides, the U.S. marshals were considered a worthy, small-scale option for enforcing court orders, and soon they were on their way from points around the country to a staging ground in Memphis, Tennessee.

James Meredith was scheduled to register for his Ole Miss classes on September 20. The state and federal governments, meanwhile, dueled in court in a flurry of actions—the state seeking injunctions to prevent his enrollment and the Justice Department fighting back. "There were other factors to take into account besides a neat, orderly sequence of court decisions," historian Walter Lord observed. "There was, in short, the legacy of a past that would not die; and this, rather than court decisions, would determine what happened next."

In preparation for Meredith's arrival on campus, Bobby Kennedy and Burke Marshall sought assurances from Governor Barnett that police would protect the black applicant. Everyone expected that a white student mob was likely to gather, and its mood was predictable. Barnett dithered for a while before finally agreeing that he, too, was interested in preventing violence. As the day approached, Mississippians were full of raw emotion. A columnist for the *Clarion-Ledger* in Jackson ridiculed Bobby Kennedy: "Little Brother has evidently concluded that the South must be forced to abandon its customs and traditions in deference to 'world opinion'—especially that of Asiatic cow-worshippers and African semi-savages not far removed from cannibalism."

* * *

On Thursday, September 20, Meredith pulled up outside the building for Continuation Studies in an unmarked green and white Border Patrol sedan, accompanied by two U.S. marshals and a Civil Rights Commission lawyer. This remote location on campus was not the usual site for registration and was chosen in hopes of eluding a crowd of student spectators—but to no avail. As Meredith stepped out of the car, two thousand young men and women jeered him, some chanting: "Go home, nigger!" A short time earlier, as the group awaited the black student, the mood was playful: Several male and female students were showing off the latest dance craze, the Twist. And in an act of mischief, a few boys, letting out a rebel yell, dashed to the flagpole and tried to pull down the Stars and Stripes and replace it with the Confederate flag; but others intervened to halt them. Now, a hundred state highway patrolmen along with a battery of law enforcement officers—sheriffs, deputies, local police, plainclothesmen—held back the boisterous throng. Reflecting widespread sentiment, a welcome sign on campus had been altered to remove a reference to *new* students in favor of a racist revision. WELCOME TO OLE MISS, it now read, *WHITE* STUDENTS REPORT TO LYCEUM ROOM 117 IMMEDIATELY AFTER CHECKING INTO DORMITORY (italics added).

In a brown suit and white shirt, Meredith climbed out of the sedan and stood in the bright sunshine for a moment amid the oak trees, gazing at the crowd. He then furrowed his brow and was escorted toward the building. Inside, the men were met by Governor Barnett, who bantered pleasantly with the federal officers and shook everyone's hand except Meredith's. Then the governor, feigning racial color-blindness, asked with good ole Mississippi humor: "Which one of you is James Meredith?" When Meredith stepped forward and said he wanted to register, Barnett refused his application and unfurled a proclamation stamped with a gold seal. St. John Barrett of the Civil Rights Commission asked the governor: "Do you realize you are placing yourself in contempt of court?" When the governor showed no regard for the possible repercussions, the federal officials, fearing that his hostility would incite the mob, decided to escort their charge off the grounds. "We hastened to our waiting car, which sped away with hordes of shouting, rock-throwing students hot on the chase," Meredith recalled. "The state troopers led us on our way north to the Tennessee line as fast as one could imagine."

87

AMERICANS SOON GRASPED, as did the White House, that the crisis taking shape in Mississippi posed the most serious conflict between state and federal authority since the Civil War. In Washington, Robert Kennedy again turned to the courts but still Governor Barnett defied the federal government in an effort to assert his state's rights. His local popularity was soaring. "He transformed himself from a bumbling politician... into the sacred incarnation of Robert E. Lee himself," Meredith said. "He became a southern superhero, and he was savoring every moment of it." Reports flowed in from the FBI and from newsmen that Barnett's rebellion was inciting the white rabble, posing a serious risk of rioting.

Throughout the weekend Bobby dueled with Barnett. "This matter must not be resolved in the street," Bobby warned the governor on the phone. The attorney general implored Barnett to make a public statement condemning violence, but the governor refused. The administration was struggling to keep the crisis from slipping out of control. To Bobby, Barnett was a puzzle impossible to solve. The attorney general regarded him "as genuinely loony." As he explained to presidential aide Arthur Schlesinger, the governor "had been hit on the head by an airplane propeller last summer and had never been the same since." Several ideas for reining in the governor were debated: One was to set up a meeting between Barnett and the president—but a similar strategy backfired for President Eisenhower during the Little Rock crisis; another was to send Vice President Lyndon Johnson, a Southerner, to Mississippi to escort Meredith to the campus—but that raised the prospect of a public humiliation for Johnson if Barnett still refused to back down; a third option was to inform Barnett that an Army division had been put on alert for deployment to Mississippi—but at this point the threat was too extreme.

Again, the attorney general turned to the courts and widened the net of contempt violations to trustees of the university for their failure to register Meredith. The trustees had ducked their duty by handing the registrar's role temporarily over to Barnett. By going after the trustees, Bobby hoped the governor would yield once he realized his actions might send others to jail. But the bullheaded Barnett did not waver; again he invoked the supremacy of Mississippi laws over federal laws and reasserted his determination to block Meredith's admission.

Next Bobby Kennedy got a federal injunction ordering Barnett not to interfere with Meredith's enrollment. And he elevated the White House presence in the matter by sending a high-ranking official, assistant attorney general for civil rights John Doar, to escort Meredith to his registration. Meredith appreciated Doar's lanky, six-foot-two presence, his "commanding, soft-spoken authority [and] classic salt-of-the earth American strength." In his memoir, Meredith recalled Doar as a man who truly believed that every American should have the same rights and full equality: "There was not a molecule of deception, guile, or hesitation and nothing tricky or shifty about Doar." Meredith described the federal civil rights man and his other protector, the burly Chief U.S. Marshal James McShane, as "two of the bravest men I have ever known." In contrast to the gangling Doar, McShane was a stout former New York Police officer known for his Irish charm who, in the words of author Walter Lord, "could perhaps best be described as a sort of tough elf."

* * *

With Doar and McShane at his side, Meredith tried to register again, on Tuesday, September 25, this time at a state government office building in Jackson, housing the offices of the university trustees who had been coerced by the courts to agree to admit the black student. But on the tenth floor of the Woolfolk Building, Meredith and his protectors encountered Governor Barnett, blocking the office doorway. Chief Marshal McShane presented Barnett with a court summons on his contempt charges but the governor brushed it aside and read a proclamation rejecting Meredith's admission. Television cameras captured the scene inside the building and the swarms of people outside. Bobby Kennedy regarded Barnett's publicity stunt as an affront both to himself personally and to the federal courts.

"Governor," he fumed when he got Barnett on the phone afterward, "you are part of the United States."

"We have been part of the United States but I don't know whether we are or not," Barnett replied.

"Are you getting out of the Union?" Bobby asked.

"It looks like we're being kicked around—like we don't belong to it."

Barnett didn't sound like a crazed rebel but rather like a forlorn politician seeking to win admiration and avoid humiliation. Bobby sensed there was a way out of the crisis with everyone saving face.

The next day, Meredith was rebuffed again, and the governor refused to take receipt of his contempt-of-court summons, which demanded he appear that Friday, September 28, in the Fifth Circuit Court of Appeals in New Orleans. Barnett was still defiant, but he could swat away court orders only so many times. The reality of his actions was beginning to sink in, and the prospect of jail frightened the sixty-four-year-old politician. The governor was now ready to make a deal, one that gave him a way out yet preserved his status as a political hero.

In a flurry of phone calls, Barnett and his advisors and Robert Kennedy and his staff gradually pieced together an outlandish theatrical solution. The governor agreed to let Meredith register, but only if it appeared to Mississippians that Barnett yielded under a personal physical threat from the federal government. Bobby hesitated. With the mood on the street already nasty, this was a dangerous proposition. But both he and Barnett were desperate to end the crisis; the longer it dragged on

In June 1940, John F. Kennedy graduated from Harvard University, a child of wealth and privilege, son of the United States ambassador to the United Kingdom. In college he had a black valet, George Taylor, who looked after his clothes and shoes and served as his chauffeur. Young Jack, an open-minded gadabout, treated Taylor as one of the boys, seeking his advice, smoking cigars together, and chatting about a mutual passion: girls. *(John F. Kennedy Presidential Library and Museum, Boston)*

Son of a prominent Baptist minister and great-grandson of a slave, Martin Luther King Jr. showed early intellectual promise, enrolling at all-black Morehouse College at age fifteen and graduating four years later, in 1948. He had a painful awakening as a young boy when the father of his two favorite playmates prohibited their friendship because King was black and his sons were white. "For the first time," King recalled years later, "I was made aware of the existence of a race problem." *(Courtesy of Morehouse College)*

Martin Luther King Jr. rose to prominence as the leader of the Montgomery Bus Boycott, which erupted in December 1955 when a black seamstress and NAACP volunteer, Rosa Parks, refused to give up her seat to a white passenger. When King and the tenacious black community ended segregation on city buses after a year-long protest, Parks and other blacks no longer had to surrender their seats to anyone and were free to sit wherever they wanted—not just in the back of the bus. King emerged from the boycott as "the number one leader" of blacks in America, observed the *Amsterdam News*. "People will follow him anywhere." *(Underwood Archives/Getty Images)*

A politician in a hurry, John Kennedy ran for president in 1960 at age forty-three, after serving as a U.S. congressman and senator. Swarmed on the campaign trail, he nonetheless had trouble wooing blacks until just before the vote, when he phoned Coretta Scott King to express his sympathies for her husband's recent jailing. The call ignited an outpouring of support from blacks that by some accounts tipped the election to Kennedy. *(John F. Kennedy Presidential Library and Museum, Boston)*

Following Kennedy's call to his wife and some behind-the-scenes activity by the candidate and his campaign manager and brother Robert, Martin Luther King Jr. was released from the maximum-security prison in Reidsville, Georgia, and reunited with his family. Kennedy's subsequent election owing to strong black turnout convinced many blacks that the president had to make good on his political debt by pursuing a strong civil rights agenda. *(Donald Uhrbrock/ The LIFE Images Collection/Getty Images)*

The 1961 Freedom Rides, aimed at desegregating bus terminals throughout the South, posed a challenge to the new president. On May 14, Southern whites set fire to a bus leaving Anniston, Alabama, and tried to trap the Freedom Riders inside. Tumbling out of the bus, the riders were beaten by a swarming mob. Slow to understand the significance of the crisis, the president remained largely silent. *(Underwood Archives/Getty Images)*

On May 20, 1961, John Lewis, a twenty-one-year-old activist, and Jim Zwerg, also twenty-one, were aboard a Freedom Ride bus that was greeted by Ku Klux Klansmen at the Montgomery, Alabama, station. Lewis was whacked on the side of the head by a wooden Coca-Cola crate. Zwerg's head was pinned between the knees of one attacker while others took turns beating him. *(Bettmann/Getty Images)*

On October 1, 1962, James Meredith walked across campus to register for classes at the University of Mississippi, flanked by Chief U.S. Marshal James McShane (left) and Assistant Attorney General John Doar. The previous night whites rioted, forcing a reluctant President Kennedy to federalize the Mississippi National Guard to restore order. *(Buyenlarge/Getty Images)*

Young children became foot soldiers for equality in Birmingham, Alabama, as Martin Luther King Jr. and other black leaders launched protests in the most segregated city in America. The controversial enlistment of children signaled the movement's rising intensity in the fight against segregation and its desire to jolt the conscience of the president. *(AP Photo/Bill Hudson)*

Birmingham fire fighters turned high-powered hoses on protesters, knocking them to the ground, lacerating the flesh, ripping clothing off their backs. *(Charles Moore/Getty Images)*

In a brutal crackdown, police called out dogs to attack nonviolent students such as high school sophomore Walter Gadsden. In Washington, President Kennedy was disgusted by the images he saw in the newspaper. As Robert Kennedy recalled: "The dogs and the hoses and the pictures with the Negroes is what created a feeling in the United States that more needed to be done." *(AP Photo/Bill Hudson)*

On Good Friday, April 12, 1963, Martin Luther King Jr. (right) was arrested along with the Reverend Ralph Abernathy and other protesters and was locked up in solitary confinement. While in prison, King wrote *Letter from Birmingham Jail*, a passionate statement of principles for the civil rights movement. *(AP Photo)*

While King sat in jail incommunicado, President Kennedy and his family celebrated Easter on Sunday, April 14, at his father's estate in Palm Beach, Florida. The following day he phoned King's wife, Coretta, to offer solace and a promise to help. *(Cecil Stoughton. White House Photographs. John F. Kennedy Presidential Library and Museum, Boston)*

Attorney General Robert Kennedy (right) with Burke Marshall, assistant attorney general in charge of the Civil Rights Division. With his quiet, thoughtful manner, Marshall won respect from both black and white leaders as he worked to bring about an agreement on desegregation and employment opportunities in Birmingham. As one ardent segregationist said of him: "There is a man who listens. I had to listen back, and I guess I grew up a little." *(AP Photo/Henry Griffin)*

On June 11, 1963, Alabama governor George Wallace stood in the schoolhouse door blocking the admission of two black students at the University of Alabama in Tuscaloosa, in defiance of a court order to integrate the institution. Deputy Attorney General Nicholas Katzenbach (right) listened as Wallace read a proclamation condemning "the unwelcome, unwanted, unwarranted" government intrusion on states' rights. President Kennedy federalized the Alabama National Guard to protect against possible rioting. *(AP Photo)*

After two and a half years of dithering on civil rights—and motivated by the latest turmoil in Alabama—President Kennedy had an epiphany. After the showdown in Tuscaloosa, the president went on live television that same evening, June 11, to address what he called a "moral crisis" in the nation and to propose civil rights legislation to ensure equal treatment for black Americans. His speech, echoing themes put forward by Martin Luther King Jr. in his *Letter from Birmingham Jail*, prompted the civil rights leader to declare that it was "one of the most eloquent profound and unequivocal pleas for justice and freedom for all men ever made by any president." *(Abbie Rowe. White House Photographs. John F. Kennedy Presidential Library and Museum, Boston)*

Thousands gathered in the capital for the March on Washington on August 28, 1963, to rally for jobs and equality and to pressure Congress to act on President Kennedy's civil rights legislation. Celebrities (left to right) Charlton Heston, Harry Belafonte, James Baldwin, and Marlon Brando joined the March. *(AP Photo)*

Jackie Robinson participated in the March on Washington. An outspoken critic of John Kennedy, he sharply revised his opinion after the president's June 11 broadcast, calling the speech "one of the finest declarations ever issued in the cause of human rights." *(Library of Congress, Prints & Photographs Division © The Estate of Roosevelt H. Carter, Roosevelt Carter LC-DIG-ppmsca-35377)*

On the steps of the Lincoln Memorial, Martin Luther King Jr. delivered his "I Have a Dream" speech before a vast crowd on the National Mall. President Kennedy watched on television in the Oval Office as King closed his speech—"Free at last! Free at last! Thank God almighty, we're free at last!"—and turned to an aide to marvel: "He's damn good." *(AFP/Getty Images)*

After the March, President Kennedy invited black leaders to the White House. "He was beside himself," recalled activist and longtime congressman John Lewis. "He was just smiling, beaming." Shaking hands with each leader, he smiled when he came to Martin Luther King Jr. and quipped with wit and sincerity: "I have a dream." *(AP Photo)*

the greater the chance of violence, and any solution seemed better than none. The men worked out the storyline and actors' roles as if creating a staged drama. The first draft had Barnett blocking Meredith from registering and the U.S. marshals escorting the student and drawing their revolvers. Another version had Meredith arriving with thirty marshals but only Chief Marshal McShane pulling out his gun—which would not be loaded. But Barnett demanded that all the marshals draw their weapons. Bobby recoiled at that. Knowing photographers would capture the scene, Barnett wanted pictures showing his surrender in the face of life-threatening federal force, thereby elevating his reputation even in defeat. If McShane alone were to draw his gun, Barnett offered, he had to point it at the governor's head. Bobby rejected that bit of theatrics, but in the end agreed to have all the marshals draw their weapons as Barnett stepped aside to allow Meredith's admission.

The script was finalized just as Meredith was on his way to the campus from Memphis, where he was staying during the ordeal; thirteen cars filled with marshals accompanied him. "I'm taking a helluva chance," Bobby told Barnett. "I'm relying on you." For his part, Barnett was in a panic: The mob on the campus had swelled to 2,500 noisy whites, with a large contingent of Ku Klux Klan members. But his greatest fear was that this secret compromise and sham confrontation would become public; if that were to happen, Barnett's political career would be over. Worse, the revelations would incite the crowd and expose him as a traitor, imperiling his own safety. "You understand," Barnett told Kennedy, "we have had no agreement." Kennedy assured him: "That's correct."

As Meredith's convoy rolled on toward the university, Barnett sweated. Finally, overcome by anxiety, he phoned Attorney General Kennedy again. "General," he said, "I'm worried. I'm nervous, I tell you. You don't realize what's going on. There are several thousand people in here in cars, trucks.... We don't know these people." The crowd, he worried, could get out of hand. "A lot of people are going to be killed," he warned. "It would be embarrassing to me." Bobby had a different emotional response to the prospect of mass killings. "I don't know if it would be embarrassing," he told Barnett. "That would not be the feeling." The attorney general then called off the charade and ordered the caravan, which was about thirty miles from the Oxford campus, to turn around and head back to Memphis.

88

WHAT BOBBY KENNEDY dreaded most now looked more likely: Federal troops were going to be needed in Mississippi. On Friday, September 28, the attorney general paid a visit to the Pentagon's War Room for discussions with General Maxwell Taylor, the chairman of the Joint Chiefs of Staff; and Cyrus Vance, secretary of the Army. By now, more than five hundred U.S. marshals—border patrolmen, prison guards, and others, a large percentage of them Southerners—were standing by at Millington Naval Air Station just north of Memphis. But the marshals alone were not sufficient to put down an outbreak of violence. The consultations in the War Room concluded that two military police battalions and a battle group from the Second Infantry should be prepared to move out from Fort Benning in Georgia, if needed. At the Justice Department, Assistant Attorney General Norbert Schlei drew up a proclamation on the troop deployment and an executive order federalizing the Mississippi National Guard; all that awaited was the president's signature.

So far, President Kennedy had hovered at the edge of the crisis. His special counsel and speechwriter Ted Sorensen, who was laid up at Bethesda Naval Hospital with stomach ulcers, encouraged him to keep away from reporters and to offer no public statements. Wishing to shield his boss from any political fallout over the crisis, Sorensen summoned his secretary to his hospital bed and dictated a memo. "Stay out of it personally for the time being," he advised the president. "The defiance [of Barnett] should be against the majesty of the United States, not John F. Kennedy." The president should hold off on any press conferences until quiet had returned to Mississippi, because "there are too many questions you should neither evade nor answer directly." In moving toward action—particularly the deployment of troops—Sorensen gave the president advice that perhaps revealed a glimpse into the White House approach on civil rights that had long frustrated and baffled black leaders. "Keep moving," Sorensen told the president, "but move slowly."

While the president maintained his cool detachment, Martin Luther

King Jr. was in Birmingham headlining the SCLC's annual national convention and strategizing ways to force the White House's hand on civil rights. The SCLC gathering focused on the many indignities in housing, schooling, income, and voting that still oppressed black lives. The organization chose to hold its convention in Birmingham, the most brutal, segregated city in America, to underscore the injustices. Two days after Meredith's latest rebuff in Mississippi, King spoke to some four hundred SCLC members in the Gaston Building auditorium. What began as a fairly ordinary King appearance suddenly turned horrific. Just as King announced that Sammy Davis Jr. would perform at a benefit in New York, a six-foot, two-hundred-pound white man rushed out of his sixth-row seat and stormed onto the stage. As King turned in surprise to face him, the bushy-haired man slugged the five-foot-seven-inch speaker in the face. Keeping true to his pledge of nonviolence, King did not fight back; he took several more blows as the audience sat in stunned silence. Then several men rushed the stage and pulled the assailant away. Later identified as a Nazi Party member, the man said he had become enraged at King's mention of Sammy Davis Jr., because the entertainer was married to a white woman; in his assailant's twisted mind, the civil rights leader deserved a beating because he approved of the mixing of the races. King suffered bruises to his jaw and neck but declined treatment and refused to press charges.

The next day, Bobby Kennedy spoke with an advisor to Mississippi governor Barnett in hopes of a breakthrough at Ole Miss. But nothing in their conversation pointed to a calming of tensions. In court the previous day, Barnett was found in contempt, ordered to admit Meredith to the university within four days or face a $10,000 fine each day afterward and possible arrest. The governor still refused to yield even though he professed not to want jail time or riots in the streets. The ruling only further fired up the masses. The local newspapers published shrieking headlines: THOUSANDS SAID READY TO FIGHT FOR MISSISSIPPI, reported the *Jackson Daily News*. The governor's constituents and rebels throughout the South were eager to rush to the governor's side: ALL SECTIONS VOICE SUPPORT OF BARNETT, the *Clarion-Ledger* declared. The Ku Klux Klan in Anniston, Alabama, site of a flaming Freedom Ride bus in May 1961, pledged to Barnett that hundreds of its members were "on a stand-by alert waiting for your call to protect the state sovereignty of Mississippi." Among the many telegrams pouring into Barnett's office was one from

Birmingham's National States' Rights Party vowing to place its people and funds "at the disposal of your supreme authority as governor." Mississippi now seemed to be sliding toward a catastrophic breakdown of law and order. His options dwindling, Attorney General Robert Kennedy reluctantly admitted: "We better get moving with the military."

At this last moment, President Kennedy finally stepped into the fray. His brother, recognizing Barnett's weakness for deal making, hoped the governor might agree to a resolution he'd actually keep if the president of the United States pressured him to do so. But the president's late gamble was largely an act of desperation against what seemed to be unstoppable momentum toward violence. Joining the president in the Oval Office at 2:30 in the afternoon were his brother, Assistant Attorney General Burke Marshall, and two close White House aides, Kenneth O'Donnell and Arthur Schlesinger. While waiting for a call to go through to Mississippi, Kennedy secretly hit a switch on his desk that signaled his secretary to turn on the Dictaphone recording system; the president had recently installed the device in the Oval Office, the Cabinet Room, and other parts of the White House to preserve his conversations for posterity. Before the governor came on the line, Bobby Kennedy quietly urged his brother on: "Go get him, Johnny boy," and the president in response comically rehearsed his lines: "Governor, this is the President of the United States—not Bobby, not Teddy, not Princess Radziwill," who was Jackie's sister, married to Prince Stanislaw Radziwill. The president's joking conveyed a serious undertone: He hoped that the prestige of the White House could bend the governor to his will.

"Hello? Hello, Governor?" the president said, the Dictaphone recording.

"All right. Yes."

"How are you?"

"Is this...?"

"This is the president," Kennedy said, amiably.

"Oh, well, Mr. President..."

"Well, I'm glad to talk to you, Governor." With no edge or sternness in his voice, the president explained: "I am concerned about this situation down there, as I know—"

Barnett interrupted: "Oh, I should say I am concerned about it, Mr. President. It's a horrible situation."

"Well, now, here's my problem, Governor."

"Yes."

"Listen," the president said, referring to Meredith, "I didn't put him in the university, but on the other hand, under the Constitution, I have to carry out the orders of the . . . carry that order out, and I don't want to do it in any way that causes difficulty to you or to anyone else. But I've got to do it. Now, I'd like to get your help in doing that."

The president maintained his geniality and appealed to reason, as was his nature, but reason held no sway in the irrational world of racial hatred in Mississippi. He listened as Barnett rattled on about wanting more time, the last thing the rapidly deteriorating situation needed. Barnett said a representative of his was planning to fly to Washington the following day for discussions with the attorney general. When the president pressed Barnett on his need to act on the contempt-of-court violation and admit Meredith within three days, the governor said he'd just have to think it over.

"You know what I am up against, Mr. President," Barnett whined. "I took an oath, you know, to abide by the laws of this state."

After the governor rambled on a bit, the president tried to bring the conversation back to the point. "Well, of course the problem is, Governor, that I've got my responsibility, just like you have yours. . . . What I want, would like to do, is to try to work this out in an amicable way. We don't want a lot of people down there getting hurt."

Barnett then praised the professionalism of the representative coming to speak to Bobby. Before signing off, the governor suddenly tried to ingratiate himself to the president. "I appreciate your interest in our poultry program," he said.

President Kennedy, uncertain what to say, stifled a laugh. "Well, we're . . ."

"Thank you so much," Barnett continued.

"Okay, Governor. Thank you."

The president had neither browbeaten Barnett nor issued an ultimatum, and the governor sounded pleased that he got off so easy. "Yes, sir. All right now."

"Bye now," the president said, ending the call.

It was a friendly conversation: Perhaps President Kennedy was too agreeable. He raised only his personal concern over the possible harm to Americans. He scarcely pressured Barnett to bring the mobs into line; indeed, he granted the governor just what he wanted—more time. The

president's reading of the governor was that he was no firebrand and could
be fairly easily bulldozed into compliance when the time came. Turning
to Bobby, he said: "You've been fighting a sofa pillow all week." Barnett,
having emerged from the conversation unscathed, no doubt felt the same
about Kennedy: The president was someone Barnett could dupe—and
that was exactly what he intended to do. Yet Bobby Kennedy remained
leery of the governor, summing him up right after the phone call: "What
a rogue!"

*　*　*

As the afternoon wore on, President Kennedy agonized over peace in
Mississippi. In another phone conversation with Barnett, at 3:15 p.m.,
he demanded to know how the governor intended to maintain law and
order, and Barnett left the president far from confident, saying he'd do
the best he could. "You just don't understand the situation down here," he
explained.

    With the mood darkening, Bobby and Barnett worked out a plan to
admit Meredith to the university. It was another stratagem to dupe the
public, but at least this one didn't require the sham brandishing of weapons. The men agreed that Barnett would go to the campus on Monday to
block Meredith's enrollment while Meredith would go to the state building in Jackson where registrars would enroll him. Barnett would then be
able to cry foul—the federal government tricked him: the deed had been
done against his will, he had fought valiantly against it but lost. Barnett
also gave assurances that several hundred highway patrolmen would
maintain order throughout the state. Speaking with Barnett at 7 p.m. on
Saturday night, President Kennedy came away believing that a satisfactory and safe conclusion was at hand.

    But had the president been in the stands that evening for the football
game between the Ole Miss Rebels and the University of Kentucky Wild-
cats at Jackson's Memorial Stadium, he would have had reason to doubt
the crisis was going to end quietly. At halftime, with Ole Miss leading
7–0, Governor Ross Barnett strode onto the field to a resounding ovation
from more than forty-one thousand spectators, many of them young men
wearing Confederate military caps. A huge Confederate flag—said to be
the largest in the world—floated across the field, carried by a battalion
of marching students. One fan feared that the crowd's roar was mighty
enough to collapse the stadium. From a microphone at the fifty-yard line,

Barnett shrieked: "I love Mississippi! I love her people! Our customs! I love and respect our *heritage*!" The fans burst into wild adulation for their governor, and Barnett was intoxicated by it. Soon afterward, he was on the phone with Bobby Kennedy, his constituents' worship of him swirling in his head, telling the attorney general that James Meredith's admission to the University of Mississippi was off: He simply could not agree to it. When one of his advisors had tried to persuade him to uphold the deal and enroll Meredith, Barnett was adamant. "I can't do it," he said. "Did you see that crowd?"

Hearing the news, John Kennedy phoned his speechwriter Ted Sorensen at Bethesda Naval Hospital: He needed some thoughts for an address to the nation. It was far from clear just yet what such a speech would say; the content and timing would evolve over the next twenty-four hours. Sorensen's initial suggestion was that the president should direct his comments to the people of Mississippi calling for their understanding and peaceful acceptance of the law. Press secretary Pierre Salinger alerted the television networks that the president wanted time for a brief broadcast at 8 p.m. on Sunday. The president realized the speech would also have to explain his reasons for the serious action he was about to undertake. With Mississippi creeping ever closer to chaos, Kennedy resigned himself to one of the toughest decisions of his presidency. The government was not going to back down; whatever Barnett's defiance, Meredith was going to show up on Monday to register. The president no longer trusted the governor's pledge, or his ability, to maintain order; so around midnight on Saturday, assistant attorney general Norbert Schlei showed up at the White House with documents authorizing the deployment of troops and the federalizing of the Mississippi National Guard. With the ranks of the state national guard filled with good ole boys, there was a question whether the men would accept the leadership of the president; the proclamation was, in many respects, a document of faith.

Seated at a table in a small, third-floor study, the president put his pen to the papers, asking Schlei: "Is this pretty much what Ike signed in 1957 with the Little Rock thing?" The Justice Department staffer explained that the language was better than Eisenhower's document; of course, the details were revised for this particular situation. But Schlei told the president, "It's essentially the same." After signing the document, the president got up, turned off the table lamp, and stood for a moment gazing toward the light in the hallway. Suddenly struck by a thought, he rapped his knuckles on the table and said: "You know, that's General Grant's table." Here was a moment of startling unfinished American history: The president had just signed an order to send the army into Mississippi—and he had done so on a piece of furniture belonging to Ulysses S. Grant, the general who led the Union Army to victory over the Confederacy in the Civil War. As Schlei started down the stairs to brief the press on what just took place, the president came sprinting back to the top balustrade and called down: "Don't tell them about General Grant's table."

89

ON SUNDAY MORNING, Robert Kennedy was back on the phone with Governor Barnett who, after having reneged on the previous staged surrender, had come up with an even more outrageous charade; in his new theatrical, the governor wanted to show himself single-handedly standing up to the aggression of the federal government and then being forced at the risk of his own life to back down. Now that federal troops were to be deployed, Barnett wanted to show up on campus with some three hundred Mississippi police and highway patrolmen, read out a proclamation rejecting Meredith, then face a similar force of Army troops with guns drawn. Only then would he step aside. Robert Kennedy rejected the plan as excessively dangerous, and when Barnett balked, the attorney general threatened him with humiliating exposure to his own people. Bobby warned that President Kennedy planned to go on television that night and disclose that the governor had made a deal with him to admit Meredith.

Barnett panicked. "That won't do at all."

Fed up, Bobby was unmoved: "You broke your word to him."

"You don't mean the president is going to say that tonight?" Barnett asked.

"He is."

Bobby had finally gotten Barnett's attention. Groveling and squirming, the governor proposed that Meredith come to the campus that Sunday afternoon when fewer people were around and get placed in a dormitory to await his registration on Monday. Barnett would announce that in the face of overwhelming force from the federal government, he was ceasing his resistance but was still going to fight Meredith's admission in the courts. Bobby gave the governor until 7:30 p.m. to make the situation clear to Mississippians, and the attorney general demanded that Barnett deploy the state Highway Patrol and other security forces to help maintain order along with the U.S. marshals who were soon to roll in.

Gearing up for a showdown, Bobby dispatched Deputy Attorney General Nicholas Katzenbach to Oxford. Flashing back to what befell another one of his men he threw into harm's way in the South—John Seigenthaler, who had been beaten unconscious in Alabama—Bobby bid Katzenbach farewell with a bit of gallows humor. "If things get rough," he quipped, "don't worry about yourself. The president needs a moral issue." While some have condemned Bobby for the callousness of the remark, Arthur Schlesinger contended that the send-off was in fact Bobby's way of expressing deep affection and concern; it was a reflection of the Kennedy penchant for humor in times of stress.

Katzenbach was to help oversee the mobilization of the marshals, a hasty deployment of about 170 men dressed in business suits, white helmets, and bright orange vests that gave them an unthreatening appearance yet robbed them of some authority. As the marshals moved onto the campus on Sunday, taking up position around the university's Lyceum administration building, they were met by at least four hundred students who threw eggs and rocks and chanted, "2-4-1-3, We Hate Kennedy." Around 6 p.m., Katzenbach went out to the Oxford airport to meet Meredith, who had flown in from Memphis "looking neat as ever and carrying a thin, tan briefcase." Meredith rode in silence toward the campus in the sedan's backseat, crushed between Katzenbach and John Doar, listening to himself referred to on the Border Patrol radio as the "subject." His convoy soon arrived at Baxter Hall, a dormitory near Lyceum, where he was installed in a room with two cots and a large, beat-up bureau. Here he was to wait out the night protected by twenty-four marshals. Like any student, he closed his door, took out his books, and started to study.

In Washington, the president postponed his speech until after Barnett spoke on statewide radio in Mississippi. But just before Barnett went on the air, word came that the state Highway Patrol were pulling out on orders of the governor, leaving the marshals to fend for themselves and preserve the peace in rapidly deteriorating conditions. The departure of the Highway Patrol sent a message to the gathering mob. The governor's personal representative on the scene, state senator George Yarbrough, tracked down Katzenbach and told him of the patrol's departure. "You have occupied this university," he declared, "and now you can have it. What happens from now on is the responsibility of the federal government."

Katzenbach recognized the betrayal and was outraged: "No, you can't do that! That would be a horrible mistake!" He stressed that all law enforcement officers had to stay; without them, violence was inevitable. "Call the governor," Katzenbach demanded. "He'll tell you that the state Highway Patrol is meant to preserve law and order here. And he has promised that they would."

At 7:30 p.m., Barnett was on the air, telling his fellow Mississippians that he was shocked to have just learned that the attorney general of the United States had sneaked James Meredith onto the campus of the University of Mississippi. He implied that he could do nothing because U.S. armed forces—the "oppressive power" of the federal government—had subdued him. Surrendering but defiant, he told his rebel state: "My heart says 'never,' but my calm judgment abhors the bloodshed that would follow." He bellowed about state sovereignty but acknowledged he had to give in to the feds' insurmountable dominance. He pleaded for order on the streets and in the same breath stirred his listeners to rebel: "I know we are now completely surrounded by armed forces and that we are physically overpowered. I know that our principles remain true, but we must at all odds preserve the peace and avoid bloodshed."

Barnett had barely finished his broadcast when Bobby Kennedy was on the line, irate over the withdrawal of the Highway Patrol. Bobby again threatened to expose Barnett's backdoor dealings with the federal government, and the governor soon had Senator Yarbrough on the phone, and Yarbrough was reversing his withdrawal of the patrolmen. In their absence the mob was emboldened, and the pretense of civil society had begun to collapse. Coke bottles set aflame with gasoline streaked through the air; a rock knocked a marshal to the ground; Molotov cocktails exploded; pipes flew toward the helmeted men. In a bid to disperse the crowd, Chief Marshal James McShane ordered his troops to strap on their gas masks and fire tear gas cartridges and hurl gas and smoke grenades.

At this moment, President Kennedy was preparing to go on air from the Oval Office. Needing a pick-me-up, the president had summoned Max Jacobson, the physician known as Dr. Feelgood, who administered amphetamine injections. Jacobson, on call for the president, had flown down on short notice from New York in a twin-engine Cessna. Speaking of the Mississippi crisis, Kennedy told the doctor: "This one is a ball-breaker." His speech had been rescheduled for 10 p.m. Washington time, 8 p.m. in Oxford. Ted Sorensen had dragged himself out of his hospital bed and come to the White House to work on a draft. But while preparing the text, Sorensen hadn't kept up with the fast-moving events on the streets in Oxford. As presidential aide Arthur Schlesinger put it, "Kennedy's speech was designed for a different occasion. It assumed that Meredith had arrived on campus in relative tranquility and appealed to white Mississippi's sense of honor."

The president was in the Oval Office about to go on the air when Robert Kennedy in the Cabinet Room next door got word from Oxford that tear gas had been fired, and a riot was in the making. He told the other aides: "I'll do something to try to stop the president." But it was too late. Inside the Oval Office, the president was already speaking into the television cameras. "Mr. James Meredith is now in residence on the campus of the University of Mississippi," the president told the nation. He explained that this fulfilled a court order permitting the admission of Meredith, and he noted that "thus far" this was accomplished without the use of the National Guard or other troops. He spoke for several minutes on the rule of law and the court process, and praised other state-supported Southern universities for already having admitted "students, regardless of race," including the universities of Virginia, North Carolina, Georgia, Florida, Texas, Louisiana, Tennessee, Arkansas, and Kentucky. And he closed by praising Mississippi for its accomplishments and courage and asking citizens of the state to uphold law and order. "It lies in your courage to accept those laws with which you disagree as well as those which you admire," the president urged. "The eyes of the nation and the world are upon you."

The speech, lasting eight minutes, contained none of the passion that Kennedy had displayed when he condemned the burning of black churches. If he were still outraged by the behavior of segregationists, he kept it hidden. Legality, not emotion, guided the president from the first words of his speech: "The orders of the court...are beginning to be carried out." And from there he spoke in pallid phrases, focusing on the law and not on the meaning or morality of segregation. He shied away from portraying himself as the nation's leader on arguably its most important domestic issue. Instead he played the role of top cop.

90

BY THE TIME President Kennedy arose from behind his Oval Office desk, Mississippi was in a state of insurrection: His anemic words stood in sharp, ironic contrast to the frenzy in the streets. His unwillingness to step forward on an issue of right and wrong had caused him to mimic the mistakes of his predecessor, Dwight Eisenhower, a failed civil rights leader; both men had refused to challenge racism on moral grounds and waited too long to act with force to uphold the Constitution and the rulings of the courts.

Now the mob's fury spread through the Mississippi campus. Newsmen and photographers were attacked for covering the rampage. A TV cameraman from Dallas staggered back to his car after a pummeling. A reporter from Louisiana and a photographer from Atlanta were beaten to the ground. When a chemistry professor tried to retrieve the photographer's camera he was knocked to the pavement. A hail of bricks, stones, and bottles—some flaming, others filled with acid—flew through the air hitting or just missing the marshals. A two-foot-long lead pipe hurtled through the air, landing on a marshal's helmet and sending him to the ground. The rioters' howls filled the darkness. More marshals arrived in a convoy of Border Patrol vehicles, while those already in place fired repeated volleys of tear gas—to little effect, because the wind carried the fumes in the wrong direction.

Deputy Attorney General Katzenbach was on the phone regularly with the White House and Justice Department, using the only communication device available in the Lyceum building, an ordinary pay phone.

"We put a dime in and made a collect call," he said. He kept two lines open, one to the attorney general and another to the president, unwilling to surrender them to the hordes of reporters needing a phone to call in their stories. At one point he had to run off but needed to keep his line open. So he told a nearby reporter: "Here, hold this phone," and the surprised newsman had a few moments with the president himself.

As the night wore on, gunfire erupted, and a wounded border patrolman fell to the ground. A student darting by had taken a bullet in the hand, raising rumors the marshals had opened fire. Edwin Guthman of the Justice Department, who was on the ground in Oxford, claimed the marshals never used their revolvers; others have said warning shots might have been fired, and some people might have been hit by marshals' bullets. Uncertainty inflamed the chaos. The body of a reporter for the French news agency Agence France-Presse was discovered on the ground near a dormitory a little distance from the main rioting, with a bullet in his back. A jukebox repairman was standing on a cinder block taking in the tumult when a bullet hit him in the forehead; he died at the scene. The marshals began to panic. Tear gas supplies were running low, and four in their ranks had been shot.

With conditions looking bleak, the Kennedys again resorted to dark humor; at one point the president said: "I haven't had such an interesting time since the Bay of Pigs." His brother the attorney general, taking responsibility for the lawlessness, joked that he was going to lose his job like former CIA director Allen Dulles, who was fired by the president after the botched Cuba invasion and was now teaching at a university. Reciting an imagined press release, Bobby said, "The attorney general announced today he's joining Allen Dulles at Princeton University" to a burst of laughter from aides.

Levity was fleeting, however. A rumor reached the White House that rampaging students had fought their way into Baxter Hall, where Meredith was lodged; in fact, a small band was lobbing bottles at the dorm building. Nonetheless, in Washington, a presidential aide voiced a horror on everyone's mind: What if the mob got to Meredith and the night ended in a lynching?

The president got Barnett on the line at the governor's mansion in Jackson. Barnett was so shattered by the turmoil in Oxford that he was unable to pick up the phone because his hands were trembling uncontrollably. But the governor wasn't so devastated he couldn't resume his fight with the president. When his daughter handed him the phone, he told Kennedy the best option now was to remove Meredith from the campus; of course, Meredith's removal would be a sign of a federal retreat and would allow Barnett to declare victory. Still hesitant to send in troops, the president advised Barnett to take charge and restore order.

"We can't consider moving Meredith as long as the, you know, there's a riot outside, 'cause he wouldn't be safe."

"Sir?" Barnett said.

Kennedy repeated himself: "We couldn't consider moving Meredith if you, if you haven't been able to restore order outside. That's the problem, Governor."

Barnett then tried to push the president, saying he'd go to Oxford himself and stand in the middle of the mob and shout through a megaphone that the president had agreed to remove Meredith. The implication was that Barnett's triumph would calm the crowd. The men then talked around each other for a while until Barnett again implored: "Mr. President, please. Can't you give an order up there to remove Meredith?"

The president lost his cool: "How can I remove him, Governor," he erupted, "when there's a riot in the street, and he may step out of that building and something happen to him? I can't remove him under those conditions.... We've gotta get somebody up there now to get order, and stop the firing and the shooting. Then you and I will talk on the phone about Meredith."

91

AT ABOUT 10 p.m. in Oxford, midnight in Washington, the president ordered the Mississippi National Guard, now under his command, to head out to the campus. Under Captain Murry Falkner, a cousin of novelist William Faulkner, some sixty-five men left the Oxford National Guard Armory in a convoy and headed to the university just a mile away. Their jeeps navigated through a hail of rocks and bottles and gunfire before the soldiers took up their positions around Lyceum. Fears that the Southern guards would refuse the president's orders were quickly dispelled: On the way to Lyceum, fourteen guardsmen had been badly injured by the mob. As Captain Falkner said: "It's hard to feel brotherly love toward someone who is trying to kill you."

The rampaging mob forced the president to take tougher action. Sinking into a morass he had wished to sidestep, Kennedy gave orders to send in troops on standby in Memphis. The 503rd Military Police Battalion was a fully integrated elite team of riot fighters; it had blacks in the ranks and black officers in command of Southern whites. The military brass suddenly worried that black riot fighters would only incite the mob, so it ordered those troops to stay at the base camp at Memphis. When Deputy Attorney General Katzenbach learned of the decision, he phoned both Bobby Kennedy and Secretary of the Army Cyrus Vance. "This is just crazy!" he told them. Segregating the troops at a time like this sent the wrong message, he believed, and it also diminished the effectiveness of the unit. The men trained together and knew each other's strengths. "Don't do it!" he urged his superiors. His pleas were ignored.

Sensing a black outcry, *Jet* magazine sent reporters out to talk to the confined soldiers. One staff sergeant said: "They wouldn't pull us back in wartime...We're professional soldiers and we're supposed to fight anywhere." A private sent a note of protest to military headquarters: "In stunned disbelief and embarrassment, in resentment and resignation," he wrote, "we stood and watched the 'white troops' move off to the 'battle' while a collective voice in our collective souls screams out 'but, this is my fight, too, this is my issue; the wrong, the hurt was done to James Meredith, my forefathers, my children and myself.'"

To the president's annoyance, the troops in Memphis weren't ready to move out immediately. After his speech, the soldiers had gone off alert believing tranquility reigned in Oxford. All they had at hand were nightsticks, and it took them hours to gather their weapons and ammunition. As the time dragged on, Kennedy became frantic. Getting Army Secretary Vance on the phone, the president screamed: "Where's the Army? Where are they? Why aren't they moving?" Vance kept offering optimistic reports to cover the delays. He told the president: "They're leaving in twenty minutes," Bobby recalled. "We'd call twenty minutes later, and they hadn't even arrived to get ready to leave." On another occasion, Vance said: "They're ready to go now." But Bobby soon learned "they hadn't been called out of their barracks to get into the helicopters yet." Vance called to say: "They're in the helicopters now," but Bobby knew "they were just forming up." When Vance said, "The first helicopter's leaving and will be there in forty minutes," Bobby knew: "The first helicopter went in the air and then circled and waited for the rest of the helicopters."

Troops of the 503rd MP Battalion finally landed by helicopter at Oxford airport at 12:30 a.m. and moved into position to back up the marshals and the National Guard. Skirmishes flared through the night, but the battle of Oxford was finally winding down, after two were killed and hundreds injured. For Bobby Kennedy the end couldn't have come soon enough; he described the long hours of September 30 as "the worst night I ever spent." At 5:30 a.m., President Kennedy turned in, having engaged in the Mississippi crisis far more than he ever anticipated. "The president of the United States, perhaps for the first time, had direct, continuous communications with a scene of violence," observed Robert Kennedy's press secretary, Edwin Guthman.

* * *

On Monday morning, October 1, James Meredith wrote, "Mississippi and I awoke to a new era." He had slept through the night, waking only now and then to the sounds of shooting and tumult. He believed he was protected and was unafraid; this was not a battle pitting white Southerners against James Meredith—it was white Mississippi against the federal government. "For that reason," he said, "I had won the war before it even started."

Just before 8 a.m., Meredith was dressed in a gray suit and red tie and ready to go to Lyceum to register for his classes. When Chief U.S. Marshal James McShane and John Doar arrived, the marshal asked the new student to put on a different tie; the blood-red one, he said, was provocative, and Meredith acquiesced. Climbing into a marshal's car, Meredith dusted the shattered glass off the seat—all the windows were broken— and rode to the registrar's office. At Lyceum, he filled out forms and paid his fees under the eye of the university registrar, Robert Ellis, who "seemed to be in a state of shock and defiance," the student recalled.

When Meredith came out of the office, he found a black janitor standing in the hallway. As he passed, the man lightly tapped the new student with his broom and stared into his eyes. "He was delivering probably one of the most important messages that I ever got at Ole Miss," Meredith wrote in his memoir. "The message was, 'You are not alone. We are looking after you twenty-four hours a day.'"

Wishing to ensure the peace and send a message to any segregationists still plotting violence, President Kennedy unleashed a massive flow of federal troops into Oxford; by week's end, thirty-one thousand soldiers were in the small town of about six thousand residents. One company commander told historian William Doyle: "We had enough men to capture the whole South." The president "must have seen a complete revolution coming," he recalled. "He must have been scared to death."

If the Battle of Oxford was a victory for blacks, it was a narrow one. The university had admitted one student and others were to follow. Integration of white universities, proceeding in a halting fashion, got a needed push. A model of grudging acceptance was taking shape and helping, however slowly, to change ingrained prejudice. Even fierce segregationist senator James Eastland of Mississippi surrendered to the implacable currents of change and enrolled his son in a recently desegregated prep school in Virginia. But the federal action in Mississippi was not framed as a battle to change minds: From beginning to end, John Kennedy sought only to maintain order and uphold the law. He expressed no outrage over the indignity of Mississippi's segregated classrooms; he did not speak out about the moral blight that segregation imposed on the character of the nation.

Having returned from Birmingham, Martin Luther King Jr. followed the rioting in Oxford on his television in Atlanta. While pleased by the admission of Meredith—he later praised Meredith's courage and "the agonizing loneliness that characterizes the life of the pioneer"—King was saddened that the president missed an opportunity to embrace the larger truths of the crisis. The president stopped short of leading the nation beyond the shackles of its racist past. Throughout the conflict President Kennedy never once spoke to Meredith; he never praised the student's ambition, nor the virtue of his quest. King gleaned nothing in the president's speech that transcended the legal issues of the Mississippi crisis. During the conflict, the president negotiated with a white supremacist who denied constitutional rights, while the courageous black student at the center of the dispute was largely ignored. In King's eyes, the blacks whose lives were at stake were made to "feel like pawns in a white man's political game."

92

IF PRESIDENT KENNEDY wanted to focus on other matters after Mississippi, he was soon handed a dreadful opportunity. On October 16, barely two weeks after the riot in Oxford, the president and the attorney general gazed in shock at aerial reconnaissance photographs showing an array of Soviet ballistic missiles in a clearing in Cuba. Bobby Kennedy—hotheaded but rarely given to cursing—cried: "Oh shit. Shit! Shit! Those sons a bitches Russians." CIA photo analysts estimated the missiles could travel more than a thousand miles and were capable of carrying nuclear warheads. The potential horror sank in: within the missiles' range and firepower lay ninety million Americans. Suddenly, the rioting in Mississippi became an infinitesimal matter beside the fear of nuclear Armageddon. But Bobby Kennedy, evidently still smarting over the Meredith showdown, offered a wisecrack to ease the tension: "Can they hit Oxford, Mississippi?"

The president and his team of advisors debated how to respond: a preemptive air strike to take out the missiles, a path favored by some hawkish generals; an invasion of Cuba, also at the top of the hawks' list; a blockade of the island, preventing further Soviet access to Cuba and offering a less belligerent response. Forced into a particularly difficult position, the president had to battle both the Soviet leadership and some of his own military chiefs aching to unleash U.S. bombs. As he told his close advisor Kenneth O'Donnell: "Those brass hats have one great advantage in their favor. If we listen to them, and do what they want us to do, none of us will be alive later to tell them they were wrong." Bobby Kennedy emerged as the wisest, most clear-sighted of the president's advisors. Arguing for the blockade, he thought it would show that the United States was serious about removing the missiles from Cuba and allow the Soviets a chance to maneuver out of the conflict and save the world from a nuclear showdown.

A lesson from the Oxford crisis hung over the Cuba deliberations. The Kennedys' frustrations with the troop deployment in Oxford raised questions about the efficiency of the U.S. military, concerns that were partly behind their hesitation to launch an air strike on Cuba. Taking out the missiles required quick, precise, and thorough action, and it was unclear whether a U.S. strike force was up to the task.

On Monday night, October 22, a solemn President Kennedy spoke to one hundred million Americans on television, revealing that the Soviet Union had missiles in Cuba capable of launching a nuclear attack on Washington, D.C., and other U.S. cities. In response, he told the nation, the United States was setting up a blockade of the island to prevent a further Soviet buildup and demanding that the existing missiles be dismantled and removed. Kennedy also sent a letter to Khrushchev through Soviet ambassador Anatoly Dobrynin, asserting that the United States would do whatever was necessary to protect its security. And a waiting game began. At first Khrushchev gave no reply, then came a belligerent letter to the White House rejecting the United States' ultimatum. In his reply, President Kennedy refused to back down. As the frightening days dragged on, the president and his men barely slept, the trauma showing on their worn faces. "The danger and concern we all felt hung like a cloud over us all," Bobby Kennedy jotted on a notepad, describing one meeting. The president's "eyes were tense, almost gray, and we just stared at each other across the table. Was the world on the brink of a holocaust and had we done something wrong?"

Bobby Kennedy went to work through back channels, just as he and the president had done with Governor Barnett, devising deals with the Soviets that would embarrass, and compromise, both sides if they became public. In private meetings with Soviet ambassador Dobrynin, Bobby brokered a secret agreement: If the Soviets withdrew their missiles, the United States would agree not to invade Cuba; but Bobby offered more: Once the crisis was over, the United States was prepared to pull its missiles out of Turkey. The current crisis was prompted in part by U.S. deployment of intermediate-range Jupiter missiles south of the Soviet Union in nearby Turkey. "The Americans had surrounded our country with military bases and threatened us with nuclear weapons," Soviet premier Khrushchev had declared, explaining his missile deployment in Cuba, "and now they would learn just what it feels like to have enemy missiles pointing at [them]." On Saturday night, October 27, Bobby laid out the American demands in a meeting with Dobrynin in his Justice Department office: The missile bases had to be removed immediately; the Soviets had to commit to this action by the next day, Sunday; if the missiles were not carted off, the United States would take action to destroy them. When Dobrynin asked about the U.S. missiles in Turkey, Bobby agreed that after a period of time they would be removed.

Back at the White House, Bobby went upstairs to the family quarters where the president was eating chicken with his close aide Dave Powers. In a gloomy recounting of his evening with Dobrynin, Bobby outlined where the crisis stood. The men agreed that there was little chance Khrushchev would respond swiftly and positively to Bobby's challenge. Plans were made for a meeting in the morning to discuss an air strike on Cuba. It was, in Powers's recollection, "the most depressing hour that any of us spent in the White House during the President's time there." But again, in the midst of that darkest moment, the president relied on humor to lighten the mood. Seeing Powers busily eating and drinking, he called out to his friend: "God, Dave, the way you're eating up all that chicken and drinking up all my wine, anybody would think it was your last meal."

"The way Bobby's been talking," Dave replied, "I thought it *was* my last meal."

On Sunday morning, to everyone's surprise, Khrushchev blinked. Speaking on Soviet radio, the premier declared: "In order to save the world, we must retreat." President Kennedy received a secret note from the Soviet premier accepting the United States' offer to remove its Jupiter missiles in several months and agreeing to keep the agreement out of the public eye.

* * *

With the world sitting on the brink of possible annihilation, President Kennedy had felt a heavy burden of personal responsibility: The fate of millions sat on his shoulders. During the crisis he had met with a group of journalists attending a foreign policy conference at the State Department and had spoken ad lib "with far deeper feelings" about the situation than anyone expected, according to his aide Kenneth O'Donnell. "I don't think it is unfair to say," the president told the journalists, "that the United States, and the world, is now passing through one of its most critical periods. Our major problem, over all, is the survival of our country, the protection of its vital interests, without the beginning of the third and perhaps the last war."

* * *

The showdown with Khrushchev matured Kennedy in powerful and unseen ways. Having followed the misguided strategy of his advisors to the Bay of Pigs catastrophe, the president this time had the fortitude to stand up to his military generals, who had insisted on immediate air strikes and an invasion; although always deliberative and self-questioning, the president emerged from the missile crisis with new political confidence; he'd found the moral courage to challenge his toughest opponents and stand on his own on matters of grave importance to the nation. These lessons would serve him well on the domestic battlefield of civil rights.

93

PRESIDENT KENNEDY'S POPULARITY soared after the Cuban missile crisis, with his approval rating hitting 74 percent. The press lauded his level-headed, firm diplomacy, and his staff glorified him. "Whatever John Kennedy felt he had to prove—determination, courage, will, the skillful use of power—he had proved it: to the world, the country, and to himself," aide Richard Goodwin observed. But still politically cautious, the president ignored pleas from black leaders to issue the promised and long-awaited executive order on housing discrimination. Listening instead to his political advisors, Kennedy refused to announce the order before the November 1962 midterm elections, fearing it could cut into Democratic success at the polls. In the election, the Democrats picked up four seats in the Senate and lost only four seats in the House. In the South, Mississippi and Alabama—the traditional white supremacist strongholds—showed the most resistance to the moderate trends sweeping the rest of Dixie. Results throughout the South, however, indicated widening opportunities to push for civil rights. Pollster Louis Harris told the president the South stood on the cusp of a new political era. "The entire Democratic Party of the South is changing rapidly into a far more moderate and liberal party," he said.

After the elections, the president finally made good on his pledge to eliminate discrimination in federal housing with a stroke of a pen—about twenty-nine months since he first broached the idea on the campaign trail in June 1960. "His desire was to make a low-key announcement that would be as little divisive as possible," his aide Ted Sorensen recalled. "He found the lowest-key time possible on the evening of November 20, 1962. It was the night before he and much of the country closed shop for the long Thanksgiving weekend." The housing order was the second part of the president's opening statement at his regular press conference; first, he brought reporters up-to-date on the missile crisis, which was still gradually playing out a month after its resolution. In announcing the executive order, which barred discrimination in government housing, the president focused on the policy and legality of the measure; he expressed no outrage over the hardships blacks faced in housing, or in any other areas of discrimination. Speaking as the nation's top bureaucrat, he said: "Our national policy is equal opportunity for all and the Federal Government will continue to take such legal and proper steps as it may to achieve the realization of this goal." There was no passion, no fire, in his voice. When asked by a reporter to elaborate, the president spoke very briefly, as if happy to dust off his hands after having taken care of a bothersome task, concluding: "In any case, it's sound public, constitutional policy and we've done it."

The president's announcement outraged Southern Democratic senators. Mississippi's John Stennis claimed the executive branch had pulled off "an audacious usurpation of power." Martin Luther King Jr. initially praised the declaration, deeming it "morally right," but after examining it more closely, he was disappointed it wasn't retroactive and that it didn't have stronger means to enforce compliance. Writing in the *Amsterdam News* in December, he said the measure was a "good-faith step in the right direction" but didn't live up to expectations.

* * *

With the approach of Christmas, the president invited a group of top black leaders to a meeting at the White House. He wanted to engage with the black activists not on matters affecting their own lives in America but on developments in distant lands: The discussion was to focus on aid for impoverished Africa. Several African countries had gained their independence from their colonial masters in the early 1960s, and Kennedy wished to encourage their progress and keep them from falling into the Soviet orbit. The leaders convening at the White House were Martin

Luther King Jr., Roy Wilkins of the NAACP, James Farmer of CORE, and Dorothy Height of the National Council of Negro Women. No one from the Student Nonviolent Coordinating Committee was invited; its activities were too aggressive for the president.

The black leaders, wishing to be a force not only in America but overseas, proposed a "Marshall Plan" for Africa, reminiscent of the economic recovery program for Europe after World War II, and the president expressed his willingness to consider it. Eager to speak on global issues, President Kennedy was generous with his time. The meeting, initially scheduled to last just a half hour, expanded into the evening. The president disappeared for a little while to fulfill his duty to light the White House Christmas tree; but then he was back. The gathering, lasting three hours, as *Jet* magazine reported, was "the longest conference ever held by Negroes with a U.S. President in the White House."

But the president's abundant time didn't make up for the absence of substantive discussion of issues dearest to the leaders' hearts: the conditions of blacks in America. While encouraged by the movement toward independence in Africa, the American activists couldn't help comparing advancement overseas to their own plight at home. Several months earlier, King had declared that "the electrifying progress being made by peoples of Africa" only highlighted "the sluggish pace of change in our own nation." At the White House, the president's visitors were either too shy, or respectful, to redirect the conversation to their immediate concerns; in the few moments devoted to domestic issues, the president reiterated that he was not going to consider civil rights legislation; he was sticking to his strategy to steer clear of such a divisive course. Afterward, the leaders fumed anonymously to *Jet* reporter Simeon Booker: "Negroes want their freedom now in America," said one. "We've got to stop begging Kennedy for this and that," said another. "We've got to start demanding our rights." Martin Luther King Jr., unafraid to put his name on his grievance, told a reporter: "[We] still have not had a strong voice from the White House dealing with the moral issues" of civil rights.

* * *

As 1962 came to an end, Martin Luther King Jr. was despondent over progress on civil rights. If the president had temporarily awakened, he was now slumbering again. In 1962, King complained in the *Nation*, "civil rights was displaced as the dominant issue in domestic politics." He conceded that the Cuban missile crisis understandably "tended to dwarf all other issues." But even still, the domestic conversation led by the White House and supported by the press concentrated on tax reform and trade legislation to the detriment of civil rights. After "thundering events in Oxford, Miss., and Albany, Ga., captured public attention," the president was once again "aloof." And following his leadership, the nation was aloof.

Playing presidential educator, King sought to instruct Kennedy on what he needed to know about the South on the eve of 1963. "The Administration," he said, "has misunderstood the forces at play." As a Southerner and a man close to the shifting tides in the region, King claimed insight that the White House lacked. In his view, the South was splitting apart: One large swath was ready for change, exemplified by a growing white chorus that recognized that progress in the modern world required integration and an end to discrimination. This prospect was not unknown to the president; it was substantially what pollster Louis Harris had already conveyed to him. "The simple and arresting truth that became clear in 1962," King explained, "is that significant elements of the South have come to see that segregation has placed the whole region socially, educationally, and economically behind the rest of the nation." The momentum for change was beginning to show up in the election of moderate leaders in several areas of the South. King did not diminish the fact that the other, white supremacist parts of the region were still "adamantly opposed to any but the most trivial alterations." Addressing the president directly, King said: "The Administration should not seek to fashion policies for [the segregationist South]; it should place its weight behind the dynamic South, encouraging and facilitating its progressive development."

King put the choice in terms the president could understand: If Kennedy wanted to lead the nation to economic invincibility, he needed to drive the South into the modern era. "The South is fissuring along a seam which divides the industrializing regions from the stagnating, backward, agricultural areas," King argued. Economic necessity was motivating the South's new social and political attitudes. If old customs produced social tensions and inadequate schools and poorly trained workers then companies were likely to be uninterested in locating there. "In short," King said, "communities have learned that they cannot live in the past and enjoy the fruits of the present." King hoped to impress upon the president that he was at a "historic crossroad." The changes in the South demanded that the administration take bold action. "In place of timorous steps for the Old South," King urged, "the government should turn to the New South."

The year 1963, King declared, could be the year of civil rights legislation: The time had arrived when the president, if he were not lethargic, could vanquish opposition in Congress to enact a historic new law that fully protected the rights of twenty million citizens. Imploring the president to reach for his better angel, King reminded him of the moral weight that lay upon his shoulders. "Throughout our history," he said, "the moral decision has always been the correct decision." Thus it was in 1776 when the nation sought to be free, and again in 1863 when Lincoln freed the slaves, and yet again in the 1940s when the world fought fascism. "The correct decision in 1963 will make it a genuine turning point in human rights," King said. "One hundred years ago a President, tortured by doubt, finally ended slavery and a new American society took shape." President Lincoln had hoped that all of America—white and black—would be free of slavery. But King lamented: "Segregation, the evil heritage of slavery, remains."

PART FIVE

"IT OFTEN HELPS ME TO BE PUSHED"

94

IN THE WINTER darkness a week before Christmas, 1962, a carload of rowdy whites breezed past the Bethel Baptist Church in Birmingham, Alabama. As the car streaked by, a bundle of at least six sticks of dynamite flew out the window. In the church basement, a dozen black children were rehearsing a Christmas play. Inside the nearby parsonage, the pastor's wife, Isabell Provitt, had just turned away from a front window. Seconds later, that window shattered, and the porch and part of the roof collapsed. The pastor's wife was thrown into a state of shock. "I felt like the house was falling in," she told a reporter for *Jet* magazine, adding she felt blessed to have moved away from the window at the last second. "If it hadn't been for God, I wouldn't be talking about it now." The blast jolted another church house nearby. Two infants asleep in the bombed houses were rushed to the hospital, their little bodies pocked by glass shards. The windows in the church basement were blown out and plaster flew off the walls; stained glass windows upstairs shattered. The young thespians at rehearsal were shaken but unhurt.

Bethel Baptist had been the base of the militant Reverend Fred Shuttlesworth; his activism was so intense he fell out of favor with his congregation and moved to a church in Cincinnati, Ohio, but he was still immersed in fighting racial injustice in Birmingham. The new pastor, V. C. Provitt, couldn't explain the bombing. "The church has been going along nicely and hasn't done anything to anybody," he observed. But even though Reverend Provitt kept a low profile, the church was still a symbol of activism.

Birmingham was known as Bombingham for its many attacks on black churches and homes and individuals—more than fifty unsolved racial bombings since the end of World War II. The attacks were a symptom of the intense bigotry and hatred in what Martin Luther King Jr. described as the most segregated city in America. But some whites were leaning toward moderation, believing that integration was inevitable and that they needed to live in peace with the black community. Some local leaders urged an end to the violence and adherence to federal law demanding admission of blacks to white schools. The city commission had declared that the community centers it had closed to prevent integration of the parks would be reopened. Local newspapers campaigned for an end to racial hostilities.

These aspirations, however, were undercut by thugs launching dynamite from cars and by the brutal tactics of Birmingham's racist public safety commissioner, Eugene "Bull" Connor, and by the state's newly elected governor, George Wallace. The new governor, scheduled to take office in January 1963, had won election on his promises of staunch defiance of the federal courts and his personal pledge to prevent black students from sullying the state's all-white campuses. If Alabama was forced to integrate its schools, Wallace was prepared for rioting as fierce as Mississippi's.

To Martin Luther King Jr. the Bethel bombing was proof of the violent, narrow-minded culture of Birmingham, a way of life that had to be confronted and changed. Seeking to reemerge as a protest leader, King had already set his sights on challenging the city's rigid segregation rules. He fired off an urgent telegram to President Kennedy signaling his impatience. Declaring that he was "shocked by the bombing," he warned: "If such acts of violence go unchecked and the Gestapo-like methods of the police officials are not halted, we may see in this city a tragic and devastating racial holocaust." His dire tone was meant to rattle the president's known aversion to bad publicity. To audiences at home and abroad, racial violence only reflected poorly on Kennedy's leadership. As King plotted his Birmingham strategy, he targeted the president as much as local officials. If real change were to come, it had to be decreed from Washington, and King had to awaken Kennedy from his slumber on civil rights.

95

IN THE SECOND week of January 1963, Martin Luther King Jr. and ten associates landed at the Savannah, Georgia, airport and headed out to a secret meeting site near the city. Two undercover FBI agents followed the group's movements. By listening in on the phone conversations of Stanley Levison, the white lawyer and close King aide, the FBI had become aware that a meeting was to take place in the area, although agents had been unable to decipher its purpose. Leaving the airport, the black leaders converged on a building near Savannah on the site of a historic Congregationalist retreat. After the Civil War, the site had housed the Dorchester Academy, a school for freed slaves. Now all that remained of the academy was a boys' dormitory, a stately two-story structure built in Georgian Revival style. The building, known as the Dorchester Center, had become a training center for nonviolent protest and voter education under the guidance of the Southern Christian Leadership Conference.

Gathering inside the dormitory, the civil rights leaders settled in to discuss a dangerous operation: a large-scale assault on segregation in Birmingham, Alabama. Among the participants in the conclave, in addition to King and Levison, were the SCLC's executive director Wyatt Walker, King's friend and prison-cell inmate the Reverend Ralph Abernathy, Jack O'Dell of the SCLC's New York office, and the Reverend Fred Shuttlesworth, the fearless authoritarian who was instrumental in targeting Birmingham for change.

Shuttlesworth, who had founded the Alabama Christian Movement for Human Rights in 1956, had fought for black equality in Birmingham for years, ignoring significant personal risk. Known to be tactless, prickly, and egocentric, he was a formidable opponent to segregationists. In his Christmas sermon at Bethel Baptist Church in 1956, he declared: "If it takes being killed to get integration I'll do just that thing, for God is with me all the way." That same night, while he was resting on his bed, talking to a church deacon, thugs lobbed six sticks of dynamite at his house. The explosion blew Shuttlesworth off the bed, shattering the frame and box springs; the mattress padding saved him, but the deacon and two of Shuttlesworth's children were injured. "I knew they were intendin' to kill me," Shuttlesworth recalled, "and yet I had the sense enough to know that I wouldn't get hurt, heard somethin' say, 'Not yet.'"

A year later, when Shuttlesworth marched his children to the all-white Phillips High School insisting that they be admitted, he was beaten to the ground by angry whites wearing brass knuckles and swinging bicycle chains and clubs. As Shuttlesworth lay nearly unconscious he heard what he deemed a divine whispering: "You can't die here. Get up. I got a job for you to do." Somehow he pulled himself onto his feet and made his way back to his car and got away, but not before the car windows were smashed and his wife had been stabbed in the hip. As historian Glenn T. Eskew has observed, Shuttlesworth's survival was regarded by the pastor himself and other activists as proof of "God's direct intervention on behalf of the civil rights struggle in Birmingham."

Bethel Baptist was bombed again the following year. A guard stationed outside the parsonage managed to grab the dynamite, drop it in the middle of the street, and run before it detonated; the blast shattered the church windows.

Shuttlesworth's ardor for reforming Birmingham society hadn't cooled after his move to Cincinnati in 1961. The rabble-rousing reverend decided that a new strategy was in order: It was necessary, he believed, to incite the irascible public safety commissioner Bull Connor to acts of brutality in order to attract wide publicity; only then might the federal government be stirred to abolish segregation. The next step in Shuttlesworth's strategy was to attract Martin Luther King Jr. and his Southern Christian Leadership Conference to help lead a news-making confrontation. "The two forces should be met," Shuttlesworth reasoned. "So it was at my invitation, my personal invitation...that Dr. King and Ralph Abernathy and the SCLC boys agreed to come in."

Inside the Dorchester Center, the men began to strategize. The SCLC's Walker laid out the master plan for the Birmingham campaign that included sit-ins, business boycotts, mass marches and jailings, and a national call for reinforcements. Particularly effective, King believed, were boycotts of white businesses. It was lamentable, he believed, that blacks were welcome to spend their money at white establishments, but if they needed to use the restroom they had to leave and find a toilet elsewhere. As King observed, "We can't all go to jail but can all keep our money in our pockets and out of the downtown merchants' pockets." If the department store owners—influential figures in Birmingham society—felt their bottom lines pinched by a boycott, they were more likely to see the wisdom in listening to black demands.

Walker labeled the Birmingham strategy Project C, for confrontation, and the leaders focused on careful, elaborate organization. Committees sprang up for telephoning, transportation, food, jail visitations. "We were sort of working like the French Underground," Walker said. Special measures were needed to keep the police and city officials from learning of the campaign's plans. "Almost anybody who was known to be connected with the movement, their phones were tapped," Walker recalled. So the leaders needed code names. "Dr. King's code name was JFK," Walker said. "Abernathy was Dean Rusk." For himself, Walker took the name Bobby Kennedy.

The Birmingham action belonged to King and Shuttlesworth and their organizations, and the two men agreed to make joint decisions. The infighting and competition that had marred the Albany movement was minimized by the absence of other black protest groups: The NAACP had been outlawed in Alabama, and the Student Nonviolent Coordinating Committee wasn't active in Birmingham. During the meeting the leaders assessed the financing of the campaign, and King was satisfied that funds existed to carry it through for several months. For King and the Southern Christian Leadership Conference, this was a make-or-break civil rights operation; its importance was impossible to overstate after the debacle of Albany. Success in Birmingham was critical, because the city was the very symbol of segregation in the South. "We knew that as Birmingham went, so would go the South," Walker recalled.

Since the president—and his conversion to the cause—were essential to the campaign's ultimate victory, the men spent considerable time at their conclave discussing the personality and politics of John F. Kennedy. Their conclusions were optimistic. As Stanley Levison explained: "It was decided that there was a kind of tacit alliance between the Federal Government—the Kennedy Administration—and the civil-rights movement; that if the civil-rights movement could arouse the country and create the demand...that this Administration would hear it and respond." Earlier administrations—President Eisenhower stood as the leading, immediate example—had conveyed to protesters that no matter what took place in the streets the president would remain unswayed, his resistance to civil rights was fixed. Not so with Kennedy, the activists believed.

Before the group disbanded, King issued a stark warning: Birmingham was a dangerous battleground. Bull Connor's disregard for black lives was well-known. "I have to tell you that in my judgment," King told his fellow activists, "some of the people sitting here today will not come back alive from this campaign. And I want you to think about it."

* * *

After their meeting, the civil rights leaders filed through the Savannah airport, again under the watchful eye of the FBI. Using a portable movie camera, agents secretly filmed King in the company of Stanley Levison and Jack O'Dell. While the agency was curious about the meeting at the Dorchester Center, it was interested in capturing those three men together. FBI files indicated that O'Dell, like Levison, had ties to the Communist Party. O'Dell had worked for the party from the late 1940s through most of the 1950s. A former merchant marine, he got involved in communist activities while a member of the National Maritime Union; he was grateful for what the party did on behalf of black sailors. By 1961, however, he had ended his efforts and had no association with the party, although he did maintain contact with some members. That same year, having come to the attention of Stanley Levison, he was hired to work for the SCLC in New York. By 1962 Levison had recognized O'Dell's talent with numbers and recommended that King expand his responsibilities.

An FBI wiretap of Levison's phone captured Levison informing O'Dell that King was in favor of his advancement in the SCLC. With open-mindedness, King had told Levison, "No matter what a man was, if he could stand up now and say he is not connected, then as far as I am concerned, he is eligible to work for me." The FBI was not as generous as King. It had already informed Robert Kennedy about O'Dell, and the administration had earlier advised King to get rid of him. But the civil rights leader had failed to heed the warning. The film footage at the Savannah airport was evidence that O'Dell was still working for King, a fact the FBI swiftly passed along to Attorney General Kennedy. Not long afterward, Kennedy aide Burke Marshall reminded King that he needed to discontinue his association with both men, Levison and O'Dell. King declined to act. Because FBI chief Hoover refused to share with the administration the documentation underpinning his reports—in fact, he had no credible facts—Marshall was unable to back up his allegations. Hoover's distortions of reality complicated the relationship between King and Kennedy and marred trust on both sides just as the Birmingham operation was taking shape.

* * *

Barely a week after the Dorchester meeting, Simeon Booker published a portrait of President Kennedy in *Jet* magazine based on interviews with several people close to him. The image was of a president still deeply conflicted on civil rights. On the one hand, Kennedy now seemed ready to respond to racial injustice. As Booker put it: "The experiences of the first two years, friends say, have convinced the President that some direction in solving racial problems—even to trying to cure basic causes—must come from the White House." That admission represented a significant step in Kennedy's evolution. He had once been like a child with his fingers in his ears blocking out noise from the black community; now he was maturing into a man who recognized that the clamor signified something important. Yet, on the other hand, the president was still blind to the magnitude of the conflict between the races. Despite the many civil rights incidents—sit-ins, Freedom Rides, rioting over James Meredith—during his first two years in office, Booker observed, "President Kennedy doesn't believe there is any serious division in the country on the racial problem."

Booker portrayed the president as unsympathetic to the core complaints about segregation and discrimination; instead, Kennedy was taking a policy approach, tackling the gap between the races on employment, health, and education standards. While certainly a worthy approach, it was also a convenient one: It allowed the president to highlight racial issues without addressing the bigoted culture of the South.

Early in 1963, the president straddled the question of equality. His political advisors saw a need to placate blacks, a voting bloc of growing importance in the coming 1964 election; at the same time, however, the administration could not favor that constituency too much, or risk alienating a wide swath of the white population, mostly in the South.

The administration was not close enough to the black community to feel the pulse of dissatisfaction: Living as a black person in America was simply not tolerable anymore, as James Baldwin starkly depicted the experience in his 1963 book, *The Fire Next Time.* "Negroes in this country," Baldwin grieved, "are taught really to despise themselves from the moment their eyes open on the world. This world is white and they are black." Baldwin had resolved in his youth to overcome the chains of white society. His voice in 1963 was the voice of many blacks impatient for their rights: "I was icily determined—more determined, really, than I then knew—never to make my peace with the ghetto but to die and go to

Hell before I would let any white man spit on me, before I would accept my 'place' in this republic."

Now had become the watchword in the fight for civil rights, as King succinctly put it in his 1963 book *Why We Can't Wait.* Capturing the spirit of that year, King warned, "Explosively, America's third revolution— the Negro revolution—had begun." But in early 1963, President Kennedy lacked the intuition to perceive what was obvious in black churches and homes and hearts. Arthur Schlesinger, the president's close advisor, writing in historical hindsight, summed up the naïveté: "The Kennedy civil rights strategy...miscalculated the dynamism of a revolutionary movement."

Martin Luther King Jr. was relentless in pushing Kennedy to discover new depths in himself. Two weeks after the Dorchester meeting, he once again blasted the president for failing to give the same passion to civil rights that he gave to other domestic issues such as steel prices. In an interview in *Look* magazine, King complained that the president had brushed off the bombing of black churches, the shooting of blacks, and the denial of voting rights: "We have not seen the kind of action that the enormity of the situation demands." Calling for White House leadership, King urged the president to go on television to discuss the moral dimensions of civil rights and "counsel the nation in this issue as he does on other issues."

96

ON FEBRUARY 12, 1963, President Kennedy welcomed more than eight hundred blacks to the White House to celebrate the birthday of Abraham Lincoln. Black entertainers, musicians, judges, businessmen, and civil rights leaders mixed with white cabinet members, Supreme Court justices, congressmen, and governors. Before the event comedian Dick Gregory had been "seen flashing his invitation at Chicago's Playboy Club," according to the Cleveland *Call and Post.* Louis Martin, the black presidential advisor behind the fest, observed that on this single day the White House hosted more black people than it had entertained altogether since the first occupant, President John Adams, took up residence there in 1800. The White House living quarters were opened up, and guests climbed to the second floor to see the recently renovated entertaining rooms and the First Lady's abundant flower arrangements. While everyone munched on shrimp Creole, hickory ham, and roast turkey, and sipped nonalcoholic fruit punches, the president and First Lady Jackie moved through the crowd greeting visitors as the Marine Band belted out the tunes.

The president had balked at Martin Luther King Jr.'s plea for a second Emancipation Proclamation and had scarcely marked the important date of January 1, when Lincoln's original proclamation had gone into effect exactly a hundred years earlier. His evasion sent a sour message to the black community, confirming the president's inaction in correcting the racial wrongs that still riddled American society. "For a minimum of ten years," Thurgood Marshall observed, "civil rights organizations throughout the country had set 1963 as the target date for the removal of discrimination against Negroes." He noted that civil rights leaders had crisscrossed the nation over those ten years preaching the importance of the centennial. "Once 1963 arrived," Marshall said, "each individual Negro realized that a hundred years after the Emancipation Proclamation they were not, in fact, free."

The Lincoln birthday bash was a blatant public relations extravaganza meant to assuage black disappointment with the administration. But from the outset the White House was only lukewarm toward the event; unwilling to commit time or resources, the White House kicked the task of organizing the evening over to the Civil Rights Commission. "No one wanted to do it," recalled Berl Bernhard, the commission's director. "It was just considered to be a big burden, and we all thought the White House ought to do it." The White House wanted all the big names to show up, anyone of any profile who had a role in the cause. Simply compiling the guest list was a headache: The commission had to manage the fragile egos and potential outbursts from anyone overlooked. "This whole civil rights issue was becoming so aggravating [and] controversial that if you missed key people," Bernhard said, "they were going to be so offended that no one knew what they might do." Most blacks eagerly took up the president's invitation. They appreciated, as Simeon Booker wrote, "that the Chief Executive was bold enough to schedule what some jokingly called 'Cullud Folks Night at the White House.'"

But several of the biggest names boycotted the event, including seventy-four-year-old A. Philip Randolph, the founder of the first black labor union, Brotherhood of Sleeping Car Porters, and dean of civil rights leaders; he was so disenchanted by Kennedy that he was considering organizing a giant march on Washington to apply pressure on the administration. Martin Luther King Jr. also declined to attend. He was courteous in rejecting the invitation, blaming it partly on his wife's latest pregnancy and partly on a prior overseas engagement. Neither excuse, however, was serious enough to keep him away from the gala if he had wanted to be there.

As part of the White House's commemoration, the Civil Rights Commission prepared a 207-page report reviewing civil rights progress over the previous hundred years, and presented it to the president before the party. Largely positive, the report noted that more people were working toward civil rights now than ever before, and the greatest developments had taken place within the past ten or fifteen years. The White House handed a copy of the report, titled *Freedom to the Free*, to every guest. Speaking briefly about the report, President Kennedy acknowledged: "We still have some length to go."

Just how far the nation had to go was abundantly apparent in the uproar over one guest in particular. President Kennedy himself had expressly forbidden the attendance of Sammy Davis Jr.; he scratched the entertainer's name from the guest list four times only to have it covertly restored each time by advisor Louis Martin. Davis was married to Swedish actress May Britt, and was therefore a potent symbol to Southerners of the horrors of integration and a politically explosive figure for the president. The two men had socialized outside the White House but were never pictured together. Most worrying for the president was the possibility that a photo of Davis and his white wife cavorting at the White House would show up in newspapers across the world; an image like that would complicate his campaign for reelection in 1964.

The entertainer had married the white actress in 1960, having agreed to postpone the wedding until after the election to lessen any political impact on Kennedy's bid for the White House. Now, three years later, neither America nor the president were any more welcoming to interracial couples. It wouldn't be until 1967 that the Supreme Court ruled in *Loving v. Virginia* that state laws prohibiting marriage between the races were unconstitutional. When the president learned that Davis and his wife arrived at the gala, he took his aides aside on the second floor, hissing: "What's he doing here?" His advisors were just as surprised as he was. "Get them out of there!" Kennedy quietly ordered. The guests were about to file downstairs for photographs. Thinking fast, the president told his aides to make sure Jackie intercepted May Britt, separating her from Davis when the flashbulbs started popping. But Jackie was enraged by the proposition and refused to go downstairs at all. His plan foiled, Kennedy sent word that the photographers were not to snap any pictures of Davis and his wife. He then calmed his wife down, and he and the First Lady joined the reception downstairs, where they posed for a photograph with eleven black leaders and Vice President Lyndon Johnson and his wife. Jackie then excused herself, saying she didn't feel well, and went back upstairs in tears. Davis was kept out of range of the photographers' cameras and caused no political controversy for the president. As Berl Bernhard remembered, "Sammy Davis, Jr., was sitting autographing all of our *Freedom to the Free* booklets as everybody was leaving and saying good-bye to everybody."

The gala garnered little newspaper coverage thanks to the strenuous efforts of press secretary Pierre Salinger to play down its significance; nothing, the administration decided, was to be gained politically by readers catching up on the event in the morning papers. The photo of the president with the black leaders ran in the features section of the *Washington Post*. Kennedy's success at censoring coverage of Sammy Davis Jr. and his wife left a mark on the guests. "The first visit of a mixed couple to the White House was not recorded for public view," lamented *Jet* reporter Simeon Booker. "A small matter, perhaps, but it was one topic that flashed brighter during those hours of the reception than the subject of Cuba.... What amused the Negro VIPs was the fact that aides to the President of the world's greatest democracy could be annoyed by such a triviality at a time of international crisis."

97

AT THE END of March, Martin Luther King Jr. flew to New York for a
secret gathering of supporters at Harry Belafonte's comfortable apart-
ment on West End Avenue. It was a star-studded crowd: actors Sidney
Poitier, Anthony Quinn, Frederic March, and Ossie Davis and his wife,
Ruby Dee; lawyer William Kunstler; a representative of Governor Nelson
Rockefeller, Hugh Morrow; the *New York Post*'s James Wechsler; and the
Amsterdam News's Jimmy Hicks. King and his wife, Coretta, had just
had their fourth child three days earlier, after which King had gone to
Birmingham to tie up loose ends for the launch of the protests the following week. But first, at the suggestion of Belafonte and Stanley Levison, he
faced a room of seventy men and women to apprise them of the strategy
for the demonstrations and to enlist their help.

Belafonte called the meeting to order at 9:30 p.m., telling the crowd
that King and Shuttlesworth were going to disclose details in strict confidence. "When they have explained what they have in mind," Belafonte
said, "we'll see how we can help them." King went first. On April 3, he
told the group, the Birmingham campaign would be launched with massive protests. The goal: the elimination of segregation in department
stores, restaurants, and all other public places; better employment opportunities; an end to police brutality; and the creation of a biracial commission to work out grievances. The campaign was originally scheduled
to begin on March 14 but, he revealed, was delayed after Birmingham
officials—in a bid to appear more moderate—had announced changes to
its city government structure; instead of commission leadership that gave
public safety commissioner Bull Connor significant power, the city put
the mayor and city council in charge. To set up the new form of government, elections for mayor were announced. Former lieutenant governor
Albert Boutwell, a moderate, was on the ballot opposed by several others
including Bull Connor. Whatever the outcome, King and the campaign
leaders had planned to launch the protests a few days after the election,
but the voting threw the mayoral race into a runoff between Boutwell

and Connor, so the demonstrations were postponed until after the run-off on April 2. Protests, it was believed, would only aid Connor's chance of election. Now, whoever won the mayor's seat, the campaign would hit the streets on April 3. In laying out the strategy, King was business-like, careful, and smart, as he often was in small settings. "If Boutwell is elected, we'll probably be criticized for not giving him a chance," he told the group. But, he observed, it was imperative for the demonstrations to move forward.

Shuttlesworth, known for his dramatics and his battle-hardened experiences, gave an emotional appeal. A veteran of Birmingham's abuses, he explained: "Birmingham's Negroes have endured too much for too long. If freedom doesn't come now, it may be too late for it ever to come." His concluding words left the group in stunned silence: "You have to be prepared to die before you can begin to live."

Shuttlesworth had already met with Birmingham businessmen, who had heard rumors of the planned boycotts and mass demonstrations. One of the city's most influential business leaders, Sid Smyer, was a die-hard segregationist who sensed the tide changing in the South. "I'm a segregationist from bottom to top," he once explained to other merchants, "but gentlemen, you see what's happening.... I'm not a damn fool.... Now, we can't win.... We can't win. We gon' have to stop and talk to these folks." But if change were to come, the businessmen didn't want it forced upon them by Martin Luther King Jr. and his cohorts. So they sat down with Shuttlesworth hoping to convince him to keep King out of Birmingham. But the conversation didn't go well. Shuttlesworth lectured the men on the suffering of the black community in Birmingham, telling them: "I'm not of a mind that this morning I came to be used by you." To prevent the demonstrations, the head of the local Sears said he'd paint over the whites-only signs on the store's toilets, and other department store owners vowed to take down the signs on their toilets and drinking fountains. But after the Sears man followed through on his promise, Bull Connor declared that removal of the signs violated city segregation laws. "The signs that did come down," Shuttlesworth said, "he made the merchants put 'em back up." Both sides—black and white—were propelling Birmingham toward a racial showdown.

After the presentations in Belafonte's apartment, the group promised an outpouring of time and money. Belafonte went to work collecting funds and organizing people; he was on the phone with King and others two or three times a day throughout the campaign. As King recalled, "It would be hard to overestimate the role this sensitive artist played." Everyone, even the reporters present at the meeting, kept the secret; before the campaign launched three days later, nothing was circulated, although word had quietly leaked out to merchants and city officials. The FBI, listening in on conversations between Stanley Levison and Jack O'Dell, had gotten an inkling in early March that something was afoot; in one conversation, Levison mentioned an upcoming campaign without revealing the city. The agency gleaned that King was heading to Birmingham and scrambled to put the pieces together.

Unwinding after the meeting, King filled his glass from the bottle of Harveys Bristol Cream that Belafonte kept on hand for him. Perhaps it was Shuttlesworth's omens, or the fact that the Birmingham showdown was days away, but King was visibly tense, even after an application of the sweet and spicy dessert sherry. Belafonte couldn't help noticing his friend's nervous facial tic: Every so often King's cheek pulled to one side. The anxious King contrasted with a large photo from the early 1960s that Belafonte prized and later hung just inside his front door—a shot of the singer and the civil rights leader snapped at the moment the duo burst into laughter over something one of them had said. The photo comforted Belafonte. "It's a good reminder," he wrote in his memoir, "that even in the movement's darkest days, we still had room for humor."

98

THE GASTON MOTEL on Fifth Avenue North was a popular resting spot for blacks in Birmingham. Built by the city's most prominent black businessman, A. G. Gaston, in 1954, it was of classic motel style, a long-and-low two stories, with outdoor corridors and stairs, and parking spaces right out front. Big-name celebrities—Harry Belafonte, Aretha Franklin, Duke Ellington, and Count Basie—spent nights at the Gaston Motel. Martin Luther King Jr., who often stayed with his younger brother A.D., took up residence this time at the Gaston Motel, turning his suite into the campaign's war room.

On Good Friday, April 12, 1963, King was in Room 30 on the second floor conducting a somber early-morning meeting with the campaign's Central Committee. It was only nine days since the launch, and this inner circle of two dozen core leaders was "overwhelmed by a feeling of hopelessness," as King remembered it. Despite the enthusiasm of the volunteers and the initial reserves of money, the Birmingham campaign was already in danger of collapse.

Hope had quickly turned to despair. The campaign's inaugural action on April 3, a coordinated series of sit-ins at whites-only lunch counters at downtown Birmingham department stores, brought only modest results at best. When protesters hit the eateries at Loveman's, Pizitz, Kress, Woolworth's, and Britt's, the workers were waiting for them. All but one counter simply closed shop—no police, no arrests, no attention-grabbing disturbance. Without publicity, there was no pressure for progress. Only at Britt's were the cops called, and twenty protesters were carted to jail. The police acted with restraint, and no white mobs intervened with clubs or bicycle chains: Bull Connor was emulating the successful tactics engineered by the patient and controlled Albany chief of police Laurie Pritchett, with whom the city of Birmingham had been consulting.

As expected, King was sharply criticized by local politicians for the timing of the protests. The new, moderate mayor, Albert Boutwell, had not even taken office yet; he'd had no opportunity to assert his influence. Boutwell himself labeled King an outsider intent on stirring "inter-racial discord." Seeking to discourage participation, he declared, "Demonstrations and sit-ins can accomplish absolutely nothing." Bull Connor's defeat in the mayoral election signaled, in many residents' view, a new racial mood in the city and the expectation that orderly, gradual change would come. But King doubted that segregation would disappear without pressure.

City officials and the powerful newspaper editor Vincent Townsend of the *Birmingham News* had gleaned what was afoot from local wiretaps of King's phone. Before the April 3 launch, Townsend had called Burke Marshall, the assistant attorney general for civil rights, and begged him to intervene to stop King. Marshall tried to track the pastor down at the Gaston Motel but didn't get past his aide, Wyatt Walker. Arguing forcefully, Marshall impressed upon Walker both his own view, and that of

Attorney General Kennedy and editor Townsend, that the new government needed some time. Walker promised to pass along the concern to King, but Marshall was skeptical he would do so.

As more sit-ins and marches and arrests disrupted city life over the next several days, many middle-class blacks and white ministers and businessmen denounced King. The city's black weekly newspaper, *Birmingham World*, called him a "glossy personality." A. G. Gaston was careful to align himself with the idea of racial progress but to distance himself from King and the disturbances; he had been generous in setting up the campaign in his motel, giving the movement a reduced rate on the suite, according to Wyatt Walker, and installing extra phones, but he did not publicly endorse its activities.

Despite the criticisms, the merchant boycott was taking root. Blacks knew all too well the injustice of segregation in the stores. As the Reverend Ed Gardner put it: "You could go downtown there in one department [of a store] and spend a thousand dollars and go to the lunch counter and be put in jail." Blacks had the potential to deliver a financial blow ahead of Easter when the stores counted on a boost from holiday spending. At King's urging, blacks resisted buying new Easter outfits and stayed away from the stores. "Buy nothing but food," King urged, adding that any black person spotted downtown carrying a department store bag wasn't "fit to be free." Department store sales in the week before Easter rose only 4 percent in Birmingham compared with the same week the previous year; that was significantly below the sales increase in Atlanta of 14 percent and in New Orleans of 22 percent. White businessmen feared the impact on their bottom lines not only of a boycott but also of the protests and potential violence. The protesters were counting on "the greed of the white merchants," Ralph Abernathy observed. "We were betting they would care more about dollars than they would about Jim Crow."

But while demonstrators volunteered for duty—and therefore jail— their numbers were not at levels that King and the leaders had hoped, and the community had not unified around the campaign. "The SCLC had expected the very presence of Martin Luther King to draw hundreds of protesters into the movement," wrote historian Glenn T. Eskew. "That had not occurred."

The protests continued nonetheless, and the arrests mounted, but national press coverage was minimal. Even when Bull Connor finally gave in to his brutal instincts and unleashed police German shepherds on peaceful demonstrators, the major newspapers buried the stories. The dogs were let loose on marchers who were streaming along Sixth Avenue North after a Palm Sunday service on April 7 singing "Hold My Hand While I Run This Race." When a black teenager drew a knife to defend himself against a snarling dog, police moved in with more dogs; protesters came to the rescue of the young man, who'd been knocked to the ground, and police swarmed in swinging their billy clubs. Twenty-six blacks were arrested and carted off in police vans. The *New York Times* ran the story on page thirty-one, while the *Washington Post* used a brief wire service report on page three. The president ignored the disturbance.

By the time of the bleak Gaston Motel meeting on April 12 about 150 protesters had been rounded up, and more than forty had been freed on bond. While the number of arrests was not attention-grabbing—the ill-fated Albany movement had more than five hundred protesters in jail in its early days—the Birmingham bail payments were enough to deplete the campaign's once-flush coffers. That meant that protesters still in jail were stuck there. And leaders didn't feel right calling for more demonstrations if the campaign could not promise to spring the volunteers from prison. Not only was the Birmingham movement failing to catch fire in town or across the country, it was unable to support its devoted followers. In the gloom of the motel room, King expressed deep distress over the financial crunch. The campaign had people in jail and "a moral responsibility to them," he recalled.

Two days earlier, Bull Connor had won a state court injunction prohibiting further demonstrations; the ruling meant that arrests would bring steeper legal costs and longer jail terms. In the first week, King had stayed off the streets—and out of jail. But, hoping to kick-start the campaign, he had vowed to march and go to prison on Good Friday. At a press conference before the Gaston Motel meeting, he declared: "We cannot in good conscience obey an injunction, which is an unjust, undemocratic and unconstitutional misuse of the legal process."

* * *

But King was torn. Everyone knew he could raise money faster than anyone else in the movement, but he couldn't do it from prison. He also had an obligation to everyone already in jail, and all the others volunteering for the lockup, to follow through on his vow to march and accept the certainty of arrest. His reputation, already suffering, was on the line. A heated discussion erupted among the two dozen men in the motel suite. Some wanted King to stay out of jail and raise money. His father, Daddy King, who had flown in from Atlanta and was always protective of his son, urged Martin to obey the injunction and avoid prison. For Reverend Abernathy, the decision was complicated because he was the only pastor of his congregation at West Hunter Street Baptist Church in Atlanta; if he joined King in a protest and went to jail, no one could lead his Easter services. Wyatt Walker, the feisty SCLC executive director, argued that King had to go to prison. "My immediate response was to break the injunction, you know, because I'm a man of action," Walker recalled. But King cooled him down. As Walker remembered: "Martin said, 'No, you have to think it through.'"

As the debate swirled around him, King fell into quiet contemplation, knowing that people were already gathering along the demonstration route to watch him march. "I sat there," he recalled, "conscious of twenty-four pairs of eyes. I thought about the people in jail. I thought about the Birmingham Negroes already lining the streets of the city, waiting to see me put into practice what I had so passionately preached." He wondered what the local community would make of him for sitting out, and he worried what the nation would think of "a man who had encouraged hundreds of people to make a stunning sacrifice and then excused himself?"

He then weighed what would happen if the money to carry on wasn't raised: The Birmingham campaign would die in ignominy just like the Albany Movement, and the protesters he had inspired to march would languish in jail. King felt his solitude. "There comes a time in the atmosphere of leadership when a man surrounded by loyal friends and allies realizes he has come face to face with himself," he thought. "I was alone in that crowded room."

As he had done in other moments of crisis, King sought time alone to pray and ruminate. Separating himself from the group, he retreated to the bedroom. Standing in the middle of the room, he reflected on "all that my life had brought me to be." His mind moved beyond the Gaston Motel, the city jail, the state line, and he meditated on the fate of the nation's twenty million blacks. A mature leader now, some eight years after he was thrust into the limelight during the Montgomery bus boycott, King grappled with what was the right course to pursue, just as he had done then. One long night at the height of the bus boycott, he had turned to God to seek guidance and courage after the latest of many racists called his home and vowed to kill him and his family; after prayer and deep soul-searching, his decision not to run but stay and fight was a turning point in his life. Again, now in the back room of the Gaston Motel suite, King stood at the precipice contemplating his future. A half hour later, he had decided on his path. He climbed out of his dark suit, his trademark attire, and pulled on a work shirt and a brand-new pair of blue jeans. When he walked back into the sitting room, some were shocked at the sight of him. His clothing exposed the change in the man. "I don't know what will happen," he told the group. "I don't know where the money will come from. But I have to make a faith act." Looking into the faces surrounding him, he said: "I've decided to go to jail....I don't know whether this Movement will continue to build up or whether it will collapse. If enough people are willing to go to jail, I believe it will force the city officials to act or force the federal government to act. So I'm going today."

King went up to his friend Ralph Abernathy, who was standing by the window, and urged him to go back to Atlanta and lead his congregation on the highest day of the Christian calendar. He then embraced his friend. In that moment Abernathy knew what King was doing: He was giving him the opportunity to ensure his own safety and do the work of God on the pulpit. But Abernathy felt a stronger calling. He didn't know what the future held for his friend—arrest, prison for months, possibly even death—but he wasn't going to leave him.

"Martin," Abernathy asked, "what are you trying to say to me?"

"I'm just saying you should be at your church on Sunday."

"Martin," Abernathy said, smiling and shaking his head, "if you're going to march, then I'm going to march, too."

In a show of strength and solidarity, the leaders joined hands and sang the movement's hymn of hope, "We Shall Overcome."

Martin Luther King Jr. looked like a new man, even if a bit awkward in his crisp blue jeans. Recognizing that retreat was now impossible, he was prepared to march past a court injunction. Andrew Young, a campaign leader, observed: "That, I think, was the beginning of his true leadership."

"Okay, then let's go," King said. "We're going to have to march. Now."

99

THE OLD MAN sat in a wheelchair in the window of Jackie Kennedy's dressing room on the second floor of the White House, peering down into the Rose Garden. His arm was "twisted grotesquely." Nearly a year and a half after his stroke, Joseph P. Kennedy was still unable to speak, although he apparently understood everything said to him. On this Tuesday before Easter, 1963, he watched in silent umbrage through the slightly parted sheer curtains as his son the president conferred honorary citizenship on Britain's former prime minister, Sir Winston Churchill. From another window on the second floor, four-and-a-half-year-old Caroline Kennedy stood in her play clothes—blue coveralls and a blue-printed blouse—gazing down on her mother and father amid a crowd of several hundred guests. Behind her was her nurse, Maude Shaw, brushing her hair and securing it neatly with a barrette.

Down in the Rose Garden under heavy clouds, President John Kennedy addressed diplomats, congressmen, government officials, and movie stars assembled to honor Churchill. Now eighty-eight years old, the former prime minister sent his son Randolph to Washington in his stead; he was at home in London watching the ceremony on the "telly"; the Relay satellite beaming President Kennedy to the British Broadcasting Company in London had been launched only four months earlier.

President Kennedy had long admired Churchill and his voluminous speeches and writings; while a Harvard student in 1939 he joined his father, then the U.S. ambassador to the United Kingdom, in Parliament's visitors' gallery as the British government grappled with the Nazi invasion of Poland. Churchill, who didn't become prime minister until May 1940, spoke passionately that day on the need to fight Adolf Hitler and the German war machine. "Churchill's speech, giving evidence of the powerful oratory that would later inspire the nation in the darkest hours of the war, left an indelible impression on Jack," historian Robert Dallek observed. John Kennedy turned his Harvard thesis on Britain's slow process of rearmament before World War II into a book called *Why England*

Slept; its title echoed *While England Slept*, the American edition of a book of speeches Churchill gave between 1928 and 1938 on Britain's failure to keep pace with Germany's military buildup. In the 1950s, early in his marriage, Kennedy and his wife were invited to join Greek tycoon Aristotle Onassis for a dinner party aboard his yacht *Christina* in the south of France, where the guest of honor was Winston Churchill. Kennedy, dressed in a white dinner jacket, hovered close to his hero throughout the evening, but the great man scarcely acknowledged him, instead spending his time in conversation with Jackie. It was devastating for Jack to be ignored by his idol. Later, alluding to Jack's white dinner jacket, Jackie teased her chagrined husband: "I think he thought you were the waiter, Jack."

Kennedy was enamored of Churchill throughout his political career. His father, however, was no admirer. Joe had favored the gentlemanly prime minister Neville Chamberlain and sided with his efforts to appease Adolf Hitler and forestall war. Joe had been a staunch isolationist. In his view, Churchill was a warmonger who hit the booze too heavily and ultimately lured America into the war. To see Churchill now lionized by his son with pomp and circumstance no doubt rankled the Kennedy patriarch. Later, over an intimate dinner at the White House, the president teased his father—good-natured ribbing was a standard of Kennedy family life—about all the men in the audience Joe had clashed with in his days as an antiwar ambassador: "All your good friends showed up, didn't they, Dad?"

* * *

Joseph Kennedy had a profound influence on his son even after his stroke. In earlier days, Joe had instructed young Jack in the ways of the world and developed him into the politician he became; after his illness, by his crippled existence, he taught his son the meaning of empathy for the struggling and less fortunate. Jack's love for his father spurred his evolution as a political leader and as a husband, father, and son. While Joe was able to visit the White House only rarely, Jack made regular trips to him in Hyannis Port and Palm Beach despite the demands of his office and surprised observers by his uncharacteristic displays of affection.

Ben Bradlee, then the Washington bureau chief for *Newsweek* and a friend of Jack's, joined the family at dinner after the Churchill ceremony and captured the Kennedy siblings' embrace of the ailing patriarch. "The evening was movingly gay, because the old man's gallantry shows in his eyes and his crooked smile," Bradlee wrote. "And because his children involve him in their every thought and action."

With the paralysis on his right side, the ambassador had trouble eating and was attended by Ann Gargan, a Kennedy cousin who had devoted her life to caring for him. Jackie also looked after him lovingly: She had an attachment to the old man that was not lost on Jack. "When [the ambassador] eats, he drools out of the right side of his mouth," Bradlee explained, "but Jackie was wiping it off quickly, and by the middle of dinner there really is no embarrassment left." As everyone ate the crabs the ambassador brought with him from Florida, Jack quipped: "I must say, there is one thing about Dad: When you go with him you go first-class." Everyone chimed their agreement and the elder Kennedy jabbed his left hand into the air concurring, and uttering "No, no, no, no"—the only words he was able to say. "Tonight," Bradlee translated, "it's a 'no' that means 'yes.'"

The old man's incapacitation unlocked emotions in his son that had been carefully guarded most of his life. It was impossible not to react to Joseph Kennedy's reversal of fortune. "He had all his life prided himself on his appearance, on his perfectly tailored business suits and leisure suits, on his military posture, and on the smile he could turn on whenever it was needed," wrote David Nasaw in his book *The Patriarch*. "He had been a handsome young man, and he'd aged gracefully into the most handsome of older men. The stroke reversed all that. He was now—and he had to have known it—a twisted, gaunt old skeleton, bound to a wheelchair, unable to make himself understood." The sight of his father compelled Jack to ruminate on fate and fairness; the man who was once the source of strength for the family—the one giving the commands—was now a gnarled dependent. The old man stirred depths of compassion in Jack. When his father phoned the White House, with the help of Ann Gargan, the president always broke away; Ann would tell him his father wanted to talk, which meant he wanted to listen to Jack. So the son told the father what was new, rattling on for a little while, and heard the *no, no, no*s in response, then signed off. The ambassador, this shell of a man, "a tragic figure—very disabled, very affected," as one of his doctors described him, through his condition matured his son. A new ritual had been put in place within the Kennedy clan. Before departing after family gatherings with Joe—whether in Hyannis Port, Palm Beach, or Washington—his children and their spouses would file past and kiss the ambassador on his forehead. The most undemonstrative of men, John Kennedy had inaugurated the custom and sometimes waited out his siblings so he could be the last one to press his lips to his father's flesh.

100

By EASTER MORNING, Coretta King was in a desperate state. She had learned on Friday that her husband, after deciding to march, was now locked up in the Birmingham jail. At home in Atlanta with their four children—the youngest, Bernice, just two weeks old—Coretta waited to hear Martin's voice on the phone reassuring her that he was safe. All she could do, as she had done on his previous imprisonments, was to await his call. All through Friday she waited, and all through Saturday, too. By Sunday, she was frantic. For the first time in her adult life, she missed church on Easter: She had stayed by the phone. Martin always called when he wound up in prison; it was a standard police procedure that allowed her to learn at least he was all right. But Birmingham was different; she knew the city's reputation for stomping on basic rights and for brutalizing blacks. She knew Birmingham had Bull Connor. This time she had not even been granted the tiny solace of a phone call. The long silence presented any number of nightmare scenarios.

* * *

After his father's visit to the White House, the president traveled to the family estate in Palm Beach to be with the ailing old man for the Easter holiday. On Good Friday, the day Martin Luther King Jr. landed in prison, Kennedy went to confession with one of his best friends, Paul Fay, a former Navy buddy known as Red for his vibrant hair color, who now served as undersecretary of the Navy. Learning of King's arrest the following day, the president was both annoyed at the civil rights leader and concerned about his treatment. He and his brother the attorney general wanted King to contain the protests—not expand them—to give the new moderate Birmingham city government a chance to address racial inequities.

But now that King was behind bars, the president phoned the assistant attorney general for civil rights, Burke Marshall, wanting to know what, if anything, the White House could do. Marshall had already heard from Wyatt Walker, the SCLC's executive director, who had phoned him at one in the morning outraged that King was being held incommunicado. Walker informed Marshall that on Friday after his arrest King had been denied a private meeting with a movement lawyer. When the lawyer had gone to the prison in the evening, he was told his conference with his client had to be conducted in front of guards. The lawyer refused and departed in protest. Walker then sent a telegram to the president begging him to intervene. He complained that both King and Ralph Abernathy were being held in solitary confinement on an arrest that violated the First and Fourteenth Amendments of free speech and equal protection under the law. "We submit that these two distinguished Americans are political prisoners and not criminals," the telegram said, adding that the inmates were deprived of even the minimum requirements of prison life: "Neither of these men have mattresses or bed linens." The president, speaking to Marshall by phone from Palm Beach, was chagrined to learn that there was nothing the federal government could do. Marshall explained to the president that the dispute was a local matter, then he informed the press: "The Federal Government has no authority to take legal action to intervene in Birmingham as the situation now stands."

* * *

Martin Luther King Jr. had spent Saturday night in solitary confinement on the sixth floor of the city prison. His friend Ralph Abernathy had been placed in similar conditions one floor below. After a dismal night, King glanced up at sunlight slanting through a window high in the cell. It was a comfort but it also reminded him that he was deprived of the daylight outside. Of his long hours in isolation, he recalled: "You will never know the meaning of utter darkness until you have lain in such a dungeon."

King and Abernathy and their small band of marchers, fewer than fifty, had run into a phalanx of police soon after they took to the street on Friday afternoon. Blacks lining the route far outnumbered the marchers, and the press, misinterpreting the large number of spectators, incorrectly reported the size of the protest. The *New York Times* declared on Saturday that "the marchers were halted...but not before more than a thousand shouting, singing Negroes had joined in the demonstration." Wyatt Walker celebrated the media misperception, describing it as a key feature in sustaining the campaign. "I used that to our advantage," he explained. He would call for protests later in the day after Negroes had returned home from work and were able to come out to watch; their presence would then confuse the press. "They would form out on the side and it would look like a thousand folks," Walker remembered.

On that Friday afternoon, King and his followers had marched up Sixth Avenue toward City Hall and into a wall of police armed with dogs. As the protesters came closer, the police allowed the snarling dogs to lengthen their leashes and lunge toward the blacks before they were yanked back at the last moment. Abernathy remembered how the marchers tried to appear cool. "We were able to maintain a certain amount of self-confidence by snapping our fingers at the dogs as if we were unconcerned with their apparent readiness to tear our throats out," he wrote in his memoir *And the Walls Came Tumbling Down.* The marchers changed course, heading to Fifth Avenue toward the downtown business district, but quickly found themselves facing another wall of police, and behind them stood Bull Connor in a Stetson hat. At his command, the officers moved in. They grabbed King and Abernathy roughly by the backs of their shirts and the seats of their pants, lifting them, and tossing them into the back of a paddy wagon for the ride to jail. The men were fingerprinted then separated. Friday and Saturday night King slept poorly on the metal slats of the bed frame, with no mattress.

* * *

On Sunday, a desperate Coretta—still without any communication from her husband—phoned Wyatt Walker and what she heard only weighed all the heavier on her. Walker explained that no one had been able to see or talk to her husband: All of Walker's phone messages left at the prison had gone unanswered; the lawyers had been denied proper access; telegrams had now been sent to the president and the attorney general.

"Wyatt, do you think if I made a statement to the press about this situation it would help?" Coretta asked.

"Do you know what I think you should do?" Walker replied. "I think you ought to call the President."

Coretta hesitated, afraid her husband would disapprove; her contacting the president might cause a complication for the Birmingham campaign that didn't occur to her. Walker agreed to ask Martin but after a while he phoned her again to say it was impossible to reach him. "You have no alternative but to call the President," he advised.

Coretta had heard President Kennedy was in Palm Beach for the Easter holiday, so she placed several calls to the White House hoping to get a Palm Beach number for him. Each time the operator turned her away, saying she had no telephone number in Palm Beach. Coretta then asked the operator to put her in touch with Vice President Johnson, but he too was away. At last, Coretta prevailed upon the operator to help her find anyone who was available; the sympathetic woman gave her the phone number for press secretary Pierre Salinger, who promised to do what he could to reach the president.

Meanwhile, Coretta's phone rang constantly: friends and associates seeking the latest news and sending their best wishes. Once when she picked up the receiver she heard the welcome voice of Harry Belafonte who had been thinking about her and the kids. She spoke frankly with him, admitting she was depressed and frazzled. She was getting many phone calls, and at the same time she was trying to look after the children and wanting to go to Birmingham to be near Martin. The Kings had several phone lines, and as Belafonte spoke to her, he heard another phone ringing and then another. He also heard the unmistakable sounds of kids racing around the house. The crisis clearly was demanding too much of Coretta—she needed help. When he asked who was taking care of the newborn, Coretta gamely said she was all right looking after the baby and the rest of the kids.

"No one's in that house with you?" Belafonte asked.

"No," she said. "It's just me."

No secretary or housekeeper? Belafonte inquired.

"No, Martin won't permit it," she answered. "He feels he can't afford the help, and if he did, people would think he was living too high."

"From this moment on," Belafonte said, "you're going to have a housekeeper and a secretary, and I want you to identify a driver who can take you wherever you need to go. And if anyone wants to know how you can afford that, you just say Harry's paying."

* * *

On Sunday, the Kennedy family's Easter services were held in the privacy of the patriarch's Spanish-style living room overlooking the Atlantic. It was a small gathering. President Kennedy, his wife, and the two kids rolled up to the estate just before 10:30 a.m. in the backseat of a white sedan driven by a Secret Service agent. Caroline, dressed in a white dress, sat on her father's lap holding an Easter bunny, and John Jr., in white shorts, was perched on his mother. As they climbed out of the car about a hundred spectators across the road applauded. Collecting in the living room in front of the large ocean windows along with the president were his father, Joe Kennedy, and his mother, Rose, and his youngest brother, Senator Edward Kennedy and his wife, Joan. Officiating was the Reverend Peter O'Donnell of nearby Saint Ann's Roman Catholic Church, with Jack serving in the role of altar boy. Beyond his usual stricken condition, the old man felt unwell, requiring the Mass to come to him. And the setting was gorgeous: Through the giant windows the sea shone brilliant blue in the morning sunlight.

* * *

In Atlanta, Coretta King's phone rang.

"Mrs. King, this is Attorney General Robert Kennedy." Coretta recognized his voice. "I am returning your call to my brother. The President wasn't able to talk to you today because he's with my father who is quite ill. He wanted me to call you to find out what we can do for you."

Coretta laid out her concerns: her husband's arrest and his silence since his jailing. The Birmingham authorities refused to allow him a phone call or private audience with his lawyer. She asked if the president might inquire after Martin's well-being. She stressed that she wasn't seeking his release; she just wanted to ensure that he was safe. She had learned that Martin was sleeping on a bare bed frame, and she informed the attorney general of that, too. Bobby offered his sympathy, noting that some local officials in Birmingham posed a special problem. "Bull Connor is very hard to deal with," he told her. "Maybe after the new city government takes over we can get something done in Birmingham. But I promise you I will look into the situation and let you know something."

Coretta thanked him, put down the phone, and resumed her waiting.

* * *

When Harry Belafonte phoned Bobby Kennedy that weekend, the conversation got heated. Belafonte complained that Bobby wasn't doing enough to ease King's "barbaric" prison conditions. Bobby reminded Belafonte that King didn't have to be in jail—he could have posted bond and left. Belafonte fired back that King's conscience would not permit him to leave prison: He was committed to nonviolent protest against inequality in Birmingham, and he was unjustly arrested. "This ain't no game," Belafonte told Bobby. "It's the real thing. Maybe it's time you open your copy of Gandhi." Bobby, unmoved, said that both he and the president were opposed to the Birmingham campaign; he made it clear that he wasn't pleased by Belafonte pressuring him to investigate King's prison accommodations. "Tell Reverend King we're doing everything we can," Bobby offered. "But I'm not sure we can get into prison reform at this moment."

Belafonte was also busy on the financial front. After the handwringing at the Gaston Motel meeting over the campaign's dwindling funds for bail, King's personal lawyer, Clarence Jones, called Belafonte. He informed the singer that there was enough money to bail out King and Abernathy, if needed, but the assets had been drained on behalf of the other protesters. Belafonte understood the dire conditions, and went to work raising money. Before the weekend was out, he had wired $50,000 to Birmingham to support the campaign and cover bail; most of it he had raised from generous donors, the rest he kicked in from his own pocket.

* * *

On Monday, Coretta waited through the morning and the afternoon for some word on Martin, but she heard nothing from Bobby Kennedy, or anyone. At around 5 p.m., the phone rang. When she picked it up, at first all she heard on the other end were the babbling sounds of her two-year-old son, Dexter. Then an operator's voice asked a little testily if Coretta couldn't get her child off the phone. Several moments later she heard a familiar Kennedy voice. "Hello, Mrs. King. I'm sorry I wasn't able to talk to you yesterday," the president said. "I understand my brother called you. I just wanted you to know that I was with my father, who is ill, and couldn't leave him." President Kennedy wanted to know how Coretta was doing and asked about newborn Bernice. When Coretta told him how anxious she was over Martin's condition the president said: "I know you'll be interested in knowing that we sent the FBI into Birmingham last night. We checked on your husband, and he's all right." Then he added: "Of course, Birmingham is a very difficult place." He discussed the problems of Birmingham then said: "I want you to know we are doing everything we can. I have just talked to Birmingham, and your husband will be calling you shortly." He told Coretta to call on him if she had any more concerns about Martin or Birmingham, and if she couldn't find him, she should try his brother or his press secretary, Salinger. Signing off, he said: "You know how to get me now."

For nearly three days, she'd had no word about her husband, and suddenly the president of the United States gave her the comfort she needed. He had made inquiries, ordered federal agents to investigate her husband's condition, and took the time to inform her personally. Although Kennedy dithered on civil rights, Coretta had no doubt he respected the dignity of every human. While political considerations often stifled him, she still believed that Kennedy was able—if pressured hard enough—to be guided by his conscience. His intervention on her husband's behalf energized the campaign and warned local officials that brutality would not be tolerated. His desire for justice gave hope to the black community. "Even though I understood that there were political overtones, I believed President Kennedy sincerely cared about what happened to us," Coretta wrote in her memoir. "There was an amazing warmth about him."

101

ON MONDAY AFTERNOON, Martin Luther King Jr. finally was allowed a visit by his lawyer. Clarence Jones had flown in from New York bearing good news. Neither he nor King knew about President Kennedy's call to Coretta. Jones brought a welcome message on the campaign's depleted coffers. While in prison King despaired over the condition of the movement, fearing its possible collapse from a lack of funds and loss of participation. Now Jones informed King that Harry Belafonte had raised $50,000 for bail bonds. "It is available immediately," Jones told King. "And he says that whatever else you need, he will raise it." King felt a massive burden slide from his shoulders. Jones saw in his face a mix of gratitude and awe and appreciation for the loyalty of friends.

While the Birmingham campaign had enjoyed a rebirth, King still faced criticism for having launched it at all. The newspapers brimmed with negative reactions to his march and jailing. The *Washington Post* condemned police brutality and praised the "valor of the Negroes who marched in protest" but added, "The wisdom of their leaders is less certain." *Time* magazine pointed out that King had "inflamed tensions" when the city was making progress in race relations, concluding the campaign was "poorly timed."

The criticism that stung King most first appeared in the *Birmingham News* on Saturday, April 13, and then was widely reported elsewhere. It came in a blistering statement by eight local white clergymen: Episcopal bishops, a Roman Catholic bishop, Methodist bishops, a Presbyterian leader, a rabbi. These clergymen, who were moderate, perhaps even liberal, in their views on race relations, called the protest campaign "unwise and untimely" and referred to King and other leaders as "outsiders." The white ministers encouraged "our own Negro community to withdraw support from these demonstrators, and to unite locally in working peacefully for a better Birmingham." King was devastated.

* * *

About thirty minutes after Coretta spoke to President Kennedy on Monday afternoon, her phone rang again, and the voice on the line filled her with relief. Martin sounded tired, his speech was sluggish, but he said he was all right. He assumed the line was tapped so he watched his words.

"I just got a call from the President and he told me you were going to call in a few minutes," Coretta told him.

"So that's why everybody is suddenly being so polite," he said.

The guards had brought in a mattress and a pillow, and told him he could take a shower. Then they had led him out of his cell, saying he was free to call his wife.

Martin chatted briefly with eight-year-old Yoki and six-year-old Marty. Then he instructed Coretta to get word of the president's phone call to Wyatt Walker so he could notify the press. Coretta promised Martin she would see him in three days, on Thursday, when she and Ralph Abernathy's wife, Juanita, were coming to Birmingham.

After the call, King arranged for a telegram to be sent to President Kennedy, thanking him for taking time out of his Easter weekend to phone Coretta. "Your encouraging words and thoughtful concern," he told the president, "gave her renewed strength to face the difficult moments through which we are now passing."

* * *

After the president's call hit the newspapers, Birmingham police chief Jamie Moore insisted there had been no White House intervention in the operations of his jail. Denying he bent to presidential power, Moore told the *Birmingham News* that Kennedy had played no part in King phoning his wife; prison officials never prohibited the civil rights leader from using the phone. "King called his wife sometime yesterday," Moore told the paper. "It was not arranged by Kennedy or anyone connected with the President. As far as I know, this was the first time he had requested a chance to call his wife." Moore said he had been unaware that Coretta had recently given birth. "That's the only reason we let him call," he said. Moore also fought back against charges that he had locked King up in solitary confinement. "Certainly King is not being and has not been held incommunicado," he declared. "This is ridiculous. Apparently some people think our jail is to be used as an office with frequent long distance calls and for press conferences. We have rules and regulations. We have to follow them when we have four hundred prisoners."

* * *

Led out of solitary confinement, Martin Luther King Jr. was taken downstairs for a few moments of fresh air. The prison yard was a dismal, treeless pen, secured on all sides by a chain-link fence with barbed wire running along the top. When he stepped into the enclosure, his spirit was suddenly lifted by the sight of his friend and fellow inmate, Ralph

Abernathy. The inmates were ordered not to talk to each other, a rule King ignored.

"Hello, Ralph," he said, smiling.

The men strolled slowly around the yard, chatting in whispers and shadowed by the guards.

"Knock it off!" a guard snarled.

"You in a cell alone?" Martin asked.

"Yeah."

"Shut up!" one of the guards barked.

They went in silence. When they tried to talk again a guard shouted at them. The two friends were nonetheless satisfied just walking side by side. "We walked around the edge of the fence, like animals, exploring the farthest reach of our cage," Abernathy recalled.

King whispered to his friend, "I'm writing a reply to…those clergymen."

"Did they give you anything to write on?"

"No," King said. "I'm using toilet paper."

102

ON TUESDAY, CLARENCE Jones returned to the prison hoping to discuss an array of questions related to the campaign, but King had only one thing on his mind: the letter he'd begun writing to the clergymen. He had been writing discreetly not only on toilet paper but on the edges of newspapers he had in his cell. Instead of going over legal matters, he wanted a commitment from Jones that he would smuggle out King's words, and supply him with the needed tools—paper, ink—to allow him to keep writing until he was finished. Over the next several days, King lost himself in the work; eventually the guards permitted him a pad of paper, and in segments his scrawled words were secretly carried out and typed up. His "Letter from Birmingham Jail," as the six-thousand-word defense became known, revealed the depth of King's inner turmoil in "its flashes of anger, pathos, and mocking irony"—qualities often absent from his other work, as historian Adam Fairclough noted. In its broad sweep, the letter was far more than a rebuttal to the clergymen; it was a statement on the passion and principles of Martin Luther King Jr. "It soon became a classic document of the civil rights movement," Fairclough explained, "its most cogent and persuasive defense of civil disobedience."

King began by noting the extraordinary nature of his literary undertaking. With a tinge of hubris, he asserted: "Seldom do I pause to answer criticism of my work and ideas." But this time he was determined to create a persuasive, moral argument for his life's purpose. He opened with a quick primer on the Southern Christian Leadership Conference, its reach across the South, and its associations with other groups, including the Alabama Christian Movement for Human Rights, the Fred Shuttlesworth organization that requested King's presence in the city. He directly refuted the clergymen's suggestion that he was an outsider who came of his own accord just to cause trouble. "I...am here because I was invited here," he wrote. "But more basically, I am in Birmingham because injustice is here." Then, conscious of his audience, he pivoted to a religious allusion: "Just as the Apostle Paul left his village of Tarsus and carried the gospel of Jesus Christ to the far corners of the Greco-Roman world, so am I compelled to carry the gospel of freedom beyond my own home town." He scolded the clergymen for their moral laxity. "You deplore the demonstrations taking place in Birmingham," he wrote. "But your statement, I am sorry to say, fails to express a similar concern for the conditions that brought about the demonstrations."

After outlining the long history of segregation, brutality, and unjust legal treatment of blacks in Birmingham, King reminded the clergymen that the movement had agreed to delay demonstrations for negotiations only to have the white leadership break its promises. As a result, the campaign began preparations for nonviolent, direct action; it trained its people in how to take blows without retaliating, how to endure the hardships of prison. He praised the virtues of nonviolence and the benefits of resolving racial discrimination through his Gandhian strategy instead of the extreme tactics advocated by other newly emerging black groups. "I have tried to stand between these two forces," he wrote, arguing that had his philosophy "not emerged, by now many streets of the South would, I am convinced, be flowing with blood."

King demolished the charge that the protests were ill-timed by observing that no one ever approved of the timing of any protest. "Frankly," King wrote with rare aggressiveness, "I have yet to engage in a direct-action campaign that was 'well-timed' in the view of those who have not suffered unduly from the disease of segregation." Speaking as much to the White House as to the Birmingham establishment, he wrote: "I must say to you that we have not made a single gain in civil rights without determined legal and nonviolent pressure." King spoke for a population tired of waiting for change; the long delay had become intolerable. "For years now I have heard the word 'Wait!' It rings in the ear of every Negro with piercing familiarity," he wrote. "This 'Wait' has almost always meant 'Never.'"

Speaking as much to the president as to his Birmingham audience, King stressed the changes underway around the world for oppressed peoples. He noted that Asian and African nations were making swift progress toward independence, "but we still creep at horse-and-buggy pace toward gaining a cup of coffee at a lunch counter." This was the kind of rhetoric capable of piercing President Kennedy's armor. While he was ever ready to proclaim America's role as a protector and promoter of freedom across the globe, the president was sensitive to criticism that America didn't live up to its own principles at home.

In wrenching imagery, King conveyed the sadness of being black in America, making clear that no white person could know the humiliation without experiencing it. He laid out the personal toll: horrific scenes of black mothers and fathers watching a mob lynch their children, of policemen cursing, kicking, and killing black citizens, of travelers sleeping in their cars because motels wouldn't sell them a bed for the night, of adults never hearing the words *Mr.* or *Mrs.* but only *boy* and *nigger.* It was this other world that King splashed before the white clergy and the president, a world of twenty million Americans "harried by day and haunted by night by the fact that you are a Negro... plagued with inner fears and outer resentments... forever fighting a degenerating sense of 'nobodiness.'" Only when the white world lived as black Americans, King explained, could it "understand why we find it difficult to wait."

Appealing to even the most hardened heart, King depicted a parent explaining racism to a daughter or son. His words harkened to his own experience as a boy when he learned that his best friends, white kids, were no longer allowed to play with him, and his mother, as sympathetic as she could be, nonetheless had to reveal realities that shattered his innocence. Speaking as a parent these many years later, King described how difficult it was to explain to a young daughter why an amusement park was closed to her because of her color and to watch her cry. It was then, King wrote, that you "see ominous clouds of inferiority beginning to form in her little mental sky, and see her beginning to distort her personality by developing an unconscious bitterness toward white people." Having welcomed his fourth child only days earlier, King might have been experiencing intense parental emotions; at the same time he was in some way channeling his own youth. After being exposed to the life-altering truth of racism, he himself grappled for a long period with his hatred of white people, learning to overcome it only by the strenuous work of religious enlightenment and deep study. In some ways, he was both parent and child as he scribbled his rage on scraps of paper in a Birmingham jail.

Both the clergymen and the president were concerned about law and order, in particular, preventing a spiral toward chaos posed by King's defiance of common customs. King's answer was simple and unassailable: The law of segregation was unjust and immoral. King built his argument along religious lines, proving that in God's eyes a law that enforced segregation was not a "law of God." He explained that a just law had to accord with God's eternal law. Segregation ordinances were unjust because, far from uplifting the black population as God's law decreed, they degraded an entire segment of God's creation. Condemning these unjust laws, King declared: "Segregation is not only politically, economically and sociologically unsound, it is morally wrong and sinful."

King denounced the clergymen for turning their back on God's injunction to fight injustice. "I have been so greatly disappointed by the white church and its leadership," he wrote. "The judgment of God is upon the church as never before." So grievous was the clergy's neglect of the disadvantaged that King had nearly come to the conclusion that the primary obstacle to black progress was not the racist White Citizen's Councils or the Ku Klux Klan "but the white moderate, who is more devoted to 'order' than to justice." In this, King tossed a dart directly at President Kennedy and his law-and-order obsession over the past two and a half years.

His final plea was for the president to embrace the role of a great man of history. "Human progress never rolls in on wheels of inevitability," he explained. "It comes through the tireless effort of men willing to be co-workers with God." The human story, in King's eyes, was not fated toward steady advancement; the flowering of civilization resulted from the conscious actions of enlightened men and women; when those actors in history abdicated their responsibility, the tides receded, flowing in the opposite direction of progress. "Now is the time," he urged the president, "to lift our national policy from the quicksand of racial injustice to the solid rock of human dignity."

103

JACKIE KENNEDY HAD kept the secret for nearly five months, partly for her own privacy and partly because of her fear that something could go wrong—things had taken a tragic turn twice before. Yet, feeling confident enough now and needing to explain her curtailed public appearances over the next few months, she allowed the White House to announce in mid-April that she and the president were expecting their third child in late August.

Pregnancy was a difficult time for Jackie: After her miscarriage in 1955 and a stillborn delivery in 1956, she had nearly lost John Jr. in 1960 when he was born three weeks early with serious respiratory problems.

In reporting her latest pregnancy, the press noted that the First Lady would curtail all her public activities over the next several months: She would spend the summer on Squaw Island near Hyannis Port; she would not join the president on a European trip in June. Her pregnancy put her in some competition with two other Kennedy wives. Prolific Ethel Kennedy, wife of Bobby, was expected to give birth to her eighth child in July, and Ted's wife, Joan, planned to deliver their third child in August. The press raised little concern over Jackie's pregnancy; nor did it probe the reasons for such a dramatic cutback in her activities. As the *Washington Post* noted, "Mrs. Kennedy is said to be in excellent health."

* * *

On Saturday, April 20, after eight days in jail, Martin Luther King Jr. and Ralph Abernathy each posted $300 bond and were freed. They tried to hold a press conference at the jail but police shooed them away. So they met reporters at the Gaston Building owned by Birmingham's leading black businessman. King had gone into jail looking quite unlike himself in blue jeans and a work shirt instead of his trademark dark suit, and on his release his appearance was also a surprise: Always clean-shaven except for his trim mustache, King now sported an eight-day-old beard. Abernathy, also scruffy-faced, explained with his typical good humor: "Lest you think we have joined the Castro brigade," he said, stroking his chin, "they took our shaving equipment from us and only brought it back this morning." His jailers urged them to shave before leaving but the inmates wanted to present an accurate picture of their time in jail. Speaking to reporters, King confirmed that he and Abernathy had been held in solitary confinement without proper bedding until President Kennedy called Coretta; he acknowledged that some guards were surly and used abusive language, but he generously offered that "on the whole, I would say the jailers were courteous." King said he and Abernathy decided to post bond so they could strategize with the campaign's leaders at a meeting over the weekend.

The movement was struggling: King's jailing failed to whip up the media locally or nationally, even after President Kennedy's intervention. While King was in prison a couple of pallid protests took place and a handful of demonstrators were arrested. The anticipated violent backlash from the white mob—the kind of bloodshed that splashed the Freedom Rides across the front pages—didn't occur. The Birmingham campaign seemed to be going the way of the failed Albany Movement, partly because Bull Connor thus far had been surprisingly restrained. Like Albany's police chief Laurie Pritchett, Connor sought to neutralize the movement by filling the prisons. In nearly three weeks of protests, some 350 demonstrators had seen the inside of a jail cell.

In King and Abernathy's absence, movement leaders had shifted their focus to voter registration, a further sign that its original plan for mass protests was proving unsustainable. The boycott of downtown department stores also was showing cracks. By the middle of King's week in jail, blacks were apparently ignoring the call to close their wallets to white merchants. The black newspaper *Birmingham World* observed that many blacks were seen shopping as usual and noted that the boycott was "meeting with less success." At the press conference following their release, Abernathy complained that the newspapers had failed to inform the public of the campaign's goals—and the importance of the protests.

Wyatt Walker sought to drum up excitement over the "Letter from Birmingham Jail," which King finished before his release, but the press paid little attention to it. The document initially got only limited circulation in mimeographed form; it was then published as a pamphlet, and later as an article in a few periodicals before it was printed in King's 1964 book, *Why We Can't Wait.* The clergymen were offended by the letter, feeling that King had denigrated their good-faith moderate efforts and portrayed them as bigots. At first, Fred Shuttlesworth also was disgruntled, complaining that King stole too much of the limelight through his "Letter." "My feeling was that the letter should have been jointly signed by all of us," he said, "simply because we had agreed to do things together."

* * *

On the same day King walked out of prison, a well-intentioned but mentally unstable Baltimore postman strode up to the White House gate to announce his own one-man protest for equal rights. William Moore was a white, thirty-five-year-old ex-Marine on a mission: Over his ten-day vacation he planned to walk from Chattanooga, Tennessee, to Jackson, Mississippi, where he hoped to deliver a letter to Governor Ross Barnett urging him to end segregation. Moore had lived in Mississippi as a child and was pained by the racism he saw in the state; just five months before his walk, he had left his wife behind in Binghamton, New York, and moved to Baltimore to be closer to the antisegregation movement.

At the White House gate, Moore asked a guard to give a letter to the president. "I am not making this walk to demonstrate either Federal or state rights but individual rights," he wrote the president. "I am doing it, among other things I feel, for the South, and hopefully to illustrate that the most basic of freedoms of peaceful protest is not altogether extinguished down there. I hope I will not have to eat these words." When the White House guard refused to accept the letter Moore dropped it in a nearby mailbox.

Six foot five and 235 pounds, Moore was a gentle, highly educated man. In the mid-1950s, he had spent two years in a state mental hospital in New

York State; he was diagnosed with schizophrenia-paranoia and had insulin shock treatments and other therapy. He kept a journal of the experience that he later used in the writing of a book titled *The Mind in Chains: The Autobiography of a Schizophrenic*. A reviewer for the *Canadian Medical Association Journal* wrote in 1958 that the book "can take its place along-side the many classics in the field." Moore had studied at several universities: Harpur College of the State University of New York, University of Southampton, England, the University of Barcelona, the Sorbonne in Paris, and Johns Hopkins University in Baltimore. "He was a restless rebel," the *Washington Post* wrote, "who loved causes and when one wasn't handy he would seek it out." Moving to Baltimore, he took a job as a fill-in mail carrier, riding to work on a small motor scooter. He became a member of the Congress of Racial Equality and joined black students and a few whites in protesting segregation at the city's Northwood Theater, landing in jail with about four hundred others. The protests led to change at the theater. In February 1963, two months before Moore took his walk, people of both races watched a movie together for the first time at the Northwood: a matinee showing of Disney's *In Search of the Castaways*.

Before setting off on his one-man march, Moore sent a letter to his wife containing an insurance policy and some personal effects. "I don't think anything will happen to me," he wrote, "but I want you to have these." He had informed the newspapers of his plans but was universally ignored. " 'Screwball' was the description used to describe him in the city rooms," *Jet* magazine wrote. After mailing his letter to the president, Moore walked back and forth in front of the White House wearing a poster board. On his chest were the words: EQUAL RIGHTS FOR ALL, and on his back: EAT AT JOE'S BOTH BLACK AND WHITE.

104

OUT OF PRISON, Martin Luther King Jr. agonized over how to revive the Birmingham campaign. "We needed more troops," offered Wyatt Walker, noting that adults just weren't turning out in large enough numbers. One solution proposed by the campaign's leaders was to throw children into the front lines of battle. The force behind the idea was James Bevel, a key strategist for the Southern Christian Leadership Conference. A twenty-seven-year-old veteran of the student movement in Nashville, he had married another Nashville student leader, Diane Nash, and had been part of the campaign to keep the Freedom Rides going after the bloodshed in Birmingham in 1961. Bevel was a volatile, charismatic figure who wore an African multicolored skull cap on his shaven head. With enthusiasm and strong reasoning, he eventually convinced King to accept the children's crusade. Bevel flooded high schools with leaflets and trained young recruits in workshops. On the night King was arrested, Walker enlisted young activists at a mass meeting attended by students and their parents. "Some of these students say they have got to go to school," he told the crowd, "but they will get more education in five days in the City Jail than they will in five months in a segregated school."

* * *

By Tuesday, April 23, William Moore had left his bus at Chattanooga, Tennessee, and hiked some twenty miles to Trenton, Georgia. Walking south wearing his signboards and pushing a small wheeled cart, Moore had encountered little trouble. On that morning he wrote a letter to the Associated Press saying that people had been "very courteous" to him. No whites had taken umbrage at his advertising for integration. In another letter also posted from Trenton, Moore told a friend: "Feeling quite secure now. But if anything ever happened, I wonder if anybody would ever know. The road is a lonely place."

Later in the day, Moore recorded in his diary that he spoke with two men somewhere near Gadsden, Alabama, who asked him about his religious and political beliefs. One of the men, Moore noted, "predicted he would never reach his destination alive." Sometime afterward, in a park along U.S. Route 11, about thirteen miles from Gadsden, the prophecy came true. A passing motorist found Moore lying dead on a patch of grass near some picnic tables, tangled up in his signboards. Two bullets from a .22-caliber rifle had pierced his head at close range. The sheriff arrested Floyd Simpson, a forty-year-old white operator of a store and filling station located about thirty miles north of the murder site; ballistics tests had been done on Simpson's rifle and on the bullets in Moore's body, but the results were never made public. Some months later, the Etowah County grand jury chose not to indict Simpson, and no one was ever convicted of the crime.

Before setting off on his doomed journey, Moore pasted a five-cent George Washington stamp on an envelope containing a letter to the famous newspaper columnist Drew Pearson. Like the rest of the press, Pearson ignored Moore until his murder. Then, devoting a column to the man and his cause, Pearson quoted Moore's letter: "I have no idea what, if anything, the press plans to do about my walk," the activist wrote. "I would feel better if I knew that if I was shot or beaten or arrested, somebody would be informed of what it was all about. . . . I hope that I can walk to Mississippi without having to ask the Kennedys to help clear a path, but I hope they will be there if I do need help. If a man cannot walk down the street or highway dressed in a sign, otherwise minding his own business, then are we not being deprived of our freedom to speak out against injustice openly?"

Moore's death galvanized members of the Congress of Racial Equality and the Student Nonviolent Coordinating Committee. Learning of the ambush, young blacks set off the following week to replicate Moore's walk from Chattanooga to Jackson. Joining the march through Ku Klux Klan–infested areas in the hill country of northwestern Georgia and northeastern Alabama was Diane Nash Bevel, the activist wife of James Bevel. She and seven others were arrested by Etowah County sheriff's deputies and charged with disturbing the peace as they approached the area where Moore was killed; they were locked up in the jail at Gadsden.

* * *

The day after Moore's murder, President Kennedy held a regularly scheduled press conference. Moore's letter had reached civil rights advisor Lee White, who informed the president of the activist's fatal journey. Speaking to reporters, the president discussed conditions in Southeast Asia and the upcoming talks between Undersecretary of State Averell Harriman and Soviet Foreign Minister Andrei Gromyko in Moscow. He took questions on population control, Cuba, the costs of sending a man to the moon, and his proposed tax cut.

No one asked him about the Birmingham campaign, or Martin Luther King Jr. Three weeks into the protests, the president hadn't commented on the unrest. A reporter asked about a Civil Rights Commission proposal to withdraw federal funds from states that deny equal rights, a proposal Kennedy had rejected as outside the bounds of White House authority. Prompted by this question, the president brought up the murder of William Moore and erupted with surprising disgust over the bigoted violence of the South. "We have the outrageous crime, from all accounts, in the state of Alabama," the president said. The murder conflicted with his ideal of America. Without mentioning Moore by name, he spoke of the "shooting of the postman," his "being assassinated on the road" while "attempting in a very traditional way to dramatize the plight of some of our citizens." He noted that while the federal government had no direct jurisdiction in the case, he had offered the services of the FBI for the investigation.

By raising the Moore murder, Kennedy underscored his dismay with conditions in the South and his frustrations in dealing with them. His final comment on Moore's killing hinted at a quiet sharpening of his will to take on the brutal and archaic practices of the South. "We are working with every legislative, legal tool at our command to insure protection for the rights of our citizens," he asserted, raising the inflammatory prospect of Congressional action, "and we shall continue to do so."

* * *

The day after the president's press conference, Attorney General Robert Kennedy and his civil rights aide, Burke Marshall, flew into Montgomery, Alabama, for a chat with the new governor, George Wallace. While troubles brewed in Birmingham, the Kennedy administration also had a crisis forming in the state capital.

Just four months in office, the tough-talking racist governor showed no signs of backing down from his campaign pledge: "Segregation now, segregation tomorrow, segregation forever"—an obvious variation on a Ku Klux Klan chant: "Here Yesterday! Here Tomorrow! Here Forever!" Wallace's inaugural address in January was a battle cry for the South, a howl of defiance against federal court orders demanding school integration; Alabama was alone in the nation in maintaining total segregation of its educational system. A showdown between the governor and the federal government was likely now that five blacks were seeking admission to the University of Alabama. Wallace was firm at his inaugural. "Let us send this message back to Washington," he declared at his swearing in, "that from this day we are standing up, and the heel of tyranny does not fit the neck of an upright man. That from this day, from this hour, from this minute, we give the word of a race of honor that we will tolerate their boot in our face no longer. And let those certain judges put that in their opium pipes of power and smoke it for what it is worth." Wallace was as determined as ever to stay true to his campaign promise to "stand in the schoolhouse door," if necessary, to block the entrance of a black student. His defiance of federal law raised the risk of white violence—and of a federal military response—on a scale even surpassing the rioting at the University of Mississippi seven months earlier.

Bobby Kennedy, needing to assess the mood in the state capital, decided to make the journey south to take the measure of the governor in person. Previewing the attorney general's visit, the *Birmingham News* portrayed the Kennedy-Wallace meeting as a clash of pugilists. In a giant headline splashed across the entire front page, the paper screamed: ROUND 1: WALLACE VS. KENNEDYS. The paper promoted the contest as "two bantam-sized scrappers" hurtling toward a "drama-packed 'eyeball-to-eyeball' confrontation."

Wallace refused to speak with Kennedy over the arrangements of his visit, and he did everything he could to ensure that his guest felt he had landed in hostile territory. State troopers in steel helmets greeted the attorney general in an intimidating show of force at the capitol building and all the way up the steps. "They had the biggest state troopers you ever saw, all guarding the way in," Bobby remembered. "And they all had big sticks." In a symbolic show of aggression, the Confederate battle flag flapped on the staff above the capitol dome. Racist leaflets had been put in circulation, referring to the "Ape Martin Luther Koon" and to "trained niggers" who needed help from Robert Kennedy and the FBI to keep "from falling off the lunch counter stools."

At the entrance to the capitol an iron star had been laid into the floor to commemorate the spot where Confederate president Jefferson Davis took the oath of office; and for Bobby Kennedy's visit, a red-and-white carnation wreath representing the state colors was placed on top of it. As Bobby's press secretary, Edwin Guthman, recalled: "A stern, middle-aged member of the United Daughters of the Confederacy, dressed in white, stood guard, arms folded, to make sure that the foot of the Attorney

General of the United States did not tread on that spot." In a surprising show of aggression, when Bobby made his way into the capitol, one of the state troopers tried out his billy club on him. "One of them...put it into my stomach," Bobby recalled, "and...belted me, hit me with the stick."

Inside Wallace's office the conversation, which the governor insisted on recording, centered around whether the attorney general planned to send troops into Alabama to enforce the federal court order to integrate the schools.

"I know you're going to use all the force of the federal government," Wallace said. "In fact, what you're telling me today is that, if necessary, you're going to bring troops into Alabama."

"No," Bobby replied, "I didn't say that."

"You didn't?" Wallace wondered. "Well, you said all the force of the federal government."

"To make sure that the orders of the court are obeyed."

"But all the force includes troops, doesn't it?"

Bobby wondered if Wallace wanted the troops to make a theatrical point like his counterpart in Mississippi. Did he want to show himself standing up to brute federal force and then having to withdraw? Even in defeat, Wallace would enjoy the adulation of his fellow Alabamans.

In a bizarre rhetorical twist, Wallace drew on the teachings of Martin Luther King Jr. to buttress his defiance against the federal government. "Well," he told Bobby, "Martin Luther King said you have a right to disobey unjust laws." But to ensure there was no confusion about Wallace's feelings toward King, the governor fulminated against the civil rights leader: "All this agitation, and all this business of this Martin Luther King, who is a phony and a fraud, marching and going to jail and all that."

The attorney general then posed a question to Wallace that suggested that he, like his brother, was beginning to gravitate toward the moral heart of the legal dispute. "You think it would be so horrifying," he asked, "to have a Negro attend the University of Alabama, Governor?"

Wallace, blind to humane considerations on race, stuck to his vow to fight the dominance of Washington: "I will never myself submit voluntarily to any integration of any school system in Alabama."

The highly anticipated face-to-face confrontation resolved nothing. As Wallace told the press afterward, he was still determined to stand in the schoolhouse door to block any black student from getting an education at a whites-only institution.

105

ON THE MORNING of May 2, Martin Luther King Jr. was holed up in Room 30 of the Gaston Motel, fielding criticism from Birmingham's black middle class, which was outraged that he would consider deploying schoolchildren in the protests. Parents, relatives, and friends of the young people challenged King on the morality of throwing children into a battle rightly belonging to the adults. The kids' safety was at stake. A. G. Gaston objected to responsible adults leading young children to face down the brutal and unpredictable Bull Connor. King was conflicted. He cringed at the possibility of a child suffering an injury, or worse. He empathized with the parents and teachers. But he also knew that young activists had been instrumental in previous movements. The Freedom Rides had been propelled and sustained by the spirit of youth. As Freedom Ride veteran John Lewis put it, "We considered it natural and necessary to involve children—adolescents—in the movement. We weren't far from being teenagers ourselves, and we shared many of the same basic feelings of adolescence: unbounded idealism, courage unclouded by 'practical' concerns, faith and optimism untrampled by the 'realities' of the adult world."

King also knew that the white community was shocked that the movement was turning black children into foot soldiers for equal rights. But these same moralists were unwilling to negotiate to change their primitive laws of discrimination; they had to be forced to the negotiating table. King understood that sending kids into the streets would draw necessary attention to the campaign and possibly awaken an indifferent White House. At an emergency meeting of the movement's leaders two days earlier, King insisted that only drastic action would keep the campaign from dying. The Reverend John Thomas Porter, who led the city's largest black congregation at the Sixth Avenue Baptist Church, was stunned by King's willingness to risk scandal. There was no denying that the movement had lost its national profile; for two weeks, nothing had appeared on the front page of the *New York Times*. Porter heard an urgency, bordering on desperation, in King's voice. "You know," King told Porter at the emergency meeting, "we've got to get something going. The press is leaving, we've got to get going."

Usually cautious and deliberative, King now peered with some abandon toward the future. He knew that to achieve real results and avoid the fate of the Albany Movement, the Birmingham campaign needed to take risks. Putting children at the forefront emphasized more than anything the hunger for social change: The fight for equal rights was in fact a fight for children; in this light their marching was not so extraordinary. King had only to ask his critics one question: Where had these protective voices been "during the centuries when our segregated social system had been misusing and abusing Negro children?"

Even if King had wanted to pull back, it was too late. On that Thursday morning— D-Day (Desegregation Day)—while King absorbed the community's complaints at the Gaston Motel, students were warming up for their march at the Sixteenth Street Baptist Church; hundreds were getting last-minute encouragement and training and were singing freedom songs, preparing to be sent out the door. For several days, students of high school age, and some much younger, had attended instructional workshops on nonviolent protest, their numbers growing daily. King and the other leaders comforted themselves in the belief that Bull Connor and his police were not so brutal that they'd purposely hurt a child. As Ralph Abernathy put it: "We had been demonstrating for more than eight years by the time we got to Birmingham; and while people had indeed been brutalized by policemen, we were reasonably certain that even the most mean-spirited cop would refrain from clubbing a very small child."

On May 2, knowing what was afoot, school principals had locked the gates to keep their charges inside but the determined and agile students crawled up and over the fences and scampered to the Sixteenth Street Baptist Church. Not even the threat of expulsion kept them inside. Some eight hundred students skipped class that day, high school students all the way down to elementary schoolkids. The worries of educators, the public resistance, the moral outrage, the potential for injury or death—none of it kept the black students from joining the cause for freedom in Birmingham. These youths were bursting with optimism and a thirst for adventure, ignoring the risks and never contemplating whether their fervor was foolhardy.

* * *

Birmingham police blocked the roads leading away from the Sixteenth Street Baptist Church. Their strategy was to contain the protests in the black section of town, allowing the students to spill into the grass-and-elm expanse of neighboring Kelly Ingram Park, and keep them away from the downtown area. Kelly Ingram Park served as a block-wide boundary dividing the black district from the downtown world of City Hall, the department stores, and whites-only lunch counters.

Bull Connor wanted to leave nothing to chance. His detectives—in plain sight and subjected to some mocking—had attended the planning sessions inside the black church; and the FBI had passed along details it had picked up. At about 1 p.m. when the first wave of about fifty buoyant young marchers filed out of the church singing "We Shall Overcome," the police were ready. The fire department also was enlisted, its trucks filling out the blockade; but the firefighters, believing the demonstrators belonged exclusively to the police, were reluctant participants.

The youngsters came out under the church's brick arch and proceeded down the front steps: girls in dresses and light sweaters; boys in slacks and walking shoes; some wore hats; some had pants held up with suspenders; and they were laughing and singing. There were high schoolers and kids as young as six, carrying handmade picket signs reading SEGREGATION IS A SIN and I'LL DIE TO MAKE THIS LAND MY HOME. One police captain stopped several dozen elementary school children and tried to talk them into stopping their protest, but none turned away.

Some kids seemed older than their years. A teenager who was forbidden by his father from joining the protest tried to explain to him why his participation was so important. As Martin Luther King Jr. later told the story, the boy apologized to his father for disobeying him, saying he'd made a pledge to the movement and he was determined to sneak out of the house even if his father tried to keep him inside. He told his father what was motivating him. "For, you see," he said, "I'm not doing this only because I want to be free. I'm doing it also because I want freedom for you and Mama, and I want it to come before you die."

As the children made their way away from the church, parents, teachers, and friends lined the streets, some watching silently, others applauding and urging the kids on. "Sing, children, sing," an elderly woman called out. The first wave headed along Fifth Avenue North closing in on Seventeenth Street, the border of white Birmingham.

Inside the church, James Bevel was arranging for subsequent deployments, smaller groups of ten and twenty, while Wyatt Walker directed his commanders on the streets by walkie-talkie. "We were sending them out this way and that way," remembered a jubilant Walker. "Oh, man, it was a great time to be alive!"

Walker had a clever strategy to draw police away from the protest routes. Under Bull Connor's orders, the entire police force had been called out to defeat the children's crusade. Deploying a certain deviousness, Walker sent small groups of men to areas far from the protest site where they called in false police alarms, siphoning officers away from the main event near the church. "I had to do what had to be done," he explained later. "I would accommodate or alter my morality . . . I felt I had no choice." Walker kept his subterfuge to himself, declining to inform Martin Luther King Jr.: "That's one thing I was very guarded about, because I knew he would not want to do that."

* * *

Some of the youngest kids, catching their first glimpse of the helmeted police, turned and ran. The others, following orders, kneeled and prayed, and were swept up and arrested. Police struggled to keep up as Bevel unleashed wave after wave of students. Some made it to the steps of City Hall before coming under arrest; others reached the edge of the downtown shopping district. As the children poured out of the church, a policeman standing near Fred Shuttlesworth asked: "Hey, Fred, how many more have you got?"

"At least a thousand more," he warned.

"God A'mighty," the cop said with a sigh.

* * *

The first children were put into squad cars; the later ones herded into paddy wagons. "The demonstrations were a bit like a picnic," wrote *Time* magazine. "The youngsters clapped and sang excitedly, and when Connor's men arrested them, they scampered almost merrily into patrol wagons." As the afternoon wore on, police filled school buses with student demonstrators. Fire hoses snaked along the streets ready to blast the kids into submission but went unused; police dogs were on the scene but they stayed in their cages. The children's crusade ended its first day peacefully with massive arrests: By four o'clock, more than five hundred kids were in jail on charges of parading without a permit, and Birmingham had hit the headlines again.

Captain Glenn V. Evans, who was commander of the uniform patrol division, retained vivid memories of the mass arrests. More than a decade later, he recalled a conversation he had with a fellow captain as they were rounding up the children and piling them into school buses for the trip to jail. "Evans," his fellow officer said, "ten or fifteen years from now, we will look back on this and we will say, 'How stupid can you be?'"

* * *

When the newspapers landed on President Kennedy's breakfast table on Friday morning, the children's crusade was spread across the front page of the *New York Times* and the *Washington Post*. In a single day, the coverage had changed its tone and volume, providing a sudden rejuvenation of the campaign. The sight of children being carted off by police shocked the president, as it did much of the nation. Kennedy feared a descent into violence. "Birmingham's Negro population today staged the largest segregation protest demonstration in the steel city's history," the *Washington Post* reported, and the demonstrations were "planned down to the finest detail." Bull Connor, stunned by the size of the protests and their military precision, had tempered his response and held his men and dogs in check. Nobody expected his restraint to last.

The first day sent a stark message to President Kennedy. Birmingham's jails were crowded with kids: seventy-five youngsters crammed into cells meant for eight adult inmates. Now that black children were swarming the streets of Birmingham to fight the white establishment and Governor Wallace in Montgomery was threatening to stand in the schoolhouse door to block black admissions, Alabama was confirming its reputation as America's number one racial battleground. And neither side seemed willing to back down. Alabama had become the latest prod to the president's conscience and his moral courage.

* * *

At a mass meeting that night, Fred Shuttlesworth declared: "The whole world is watching Birmingham tonight." King was confident that Birmingham had captured President Kennedy's attention. Moreover, the city's blacks had awakened. Two thousand people packed into the Sixth Avenue Baptist Church to celebrate the day's success and to plan follow-up demonstrations on Friday, which James Bevel had dubbed Double D-Day. After waffling on the deployment of children, King had now embraced it. Speaking to the crowd, he praised the kids' accomplishment. He recognized that previous civil rights campaigns were propelled by the energy of students and that an injection of youthful idealism was just what the Birmingham movement needed. "I have been inspired and moved today," he told the congregation. "I have never seen anything like it."

106

ON FRIDAY, BULL Connor was prepared for the onslaught of "our little folks," as Fred Shuttlesworth described the young protesters pouring out of the Sixteenth Street Baptist Church in the afternoon. Arrayed against the youngsters was a massive force of police and firefighters, their squad cars and fire trucks forming barricades in the road. Officers stood at the ready armed with truncheons, and guns holstered on their hips. Firefighters had their high-pressure hoses unfurled, prepared to blast the children into retreat. Connor's aim this time was to disperse the students instead of arresting them—the jails were already packed—and prevent them from reaching downtown.

In the morning, Martin Luther King Jr. had met with movement leaders to plot strategy and try to mollify critics from the black community. A. G. Gaston urged King to "let those kids stay in school." King was not swayed, telling newsmen: "We are ready to negotiate. But we intend to negotiate from strength." He said if city leaders met some of the campaign's minimum demands, he'd consider halting the demonstrations. "But we want promises, plus action," he demanded.

King's tough talk, suddenly from a position of power, was backed by a flood of youngsters into the streets. The first group of sixty kids flowed out the double oak doors of the church down the steps toward Kelly Ingram

Park, which was lined by about four hundred parents, friends, office workers, and some rabble-rousers. The kids scampered along, chanting: "We're going to walk, walk, walk." And: "Freedom...Freedom... Freedom." Some fifteen hundred schoolkids were still inside the church awaiting their orders, emerging at intervals from the oak doors in small groups and fanning out in different directions from those who marched before them. Some were arrested quickly. Others carried on down Fifth Avenue along the edge of Kelly Ingram Park toward Seventeenth Street. Connor was adamant that no black marcher was going to cross Seventeenth Street into white Birmingham. His initial tool of persuasion was the fire hose. Knowing the fire department disapproved of hosing citizens into submission, Connor nonetheless gave the command: "Turn 'em on, or go home," he ordered the fire chief.

* * *

Years later, Police Captain Evans was still distraught over his role in quelling the protests. A high-ranking Birmingham police officer, he didn't share the bigotry of many fellow cops and other local citizens. He empathized with blacks over the conditions they had to endure in the city. He had witnessed one unfortunate and common black experience, and had never forgotten it. He was on a bus heading into work when a young woman came aboard with a little boy no more than four years old. The mother helped the boy onto the bus then stopped to pay the driver; by the time she'd finished the boy had sat down in front of Evans, not knowing he was in violation of strict segregation laws requiring that he get off the bus and go sit in the back. Nervous, the woman snatched the boy off the seat and scolded him: "Come on, you can't sit there."

In retelling this incident years later, Evans's voice broke and his eyes welled with tears. "Well, it did something to me just as a human being, not as a police officer. I said to myself...How do you explain to a child? And I came to the conclusion there wasn't any way to explain it....What's going to happen later when this child remembers this incident? And children *do* remember."

* * *

At Connor's command, water burst from the fire hoses, bombarding the children, knocking them to the ground and spinning them down the street. To fight the high-powered blasts, some kids joined hands trying to keep their balance in a human chain. But the torrents were too fierce; upon impact the kids whirled one way then the other, dragging their comrades down. To enhance the force, firefighters funneled the flow of two hoses into one nozzle, packing it with such ballistic fury it dislodged bricks from buildings. These jets were directed at the children, driving across their bodies, lacerating their flesh, tearing clothing off their backs; hitting the elm trees in Kelly Ingram Park, the blasts ripped off the bark. The children, knocked to the pavement, crawled away and ran back to the church, or just kept running. Some struggled to their feet with bloody noses and gashes on their faces.

Watching the assault from the sidelines, the spectators turned into a warlike mob, hurling bricks at the firefighters; bottles flew, glass shattered, people cursed and screamed. The streets were igniting into a riot. Bull Connor now had an excuse to bring in his dogs. True to character, he delivered just what King and the campaign's organizers wanted: He supplied the evening television news and tomorrow's newspapers with searing images of blacks under attack in their own country by white policemen with snarling German shepherds. The highly publicized racial crisis focused the city and the nation on the need for change. In the spirit of rebellion, Wyatt Walker was grateful for Bull Connor. "Birmingham would have been lost if Bull had let us go down to the City Hall and pray," Walker said later. "He was the perfect adversary. Connor wanted publicity, he wanted his name in the paper."

At Connor's order, police moved in behind their canines on tight leashes. The officers and the dogs pressed into the crowd, sending people fleeing. With satisfaction, Connor shouted to an officer: "Look at those niggers run." But some stood their ground. Boys taunted the dogs by flapping their shirts at them and barking. A photographer from *Life* magazine, Charles Moore, was on the scene when a block of concrete flew through the air and landed on his ankle. Despite his wound he stayed in the center of the fray, snapping photos in Kelly Ingram Park. He captured thirty-four-year-old Henry Lee Shambry as he tried to cross the park. In one shot, a German shepherd tore at the seat of Shambry's pants; in another, the dog ripped his pants leg off as Shambry, in a fedora and gazing down at the animal, tried to pull away. Shambry broke free with dog bites on his arm, leg, and hip.

Another photographer, Bill Hudson of the Associated Press, was in the center of the action, with thoughts of "making pictures and staying alive" and "not getting bit." When a six-foot high school sophomore, Walter Gadsden, crossed into his viewfinder, Hudson clicked off a series of shots. In one image, the lanky Gadsden was upright as a uniformed officer in round shades and a narrow tie yanked on the boy's sweater; at the same time a German shepherd lunged toward Gadsden's stomach with mouth open, fangs bared. A second image showed Gadsden leaning forward as the dog yanked on his sweater in front while the hand of an officer pulled on the back. Although no one was seriously injured and the dog attacks were fairly isolated, the images sent a horrific message across the nation, cementing into the American consciousness the brutal treatment of blacks in the South. King and his child soldiers were winning the propaganda war.

* * *

In Washington, mild-mannered Burke Marshall kept close watch on the Birmingham crisis. As the Justice Department's representative on civil rights matters, Marshall had contacts on both sides of the conflict: the city's white officials and newspaper publishers and the black leaders, including Martin Luther King Jr. He had already won some respect from the city's white establishment for urging King to postpone the demonstrations after the mayoral elections, conversations local officials captured on King's wiretapped phone.

After trying to reach King several times, Marshall finally spoke to him toward the end of the day and urged him to call off the demonstrations in light of the violence. But Marshall's plea only emboldened King, who sensed that the Birmingham movement had rattled the White House. With conditions tense, city officials were feeling pressed to negotiate but wanted to avoid caving in at all costs. In Marshall's view, the administration had no choice but to intervene. In a late afternoon meeting at the Justice Department, Attorney General Kennedy asked, "Do you think you should go down there?"

Marshall replied: "I think I should."

As he told an interviewer the following year: "I was off within half an hour."

* * *

At a mass meeting at the Sixteenth Street Baptist Church on Friday evening, King addressed hundreds of kids and their parents. Everyone was relieved that the swarms of young students had faced down police and fire hoses and dogs and eked by with only minor injuries. Fears over their future safety were mixed with glee over the day's success. In a statement late Friday, Attorney General Robert Kennedy condemned the use of kid protesters. "An injured, maimed, or dead child is a price that none of us can afford to pay," he said. The federal government could do little to protect the children from the brutal response of Bull Connor and recognized that the best hope was to encourage negotiation. "A lot turned on the success of Burke's efforts," Bobby Kennedy recalled. The attorney general pleaded with black leaders to give the incoming mayor, Albert Boutwell, time to act, and Boutwell told newsmen that upon assuming office he would give "immediate and determined attention" to the city's racial difficulties. Echoing the attorney general, he denounced black leaders for endangering children.

At Friday's mass meeting, King ignored all the criticism. He urged parents not to worry about their children, either the ones already in jail or the others heading out into the streets for another round of demonstrations on Saturday. "They are suffering for what they believe," he told the crowd, "and they are suffering to make this nation a better nation." Speaking as a pastor, King assured these worried souls that the children's bravery in the streets and in jail was a path to their spiritual elevation. The children had given the movement a moral power and had engaged the sympathies of Americans everywhere, in Birmingham and in the White House. "Looking back," King wrote later, "it is clear that the introduction of Birmingham's children into the campaign was one of the wisest moves we made. It brought a new impact to the crusade, and the impetus that we needed to win the struggle."

107

ON SATURDAY, MAY 4, the morning papers captured frozen images of what the television news broadcasts had streamed over the airwaves the previous night: fire hoses blasting young blacks down the pavement and snarling dogs snapping at their clothing. At the White House President Kennedy gazed in disgust at the front pages. One photo in particular caught his attention: high schooler Walter Gadsden standing tall as a ferocious German shepherd lunged for his stomach. Photos like that drove the president to conclude that dramatic action was needed to resolve racial strife in the South. He and his brother the attorney general had begun considering a route toward civil rights legislation.

As Bobby explained to the president, the federal government had few, if any, avenues of legal intervention in the local situation; at the same time, constitutional protections for blacks weren't working, "so therefore, what was acceptable was to try to get to the heart of the problem." In their private conversations, the president and the attorney general focused on the practicalities of changing the civil rights landscape. Both men understood the moral considerations of racial equality, but they steered clear of that discussion. Their conversations on legislation were conducted somewhat in brotherly unspoken language. "Perhaps because we were brothers, or whatever it might be, we didn't make speeches to each other or even discuss the fact which was obvious—I mean, the conclusion that legislation was necessary," Bobby recalled. That President Kennedy even engaged in serious conversation about civil rights legislation was a sign of how far he'd come from his previous knee-jerk rejection of the notion. He still blanched, however, at the political battle and potential harm a push for civil rights legislation might have on the rest of his agenda, not to mention on his bid for reelection in 1964. He wasn't yet entirely sold on taking the lead on civil rights, but something was no doubt stirring in him. He and Bobby knew the national mood was shifting. "What Bull Connor did down there, and the dogs and the hoses and the pictures with the Negroes," Bobby recalled, "is what created a feeling in the United States that more needed to be done."

* * *

On Saturday, as King launched another wave of protests in Birmingham and Burke Marshall began frantic negotiations with black and white leaders in the city, the president held a previously scheduled meeting with about twenty members of the Americans for Democratic Action. Speaking to the liberal lobbying group, he sounded frustrated and politically hemmed in, unable to confront conditions in Birmingham with the resolve he knew they required. "Birmingham is the worst city in the South," he said. "They have done nothing for the Negroes in that community, so it is an intolerable situation." He referred repeatedly to the undesirable possibility that federal troops would be needed, if matters got out of hand. "This may be the only way these things come to a head," he admitted.

His thoughts were disjointed; the president bounced from one subject to the next. One minute, he fretted over the economy and its potential decline; the next, he touted his progress on civil rights; another moment, he described the opposition in Congress to aspects of his domestic agenda; at another, he laid into newspaper columnists who took him to task on civil rights yet themselves dined at the whites-only, male-only Metropolitan Club while he had forced the Cosmos Club to change its policy of segregation. He did not mention the possibility of comprehensive civil rights legislation, although he addressed efforts to gain a voting rights law as a way to change the South through the ballot box.

In the tone of his voice and the hopscotching of his remarks, the president seemed a man still searching for a path forward, a man seeking a way to salve his conscience on civil rights. He seemed particularly moved by the photo of the dog attacking the young student. "I think it's terrible, the picture in the paper," he said. "The fact of the matter, that's just what Connor wants." Later, Arthur Schlesinger described the president as reacting even more strongly to the photo; in Schlesinger's telling, Kennedy told the ADA group that the picture had made him "sick." Whatever the president's actual language, he conveyed that the images from Birmingham revolted him.

When one of the ADA members said he wanted the president to assert stronger moral leadership on equal rights, Kennedy bristled. "Let me just say about the civil rights business," he began. "We have done not enough because the situation is so desperate. But we have shoved and pushed and . . . there is nothing that my brother has given more time to." Then, in a sudden show of empathy, the president revealed that he had indeed contemplated Southern conditions and even imagined what it was like to be black in America. "I quite agree," he said, "if I were a Negro I would be awfully sore."

108

SEEKING TO CALM tensions and bring opposing parties to the negotiating table, Burke Marshall moved through an unsettled city on the edge of a storm. The Birmingham movement now traveled along two tracks simultaneously: In indoor meeting rooms, the Kennedy administration, through Marshall, was racing to get blacks and whites to understand each other, while out on the street, young protesters didn't let up. King and his fellow leaders sought to keep the protests peaceful, launching young activists on Saturday from two churches in small groups without signs; the strategy was to sneak the teenagers quietly past police so they could link up at the designated target: City Hall. But most were arrested; only a few slipped through. More troubling to police than the smiling children were the spectators, now numbering more than a thousand, who had amassed under the elms in Kelly Ingram Park. Some taunted officers by yelling, waving their arms, and dancing, and were answered by a high-powered blast from a fire hose. The mob became belligerent: Rocks and bottles flew at police and firemen as the water cannons unleashed their fury. Blacks on rooftops rained bricks and other debris down on the scene.

With conditions veering toward anarchy, James Bevel emerged with another pastor to confront the mob. "We don't want a riot," Bevel warned. "Lives could be lost." He'd seen at least two dozen black men with guns, and he did not want anyone untrained in peaceful protest to undermine the nonviolent movement. The pastors begged the crowd to go home. "We don't want any trouble," Bevel shouted through a borrowed police bullhorn. "The only way you can help our movement now is to get back." The pleas and the hoses eventually dispersed the mob but not before two hundred blacks were arrested, 111 of them children under the age of sixteen. In all, more than 1,600 had been carted to jail since the protests began on April 3.

* * *

On Sunday, Martin Luther King Jr. was back at his church, Ebenezer Baptist, in Atlanta to preach to his congregation, while Burke Marshall met with white merchants and businessmen in Birmingham in search of a resolution. King optimistically predicted that blacks were on the verge of new freedoms in Birmingham. "In a few days," he told the Atlanta congregants, "we will have everything we are asking and maybe more."

Although King wasn't present to see it, a showdown that some described as a miracle took place in Birmingham on that same Sunday and seemed to confirm his hope. After a mass meeting at Birmingham's New Pilgrim Baptist Church, some two thousand well-attired marchers moved quietly up Sixth Avenue where they confronted paddy wagons, fire hoses, and lines of police. The demonstrators hoped to hold a prayer vigil at the city jail for the many imprisoned children. When they approached a barricade preventing them from passing from the black district into the city's white area, Bull Connor stepped boldly forward.

A standoff ensued. Captain Glenn Evans asked the marchers to proceed no farther and instead return to the church. At the head of the march, the Reverend Charles Billups, a veteran of Birmingham's racial battles, knelt in prayer, and immediately the long column behind him followed his lead, blacks in their Sunday best dropping to their knees on the pavement in silence one after the other. Stunned, Bull Connor watched with growing fury. Billups got to this feet and hollered at the forces arrayed against them: "Turn on your water, turn loose your dogs, we will stand here till we die." As the protesters braced for the attack, some trembling, one even fainting, no water jets blasted from the nozzles. No snarling dogs leapt into the crowd. In a rage, Bull Connor barked at his men: "Dammit. Turn on the hoses." But his soldiers defied his orders. Writing later, King depicted the scene: "What happened in the next thirty seconds was one of the most fantastic events of the Birmingham story," he wrote in *Why We Can't Wait*. The firemen trained their hoses on the marchers, many of whom were on their knees. And something amazing happened. "Connor's men, as though hypnotized, fell back," King wrote, "their hoses sagging uselessly in their hands." Without incident, the marchers carried on into a nearby blacks-only park and held a prayer service.

William Kunstler, the civil rights activist and lawyer, was spellbound by the muted drama of that Sunday afternoon. "Until Birmingham, I was not certain that I really believed that good could triumph over evil," he wrote in his memoir, *Deep in My Heart*. But, he added, that one victory over Bull Connor by blacks praying in the street "helped to change my mind."

109

THE PROTESTS CHANGED national sentiment. Before Birmingham, only 4 percent of Americans polled believed civil rights was the country's most urgent issue; after Birmingham, that figure jumped to 52 percent.

Burke Marshall, sensitive to the pain of racial change, tried to ease the white community to a new understanding. He listened to businessmen and local leaders and gently prodded them to sit down with black activists. Chief among black demands were total desegregation of Birmingham stores—lunch counters, restrooms, fitting rooms—immediate improvement of employment opportunities, dropping charges against those arrested, establishment of a biracial Birmingham committee to work out future grievances. Marshall hinted that King was willing to bend on some of these proposals, which gave the white men room to maneuver. At all hours of the day and night the assistant attorney general for civil rights shuttled back and forth between the white and black leaders to keep the conversation going, clarifying issues, seeking any grounds for agreement; if the men kept talking, he hoped at some point he could bring them together for substantive negotiations.

Marshall walked a very fine line: The businessmen believed they were being forced into abandoning their vaunted history of white supremacy and were suspicious of the Kennedy administration. President Kennedy was criticized and mocked in local newspapers in cartoons, columns, and editorials. The resistance of white Birmingham to both Kennedy and King proved almost insurmountable. "At the start, there was nothing," Marshall recalled. "The politicians in Birmingham were not in a position to make any sort of accommodation with Martin King. They wouldn't talk to him. They wouldn't talk to anybody that *would* talk to him." Marshall targeted whites who had a personal interest in resolving the conflict: those affected by the business boycott and by the disturbances in the street.

At the same time, black leaders turned up the heat, knowing that the white community would bend only under massive pressure. On Monday,

May 6, the movement sent out more than a thousand kid marchers, and nearly all were arrested. A black spectator tossed a Coke bottle that grazed the foot of an officer, setting off an aggressive water cannon and police response. Far from coming together, the city was fracturing. By the end of the day, the number of people filling Birmingham's overcrowded jails had climbed to nearly 2,500.

Amid the tensions, Marshall accelerated his shuttle diplomacy; he met separately with Martin Luther King Jr. and old-time segregationist Sid Smyer, Birmingham's most influential businessman who, as reluctant as he was, knew the time for change had come. Smyer needed a good-faith gesture from King—a halt in the demonstrations—to get a dialogue going with the white community. He got his fellow businessmen to agree that in return for a pause in the protests they would move to desegregate department stores and lunch counters; and then real conversations on other demands could begin. But black leaders rejected the proposal as "too little and too late."

Tuesday, Marshall was at it again, meeting with Smyer and the merchants early in the morning. Some of the white businessmen had received phone calls from President Kennedy and his brother urging them to go further to bring blacks to the negotiating table. The merchants agreed to promote some of their lowest-level black employees to store clerks and to desegregate all store facilities. But King was unimpressed, telling reporters that the demonstrations would continue until the demands were met. "At this point," he said, "I would not say that negotiations have been satisfactory." He was pleased that nonviolent protest had filled the jails. By sitting behind bars, the young protesters tugged on the conscience of the community and the nation. "Activities which have taken place in Birmingham over the last few days, to my mind, mark the nonviolent movement coming of age," he told reporters. "This is the first time in the history of our struggle that we have been able, literally, to fill the jails. In a very real sense, this is the fulfillment of a dream."

Nonviolence was soon tested. When the student marchers fanned out into the streets on Tuesday, they were swamped by a huge crowd numbering as many as three thousand. The mob, untrained in Gandhian nonviolence, erupted in rioting. Rocks and bottles battled fire hoses mounted on tripods. One of the high-powered nozzles flew out of control, its blistering spray ripping into two police officers, fracturing the ribs of one and injuring the legs of the other. Police and highway patrolmen stormed the area. Blacks were chased down and beaten with billy clubs. An armored car rolled in like a tank. "We've just started to fight, if that's what they want," Bull Connor declared. "We were trying to be nice to them but they won't let us be nice." Few arrests were made, because there was nowhere to put new inmates.

When the Reverend Fred Shuttlesworth stepped outside the Sixteenth Street Baptist Church to check on the scene, he was slammed against a stone wall by water-cannon fire. Carried inside with chest injuries, he was soon in an ambulance heading to the hospital. Bull Connor gloated over taking out his longtime opponent. "I waited a week to see Shuttlesworth get hit with a hose," he said. Connor's only regret was that he wasn't there to see it and had to learn about it secondhand. "I wish they'd carried him away in a hearse," he told a reporter.

In response to the chaos, Governor Wallace told the opening session of the state legislature that he was "beginning to tire of agitators, integrationists, and others who seek to destroy law and order in Alabama." Wallace ordered 250 highway patrolmen into Birmingham. He also sent Brigadier General Henry Graham of the Alabama National Guard to the city, although the governor did not indicate whether Alabama troops would follow. Graham had overseen martial law in Montgomery during the Freedom Ride riots in 1961.

Both sides—whites and blacks—complained to the president. Clarence Hanson, the publisher of the *Birmingham News*, printed a rambling editorial on the front page in the form of a telegram to the president that begged for an end to the demonstrations. He blamed Kennedy for inspiring blacks to challenge white society in Alabama. "Mr. President, it is our sincere belief that you, too, have a responsibility for this crisis," Hanson wrote. "We recall that in the past some of these same demonstration leaders have met with you, presumably to discuss their problems and their goals." On the other side, Roy Wilkins, the executive secretary of the NAACP, urged blacks throughout the country to send telegrams to the White House in support of Birmingham's desegregation movement. He called on his organization's branches in a hundred key cities to organize sympathy pickets for the protesters in Alabama.

In a letter to the president, baseball star Jackie Robinson charged that civil rights progress had collapsed during his administration. "The pace at which our country is moving toward total equality for all peoples is miserably slow," he said. The "atrocities" inflicted on blacks in the South were "disgusting," he added, noting: "The revolution that is taking place in this country cannot be squelched by police dogs or high power hoses." He then raised a sensitive point for the president: perceptions of America overseas. Quoting a news report from Ghana that said "America's greatness is meaningless as long as racial discrimination continues," Robinson asked: "How can those newly formed governments of Africa possibly be expected to emulate our way of life," when brutal conditions exist in Alabama? Recalling other times the president had acted courageously, Robinson challenged him: "I must state bluntly that there will be grave doubts as to the sincerity of your administration, unless you face this issue in the forthright manner with which you handled the steel industry and the Cuban situation."

* * *

On Tuesday afternoon, Sid Smyer convened a meeting with eighty-nine of the city's community and industry leaders, including the so-called Big Mules who headed local steel, insurance, banking, and utilities operations. The men gathered inside the opulent conference room at the Chamber of Commerce as sirens screamed outside. Burke Marshall recalled that during the meeting "reports would come in from the police chief and the sheriff that they didn't think they could handle the situation for more than a few more hours. It was very tense." One business leader immediately proposed that they call the governor, have him declare martial law, and send in the Alabama National Guard to stamp out the demonstrations. It seemed an understandable request given the sounds of chaos just outside. But Smyer rejected the hard line. He tried to talk sense to the men, telling them it was time to compromise on segregation. Smyer, as staunch a segregationist as any of them, saw the world changing around him, and if the business community in Birmingham wanted to keep pace it had to adapt.

Smyer then called on Marshall to speak. In his usual subdued tone, Marshall explained that martial law was not the answer; it only postponed the inevitable. The black community was likely to keep protesting until its rights were granted. The businessmen had already offered some concrete proposals on integrating the department store facilities and on hiring. Now, Marshall told the men, "they had a solution in their hands," if they would endorse certain changes in the way they did business. Marshall had proved an honest broker; he persuaded without demanding. "Rarely did he inject himself into the settlement of the community's problem," observed Chuck Morgan, a white, liberal Birmingham lawyer. "But he was there and the presence of the United States coupled with his quiet skill helped bring forth Birmingham's abstainers, its business community."

As the afternoon wore on, the men gradually fell into line. Vigorous debate produced a vague resolution outlining some reforms; it passed a vote with only three dissents and was left to a committee to work out the tough details of Birmingham's new acceptance of black rights. Outside the conference room, Marshall immediately phoned Robert Kennedy, who was sitting with his brother in the Oval Office. President Kennedy got on the line and Marshall gave him the news directly. "I told the president that the meeting had worked and that I thought we were going to have a solution the next day," he recalled.

110

WHILE MASS MEETINGS filled three churches on Tuesday evening, black and white negotiators were in the offices of a downtown insurance company to iron out the details of an agreement, with Burke Marshall looking on. Birmingham's white establishment had refused to invite Martin Luther King Jr., still deemed an outside agitator—on this night, he rallied the crowd at the Sixteenth Street Baptist Church. The negotiators agreed on a time frame for desegregation and for boosting black employment, but insurmountable snags prevented a consensus on dropping charges against the demonstrators and forming a biracial commission to tackle future issues. The group broke up without a full resolution, and another, smaller team, continued talking until three in the morning at another location. In the marathon session, both sides finally yielded.

On Wednesday morning, each group prepared to announce the

settlement to their constituents. The agreement hinged on the black leaders calling off their protests in return for a variety of actions by the business and political communities: desegregation of the department store fitting rooms within three days, lunch counters within sixty days, removal of segregation signs on washrooms, restrooms, and drinking fountains within thirty days, a meeting with the new city government once it was in place, new employment opportunities within sixty days, and establishment of a white committee to liaison with blacks. Despite all the white concessions, the proposal reflected a significant black compromise: Originally the alliance between King's Southern Christian Leadership Conference and Shuttlesworth's Alabama Christian Movement for Human Rights planned no end to the marches until all its demands were met. To do otherwise was to surrender the power of protest on promises from a white community that had reneged on its pledges many times in the past. Now, the movement's leadership agreed to stop the protests on the expectation that the white businessmen would sign on to their side of the agreement.

The black committee presented the proposal to King at the home of John Drew, a real estate and insurance executive and one of Birmingham's black elites. King listened while the group loudly debated the provisions. He had come to appreciate Burke Marshall's subtle influence; at first he had been wary of the administration's envoy but he'd grown to trust and respect him. Marshall had come not merely to impose an unfair truce on blacks, as King had first worried; but rather, with patience and an open mind, he had helped both races navigate their own deep-seated biases. Through their own efforts, blacks and whites together had fashioned a platform on which to build a new future. King recalled an ardent segregationist saying of Marshall: "There is a man who listens. I had to listen back, and I guess I grew up a little." King saw the virtues of the agreement and gave his approval.

Delighted by the progress, Marshall arrived at Drew's home and began preparing to release the news. He informed the White House that President Kennedy could announce the truce at his regularly scheduled press conference in Washington later in the day. Simultaneously King himself would go before reporters in Birmingham. The prestige of the president, the reputation of Martin Luther King Jr., and the integrity of the white community were all on the line. America stood on the verge of a groundbreaking step in racial progress. All seemed to be proceeding just as planned until Fred Shuttlesworth, still wobbly from his fire-hosing, suddenly burst into Drew's living room. Still wearing his patient's wristband, he had raced out of the hospital when he heard of the agreement. "Kennedy was all set to announce in Washington and King in Birmingham that the demonstrations were gon' be called off, but I had to veto that," Shuttlesworth recalled. He was not only outraged by the agreement—made without his consultation—he was also offended that King hadn't found time to visit him in the hospital. Shuttlesworth had been administered "three hypos," as he called the shots of sedative in his system, and he was groggy; he described himself as "reelin' and rockin'." For a moment he lost focus. When King told him, "Fred, we've got to call the demonstrations off," Shuttlesworth was so light-headed he didn't quite catch it.

"Say that again, Martin," he asked.

"We've got to call the demonstrations off."

Shuttlesworth was clearly confused and in pain, but he was so furious he pushed right through it, laying into King. "My language probably wasn't as sweet as it shoulda been," he admitted. To Shuttlesworth, the agreement didn't assure victory: The movement was giving up only on the word of the white community. "You and I promised that we would *not* stop demonstrating until we *had* the victory," he reminded King. "And if you call it off or Mr. Kennedy calls it off, with the last little ounce of strength I got, I'm gonna get back out and lead." Abernathy tried to calm him, to no effect. Shuttlesworth suspected that King had been charmed by President Kennedy and his effective emissary, Burke Marshall, and now there was no turning him around. Despondent, he told King to go ahead and have his press conference, but that, too, was a betrayal of their partnership in the campaign. "We wasn't supposed to have press conferences, 'cept joint," he reminded King. "I'm goin' back to my bed. I already gave you my answer."

In another room, an associate of Marshall's was heard speaking on the phone. A line had been kept open to the White House to provide immediate updates. "We hit a snag—the frail one," the voice said, meaning Shuttlesworth. "The frail one is hanging up. Looks like it won't go through."

"Wait, wait, Fred," King said.

Before he could say another word, Shuttlesworth was out the door.

111

UNABLE TO REVERSE course, a fretful Martin Luther King Jr. went ahead with his press conference, announcing a postponement of the demonstrations while the agreement was fully ratified by the white negotiators. Fred Shuttlesworth, having been cajoled back into the fold, sat at King's side. "Fred was under a great deal of strain," explained Wyatt Walker. "He was not physically well. He saw Birmingham as something which he built with spit and Scotch tape. And he did." Walker conceded that the Birmingham campaign never would have happened without Shuttlesworth's Alabama Christian Movement for Human Rights. Shuttlesworth was known for his ravings, but he also had a deep love and respect for King, which ultimately brought him around. Narcotics may also have played a role. An SCLC member may have sneaked a sedative into Shuttlesworth's coffee, changing his mood and cooling his opposition. Nonetheless, Shuttlesworth managed to wrest a compromise from King: Instead of announcing a complete end to the protests, King said the marches were off for one day only while final touches were put on the agreement. If the white community didn't sign off on the settlement, protesters were again going to take to the streets.

* * *

In Washington, President Kennedy stepped before reporters at his news conference. Now, more than at any time in his presidency, he was preoccupied by civil rights. When he had grappled with the rioting at Ole Miss, he had not yet appreciated how profound and consequential the issue of racial equality was to American life. But having presided over the bloodshed of the Freedom Rides, and the unrest in Mississippi, and now the resolve of the black community in Birmingham, the president was nearing a personal turning point. As he began his statement, his public face was presidential: engaged, impartial, and encouraging.

"I am gratified to note the progress in the efforts by white and Negro citizens to end an ugly situation in Birmingham, Alabama," he began. He spoke briefly of the administration's efforts to uphold the law and enforce court decisions. Then he returned to the agreement and highlighted the suffering blacks endured in Birmingham. "Our efforts have been focused on getting both sides together to settle in a peaceful fashion the very real abuses too long inflicted on the Negro citizens of that community." He praised the business community for responding in "a constructive and commendable fashion" and for pledging to take "substantial steps [that] would begin to meet the justifiable needs of the Negro community." He also commended the black leaders for suspending the demonstrations. "While much remains to be settled before the situation can be termed satisfactory," the president observed, "we can hope that tensions will ease and that this case history which has so far only narrowly avoided widespread violence and fatalities will remind every State, every community, and every citizen how urgent it is that all bars to equal opportunity and treatment be removed as promptly as possible."

112

BIRMINGHAM DID NOT look like a city moving away from crisis: The streets were lined with state troopers and city police; the Sixteenth Street Baptist Church was packed with students determined to hit the pavement again should the settlement unravel. One powerful and unrestrained member of the white community, Bull Connor, despised the agreement and was prepared to fight it with all of his considerable resources. He was dismissive of the white negotiating committee. "They haven't talked to Bull Connor," he told a reporter. Asked if the merchants were empowered to speak for him, he shouted: "No sir! No sir!"

Not long after the president left the podium in Washington, a local judge—with Bull Connor's full encouragement—suddenly increased the amount of bail that Martin Luther King Jr. and Ralph Abernathy had to pay to stay out of jail while appealing their convictions for unlawful parading on Good Friday. Unable to pull together the $2,500 each, vastly more than the original bond of $300, the two men were carted off to jail.

Their imprisonment lit a fuse in the black community, and that might have been exactly what Connor and the judge had hoped to do: ignite black fury, spur more marches, perhaps incite a riot, and thereby kill the agreement. Word quickly reached Washington, alarming the Kennedys; not only was bond money needed for the two leaders, King was now demanding the release of some two thousand other protesters. The sudden hike in King's bond burden set Bobby Kennedy to work behind the scenes to round up the cash.

Predictably Fred Shuttlesworth flew into a rage over King's jailing; he pulled on his "marching shoes" and lifted himself off his bed at the Gaston Motel intent on leading young protesters into battle: In his view, the moratorium on marches was over. But before he could get out the door, Justice Department staffer Joseph Dolan asked him to wait a moment. Dolan, who had accompanied Marshall to Birmingham, phoned Robert Kennedy and spoke quietly into the receiver: "Fred's sort of gone off the deep end. Could you try to calm him down?" Taking the phone, Shuttlesworth listened as the attorney general reasoned with him. No one revealed what was said between the two men, but by the time Shuttlesworth handed back the phone, he had agreed to give the process more time.

* * *

In New York, the phone rang in Harry Belafonte's Upper West Side apartment. On the line was Robert Kennedy, who was frantic to get King and Abernathy out of jail. "Could I send down $5,000 myself to bail out the two of them?" Kennedy asked Belafonte, only half joking. He was desperate to salvage the Birmingham agreement any way he could. "The only problem is," Belafonte told him, "I'm not sure the SCLC will use it." He explained that King was now adamant about staying in jail himself until all the young protesters were free. With the agreement on the line, Kennedy was clearly annoyed by King's ploy; his continued incarceration could only inflame the black community. Besides, King was crucial to ironing out last-minute snags in the settlement. If the settlement collapsed, Birmingham could explode. The attorney general hung up the phone, telling Belafonte he'd come back to him: He had another strategy to save the day.

In moments, Bobby had A. G. Gaston on the line. As a prominent

Birmingham businessman, Gaston had a strong motive to seal the agreement without further delay and therefore to get King out of jail. Soon, Gaston was at the jail handing over $5,000 in bond money. Even if King and Abernathy wanted to remain locked up, their bond had been paid and they had no choice. They were escorted out of the jailhouse. In New York, Belafonte and lawyer William Kunstler were also scrambling to raise the funds, and Kunstler had booked himself a 2 a.m. flight from Newark, New Jersey, to Birmingham to deliver the cash. "To my surprise," Kunstler observed, "I found that there was a lot of available cash around New York late at night." With the money in hand, he was about to depart for the airport when the phone rang, and Wyatt Walker reported that Gaston had beat them to the rescue. As Kunstler recalled: "Belafonte and I spent the rest of the night returning the money to the people who had lent it to us."

113

ON THURSDAY, MAY 9, as tensions escalated in Birmingham, Ben Bradlee of *Newsweek* had dinner at the White House. The one-day moratorium on protests had passed and still no agreement had been finalized. Martin Luther King Jr. extended the deadline, to Fred Shuttlesworth's annoyance. The two original partners in the Birmingham campaign now had different goals: King was taking a conciliatory approach; he was willing to compromise to gain victory, and he hoped to claim Birmingham as a badge of his new leadership. Shuttlesworth, his combativeness in stark contrast to King's studied calm, fumed at the faithlessness of the white community; he wanted to send marchers back into the street to pressure the city's political and business leaders to surrender.

The internal battles of the black leadership in Birmingham were far removed from the dinner conversation at the White House. Dining with the president and Jackie were Bradlee and his wife, Tony, Teddy Kennedy, Robert Kennedy, and the patriarch, Joseph Kennedy Sr., who was assisted by cousin Ann Gargan. "Old Joe was unchanged," Bradlee noted. "It took us a few minutes to get used to his 'no, no, no' again, but we did." President Kennedy was headed to Ireland in June to explore his heritage. He planned to visit the region of his ancestors in County Wexford, with a jaunt to the nearby port of New Ross; it was from New Ross that his great-grandfather had set sail for America during the potato famine of the mid-nineteenth century. At dinner, he "noted with pride that he and his brothers and sisters were 100 percent Irish," Bradlee recalled. The president then joked about how "mongrelized" others at the table were: Bradlee had English, German, and Polish ancestors, and both Tony and Jackie had English and French blood. "He changed the subject," Bradlee noted, "when we pointed out that if Jackie were all that 'mongrelized,' so were Caroline and John."

If there was any outward sign of the crisis in Birmingham, it was in Bobby's distraction and his absence from the table. A crucial sticking point in reaching a final accord was the release of the 790 schoolchildren still in prison; the required bond at $300 each totaled about $237,000. Bobby spent the dinner on the phone trying to drum up the cash, chiefly from trade and labor unions: the AFL-CIO, the steelworkers, the auto workers. Their slush funds were brimming with ready cash.

* * *

Harry Belafonte was also on the phone with Bobby Kennedy that night, helping to chase down the cash. Impressed by the attorney general's commitment, Belafonte noticed a transformation coming over the younger Kennedy. "I felt that at last I'd found his moral center, just as Martin had predicted we would," Belafonte recalled. King was fielding calls from Belafonte about the funds, and he, too, was impressed with Bobby's effort. King "now sensed that Bobby was doing all he could to resolve the crisis by bailing out the children." While the president enjoyed his dinner, Bobby had rounded up $80,000 from the AFL-CIO, and $40,000 from the United Steelworkers. He phoned Belafonte to check on his progress securing $50,000 from the New York transportation workers' union. While the men were talking, the apartment intercom rang, and Belafonte went to answer it.

"I'll wait on the line," Bobby said.

When Belafonte opened the door, a courier from the transportation union greeted him with a satchel containing $50,000 in cash.

Returning to the phone, Belafonte told Kennedy: "Okay, it's in my hands."

* * *

In his search for cash, Belafonte was also in contact with Nelson Rockefeller's assistant, journalist turned speechwriter Hugh Morrow. Belafonte had enlisted Martin Luther King Jr.'s lawyer, Clarence Jones, to work with Morrow in securing the funds.

When Jones phoned Morrow on Thursday night, he got the good news.

"Mr. Rockefeller would like to help," Morrow told Jones.

Jones was instructed to meet Rockefeller and Morrow at the Chase Manhattan Bank on Forty-Seventh Street and Sixth Avenue. Understanding the urgency, the governor agreed to meet at the bank after hours. When Jones questioned how the transaction could be done at that time, Morrow said simply: "Please, Mr. Jones, just meet us at the bank."

Arriving at the location as instructed, Jones was escorted by a guard to a downstairs vault where he found Rockefeller and Morrow. A few spins of the combination lock opened the thick vault door revealing stacks of dollar bills wrapped in cellophane. "I mean I'm an educated Negro," Clarence recalled, "but I sure never stood in front of an open bank vault door before." Rockefeller, the grandson of John D. Rockefeller, cofounder of Standard Oil, entered the vault, picked up a couple stacks of bills, and set them on a table in front of Jones. "I hope this is enough," he said.

Morrow explained that now strict secrecy was required. Rockefeller had much to lose if his donation on behalf of jailed black protesters became public. He did not want to be accused of trying to buy black votes in his expected run for the 1964 Republican nomination for president.

The secret, it turned out, was a big one. Referring to the cellophane packages on the table, Morrow told Jones: "It's a hundred thousand dollars."

The movement now had more than enough bond money to free the jailed children.

114

BY FRIDAY MORNING, May 10, the agreement had been hammered out and the cash was making its way to the city's bond clerks. The press conference to announce the settlement was postponed until Martin Luther King Jr. was satisfied the money had been secured and the jails had been emptied and the children were back in the arms of their parents. In the afternoon, King, Ralph Abernathy, and Fred Shuttlesworth sat at a table on the patio of the Gaston Motel and faced reporters. The three men, dressed in suits and ties, looked drawn, but no one was as exhausted and wobbly as Shuttlesworth, still weak from his hammering by a fire hose; he had been promised the opportunity to speak first.

"The city of Birmingham has reached an accord with its conscience," Shuttlesworth said, reading from a statement. "Birmingham may well offer for Twentieth Century America an example of progressive racial relations; and for all mankind a dawn of a new day, a promise for all men, a day of opportunity, and a new sense of freedom for all America." The agreement held that lunch counters, fitting rooms, and drinking fountains would be desegregated within ninety days; blacks would be hired as clerks and salesmen within sixty days, and would be eligible throughout industrial Birmingham for jobs previously denied them; everyone in jail on charges related to protesting would be released; communications between white and black citizens would be established to prevent the need for further protests.

King declared the day a triumph for both races and stressed that this moment was not an end but a beginning. "Though we have come a long way, there is still a strenuous task before us and some of it is yet uncharted," he said. In spreading credit for the victory, he went out of his way to praise Shuttlesworth. "Without question, of course, the name of Fred Shuttlesworth stands clear as the magic name in this Magic City," King told reporters. King praised the members of Shuttlesworth's Alabama Christian Movement for Human Rights and the thousands of children and adults who risked their safety, and the white community, which he described as "men of good will." The final glory went to God: "For He has clearly been at work among us. And it is He alone who has finally gained the victory for all His children." Before the men could close the press conference Shuttlesworth collapsed and was whisked away by ambulance to a segregated hospital.

For both sides, the agreement was founded on hope, rather than fact: Blacks accepted less than they had originally wanted; in place of immediate and measurable action on their rights, they got promises; and the white community, never having wanted to surrender at all, had pledged to make changes as long as protesters stayed off the streets. The cautious words of all the leaders gave the sense of a lull in the crisis rather than any permanent cooperation. King urged his followers to avoid celebrating the moment as a "victory for the Negro. It is rather a victory for democracy and the whole citizenry of Birmingham—Negro and white." Knowing that Birmingham sat upon a fragile peace, King pleaded with the black community: "This is the time we must evince calm dignity and wise restraint. Emotion must not run wild. Violence must not come from any of us." And, he added, no gloating: "As we stand on the verge of using public facilities heretofore closed to us, we must not be overbearing and haughty in spirit. We must be loving enough to turn an enemy into a friend."

In the white community, deep misgivings simmered. Knowing that white acquiescence, grudging as it may have been, was essential, businessman Sid Smyer tried to appeal to reason. "It is important that the public understand that the steps we have taken were necessary to avoid a dangerous and imminent explosion," he said. "Now that peace has returned to our community, it is up to all to help preserve it by doing nothing which would destroy it."

* * *

In Washington, the Kennedys were relieved. Most pleasing to the president and the attorney general, the crisis had dissolved without direct federal intervention: The local community resolved its problems on its own. The only federal presence was the unobtrusive, guiding hand of Burke Marshall. King praised Marshall in front of the Birmingham media for bringing the two sides together. "He made the dialogue possible," he explained.

Marshall returned to Washington on Friday and joined Robert Kennedy at a press conference, where the attorney general lavished praise on his assistant. "If it hadn't been for his efforts," Kennedy said of Marshall, "the situation in Birmingham would be far different tonight."

* * *

For the moment, Birmingham was quiet. But the Kennedys had no illusions that the city reflected a larger problem throughout the South and across the country. The president and the attorney general recognized the likelihood of repeated racial confrontation and that the federal government had to set the country on a new course. "I don't know what discussion the President and the Attorney General had," Marshall observed. "But I think as I came back...everybody's mind was turned to the future and they thought this pattern of Birmingham had been established, that it would recur in many other places." President Kennedy was searching for a path forward, and he knew that racial unrest was something "he had not only to face up to himself, but somehow bring the country to face up to and resolve." The president began seeking recommendations from his brother the attorney general on what far-reaching solution was possible. Their discussions about civil rights legislation now became more serious.

115

WHITE-ROBED EXTREMISTS CONGREGATED on Saturday, May 11, at Moose Club Park in Bessemer, Alabama, a Ku Klux Klan stronghold several miles outside of Birmingham. They had poured in from Georgia, South Carolina, Tennessee, and Mississippi for a picnic and barbecue with local families and a rally for racism. Speaking to the crowd, Imperial Wizard Robert Shelton sought to reel in new recruits and drum up support for the Klan's violent resistance to the Birmingham agreement. He attacked the movement's black leaders in vile language and tried to whip up a united front, alleging a conspiracy between blacks and white businessmen. His cries were met largely by silence. Unwilling to surrender to the cool reception, Shelton tried to stir the crowd to hoot rebel yells. "Let's stand back and yell for the white people of Alabama," he prompted. But barely a murmur came in reply. The families out for a barbecue might have nursed similar fears about integration, but their restraint was telling. "Shelton's inability to rev up this family crowd was perhaps the truest reflection of the sea change that had been inspired by Birmingham that week," historian Diane McWhorter wrote in her book *Carry Me Home*. "In the growing consensus that segregation had to go, the Klan was losing its mainstream appeal and shrinking into a purely terrorist cell."

* * *

Birmingham cop Ben Allen got word that the Klan was planning to retaliate against the agreement, and its target was Martin Luther King Jr. "I had information," Allen explained, "that the Gaston Motel in Birmingham was gonna be dynamited at a given hour from an informer that had never given me wrong information before." A white Southerner, Allen took his duty to protect the public seriously, although his efforts were constrained under the perverse leadership of Alabama's law-enforcement officials. Allen informed Albert Lingo, head of the Alabama Highway Patrol. Appointed by Governor George Wallace, businessman Lingo had almost no experience in law enforcement; his only exposure was in the 1930s when he secured a short stint as a highway patrolman. Far more important to Wallace was that Lingo was a like-minded racist, known as "hell on niggers" and a man with an appetite for confrontation. Taking over the highway patrol, which he renamed the Alabama State Troopers, he insisted that every patrol car display a Confederate flag on its bumper. Allen described him as paranoid and unstable. He had troopers "body guardin' him, carrying Thompson submachine guns." And according to Allen, Lingo was "takin' pills by the handful. . . . Just a whole handful of tranquilizers."

When Allen alerted Lingo to the Klan danger, the chief said he would take care of it, but to Allen, the clear implication was that Lingo would do nothing to stand in the way. Lingo had already ordered all troopers out of Birmingham, a sign that if rioting were to erupt, he was going to let it play out, on the expectation that blacks would suffer the worst of it.

Laurie Pritchett, the Albany, Georgia, police chief who had so effectively shut down Martin Luther King Jr. and the protests in his city, was in Birmingham to advise local officials. But Bull Connor, for one, turned a deaf ear to him: He had no intention of performing genuine law-enforcement duties. When Pritchett encouraged Birmingham police to set up a visible presence outside King's lodgings at the Gaston Motel, Connor dismissed the notion, declaring he wasn't going to "guard that nigger son-of-a-bitch." Connor also ignored Pritchett's warning about the repercussions of an attack on King: "Bull," Pritchett told him, "you got the Ku Klux Klan just over the mountain here holding a meeting. They're going to blow King up. And if anything ever happens to him, wherever he's at, the city's going to burn. Cities all over this Untied States are going to burn."

* * *

The operator at the Gaston Motel answered a call at 8:08 p.m. from a white man who wanted to know if King had a room there; then he divulged his real reason for calling: King, he informed the operator, was going to get gunned down. A few minutes later another voice wondered if the operator had a casket for King, assuring her that if bullets failed, dynamite would get him. The motel's proprietor, Ernest Gibson, phoned police, the sheriff, and the FBI.

* * *

The Gaston Motel wasn't the only target that night. A thirty-nine-year-old black Navy veteran named Roosevelt Tatum was outside the house of A. D. King, the brother of Martin Luther King Jr. and a leading propo-nent of the protests, when an explosion erupted beside the front porch. The blast ripped bricks off the walls, caved the roof in, and hurled the front door deep into the house. A shrub in the garden was ripped out of the earth. Tatum later claimed that he had seen a police car, Car 49, roll up to King's house and shut off its headlights. An officer got out, crossed the lawn, and tossed something near the porch. He jumped back inside as the car pulled away. Something else then flew out of the driver's window and landed on the lawn. The bomb on the lawn detonated with limited force, followed by the second, stronger blast near the porch. After the first explosion, Tatum ran toward the house to warn the people inside and when the second blast came, he was thrown backward, landing against a fire hydrant. A. D. King and his five children were in bed; his wife,

Naomi, was in the living room. At the sound of the first blast, everyone hurried out the back of the house, escaping the second, more serious concussion.

With Mother's Day falling the next day, Sunday, May 12, Wyatt Walker was eager to see his wife, Ann, and his four children. He hadn't been home since March, before the campaign had begun, and told Ann he'd see her that weekend now that the agreement was sealed. But King asked him to stay in Birmingham.

"I promised Ann I was coming," Walker told King.

"Well," King offered, "do you want her to come over?"

Walker was excited by the prospect but reminded King that she was looking after their four children.

"Fly her over with the four children," King proposed, saying the Southern Christian Leadership Conference would pick up the tab. "This is our responsibility."

Walker and his family were now lodged at the Gaston Motel. At about 10:30 p.m., as Walker was about to turn in for the night, a student leader pounded on the door. Tired, and in a foul temper, Walker didn't want to be bothered. "I admit I was nasty," he recalled. But he pulled on his clothes and was out the door as soon as the messenger delivered the news: "A.D.'s house has been bombed!"

By the time Wyatt Walker ran up, a throng of angry blacks had converged on the house. "People were in a real bad mood," he recalled. No one in the mob was surprised that white extremists had lashed out: Bombingham was living up to its reputation. A few blacks in the crowd were singing "We Shall Overcome." But many others, armed with bricks, were aching to fight back. A.D. was younger than his brother Martin and more volatile, but the crisis brought out the best in him, as historian Taylor Branch noted: "From somewhere within A. D. King—temperamental, hard-drinking, insecure in the shadow of his famous brother—the shocks of the night drew out his finest moments of the movement years." He tried to defuse the anger, begging spectators through a bullhorn to drop their bricks and turn to nonviolence.

* * *

After warning Lingo of the Gaston Motel plot, officer Ben Allen spent the evening sipping coffee in the kitchen of a state senator. He was filling the senator in on his discussions with the head of the state troopers when the window rattled in its frame. To his chagrin, he knew instantly that his informant had once again passed along accurate intelligence. "There's your bomb," he told the senator.

* * *

In the humid, heavy air, sounds carried far in Birmingham. Out at A. D. King's house, Wyatt Walker heard the blast, too, and knew with a panic what it was.

"That's the motel," he said, immediately worried about his wife and kids. He was amazed that A. D. King and his family had escaped unscathed. "How they got out alive I'll never know," he said. "You talk about miracles. I've seen so many miracles in this movement." He hoped for another miracle at the Gaston Motel. He called over there and spoke to a waitress who was hysterical; the place had indeed been bombed, and there were injuries, possibly even deaths. He raced back to the motel. "All the way... my heart's in my mouth," he recalled. "I don't know how I got back. But I got back."

The bars and pool halls and nearby neighborhoods had emptied; blacks were running through the streets to the Gaston Motel. People said four white men launched a dynamite bomb from their car and sped away. It knocked out a wall, shattered windows, and ripped apart the motel office just below Room 30, the suite where Martin Luther King Jr. usually laid his head. The mob outside sought blood and vengeance.

Scrambling to locate his wife and kids, Walker was overjoyed to find them unharmed. Only four people were injured, none seriously. Martin Luther King Jr. was safe, long gone from the motel. He and Ralph Abernathy, taking a breather after working out the agreement, had flown back to Atlanta to preach at their churches' Sunday services. The bombers mistakenly believed that the men were at a dinner at the motel attended by both blacks and whites celebrating the settlement. "No one had the slightest doubt that the explosion was intended to kill us," Abernathy observed.

116

ALTHOUGH LIVES WERE spared, the night was disintegrating. At the site of the first bombing, A. D. King stood outside his home and shouted through a bullhorn at a seething mob: "Why must you rise up to hurt our cause? You are hurting us, you are not helping." The mob's answer was to hurl rocks and bottles at police and firefighters arriving on the scene. Some rioters wielding knives and ice picks slashed the tires of the patrol cars and fire trucks.

Around the Gaston Motel, some twenty-five hundred blacks rampaged, tipping cars and setting them ablaze, shattering store windows and looting. When police arrived, there were cries of "Kill 'em! Kill 'em!"

Orange flames leapt into the night sky as rioters set fire to white-owned stores in the neighborhood; indiscriminate in its fury, the mob also burned black homes and ransacked black-owned liquor stores. These weren't King's soldiers, the young protesters and older students well schooled in nonviolence, but rather long-suffering ghetto dwellers, scarred by the brutality regularly inflicted on them by police and white society, and invisible until they expressed their rage by torching their own community.

Alabama's unruly law-enforcement leaders, Bull Connor and Albert Lingo, responded with massive force. Connor sent in his armored white tank Sunday morning, Mother's Day, at 12:45 a.m., followed by hundreds of Lingo's state highway patrolmen. Friction flared between Birmingham's police chief, Jamie Moore, and Lingo, who arrived in a riot squad hard hat to command his troopers, armed with shotguns and carbines. "Will you please leave," Moore implored Lingo. The local police under his command were for the most part trying to contain the rioters without an excessive crackdown. "We don't need any guns down here," Moore told Lingo. "You all might get somebody killed."

Lingo, toting an automatic shotgun, was eager to demonstrate his toughness. Perhaps referring to his own weapon, he shouted back: "You're damned right it'll kill somebody."

A. D. King arrived on the scene from his own bombed house at around 1:30 a.m. and begged rioters to disperse. "We're not mad at anyone," he shouted through a bullhorn. "Father, forgive them for they know not what they do." He pleaded with the enraged blacks not to adopt the violent tactics of the white man. A squad of auxiliary officers under the command of the state troopers converged on the area dressed in sports shirts and helmets, with double-barreled shotguns slung over their shoulders. Along with the troopers, armed with their guns and billy clubs, the auxiliaries chased blacks into the motel. Reporting from outside, Claude Sitton of the *New York Times* noted: "The 'thonk' of clubs striking heads could be heard across the street."

* * *

The streets finally calmed by 4:30 a.m., and as Mother's Day dawned, quiet had descended over Birmingham like the aftermath of a wartime bombing. The unrest had spread over a twenty-eight-block area. By the end, fifty people had been injured, including Wyatt Walker. He was hit on the ankle by a flying brick while trying to talk sense to the mob, and his wife, Ann, was clubbed by a trooper wielding a gun butt. One policeman was stabbed. Scores of cars and police vehicles were destroyed, some were burned, and six small stores and a two-story apartment house went up in flames.

On Mother's Day two years earlier, white vigilantes clubbed and kicked Freedom Riders at the Trailways bus station in Birmingham; this time, the only whites engaged in violence were the extremists who set off the bombs and the troopers, egged on by their lawless commanders responding to black rage. This absence of the wider white population suggested a turning point in racial relations. Writing in his book *Why We Can't Wait*, Martin Luther King Jr. observed that if the Birmingham campaign had been launched a year or two earlier, the white mob would have assisted Bull Connor and Al Lingo in attacking blacks. But something significant had changed. White Birmingham had restrained itself and recognized the larger forces at work—not unlike the businessmen who had come to an agreement with black leaders. To King, it was "powerfully symbolic of shifting attitudes in the South.... This neutrality added force to our feeling that we were on the road to victory."

117

IN THE AFTERNOON on Mother's Day, 1963, President John Kennedy touched down on the South Lawn of the White House in a United States Army helicopter, cutting short his weekend stay at Camp David. Attorney General Robert Kennedy rolled up in his Ford Galaxie convertible packed with three aides and his dog, Brummus. The men congregated inside the Oval Office along with four top figures from the military for an emergency meeting on Birmingham. The president, seated in his rocking chair, listened as Bobby began the proceedings.

"Now, have you got what happened last night?" he asked his brother. "You want to hear a few things?"

"Okay," the president said.

Bobby outlined the bombings, the brick throwing, the arrival of the troopers—"they started shoving people around, sticking their guns into people, and hitting them with billies"—which intensified the anger of the blacks so "it was very close to becoming complete chaos." Bobby described the fires, the injuries, and finally the mob dispersing at daybreak. He described the anxieties of Wyatt Walker, whose wife "had headaches all day" after getting whacked by the butt of a rifle. Walker told Bobby the situation was "completely out of hand." On Sunday night, Walker said, blacks under cover of darkness were going to go after law enforcement— what he called "head-hunting"—aimed at shooting and killing police.

The Oval Office conversation debated whether more violence was on the way, whether federal troops were needed to maintain law and order, and whether the agreement between blacks and Birmingham businessmen was in danger of blowing up. Views were offered by the President's Justice Department aides and his military advisors, including Defense Secretary Robert McNamara. Burke Marshall was present, having helicoptered in from his farm in West Virginia, where he was resting after his diplomatic feats in Birmingham.

A man not in the room but much on President Kennedy's mind was Martin Luther King Jr. The president wanted to know what King was thinking, what his plans were, what he expected of the administration. Burke Marshall had spoken to King and had filled in Bobby about their conversation. Bobby told the president that King was now rushing back to Birmingham in hopes of preventing another night of violence. King planned an evening rally, Bobby said, where "he is going to ask all the Negroes to go back home and stay home tonight and stay off the streets." He was going to stress that violence should play no role in their campaign and that they should pray for those who caused trouble the previous night. Bobby expected King to have some sway over those who heard his words, but his influence on the community at large was questionable.

While the men in the room discussed the logistics of a federal troop deployment, the president kept turning the conversation back to King. He seemed willing, even eager, to work with the civil rights leader to ensure calm in the streets and to preserve the settlement on black rights in the city. Kennedy was concerned that sending troops would provoke a backlash from the white establishment. "They might tear up that paper agreement they made," Kennedy said. Sensitive to the black perspective, the president added: "You'd have the Negroes knocked out again without getting the agreement." He then drew King's name into the conversation. "What is King? I mean King has said that we should issue a statement . . ."

Bobby Kennedy then turned the discussion back to a strategy on troop deployment. But as several men in the room, including Defense Secretary McNamara, laid out the details on how a deployment would work, the president grew restless and cut them off. He wanted to know from Burke Marshall about the tenor of his conversations with Martin Luther King Jr.

"I talk to him freely," Marshall said. "I'll tell you what he intends to do, Mr. President." He reiterated that King was speaking at a rally that evening. "Tomorrow, he intends to go around the city and visit pool halls and saloons and talk to the Negroes and preach against violence."

The president wanted to know if King expected rioting again, but Marshall said they hadn't discussed it. As he weighed whether troops were needed, the president wanted King's opinion. He asked Marshall to get King on the phone immediately and sound him out on the potential for violence that night. Marshall should not, the president said, imply the White House was contemplating troop deployment. "I think you ought to look like you're talking just on your own, without saying we're considering it," the president advised him.

Kennedy then returned to King's recommendation that he speak to the nation—and by implication to Birmingham—stressing the government's concern, and its determination to preserve the peace and the agreement on desegregation. "He wants me to make a statement," he reiterated. The president had brought to the meeting a stack of papers, among which were copies of King's recent comments. Selecting one of the pages, Kennedy read that King didn't want the bombings to jeopardize the agreement, a sentiment the president shared. "Now there's one other thing," Kennedy said, shuffling through the papers, "where he's asked me to make a statement." He then read a portion of a United Press International news report in which King was quoted making a direct appeal to the president: He "said today the new outbursts would make it mandatory to take a forthright stand against the indignities which Negro citizens still face."

King's demands—and his nonviolent tactics—were far more attractive to the White House than those of Malcolm X, the leader of the emerging Black Muslim movement. Malcolm X urged blacks to fight back against white brutality and oppression. As he told the press after police and their dogs attacked blacks in Birmingham: "We believe that if a four-legged dog or a two-legged dog attacks a Negro he should be killed. We only believe in defending ourselves against attack." Such sentiments sent tremors through the White House. If the Kennedy administration didn't address the grievances, it risked driving young activists into the arms of the Black Muslims. In the Oval Office meeting, Bobby observed that the police brutality in Birmingham "could trigger off a good deal of violence around the country" and prompt blacks to "start following the ideas of the Black Muslims." King opposed the Black Muslims just as much as the Kennedys did. Speaking to the *Boston Globe* during the Birmingham crisis, King warned of the "dangerous overtones" of the Black Muslims. "If this movement grows," he said, "it can create an atmosphere for a great deal of bitterness and hatred, and can bring about a nightmarish situation in any big city in this country."

By the end of the meeting, President Kennedy had decided he needed to speak to the nation. He and Bobby agreed that he should both condemn the bombings by white extremists and urge blacks to stay off the streets. "You can make a pretty strong statement, I think, this time," Bobby said.

Burke Marshall, just off the phone with King, said that he asked the civil rights leader for his advice on any public remarks by the president.

But King didn't have much to offer: He just hoped the president would steer people away from violence and call on "everyone to be decent and respect law and order." King said that as long as there were no more bombings or other incidents, he expected the community to stay calm. But if Birmingham's businessmen reversed themselves and rejected the agreement, King warned, "I can't control the people."

* * *

Shortly before 9 p.m., President Kennedy reviewed the statement he planned to deliver on live television. His brother, working with Burke Marshall and two other aides in the Cabinet Room, had labored over the language. "One of the great moral issues of our time is achievement of equal opportunity for all citizens," the president read to himself. "There are problems which must concern all of us and to which all of us have a moral obligation to put right."

Those were strong words: The president had never framed the struggle for civil rights as a moral cause. Such language would reverberate in the streets and in Congress. As the television camera was pushed into place, the president considered the consequences. Although Birmingham had penetrated his conscience, he was still more comfortable appealing to reason and respect for law than moralizing about rights. He didn't yet have the courage to challenge the fundamental beliefs of Southern whites. He called in his trusted speechwriter Ted Sorensen to change the text.

When he went on the air, the president spoke for barely a minute. His face framed in a tight camera shot, he read the statement as if seeing it for the first time, his eyes flicking down to the page then up again. He began by saying he was "deeply concerned" about events in Birmingham. He then reported that A. D. King's house and the Gaston Motel both were bombed and that rioting ensued, with damage, injuries, and evidence of brutality. He said the government was prepared to do whatever was necessary "to preserve order, to protect the lives of its citizens, and to uphold the law of the land." He then praised the Birmingham agreement as "a fair and just accord" and vowed that the federal government would not allow it "to be sabotaged by a few extremists on either side." He highlighted the efforts of Birmingham's citizens—black and white—in reaching the settlement, declaring that the outcome was "a tribute to the process of peaceful negotiation and to the good faith of both parties." He called upon residents of Birmingham "to realize that violence only breeds more violence, and that good will and good faith are most important now." In conclusion, he made clear his willingness to use force to maintain order and to ensure the settlement was enacted: He was dispatching troops trained in riot control to military bases near Birmingham, and he was taking preparatory steps for federalizing the Alabama National Guard should their deployment become necessary.

Without any mention of the moral implications of racism, the president nonetheless delivered a strong, forceful endorsement of desegregation and equal rights; he also conveyed that he would brook no more violence from the black community.

118

BIRMINGHAM FELL QUIET for a couple weeks after President Kennedy moved federal troops nearby. King's exhortations to the blacks of Birmingham in churches, pool halls, and bars helped preserve the peace. But reverberations of Birmingham were rocking other cities around the country: Demonstrations erupted in Jackson, Mississippi, and Raleigh, North Carolina, and spread to the North. Black Muslims sparked violent clashes in Harlem, and protests flared in Philadelphia, Chicago, Syracuse, and New Rochelle.

Attorney General Robert Kennedy, wishing to understand the roots of the unrest, particularly in the North, invited author James Baldwin to Hickory Hill for breakfast on May 23. Harry Belafonte noticed lately that Bobby was searching for answers. As Belafonte described it, Bobby's "conscience was struck in a way that he had to just wrestle and wrestle and wrestle." Bobby admired Baldwin's work but he was troubled by the author's portrayal of the hopelessness of black life in America. In the *New Yorker* six months earlier, Baldwin wrote: "The brutality with which Negroes are treated in this country simply cannot be overstated. A Negro just cannot *believe* that white people are treating him as they do; he does not know what he has done to merit it." In the piece "Letter from a Region in My Mind," which was subsequently published as the book *The Fire Next Time*, Baldwin contended that the nation and its vaunted mythology of the American Dream were doomed if blacks remained excluded from the benefits of white society. He grieved over the ill treatment of black soldiers both on the battlefield and at home. Although the black soldier put his life on the line for his country, he was still called a nigger and on his return from war was denied an equal chance for a decent life. "Search, in his shoes, for a job, for a place to live; ride, in his skin, on segregated buses; see, with his eyes, the signs saying 'White' and 'Colored,' " Baldwin wrote. The war was "a turning point in the Negro's relation to America," he believed. "To put it briefly, and somewhat too simplistically, a certain hope died."

During their brief breakfast in Bobby's large brick home in McLean, Virginia, the attorney general and the writer had an illuminating chat about urban life and black conditions. "We had a very nice meeting," Bobby said later. But Baldwin's plane had been late and Bobby had a meeting at the Justice Department, so they didn't have the full conversation the attorney general had hoped. Bobby wanted to hear more.

In Belafonte's view, Bobby was having an intellectual growth spurt; he was seeking a deep awareness of black disaffection, as if he were asking himself, "What is really the cause of this? Because obviously I've missed something here, and I don't like missing anything. I need to know." To Belafonte, Bobby was undergoing "one of the most profound transformations I have ever met in any human being.... He was moving towards a new moral horizon.... I found in Bobby Kennedy a man wrestling with profound moral questions and always coming down on the right side of the answer." Having had to cut short his breakfast with Baldwin, Bobby asked if they could continue the conversation the following day in New York. "Why don't you get a couple of your friends together," Bobby said, "and maybe we could meet and talk."

Baldwin agreed, and phoned Belafonte.

"What's the agenda?" the singer wanted to know.

"There's so much anger out there in the black community," Baldwin explained. "Bobby wants to understand that anger better, to know how to respond."

* * *

The next day, a small group of black intellectuals and activists gathered in the Kennedy apartment in Manhattan, at 24 Central Park South, where in 1960 Martin Luther King Jr. first met face-to-face with presidential candidate John Kennedy. The visitors sipped cocktails and munched on hors d'oeuvres and a light buffet. King was absent from the off-the-record gathering of black luminaries: writer James Baldwin, singer Harry Belafonte, psychologist Kenneth Clark, playwright Lorraine Hansberry, who wrote *A Raisin in the Sun*, singer Lena Horne, Chicago Urban League director Edwin Berry, and King's attorney, Clarence Jones. Also invited was twenty-four-year-old Jerome Smith, a field-worker for the Congress of Racial Equality, who had spent considerable time in prison for his protests and had suffered brutally on the front lines of the Freedom Rides. In November 1961, he had rolled into McComb, Mississippi, on a Freedom Ride bus and was attacked after being denied service in the terminal's whites-only waiting room. A thug screaming, "I'll kill him," knocked him to the ground as others joined in smashing his head into the pavement. At the time, Smith was a confirmed adherent of King's philosophy of nonviolence. Two years later, he was in New York for medical treatment for the lingering repercussions of his beating, and like many young blacks he now could barely suppress his anger at the white world and the slow progress from the Kennedy administration. Among young activists, Smith "had probably spent more months in jail and been beaten more often than other CORE members," according to a report prepared by the organization.

Bobby Kennedy, who was joined by his press secretary, Edwin Guthman, and Assistant Attorney General Burke Marshall, hoped to convince the group that the president was determined to produce real results on civil rights; the administration had worked secretly on behalf of the movement—the latest example being Bobby's efforts to round up cash for Birmingham bail payments—and was already discussing the possible shape of civil rights legislation; but most black leaders knew very little of these activities, if anything at all.

Kennedy and Marshall arrived at the apartment after a disagreeable morning at the Waldorf Astoria hotel with the owners of national department store chains including Woolworth's, J. C. Penney, and Sears. Trying to lay the groundwork for civil rights legislation, the attorney general was privately measuring sentiment among the store owners; he urged them to desegregate their dining facilities in the South, a proposal that displeased the businessmen. "I guess they thought the devil incarnate had arrived in New York and they were asked to meet with him," Bobby recalled.

Leaving the wary owners behind, Bobby showed up at his father's apartment overlooking Central Park only to confront the other side of the racial divide. After the buffet, he thanked his guests for coming and trumpeted the administration's contributions to the movement. Noting the danger of Malcolm X and his violent brand of protest, the attorney general urged blacks and whites to cooperate in a patriotic struggle. As Bobby spoke, young Jerome Smith's temper was rising. "I don't know what I'm doing here, listening to all this cocktail-party patter," he suddenly exploded. "What you're asking us young black people to do is pick up guns against people [in other countries] while you have continued to deny us our rights here."

Baldwin interrupted, asking if Smith would ever take up arms in defense of America. The look on Smith's face was startling, Baldwin recalled, as the angry activist declared: "Never! Never! Never!"

"You will not fight for your country?" Bobby replied. "How can you say that?"

Enraged, Smith exclaimed: "I want to vomit being in the same room as you."

Shocked and offended, Bobby turned away. And, in doing so, he found himself facing the other guests—those he thought were, as Baldwin put it, "the reasonable, responsible, mature representatives of the black community." Among that mature group was Lorraine Hansberry, who said she felt sick, too. "You've got a great many accomplished people in this room, Mr. Attorney General," she said. Gesturing toward Smith, she added: "But the only man who should be listened to is that man over there."

Smith had only begun his tirade. He laid into Bobby for his ignorance about what was truly going on with young blacks. "You don't have no idea what the trouble is. I'm close to the moment where I'm ready to take up a gun," he fumed. "I've seen what government can do to crush the spirit and lives of people in the South."

Smith's outburst was all the more poignant because, as Baldwin explained, the young activist stammered when upset. Smith told Bobby that he had given up on nonviolence, along with many other blacks he knew. If police ever attacked him again, he said, he'd know what to do with his own gun: "When I pull the trigger, kiss it good-bye."

Young Smith emboldened the others and, in the words of Kenneth Clark, gave rise to "the most intense, traumatic meeting in which I've ever taken part." From Kennedy and Marshall's perspective, it was a gang assault, an unloading of pent-up black anger and frustration. "They all started sort of competing with each other in attacking us, the President, the federal government, and the whole system of government in addition to the United States," Marshall recalled. When Bobby tried to explain his approach on civil rights or the administration's goals, he was shouted down; if he sought common ground for discussion, no one wanted to hear. "You can't talk to them the way you can talk to Martin Luther King or Roy Wilkins," Bobby recalled later. "They didn't want to talk that way. It was all emotion, hysteria—they stood up and orated—they cursed— some of them wept and left the room."

Lorraine Hansberry explained that deep-seated anger was driving blacks from King's nonviolence toward extreme militancy. She spoke fervently in what Bobby described as "poetical terms" about the way white society was castrating blacks, preventing them from ever improving their position in America. "Lorraine Hansberry said that they were going to go down and get guns," Bobby recalled, "and they were going to give the guns to people on the street, and they were going to start to kill white people."

The perception was that Bobby Kennedy, his brother the president, and all of white America lacked an understanding of the indignities blacks suffered. Kenneth Clark didn't believe that the attorney general harbored racist feelings; the problem was Bobby's inability to put himself in the position of a black man. "He did, in fact, represent about the best that white America had to offer, but this was tragic because he did not have empathy," Clark said. Bobby's attempt fell flat when he tried to equate his family's discrimination as immigrant Irish Catholics with the bigotry blacks endured. He said that in a few generations the Kennedys had produced a president of the United States. "You should understand that this is possible," he told the group, "that in the next fifty years or so, a Negro can be president." Baldwin was unimpressed with that reasoning. "Your family has been here for three generations," he shot back. "My family has been here far longer than that. Why is your brother at the top while we are still so far away? That's the heart of the problem."

No one in the room was willing to give Bobby or the administration any credit for advancing civil rights. Belafonte, of course, knew about Bobby's behind-the-scenes drive to drum up bail money; and Clarence Jones knew about the Kennedys' efforts on behalf of Martin Luther King Jr. When Bobby pointed out to the people in the room that the administration worked with King on various matters, "they'd laugh at that and say, 'That's not true.'" Finally he gave up. "Bobby became more silent and tense, and he sat immobile in the chair," Clark recalled. "He just sat, and you could see the tension and the pressure building in him." After about two and a half hours, the attorney general called an end to the meeting. Later Bobby told his press secretary that Harry Belafonte came up to him before leaving and admitted: "Of course you've done more for civil rights than anyone else."

"Why didn't you say this to the others?" Bobby wanted to know.

Belafonte was in a tough position. "I couldn't say this to the others," he answered. "It would affect my position with these people. . . . If I sided with you on these matters then I would become suspect." King's lawyer, Clarence Jones, also quietly spoke to Bobby as the others were leaving. "I just want to say that Dr. King deeply appreciates the way you handled the Birmingham affair," he told the attorney general. Bobby was upset that Jones had remained silent. "You watched these people attack me over Birmingham," he replied. "There is no point in your saying this to me now." Later Bobby told an interviewer why he believed Jones didn't defend him during the verbal assault; Jones was in the same sticky position as Belafonte was in front of the other blacks. "He didn't dare," Bobby said.

Stung by the flogging, Bobby believed it was unfair to dismiss the actions of the Kennedy administration, especially in light of the inertia of most every other president. If the encounter proved anything, it was that a vast gulf existed between black and white America, and it was expanding, with potentially catastrophic consequences for the nation.

* * *

Two days after the secret meeting, Bobby Kennedy read all about it on the front page of the *New York Times*, apparently leaked to the newspaper by James Baldwin. In the piece, Baldwin stressed that Kennedy failed to grasp the depth of the racial problem in America, and he called the White House approach "totally inadequate." A week later Baldwin invited another *Times* reporter into his tiny apartment in Greenwich

Village on "a street populated by Negroes and Puerto Ricans" to elaborate on the urgency of the moment. The reporter seemed surprised to see that an American writer of such renown was living in such a cramped, dimly lighted space. The two-room apartment had "a combination living room-bedroom" crowded with a bed, chairs, lamps, a bookcase, a desk with a typewriter, piles of music records, and worn carpeting. "A window faces a dreary air shaft, but no outside light penetrates the room," observed the reporter, adding it was a "dismal setting for...one of the great creative artists of this country." Baldwin warned of racial conflagration but refused to give in to hopelessness. "The Birminghams cannot be stopped," he said. "They can happen in New York and elsewhere in the country. There is drift and danger today." But he added: "Despair is a sin. I believe that. It is easy to be bleak about the human race, but there are people who have proved to me that we can be better than we are."

* * *

The takedown Bobby suffered in Manhattan caused him to look inward. He redoubled his effort to understand the black plight and to do what he could in his position to ameliorate it. John Maguire, a white Alabaman who abandoned his teenage racism and became a religion professor and Freedom Rider, watched what he called the "pilgrimage of Robert Kennedy" during the civil rights movement. Bobby's journey through the era took him from the beating of his aide and friend John Seigenthaler in Montgomery, Alabama, to the rioting in Oxford, Mississippi, to the dogs and fire hoses in Birmingham, and finally to his cocktail-party confrontation in Manhattan. "The meeting with James Baldwin was crucial," Maguire observed.

After that experience, Bobby tried to comprehend the depths of rancor that provoked the outbursts. After a couple days, he was still shocked by Jerome Smith's refusal to fight in any war for America; to hear Smith vehemently reject patriotism startled Bobby. "He had never heard an American citizen say he would not defend the country and it troubled him," explained Bobby's press secretary, Edwin Guthman. Gradually Bobby's attitude toward the meeting began to change. Perhaps recalling what Baldwin had written about the sour welcome given to black war veterans returning home, Bobby tried to see America through Smith's eyes. He spent long periods contemplating the circumstances that gave rise to Smith's profound bitterness. Finally he admitted to Guthman: "I guess if

I were in his shoes, if I had gone through what he's gone through, I might feel differently about this country."

This realization—this understanding through empathy—motivated Bobby and made justice for the black community a matter of urgency. "After Birmingham, it was unacceptable to him that Congress would not pass legislation," recalled John Doar, an assistant attorney general for civil rights. "I remember that he insisted in a conference with President Kennedy and Vice President Johnson that until Congress acted and passed legislation, the situation was just unacceptable to an American civilization...to this country." The black psychologist Kenneth Clark, who participated in the rancorous meeting in Manhattan, reevaluated his opinion of the attorney general. "I did not become an avid Bobby Kennedy devotee or fan, but I respected the complexity of the man," he said. Bobby had done "a double take," Clark realized, "some serious rethinking." Speaking after Bobby's assassination in 1968, Clark mused: "Had he lived, he really would have demonstrated a rare combination of courage, clarity, and concern about the same issues that concerned me." In late May 1963, while the president still hadn't found his voice, Bobby took on black rights as a moral cause and by his words and his example urged his brother the president to do the same.

119

YOU HEARD IT in black communities, read it in the newspapers, and saw it on streets flaring with unrest. The Kennedy administration was still scorned for moving too slowly on civil rights. The president's public statements were vague proclamations that only called for more patience. On May 18, President Kennedy traveled to Vanderbilt University in Nashville, Tennessee, and spoke "forthrightly about civil rights," as the *New York Times* put it, but offered nothing new. He called on educated men and women to reject prejudice and violence and to accept the rule of law, noting vaguely "that debate will go on, and those rights will expand." Some critics saw the president's fainthearted remarks as an unwillingness to lead—a failure by John Kennedy to live up to his potential. "Both Kennedys are tremendously intelligent and sensitive people. They have shown the ability to grasp deep knowledge of other situations involving the nation's welfare," wrote Jackie Robinson in the black newspaper *Chicago Defender*. "It is hard to understand why they find it so difficult to understand our basic human yearnings." *Jet* magazine challenged the president to find the political courage to produce lasting change. "The president must take a much stronger stand—despite the political hazards of annoying the most powerful Dixie vote bloc on Capitol Hill—if he expects harmony to return to the racial front in all parts of the nation."

Just as Birmingham quieted, another challenge loomed in Alabama: Governor George Wallace had already declared his intention to defy court-ordered desegregation of the University of Alabama in early June by standing in the schoolhouse door, if necessary. "Dammit," he cried, "send the Justice Department word, I ain't compromising with anybody. I'm gonna make 'em bring troops into this state." The president was firm but noncommittal about how far he would go to ensure the university's desegregation. During a press conference near the end of May, he said he did not want to use federal marshals or troops, and he was sure the governor wouldn't want that, either. "But I am obligated to carry out the court order," he told reporters. He was just as vague when asked whether any new legislative efforts were likely as a result of the turmoil in the South. The best he could offer was that Birmingham was stirring him to consider a variety of possible legislative remedies. "I would hope that we would be able to develop some formulas so that those who feel themselves—or who are, as a matter of fact—denied equal rights would have a remedy," he said.

Demonstrators were not assuaged. Headlines in the black press highlighted the nation's plunge into racial chaos. Three days after the president's press conference, the *Baltimore Afro-American* screamed: PICKETS IN SEVEN CITIES PUT SOUTH IN UPROAR, noting a wave of arrests that accompanied the protests. In the first week of June, demonstrations erupted coast to coast, North and South, in California, Michigan, Florida, Virginia, Louisiana, Oklahoma, Kentucky, and Tennessee.

By the end of May, a troubling realization settled over the White House: Racial strife, far from abating, was intensifying. As arrests multiplied, President Kennedy realized the black revolution was spinning out of control.

In response, he moved tentatively toward a dramatic solution. His aides began drafting legislation that would give the government the power to speed up integration of public facilities and schools. The president realized that action in Congress was necessary, because Southern states easily subverted constitutional requirements on desegregation, and court efforts were circuitous and time-consuming. But he was still cautious about moving precipitously; he deliberated, he made no announcement. First he sought to build a consensus among political leaders and businessmen around the country. He invited nine Democratic governors to lunch at the White House and urged them to move forward on providing equal opportunity to blacks in their states; he called for a conference in early June at the White House of hundreds of owners and managers of theaters, hotels, variety stores, and drugstore chains that had outlets in the South. In a telegram to the businessmen, he said, he wanted to discuss the "difficulties experienced by minority groups in many of our cities in securing employment and equal access to facilities and services generally available to the public."

Details gradually trickled out about how legislation might work. The law would prohibit discrimination by hotels, stores, restaurants, theaters, and other businesses that operate across state lines and would give the government authority to sue to stop such action. The Kennedy administration hoped the legislation would address black anger over segregated lunch counters and other public facilities. But the president repeatedly delayed announcing the bill. As the White House defended itself, arguing that care and deliberation were needed so the legislation would not fail in Congress, critics continued to tear into the pace of presidential action. In a phone conversation with Harry Belafonte, Martin Luther King Jr. warned that the Kennedys were going to face a lot more heat "if the President keeps dawdling on that civil rights bill."

120

AFTER THE SUCCESS in Birmingham, Martin Luther King Jr. set off on a whirlwind series of speaking engagements around the country to raise money for the Southern Christian Leadership Conference. Huge crowds greeted him in Cleveland, Chicago, Louisville, and Los Angeles. At every stop, he turned up the heat on President Kennedy. In Los Angeles, he warned of the dangerous impatience of the black population and called on the president to demonstrate just how courageous he was in the battle for civil rights. "I think that if the Governor of Alabama will present his body by standing in the door to preserve an evil system," King told the crowd, "then President Kennedy ought to go to Tuscaloosa and personally escort the student into the university with *his* body! And I think that would be a magnificent witness for what this nation stands for." Hollywood celebrities competed to befriend the civil rights leader and to hand over contributions to his organization. Burt Lancaster hosted a fundraiser at his Beverly Hills home where the likes of Paul Newman, Lloyd Bridges, and Marlon Brando circulated and wrote checks. From his Los Angeles rally attended by nearly fifty thousand people and the Lancaster reception, the SCLC pulled in more than $100,000. In Chicago, performances by gospel star Mahalia Jackson and twenty-one-year-old Aretha Franklin helped raise $40,000.

Without any firm action yet on legislation, famed journalist Walter Lippmann took both the president and Congress to task. "For the most part, they are the spectators," he wrote in *Newsweek*, "some of them in the cheering section and others in the booing section." The *Call and Post*, a black paper in Cleveland, looked to the president and Congress for action and was left wanting. "This ... isn't leadership," it said. "It is, to say the least, cowardly, dodging and hopefully ducking."

To pressure the president, King began to consider a tactic first proposed by the civil rights leader A. Philip Randolph. "Philip keeps talking about a march on Washington," King told Harry Belafonte on the phone. "It sure would bring the movement right to the President's door. Maybe it's time." Back in January, seventy-four-year-old Randolph had asked his friend the civil rights strategist Bayard Rustin to draw up a plan for thousands of blacks to descend on Washington. Rustin came back with a three-page memorandum proposing a march to draw attention to the "economic subordination" of blacks and to call for more jobs and for economic justice. The goal was to attract one hundred thousand marchers. King delighted in the prospect of a huge march on Washington and, according to historian Adam Fairclough, he "borrowed, revived, and transformed Randolph's idea [and] shifted the focus from jobs to civil rights. He also supplied the drive and sense of purpose to make the event succeed." Big-name stars such as Paul Newman and Marlon Brando were enlisted. It was decided that August was the soonest the plan could be put in motion. In a phone call to Stanley Levison, which was picked up by FBI wiretaps of Levison's line, King stressed that if one hundred thousand marchers converged on Washington, President Kennedy would have to pay attention.

Emboldened, King sought to see the president in person. He shot off a telegram asking for a conference with him and the attorney general "to discuss the crisis in race relations." He decried the "snail like pace of desegregation" in the South and proposed visiting the White House "to discuss with you some of the problems we are facing in the South and some of the specific measures that may avert a national calamity." Noting the urgency, King offered three dates when he was free during the next week. The administration had discussed inviting in black leaders to apprise them of its efforts on legislation and other civil rights matters. The White House decided it was wiser to see white business leaders first to avoid appearing biased toward the black side. And before meeting with King, the president preferred to ask in other black leaders; or, perhaps, King could join in a group visit. But meeting alone with him was out of the question: He was too controversial. "The trouble with King is," the president explained during an Oval Office meeting, "everybody thinks he's our boy anyway. So everything he does, everybody thinks we stuck him in there. So we ought to have him well surrounded." Kennedy was sensitive to perceptions of King's radicalism. "King is so hot these days," he said, "that if it looks like Martin's coming to the White House, I'd like to have some Southern governors or mayors or businessmen in first." In contrast to King's earlier telegrams to the president when a reply was left hanging for months, the White House responded quickly. But as often happened, King was informed that the president was simply too busy to meet with him.

As Kennedy dawdled, the textile and tobacco town of Danville, Virginia, erupted in protest, prompting some of the most vicious police brutality yet. The southern Virginia town on the North Carolina border, where Jefferson Davis retreated with his cabinet at the end of the Civil War, had been largely free of racial unrest until early June. Since then hundreds had been arrested during protests demanding immediate, total desegregation. On June 10, about 150 blacks took to the streets, marching on City Hall—where they found all the doors locked—and then moved on through the downtown area. Mayor Julian Stinson had gone on the radio to warn protesters that the city planned a vigorous police response. "Our patience is just about at an end," he said. "We will hose down the demonstrators and fill every available stockade." He was true to his word. Firemen trapped the protesters in a narrow alleyway and blasted them with their ferocious water cannons, knocking many to the ground. Policemen, along with deputized local citizens, moved in with nightsticks and beat the protesters sending forty-seven to the hospital, two with serious injuries. Thirty-five protesters were arrested. In a telegram to the White House, Martin Luther King Jr. said he was outraged over the "beastly conduct of law enforcement officers at Danville," warning the president and attorney general that "the Negro's endurance may be at a breaking point." As he had on so many occasions, King tried to get the president to see that black justice required something beyond the typical law-and-order response. "I ask you in the name of decency and Christian brotherhood to creatively grapple with Danville's and the nation's most grievous problem." And he begged the president for a "just and moral" solution.

King urged the president to do a series of fireside chats as Franklin Roosevelt did on radio in the 1930s and 1940s during the Depression and World War II. Through televised fireside chats, King believed, Kennedy could rally the nation around civil rights. But the president dismissed the idea. "I don't have Franklin Roosevelt's voice," he told a visitor to the White House. "I've always thought that a half hour speech on television is pretty disastrous."

121

ON JUNE 11, Governor George Wallace stood in the schoolhouse door on the campus of the University of Alabama in Tuscaloosa awaiting the arrival of two black students. As the temperature hovered near one hundred degrees the governor, as promised, intended to block the registration

of Vivian Malone and James Hood. His director of public safety, Albert
Lingo, had called out 150 helmeted state troopers who now lined the
campus walkways. Nearly as many newsmen were on hand to capture
the showdown. Here was the president's and the nation's latest civil rights
crisis playing out before the television cameras. As Wallace began his
day of defiance, Robert Kennedy encouraged his brother to go on television to announce the administration's plans for civil rights legislation. But
the president held back: The situation in Alabama was too uncertain. His
political aides worried about a backlash if he became too immersed in
civil rights advocacy.

In the late morning, Deputy Attorney General Nicholas Katzenbach
emerged from a sedan on campus and strode up to the governor, who
stood at a lectern at an auditorium doorway. The governor was dressed
in a light gray suit, blue shirt, and narrow tie with a gold tie clip; around
his neck he wore a microphone connected to a public address system. A
man of theatrics, the governor had rehearsed a performance to play to his
segregationist constituency. Katzenbach approached him alone without
the enrolling black students and asked Wallace for his assurance that he
would do his constitutional duty and step aside—that he would not bar the
admission of the students. Wallace didn't budge and insisted on reading
a statement. Filmmaker Robert Drew captured the drama in a remarkable documentary called *Crisis* that had cameras running simultaneously
in Tuscaloosa and Washington as the showdown developed. In Washington, Attorney General Kennedy and his aides monitored the scene from
a speakerphone in his office, while Governor Wallace in Tuscaloosa
read his verbose statement condemning the Justice Department action.
"The unwelcome, unwanted, unwarranted and force-induced intrusion
upon the campus of the University of Alabama today of the might of the
Central Government," Wallace rambled from his prepared text, "offers a
frightful example of oppression of the rights, privileges, and sovereignty
of this state by officers of the Federal Government." The film cut to the
attorney general's office and then back to Tuscaloosa as Wallace concluded: "I hereby denounce and forbid this illegal and unwarranted action
by the Central Government."

Katzenbach, waiting patiently through the governor's tirade, replied:
"Governor Wallace, I take it from that statement that you are going to
stand in that door and that you are not going to carry out the orders of this
court and that you are going to resist us from doing so. Is that correct?"

"I stand according to that statement."

"You stand upon that statement," Katzenbach echoed. "Governor, I am not interested in a show. I don't know what the purpose of this show is. I am interested in the orders of these courts being enforced. That is my only responsibility here. I would ask you once again—the choice is yours." Then he turned tough, telling the governor that if he did not step aside, the government would take the necessary actions to ensure that the court orders were enforced. Katzenbach told Wallace in no uncertain terms that the students would be registered immediately and would attend classes the following day. The governor was silent, listening with his head thrown back, his chin jutting out, and his lips pursed.

Leaving Wallace, Katzenbach went to the car to get prospective student Vivian Malone and escorted her along a walkway toward a women's dormitory, where she entered unhindered. In Washington, Attorney General Kennedy listened to a live radio report of the unfolding events. When he heard that Malone had gone into the dorm and that the other prospective student, James Hood, was headed to his, Bobby turned to face the documentary camera and broke into a small smile that was full of relief and supreme satisfaction.

But the standoff wasn't over. The governor remained defiant, and the inflamed local population posed a riot risk now that blacks were on campus. Fearing the worst, the attorney general advised his brother to sign a proclamation federalizing the Alabama National Guard. By late afternoon, some six hundred troops under federal command, outfitted in green fatigues and carrying M1 rifles, marched onto the campus. Amid the sweltering temperatures, Governor Wallace had gone inside the auditorium to cool down. Before taking up his position again in the doorway, the governor stood erect while an aide straightened out his tie. Then he denounced what he called a trend toward "military dictatorship." But the fight was over—the president's show of force was too much. Wallace, in effect, surrendered, walked swiftly to his car, and was driven off the campus. Minutes later, Malone and Hood walked up to the auditorium and proceeded through the unlocked door to register for their classes.

* * *

In the White House, the president followed the confrontation and its resolution with his advisor and speechwriter Ted Sorensen. By the time Wallace disappeared it was nearly 5 p.m., the entire day having been taken up by his showmanship. "As Wallace left the doorway," Sorensen recalled, "the president turned around and said to me, 'I think we'd better give that speech tonight.'" Sorensen was taken aback. "What speech?" he wondered. White House aides had discussed civil rights strategy and the outlines of legislation for a couple weeks, and there was talk about the president addressing the nation. "But no decision had been made," Sorensen recalled, "and no draft had been prepared." Bobby also remembered that the president made a snap decision. Some threshold had been crossed; some epiphany had been reached. "I think he just decided that day," Bobby recalled. "I think he called me up on the phone and said that he was going to do it that night."

The president wanted to go on air at 8 p.m., and he wanted to deliver a major civil rights speech; he was determined to speak on black rights in a manner he had never done before—in language no president had uttered. Prepared text or no prepared text, he was going to announce civil rights legislation. With the nation's streets boiling daily with blacks impatient for change, he grasped the urgency for a remedy. It was palpable in the Oval Office debates on the administration's next step. "At those meetings, the point was made over and over and over again that this problem faced all of us and was going to get worse during the summer," Burke Marshall recalled. "It really...had to be faced up to." The president's political advisors opposed his speaking out publicly, while Robert Kennedy argued in its favor. But the president's aides were no match for the president's brother; no one could defeat Robert Kennedy once his mind was set. He was adamant: the president had to introduce legislation and had to do it in a television address. "He felt it, he understood it, and he prevailed," Marshall said.

Usually fearful of powerful Southern senators and the havoc they could wreak on his domestic agenda, the president on that Tuesday evening in June was prepared to ignore politics. After dithering for two and a half years, he was ready to respond to the pleas of Martin Luther King Jr. and to the determination and courage of thousands of blacks. "Recognizing the call of history," early King biographer Lerone Bennett Jr. wrote, "Kennedy made an abrupt turn and accepted the mantle of moral leadership King had urged upon him." The president's advisors were alarmed over the president taking a moral stand on black equality. "They thought that would involve him much more [in civil rights] as a person and that it would lose him political support in 1964," Marshall explained. But once he had made the decision, Marshall added, "I don't think the president... ever intended not to [do it] for a minute."

President Kennedy instructed his press secretary, Pierre Salinger, to alert the television and radio networks that he wanted airtime. For a man of deliberation, the president was acting with unusual impulsiveness. Afterward, he explained what came over him. "I may lose the legislation, or I may even lose the election in 1964," he told his commerce secretary, Luther Hodges. "But there comes a time when a man has to take a stand and history will record that he has to meet these tough situations and ultimately make a decision."

* * *

Under pressure, Sorensen went off to frame words that would match the moment. Normally, he'd have weeks to coddle the language for a speech of this magnitude; a major domestic statement typically went through various hands for review and comment, and careful dissection. But this time the president took the lead. He was eager to hear input from Sorensen and a few others, but he seemed to know what he wanted to say and how he wanted to say it. Sorensen barely had three hours. "I could not draw upon a previous Kennedy civil rights speech file, because there was no such file," Sorensen remembered. "But I had a memory full of JFK's remarks during the campaign, plus issues and proposals we hoped to cover in the legislation." When Sorensen grumbled about how little time he had, Bobby Kennedy said, "Don't worry, we have a lot of good material over at the Justice Department that we can send to you."

As chief speechwriter, Sorensen wanted to assert control over the process and to guarantee that his words were the ones that came from the president's mouth. But with the president's and Bobby's active involvement—and the limited time—Sorensen had a tough time protecting the speech's development. In anticipation of this moment, Bobby had already had a draft prepared by a talented new Justice Department speechwriter. Richard Yates had attracted Bobby's attention when he published an acclaimed novel, *Revolutionary Road*, in 1961; the book created a dark portrait of suburban life in the 1950s as a way to probe the state of American culture. In his draft of the speech, Yates composed an eloquent and poignant portrayal of black life: the oppression, prejudice, poverty, and demoralization in the ghetto. His language was harsh, far too dark for President Kennedy; but his themes were in line with the president's perception for the speech: the difficulty of black conditions, the morality of equal rights, and the introduction of legislation. Sorensen ignored Yates's contribution, and by 7:30 p.m., a half hour before airtime, he still had no draft of his own.

Working on a parallel path, Bobby Kennedy sat down with the president and Burke Marshall in the Cabinet Room around 7 p.m. to scratch out some ideas of their own. When Ted Sorensen came in with a draft, Bobby rejected it, and Sorensen took notes as the president and the attorney general hashed out some thoughts. Then, he returned to his desk to get back to work. "The president and I stayed there for about twenty minutes," Bobby recalled. The men brainstormed themes and language. At one point, the president turned to Marshall. "Come on. Come on now, Burke," he said. "You must have some ideas."

Cameras were rolled in and tested in the Oval Office. The president was moving quickly toward airtime. "He thought he was going to have to do it extemporaneously," Bobby recalled. Neither the president nor the attorney general was terribly worried about a bit of ad-libbing. Both knew the president had the personal style to pull it off. But he needed an outline, some structure, and a few eloquent words at hand.

So the brothers went to work in the Cabinet Room. "The two of us talked about what he'd say," Bobby remembered. "He made notes...on the back of an envelope or something, outlining and organizing." At four minutes to eight, Sorensen still hadn't delivered a text; his secretary was typing up his handwritten draft when the president suddenly appeared in his office. "It was the only time in my three years in the White House that JFK came to my office to ask about a speech," Sorensen recalled. "Don't worry," Sorensen told the president. "It's in the typewriter now." For a man moments away from facing a live audience without a text, Kennedy was remarkably cool. "Oh," he joked, "I thought I was going to have to go off the cuff on national television." Moments before airtime, Sorensen came back to the Cabinet Room and presented his work. The president looked it over; the speech had most of what he wanted—it wasn't entirely there—he scratched out parts, scribbled in his own thoughts. But he knew he was going to have to wing it in parts.

* * *

In the Oval Office, a minilectern had been placed on the desk with a microphone on either side, and a glass of water was within reach. The president took his seat and did a quick camera test, noticing something he didn't like on the monitor. "The camera ought to be brought up," he said. While the technicians fixed the angle, the president gave his text one more look, scribbling here and there. At 8 p.m., the president addressed the nation: "Good evening, my fellow citizens." He was visible on television screens across America in a tight head-and-shoulders shot, looking crisp in a white shirt, narrow tie, and a handkerchief poking from his jacket pocket; two flags standing either side of him gave a sense of symmetry, and the tips of the two microphones appeared at the bottom of the frame. As he spoke, the camera slowly zoomed in, enhancing the gravity and importance of his words. His first topic of business was that afternoon's news, the successful admission to the University of Alabama, as he put it, "of two clearly qualified young Alabama residents who happened to have been born Negro." Without mentioning Governor Wallace, he noted that the students' admission came after "a series of threats and defiant statements" and in the presence of the Alabama National Guard. His tone suggested that enrollment of these two black students should not have provoked such histrionics from the governor and should not have required deployment of the National Guard. The president praised the Alabama students on campus for peacefully accepting this turning point in racial relations.

* * *

In Atlanta, Martin Luther King Jr. had settled in front of the television with his friend the Reverend Walter Fauntroy. Belafonte was tuned in. Jackie Robinson, so long a critic of the president, sat in anticipation. John Lewis, the young activist and veteran of the Freedom Rides, had closely followed the Birmingham protests and felt it was "head-spinning, in a way, to watch Wallace's stand and the President's speech on the same day. I'll never forget watching him that night."

* * *

On the television screen, the president asked the nation to take a lesson from the scenes in Alabama; he challenged Americans to be better, drawing on words that were in many ways about himself and his own journey that had brought him to this point: "I hope that every American, regardless of where he lives, will stop and examine his conscience about this and other related incidents." He reminded his listeners that America "was founded on the principle that all men are created equal, and that the rights of every man are diminished when the rights of one man are threatened."

Here in front of a live national audience, John Kennedy was answering the call of his own conscience. Historian James MacGregor Burns had wondered whether Kennedy had the mettle for moral leadership. In a biography published in 1960 before Kennedy took office, Burns found the then presidential candidate intellectual and charming but perhaps lacking the character to lead the nation in extraordinary times. The historian quoted Franklin Roosevelt as saying the presidency "is pre-eminently a place of moral leadership. All our great Presidents were leaders of thought at times when certain historic ideas in the life of the nation had to be clarified." Kennedy was yet to prove himself, Burns concluded: "Whether he would bring passion and power would depend on his making a commitment not only of mind, but of heart, that until now he had never been required to make." Burns was sympathetic to the candidate and optimistic about his personal evolution, noting: "His life seems to show a steady growth into commitment from a position of detachment."

As he spoke into the television camera that June evening, the president was becoming the man Burns had envisioned: He revealed a passion and commitment to civil rights that he had never before shown. Like his brother Bobby he had finally come to view the black predicament through the eyes of a black citizen. "If an American, because his skin is dark, cannot eat lunch in a restaurant open to the public, if he cannot send his children to the best public school available, if he cannot vote for the public officials who will represent him, if, in short, he cannot enjoy the full and free life which all of us want," the president told the country, "then who among us would be content to have the color of his skin changed and stand in his place? Who among us would then be content with the counsels of patience and delay?"

Martin Luther King Jr. was present in the president's voice, in his words, and in his conscience. Intentionally or not, Kennedy had absorbed the language and themes of King's "Letter from Birmingham Jail," a copy of which had been delivered to the White House. King had written the letter as much to President Kennedy as to its ostensible targets, the white clergymen who were critical of King and the Birmingham movement. In it, King asked his readers to see through black eyes: Imagine, he proposed, if you had a relative who was lynched, or if you were beaten by the police, or if your child was denied the opportunity to go to an amusement park, or if you were humiliated daily by WHITE and COLORED signs on water faucets and restrooms and dining rooms; then it would be hard as President Kennedy remarked, to be patient about change. As Barnard professor Jonathan Rieder observed, the president's speech "was full of echoes" of King's "Letter from Birmingham Jail." "In a powerful sense, King and the movement were the authors of the president's oratory." The president had read King's lament over black impoverishment as the civil rights leader expressed it in the "Letter": "Twenty million Negro brothers, smothering in an airtight cage of poverty in the midst of an affluent society." In his speech Kennedy highlighted that predicament, spelling out for America that a black baby born in the same place on the same day as a white baby was half as likely to complete high school; was twice as likely to become unemployed; was destined to have a life expectancy seven years shorter than the white baby's; and was likely to earn half as much as that white baby. "Throughout the speech," Rieder noted, "Kennedy seemed to be channeling the 'Letter from Birmingham Jail.'"

In this address two and a half years into his term, the president found his moral voice, his commitment of mind and heart. Without hesitation or equivocation, he embraced black justice. As his aide Arthur Schlesinger put it: "Kennedy now responded to the Negro revolution by seeking to assume its leadership." Martin Luther King Jr., watching in Atlanta, heard the president frame the civil rights dilemma just as he had begged him to understand it. "We are confronted primarily with a moral issue," Kennedy said. "It is as old as the scriptures and is as clear as the American Constitution." Departing from his previous emphasis on law and order, the president reached a higher moral ground on this issue than he ever had. "The fires of frustration and discord are burning in every city, North and South, where legal remedies are not at hand," he said. As the nation's leader he again peered through the eyes of the aggrieved. "Redress is sought in the streets, in demonstrations, parades, and protests which create tensions and threaten violence and threaten lives. We face, therefore, a moral crisis as a country and as a people. It cannot be met by repressive police action. It cannot be left to increased demonstrations in the streets. It cannot be quieted by token moves or talk. It is time to act in the Congress, in your State and local legislative body and, above all, in all of our daily lives."

Hearing the president, Lewis sensed a momentous change. "Just five months earlier, at a meeting in early January with Dr. King," he recalled, "Kennedy had told King that the administration had no plans to propose any civil rights legislation in 1963. Now here he was, on national television, announcing his intention to send to Congress the most sweeping civil rights bill in the nation's history."

After revealing his intention to send legislation to Congress, the president called on every citizen to push the country forward and to treat each other as equals. "This is one country. It has become one country because all of us and all the people who came here had an equal chance to develop their talents," he said. "We cannot say to 10 percent of the population that you can't have that right; that your children cannot have the chance to develop whatever talents they have; that the only way that they are going to get their rights is to go into the streets and demonstrate. I think we owe them and we owe ourselves a better country than that."

In Atlanta, Martin Luther King Jr. jumped out of his seat, elated. "Walter," he cried to his friend, "can you believe that white man not only stepped up to the plate, he hit it over the fence!" Harry Belafonte, deeply moved, spent the evening on the phone with his friends. "We couldn't have asked for a more strongly worded declaration," he recalled in his memoir. "Martin was in tears. So were a lot of other people I talked to that night. So was I."

Jackie Robinson, long dissatisfied with the president, sharply revised his opinion. He sent a glowing telegram to the White House. "Thank you for emerging as the most forthright President we have ever had and for providing us with the inspired leadership that we so desperately needed," Robinson wrote. "I am more proud than ever of my American heritage," Robinson wrote. In a newspaper column drafted the following day, the baseball star went public with his praise. "As an American citizen," he began, "I am deeply proud of our President. In my opinion, the address which Mr. Kennedy made to the American people on the color question is one of the finest declarations ever issued in the cause of human rights." Robinson reminded readers of his earlier criticism of the president then declared his change of heart. "I must state now that I believe the President has come through with statesmanship, with courage, with wisdom and absolute sincerity," he wrote, adding that Kennedy had now done everything Robinson hoped he would do.

After the speech, Martin Luther King Jr. rushed out a telegram to the White House calling the address "one of the most eloquent profound and unequivocal pleas for justice and freedom for all men ever made by any president." Finally, King had heard the Kennedy voice that he had hoped to hear for so long. "You spoke passionately to the moral issues involved in the integration struggle. I am sure that your encouraging words will bring a sense of hope to the millions of disinherited people of our country. Your message will become a hallmark in the annals of American history."

The president's Southern foes in Congress rose up in opposition. Led by the powerful Democratic senator Richard Russell of Georgia, seventeen senators conferred for an hour and a half the next day to strategize on how to derail the president's legislation. Afterward, Russell vowed to block any civil rights bill with "every means and resource at my command." He said he was "shocked" by the president's speech and asserted that attempts to end segregation were steps toward Communism. The president, he said, was threatening Congress when he declared that a failure to pass legislation could provoke violence in the streets. His language "may intimidate a few weak-kneed people," Russell said, adding that "those who would be intimidated have no business in positions of power." Former president Dwight Eisenhower, who was condemned for his inaction on civil rights during his administration, offered President Kennedy no support for his legislation. After meeting with Kennedy and Vice President Johnson for more than an hour the day after the speech, Eisenhower dodged newsmen and slipped out of the White House without commenting. Earlier he met with Republican congressmen over breakfast and reportedly told them to work for voting rights legislation. But he said "passing a whole bundle of laws" was not going to solve the country's civil rights problems, according to a congressman who attended the breakfast. "No one can be sure he's got the right answer," Eisenhower said of President Kennedy's legislative proposal.

* * *

Back in 1954 and 1955 when he wrote *Profiles in Courage*, John Kennedy had an idealized view of courageous politicians who defied sharp opposition to take action they deemed was right. And he had a vision

of himself as a member of their ranks, although for most of his political career his place among them was largely imaginary. He had moved
only with tentative steps on civil rights, and for every advance there was
a measurable retreat. But over the months and years of his presidency,
he grew almost imperceptibly as a politician, a president, and a man. As
those who met him often observed, the president was a good listener. The
British philosopher Isaiah Berlin once good-naturedly complained: "He
exhausts you by listening." Although often appearing distant, the president was sublimely attentive; he absorbed information, asked questions,
and weighed the answers. On civil rights, he listened to Martin Luther
King Jr., to his brother Robert, to his conscience. He keenly observed the
rising black unrest and the barbarity of the white response. The nation also
was listening and evolving; in the wake of Birmingham more than half of
Americans believed that civil rights was the nation's most urgent issue,
up from less than 5 percent before the demonstrations. The president had
the political capital to address an injustice that for too long contradicted
an American principle. By acting on civil rights, he not only asserted his
political will, he also lifted the nation onto a higher moral plane. At last
he had risen to the ideal he had envisioned for himself when he wrote
Profiles in Courage. "A man does what he must," Kennedy asserted nearly
a decade earlier, "in spite of personal consequences, in spite of obstacles
and dangers and pressure—and that is the basis of all human morality."

122

THAT TUESDAY EVENING, President Kennedy had altered the rhetorical
battlefield and injected hope into the hearts of millions of blacks across
the country. But Medgar Evers, the field secretary of the NAACP in Jackson, Mississippi, knew the struggle was far from over. Like other cities,
Jackson had erupted in protest since Birmingham—and with a militancy
uncommon for the city's blacks. "Ten years ago you couldn't pay a Negro
to go downtown and challenge the law the way he's doing here now," the

president of Jackson State College, an all-black institution, told the *Washington Post*. "And these Negroes now are even unafraid of guns staring them in the face." At the end of May, Evers had organized a march of young students, some from grade school, that was met by police wielding nightsticks and riot guns. Officers acting, in Evers's words, like "storm troopers" out of "Nazi Germany" arrested some six hundred children. The following day, the executive secretary of the NAACP, Roy Wilkins, came to Jackson to join Evers in a protest over segregated lunch counters at Woolworth's; both men were arrested along with another hundred schoolchildren. Evers's skills as an organizer made him a powerful target for the city's extremists.

On the night of the president's address, Evers attended a mass meeting at a local church then visited a black lawyer for a strategy session before heading back to his tidy brick-and-green-paneled home. His wife, Myrlie, had allowed their three young children, aged ten, eight, and three, to stay up late to hear their father's view of the president's speech. A little after midnight, the thirty-seven-year-old Evers drove up to the house in his 1962 light blue Oldsmobile. Inside the car were a stack of sweatshirts with a cry printed across the chest: JIM CROW MUST GO. Evers crossed toward the house under the bright lights of the carport as a sniper hidden in a honeysuckle thicket about two hundred feet away took aim through a telescopic sight on his .30-06 rifle.

Evers knew, as both a Southern black man and as a protest organizer, that he walked in danger. From a young age he'd witnessed the ugliness of white brutality. At fourteen, he had stared in horror at the body of his father's friend, who had been lynched for supposedly insulting a white woman. In 1958, when he refused to sit in the rear of a bus in Meridian, Mississippi, he was hauled off for questioning by local police; afterward, he got onto another bus and again sat in the front and was punched in the face by a white man. In 1961, when he applauded a sit-in defendant in court, a policeman pistol-whipped him. Once he had heard anonymous voices on his phone warn him that he had only hours to live, the caller knocking the cylinder of his revolver into the mouthpiece and telling Evers, "This is for you." In recent weeks, the threats had escalated. The previous weekend, two whites tried to run him down in their car in front of the NAACP headquarters in Jackson; he jumped out of the way to the laughter of white spectators on the sidewalk. "This is what you must face to get free in Mississippi," he told a reporter at the time. He recently had a Molotov cocktail land on his carport and several times during the previous week had picked up his phone to hear someone say: "We're going to kill you."

Evers had served in the U.S. Army during World War II and returned home angry at the freedoms denied to blacks who risked their lives for the country. He wanted to fight back violently against his white oppressors. "We wanted to go home, arm ourselves and fight it out," he recalled. "I had earlier thought that maybe Negroes should form a black shirt gang to deal with the Ku Klux Klan. I was very violent in my thoughts then." But at the urging of his mother he turned away from violence and relied on peaceful protest and the courts. His mother, he said, "prevailed on us the need to act in goodness and mercy no matter what happens. I agreed with her then and have ever since." Seeking to improve himself, Evers graduated with a business degree from Alcorn Agricultural and Mechanical College, an all-black institution established in 1871 to educate former slaves. For a while, he worked as an insurance salesmen but then found his calling with the NAACP. By 1963, he had been married to Myrlie for twelve years. In early June, amid the wave of threats against him, he told a newspaper reporter: "If I die it will be in a good cause."

Now, a few hours after the president's speech, Evers approached his house, his white dress shirt illuminated in the carport lights. A gunshot rang out, and a bullet passed through Evers's back just below the right shoulder blade; it smashed through the front window of the house, ricocheted off the refrigerator, and hit a coffeepot. Evers managed to stagger a few steps toward the doorway before collapsing. A neighbor, hearing the blast, looked out his bedroom window and saw Evers crumpled on the carport. The screaming of the Evers children—"Daddy! Daddy! Daddy!"—awoke another neighbor. When police arrived, they helped neighbors lift Evers into a station wagon that sped toward the hospital. In the car, he struggled to sit up then weakly uttered his last words: "Turn me loose." An hour later, at 1:14 a.m., he was dead.

* * *

Medgar Evers's murder—jolting the nation just hours after President Kennedy's speech—was a somber reminder that racial progress comes grudgingly, if at all, and only through endless suffering. No one—not

President Kennedy or Martin Luther King Jr.—had any illusions that a single speech, a single law, or a single protest could change bigoted behavior. As the president explained in his speech that evening, "Law alone cannot make men see right." Martin Luther King Jr. had underscored this point two years earlier speaking in Chester County, Pennsylvania. "Now, people will say, 'You can't legislate morals.' Well, that may be true," he told a crowd in June 1961 at Lincoln University, the nation's first degree-granting black college. If a man's beliefs could not be improved by legislation, King reasoned, laws at least had to be obeyed. "It may be true that the laws can't make a man love me," he said, "but it can keep him from lynching me, and I think that's pretty important also."

123

ON JUNE 22, thirty leaders of the civil rights movement gathered at the White House to meet with President Kennedy. It was the first time during his administration that the president agreed to sit down with top black figures for a strategy session on civil rights. Facing a fierce battle over his civil rights legislation, he needed cooperation from the black community. The protests had to stop: Unrest in the streets would only impair the bill's chances of success in Congress. Among the black leaders around the table in the Cabinet Room were Martin Luther King Jr., Roy Wilkins, A. Philip Randolph, James Farmer, and John Lewis. Reflecting the president's seriousness, top administration officials were also present, including Attorney General Robert Kennedy and Vice President Lyndon Johnson. Wilkins remembered that during the discussion one of Bobby Kennedy's young daughters pranced into the room and climbed onto his lap "where she sat for ten minutes or so, putting her tiny fingers to his face. Finally, he lifted her gently and carried her out."

The president had sent his legislation to Congress three days earlier. It was comprised of seven parts that tackled voter literacy tests, discrimination in public accommodations such as hotels and restaurants, and discrimination in federal employment; it gave the attorney general power to file lawsuits to desegregate public schools; it established an organization to resolve racial disputes; it extended the existence of the Civil Rights Commission; and it allowed the U.S. government to stop funding state and local programs that discriminated.

Opposition to the bill was stiff and its fate uncertain. When the president said he needed black protesters off the streets, A. Philip Randolph replied: "The Negroes are already in the streets." He pointed out that most important was how they conducted themselves. "Is it not better that they be led by organizations dedicated to civil rights and disciplined by struggle," he reasoned, "rather than to leave them to other leaders who care neither about civil rights nor about non-violence?" The president's aide Arthur Schlesinger recalled that the seventy-four-year-old Randolph spoke with "quiet dignity which touched Kennedy." The president agreed that the street demonstrations had had a powerful impact, forcing him to act faster than he might have otherwise, and now forcing Congress to consider legislation. "This is true," he said. "But now we are in a new phase, the legislative phase, and results are essential. The wrong kind of demonstration at the wrong time will give those fellows a chance to say that they have to prove their courage by voting against us."

The black leaders were eager to launch a massive march on Washington in August. The president strongly discouraged the idea, arguing that announcing a march before his bill had even reached Congress was a form of intimidation. "We want success in Congress, not just a big show at the Capitol," he told the gathering. "Some of these people are looking for an excuse to be against us. I don't want to give any of them a chance to say, 'Yes, I'm for the bill, but I'm damned if I will vote for it at the point of a gun.'"

The president outlined the steep hurdles facing the legislation in Congress. Then, Lyndon Johnson, the master of moving bills through the body, elaborated, ticking off the number of votes in favor and against and the votes that still had to be wrangled. The president interjected that failure to win Congress would have far-reaching ramifications. Privately he agonized over taking on the Senate. As Bobby said, "There was a good deal of soul searching that went into the decision about sending up the legislation," and afterward the president constantly questioned himself. "He would ask me every four days, 'Do you think we did the right thing?' " Bobby recalled. "Look at the trouble it's got us in." But the president never wavered after taking the action: His commitment was total, and his doubts were always framed "in a semi-jocular way," Bobby said.

Martin Luther King Jr. spoke little and held his comments until close to the end of the two-hour session. When he finally spoke, he strongly supported the March on Washington as a way to channel grievances through nonviolence. "It may seem ill-timed," he told the president. "Frankly, I have never engaged in any direct action movement which did not seem ill-timed. Some people thought Birmingham was ill-timed." To which the president replied drily: "Including the attorney general." As the meeting wound down, the conversation turned to the issue of Birmingham and police brutality, and President Kennedy shocked the room when he said: "You may be too hard on Bull Connor." Wilkins recalled hearing murmurs around the table before the president offered his sardonic follow-up: "After all, Bull has probably done more for civil rights than anyone else."

* * *

Although he invited black leaders to the White House, the president was still circumspect around them, particularly in his interaction with Martin Luther King Jr. Before the group meeting, he had a few private moments with King, at 10:10 a.m., according to the White House appointments log that historian Taylor Branch dug up. Some twenty minutes before the 10:30 a.m. gathering, the president invited King to take a stroll in the Rose Garden. They had come a long way together: first, Kennedy's call to Coretta during the campaign; then, the acrimony of the past two years and the disappointment each had in the other, King wishing Kennedy would move faster on equal rights, and Kennedy wishing King would contain the protests. Now, by some appearances, the two leaders had found grounds for trust. So it came as a surprise to King when the president delivered an alarming message as they walked together in the fresh air of the Rose Garden.

"I assume you know you're under very close surveillance," the president told King. It quickly became clear that Kennedy was talking about King's relationship with Stanley Levison, his trusted advisor and suspected communist, whose phone was tapped. The president advised King not to discuss important subjects in phone calls with Levison, because FBI chief J. Edgar Hoover regarded the white lawyer as "a conscious agent of the Soviet conspiracy."

King immediately wondered, as he later told his aide Andrew Young, whether the Oval Office was bugged by the FBI. Why else had Kennedy guided King outside to engage in this dialogue? "Martin came back saying that the President was afraid to talk in his own office," Young recalled, "and he said—he was kinda laughing about it—he said, 'I guess Hoover must be buggin' him too.'" Hoover had been funneling reports about King and Levison to the administration; the FBI had kept both Kennedys apprised of the movement's discussions during the Birmingham protests, and on June 3 had delivered a nine-page memo to the attorney general on Levison's influence on King. On June 17, Robert Kennedy phoned Hoover to discuss suspicions about King, according to David Garrow's investigation of the FBI's strategy to destroy the civil rights leader. At one point in their garden stroll, the president put his hand on King's shoulder and mentioned both Levison and Jack O'Dell, the staffer in the New York office of the Southern Christian Leadership Conference. "They're Communists," he warned. "You've got to get rid of them." He explained that Senate opponents of the civil rights legislation will do anything to derail it; they had already claimed the bill was a communist plot. "If they shoot you down," the president continued, "they'll shoot us down too—so we're asking you to be careful."

King leapt to Levison's defense. "I know Stanley," he said, "and I can't believe this. You will have to prove it."

The president said he'd have Burke Marshall get the proof and pass it on to King. But if this claim of Hoover's was like the others, there were no documents to prove anything, because they didn't exist, and in their absence the FBI chief simply asserted that the material was too sensitive to let out of his grasp.

Hoover's shadow hung over the Rose Garden chat in another way. "You've read about Profumo in the papers?" the president asked. Kennedy was obsessed by a sex scandal that erupted in June and brought down Britain's minister of war, John Profumo. The government of Prime Minister Harold Macmillan was rocked by revelations that Profumo had been cavorting with prostitutes and possibly compromising national security. "Kennedy had devoured every word written about the Profumo case," newsman and Kennedy friend Ben Bradlee recalled. "It combined so many of the things that interested him: low doings in high places, the British nobility, sex, and spying." During a dinner at the White House, the Bradlees and the Kennedys played a game of speculation: Who might be the hidden Profumo in his own administration? They threw out names; no culprit ever emerged. In discussing the Profumo case with King, Kennedy put it in the context of the potential damage done to Macmillan's government; the prime minister had put himself at risk by trying to protect his war minister, Profumo. "That was an example of friendship and loyalty carried too far," Kennedy told King. "Macmillan is likely to lose his government because he has been loyal to a friend. You must take care not to lose your cause for the same reason."

The renewed Communism charges against Levison and, by association, King, may have partly explained why the civil rights leader was subdued in the meeting immediately following his Rose Garden chat with the president. King had been blindsided just when he ought to have been rejoicing at the president's introduction of legislation and at his invitation to the White House.

After the meeting, King went before reporters and showed no sign that he was yielding to presidential pressure. While he abhorred violent protests, he asserted that demonstrations would not end as long as segregation and discrimination existed. He hinted that a large-scale march on Washington was still likely despite the president's wish to quash it. "I made it very clear," King told the press, "we could not in all good conscience call off any massive demonstrations until the problems that brought these demonstrations into being are solved."

124

SETTLED IN ON Squaw Island for the summer, Jackie Kennedy passed the days reading, boating, strolling, and painting. Her pregnancy progressed smoothly, and her husband visited regularly. The president traveled to Europe in late June, where he spoke stirringly at the Berlin Wall, declaring, *"Ich bin ein Berliner*—I am a Berliner," and returning home he landed in a Marine Corps helicopter at the Kennedy compound in Hyannis Port to Jackie and the kids awaiting him on the lawn. After two weeks away from each other, the presidential couple embraced in a rare show of public affection. In July, as Jackie awaited her own baby, Robert Kennedy's wife, Ethel, gave birth to their eighth child. Troubled by her precarious pregnancies and births, Jackie envied the prolific and athletic Ethel. In biographer Christopher Andersen's telling, Jackie once sniped that Ethel "drops kids like rabbits... She's the baby-making machine— wind her up and she becomes pregnant."

If everything went as planned, Jackie intended to leave Cape Cod in late August to deliver her baby by Cesarean section in early September at Walter Reed Army Medical Center in Washington. But given her past complications, the hospital at Otis Air Force Base was on alert for any emergency. Just twelve minutes by car from Squaw Island, even less by helicopter, the hospital had spruced up a wing in case it was needed. The area prepared for Jackie was inside Building 3703, a one-story, wooden structure, with a delivery room, six bedrooms, two lounges, a kitchen, and a nursery.

* * *

On Wednesday morning, August 7, Jackie was at the stables in Osterville, not far from her Squaw Island home, watching Caroline's riding lesson when she turned to her Secret Service agent Paul Landis and said: "Mr. Landis, I don't feel well. I think you better take me back to the house." Another agent stayed behind to look after Caroline, while Landis drove cautiously but quickly over a bumpy, winding two-lane road, with the First Lady imploring him to go faster. At the house, they were met by her doctor, John Walsh, who had taken up residence on Cape Cod for the summer to be nearby. A quick examination revealed that for the fourth time out of her five pregnancies things weren't going right. Her latest child was on its way five and a half weeks early. In minutes, Jackie and the doctor were aboard a helicopter whirring toward Otis Air Force Base hospital.

By 1 p.m., Jackie had delivered a four-pound, ten-and-a-half-ounce boy by Cesarean section. Like all early infants, he was struggling to breathe. Care for premature babies in 1963 was nowhere near the level it is today; had the child been born today he would have had the benefit of ventilators and neonatal intensive care units and would have had a 95 per- cent likelihood of surviving. Under the state of medicine in his day, his fate was dangerously uncertain. All that could be done was to place him in an oxygen-pumping incubator called an Isolette.

President Kennedy arrived by jet at Otis Air Force Base at 1:25 p.m., and was soon inside Building 3703. He was briefed on the baby's condition, and visited briefly with a groggy Jackie. He then asked the base chaplain to baptize the baby at once; the infant was christened Patrick Bouvier Kennedy, after the president's grandfather and Jackie's father.

Patrick's battle for life played out in newspapers and on television both at home and abroad. Americans huddled by their radios listening for updates. To many, the mystique of the Kennedys meant that luck was on Patrick's side. In that spirit, the *Boston Globe* declared: HE'S A KENNEDY—HE'LL MAKE IT.

Dr. James Drorbaugh, one of the nation's leading experts on infant respiratory ailments, rushed to Otis from Children's Medical Center in Boston to find that Patrick was fighting hard for each breath. Dr. Drorbaugh quickly laid plans to transport Patrick to Children's where, he believed, better care awaited. Just before 6 p.m., Kennedy's press secretary, Pierre Salinger, appeared before reporters in front of the lime-green, single-story building to announce the transfer. A caravan led by a state police escort set off, passing mobs of Cape Cod well-wishers and, one hour and eighteen minutes later, arrived at Children's.

That evening, the president conferred with Patrick's doctors on the fifth floor of Farley Building at Children's Medical Center. There were at least a half-dozen physicians applying the latest knowledge in premature infant care. They were acutely aware that Patrick's ailment, hyaline membrane disease, was the number one killer of babies born before full term, responsible at the time for twenty-five thousand deaths a year. Premature babies have difficulty breathing because they do not have enough of a substance called surfactant in their lungs to help the air sacs expand and stay open. As a result, an insufficient amount of oxygen gets into the bloodstream, possibly causing damage to the brain and other tissues. Treatment options were minimal—mostly just a heat-controlled incubator and lots of attention. The critical period was the first forty-eight hours of life—if the baby could struggle his way through that delicate time, odds of his survival improved, but were still only about 40 to 50 percent.

By 2 p.m. the next day, August 8, the news was grim: Doctors were preparing for a last-ditch effort to save the fragile child. They had decided to place him in a hyperbaric chamber to force oxygen into his lungs. The chamber, located in the hospital basement, was a steel device thirty-one feet long and eight feet in diameter that press secretary Salinger described as similar to a submarine with air vents and pressurized doors and a window to see the patient inside. Not wanting to worry Jackie, the president ordered that she not be told of the seriousness of the situation.

Patrick was placed inside the chamber in the hospital basement at 4:41 p.m. where doctors in pressurized suits tended to the day-and-a-half-old infant; but Patrick was struggling to draw enough oxygen into his lungs and nourish the rest of his tiny body. The president decided he wanted to be near his son, so he took over a vacant fourth-floor room. His friend Dave Powers bunked in with him, sleeping on a cot beside the president's bed.

Throughout the night, Patrick's condition deteriorated. At 2 a.m., a Secret Service agent awakened Powers, who roused the president. Bobby Kennedy, who had come into Boston, was awakened at his hotel. For the next two hours, the three men kept a vigil in the basement, peering through a small window into the chamber. The president paced back and forth, stopping now and then to see a jarring sight: his tiny son inside the monstrous steel chamber with doctors in their pressurized suits fussing about.

At about 4 a.m., the doctors had to admit that they could not stop the inevitable. The doctors, the president, the attorney general all were powerless to help the struggling infant. Little Patrick Bouvier Kennedy was fading. The baby was carried out of the chamber and placed in his father's arms, still alive. With Powers and Bobby at his side, John Kennedy cradled his son as the frail newborn took his last labored breaths. After a brief thirty-nine hours and twelve minutes of life, Patrick was gone. "He put up quite a fight," the president said softly. "He was a beautiful baby."

* * *

Jackie was too weak to attend the Mass and burial. On doctor's orders, she was to have no visitors during that period; she sobbed and prayed silently on her own in her hospital room, with her doctor at her side. The private Mass for Patrick was held at 10 a.m., on Saturday, August 10, in the small chapel at the residence of Richard Cardinal Cushing. The mourners—in all, twelve Kennedy family members—arrived in five black limousines. Inside the chapel little Patrick lay in a white gown in a small, white casket covered, at the request of his mother, in a blanket of white flowers. After the Mass, the president was the last one to leave the chapel. Overwhelmed with grief, he shed "copious tears," Cardinal Cushing remembered later. The distraught father was in no hurry to go. As the others filed out, he stayed behind. "He literally put his arms around that casket" like he was going to carry it out, the cardinal recounted in an oral history. "I said, 'Come on, Jack. Let's go. God is good.'"

* * *

Patrick had changed the president as a husband and father. Everybody close to him noticed it. He and the First Lady shared a deeper affection for each other. "The death of the infant was one of the hardest moments in the lives of both President and Mrs. Kennedy," Salinger recalled. "The White House had brought about a closeness in their relationship, a wider understanding of one another. The death of their baby brought them even closer." After Patrick's burial, Kennedy visited with Jackie alone in her room and recounted for her the beauty of the Mass and the loveliness of the white flowers she requested for the coffin. They cried together.

He wasn't shy about his new tenderness toward Jackie. "After the death of Patrick, the other agents and I noticed a distinctly closer relationship, openly expressed, between the president and Mrs. Kennedy," agent Clint Hill recalled. "I first observed it in the hospital suite at Otis Air Force Base, but it became publicly visible when Mrs. Kennedy was released from the hospital." A telltale clue on that day a week later, Hill said, was that the president and First Lady emerged holding hands. "It was a small gesture, but quite significant to those of us who were around them all the time. Prior to this, they were much more restrained and less willing to express their close, loving relationship while out in public."

125

ON THE NIGHT of August 27, 1963, a half-moon rose over the reflecting pool and the Lincoln Memorial and the Washington Monument, glowing on a vast, empty space, the quiet broken by the sound of hammering on the television platforms. A technician testing the loudspeakers sent his voice out over the mall: "Final audio, one, two, three, four." A group of black out-of-towners climbed the steps of the memorial to the sixteenth president and wandered into the north chamber. A middle-aged couple, the man with his arm around the shoulders of the woman, softly read the lines inscribed in the wall from Lincoln's second inaugural: "If we shall suppose that American slavery is one of the offenses which, in the providence of God, must needs come, but which, having continued through His appointed time, He now wills to remove..."

Over at the White House, President Kennedy was still in mourning over the loss of Patrick, barely two weeks earlier. His son's death was the latest personal trauma—after the Bay of Pigs disaster, his father's incapacity, and his own fragile health—that had softened him. His emotional engagement and his consideration of his wife's sorrow blunted "stories of the formidable Kennedy family reputation for ruthlessness, all-conquering efficiency and ambition," the *Boston Globe* observed. The president's conduct prompted a *Globe* commentator to suggest "a widespread reappraisal of his character.... The image is of a man more warmhearted, more considerate, more kind." His emotional growth had spilled over into the actions of his administration: His championing of the black cause was of a piece with his personal development.

On this night before the massive March on Washington, the president was anxious but hopeful that peace would prevail. Tens of thousands of people were descending on the capital to support civil rights and equal job opportunities. They were to gather, possibly 100,000 or 200,000 in all, packed in between the memorial and monument, around the reflecting pool. The president knew that the march was not targeted at him but at Congress in a bid to accelerate work on his new legislation. Violence would be catastrophic for the nation and for the future of the legislation.

The ten chairmen of the march, including Martin Luther King Jr.— leaders of civil rights, labor, and religious organizations—had issued a plea for participants to be peaceful. Racist groups were expected to land in Washington. March organizers urged their followers to resist provocations and to remain disciplined and nonviolent. As they strolled the streets of Washington, blacks were encouraged to walk tall, to carry their heads high. In a statement, the leaders offered their hope for the march: "It will be orderly, but not subservient. It will be proud, but not arrogant. It will be nonviolent, but not timid.... It will be outspoken, but not raucous."

The capital could handle huge crowds. Far larger throngs swarmed into town for the presidential inauguration every four years. Planners knew exactly what to do, but this was different. At other events, hordes poured in as spectators, a passive group easier to control; this time, the crowds were participants. And the capital had only two months to prepare; inauguration planning usually began at least a year before the event. Most significant, however, was the uncertainty attached to the march. The purpose of the event, black rights, suggested conflict. The march came after years of unrest and bloodshed in cities across the country, and racial turmoil was intensifying just as the buses, trains, and planes full of marchers were arriving in the capital.

Every precaution had been taken. The downtown area was divided into five police commands, with nearly two thousand officers on duty backed by more than five thousand District of Columbia National Guard troops, firemen, civilian reservist police, and National Park Service police. Some four thousand soldiers and marines were on alert at nearby military bases. First-aid stations, ambulances, food and drink stands, and water trucks would be in position. With the temperature expected to sizzle above eighty degrees, fire hydrants were being converted into drinking fountains. Bayard Rustin, energetic organizer of the undertaking, oversaw the tiniest details. Toilets, many toilets, were a top priority, in his view. "Now we cawn't have any disorganized pissing in Washington," he said in his somewhat affected British accent. Some black leaders, particularly NAACP head Roy Wilkins, opposed Rustin taking a central role in the march; Rustin was a controversial figure and a potential target of civil rights opponents. Among Wilkins's worries was that Rustin was gay and could be attacked for his morals. "It was not just Rustin's sexual orientation that disturbed Wilkins," John Lewis explained. "There was also his status as a conscientious objector, and his controversial involvement over the years with the Communist Party." Nonetheless, master strategist and organizer that he was, Rustin was a leading force in skillfully piecing together the many parts of the march.

* * *

With the morning light, the capital flew into action. "Truck convoys of regular Army troops and Marines criss-crossed the city—fighting men racing to take up strategic positions," *Jet* magazine reported. "On Capitol Hill, police rimmed the legislative buildings, standing five feet apart.

In downtown Washington, every street corner was dotted with District police and National Guardsmen. Sure, there was an occasional smile, but the attitude was, 'Don't start nuttin', buddy.' "

Throngs flowed onto the mall in orderly fashion. By 10 a.m., some forty thousand people populated the slopes around the monument. And the marchers kept coming: An hour later, some ninety thousand people had poured in. Many carried placards: FREE IN '63 and WE MARCH TOGETHER, CATHOLICS, JEWS, PROTESTANTS and WE DEMAND AN END TO POLICE BRUTALITY NOW! The blind were led by guide dogs, and the young came on roller skates. Seventy-four members of the American Nazi Party staked out territory near the monument and were quickly surrounded by two hundred police and National Guardsmen, barricading them from the marchers; the Nazis eventually gave up and went home. As the crowd swelled the mood turned festive: Schoolchildren clapped their hands and sang freedom songs. With the temperature climbing, blacks and whites in a celebration of integration drank together from rows of temporary water faucets.

* * *

Twenty-three-year-old student activist John Lewis had been elected chairman of the Student Nonviolent Coordinating Committee just a week before the June meeting of black leaders with President Kennedy. "It was mind-blowing," he said, to attend that White House meeting; and now he was an invited speaker at the March on Washington. He had prepared a militant speech condemning "cheap political leaders" for their "immoral compromises." He spoke of a black revolution not waiting for the president, the Justice Department, or the Congress to act, but rather taking matters into its own hands. Blacks would march not only on Washington, he vowed, but "we will march through the South, through the heart of Dixie, the way Sherman did." He called President Kennedy's legislation "too little and too late."

Inside the White House, Lewis was considered too extreme. "This was a very radical speech," Burke Marshall observed. Bobby Kennedy added, "It was a bad speech." The address risked disrupting the program: According to Marshall, the archbishop of Washington, Patrick A. O'Boyle, who was to give the invocation, refused to show up unless Lewis softened his words. The march's leaders, fearing controversy and wishing to avoid upsetting their nascent alliance with the White House, badgered Lewis until he toned down his language. He reluctantly removed several passages—"cheap," "through the heart of Dixie, the way Sherman did," "too little and too late"—but he still believed the speech was fiery.

By the time he arrived at the Lincoln Memorial, Lewis was in awe of what was unfolding before him. "I was stunned as I climbed up the steps to the speakers' platform," he recalled. "My thought, looking out at that vast scene, was, We are here. We, the people, are *here*. It was fascinating to see the collage of famous faces, Josephine Baker climbing up on the stage near me; Jackie Robinson over there telling a reporter, 'We cannot be turned back!'; Paul Newman turning away from the celebrity section, preferring to watch from the crowd; Marlon Brando sitting on stage, twirling an electric cattle prod in his hands as a symbol of police brutality." And there were other stars: Dick Gregory, Sidney Poitier, Lena Horne, Ossie Davis, Charlton Heston, Sammy Davis Jr., Diahann Carroll, Harry Belafonte.

Famous musicians sang of protest and hope: Joan Baez performed "We Shall Overcome"; Peter, Paul and Mary harmonized "If I Had a Hammer"; Bob Dylan, tooting on his harmonica with Baez at his side, offered a musical ode to Medgar Evers, "Only a Pawn in Their Game."

The program was interdenominational: The archbishop of Washington gave the invocation, and a Presbyterian minister and two rabbis delivered remarks. Other speakers included Walter Reuther, president of the United Auto Workers, James Farmer, the head of CORE, Roy Wilkins, NAACP executive secretary, A. Philip Randolph, the director of the march, Myrlie Evers, widow of Medgar Evers, and Martin Luther King Jr.

* * *

At the White House, President Kennedy settled in front of a television in the Oval Office. He had been inside the White House all day, having met earlier with foreign policy advisors to discuss Vietnam. At one point he had climbed to the third floor to gaze out on the mall from the Solarium with White House doorman Preston Bruce.

Bruce, lean and courtly in his dark suit and trim white mustache, had served in the White House for ten years under both Eisenhower and Kennedy. Besides greeting White House guests, he served in a quasi valet capacity, bringing items to the president, delivering briefing papers, and escorting the president to White House dinners and events. Often working in the family quarters, Bruce developed an easy familiarity with the president; and the president drew Bruce close to the family. Sometimes Bruce joined the president and First Lady for movies in the White House theater. When Bruce's son was appointed principal of a school in Vermont at age twenty-four, the president asked the proud father to bring his son in for a chat; when the president learned that the young man was visiting his father, he interrupted his schedule and spent twenty-five minutes with him. With his casual wit, Kennedy made Bruce feel an integral part of the White House. The doorman often heard the president say to visitors: "Bruce, he runs the place."

That afternoon, as marchers swarmed the mall, this son of a sharecropper stood with the president of the United States listening to the crowd below singing "We Shall Overcome." Years later, Bruce recalled that an emotional John Kennedy gripped the windowsill so firmly his knuckles blanched. "Oh, Bruce," he told the doorman, "I wish I was out there with them."

In the Oval Office, President Kennedy watched on television as King stepped before a bank of microphones. From the Montgomery bus boycott to the Birmingham movement, and after many battles with the president, King now spoke in the backyard of the White House with some two hundred thousand men, women, and children riding on his words, gazing upon him as the nation's preeminent black leader. His had been a long, precarious journey to his biggest stage yet.

For most of his speech, King relied on a prepared text and, while his voice was strong and his words eloquent, his message in some ways was not connecting with the masses below. John Lewis, who had heard King many times, felt something was lacking. "As he moved toward his final words, it seemed that he, too, could sense that he was falling short," Lewis recalled. "He hadn't locked into that *power* he so often found."

It was at that moment that the gospel singer Mahalia Jackson called out to King from her seat just behind him. She had preceded him on stage, stirring the crowd with her a cappella spiritual "I Been 'Buked and I Been Scorned." Now, she urged him: "Tell 'em about the dream, Martin." Anyone close to King, anyone who had conversations with him, or who had heard him speak, was aware of his dream. He had spoken of it on other stages; only a week earlier he had told an audience of insurance executives in Detroit about his dream. Now he set aside his prepared words and became the fiery, sublime preacher he was, and delivered the words that defined the march, the historical moment, and the fundamental yearning at the heart of the civil rights movement.

* * *

"So even though we face the difficulties of today and tomorrow I still have a dream," he said. "I have a dream that little children will one day live in a nation where they will not be judged by the color of their skin but by the content of their character."

King raised his voice calling for a union of blacks, whites, Jews, Gentiles, Protestants, and Catholics. And he dreamed that all men would "be able to join hands and sing in the words of the old Negro spiritual, 'Free at last! Free at last! Thank God almighty, we're free at last!'"

* * *

In the Oval Office, President Kennedy watched with total absorption. He had never been inside a church when Martin Luther King Jr. was on the pulpit; he had never sat through an entire King speech; he had never witnessed the rolling cadence and rhythm in its fullness. The preacher had dazzled the president. Turning to his aide Lee White, Kennedy was in awe: "He's damn good," he said. Robert Kennedy later seconded that, marveling, "Boy, he made a helluva speech." President Kennedy was a man who had hit rhetorical highs himself, and he appreciated eloquence: He knew he had just seen a performance for the ages.

* * *

Soon after King's speech, the marchers exited in waves. With hardly a hitch, the buses and trains pulled out, and Washington was rapidly drained of the human tide that had washed in. "At 9 p.m.," the *New York Times* reported, "the city was as calm as the waters of the Reflecting Pool between the two memorials."

The day began and ended smooth and peaceful. "There was no violence, no flare-ups," reported *Jet* magazine. Observers noted the dignity of the marchers. "It was an answer to the scoffers hoping for the worst," wrote the *Washington Post*. "All the dire forebodings about what might happen with such an influx of people were put to naught." The Reverend Charles Billups, who rode into town with a busload of Alabama blacks, already was thinking of how this chapter would read in school textbooks. "The only weapon we have is protest," he said. "This ride isn't going to be a waste of time. I think this march will be remembered indefinitely." James Reston of the *New York Times* placed King in the historical tradition of America's great reformers: "Roger Williams calling for religious liberty, Sam Adams calling for political liberty, old man Thoreau denouncing coercion, William Lloyd Garrison demanding emancipation, and Eugene V. Debs crying for economic equality." King's cry "I have a dream" was a similar cry for American rights and liberty. But as Reston wondered: "The question of the day, of course, was raised by Dr. King's theme: Was this all a dream or will it help the dream come true?"

The president was grateful the day had passed without incident. In a statement afterward, he praised "the deep fervor and the quiet dignity" of the thousands of participants "both Negro and white," saying that the desire to gain equal treatment and opportunity was "neither novel nor difficult to understand." He put opponents on notice: "What is different today," he explained, "is the intensified and widespread public awareness of the need to move forward in achieving these objectives."

In a spirit of accomplishment, the president welcomed the black leaders to the White House after the event, "relief written all over his face," Roy Wilkins recalled. He greeted the men and shook their hands, saying, "You did a superb job of making your case." John Lewis remembered the president standing at the door to the Oval Office speaking to each man: "He was beside himself. He was just smiling, beaming like a proud father that everything had gone so well." When he came to Martin Luther King Jr., the president smiled and said in a tone that rang at once with wit and sincerity, "I have a dream."

As the leaders gathered around the long table in the Cabinet Room, President Kennedy learned that none of them had had time to eat all day. A. Philip Randolph politely asked, "Mr. President, I wonder if I could have just a glass of milk." Along with Randolph's milk, Kennedy ordered coffee, tea, canapés, and sandwiches brought in for everyone. Over the next hour they discussed both the march and the outlook for the civil rights bill. John Lewis, who was on his second visit to the White House, noticed that President Kennedy and Martin Luther King Jr. had a newfound respect and admiration for each other. It was as if each man had recognized in this moment the working out of their complicated relationship. Lewis sensed that Kennedy understood King's powerful role in the day's success. "I felt that he believed that Martin Luther King Jr., his presence, his speech,...helped him make a mass assembly of humanity so peaceful and so orderly." And King welcomed the recognition. "You could tell he was just overjoyed," Lewis recalled. "He was very happy and proud—not grinning but really beaming."

This White House meeting was not predestined. The journey of the civil rights movement was uncertain, lurching in one direction, then another, and then turning, backtracking, then thrusting forward again. It had arrived at this historic moment in large measure by the determination of these two indomitable figures. Sitting at that long table in the Cabinet Room, John Lewis realized that John F. Kennedy and Martin Luther King Jr. were now interwoven in any discussion of civil rights. Absorbing the optimism of the day, Lewis distilled the Kennedy-King relationship: "It was like history and fate and inspiration just sort of came together."

Epilogue

THE MARCH ON Washington, sadly, was no Hollywood ending. Just two weeks later, on September 15, the Sixteenth Street Baptist Church in Birmingham, Alabama, held a Youth Day celebration. "The Sixteenth Street Baptist Church was the city's most elegant black church," historian and Southern native Diane McWhorter explained. "Church clothes were, as white people knew, the acme of the Negro wardrobe, and Sixteenth Street was a continual fashion show." For Youth Day, fourteen-year-old Carole Robertson wore medium-high heels for the first time. Shy Addie Mae Collins, also fourteen, was an usher in a white dress, and her twelve-year-old sister, Sarah, was also in her finest. Saxophonist and honor student Cynthia Wesley, fourteen years old, showed up all in white, and eleven-year-old Denise McNair, who had a dog named Whitey, wore a plaid purple dress and had her hair up in a French twist with a gold barrette. A little before 10:30 a.m., the five girls scampered downstairs to the women's lounge for some primping before the 11 a.m. service.

Robert Chambliss, nicknamed "Dynamite Bob" for his role in many Birmingham bombings, made his own elaborate preparations for Youth Day. A Ku Klux Klansman, he had been heard numerous times declaring his one hope for Sixteenth Street Baptist: "They ought to blow that church up." In her book *Carry Me Home*, McWhorter depicted Chambliss as a "bandy-legged figure"; whose face "was perpetually ruddy, his eyes an intense, deep-in-the-head blue, and his mouth seemed on the verge of a pucker, as if he had been weaned on moonshine." According to McWhorter, Chambliss also had a "tendency to sexually fondle his nieces and nephews." On September 4, Dynamite Bob showed up at a store in Blossburg, Alabama, about fifteen miles north of Birmingham and left with a case of dynamite containing about 140 sticks. The store's owner didn't know Chambliss's real purpose in buying all that dynamite but he had his own ideas, telling his regular customer: "If you are going to blow up some niggers, I will throw in a few extra sticks."

The morning of September 15 was cool and overcast. Disguising himself as an old man wearing a hat and walking with a cane, Chambliss climbed into a turquoise Chevrolet with Confederate flags flapping on the antenna. He drove to Sixteenth Street Baptist with three other Klansmen. Dynamite Bob figured about twenty sticks would do the job. Working quickly, the men placed the bulky package outside the front of the church at the basement entrance; it was connected to a crude timing device that would detonate the dynamite later in the morning around the time the church was filled with kids and their parents.

At 10:22 a.m., when the girls were in the downstairs lounge, the dynamite erupted with a thundering blast: The church quaked, walls collapsed, doors blew open, the rafters tumbled down, flames shot into the sky. Outside chunks of stone rocketed through parked cars. A passing driver was knocked unconscious when his windshield shattered. Pieces of brick shaved leaves off of trees in Kelly Ingram Park some two hundred feet away.

Inside the church, a teacher screamed: "Lie on the floor! Lie on the floor!" A skylight crashed onto the pulpit. A stained glass window blew out, erasing the face of Christ. A brick and stone wall collapsed onto the women's lounge. Parishioners dug bare-handed through the rubble in a haze of dust and debris and came upon the bodies of four little girls. The horror was unimaginable: One girl had been decapitated. The only sign of life was a weak voice calling out: "Addie? Addie? Addie?" It was twelve-year-old Sarah Collins hoping to hear her big sister calling back.

* * *

As the blast reverberated through the community, black youths converged on the church and hurled rocks at police. Three hundred highway patrolmen swept in under the command of the Alabama director of public safety, Albert Lingo. A black sixteen-year-old fleeing the scene was shot in the back and died. Two sixteen-year-old white Eagle Scouts fired a pistol at two blacks riding by on a bicycle; a thirteen-year-old balancing on the handlebars was killed.

Martin Luther King Jr. was about to preach at Ebenezer Baptist Church in Atlanta on that Sunday morning when he heard of the bombing. Overcome by grief, he sent an angry telegram to President Kennedy and immediately made plans to go to Birmingham. "The savage bombing of the 16th Street Baptist Church this morning," he told the president, "is another clear indication of the moral degeneration of the state of Alabama and Governor George Wallace." Throughout September, Governor Wallace—still stinging from his humiliation at the University of Alabama—had tried to block black students from enrolling in several public schools that were under court orders to desegregate; he backed his efforts with the Alabama National Guard and with incendiary warnings of violence if the blacks were admitted. Cracking down on Wallace's defiance, President Kennedy snatched the National Guard out of his control, federalizing those troops, and on September 10 twenty black students walked onto previously all-white campuses. Wallace clung to his inflammatory rhetoric, crowing against integration and inciting whites to violence. In his telegram, King told the president that he would plead with his people to stay calm "in the face of this terrible provocation. However," he added, "I am convinced that unless some steps are taken by the federal government to restore a sense of confidence in the protection of life, limb and property my pleas shall fall on deaf ears and we shall see the worst racial holocaust this nation has ever seen after today's tragedy."

The president sent a helicopter for Burke Marshall, who was spending the weekend at his farm in West Virginia, and the civil rights aide was soon on his way to Birmingham. In a statement, President Kennedy expressed his "deep sense of outrage and grief over the killing of the children." Then targeting Wallace, without mentioning him by name, the president added: "It is regrettable that public disparagement of law and order has encouraged violence which has fallen on the innocent."

Arriving in Birmingham, King indicted Wallace for the actions of the extremists. "The governor said things and did things that caused these people to feel that they were aided and abetted by the highest officer of the state," he told Claude Sitton of the *New York Times.* "The murders of yesterday stand as blood on the hands of Governor Wallace."

* * *

And so it went. Progress on civil rights was stymied by a hatred that simply wouldn't die. Leadership obviously played an enormous role. On one side was George Wallace, and others like him, with a hardened, unyielding conscience who confirmed the biases of his followers; and on the other was John Kennedy, who had an aptitude for enlightenment and empathy, qualities he hoped to inspire in the country at large. But with his assassination on November 22, 1963, his leadership on civil rights was never to be fully realized. His loss was the loss of hope for many blacks. Martin Luther King Jr. grieved over what might have been. Kennedy "was at his death undergoing a transformation," King believed, "from a hesitant leader with unsure goals to a strong figure with deeply appealing objectives." King made a remarkable admission in early 1964 that he had planned to break with his long-standing policy during presidential campaigns. Believing that "a new stage in civil rights has been reached," King acknowledged that "had President Kennedy lived, I would probably have endorsed him in the forthcoming election."

* * *

What John Kennedy began, his successor, Lyndon Johnson, completed. In his first speech after the assassination to a joint session of Congress on November 27, 1963, President Johnson said: "No memorial oration or eulogy could more eloquently honor President Kennedy's memory than the earliest possible passage of the civil rights bill for which he fought so long. We have talked long enough in this country about equal rights. We have talked for one hundred years or more. It is time now to write the next chapter, and to write it in the books of law." Under Johnson's guidance the Civil Rights Act was passed in 1964, followed by the Voting Rights Act in 1965.

* * *

The 1960s was a mix of optimism and menace. Color televisions, flashy cars with tail fins, and landings on the moon competed with warfare in distant jungles and assassinations at home. Even the hopeful Martin Luther King Jr. was deeply discouraged by late in the decade, believing that the war in Vietnam was destroying America and holding back progress in racial equality. In 1967, he told a television reporter that in some ways the dream he had in 1963 had "turned into a nightmare." On April 3, 1968, he spoke in Memphis, Tennessee, in support of a sanitation workers' strike. Feeling sick that night, he hadn't intended to appear but left his motel at the urging of his friend Ralph Abernathy and took the stage at the Mason Temple. His oratory, as it so often did, hit a bright note; but embedded in his words was a dire prophecy. At the close of his speech, he told the crowd: "I've been to the mountaintop." *Yeah*, the audience said back to him, applauding. "Like anybody, I would like to live a long life." But, he said, the length of his life didn't matter; he wanted to do what God had called upon him to do. "I've seen the Promised Land," he told the crowd. "I may not get there with you. But I want you to know tonight…that we, as a people, will get to the Promised Land." He was happy, he declared; he had no worries, he feared no man. "Mine eyes have seen the glory of the coming of the Lord."

The next day, when King was standing on the balcony of the Lorraine Motel in Memphis, an assassin's bullet pierced his cheek and severed his jugular vein. His rich, instructive voice was silenced. Robert Kennedy, by then a strong advocate for social justice, was running for the Democratic presidential nomination; he was flying to Indianapolis to speak in a ghetto when he learned of the shooting. By the time he got to the city, word reached him that Martin Luther King Jr. was dead. His aides and his wife, Ethel, all tried to dissuade Bobby from going into the ghetto. The police chief feared a riot. But Bobby was adamant. Sending Ethel back to the hotel, he went along accompanied by a couple aides; his police escort, expecting a night of mayhem, pulled back before Bobby got to the site. Bobby carried on and entered an open lot bordered by tenements where a crowd awaited him. He asked an aide if the people had heard about King and learned that the news hadn't reached them. So, bundled in an old overcoat that had belonged to his dead brother, he climbed onto a flatbed truck and took it upon himself to inform them. "I have some very sad news for all of you," he told the crowd of about two thousand blacks who had waited an hour for him, "and, I think, sad news for all of our fellow citizens, and people who love peace all over the world; and that is that Martin Luther King was shot and was killed tonight in Memphis, Tennessee." There were cries of disbelief. Bobby pulled out of his pocket a few notes he had scribbled down on his way, but as he continued speaking he barely referred to them. He spoke of King's special dedication to his fellow man, to love, and to justice. "What we need in the United States is not division," Bobby said, "what we need in the United States is not hatred; what we need in the United States is not violence and lawlessness, but is love, and wisdom, and compassion toward one another, and a feeling of justice toward those who still suffer within our country, whether they be white or whether they be black." He sympathized with the feelings of bitterness and revenge that might have filled many in the crowd; and he asked that everyone try to "make gentle the life of this world." And there, confronting a crowd of angry blacks living in tenements, Bobby quoted lines from the Greek playwright Aeschylus that soothed him during his darkest nights after his brother's assassination.

> *Even in our sleep, pain which cannot forget*
> *falls drop by drop upon the heart,*
> *until, in our own despair,*
> *against our will,*
> *comes wisdom*
> *through the awful grace of God.*

America exploded that night with riots in 110 cities, leaving thirty-nine people dead and more than 2,500 injured. Indianapolis was quiet. But something broke that night. Richard Goodwin, advisor and friend to the Kennedys, captured the difference between the assassinations of the president and Martin Luther King Jr. "The murder of John Kennedy was stupefying, an eye-scorching blast from a cloudless sky," he wrote in his memoir, *Remembering America.* "A grieving country had halted for a moment, then moved toward the destiny he had come to represent—more, perhaps, in death than in life." Goodwin noted that the New Frontier of the Kennedy days was followed by Johnson's Great Society, the War on Poverty, and some civil rights strides. "But this murder was different. Martin Luther King's death did not pour fresh energy into black demands, arouse the accommodating sympathies of a country. It left only emptiness." Goodwin suggested that race of course played a role. "Kennedy was white and King was black," he observed. "But more important were the times." The innocence and hope of the early sixties was giving way to something else later in the decade. "It was 1968 not 1963," Goodwin noted. "We had already begun to shatter that collective self—the bonds of American community—and move toward the self-regarding individualism that would dominate approaching decades."

That night in Indianapolis, Bobby Kennedy was unable to sleep. He wandered through the corridors of his hotel to his aides' rooms. On one stop, the aide said, he heard Bobby utter the name of his brother's assassin for the first time; but he called him Harvey Lee Oswald, and the aide believed that that name, which had incorrectly been reported in early radio reports, had stuck in Bobby's head through the years. Later in the night, he wandered into another aide's room and admitted to what was troubling him. "That could have been me," he said of King's assassination.

And two months later, after winning the California Democratic primary, Bobby told a raucous crowd at the Ambassador Hotel in Los Angeles, "We are a great country, an unselfish country, and a compassionate country....So my thanks to all of you, and now it's on to Chicago, and let's win there." The Illinois primary was a week away, and the Democratic National Convention was coming in August in Chicago. Bobby left the podium in his blue pin-striped suit and white shirt, with a daub of actor's makeup on his forehead, covering a bruise he'd gotten in the Pacific Ocean in the morning; he was staying at filmmaker John Frankenheimer's place in Malibu and had dived into the sea to grab his nearly thirteen-year-old boy, David, who was struggling in a strong undertow, and Bobby scraped his forehead on the sea floor. Now he stood in a narrow corridor shaking hands with the hotel's kitchen staff. The place was filled with good cheer until the sound of a snub-nosed .22-caliber pistol changed everything: six pops, and Bobby was on his back on the floor with a bullet in his brain.

With a cruel irony, Bobby had calmed the crowd in Indianapolis after the killing of Martin Luther King Jr. in words of prophecy for not only himself but for America in the decades ahead. "We can do well in this country," he had told the restless blacks. "We will have difficult times. We've had difficult times in the past...and we will have difficult times in the future." And in a final note, he added: "It is not the end of violence; it is not the end of lawlessness; and it's not the end of disorder."

* * *

In the past fifty years, after the promise of racial equality emerged in the early 1960s, America has stumbled backward. The progress implied by integration and voting rights legislation in the sixties and by the flowering of new freedoms—political, racial, sexual—has stalled. We have achieved what Bobby Kennedy had predicted long ago: In Barack Obama we have had a black president. But in alarming numbers, police in recent years have killed black men under suspicious circumstances. The names Eric Garner, Michael Brown, Tamir Rice, Freddie Grey have become part of our culture in discussions of deadly police brutality. Despite the Supreme Court's *Brown v. Board of Education* ruling in 1954, America has still failed to end school segregation. The proportion of schools intensively segregated—meaning they contained more than 90 percent of low-income students and students of color—more than doubled between 2001 and 2014. Meanwhile, states across the country—Texas, North Carolina, Wisconsin, Ohio, Kansas—made it more difficult over the years for minorities to vote; gradually, some of those obstructions were reduced but only through a series of court actions.

What was true in 1963, sadly, seems true today, as James Baldwin described in *The Fire Next Time* more than fifty years ago. "There is simply no possibility of a real change in the Negro's situation without the most radical and far-reaching changes in the American political and social structure," he wrote. "And it is clear that white Americans are not simply unwilling to effect these changes; they are, in the main...unable even to envision them. It must be added that the Negro himself no longer believes in the good faith of white Americans—if, indeed, he ever could have."

As bleak as conditions sometimes looked to him in the early years, Martin Luther King Jr. resisted such pessimism. His experience through 1963 suggested that it was possible to speak truth to power and to have the president of the United States listen. After King repeatedly badgered Kennedy about the moral crimes inflicted on the black community, the president finally acted. "He had the vision and wisdom to see the problem in all of its dimensions and the courage to do something about it," King observed. But it was never easy to enlighten the president. In the role of activist, pastor, and educator, King had to be relentless. As he once insisted, "I never wanted—and I told him this—to be in the position that I couldn't criticize him if I thought he was wrong." And President Kennedy, in a sign of open-mindedness, admitted to King: "It often helps me to be pushed."

ACKNOWLEDGMENTS

My wife, Suzanne, has contributed in innumerable ways, visible and invisible, to this book, as she did on my previous one. *Kennedy and King*, to her regret, didn't require her to do research in French and translate stacks of French newspapers and documents—a task she loves and one she undertook for *Little Demon in the City of Light*. This time, her researching was no less prodigious. She spent hours at the Library of Congress digging up mountains of news reports from many publications, invaluable for understanding the mood of the early civil rights movement and the public persona of President Kennedy. She was a wise ear as this project developed, offering insight into its themes and approach. She was a first eye on the text, raising thoughtful questions and pointing out stumbles. With patience I could never muster, she prepared the source notes with meticulous care, a time-consuming, arduous task that no one can truly appreciate unless you've done it. She plunged into another demanding task: navigating various rights issues, a challenge requiring steadfast attention to detail that she accomplished with speed and intelligence. She also researched and compiled a tremendous selection of photos, only a handful of which made it into the book because of space and expense. In the later stages of editing, she sat by my side combing the manuscript, fixing large and small errors and offering helpful touches on language. Driven by her terror of inaccuracy, she is a tenacious fact-checker. If *Kennedy and King* gets things right, it's due to her; if it gets anything wrong, I am entirely to blame. In sum, as always, she has been a force for calm amid the personal and professional insanity that writing a book places on a family and a relationship. My gratitude to her is as deep as my love.

My thanks go to friends and colleagues at the *Washington Post*, who have aided this project in both spiritual and concrete ways: Marty

Baron, who creates an atmosphere of excellence that infuses every aspect of a *Post* staffer's professional life; Tracy Grant, Adam Kushner, Eddy Palanzo, Ron Charles, Nora Krug, Tim Smith, Richard Aldacushion, Juliet Eilperin, David Nakamura, Karen Heller, Geoff Edgers; and the many others who love talking about books and ideas for book projects.

I'm grateful to others for their thoughts and assistance: Alexandra Dahne at the University of California Press, Abigail Malangone at the JFK Library, Sarah Pratt at the Martin Luther King Jr. Archive at Boston University's Howard Gotlieb Archival Research Center, Joellen ElBashir of the Moorland-Spingarn Research Center at Howard University, Brenda Jones, Helen O'Donnell, and Bill Silbert. Thanks also go to several historians who offered their insights on the project: Robert Dallek, Matt Dallek, Douglas Brinkley, and David Garrow.

My writing life, and this book in particular, owes much to my agent, the always sensible and unflappable Dan Lazar at Writers House, and to the gracious and helpful staff there. I'm indebted to Paul Whitlatch, a superlative editor at Hachette, for his encouragement, guidance, and careful hand on the manuscript, and to Michelle Aielli, Lauren Hummel, and Kara Thornton. I learned a lot about copyright from the wise legal counsel of John Pelosi.

Finally, back to my family. I want to thank our kids, Katie and Ben, who have grown up under the strange intensity that book writing imposes on a household and have endured it with their usual intelligence, patience, and curiosity.

NOTE ON SOURCES

As the John F. Kennedy–Martin Luther King Jr. era recedes further into history, sadly many of the men and women closest to them have been lost. Researching this book meant mining the voluminous existing material: interviews, memoirs, newspaper coverage, letters, and other documents in archives, along with conducting new conversations with a few principals of the era. Also of immeasurable value were the masterful works on Kennedy and King and the men and women around them that have laid the foundation for all succeeding efforts. This book has drawn insight, inspiration, and guidance from the towering contributions of Raymond Arsenault, Taylor Branch, Nick Bryant, Thurston Clarke, Peter Collier and David Horowitz, Robert Dallek, Glenn Eskew, Adam Fairclough, David Garrow, Doris Kearns Goodwin, David Nasaw, Arthur Schlesinger, Ted Sorensen, Evan Thomas, and Diane McWhorter, among others. Many participants in the major events of the era have written compelling memoirs that gave me a sense of time and place and detail, among them: Ralph Abernathy, James Baldwin, Harry Belafonte, Simeon Booker, Ben Bradlee, Richard Goodwin, Edwin Guthman, Clint Hill, Coretta Scott King, Martin Luther King Jr., William Kunstler, John Lewis, Evelyn Lincoln, Kenneth O'Donnell and David Powers, Ted Sorensen, Roy Wilkins, and Harris Wofford. I'm indebted to Jean Stein and George Plimpton for their fine work on first-person recollections of Robert Kennedy, and to Howell Raines for his incomparable collection of civil rights oral histories. I'm grateful for the time I had with Harris Wofford and John Lewis to hear their perspectives.

Archival research has taken me to the John F. Kennedy Presidential Library and Museum and to the Martin Luther King Jr. Archive at Boston University's Howard Gotlieb Archival Research Center. The nature of historical research has changed profoundly in recent years as archives place an abundance of material online. The digital revolution has speeded the process of research and provided remote access to essential material miles away. The John F. Kennedy Library has made remarkable progress in digitizing a range of documents: letters, telegrams, original drafts of speeches, and hundreds of oral histories. The oral history program, undertaken in the dark days soon after John Kennedy's assassination with strong encouragement from Jacqueline Kennedy and Robert Kennedy, has provided a rich trove of first-person recollections. Fresh readings of the oral histories provide new interpretations to stories we thought we already knew. A spectacular ongoing project that puts hundreds of Martin Luther King Jr. documents at researchers' fingertips is the Martin Luther King, Jr. Papers Project under the sponsorship of Stanford University, with the support of the King Estate and the cooperation of the King Center in Atlanta. This massive undertaking, led by Clayborne Carson, has so far produced seven thick volumes of perfectly organized and annotated documents. These books, published by the University of California Press, are a researcher's dream.

NOTES

Abbreviations: Associated Press (AP), John F. Kennedy Library (JFKL), John F. Kennedy Library Oral History Program (JFKLOHP), the *New York Times* (*NYT*), United Press International (UPI), the *Washington Post* (*WP*)

"To Teach a President"

x   **"their heirs, their grandsons":** John F. Kennedy, "Report to the American People on Civil Rights, June 11, 1963, JFKL, https://www.jfklibrary.org/Asset-Viewer/LH8F_0Mzv0e6 Ro1yEm74Ng.aspx.

x   **"The very being":** John Lewis, recorded interview with author, April 20, 2016.

x   **"We saw two":** Martin Luther King Jr., recorded interview by Berl Bernhard, March 9, 1964, 6, 17, JFKLOHP.

xi   **"Leaders have choices":** Margaret MacMillan, *History's People*, CBC Massey Lectures (Toronto: House of Ananci, 2015), 9.

xi   **"It's a difficult":** "It's a Difficult Thing to Teach a President," *Look*, Nov. 17, 1964, 62.

PART ONE: *Two Men, Two Worlds*

3   **"Many are distrustful":** Memo from Sorensen to RFK, undated, RFKPAF Box 34, Nicholas Andrew Bryant, *The Bystander: John F. Kennedy and the Struggle for Black Equality* (New York: Basic Books, 2006), 127.

3   **"a friend of":** Associated Press, "Alabama Governor Endorses Kennedy," *NYT*, June 17, 1959, 38.

4   **"I said to":** Arnold Rampersad, *Jackie Robinson: A Biography* (New York: Alfred A. Knopf, 1997), 324.

4   **"We shall never be":** Rampersad, *Jackie Robinson: A Biography*, 325.

4   **"In this endeavor":** Jackie Robinson letter to Vice President Nixon, March 19, 1957; Nixon Library, https://www.nixonlibrary.gov/forkids/edu_programing/HistoryDay2010/ Civil%20Rights/16.%2003-19-1957,%20Pre-Pres.%20Papers,%20VP%20General%20 Correspondence%20Robinson.%20Jackie-Rock-n-Roll%20Club%20of%20South%20 America,%20Box%20649.pdf.

4   **"If it should":** Jackie Robinson column, *New York Post*, Dec. 30, 1960.

4   **"strongly in favor":** Michael G. Long, ed., *First Class Citizenship: The Civil Rights Letters of Jackie Robinson* (New York: Times Books, 2007), 83–84.

5 **"Sen. Kennedy won":** "Kennedy Faces Key Race Test in Maryland Primary Vote," *Jet*, April 21, 1960, 7.

5 **"shoo-in":** Earl Mazo, "Nixon Says Kennedy Could Be Shoo-In," *Boston Globe*, April 12, 1960.

5 **"I must repeat":** Jackie Robinson, *New York Post*, April 8, 1960.

5 **"We're in trouble":** Harris Wofford, *Of Kennedys and Kings: Making Sense of the Sixties* (Pittsburgh, PA: University of Pittsburgh Press, 1980), 47.

5 **"He felt that":** George A. Smathers, recorded interview by Don Wilson, on July 10, 1964, 6F, JFKLOHP.

6 **"Protestants . . . need apply":** Joe McCarthy, *The Remarkable Kennedys* (New York: Popular Library, 1960), 26.

6 **"Those narrow-minded bigoted":** Peter Collier and David Horowitz, *The Kennedys: An American Drama* (New York: Summit Books, 1984), 44.

7 **"It's an indelible":** Nigel Hamilton, *JFK: Reckless Youth* (New York: Random House, 1992), 55.

7 **"We did grow":** Robert F. Kennedy, recorded interview #5 by Anthony Lewis, Dec. 4, 1964, 342–343, JFKLOHP.

7 **"nigger place":** Michael O'Brien, *John F. Kennedy: A Biography* (New York: Thomas Dunne Books, 2005), 364.

8 **"I never saw":** Arthur Krock, recorded interview by Charles Bartlett, on May 10, 1964, 17–18, JFKLOHP.

8 **"We didn't lie":** RF Kennedy Oral History #5, 342.

8 **"We were good":** George H. Taylor, recorded interview #1 by Sal Micciche, on May 7, 1964, 15, JFKLOHP.

8 **"Taylor, how'd I":** Ibid., 10.

9 **"He'd say, 'Come":** Ibid.

9 **"It was easy":** Theodore C. Sorensen, *Kennedy* (New York: Harper & Row, 1965), 18.

9 **"If I walked":** Doris Kearns Goodwin, *The Fitzgeralds and the Kennedys* (New York: Simon & Schuster, 1987), 707.

10 **"As of . . . with you":** George H. Taylor, recorded interview #2 by Sheldon Stern, Aug. 12, 1977, 8, JFKLOHP.

10 **"They're all giving":** Ibid., 9.

10 **"George, you're thin-skinned":** Ibid., 10.

10 **"They don't have":** Ibid.

10 **"One of . . . but work":** "Young Kennedy Hard Worker," *WP*, Dec. 21, 1946, 7.

11 **"We weren't thinking":** Edwin O. Guthman and Jeffrey Shulman, eds., *Robert Kennedy: In His Own Words: The Unpublished Recollections of the Kennedy Years* (New York: Bantam Books, 1988), 68.

11 **"Northern pols were . . . I'm Jack Kennedy":** Bryant, *The Bystander*, 25.

11 **"That young American":** Robert Dallek, *An Unfinished Life: John F. Kennedy 1917–1963* (New York: Back Bay, 2013), 153.

12 **"When we talk":** Gould Lincoln, "Kennedy Trying to Get Vote for District of Columbia Residents," *Boston Globe*, Jan. 28, 1950.

12 **"attitudinizing liberals":** Joseph W. Alsop, recorded interview by Elspeth Rostow, June 26, 1964, 73, JFKLOHP.

12 **"When he came":** Kenneth P. O'Donnell, David F. Powers, and Joe McCarthy, *"Johnny, We Hardly Knew Ye": Memories of John Fitzgerald Kennedy* (New York: Pocket Books, 1973), 89.

13 **"at least one-half":** Sorensen, *Kennedy*, 42.

13 **"Those who knew . . . nothing":** Ibid., 42.

13 **"He went along...of the time":** Rose Fitzgerald Kennedy, *Times to Remember* (New York: Doubleday, 1995), 175.

13 **"The point is":** Dallek, *An Unfinished Life*, 154.

13 **"It had taken":** Ibid.

14 **"billowing felt skirt":** Bryant, *The Bystander*, 39–40.

15 **"Generations of Southerners":** Dan Wakefield, "Respectable Racism," *Nation*, Oct. 22, 1955, 339.

16 **"It isn't the matter":** Samuel Gandy, "Nation Asked to Help Boycotters," *Journal and Guide* (Norfolk, VA), July 28, 1956, 9.

16 **"So far from":** W. J. Cash, *The Mind of the South* (New York: Vintage, 1969), x.

16 **"A youthful 34":** Elizabeth Maguire, "Surely He'll Need a First Lady—If!" *WP*, March 2, 1952, 55.

16 **"capital's most eligible bachelor":** John Harris, "Most Eligible Bachelor? It's Martin, Says Kennedy," *Boston Globe*, March 1, 1953.

17 **"I'd be very happy":** Dallek, *An Unfinished Life*, 178.

17 **"No attribute he":** Sorensen, *Kennedy*, 23.

18 **"Joe Kennedy not":** O'Brien, *John F. Kennedy*, 265.

18 **"Getting to know":** O'Donnell, Powers, and McCarthy, *"Johnny, We Hardly Knew Ye,"* 107.

19 **"this little boy":** Theodore H. White, "For President Kennedy: An Epilogue," *Life*, December 6, 1963, available at https://www.jfklibrary.org/Asset-Viewer/Archives/THWPP-059-009.aspx.

19 **"He saw her...performances":** D. K. Goodwin, *The Fitzgeralds and the Kennedys*, 770.

19 **"one of those dream-perfect":** O'Donnell, Powers, and McCarthy, *"Johnny, We Hardly Knew Ye,"* 108.

19 **"It was enough":** D. K. Goodwin, *The Fitzgeralds and the Kennedys*, 771.

19 **"I used to tell":** Ibid., 772.

20 **Earlier in the year:** Ibid., 774.

20 **"I'd rather be":** O'Donnell, Powers, and McCarthy, *"Johnny, We Hardly Knew Ye,"* 113.

21 **"I have here":** Burt Hirschfeld, *Freedom in Jeopardy: The Story of the McCarthy Years* (New York: Julian Messner, 1969), 48.

21 **"I think that the stories":** Arthur M. Schlesinger, Jr., *A Thousand Days* (Boston: Houghton Mifflin, 1965), 12.

21 **"He referred to":** Ibid.

22 **"Hell," Kennedy told:** Ibid.

22 **"Oh, hell, you can't fight":** Dallek, *An Unfinished Life*, 189.

22 **"McCarthyism simply did":** Schlesinger, *A Thousand Days*, 12.

22 **"I agree that many":** Dallek, *An Unfinished Life*, 191.

23 **"I was just darned sick":** James MacGregor Burns, *John Kennedy: A Political Profile* (New York: Harcourt, Brace, 1960), 157.

23 **"I never said":** Dallek, *An Unfinished Life*, 191.

23 **"You know, when":** Charles Spalding, recorded interview by John F. Stewart, March 14, 1968, 35, JFKLOHP.

23 **"A man who does":** Bryant, *The Bystander*, 47.

24 **"Robert Kennedy tells":** Schlesinger, *A Thousand Days*, 86.

24 **"Unable to sleep":** O'Donnell, Powers, and McCarthy, *"Johnny, We Hardly Knew Ye,"* 115.

25 **"Many assumed that":** Sorensen, *Kennedy*, 68.

25 **"In choosing to write":** D. K. Goodwin, *The Fitzgeralds and the Kennedys*, 777.

25 **"eyes shone with":** O'Brien, 804; citing Arthur Schlesinger Jr., "On JFK: An Interview with Isaiah Berlin," *New York Review of Books*, Oct. 22, 1998, 31.

25 **"The stories of"**: John F. Kennedy, *Profiles in Courage* (New York: Harper & Row, 1961), 246.

25 **"splendidly readable"**: Charles Poore, "Books of the Times," *NYT*, Jan. 7, 1956, 15.

26 **"He was the"**: Bill Cunningham, "Kennedy Rates as Real Victor," *Boston Herald*, Aug. 18, 1956, 1.

26 **"Senator Kennedy came"**: "Party's Film Aids Kennedy's Drive," *NYT*, Aug. 4, 1956, 13.

26 **"and learned that"**: O'Donnell, Powers, and McCarthy, *"Johnny, We Hardly Knew Ye,"* 109.

26 SEN. KENNEDY ON: Winzola McLendon, "Sen. Kennedy on Mediterranean Trip Unaware His Wife Has Lost Baby," *WP*, Aug. 25, 1956, 1.

27 **"You better haul"**: Ralph G. Martin, *A Hero for Our Time: An Intimate Story of the Kennedy Years* (New York: Macmillan, 1983), 123.

27 **"When I'd tell him"**: Paul B. Fay Jr., *The Pleasure of His Company* (New York: Harper & Row, 1966), 54.

27 **"Now, Lem, tell me...anything else"**: Christopher Andersen, *Jack and Jackie: Portrait of an American Marriage* (New York: Avon Books, 1996), 188.

27 **undisclosed case of Addison's disease:** D. K. Goodwin, *The Fitzgeralds and the Kennedys*, 745.

27 **"between May 1955"**: Dallek, *An Unfinished Life*, 212.

27 **"Jack is the greatest attraction"**: D. K. Goodwin, *The Fitzgeralds and the Kennedys*, 792.

28 **"like a method actor"**: Collier and Horowitz, *The Kennedys*, 235.

29 **"I didn't know why"**: Harry Belafonte with Michael Shnayerson, *My Song: A Memoir* (New York: Alfred A. Knopf, 2011), 214.

29 **"Once you say"**: Sorensen, *Kennedy*, 13.

29 **"very persistent and very insistent"**: Harry Belafonte, recorded interview with Vicki Daitch, May 20, 2005, 7, JFKLOHP.

29 **"He kept calling"**: Belafonte, *My Song*, 214.

29 **"I tell you"**: Ibid.

29 **"his home away"**: Ibid., 194.

30 **"In the end,"**: Ibid., 11.

30 **"I wasn't nonviolent by nature"**: Ibid., 150.

30 **"I would come...my personal anger"**: Ibid.

30 **"I am sure...as my neighbors"**: Eleanor Roosevelt, "My Day," column, Oct. 20. 1958, available at *The Eleanor Roosevelt Papers Digital Edition* (2008), https://www.gwu.edu/~erpapers/myday/displaydoc.cfm?_y=1958&_f=md004254.

30 **"When we tried"**: Belafonte, *My Song*, 192.

31 **"He was kind of"**: Harry Belafonte Oral History Interview JFK#1, May 20, 2005, 7.

32 **"Doctor, I don't know"**: Bryant, *The Bystander*, 24–25.

32 **"I understand that you"**: Belafonte, *My Song*, 214.

33 **"I was quite forthright"**: Harry Belafonte Oral History Interview JFK#1, 8.

33 **"Not once in his disquisition"**: Belafonte, *My Song*, 214.

33 **"I am somewhat...in your thinking"**: Harry Belafonte Oral History Interview JFK#1, 8.

33 **"You're making a big mistake"**: Belafonte, *My Song*, 215.

33 **"Why, he asked"**: Ibid.

33 **"The time you've spent...our people"**: Belafonte Oral History JFK #1, 8.

34 **"Kennedy, I told him"**: Belafonte, *My Song*, 215.

34 **"The cop in the"**: Baldwin, *The Fire Next Time* (New York: Dell, 1963), 32.

34 **"as cheerless as"**: James Baldwin, "Letter from Harlem," in *Reporting Civil Rights, Part One: American Journalism 1941–1963* (New York: Library of America, 2003), 514.

35 **"The only way"**: Ibid., 516.

35 **"You just wait":** Lerone Bennett Jr., *What Manner of Man: A Biography of Martin Luther King, Jr.* (Chicago: Johnson, 1964), 17.

36 **"None of us seriously":** Ibid., 19.

36 **"were white and I":** Ibid.

36 **"Here for the...of it before":** "An Autobiography of Religious Development," Nov. 22, 1950, in Clayborne Carson, ed., *The Papers of Martin Luther King, Jr.*, vol. 1, *Called to Serve, January 1929–June 1951* (Berkeley, CA: University of California Press, 1992), 362 (hereafter cited as *Called to Serve*).

36 **"I was determined":** Ibid.

36 **"I don't care...accept it":** Martin Luther King, Jr., *Stride Toward Freedom: The Montgomery Story* (San Francisco: Harper & Row, 1986), 19.

37 **"All right boy...listen to you:** Ibid., 20.

37 **"The King family":** Carson, *Called to Serve*, 19 n. 59.

38 **"gracious manners, captivating smile":** Ibid., 18.

38 **"I had no natural talent":** Ibid., 19.

38 **"To prepare a child":** Ibid., 29.

39 **"We cannot have...for all people":** Ibid., 110.

39 **"It was the angriest":** *"Playboy* interview: Martin Luther King," *Playboy*, Jan. 1965, 66.

39 **"Religion for me":** "An Autobiography of Religious Development," in Carson, *Called to Serve*, 363.

39 **"It was my duty":** Ibid., 362.

39 **"No matter what flavor":** C. S. King, *My Life with Martin Luther King, Jr.* (New York: Holt, Rinehart and Winston, 1969), 33.

40 **"His conscience was":** Ibid., 61.

40 **"moral obligation":** M. L. King, *Stride Toward Freedom*, 21.

40 **"Finally we agreed":** Ibid.

41 **"Even in 1954":** C. S. King, *My Life with Martin*, 97.

41 **"Martin and I":** Ibid.

42 **"Acquiescence...coward":** M. L. King, *Stride Toward Freedom*, 212.

42 **"You ought to":** Ibid., 37.

42 **"niggers," "black cows":** Ibid., 40.

42 **"Many unconsciously...personality":** Ibid., 37.

42 **"I had had problems...from the bus":** Howell Raines, *My Soul Is Rested: The Story of the Civil Rights Movement in the Deep South* (New York: Penguin, 1983), 40.

43 **"Don't ride the bus":** Clayborne Carson, ed., *The Papers of Martin Luther King, Jr.*, vol. 3, *Birth of a New Age, December 1955–December 1956* (Berkeley, CA: University of California Press, 1997), 67 (hereafter *Birth of a New Age*).

43 **"the hottest story":** Interview with E. D. Nixon in Taylor Branch, *Parting the Waters: America in the King Years 1954–63* (New York: Simon & Schuster, 1989), 133.

43 NEGRO GROUPS READY BOYCOTT: Ibid.

43 **"That awesome conscience":** C. S. King, *My Life with Martin*, 114.

43 **"We were simply saying":** M. L. King, *Stride Toward Freedom*, 51.

43 **"I still had doubts":** Ibid., 52.

44 **"Martin, Martin...fully awake":** Ibid., 53–54.

44 **"Well, if you think I can":** David J. Garrow, *Bearing the Cross: Martin Luther King, Jr., and the Southern Christian Leadership Conference* (New York: William Morrow, 1986), 22.

44 **"Idealists would...than glory":** Branch, *Parting the Waters*, 137.

45 **"My feets is tired":** "23 March 1965: Address at the Conclusion of the Selma to Montgomery March," in *Martin Luther King, Jr. and the Global Freedom Struggle*, Stanford University,

http://kingencyclopedia.stanford.edu/encyclopedia/documentsentry/doc_address_at
_the_conclusion_of_selma_march.1.html.

45 **"soft-spoken man...convictions":** "Battle Against Tradition: Martin Luther King Jr.,"
NYT, March 21, 1956, 28.

45 **"We hold these truths...the White House":** "National Grapevine: Declaration of Segregation," *Chicago Defender*, March 17, 1956, 2.

45 **"Nigger, we are tired":** Martin Luther King Jr., "Why Jesus Called a Man a Fool,"
*A Knock at Midnight: Inspirations from the Great Sermons of Rev. Martin Luther
King Jr.*, Stanford University Libraries, https://swap.stanford.edu/20141218230003/
http://mlk-kpp01.stanford.edu/kingweb/publications/sermons/670827.000_Why_Jesus
_Called_a_Man_a_Fool.html.

46 **"They can be":** M. L. King, *Stride Toward Freedom: The Montgomery Story*, 134.

46 **"I was ready":** Ibid.

46 **"But now I...face anything":** Ibid., 134–135.

46 **"We cannot solve...radiant assurance":** Ibid., 137–138.

47 **"I have reached":** Ibid., 145.

47 **"lacked the moral":** Ibid., 144.

47 **"For the first time":** Ibid., 129.

47 **"A once fear-ridden":** Ibid., 146.

48 **"God struggles with":** Ibid., 171.

48 **"Do not deliberately":** Ibid., 164.

48 **"The Negroes along":** Enoc P. Waters, "Klan Parades in Montgomery: Race Haters
Boil over Bus Ruling," *Chicago Defender*, Nov. 15, 1956, 1.

48 **"Any time...saved to run":** Raines, *My Soul Is Rested*, 154–155.

49 **"We know why":** L. D. Reddick, *Crusader Without Violence: A Biography of Martin
Luther King, Jr.* (New York: Harper & Brothers, 1959), 157.

49 **"In little more":** "The South: Attack on the Conscience," *Time*, Feb. 18, 1956, 17.

49 **"Today...for this people":** Ethel L. Payne, "The South's New Hero," *Chicago
Defender*, Feb. 15, 1956, 8.

49 **"a natural born...thirsty for leadership":** Ethel L. Payne, "The South at the Crossroads: The Story of Rev. Martin L. King," *Chicago Defender*, May 19, 1956.

50 **"segregation is evil...of full citizenship":** King testimony to DNC platform, Aug. 11,
1956, in Carson, *Birth of a New Age*, 337.

50 **"From our first":** Wofford, *Of Kennedys and Kings*, 115.

50 **"Nonviolent direct...use of symbolic acts":** Ibid., 117.

50 **"Give us the ballot":** Martin Luther King Jr., "Give us the Ballot," Address at the Prayer
Pilgrimage for Freedom, May 17, 1963, *Martin Luther King Jr. and the Global Freedom
Struggle*, http://kingencyclopedia.stanford.edu/encyclopedia/documentsentry/doc_give_us
_the_ballot_address_at_the_prayer_pilgrimage_for_freedom.1.html.

50 **"the number one leader":** James Hicks, "King Emerges as Top Negro Leader," *New
York Amsterdam News*, June 1, 1957, 1.

51 **"Man on the Go":** " 'Man on the Go,' " *Jet*, July 17, 1958, 14–15.

51 **"King's colleagues felt":** Reddick, *Crusader Without Violence*, 179.

51 **"the hideous piety":** James Baldwin, "The Dangerous Road Before Martin Luther
King," *Harper's*, Feb. 1961, 34.

51 **"not like any preacher":** Ibid., 33.

51 **"I am called":** Belafonte, *My Song*, 150.

51 **"I need your help":** Ibid., 149.

51 **"get the hell away...Let's go":** Reddick, *Crusader Without Violence*, 226.

52 **"Gal...darling":** Ibid.

52   **"just another publicity stunt"**: Branch, *Parting the Waters*, 242.
52   **"to find out...KING"**: FBI memo, in Carson, *Birth of a New Age*, 96.
53   **"Little did I know"**: Clayborne Carson, ed., *The Papers of Martin Luther King, Jr.*, vol. 5, *Threshold of a New Decade, January 1959–December 1960* (Berkeley, CA: University of California Press, 2005), 328–329 (hereafter *Threshold of a New Decade*).
53   **"The time has...tangible gains"**: Press release on leaving Montgomery; Ibid., 330–331.
54   **"Wherever M.L. King, Jr....races"**: "Vandiver Says Rev. King Not 'Welcome' Here," *Atlanta Daily World*, Dec. 2, 1959, 2.
54   **"not coming to cause"**: Garrow, *Bearing the Cross*, 128.
54   **"My enemies have previously"**: C. S. King, *My Life with Martin*, 185.
54   **"I don't even wish"**: Garrow, *Bearing the Cross*, 129.
55   **"I had never seen"**: C. S. King, *My Life with Martin,* 186.
55   **"those who dare...social life"**: "Alabama vs. Martin Luther King," *Chicago Defender*, March 1, 1960, 10.
55   **"The verdict represents"**: "King Acquitted; Sees 'New Hope For South': All-White, Male Jury Hailed For Verdict," *Chicago Defender*, May 30, 1960, 1.
55   **"He did not look...eradicate it"**: Baldwin, "The Dangerous Road," 39.
56   **"kind and attentive"**: Ibid., 40.
56   **"I'm sure I've...I forget to"**: Garrow, *Bearing the Cross*, 164.
57   **"I would hesitate"**: "Mrs. Roosevelt Lauds Humphrey," *NYT*, Dec. 8, 1958, 34.
57   **"None of this is true...until the North changes"**: James Baldwin, "Fifth Avenue, Uptown," *Esquire*, July 1960; later published as "Letter from Harlem," in *Reporting Civil Rights, Part One*, 519.
58   **"he would compromise"**: M. L. King Oral History #1, 6.
58   **"He agreed...of leadership"**: Ibid., 2.
58   **"He felt that"**: Ibid.
58   **"I was very frank...position"**: Ibid., 1, 3.
59   **"The sit-in"**: Ibid.
59   **"willingness to learn more"**: Ibid., 2.
59   **"He had a long...for freedom"**: Ibid., 3.
59   **"depthed understanding"**: Wofford, *Of Kennedys and Kings*, 46.
59   **"made some progress"**: Branch, *Parting the Waters*, 314.
59   **"impressed by the forthright"**: M. L. King to Bowles, June 24, 1960, in Carson, *Threshold of a New Decade*, 478.
60   **"no sparks on either side"**: Belafonte, *My Song*, 215.
60   **"The stage had been"**: Ibid., 216.
60   **"strong moral leadership"**: Statement of Senator John F. Kennedy following a meeting with the Executive Committee of the New York State Liberal Party, New York, June 23, 1960, John F. Kennedy Speeches, JFKL, https://www.jfklibrary.org/Research/Research -Aids/JFK-Speeches/New-York-State-Liberal-Party_19600623.aspx.
60   **"without a single Southern"**: Leo Egan, "Kennedy Assures Liberals He Seeks No Help in the South," *NYT*, June 24, 1960, 1.
61   **"essentially a moral...to sit down"**: Remarks of Senator John F. Kennedy at Luncheon in Honor of African Diplomatic Corps, June 24, 1960, John F. Kennedy Speeches, JFKL, http:// www.jfklibrary.org/Research/Research-Aids/JFK-Speeches/African-Diplomatic-Corps -Washington-DC_19600624.aspx.
61   **"After a long, unwise...Negro population"**: "Kennedy's Racial Stand," *Chicago Defender*, June 28, 1960, 10.
61   **"Although I appreciated"**: Rampersad, *Jackie Robinson: A Biography*, 345.
62   **"Look, Senator"**: Ibid.

62   **"for an end":** Martin W. Sandler, ed., *The Letters of John F. Kennedy* (New York: Bloomsbury Press, 2013), 190.

62   **"more evidence…in the eye":** Letter, Jackie Robinson to Senator Kennedy, July 6, 1960, Letters of Support and Advice, 1960: 30 June–14 July, undated, JFKL, http://www.jfk library.org/Asset-Viewer/Archives/JFKCAMP1960-1104-022.aspx.

62   **"impressive man…catch up":** Jackie Robinson, *New York Post*, July 6, 1960, 34.

63   **"the condescending smile":** Carson, *Threshold of a New Decade*, 467.

63   **"single candidate":** Ibid., 468 n. 5.

63   **"I'm still not sure":** Bryant, *The Bystander*, 141.

63   **"small crush":** Ibid., 118.

63   **"Vel, it would be":** Ibid., 141.

63   **"perfunctory":** Elise Carper, "Kennedy in Rights Talk Applauded and Booed," *WP*, July 11, 1960, 9.

64   **"We meet on…White House":** Remarks of Senator John F. Kennedy at NAACP Rally, Los Angeles, California, July 10, 1960, John F. Kennedy Speeches, JFKL, http://www .jfklibrary.org/Research/Research-Aids/JFK-Speeches/Los-Angeles-CA-NAACP -Rally_19600710.aspx.

64   **"The cause of…hands":** Address at NAACP Mass Rally for Civil Rights, July 10, 1960, in Carson, *Threshold of a New Decade*, 485.

65   **"all out"…"blank check":** Bryant, *The Bystander*, 143.

65   **"I want to say":** Schlesinger, *A Thousand Days*, 34.

65   **"I think it's the most":** "Kennedy out of Favor with Negro, King Says," *Montgomery Advertiser*, July 14, 1960, in Carson, *Threshold of a New Decade*, 482.

65   **"I was certainly…the Negro question":** Interview by Zenas Sears, on "For Your Information," broadcast on Atlanta radio station WAOK, Nov. 6, 1960, in Carson, *Threshold of a New Decade*, 552.

66   **"better qualified":** Jackie Robinson Joins Nixon Campaign Drive," *NYT*, Sept. 3, 1960, 37.

66   **"Just how important":** Robert G. Spivack, "Watch on the Potomac: The Negro Vote," *Chicago Defender*, Sept. 28, 1960, 12.

66   **Soon after Robinson:** Garrow, *Bearing the Cross*, 142–143.

66   **"he was the best…civil rights":** M. L. King Oral History #5, JFKL.

PART TWO: *A Call to Coretta*

71   **"The plan was":** Raines, *My Soul Is Rested*, 89.

72   **"bullheaded"…"ended up":** Martin Luther King, Sr., with Clayton Riley, *Daddy King: An Autobiography* (New York: William Morrow, 1980), 160.

72   **"Jealousy among Negro":** Garrow, *Bearing the Cross*, 124.

73   **"They viewed that":** Raines, *My Soul Is Rested,* 87–88.

73   **"All we're asking":** Ibid., 88.

73   **"literally shamed him":** Ibid., 426.

74   **"Well, Martin…ten o'clock":** Ibid., 90.

74   **"I cannot in all":** UPI, "Won't Make Bail," *New Journal and Guide*, Oct. 22, 1960, B1.

74   **"moral obligation":** Carson, *Threshold of a New Decade*, 524.

74   **"It is our sincere":** "King Opens New Integration Fight," *Chicago Defender*, Oct. 22–28, 1960.

75   **"What an incompetent":** Harris Wofford, recorded interview #1 with Berl Bernhard, Nov. 29, 1965, 17, JFKLOHP.

75   **Morris Abram** information from http://www.momentmag.com/remembering-morris -abram/ and Morris B. Abram, *The Day Is Short: An Autobiography* (New York: Harcourt Brace Jovanovich, 1982).

75   **"her promised day"**: Abram, *The Day Is Short*, 126.

75   **"Senator Kennedy did...soon as possible"**: Wofford, *Of Kennedys and Kings*, 14.

76   **"Take her with...interest and concern"**: Abram, *The Day Is Short*, 126.

76   **"Yeah, come down"**: Ibid., 127.

76   **"rugged decency...wits to survive"**: Ibid., 94.

76   **"Only one white"**: M. L. King, Sr., *Daddy King*, 121.

77   **"He addressed black"**: Ibid.

77   **"Sit down and hold on"**: Wofford, *Of Kennedys and Kings*, 14.

77   **"This is Bill Hartsfield"**: Ibid., 14.

77   **"Hartsfield said *what*?"**: Ibid.

78   **"As a result"**: Ibid., 15.

78   **"I somehow did not"**: C. S. King, *My Life with Martin*, 192.

79   **"I find the defendant"**: Ibid., 193.

79   **"Corrie, dear...this time"**: C. S. King, *My Life with Martin*, 193–194. Branch, *Parting the Waters*, 358.

80   **"Through contacts around the state"**: M. L. King, Sr., *Daddy King*, 174.

80   **"This seemed more"**: C. S. King, *My Life with Martin*, 194.

80   **"I knew that it was"**: Ibid., 195.

81   **"Neither my child"**: Harold Paulk Henderson, *Ernest Vandiver: Governor of Georgia* (Athens, GA: University of Georgia Press, 2000), 252 n. 13.

81   **"Kennedy is deeply concerned"**: Dean Gordon B. Hancock, "Between the Lines: Sizing Up Kennedy," *Atlanta Daily World*, Aug. 2, 1960, 6.

81   **Promise from Kennedy re: troops**: Ibid., quoting Vandiver Oral History, 26.

81   **"Governor...call me back"**: Jack Bass, *Taming the Storm: The Life and Times of Judge Frank M. Johnson, Jr. and the South's Fight over Civil Rights* (New York: Doubleday, 1993), 170.

82   **"surprised...of my interest"**: President Kennedy's Letter to Georgia governor Ernest Vandiver, October 26, 1960, JFKL, http://www.jfklibrary.org/Research/Research-Aids/Ready-Reference/JFK-Fast-Facts/Vandiver-Letter.aspx.

83   **"arrest and imprisonment"**: "King's Imprisonment Stirs U.S.-Wide Wave of Criticism," *Atlanta Constitution*, Oct. 27, 1960, 10.

83   **"I wish to protest"**: "Georgia Refuses to Free Dr. King," *NYT*, Oct. 27, 1960, 22.

83   **"speak out against...as a people"**: Carson, *Threshold of a New Decade*, 38 n. 195.

83   **"tears of frustration...deserve to win"**: Rampersad, *Jackie Robinson: A Biography*, 351.

84   **"terribly disappointed"**: Ibid., 352.

84   **"I know this...power of endurance"**: Carson, *Threshold of a New Decade*, 531.

85   **"She told my wife"**: Wofford Oral History #1, 23.

85   **"They are going to kill him"**: Wofford, *Of Kennedys and Kings*, 11.

85   **"What Kennedy ought...perfect"**: Ibid., 17.

85   **"All right...me *her* number"**: Branch, *Parting the Waters*, 361–362.

86   **"I'll go right straight"**: Wofford Oral History #1, 24.

86   **"I wasn't sure"**: Ibid., 24.

86   **"I felt my job"**: Helen O'Donnell, and Kenneth O'Donnell, Sr., *The Irish Brotherhood: John F. Kennedy, His Inner Circle, and the Improbable Rise to the Presidency* (Berkeley: Counterpoint, 2015), 403.

86   **"While I am sympathetic...could be a mess"**: Ibid., 402.

86   **"I never use"**: Ibid.

87   **"Unlike others...against it"**: Ibid., 402–403.

87   **"You know...all the blame"**: Ibid., 403.

87   **"Jack...stand behind him"**: Scott Stossel, *Sarge: The Life and Times of Sargent Shriver* (Washington: Smithsonian Books, 2004), 164.

87 **"Negroes don't expect...will be killed"**: Ibid.

88 **"That's a pretty good...that be okay?"**: Ibid., 165.

88 **"Good morning, Mrs. King...call on me:** C. S. King, *My Life with Martin*, 196.

88 **"I would appreciate"**: Ibid., 196.

88 **"You just lost"**: Stossel, *Sarge,* 165.

89 **"If Kennedy has"**: Wofford, *Of Kennedys and Kings*, 19.

89 **"When she said"**: Ibid.

89 **"feel good that...out of jail"**: Anthony Lewis, "Kennedy Phoned to Express Concern, King's Wife Says," *Atlanta Constitution*, Oct. 27, 1960, 14.

89 **"Bobby landed on me"**: Sargent Shriver, recorded interview by Anthony Shriver, "Kennedy's Call to King: Six Perspectives," Georgetown University, 1988, 33, JFKL.

89 **"with fists tight"**: Wofford, *Of Kennedys and Kings*, 19.

89 **"Do you know"**: Ibid.

90 **"I think I should...out of it"**: "Robert Kennedy Secures the Release of Martin Luther King Jr. from Prison 10/1960," NBC News transcript, NBC Learn K-12, May 28, 1993, http://indiana.nbclearn.com/portal/site/k-12/flatview?cuecard=1783.

90 **"She is a friend"**: Reese Cleghorn, "Kennedy Pledges Aid to Rev. King," *New York Post*, Oct. 27, 1960, 4.

90 **"I understand from"**: Transcript of television news footage, in Carson, *Threshold of a New Decade*, 535, 2.

91 **"For him to be that courageous"**: Reese Cleghorn, "From Ga.—Tribute to a Candidate," *New York Post*, Oct. 28, 1960, 2.

91 **"morally wise"..."I hold Senator Kennedy"**: Wofford, *Of Kennedys and Kings*, 22.

91 **"And yet, when this moment"**: M. L. King Oral History #1, 12.

91 **"I stood listening...joy—and hope"**: Pat Watters, *Down to Now: Reflections on the Southern Civil Rights Movement* (New York: Random House, 1971), 54.

92 **"It just can't...do you mean"**: Jean Stein, *American Journey: The Times of Robert Kennedy / Interviews by Jean Stein*, edited by George Plimpton (New York: Harcourt Brace Jovanovich, 1970), 93–94.

93 **"It just burned"**: Ibid., 94. John L. Seigenthaler, recorded interview #2 by Ronald Grele, Feb. 21, 1966, 233–4, JFKLOHP.

93 **"I was so"**: Stein, *American Journey*, 93.

93 **"screwing up my"**: Wofford, *Of Kennedys and Kings*, 21.

93 **"I called the judge"**: R. F. Kennedy Oral History #5, 348.

94 **"I talked to the governor"**: Ibid., 347.

94 **"Can't you just say"**: Wofford, *Of Kennedys and Kings*, 22.

94 **"swamped"**: Bruce Galphin, "His Call Misinterpreted Robert Kennedy Says," *Atlanta Constitution*, Nov. 1, 1960.

94 **"Louis...honorary Brother!"**: Wofford, *Of Kennedys and Kings*, 22.

95 **"a member of...Ted's name mentioned"**: "Dr. King Released Pending His Appeal," *NYT*, Oct. 28, 1960, 12.

95 **"Many Harlemites were"**: Ted Poston, "How Harlem Reacts to Case of Rev. King," *New York Post*, Oct. 28, 1960, 2.

95 **"Mr. Nixon, in his refusal"**: Ibid.

95 **"This must be pretty hard"**: AP, "Judge Alters Decision, King Free on Bond," *Hartford Courant*, Oct. 28, 1960.

96 **"I had expected...in his lap"**: Wofford, *Of Kennedys and Kings,* 23.

96 **"Imagine Martin Luther King"**: Ibid., 28.

96 **"get King to announce"**: Abram, *The Day Is Short*, 131.

96 **"Sometimes I think":** Levison, letter to King Oct. 13, 1960, in Carson, *Threshold of a New Decade*, 518.

97 **"what is lost":** Ibid.

97 **"If you anoint":** Belafonte, *My Song*, 218–219.

97 **"You just don't understand...pay your debt":** Branch, *Parting the Waters*, 369.

97 **"It's true we":** Belafonte, *My Song*, 219.

98 **"The problem was":** Louis Martin, recorded interview by Anthony Shriver, "Kennedy's Call," 58, 61.

98 **Negro newspapers:** "Admit Negro Vote for Jack Whipped Nixon," *Chicago Defender*, Nov. 19, 1960, 12.

98 **"innumerable letters":** Ruth Jenkins, "Intervention helped Kennedy says King," *Baltimore Afro-American*, Nov. 12, 1960, 1.

98 **"sought to intervene":** "Dr. King Released Pending His Appeal," *NYT*, Oct. 28, 1960, 12.

98 **staff resignations:** "R.F. Kennedy's Part in King Case Scored," *NYT*, Oct. 29, 1960, 12.

98 **"the whole performance":** "The South: Swift Deliverance," *Time*, Nov. 7, 1960, 30.

98 **"to be gaining...Southern states":** Claude Sitton, "Gains by Kennedy Appear in South: Senator is Reported Cutting Nixon Lead," *NYT*, Oct. 30, 1960, 60.

99 **"However supportive people":** Martin, "Kennedy's Call," JFKLOPH, 58.

99 **"Suddenly, civil rights":** Mark Stern, *Calculating Visions: Kennedy, Johnson & Civil Rights* (New Brunswick, NJ: Rutgers University Press, 1992), 35.

99 **"the motivation...according to Bobby":** Ibid., 37.

99 **"It was not just Dr. King":** "The Case of Martin Luther King," available in "Statement on Presidential Endorsement," The Martin Luther King, Jr. Papers Project, Stanford University, http://kingencyclopedia.stanford.edu/primarydocuments/Vol5/1Nov1960_StatementonPresidentialEndorsement.pdf.

100 **"America was on trial":** Ibid.

100 **"I earnestly and...our Nixon buttons":** Ibid.

100 **"In this dramatic...Heart, Senator Kennedy":** Ibid.

100 **"I stood outside":** Sargent Shriver, in "Kennedy's Call," 25.

101 **"One cannot identify":** Theodore H. White, *The Making of the President 1960* (New York: Atheneum, 1961), 352–353.

101 **"Some Negro political":** Ibid., 386.

101 **Nationwide:** "Election of 1960," The American Presidency Project, http://www.presidency.ucsb.edu/showelection.php?year=1960.

102 **"Negroes in Northern":** Anthony Lewis, "Negro Vote Held Vital to Kennedy," *NYT*, Nov. 27, 1960, 51.

102 **"But," Lewis noted:** Ibid.

102 **"no comment":** Jonathan Aitken, *Nixon: A Life* (Washington, DC: Regnery, 1993), 281.

102 **"fundamentally unjust":** Anthony Lewis, "Protest over Dr. King's Arrest Was Drafted for President's Use," *NYT*, Dec. 15, 1960, 30.

102 **"Had this recommendation":** Richard Nixon, *Six Crises* (New York: Simon & Schuster, 2013), 363.

103 **"getting a bum...to do so":** Ibid., 362.

103 **"I could have become":** Simeon Booker, "Richard Nixon Tells: What Republicans Must Do to Regain the Negro Vote," *Ebony*, April 1962, 47.

103 **"couple of phone calls":** Felix Belair Jr., "President Rueful on the Negro Vote," *NYT*, Dec. 14, 1960, 24.

104 **"had an instinctive":** Schlesinger, *A Thousand Days*, 110.

104 **"The call to Mrs. King"**: Ibid., 74.

104 **"It was said...at Reidsville"**: M. L. King Sr., *Daddy King*, 176.

104 **"There are those moments"**: M. L. King Oral History #1, 11, JFKL.

105 **"King, by that time...respect for us"**: Sam Proctor, interview with Anthony Shriver, 1988, "Kennedy's Call," 89.

PART THREE: *"Tomorrow May Be Too Late"*

109 **"There's the white...not the same man"**: O'Donnell and O'Donnell, *The Irish Brotherhood*, 43.

109 **"the meeting of...calls the dance"**: White, *The Making of the President 1960*, 397.

110 **"I can assure"**: President-elect John F. Kennedy at Hyannis Armory, Nov. 9, 1960, YouTube, https://www.youtube.com/watch?v=8DvBSM99eKQ (accessed Nov. 20, 2015).

110 **"spoke evenly, with"**: White, *The Making of the President 1960*, 380.

110 **"I should submit"**: Carson, *Threshold of a New Decade*, 573.

111 **"Segregation is wrong...are morally wrong"**: Ibid., 575.

111 **"We have seen something"**: Ibid., 568.

111 **"On the civil rights issue"**: "A Talk with Martin Luther King, Jr." Ithaca, NY, Dec. 1960; *Dialogue*, a Cornell publication; recounting Q&A of Nov. 13, 1960, in Ibid., 551.

111 **"Now, there were...has been impressive"**: Ibid.

112 **"in the coming months...coming months and years"**: John F. Kennedy, "The Presidency in 1960—National Press Club, Washington, DC., Jan. 14, 1960," The American Presidency Project, http://www.presidency.ucsb.edu/ws/?pid=25795.

112 **"the immense moral"**: Remarks of Senator John F. Kennedy at NAACP Rally, Los Angeles, CA, July 10, 1960, John F. Kennedy Speeches, JFKL, http://www.jfklibrary.org/Research/Research-Aids/JFK-Speeches/Los-Angeles-CA-NAACP-Rally_19600710.aspx.

113 **"I have spoken...in this field"**: "A Talk With Martin Luther King, Jr.," in Carson, *Threshold of a New Decade*, 568.

113 **"He could have at least"**: Carson, *Threshold of a New Decade*, 550.

114 **"Publicly, the Eisenhower"**: Branch, *Parting the Waters*, 236.

114 **"He was very honest"**: M. L. King Oral History #1, 14.

115 **"You're from the"**: John Seigenthaler, recorded interview #3 by Ronald Grele, Feb. 22, 1966, 323, JFKLOHP.

115 **"unvarnished...completely"**: Ibid., 324–325.

115 **"It was good"**: Wofford, *Of Kennedys and Kings,* 164–165.

115 **"My illusions faded"**: Roy Wilkins with Tom Mathews, *Standing Fast: The Autobiography of Roy Wilkins* (New York: Viking, 1982), 279.

116 **"This simply floored"**: Roy Wilkins, recorded interview by Berl Benheim, Aug. 13, 1964, 4, JFKLOHP.

116 **"was giving away...legislation was out"**: Wilkins, *Standing Fast*, 279.

116 **"atmosphere of super-caution"**: Russell Baker, "Kennedy Tactics Disturb Wilkins," *NYT*, Dec. 29, 1960, 13.

116 **"the power, the will"**: Ibid.

117 **"right direction"..."all deliberate speed...time is now"**: Ibid.

117 **"easy and sophisticated"**: Wofford, *Of Kennedys and Kings*, 128.

117 **"some of the"**: Claude Sitton, "Dr. King, Symbol of the Segregation Struggle," *NYT*, Jan. 22, 1961, SM10, 72.

117 **"I wondered if"**: Roy Wilkins Oral History, 5.

118 **"He didn't assail it"**: Ibid.

118 **"Why don't you"**: Ibid.

118 **"Through all the years"**: Wilkins, *Standing Fast*, 272.

119 **"Did you see...get right on it"**: Richard N. Goodwin, *Remembering America: A Voice from the Sixties* (Boston: Little, Brown, 1988), 4.

119 **"This is the most"**: Roy Wilkins Oral History, 6, JFKL.

120 **"All these gestures"**: Wilkins, *Standing Fast*, 281.

120 **"sellout...going to overflow"**: Wofford, *Of Kennedys and Kings*, 138–139.

120 **"The president"**: Ibid., 139.

121 **"the representatives from"**: Gilbert Fite, *Richard Russell, Jr.: Senator from Georgia*, (Chapel Hill, NC: University of North Carolina Press, 2002), 377.

121 **"our Southland from"**: Bryant, *The Bystander*, 194.

121 **"Of the thirty-six"**: Ibid., 195.

121 **"predominately liberal in"**: Russell Baker, "Democratic Edge is Pared to 64–36," *NYT*, Nov. 10, 1960, 38.

121 **"jumps right in"**: Bryant, *The Bystander*, 195.

122 **"The good [Southern] ones"**: Ibid., 193–194, quoting Ralph McGill Oral History, 4–5.

122 **"overawed...never confronted directly"**: Ibid., 193.

122 **"No amount of"**: Sorensen, *Kennedy*, 475.

122 **"There is no"**: Schlesinger, *A Thousand Days*, 709.

123 **"intolerably slow pace"**: Martin Luther King, Jr., "Equality Now: The President Has the Power," *Nation*, February 4, 1961, in Clayborne Carson, ed., *The Papers of Martin Luther King, Jr.*, vol. 7, *To Save the Soul of America: January 1961–August 1962* (Oakland, CA: University of California Press, 2014), 140 (hereafter cited as *To Save the Soul*).

123 **"take the offensive"**: Ibid., 141.

123 **"moral persuasion"**: Ibid., 144.

123 **"Even in the hard"**: Ibid., 144.

123 **"a method of securing"**: Ibid., 149.

123 **"thousands of courageous"**: Ibid., 149.

123 **"I think he has"**: "Self-Portrait of a Symbol: Martin Luther King" from *The Mike Wallace Interview*, Feb. 7–8, 1961, in Carson, *To Save the Soul*, 161.

124 **"A funny man"**: Wofford, *Of Kennedys and Kings*, 143.

124 **"very thoughtful, quiet"**: Garrow, *Bearing the Cross*, 116–117.

124 **"winning...or warm"**: Baldwin, "The Dangerous Road," 33–34.

125 **"If, for instance"**: M. L. King, "Equality Now," 145.

125 **"dangerous"**: R. F. Kennedy, recorded interview #6 with Anthony Lewis, Dec. 6, 1964, 433, JFKLOHP.

125 **"psycho"**: Arthur Schlesinger Jr., *Robert Kennedy and His Times* (Boston: Houghton Mifflin, 1978), 260.

125 **"We had to engage"**: Ibid., 353.

125 **"I really was...they would do"**: Belafonte, *My Song*, 226–227.

126 **"a high moral purpose"**: Remarks of the President at the meeting in the Cabinet Room of the President's Committee for Equal Employment Opportunity, April 6, 1961, Asst. Atty. General Files, http://www.jfklibrary.org/Asset-Viewer/Archives/BMPP-033-008.aspx.

126 **"How could anybody"**: R. F. Kennedy Oral History #5, 399.

126 **"If it is at all"**: Carson, *To Save the Soul*, 175.

127 **"Such a meeting"**: Garrow, *Bearing the Cross*, 154.

127 **"national liberation movements"**: Osgood Caruthers, "Victory Seen by Russian: Khrushchev Sees Ultimate Victory," *NYT*, Jan. 19, 1961, 3.

127 **"this difficult and potentially"**: "Transcript of the President's News Conference on World and Domestic Affairs," *NYT*, March 24, 1961, 8.

127 **"The security of"**: Ibid.

127 **"present international situation"**: Branch, *Parting the Waters*, 404.

128 **"Whoever had listened"**: Wofford, *Of Kennedys and Kings*, 216.

129 **"the most self-effacing"**: Branch, *Parting the Waters*, 406.

129 **"a saint or"**: Ibid.

129 **"to cultivate him…you call"**: Ibid., 407.

129 **"he was so upset"**: Amanda Smith, ed., *Hostage to Fortune: The Letters of Joseph P. Kennedy* (New York: Viking, 2001), 697–698.

130 **"It's good to see…open to you,"**: M. L. King Oral History #1, 15.

130 **"King seemed somehow"**: Lerone Bennett, Jr., *What Manner of Man: A Biography of Martin Luther King, Jr.* (Chicago: Johnson, 1964), 117.

131 **"We expect you…asserting our rights"**: James Farmer letter to President Kennedy, April 26, 1961; JFKL, http://www.jfklibrary.org/Asset-Viewer/Dt0GtQ5k8kyp3fVHo9Y-tg.aspx.

131 **"We got no reply"**: Raines, *My Soul Is Rested*, 110.

132 **"We planned the Freedom"**: Farmer interview in Garrow, *Bearing the Cross*, 156.

132 **"An international crisis"**: Ibid.

132 **"The real test"**: Wilkins, *Standing Fast*, 283.

132 **"Okay…call me"**: Branch, *Parting the Waters*, 413.

133 **"spacious as a telephone"**: "Shepard's Ride," *NYT*, May 7, 1961, E1.

133 **"astonishing…sensational"**: Ibid.

133 **"I want to pay"**: Associated Press, "Kennedy's and Shepard's Remarks," *NYT*, May 9, 1961, 35.

134 **"He was well down"**: James Reston, "Symbol of the Nation," *NYT*, May 9, 1961, 35.

134 **"for symbolic purposes"**: Richard Paul and Steven Moss, *We Could Not Fail: The First African Americans in the Space Program* (Austin: University of Texas Press, 2015), 90.

134 **"Danger he took…and natural man"**: Reston, "Symbol."

135 **"Back up and"**: Claude Sitton, "Georgia Students Riot on Campus; Two Negroes Out," *NYT*, Jan. 12, 1961, 1.

135 **"in the interest"**: Ibid.

135 **"Several students shouted"**: Claude Sitton, "Tension Declines in Georgia Crisis," *NYT*, Jan. 18, 1961, 28.

136 **"They have told…the rule of law"**: "Kennedy, Robert F.: Address for Law Day Exercises of the University of Georgia Law School, 6 May 1961," Papers of John F. Kennedy, JFKL, http://www.jfklibrary.org/Asset-Viewer/Archives/JFKWHSFHW-014-013.

138 **"enthusiastic"**: Anthony Lewis, "Robert Kennedy Vows in Georgia to Act on Civil Rights," *NYT*, May 7, 1961, 1.

138 **"applauded warmly"**: James E. Clayton, "US Vows Firm Fight on Rights," *WP*, May 7, 1961, A1.

138 **"sincere desire"**: AP, "Jackie Robinson Lauds Speech of Robert Kennedy," *WP*, May 21, 1961, A3.

138 **"courageous, frank and all-embracing"**: "Editorials: The 'Voice' Has Spoken," *Pittsburgh Courier*, May 20, 1961, 8.

138 **"a tall, blonde…the late afternoon"**: Charlayne Hunter, "A Walk Through a Georgia Corridor," *Urbanite*, June 1961, in *Reporting Civil Rights, Part One*, 596.

138 **"Maybe I am…or as friends"**: Ibid., 596–597.

139 **"Okay, look, if"**: Raines, *My Soul Is Rested*, 335.

139 **"After that, I"**: Ibid., 336.

139 **"will without question"**: R. F. Kennedy, "Address for Law Day."

140 **"I almost fell"**: Charlayne Hunter-Gault, "Georgia of 24 Years Ago on My Mind," *NYT*, June 14, 1988, A4.

140 **"with them morally"**: Peter Maas, "Robert Kennedy Speaks Out," *Look*, March 28, 1961, 24.

141 **"I have every...on that":** Raines, *My Soul Is Rested*, 111.

141 **"Members of a biracial":** UPI, "Biracial Unit Tells of Beating in the South," *NYT*, May 11, 1961, 25.

142 **"I've gotten word":** Simeon Booker and Carol McCabe Booker, *Shocking the Conscience: A Reporter's Account of the Civil Rights Movement* (Jackson, MS: University Press of Mississippi, 2013), 189.

142 **"There, somebody will":** Raines, *My Soul Is Rested*, 112.

142 **"I must confess":** Ibid.

142 **"brave but also reckless":** Adam Fairclough, *To Redeem the Soul of America: The Southern Christian Leadership Conference and Martin Luther King, Jr.* (Athens, GA: University of Georgia Press, 1987), 78.

142 **"seemed strangely ambivalent":** Ibid., 57–58.

142 **"leadership seemed less":** Ibid., 58.

143 **"full equality":** Claude Sitton, "Wave of Negro Militancy Spreading over the South," *NYT*, May 14, 1961, 1.

143 **"The lack of progress...barriers to freedom":** Ibid., 76.

144 **On that Mother's Day:** Attiyya Anthony, "Fifty Years on, JFK's Legacy lives in Palm Beach," *Sun Sentinel* (Fort Lauderdale, FL), November 20, 2013, http://articles.sun-sentinel.com/2013-11-20/news/fl-palm-jfk-compound-20131120_1_rose-kennedy-joseph-kennedy-peanut-island.

144 **"Freedom will come":** Merriman Smith, "Kennedy Tells Foes of Castro Their Land May Soon Be Free," *WP*, May 16, 1961, A2.

145 **"like a rabbit":** Raines, *My Soul Is Rested*, 113.

146 **"I got whacked":** Ibid.

146 **"unless we get these niggers":** Simeon Booker, "Eyewitness Report on Dixie Freedom Rides: Jet Team Braves Mob Action," *Jet*, June 1, 1961, 14.

147 **"We made an astounding":** Raymond Arsenault, *Freedom Riders: 1961 and the Struggle for Racial Justice* (Oxford, UK: Oxford University Press, 2006), 153.

147 **"responded by simply saying":** James Peck, *Freedom Ride* (New York: Black Cat, 1962), 98.

148 **"served notice that...President must speak":** Telegram dated May 14, 1961, from James Farmer to President Kennedy, JFKL, http://www.jfklibrary.org/Asset-Viewer/x6Nf7QL6FEavCAYE0y9Byw.aspx.

149 **"I couldn't believe":** Booker and Booker, *Shocking the Conscience*, 197–198.

149 **"One passenger was...time, the President":** Arsenault, *Freedom Riders*, 165.

150 **"They were sickened...black America":** John Lewis with Michael D'Orso, *Walking with the Wind: A Memoir of the Movement* (New York: Simon & Schuster, 1998), 178.

150 **"refreshed from his four-day":** E. W. Kenworthy, "Kennedy Talk with Khrushchev Back and Opposed in Capital," *NYT*, May 16, 1961.

150 **beatings:** Arsenault, *Freedom Riders*, 166.

150 **"None of them...to the White House":** Lewis, *Walking with the Wind*, 144.

151 **"The people at":** Raines, *My Soul Is Rested*, 114.

151 **"The attorney general":** Booker and Booker, *Shocking the Conscience*, 198.

151 **"It was the first time":** Ibid.

151 **"sole purpose":** John M. Patterson, recorded interview by John Stewart, May 26, 1967, 33, JFKLOHP.

151 **"I liked the man":** Ibid., 5.

152 **"he would ask me":** Ibid., 31.

152 **"The whole world":** Booker and Booker, *Shocking the Conscience*, 199.

152 **"The citizens of":** UPI, "Bi-racial Bus Trip Ends," *Chicago Daily Tribune*, May 16, 1961, 14.

152 **"Do you know...on their way":** Transcript of Kennedy-Cruit conversation, May 15, 1961, RFK Papers, quoted in Schlesinger, *Robert Kennedy and His Times*, 296.

153 **"the most basic...not a choice":** Lewis, *Walking with the Wind*, 143.

153 **"I understood that":** Ibid., 133.

154 **"Everything he did":** Ibid.

154 **"The first thing":** Ibid., 83–84.

154 **"You realize...movement is dead":** James Farmer, *Lay Bare the Heart: An Autobiography of the Civil Rights Movement* (New York: Arbor House, 1985), 203.

154 **"It was a little":** Lewis, *Walking with the Wind*, 144.

155 **"No sooner had we":** Peck, *Freedom Ride,* 101.

155 **"It's pretty bad":** John L. Seigenthaler Oral History JFK #3, 432.

155 **"He thought that":** Ibid., 433.

155 **"This is a trap":** Booker and Booker, *Shocking the Conscience*, 200.

155 **"sad befuddled group":** Seigenthaler Oral History JFK #3, 434.

155 **"We want to get":** Ibid., 436.

155 **"We have another":** Ibid., 435–436.

155 **"You don't want":** Ibid.

156 **"When I give you...as possible":** Ibid., 437.

156 **"The sweat in our":** Booker and Booker, *Shocking the Conscience*, 200.

156 **"I got on with":** Seigenthaler Oral History JFK #3, 437.

156 **"Do you know...get somebody through":** Ibid., 439.

157 **"It was not until":** Lewis, *Walking with the Wind*, 147.

157 **"He was short":** Ibid., 148.

157 **"He couldn't stand":** Burke Marshall, recorded interview by Louis Oberdorfer, May 29, 1964, 13, JFKLOHP.

158 **"As you know":** Ibid., 5.

158 **"It was explained":** Ibid., 6.

158 **"imagine any set":** "Transcript of the President's News Conference," *NYT*, July 18, 1957, 12.

158 **"The President was a very":** B. Marshall Oral History #1, 6.

159 **"He realized there":** Ibid., 8–9.

159 **"A midnight ride":** Lewis, *Walking with the Wind*, 149.

159 **"This is where":** Ibid., 150.

161 **"launched into a diatribe...marshals into Alabama":** Seigenthaler Oral History JFK#3, 443–445.

161 **"The United States government":** Ibid.

161 **"The state of Alabama...provide them safety":** Ibid., 448–449.

162 **"Well, now I'll tell...Alabama highway patrol":** Ibid., 449.

162 **"Will he issue":** Ibid., 450.

163 **"I thought I'd":** Ibid., 453.

164 **"We just got out":** Stuart L. Loory, "Alabama Racist Mob on a Rampage; U.S. Rushes In Force of 400 Officers," *New York Herald Tribune*, May 21, 1961, 26.

164 **"Someone grabbed my briefcase":** Lewis, *Walking with the Wind*, 156.

164 **"Oh, there are fists":** Edwin Guthman, *We Band of Brothers* (New York: Harper & Row, 1971), 171.

165 **"permanent damage that shortened his life":** Arsenault, *Freedom Riders*, 214.

165 **"I'll shoot the next man":** Ibid., 215.

165 **"We ain't arranging":** Loory, "Alabama Racist Mob on a Rampage," 27.

165 **"You're a rotten":** Ibid.

165 **"I really don't know":** Ibid.

165 **"suitcases and bags":** Seigenthaler Oral History JFK #3, 454.

166 **"That's a fellow":** Ibid., 455.

166 **"Are you hurt?...I'm with her":** Ibid., 456.

166 **"Who the hell...a federal man":** Ibid., 458.

167 **"if you got":** Evan Thomas, *Robert Kennedy: His Life* (New York: Touchstone, 2002), 184.

167 **By the afternoon:** Anthony Lewis, "Force Due Today; Agents to Bear Arms," *NYT*, May 21, 1961, 1.

167 **"What happened...Get out":** Seigenthaler Oral History JFK #3, 458–459.

168 **"middle-aged, fat":** Arsenault, *Freedom Riders*, 227.

168 **"I wonder which side":** Thomas, *Robert Kennedy*, 130.

168 **"I think Bob changed...and been hit":** Stein, *American Journey*, 103.

169 **"How are you...elected":** Seigenthaler Oral History JFK #3, 459–461.

169 **"deepest concern...outbreaks":** "Texts on the Montgomery Riots," *NYT*, May 21, 1961.

170 **"As these events":** Wofford, *Of Kennedys and Kings*, 153.

170 **"this Goddamned civil rights mess":** Richard Reeves, *President Kennedy: Profile of Power* (New York: Simon & Schuster, 1993), 126; the footnote indicates five aides heard him use the phrase.

170 **"Stop them! Get":** Ibid., 125.

170 **"I don't think":** Schlesinger, *Robert Kennedy and His Times*, 295.

170 **"assistant president":** Thomas, *Robert Kennedy*, 137.

170 **"Bob became a":** Stein, *American Journey*, 95.

170 **"the president's personal...vehicles in Alabama":** "Texts on the Montgomery Riots."

170 **"four-letter words":** Raines, *My Soul Is Rested*, 309.

171 **"We have the men...incidents":** AP, "Text of Statement Issued by Gov. John Patterson," *NYT*, May 21, 1961, 78.

171 **"We had a national":** Lewis, *Walking with the Wind*, 176.

171 **"The outrage generated":** Ibid., 175.

171 **"You may inform...cause of justice":** *Montgomery Advertiser*, May 21, 1961.

173 **"Fifty marshals...the United States":** Raines, *My Soul Is Rested*, 309.

174 **"Will you make...these people are":** Guthman, *We Band of Brothers*, 172–173.

174 **"We don't need your":** Arsenault, *Freedom Riders*, 228; citing *Birmingham Post-Herald*, May 22, 1961.

175 **"It was not easy":** Lewis, *Walking with the Wind*, 159.

175 **"these gallant but":** Murray Kempton, "Tear Gas and Hymns," in *Reporting Civil Rights, Part One*, 580.

176 **"He wanted to":** Lewis, *Walking with the Wind*, 159.

176 **"Nigger King":** Arsenault, *Freedom Riders*, 231. Also in Branch, *Parting the Waters*, 458.

176 **"Let's clean the niggers":** Arsenault, *Freedom Riders*, 233.

177 **"Nobody is singing":** Kempton, *America Comes of Middle Age*, 581.

177 **"Bless all those cowards":** Ibid., 582.

177 **"He was Southern":** Arsenault, *Freedom Riders*, 236.

177 **"At one point":** Schlesinger, *Robert Kennedy and His Times*, 298.

178 **"panicky...very dangerous":** B. Marshall Oral History #1, 28.

178 **"the fear in":** Ibid., 30.

178 **"Martin Luther King was":** R. F. Kennedy Oral History #5, 378.

178 **"as long as he":** Ibid., 379.

178 **"He rather berated":** R. F. Kennedy Oral History JFK #5, 379.

179 **"I felt that he":** M. L. King Oral History #1, 16.

179 **"Somewhere in this man":** Belafonte, *My Song*, 233.

179 **"I just talked...basement downstairs":** Kempton, *America Comes of Middle Age*, 582.

180 **"We had information":** Patterson Oral History #1, 35.

180 **"Now you got":** Ibid., 36.

181 **"Through our scientific":** Address at Freedom Riders Rally at First Baptist Church, May 21, 1961, in Carson, *To Save the Soul*, 228.

181 **"These courageous freedom riders":** Ibid., 228.

181 **"America's chief moral dilemma":** Ibid.

181 **"The deep South":** Ibid., 229.

182 **"His consistent preaching...forces of violence":** Ibid., 229.

182 **"The troops, which...like the enemy":** Lewis, *Walking with the Wind*, 161.

182 **"outside agitators...laws and customs":** "Proclamation by Gov. John Patterson, Declaring a State of Martial Rule in Montgomery," May 21, 1961, Alabama Dept of Archives & History, http://digital.archives.alabama.gov/cdm/ref/collection/voices/id/.

183 **"Bob held the phone":** Guthman, *We Band of Brothers*, 177.

183 **"Now, Reverend":** Ibid., 178.

183 **"Who's Kelsey?":** Reeves, *President Kennedy*, 131.

183 **"Have you ever":** R. F. Kennedy, Oral History #5, 380.

184 **"Now, John...survive politically":** Guthman, *We Band of Brothers*, 178.

185 **"The current toward":** AP, "Kennedy Is Praised," *NYT*, May 23, 1961, 27.

185 **"Sure...about the Freedom Riders":** Wofford, *Of Kennedys and Kings*, 126.

186 **"Who the hell...sensitive he was":** Ibid.

187 **"There was a certain":** David Halberstam, *The Children* (New York: Random House, 1998), 327.

187 **"cooling-off period":** Farmer, *Lay Bare the Heart*, 205.

187 **"The Nashville Student":** Ibid.

187 **"Please tell the":** Ibid., 206.

187 **"I'm on probation":** Lewis, *Walking with the Wind*, 163.

188 **"I think...I":** Ibid., 164.

188 **"De Lawd!":** Ibid.

188 **"There couldn't have":** Ibid.

188 **"But now his position":** Ibid.

189 **"It's a matter of conscience...moral, legal and peaceful":** Guthman, *We Band of Brothers*, 154–155.

190 **"I'm deeply appreciative":** Ibid., 155.

190 **"I am different than my father":** Ibid.

190 **"It would be wise...to his mission":** "Attorney General's Pleas," *NYT*, May 25, 1961, 25.

191 **"not the way":** James E. Clayton, "Robert Kennedy's Aim in South: To Uphold Law, But Take No Sides," *WP*, May 27, 1961, A1.

191 **"He does not feel":** Ibid., A4.

191 **"These are extraordinary times":** "President Kennedy's Special Message to the Congress on Urgent National Needs, May 25, 1961," JFKL, http://www.jfklibrary.org/Research/Research-Aids/JFK-Speeches/United-States-Congress-Special-Message_19610525.aspx (accessed March 14, 2016).

191 **"The great battleground...safely to the earth":** Ibid.

192 **"Personally," he said, "I don't care":** "A Statement by Commissioner Hesburgh," Report: 1961 U.S. Commission on Civil Rights Report Book 5: Justice, U.S. Commission on Civil Rights, Washington, DC, 1961, 168, https://www.law.umaryland.edu/marshall/usccr/documents/cr11961bk5.pdf.

192 **"very commendable":** "Parisians Await Mrs. Kennedy," *NYT*, May 31, 1961, 5.

192 **"I do not...have enjoyed it":** President Kennedy, news conference, Palais Chaillot, Paris; June 2, 1961; JFKL, http://www.jfklibrary.org/Research/Research-Aids/Ready-Reference/Press-Conferences/News-Conference-12.aspx (accessed March 14, 2016).

192 **"I'd like to"**: AP, "First Lady Wins Khrushchev, Too," *NYT*, June 4, 1961, 1.

193 **"fat as a sausage"**: Reeves, *President Kennedy*, 159.

193 **"Not too well"**: Ibid.,166–167.

193 **"It is up to the U.S."**: Dallek, *An Unfinished Life*, 413.

193 **"somber...obliteration of mankind"**: Schlesinger, *A Thousand Days*, 374.

195 **"to move freely...the Freedom Riders"**: JFK Press Conference, July 19, 1961, in George W. Johnson, ed., *The Kennedy Presidential Press Conferences* (New York: Earl M. Coleman, 1978), 123–124.

195 **"necessary to create...color-blind"**: "Robert Kennedy Asks I.C.C. to End Bus Segregation," *NYT*, May 30, 1961, 1.

196 **"the Irish were"**: Stanley Meisler, "Negro Can Be U.S. President Atty.-Gen. Says," *WP*, May 27, 1961, A4.

196 **"Experts considered the"**: Branch, *Parting the Waters*, 478.

196 **"Here was a classic"**: Stein, *American Journey*, 103.

196 **"Public relations is..."**: King Letter to Courlander, Oct. 30, 1961, in Carson, *To Save the Soul*, 315.

197 **"After the Freedom Rides"**: M. L. King Oral History #1, 22.

197 **"The sit-ins and"**: Thurgood Marshall, recorded interview by Berl Bernheim, April 7, 1965, 8, JFKLOHP.

PART FOUR: *"Pawns in a White Man's Political Game"*

201 **"He'd ask for"**: Wofford, recorded interview #3 by Larry Hackman, February 3, 1969, 133, JFKLOHP.

201 **"I got tired"**: Wofford, *Of Kennedys and Kings*, 166.

201 **"Kennedy had a touch...about civil rights"**: Wofford Oral History #3, 134.

202 **"Just as Abraham Lincoln"**: Press release, statement, June 5, 1961, in "The Negro and the American Dream," address at Memorial Auditorium, Dec. 30, 1960, in Carson, *To Save the Soul*, 244.

202 **By March 1957, the FBI:** David J. Garrow, *The FBI and Martin Luther King, Jr.* (New York: Penguin Books, 1981), 42.

203 **"We never put any"**: William C. Sullivan, *The Bureau: My Thirty Years in Hoover's FBI* (New York: Norton, 1979), 50.

203 **"I would rather"**: Hugh Sidey, "The Presidency: L.B.J., Hoover and Domestic Spying," *Time*, Feb. 10, 1975, 16.

203 **"Dr. King, you"**: Wofford Oral History #3, 139.

203 **"Yes—yes"**; Wofford, *Of Kennedys and Kings*, 128.

204 **"I've just got"**: Wofford Oral History #3, 139.

204 **"listened very sympathetically"**: Press Conference after Meeting with John F. Kennedy, Oct. 16, 1961, in Carson, *To Save the Soul*, 308.

204 **"not Kennedy's style"**: Wofford, *Of Kennedys and Kings*, 128.

204 **"gave every indication"**: Wofford Oral History #3, 138.

204 **"But, believe me"**: Ibid.

204 **"a stroke of"**: Kennedy-Nixon debate, Oct. 7, 1960, JFKL, http://www.jfklibrary.org/Research/Research-Aids/JFK-Speeches/2nd-Nixon-Kennedy-Debate_19601007.aspx.

204 **"Many things can"**: Remarks of Sen. John F. Kennedy, Oct. 12, 1960, National Conference on Constitutional Rights and American Freedom, New York; JFKL, http://www.jfklibrary.org/Research/Research-Aids/JFK-Speeches/Constitutional-Rights-Conference-NYC_19601012.aspx.

204 **"Send them to Wofford!"**: Wofford, *Of Kennedys and Kings*, 124.

204 **"What disappointed me most":** Ibid., 124.

205 **"I would like you":** *El Mundo*, Feb. 16, 1962, in Carson, *To Save the Soul*, 417 n. 14.

205 **"fruitful and rewarding":** Press Conference after Meeting with John F. Kennedy, Oct. 16, 1961, in Carson, *To Save the Soul*, 308.

205 **"As long as...such an order":** Ibid., 310.

205 **"too much to ask":** Ibid., 309.

205 **"But," he added,":** Ibid.

206 **"My feeling is that":** M. L. King Oral History #1, 19.

206 **"He was afraid politically":** Ibid.

206 **"this didn't mean that":** Wofford Oral History #1, 18.

206 **"has the understanding":** Wofford, *Of Kennedys and Kings*, 128–129.

207 **"America's third revolution":** Martin Luther King Jr., *Why We Can't Wait* (New York: Signet Classic / Penguin Group, 2000), 1.

207 **"How many people":** Ibid., 7.

207 **"Distressed that our city":** King telegram to Hartsfield, Nov. 1, 1961, in Carson, *To Save the Soul*, 320.

208 **"It's all done":** Hedrick Smith, "Segregation Stronghold," *NYT,* August 16, 1962, 18.

208 **"The fat, drawling":** Adam Fairclough, *Martin Luther King, Jr.* (Athens, GA: University of Georgia Press, 1995), 69.

209 **"I don't want a man":** Claude Sitton, "Negroes' Unrest Grows in Georgia," *NYT*, Dec. 16, 1961, 18.

209 **"Pritchett conducted arrests":** Ralph David Abernathy, *And the Walls Came Tumbling Down: An Autobiography* (New York: Harper & Row, 1989), 226.

209 **By December 13:** AP, "Albany Ga. Jails 267 Youths," *NYT,* Dec. 13, 1961, 51.

209 **"I had made":** Raines, *My Soul Is Rested*, 361–362.

210 **"It might not be":** David Miller, "Non-Violence: Police Chief and Minister," *New York Herald Tribune*, Dec. 18, 1961, 21.

211 **"By the time":** Abernathy, *And the Walls Came*, 206.

211 **"Which of the pastors":** Ibid.

211 **"who are telling us":** Address at Albany Movement mass meeting at Mt. Zion Baptist Church, Dec. 15, 1961, in Carson, *To Save the Soul*, 343.

212 **"Be here at seven o'clock":** Bruce Galphin, "Albany Balks at Truce Price," *Atlanta Constitution*, Dec. 16, 1961, in Carson, *To Save the Soul*, 25 n. 137.

212 **"Tell the children":** "Integration: 'Albany Movement,'" *Newsweek,* Dec. 25, 1961, 18.

212 **"the yearning of":** "The World," *NYT*, Dec. 17, 1961, E1.

212 **"shocking and deplorable":** L. Joseph Overton to Robert Kennedy, Dec. 18, 1961, Department File 144-101-19M-9, in Carson, *To Save the Soul*, 26 n. 148.

213 **"meanest man in":** "Rev. King Meets 'Meanest Man in the World' in Jail," *Jet*, Jan. 4, 1962, 46.

213 **"Then and only...communism and tyranny":** Telegram dated December 13, 1961, from Martin Luther King Jr. to President Kennedy, Dec. 13, 1961, JFKL, http://www.jfklibrary.org/Asset-Viewer/9EKJbHBCsEaVSQuCdwdigA.aspx.

213 **"I would not want":** "Dr. King Is Freed," *NYT*, Dec. 19, 1961, 24.

214 **"Negroes had been":** Ibid.

214 **"one of the":** David Miller, "A Loss for Dr. King—New Negro Roundup: They Yield," *New York Herald Tribune*, Dec. 19, 1961, 1.

214 **"Looking back over":** "Man of the Year: Never Again Where He Was," *Time*, Jan. 3, 1964, 15.

214 **The president and the attorney general:** In Bryant, *The Bystander*, 281; citing *Atlanta Journal*, Dec. 19, 1961, *New York Herald Tribune*, Dec. 19, 1961, *New Republic*, July 20, 1963.

215 **"coughing and unable":** David Nasaw, *The Patriarch: The Remarkable Life and Turbulent Times of Joseph P. Kennedy* (New York: Penguin, 2012), 776.

215 **" 'hot line' was flashing":** Ibid.

215 **"Now, suddenly, on…heard or saw":** Ibid., 777.

215 **"First, his high…sense of compassion":** Benjamin C. Bradlee, *Conversations with Kennedy* (New York: W. W. Norton, 1975), 142–143.

216 **"As the year":** Martin Luther King, Jr., "Report on Civil Rights: Fumbling on the New Frontier," *Nation*, March 3, 1962, 190.

216 **"While the president…purpose":** Ibid.

216 **"can be confident":** Ibid., 192.

216 **"The President has":** Ibid., 193.

216 **"He wanted it proved…off our back":** Sullivan, *The Bureau*, 135.

217 **"On January 8, 1962":** Carson, *To Save the Soul*, 33.

218 **"My tendency is":** SAC, New York, to Hoover, March 30, 1962, Bureau File 100-106670-33, in Carson, *To Save the Soul*, 428.

218 **"careful consideration":** O'Brien to M. L. King, April 5, 1962, in Carson, *To Save the Soul*, 429.

218 **"That Communist agent":** Branch, *Parting the Waters*, 584.

219 **"You had almost 50 percent":** R. F. Kennedy Oral History #5, 394.

220 **"I went down…carefully and closely":** Seigenthaler Oral History #3, 465.

220 **"directly in the eye":** Garrow, *The FBI and Martin*, 44.

220 **"I didn't have the feeling":** Seigenthaler Oral History #3, 466.

221 **"Marshall could not":** Wofford, *Of Kennedys and Kings*, 216.

221 **"Unfortunately," historian David Garrow:** Garrow, *The FBI and Martin*, 47.

221 **"depressed and dumbfounded…to trust Hoover":** Wofford, *Of Kennedys and Kings*, 216.

222 **"something more intellectual":** "To Coretta Scott," July 18, 1952, *Martin Luther King, Jr. and the Global Freedom Struggle*, Stanford University, http://kingencyclopedia.stanford.edu/encyclopedia/documentsentry/to_coretta_scott1.1.html.

222 **"I imagine you":** Ibid.

222 **"In reading such Communist…wheel of the state":** Martin Luther King, Jr., *Stride Toward Freedom*, 92–93.

223 **"If an FBI man…of the land":** "Dr. King Says F.B.I. in Albany, Ga., Favors Segregationists," *NYT*, Nov. 19, 1962, 21.

223 **"long and slow…to self-destruction":** Peter Kihss, "Dr. W. E. B. DuBois Joins Communist Party at 93," *NYT*, Nov. 23, 1961, 5.

223 **"There can be no doubt":** Letter from M. L. King to Edward Ball, Dec. 14, 1963, in King Center in Atlanta, in Branch, *Parting the Waters*, 563.

224 **"King was fairly low":** Wofford, recorded interview #2 by Larry Hackman, on May 22, 1968, 57, JFKLOHP.

224 **"The inaugural festivities":** "But They Take No Action: Negro Leaders in Big Numbers at Inauguration," *Pittsburgh Courier*, Jan. 28, 1961, 13.

225 **"The general assumption":** E. W. Kenworthy, "Cosmos Club in Capital Rejects Rowan, Rusk Aide, as Member," *NYT*, Jan. 10, 1962, 1.

225 **"It is my judgment":** Kenworthy, "More Leave Club over Rowan Bar," *NYT*, Jan. 11, 1962, 17.

225 **"It is my understanding":** Carl T. Rowan, *Breaking Barriers: A Memoir* (Boston: Little, Brown, 1991), 205.

225 **"Your statement was":** Ibid., 205.

225 **"What JFK managed…pride in ourselves":** Booker and Booker, *Shocking the Conscience*, 178–179.

226 **"It will take":** Wofford, *Of Kennedys and Kings*, 125.

227 **"a document we consider"**: Address at the Formation of the Gandhi Society for Human Rights, May 17, 1962, in Carson, *To Save the Soul*, 459.

227 **"a great deal of interest"**: Wallace Terry, "Race Group to Stress Gandhi Non-Violence," *WP*, May 18, 1962, A2.

227 **"grotesque array...forebears had been"**: Address at the Formation of the Gandhi Society, 460.

227 **"Just as Abraham Lincoln"**: Ibid., 459.

228 **"This is my rocker"**: Ralph G. Martin, *A Hero for Our Time: An Intimate Story of the Kennedy Years* (New York: Macmillan, 1983), 436.

228 **"like flesh with sequins"**: O'Brien, *John F. Kennedy*, 697.

228 **"I can now retire"**: Marilyn Monroe Sings Happy Birthday to President Kennedy," Marilyn Monroe Film Archives, YouTube, https://www.youtube.com/watch?v=qvoqK6aLE2E.

229 **"better to go to jail"**: Press release, July 10, 1962, in Carson, *To Save the Soul*, 510.

229 **"There is something...cause and purpose"**: "Albany Jail Diary from 10 July to 11 July 1962," Ibid., 515.

229 **"companionship of roaches...hole"**: Ibid., 514.

229 **"conscience of the...the nation"**: Ibid., 514–515.

229 **"calm and sweet...help the people"**: Albany Jail Diary, Tuesday, July 10, 1962, in Carson, *To Save the Soul*, 515.

230 **"President Kennedy seemed"**: Marie Smith, "JFK Keeps Eye on the Ball—Skips Parties," *NYT*, July 12, 1962, C19.

230 **"the first wave...now or never"**: Claude Sitton, "Protest in Georgia," *NYT*, July 12, 1962, 18.

230 **"win this battle...no retreat"**: Shuttlesworth to M. L. King, July 20, 1962, in Carson, *To Save the Soul*, 39.

231 **"He was worried"**: B. Marshall Oral History #3, 70.

231 **"interest in her husband's"**: Cabell Phillips, "Kennedy Requests Report on Dr. King," *NYT*, July 12, 1962, 18.

231 **"They were imposing...on the streets"**: B. Marshall Oral History #3, 70.

232 **"a cell of professional...most implacable foe"**: Claude Sitton, "Negro Groups Split on Georgia Protest," *NYT*, Dec. 18, 1961, 31.

232 **"The damn media"**: A 1986 interview with Gray, quoted in Branch, *Parting the Waters*, 603.

233 **"an unidentified, well-dressed"**: Claude Sitton, "Dr. King Is Freed Against His Will," *NYT*, July 13, 1962, 10.

233 **"there were indications"**: Ibid.

233 **"reasonable"**: Ibid.

233 **"Dr. King's release"**: In Branch, *Parting the Waters*, 607, citing *Albany Journal*, July 12, 1962.

234 **"lately, some of...organizational ability"**: "Spokesman for Negroes: Martin Luther King Jr.," *NYT*, July 16, 1962, 35.

234 **"officials met at"**: Sitton, "Dr. King Is Freed."

234 **"subtle and conniving"**: Address Delivered at Mass Meeting at Shiloh Baptist Church, July 12, 1962, in Carson, *To Save the Soul*, 518.

234 **"saying one thing"**: Ibid., 524.

234 **"long history of double-talk"**: Ibid., 521.

235 **"We band ourselves"**: Ibid., 521–522.

235 **"The City Commission...now"**: AP, "Georgia Mayor Rejects Parley with Negroes," *NYT*, July 17, 1962, 16.

235 **"They tricked us...than ever before"**: Address Delivered at Albany Movement Mass Meeting at Shiloh Baptist Church, July 16, 1962, in Carson, *To Save the Soul*, 524.

235 **"This is what":** Ibid., 524–525.

235 **"Now, since they...committed this minute":** Ibid., 525.

236 **"in the interest":** To Albany City Commission and Ada D. Kelley, July 17, 1962, in Carson, *To Save the Soul*, 526.

236 **"the first step...we'll be back":** Claude Sitton, "Negroes Pushing Tests in Georgia," *NYT*, July 18, 1962, 30.

237 **"Victor Hugo once":** M. L. King, Address Delivered to the National Press Club and Question and Answer Period, July 19, 1962, in Carson, *To Save the Soul*, 528.

237 **"sweep of positive":** Martin Luther King, Jr, "Fumbling on the New Frontier," *Nation*, March 3, 1962, 415.

237 **"you cannot legislate":** M. L. King, Address to National Press Club, 529.

237 **"The habits...segments of life":** Ibid.

237 **"The method of nonviolent":** Ibid., 531.

238 **"This is where nonviolence":** Ibid.

238 **"We will take direct":** Ibid., 531–532.

238 **"a dream of":** Ibid.

238 **"There is still":** Ibid.

239 **"Injunctions, various legal":** Don McGee, "Court Bars Rallies in Albany, Ga.," *WP*, July 22, 1962, A4.

239 **"I don't want those pinks":** Anne Emanuel, *Elbert Parr Tuttle: Chief Jurist of the Civil Rights Revolution* (Athens, GA: University of Georgia Press, 2011), 236.

239 **"I was...injunction":** M. L. King Oral History, JFK #1, 25.

239 **"I know it was":** Ibid.

240 **"Ironically, one of the chief":** "The Nation: Command Shifts," *NYT*, July 22, 1962.

240 **"Some of these":** M. L. King Oral History, JFK #1, 26.

240 **"I would go along":** Ibid., 25.

240 **"I've heard about...high noon! Now!":** Claude Sitton, "Negroes Defy Ban, March in Georgia," *NYT*, July 22, 1962, 1.

240 **"I'm gonna keep":** Paul Harvey, ed., *The Columbia Documentary History of Religion in America Since 1945* (New York: Columbia University Press, 2005), 153.

241 **"Well, Rev, you...under arrest":** Sitton, "Negroes Defy," 32.

241 **"The city of Albany":** Charles Aldinger, "Court Injunction in Albany Seen as Invitation to Violence," *WP*, July 23, 1962, A22.

241 **"a vigorous stand...aspects of this problem":** UPI, "Critical of the President," *NYT*, July 23, 1962, 13.

242 **"Martin was about":** Adam Fairclough, *To Redeem the Soul*, 103. Judith Martin interview, March 15, 1972, 6–7, MLK Center for Non-Violent Social Change.

243 **"inhumane treatment and":** King, Letter to Robert Kennedy, July 23, 1962, in Carson, *To Save the Soul*, 547.

243 **"this morning something happened":** King, Address Delivered at Albany Movement Mass Meeting, July 25, 1962, in Carson, *To Save the Soul*, 551.

243 **"a sober and...be postponed":** To Albany City Commission and Asa D. Kelley, July 24, 1962, in Carson, *To Save the Soul*, 548.

243 **"lawbreakers":** Claude Sitton, "Albany, Ga., Police Break Up Protest by 2,000 Negroes," *NYT*, July 25, 1962, 22.

244 **"I say all of this":** King, Address Delivered at Albany Movement Mass Meeting, July 25, 1962, in Carson, *To Save the Soul*, 551.

244 **"The most potent":** Ibid., 552.

244 **"Did you see":** Claude Sitton, "Dr. King Sets a Day of Penance After Violence in Albany, Ga.," *NYT*, July 26, 1962, 13.

244 **"We abhor violence":** Ibid.

245 **"All of these things":** King, Press Conference Denouncing Violence in Albany, July 25, 1962, in Carson, *To Save the Soul*, 554.

245 **"who are well-grounded":** Ibid.

245 **"We want to talk...power of souls":** Pat Watters, *Down to Now: Reflections on the Southern Civil Rights Movement* (New York: Random House, 1971), 214.

246 **"Do you know...in action":** Ibid., 215–216.

246 **"It was not the words":** Ibid., 217.

246 **"there was no":** Ibid.

246 **"Folks," he said...to do that:** Abernathy, *And the Walls Came*, 221.

247 **"Look at this...hotter":** Ibid., 222.

248 **"Somehow, he just got":** B. Marshall Oral History #3, 70.

248 **"We discussed it":** Ibid.

248 **"We want our colored...some of you":** Anecdote and quotes from Claude Sitton, "Sheriff Harasses Negroes at Voting Rally in Georgia," *NYT*, July 27, 1962, 1, 9.

249 **"You don't know...a damn nigger":** Bryant, *The Bystander*, 322, citing *Nation*, Dec. 1, 1962.

249 **"that something had":** Martin Luther King, "Rev. M.L. King's Diary in Jail: Integration Leader Wary of Being Tricked out of Jail," *Jet*, Aug. 23, 1962, 17.

249 **"let down...city of Albany":** Milton Bracker, "Albany, Ga., Fight to Continue, Dr. King's Spokesman Pledges," *NYT*, July 30, 1962, 12.

249 **ALBANY, GA., A..."needs a push":** Gerald Grant, "50 Pickets at the White House to Protest Dr. King's Arrest; Petitions Started," *WP*, July 29, 1962, A6.

250 **"Let me say...point of view":** Johnson, *The Kennedy Presidential Press Conferences*, 356.

251 **"Gratified by directness":** King telegram to JFK, August 2, 1962, in Carson, *To Save the Soul*, 568.

251 **"inappropriate...or federal injunctions":** "Mayor Bars Talks with Dr. King," *NYT*, Aug. 2, 1962, 15.

251 **"two ambitious Bostonians":** Bryant, *The Bystander*, 324, citing *Albany Herald*, Aug. 10, 1962.

252 **"with clean hands":** Hedrick Smith, "U.S. Intervenes on Negroes' Side in Georgia Case," *NYT*, Aug. 9, 1962, 1.

252 **"an affront to":** Ibid.

252 **"vindicated...of the problem":** Ibid.

253 **"these ordinances have":** Hedrick Smith, "Dr. King Set Free After Conviction," *NYT*, Aug. 11, 1962, 41.

253 **"Segregation is on":** Hedrick Smith, "Dr. King Speaks to 1,000 in Albany," *NYT*, Aug. 14, 1962, 16.

253 **"indefinitely, in the":** Milton L. Carr, "Libraries, Parks Shut by Albany," *WP*, Aug. 12, 1962, A6.

254 **"The present action...and the nation":** Nashville *Tennessean*, Aug. 12, 1962, available at "Albany Police Lock City Parks, Library," http://tennessean.newspapers.com/search/#query=Albany+Police+Lock+City+Parks%2C+Library.

254 **"They saw no":** Abernathy, *And the Walls Came*, 223.

254 **"After ten months":** Diane McWhorter, *Carry Me Home: Birmingham, Alabama, The Climactic Battle of the Civil Rights Movement* (New York: Simon & Schuster, 2012), 270.

254 **"The church is burned":** "Negroes' Church Burns in Georgia," *NYT*, Aug. 16, 1962, 18.

254 **"I think it...the right to vote":** Ibid.

255 **"holds the Negro":** "Albany, Ga., Hears Negro Pleas But Refuses to Take Any Action," *NYT*, Aug. 16, 1962.

255 **"We'll continue, to":** Ibid., 18.

255 **"Direct action, for":** Wilkins, *Standing Fast*, 286.

255 **"In fact," Abernathy:** Abernathy, *And the Walls Came*, 224.

256 **"We are asking":** M. L. King to Ralph Lord Roy, Aug. 22, 1962, in Carson, *To Save the Soul*, 604.

256 **"This looks like":** "Religion: Act of Belief," *Time*, September 7, 1962, 45.

256 **"Is everybody bashful...in jail":** Claude Sitton, "Albany, Ga., Jails 75 in Prayer Vigil," *NYT*, Aug. 29, 1962, 14.

256 **"arouse the conscience":** Martin Luther King Jr. telegram to John F. Kennedy, August 31, 1962; Papers of John F. Kennedy, JFKL, http://www.jfklibrary.org/Asset-Viewer/ XADqOAhcTEGz1E1QAxJEMw.aspx.

256 **"We are all agreed":** UPI, "Clerics in Albany Jail Urge Kennedy to Help," *WP*, Sept. 3, 1962, A6.

256 **"the rights of all":** RFK response, Sept. 2, 1962, in Carson, *To Save the Soul*, 606.

257 **"a callous exercise":** "Soviet Arms to Cuba," *NYT*, Sept. 3, 1962, 14.

257 **"We have been saying":** Tad Szulc, "Modernized Army Called Cuba's Aim," *NYT*, Sept. 3, 1962, 1.

257 **"there is also":** Dallek, *An Unfinished Life*, 537, citing *Foreign Relations of the States*, by U.S. Department of State / FRUS: Cuba, 1961–62, 1002-10.

257 **"the United States":** Arthur J. Olsen, "Boats off Cuba Fire at U.S. Navy Plane; Havana Cautioned," *NYT*, Sept. 1, 1962, 2.

258 **"be prevented by whatever":** Carroll Kilpatrick, "President Warns U.S. Will Bar Any Aggressive Action," *WP*, Sept. 5, 1962, A6.

258 **"provocations which might":** Seymour Topping, "Kennedy Assailed," *NYT*, Sept. 12, 1962, 1.

258 **"Have you ever":** Jackie Robinson, "It's Sad to Watch a House of God Die," *New York Amsterdam News*, Sept. 22, 1962, in Michael G. Long, ed., *Beyond Home Plate: Jackie Robinson on Life After Baseball* (Syracuse, NY: Syracuse University Press, 2013), 75–76.

258 **"We must not only":** Ibid., 77.

259 **"as a Baptist":** Nelson Rockefeller to Robinson, Sept. 19, 1962, in Long, *First Class Citizenship*, 152.

259 **"Nazi-like reign of terror...mockery of democracy":** UPI, "2 Negro Churches Burned in Georgia," *WP*, Sept. 10, 1962, A1.

259 **"If Negroes are":** AP, "Dr. King Asks U.S. to Act, Fears Riots," *WP*, Sept. 13, 1962, A18.

260 **"There ain't but":** Claude Sitton, "Georgia Primary Won by Moderate," *NYT*, Sept. 13, 1962, 20.

260 **"inflammatory...directly linked":** Ibid.

260 **"Rash talk":** President News Conference, Sept. 13, 1962, in Johnson, *The Kennedy Presidential Press Conferences*, 384.

260 **"Mr. President":** Ibid., 387.

260 **"I don't know...we shall do that":** Ibid.

261 **"livid with rage":** Dallek, *An Unfinished Life*, 484, citing O'Donnell tapes.

261 **"He fucked me":** Reeves, *President Kennedy*, 296; also Dallek, *An Unfinished Life*, 484.

261 **"You double-crossed me":** Ibid.

261 **"Businessmen were all":** Dallek, *An Unfinished Life*, 484.

262 **"wholly unjustifiable":** President News Conference, April 11, 1963, in Johnson, *The Kennedy Presidential Press Conferences*, 265.

262 **"Righteous indignation...bitter denunciation":** "Editorial Views Across the Nation on Steel Price Rise and Kennedy's Criticism," *NYT*, April 13, 1962, 20.

262 **"One thing is...get angry again":** Jackie Robinson column, *New York Amsterdam News*, May 5, 1962.

262 **"had crossed an":** Bryant, *The Bystander*, 328.

263 **"The Albany Movement...more heartfelt involvement":** Ibid., 327.

263 **"reign of terror...as well as outrageous":** "*Jet* Editorial: JFK Should Act to Stop Terror Against Negroes," *Jet*, Sept. 27, 1962, 10.

263 **"antipathy to nationally...education and persuasion":** Howard Zinn, "Reluctant Emancipator," *Nation*, Dec. 1, 1961, 376.

264 **"When God made":** Walter Lord, *The Past That Would Not Die* (New York: Harper & Row, 1965), 141.

264 **"Nobody handpicked me":** John Bowers, "James Meredith at Columbia Law," *New York Herald Tribune*, April 3, 1966.

264 **Meredith background from** Lord, *The Past That Would*, 36.

265 **"evil and illegal":** Schlesinger, *Robert Kennedy and His Times*, 318.

265 **"No school will be":** AP, "Barnett Defies Federal Court on Mississippi U Integration," *NYT*, Sept. 14, 1962, 15.

266 **"On this 100th":** Lloyd L. General, "Where is Negro After 100 Years?" *Chicago Defender*, Sept. 29, 1962.

266 **"ceaseless rebellion...his political balance":** Thomas Buckley, "Dr. King Decries Civil Rights Pace; Prods U.S. in Speech Here at Emancipation Fete," *NYT*, Sept. 13, 1962, 38.

266 **"Administration aides said":** "National Report: JFK Sets Major Rights Address for September," *Jet*, May 31, 1962, 3.

267 **"painfully slow":** Buckley, "Dr. King Decries."

267 **"Like the Proclamation":** "Remarks Recorded for Emancipation Proclamation Centennial Ceremony, Lincoln Memorial, 22 September 1962," JFKL, http://www.jfklibrary.org/Asset-Viewer/Archives/JFKPOF-040-014.aspx.

267 **"he didn't look happy":** Berl I. Bernhard, recorded interview #2 by John Stewart, July 23, 1968, 54, JFKLOHP.

268 **"reaffirm democracy by...of freedom real":** Martin Luther King, Jr, "Emancipation Proclamation," *New York Amsterdam News*, Nov. 10, 1962.

268 **"There were other...what happened next":** Lord, *The Past That Would*, 144.

269 **"Little Brother has":** Ibid., 149.

269 **"Go home, nigger":** Claude Sitton, "Negro Rejected at Mississippi U," *NYT*, Sept. 21, 1962, 13.

269 **WELCOME TO OLE MISS:** AP wire photos in Robert S. Bird, "The Day: A Lone Student, A Guarded Campus," *New York Herald Tribune*, Sept. 20, 1962, 1.

270 **"Which one of you":** James Meredith and William Doyle, *A Mission from God: A Memoir and Challenge for America* (New York: Atria Books, 2012), 93.

270 **"Do you realize":** Guthman, *We Band of Brothers*, 186.

270 **"We hastened to":** Meredith and Doyle, *A Mission from God*, 94.

270 **"He transformed himself":** Ibid., 89.

270 **"This matter must":** Guthman, *We Band of Brothers*, 187.

271 **"as genuinely loony":** Schlesinger, *Robert Kennedy and His Times*, 318.

271 **"commanding, soft-spoken":** Meredith and Doyle, *A Mission from God*, 96.

271 **"There was not...ever known":** Ibid.

271 **"could perhaps best":** Lord, *The Past That Would*, 145.

272 **"Governor," he fumed...belong to it":** Schlesinger, *Robert Kennedy and His Times*, 318.

273 **"I'm taking a...That's correct":** Bryant, *The Bystander*, 337, citing conversation in Burke Marshall papers.

273 **"General," he said...these people":** Ibid.

273 **"A lot of people...the feeling":** Schlesinger, *Robert Kennedy and His Times*, 319.

274 **"Stay out of it...but move slowly":** Ted Sorensen, *Counselor: A Life at the Edge of History* (New York: Harper, 2009), 274–275.

275 **THOUSANDS SAID READY...SUPPORT OF BARNETT:** Lord, *The Past That Would*, 175.

275 **"on a stand-by":** Ibid., 184.

276 **"at the disposal":** Ibid.

276 **"We better get moving":** Guthman, *We Band of Brothers*, 197.

276 **"Go get him...Princess Radziwill":** Schlesinger, *Robert Kennedy and His Times*, 320.

276 **"Hello? Hello, Governor?...Bye now":** Conversation found in Ted Widmer, comp., *Listening In: The Secret White House Recordings of John F. Kennedy* (New York: Hyperion, 2012), 101–106.

278 **"You've been fighting...What a rogue!":** Schlesinger, *Robert Kennedy and His Times*, 321.

278 **"You just don't":** William Doyle, *An American Insurrection: The Battle of Oxford, Mississippi, 1962* (New York: Doubleday, 2001), 111–112.

279 **"I love Mississippi!":** Ibid., 113.

279 **"I can't do it":** Doyle, citing his own interview, in *An American Insurrection*, 113.

279 **"Is this pretty":** Norbert A. Schlei, recorded interview by John Stewart, Feb. 20–21, 1968, 14, JFKLOHP.

280 **You know, that's...Grant's table":** Ibid., 15.

280 **"That won't do...He is":** Guthman, *We Band of Brothers*, 200.

281 **"If things get rough":** Schlesinger, *Robert Kennedy and His Times*, 322.

281 **"2-4-1-3":** Lord, *The Past That Would*, 202.

281 **"looking neat as":** Ibid., 203.

282 **"You have occupied...that they would":** Doyle, *An American Insurrection*, 144.

282 **"oppressive power...avoid bloodshed":** Ibid., 145.

283 **"This one is":** Reeves, *President Kennedy*, 364.

283 **"Kennedy's speech was":** Schlesinger, *Robert Kennedy and His Times*, 323.

283 **"I'll do something":** Nicholas deB. Katzenbach, recorded interview #2 by Larry Hackman, Nov. 29, 1964, 109, JFKLOHP.

283 **"Mr. James Meredith...are upon you":** "President's Original Speech with Notes: The James Meredith Case," Integrating Ole Miss: A Civil Rights Milestone, JFKL, http://microsites.jfklibrary.org/olemiss/confrontation/doc10.html.

284 **"The orders of...":** Ibid.

285 **"We put a...this phone":** Katzenbach Oral History #2, 108–109.

285 **"I haven't had...at Princeton University":** Jonathan Rosenberg and Zachary Karabell, *Kennedy, Johnson, and the Quest for Justice: The Civil Rights Tapes* (New York: W. W. Norton, 2003), 66.

286 **"We can't consider...about Meredith":** Doyle, *An American Insurrection*, 194–195.

287 **"It's hard to feel":** Lord, *The Past That Would*, 223.

287 **"This is just":** Doyle, *An American Insurrection*, 284.

287 **"They wouldn't pull...children and myself":** Simeon Booker, "Negro GI's, White Marshals Praised for Routing Miss. Mobs," *Jet*, Oct. 18, 1962, 24.

287 **"Where's the Army?"** Bryant, *The Bystander*, 349, quoting White House conversations.

287 **"They're leaving in...of the helicopters":** R. F. Kennedy Oral History #5, 482.

288 **"the worst night":** Lord, *The Past That Would*, 228.

288 **"The president of":** Guthman, *We Band of Brothers*, 99.

288 **"Mississippi and I awoke...even started":** Meredith and Doyle, *A Mission from God*, 143.

288 **"seemed to be in":** Ibid., 147.

288 **"He was delivering":** Ibid.

289 **"We had enough men"**: Doyle, *An American Insurrection*, 272.
289 **"the agonizing loneliness"**: King, "Letter from Birmingham Jail," in *Why We Can't Wait*, 83.
289 **"feel like pawns"**: "It's a Difficult Thing."
290 **"Oh shit. Shit!"**: Dino A. Brugioni, *Eyeball to Eyeball: The Inside Story of the Cuban Missile Crisis* (New York: Random House, 1992), 223.
290 **"Can they hit"**: Schlesinger, *Robert Kennedy and His Times*, 506.
290 **"Those brass hats"**: O'Donnell, Powers, and McCarthy, *"Johnny, We Hardly Knew Ye,"* 368–369.
291 **"The danger and…something wrong"**: Schlesinger, *Robert Kennedy and His Times*, 514.
291 **"The Americans had"**: Raymond Garthoff, "Reflections on the Cuban Missile Crisis: Khrushchev, Nuclear Weapons, and the Cuban Missile Crisis," Cold War International History Project, Winter 1998, 10.
292 **"the most depressing"**: O'Donnell, Powers, and McCarthy, *"Johnny, We Hardly Knew Ye,"* 394.
292 **"God, Dave…my last meal"**: Ibid.
292 **"In order to save"**: Thomas, *Robert Kennedy*, 230.
292 **"with far deeper…the last war"**: O'Donnell, Powers, and McCarthy, *"Johnny, We Hardly Knew Ye,"* 365.
293 **"Whatever John Kennedy"**: R. N. Goodwin, *Remembering America*, 218.
293 **"The entire Democratic"**: Bryant, *The Bystander*, 359, quoting a memorandum from Louis Harris to JFK, Nov. 19, 1962. JFKL President's Office Files Box 30.
294 **"His desire was"**: Sorensen, *Kennedy*, 482.
294 **"Our national policy"**: President News Conference, Nov. 20, 1962, in Johnson, *The Kennedy Presidential Press Conferences*, 403.
294 **"In any case"**: Ibid., 407.
294 **"an audacious usurpation"**: UPI, "Dr. King Hails Housing Order," *NYT*, Nov. 21, 1962.
294 **"morally right"**: Ibid.
294 **"good-faith step in the right direction"**: Martin Luther King Jr., "JFK's Executive Order," *New York Amsterdam News*, Dec. 22, 1962, 13.
295 **"the longest conference"**: Simeon Booker, "JFK in Record, 2-Hour Confab With 6 Top Negro Leaders," *Jet*, Jan. 3, 1963, 6.
295 **"the electrifying progress"**: Carson, *To Save the Soul*, 307–308.
295 **"Negroes want their freedom…with the moral issues"**: Bryant, *The Bystander*, 363.
295 **"civil rights was…aloof"**: Martin Luther King Jr., "A Bold Design for a New South," *Nation*, March 30, 1963, 259.
296 **"The Administration…progressive development"**: Ibid., 260.
296 **"The South is…the New South"**: Ibid., 261.
297 **"Throughout our history…remains"**: Ibid.

PART FIVE: *"It Often Helps Me to Be Pushed"*

301 **"I felt like…about it now"**: "Bomb Terror Returns to B'ham," *Jet*, Jan. 3, 1963, 9.
301 **"The church has"**: AP, "Negro Church Bombing in Birmingham Probed," *WP*, Dec. 16, 1962, A6.
302 **"shocked by the bombing…racial holocaust"**: Telegram dated Dec. 15, 1962, from Martin Luther King, Jr. to President Kennedy, JFKL, Presidential Papers, White House Central File, Subject File, https://www.jfklibrary.org/Asset-Viewer/6F3fjCmU7Em6I4755O427w.aspx.
303 **"If it takes"**: Glenn T. Eskew, *But for Birmingham: The Local and National Movements in the Civil Rights Struggle* (Chapel Hill, NC: University of North Carolina Press, 1997), 131.

303 **"I knew they were":** Raines, *My Soul Is Rested*, 154.

303 **"You can't die here":** Ibid.

304 **"God's direct intervention":** Eskew, *But for Birmingham*, 141.

304 **"The two forces":** Raines, *My Soul Is Rested*, 155.

304 **"We can't all":** Fairclough, *To Redeem the Soul*, 120.

304 **"We were sort of":** Wyatt Tee Walker, recorded interview by John H. Britton, Oct. 11, 1967, 54, Civil Rights Documentation Project, Ralph J. Bunch Collection, Moorland-Springarn Research Center, Howard University.

305 **"Almost anybody who":** Ibid., 64.

305 **"We knew that as":** Ibid., 52.

305 **"It was decided…and respond":** Stein, *American Journey*, 114.

305 **"I have to tell you…think about it":** Ibid., 115.

306 **"No matter what":** Garrow, *Bearing the Cross*, 200–201.

307 **"The experiences of":** Simeon Booker, "JFK Says Nation Not Seriously Divided on Racial Question," *Jet*, Jan. 17, 1963, 7.

307 **"President Kennedy doesn't":** Ibid., 6.

307 **"Negroes in this country":** Baldwin, *The Fire Next Time*, 39–40.

307 **"I was icily":** Ibid., 37.

308 **"Explosively, America's third revolution":** M. L. King, *Why We Can't Wait*, 1.

308 **"The Kennedy civil rights strategy":** Schlesinger, *Robert Kennedy and His Times*, 317.

308 **"We have not seen…on other issues":** "King Wants JFK to Do More for Civil Rights," *Chicago Daily Defender*, Jan. 29, 1963, 5.

308 **"seen flashing his invitation":** Dan Day, "In the Nation's Capital: Negro Dems at White House," *Call and Post* (Cleveland, OH), Feb. 16, 1963, 3C.

309 **"For a minimum…in fact, free":** Thurgood Marshall Oral History #1, 16.

309 **"No one wanted":** Berl I. Bernhard Oral History #2, 53.

309 **"This whole civil rights":** Ibid., 55.

310 **"the Chief Executive":** Simeon Booker, *Black Man's America* (New York: Prentice-Hall, 1964), 34.

310 **"We still have":** Carroll Kilpatrick, "Rights Fight at Peak, Is Report to President," *WP*, Feb. 13, 1963, A1.

311 **"What's he doing here?":** Reeves, *President Kennedy*, 464.

311 **"Sammy Davis, Jr.":** Berl I. Bernhard Oral History #2, 54.

311 **"The first visit…international crisis":** Booker, *Black Man's America,* 35.

312 **"When they have explained":** William M. Kunstler, *Deep in My Heart* (New York: William Morrow, 1966),174.

313 **"If Boutwell is":** Ibid.

313 **"Birmingham's Negroes have":** Ibid., 175.

313 **"You have to be prepared":** M. L. King, *Why We Can't Wait*, 44.

313 **"I'm a segregationist":** Raines, *My Soul Is Rested*, 145.

313 **"I'm not of a mind…put 'em back up":** Ibid.

314 **"It would be hard":** M. L. King, *Why We Can't Wait*, 44.

314 **"It's a good reminder":** Belafonte, *My Song*, 247.

315 **"overwhelmed by a feeling":** M. L. King, *Why We Can't Wait*, 59.

315 **"inter-racial discord…accomplish absolutely nothing":** Eskew, *But for Birmingham*, 222.

316 **"glossy personality":** Fairclough, *To Redeem the Soul*, 118.

316 **"You could go downtown":** Raines, *My Soul Is Rested*, 139.

316 **"Buy nothing but food":** Fairclough, *To Redeem the Soul*, 120.

316 **Comparison of Easter sales figures in:** Ibid.

316 **"the greed of...about Jim Crow"**: Abernathy, *And the Walls Came*, 248.

316 **"The SCLC had"**: Eskew, *But for Birmingham*, 227.

317 **"a moral responsibility"**: M. L. King, *Why We Can't Wait*, 59.

317 **"We cannot in good conscience"**: UPI, "King Says He'll Ignore Court Ban on Actions," *WP*, April 12, 1963, A6.

318 **"My immediate response...think it through"**: Walker Oral History #1, 61.

318 **"I sat there...himself"**: M. L. King, *Why We Can't Wait*, 59–60.

318 **"There comes a...crowded room"**: Ibid., 60.

318 **"all that...faith act"**: Ibid.

319 **"I've decided to...going today"**: C. S. King, *My Life with Martin*, 222–223.

319 **"Martin," Abernathy asked,..."to march, too"**: Abernathy, *And the Walls Came*, 249.

319 **"That, I think"**: Eskew, *But for Birmingham,* 240.

319 **"Okay, then let's go"**: Abernathy, *And the Walls Came*, 249.

320 **"twisted grotesquely"**: Nasaw, *The Patriarch*, 780.

320 **"Churchill's speech, giving"**: Dallek, *An Unfinished Life*, 58.

321 **"I think he thought"**: William Douglas-Home, recorded interview by Joseph O'Connor, Oct. 28, 1966, 16, JFKLOHP.

321 **"All your good friends"**: Bradlee, *Conversations with Kennedy*, 168.

321 **"The evening was...and action"**: Ibid.

322 **"When [the ambassador]"**: Ibid., 169.

322 **"I must say"**: Ibid.

322 **"Tonight"**: Ibid.

322 **"He had all his life...understood"**: Nasaw, *The Patriarch*, 782.

322 **"a tragic figure"**: Ibid., 779.

324 **"We submit that these two"**: Telegram from Wyatt Tee Walker to JFK, April 13, 1963, JFKL, https://www.jfklibrary.org/Asset-Viewer/QNcJq269vUai2GG_ZyI0Ag.aspx.

324 **"The Federal Government"**: Jack Raymond, "President Phones Justice Aide On Negroes' Jailing in Alabama," *NYT*, April 14, 1963, 46.

324 **"You will never know"**: M. L. King, *Why We Can't Wait*, 61.

325 **"the marchers were"**: Foster Hailey, "Dr. King Arrested at Birmingham," *NYT*, April 13, 1963, 1.

325 **"I used that"**: Walker Oral History #1, 62.

325 **"They would form"**: Ibid., 61.

325 **"We were able"**: Abernathy, *And the Walls Came*, 251.

326 **"Wyatt...the President"**: C. S. King, *My Life with Martin*, 224.

326 **"You have no alternative"**: Ibid., 224.

326 **"No one's in...say Harry's paying"**: Belafonte, *My Song*, 257.

327 **"Mrs. King, this is"**: C. S. King, *My Life with Martin*, 225–226.

327 **"Bull Connor is"**: Ibid., 226.

328 **"barbaric"**: Belafonte, *My Song*, 258.

328 **"This ain't no game"**: Ibid., 259.

328 **"Tell Reverend King"**: Ibid., 258.

328 **"Hello, Mrs. King"**: C. S. King, *My Life with Martin*, 226.

329 **"I know you'll be"**: Ibid., 227.

329 **"I want you"**: Ibid.

329 **"Even though I understood"**: Ibid., 228.

330 **"It is available"**: M. L. King, *Why We Can't Wait*, 63.

330 **"valor of the Negroes"**: "Handwriting on the Wall," *WP*, April 14, 1963, E6.

330 **"inflamed tensions"..."poorly timed"**: "The South: Poorly Timed Protest," *Time*, April 19, 1963, 30.

330 **"unwise and untimely...better Birmingham":** "White Clergymen Urge Local Negroes to Withdraw from Demonstrations," *Birmingham News*, April 13, 1963, 2.

330 **"I just got a call...so polite":** Garrow, *Bearing the Cross*, 244.

331 **"Your encouraging words":** Telegram dated April 16, 1963, from Martin Luther King Jr. to President Kennedy, JFKL, Papers of John F. Kennedy, Presidential Papers, White House Central File, Subject File, https://www.jfklibrary.org/Asset-Viewer/1yZGXj36Hk-XnqdshlIuoA.aspx.

331 **"King called his wife...four hundred prisoners":** "Moore Says Kennedy Didn't Arrange Call," *Birmingham News*, April 16, 1963, 2.

332 **"Hello, Ralph":** Abernathy, *And the Walls Came*, 253.

332 **"You in a cell":** Ibid.

332 **"We walked around":** Ibid., 254.

332 **"I'm writing a reply":** Ibid.

332 **"its flashes of...defense of civil disobedience":** Fairclough, *To Redeem the Soul*, 124.

333 **"Seldom do I pause":** M. L. King, *Why We Can't Wait*, 64.

333 **"I...am here...is here":** Ibid., 65.

333 **"Just as the Apostle...home town":** Ibid.

333 **"You deplore...the demonstrations":** Ibid.

333 **"I have tried":** Ibid., 75.

334 **"Frankly...disease of segregation":** Ibid., 68–69.

334 **"I must say...nonviolent pressure":** Ibid., 68.

334 **"For years now...":** Ibid., 69.

334 **"but we still":** Ibid.

334 **"harried by day":** Ibid., 70.

335 **"see ominous clouds":** Ibid., 69.

335 **"law of God":** Ibid., 70.

335 **"Segregation is not only":** Ibid., 71.

335 **"I have been so greatly":** Ibid., 78.

335 **"The judgment of":** Ibid., 80.

335 **"but the white moderate":** Ibid., 73.

336 **"Human progress never":** Ibid., 74.

336 **"Now is the time":** Ibid., 75.

336 **"Mrs. Kennedy is said":** Carroll Kilpatrick, "Kennedys Expect Their Third Child in August," *WP*, April 16, 1963, A1.

337 **"Lest you think":** Foster Hailey, "Dr. King Leaves Birmingham Jail," *NYT*, April 21, 1963.

337 **"on the whole":** Ibid., 70.

338 **"meeting with less success":** Eskew, *But for Birmingham*, 249; *Birmingham World*, April 17, 1963.

338 **"My feeling was":** Raines, *My Soul Is Rested*, 161.

338 **"I am not making":** "Ambushed in Ala., White Postman Dies Advancing Cause of Negroes," *Jet*, May 9, 1963, 14.

339 **"can take its place":** Ibid., 18.

339 **"He was a":** William Chapman, "Slain Hiker Was Restless Rebel Who Would Seek Out a Cause," *WP*, April 25, 1963, A3.

339 **"I don't think anything":** AP, "White Foe of Segregation Slain on a Protest Trek in Alabama," *NYT*, April 25, 1963, 20.

339 **"'Screwball' was the":** "Ambushed in Ala.," 16.

339 **"We needed more troops":** Walker interview, Oct. 11, 1967, 62.

340 **"Some of these":** Eskew, *But for Birmingham*, 242–243.

340 **"very courteous"**: AP, "White Foe of Segregation."

340 **"Feeling quite"**: Chapman, "Slain Hiker."

340 **"predicted he would"**: UPI, "Alabama Jury Refuses to Indict in Murder of Hiking Postman," *NYT*, Sept. 14, 1962, 11.

341 **"I have no idea...injustice openly"**: Drew Pearson, "My Letter from Doomed Mailman," *WP*, April 30, 1963, B23.

342 **"We have the...continue to do so"**: President Kennedy's News Conferences, News Conference 54, April 24, 1962, JFKL, https://www.jfklibrary.org/Research/Research-Aids/Ready-Reference/Press-Conferences/News-Conference-54.aspx.

342 **"Segregation now, segregation"**: "News from Alabama," *NYT*, Feb. 23, 1963, 6.

342 **"Let us send"**: AP, "North Denounced by Gov. Wallace," *NYT*, Jan. 15, 1963, 9.

343 **"stand in the schoolhouse"**: AP, "Ex-Judge and Alabama State Senator Face Tuesday Runoff for Governor," *WP*, May 28, 1963, A2.

343 ROUND I: WALLACE..."**confrontation"**: James Free, "Round 1: Wallace vs. Kennedys," *Birmingham News*, April 24, 1963, 1.

343 **"They had the biggest"**: R. F. Kennedy Oral History #6, 518.

343 **"Ape Martin...stools"**: McWhorter, *Carry Me Home*, 344.

343 **"A stern, middle-aged"**: Guthman, *We Band of Brothers*, 208.

344 **"One of them"**: R. F. Kennedy Oral History #6, 518.

344 **"I know you're...troops, doesn't it?"**: Guthman, *We Band of Brothers*, 209.

344 **"Well,...unjust laws"**: McWhorter, *Carry Me Home*, 345.

344 **"All this agitation"**: Jonathan Rieder, *Gospel of Freedom* (New York: Bloomsbury, 2013), 134.

344 **"You think it...system in Alabama"**: Guthman, *We Band of Brothers*, 208.

345 **"We considered it"**: Lewis, *Walking with the Wind*, 196–197.

346 **"You know...get going"**: Eskew, *But for Birmingham*, 261.

346 **"during the centuries"**: King, *Why We Can't Wait*, 86.

346 **"We had been"**: Abernathy, *And the Walls Came*, 262.

347 SEGREGATION IS A SIN: Branch, *Parting the Waters*, 757.

347 I'LL DIE TO: McWhorter, *Carry Me Home*, 349.

347 **"For, you see,"**: M. L. King, *Why We Can't Wait*, 87.

347 **"Sing, children, sing"**: Foster Hailey, "500 Are Arrested in Negro Protest at Birmingham," *NYT*, May 3, 1963, 1.

348 **"We were sending"**: Walker Oral History #1, 63.

348 **"I had to do...to do that"**: Garrow, *Bearing the Cross*, 248.

348 **"Hey, Fred...A'mighty"**: McWhorter, *Carry Me Home*, 349; and Branch, *Parting the Waters*, 757, quoting police notes on a May 2, 1963, mass meeting.

348 **"The demonstrations were"**: "Dogs, Kids and Clubs," *Time*, May 10, 1963, 19.

349 **"Evans...can you be?"**: Raines, *My Soul Is Rested*, 171.

349 **"Birmingham's Negro population"**: Robert Gordon, "Waves of Young Negroes March in Birmingham Segregation Protest," *WP*, May 3, 1963, A1.

349 **"The whole world"**: Branch, *Parting the Waters*, 757, citing police memo from May 2, 1963.

350 **"I have been inspired"**: McWhorter, *Carry Me Home*, 350; Eskew, *But for Birmingham*, 265; and Branch, *Parting the Waters*, 757–758, all referencing a police report on the May 2, 1963, mass meeting.

350 **"our little folks"**: Eskew, *But for Birmingham*, 265.

350 **"let those kids"**: McWhorter, *Carry Me Home*, 350.

350 **"We are ready"**: Foster Hailey, "Dogs and Hoses Repulse Negroes at Birmingham," *NYT*, May 4, 1963, 1.

351 **"We're going"**: "Fire Hoses and Police Quell Birmingham Segregation Protest," *WP*, May 4, 1963, A1.

351 **"Turn 'em on"**: McWhorter, *Carry Me Home*, 351.

351 **"Come on...children *do* remember"**: Raines, *My Soul Is Rested*, 172.

352 **"Birmingham would have"**: Garrow, *Bearing the Cross*, 251.

352 **"He was the perfect"**: Ibid.

352 **"Look at those niggers"**: "Fire Hoses," A1.

352 **"making pictures...not getting bit"**: McWhorter, *Carry Me Home*, 354.

353 **"Do you think...half an hour"**: B. Marshall Oral History #5, 97.

354 **"An injured, maimed"**: UPI, "Robert Kennedy Warns of 'Increasing Turmoil,'" *NYT*, May 4, 1963, 8.

354 **"A lot turned on"**: R. F. Kennedy Oral History #5, 495.

354 **"immediate and determined attention"**: Hailey, "Dogs and Hoses," 1.

354 **"They are suffering"**: Branch, *Parting the Waters*, 763.

354 **"Looking back...win the struggle"**: M. L. King, *Why We Can't Wait*, 86.

355 **"so therefore, what"**: R. F. Kennedy Oral History #5, 497.

355 **"Perhaps because we were"**: Ibid., 496.

355 **"What Bull Connor"**: Ibid.

355 **"Birmingham is the worst...to a head"**: Widmer, *Listening In*, 112.

356 **"I think it's"**: Ibid.

356 **"sick"**: Schlesinger, *A Thousand Days*, 959.

356 **"Let me just...awfully"**: Widmer, *Listening In*, 113.

357 **"We don't want"**: AP, "1000 Defy Police in Birmingham," *WP*, May 5, 1963, A1.

357 **"We don't want any...get back,"**: Ibid.

358 **"In a few days"**: Garrow, *Bearing the Cross*, 251, citing *Atlanta Constitution*, May 6, 1963.

358 **"Turn on your water"**: Foster Hailey, "Birmingham Talks Pushed; Negroes March Peacefully," *NYT*, May 6, 1963, A1.

358 **"Dammit. Turn on"**: M. L. King, *Why We Can't Wait*, 90.

358 **"What happened...in their hands"**: Ibid.

358 **"Until Birmingham"**: Kunstler, *Deep in My Heart*, 190.

359 **"At the start"**: Stein, *American Journey*, 115.

360 **"too little and"**: Claude Sitton, "Birmingham Jails 1,000 More Negroes," *NYT*, May 7, 1963.

360 **"At this point"**: Claude Sitton, "Rioting Negroes Routed by Police," *NYT*, May 8, 1963, 28.

360 **"Activities which have...of a dream"**: Ibid.

361 **"We've just started"**: Ibid.

361 **"I waited a week"**: Ibid.

361 **"beginning to tire"**: Ibid.

361 **"Mr. President, it is"**: "A Telegram to the President," *Birmingham News*, May 7, 1963, 1.

361 **"The pace at which...and the Cuban situation"**: Long, *First Class Citizenship*, 168–169.

362 **"reports would come in"**: B. Marshall Oral History #5, 101.

362 **"they had a solution"**: Ibid., 102.

363 **"Rarely did he inject"**: Eskew, *But for Birmingham*, 274.

363 **"I told the president"**: B. Marshall Oral History #5, 102.

364 **"There is a man who"**: M. L. King, *Why We Can't Wait*, 92.

365 **"Kennedy was all set"**: Raines, *My Soul Is Rested*, 157.

365 **"three hypos...reelin' and rockin'"**: Ibid., 158.

365 **"Fred, we've got...it shoulda been"**: Ibid., 159.

365 **"You and I"**: Ibid.

365 **"We wasn't supposed"**: Ibid., 160.

365 **"We hit a snag"**: Ibid.

365 **"Wait, wait, Fred"**: Ibid.

366 **"Fred was under"**: Walker Oral History Interview, 82.

366 **"I am gratified...promptly as possible"**: "President Kennedy's News Conferences, News Conference 55, May 8, 1963," JFKL, https://www.jfklibrary.org/Research/Research-Aids/Ready-Reference/Press-Conferences/News-Conference-55.aspx.

367 **"They haven't talked...No sir!"**: Claude Sitton, "Hurdles Remain: Negroes Warn of New Protests Today If Parleys Fail," *NYT*, May 9, 1963, 17.

368 **"marching shoes"**: Eskew, *But for Birmingham*, 289.

368 **"Fred's sort of gone"**: McWhorter, *Carry Me Home*, 399.

368 **"Could I send...use it"**: Belafonte, *My Song*, 262.

369 **"To my surprise"**: Kunstler, *Deep in My Heart*, 192.

369 **"Belafonte and I"**: Ibid., 192–193.

370 **"Old Joe"**: Bradlee, *Conversations with Kennedy*, 189.

370 **"noted with pride...Caroline and John"**: Ibid., 190.

370 **"I felt that...the children"**: Belafonte, *My Song*, 262.

370 **"I'll wait on"**: Ibid., 262.

371 **"Mr. Rockefeller would"**: Ibid., 263.

371 **"Please, Mr. Jones"**: Ibid.

371 **"I mean I'm"**: Ibid.

371 **"I hope this"**: Ibid.

371 **"It's a hundred"**: Ibid.

372 **"The city of Birmingham"**: Claude Sitton, "Birmingham Pact Sets Timetable for Integration," *NYT*, May 11, 1963, 8.

372 **"Birmingham may well"**: "Negro Leaders' Statements on Birmingham Accord," *NYT*, May 11, 1963, 8.

372 **"Though we have come...all His children"**: Ibid.

373 **"a victory...into a friend"**: Ibid.

373 **"It is important"**: Sitton, "Birmingham Pact."

373 **"He made the dialogue"**: "Negro Leaders.'"

374 **"If it hadn't been"**: Anthony Lewis, "Accord Pleases Robert Kennedy," *NYT*, May 11, 1963, 1.

374 **"I don't know what...and resolve"**: B. Marshall Oral History #5, 102.

375 **"Let's stand back"**: McWhorter, *Carry Me Home*, 407.

375 **"Shelton's inability to...terrorist cell"**: Ibid., 408.

375 **"I had information"**: Raines, *My Soul Is Rested*, 177.

375 **"hell on niggers"**: Dan T. Carter, *The Politics of Rage* (New York: Simon & Schuster, 1995), 125.

375 **"body guardin' him"**: Raines, *My Soul Is Rested*, 176.

375 **"takin' pills by the"**: Ibid., 176.

376 **"guard that nigger"**: Branch, *Parting the Waters*, 793.

376 **"Bull," Pritchett told**: Fred Powledge, *Free At Last? The Civil Rights Movement and the People Who Made It* (Boston: Little, Brown, 1991), 512.

376 **Gaston Motel information**: from McWhorter, *Carry Me Home*, citing a police memo on "Bomb Threats" (in her notes on 661).

377 **"I promised Ann...responsibility"**: Walker Oral History #1, 69.

377 **"I admit"**: Ibid., 70.

377 **"People were in"**: Ibid.

377 **"From somewhere within"**: Branch, *Parting the Waters*, 794.

378 **"There's your bomb"**: Raines, *My Soul Is Rested*, 178.

378 **"That's the motel...movement"**: Walker Oral History #1, 70–71.

378 **"All the way"**: Ibid., 71.

378 **"No one had the slightest"**: Abernathy, *And the Walls Came*, 270.

379 **"Why must you"**: McWhorter, *Carry Me Home*, 409.

379 **"Kill 'em! Kill 'em!"**: Claude Sitton, "50 Hurt in Negro Rioting After Birmingham Blasts," *NYT*, May 13, 1963, 1.

379 **"Will you please...might get somebody killed"**: Ibid.

379 **"You're damned right"**: Ibid.

380 **"We're not mad...across the street"**: Ibid.

380 **"powerfully symbolic of...road to victory"**: M. L. King, *Why We Can't Wait*, 90.

381 **"Now, have you...with billies...complete chaos"**: Rosenberg and Karabell, *Kennedy, Johnson, and the Quest*, 96.

381 **"had headaches all day...head-hunting"**: Ibid., 97.

382 **"he is going"**: Ibid.

382 **"They might tear up...issue a statement"**: Ibid.

382 **"I talk to...preach against violence"**: Ibid., 101.

382 **"I think you...against the indignities"**: Ibid., 102.

383 **"which Negro citizens still face"**: McWhorter, *Carry Me Home*, 421.

383 **"We believe that if"**: M. S. Handler, "Malcolm X Starting Drive in Washington," *NYT*, May 10, 1963, 14.

383 **"could trigger...the Black Muslims"**: Rosenberg and Karabell, *Kennedy, Johnson, and the Quest*, 98.

383 **"dangerous overtones...in this country"**: Robert S. Bird, "Civil Rights Demands: ALL...NOW...HERE," *Boston Globe*, May 7, 1963, 7.

383 **"You can make"**: Rosenberg and Karabell, *Kennedy, Johnson, and the Quest*, 102.

384 **"everyone to be"**: Ibid., 104.

384 **"I can't control the people"**: Ibid.

384 **"One of the great"**: Bryant, *The Bystander*, 394, quoting draft statement from JFKL presidential papers.

384 **"deeply concerned...most important now"**: "181—Radio and Television Remarks Following Renewal of Racial Strife in Birmingham, May 12, 1963," John F. Kennedy, American Presidency Project, http://www.presidency.ucsb.edu/ws/?pid=9206.

385 **"conscience was struck"**: Belafonte Oral History JFK #1, 14.

385 **"The brutality with"**: Baldwin, *The Fire Next Time*, 94–95.

386 **"Search, in his...a certain hope died"**: Ibid.

386 **"We had a very nice meeting"**: Robert Kennedy, recorded interview #7 by Anthony Lewis, Dec. 22, 1964, 585, JFKLOHP.

386 **"What is really"**: Belafonte Oral History JFK #1, 14.

386 **"one of the most...right side of the answer"**: Ibid.

386 **"Why don't you get"**: Stein, *American Journey*, 119.

386 **"What's the agenda?"**: Belafonte, *My Song*, 266.

387 **"I'll kill him"**: Arsenault, *Freedom Riders*, 465.

387 **"had probably spent"**: Schlesinger, *Robert Kennedy and His Times*, 331.

388 **"I guess they thought"**: Guthman and Shulman, *Robert Kennedy in His Own Words*, 181.

388 **"I don't know what"**: Belafonte, *My Song*, 267.

388 **"Never! Never! Never!"**: Stein, *American Journey*, 120.

388 **"You will not fight"**: Belafonte, *My Song*, 268.

388 **"I want to vomit"**: Bryant, *The Bystander*, 403.

388 **"the reasonable, responsible"**: Stein, *American Journey*, 119.

388 **"You've got a great many":** Ibid.

388 **"You don't have no idea":** Bryant, *The Bystander*, 403.

389 **"When I pull":** Ibid., 121.

389 **"the most intense":** Schlesinger, *Robert Kennedy and His Times*, 335, citing his own interview with Clark.

389 **"They all started sort":** R. F. Kennedy Oral History #7, 586.

389 **"You can't talk to them":** Ibid., 587.

389 **"poetical terms":** Guthman and Shulman, *Robert Kennedy in His Own Words*, 225.

389 **"Lorraine Hansberry said":** Ibid.

389 **"He did, in fact":** Stein, *American Journey*, 121–122.

389 **"You should understand":** Ibid., 122.

389 **"Your family has been here":** Schlesinger, *Robert Kennedy and His Times*, 332–333.

390 **"they'd laugh at that":** Guthman and Shulman, *Robert Kennedy in His Own Words*, 224.

390 **"Bobby became more silent":** Stein, *American Journey*, 120.

390 **"Of course, you've... would become suspect":** Schlesinger, *Robert Kennedy and His Times*, 333–334.

390 **"I just want":** Ibid., 333.

390 **"You watched these... to me now":** Ibid., 333.

390 **"He didn't dare":** Guthman and Schulman, *Robert Kennedy in His Own Words*, 224.

390 **"totally inadequate":** Layhmond Robinson, "Robert Kennedy Fails to Sway Negroes at Secret Talks Here," *NYT*, May 26, 1963, 59.

391 **"a street populated by Negroes":** M. S. Handler, "James Baldwin Rejects Despair Despite Race 'Drift and Danger,' " *NYT*, June 3, 1963, 1.

391 **"a combination living room-bedroom":** Ibid.

391 **"A window faces":** Ibid., 19.

391 **"dismal setting":** Ibid., 1.

391 **"The Birminghams cannot... today":** Ibid.

391 **"Despair is a sin":** Ibid.

391 **"pilgrimage of Robert Kennedy":** Stein, *American Journey*, 124.

391 **"The meeting with James":** Ibid., 125.

391 **"He had never heard":** Guthman, *We Band of Brothers*, 221.

391 **"I guess if":** Ibid.

392 **"After Birmingham, it":** Stein, *American Journey*, 122.

392 **"I did not become... that concerned me":** Ibid.

392 **"forthrightly about civil rights":** Tom Wicker, "Kennedy, in South, Hails Negro Drive for Civil Rights," *NYT*, May 19, 1963, 1.

392 **"that debate will go on":** Remarks at Vanderbilt University, May 18, 1963, 5, JFKL, https://www.jfklibrary.org/Asset-Viewer/Archives/JFKPOF-044-020.aspx.

393 **"Both Kennedys are... basic human yearnings":** Jackie Robinson, "Top Personalities Talk Vital During Crisis," *Chicago Defender*, June 8, 1963, 8.

393 **"The president must":** "Ticker Tape U.S.A.," *Jet*, June 13, 1963, 12.

393 **"Dammit,... send the Justice":** Carter, *The Politics of Rage*, 118.

393 **"But I am obligated":** President News Conference, May 22, 1963, in Johnson, *The Kennedy Presidential Press Conferences*, 506.

393 **"I would hope":** Ibid., 513.

393 PICKETS IN SEVEN CITIES: "Pickets in Seven Cities Put South in Uproar: Protests Mount," *Baltimore Afro-American*, May 25, 1963, 1.

394 **"difficulties experienced by minority":** Tom Wicker, "President Bids Governors Lead Rights Campaign," *NYT*, May 30, 1963, 1.

394 **"if the President keeps":** Belafonte, *My Song*, 270.

395 **"I think that if the Governor"**: Branch, *Parting the Waters*, 805, quoting from Tape 475a, PRA, Pacific Radio Archives, Los Angeles.

395 **"For the most part, "**: Walter Lippmann, "The Racial Crisis," *Newsweek*, May 27, 1963, 23.

395 **"This...isn't leadership"**: William Walker, "Down the Big Road," *Call and Post* (Cleveland, OH), May 25, 1963, 2C.

395 **"Philip keeps talking"**: Belafonte, *My Song*, 270.

395 **"economic subordination"**: Garrow, *Bearing the Cross*, 266.

395 **"borrowed, revived, and transformed"**: Fairclough, *To Redeem the Soul*, 150.

396 **"to discuss the crisis...a national calamity"**: Telegram dated May 30, 1963, from Martin Luther King Jr. to Attorney General Robert Kennedy, JFKL, https://www.jfklibrary .org/Asset-Viewer/4HqZ_AyLF0KpEIThASKhgQ.aspx.

396 **"The trouble with King"**: Rosenberg and Karabell, *Kennedy, Johnson, and the Quest*, 125.

397 **"Our patience is"**: Charles E. Flinner, "Hoses Used on Negroes in Danville," *WP*, June 11, 1963, A1.

397 **"beastly conduct...just and moral"**: Branch, *Parting the Waters*, 822.

397 **"I don't have"**: Meeting with Americans for Democratic Action, May 4, 1963, Miller Center, Univ. of Va., tape 85.1, at 40:10.

397 **"I've always thought"**: Ibid., at 49:26.

398 **"The unwelcome, unwanted"**: Robert Drew, director, *Crisis: Behind a Presidential Commitment*, Oct. 21, 1963, The Robert Drew Collection.

398 **"I hereby denounce"**: Ibid.

398 **"Governor Wallace, I...the choice is yours"**: Ibid.

399 **"military dictatorship"**: Sitton, "Governor Leaves," *NYT*, June 12, 1963, 20.

400 **"As Wallace left"**: Sorensen, *Counselor*, 278.

400 **"I think he just decided"**: Andrew Cohen, *Two Days in June* (Toronto: McClelland & Stewart, 2014), 330.

400 **"At those meetings"**: Guthman and Shulman, *Robert Kennedy in His Own Words*, 180.

400 **"He felt it, he understood"**: O'Brien, *John F. Kennedy*, 838.

400 **"Recognizing the call"**: Bennett, *What Manner*, 157.

400 **"They thought that...for a minute"**: B. Marshall Oral History #5, 109.

401 **"I may lose"**: Luther H. Hodges, recorded interview #3 by Dan Jacobs, May 18, 1964, 104, JFKLOHP.

401 **"I could not draw"**: Sorensen, *Counselor*, 279.

401 **"Don't worry, we"**: Ibid.

402 **"The president and I...extemporaneously"**: B. Marshall Oral History #5, 110.

402 **"The two of us talked"**: Guthman and Shulman, *Robert Kennedy in His Own Words*, 200.

402 **"It was the...on national television"**: Sorensen, *Counselor*, 280.

403 **"The camera ought"**: Cohen, *Two Days in June*, 330.

403 **"Good evening, my fellow...statements"**: John F. Kennedy, "Report to the American People on Civil Rights, June 11, 1963, JFKL, https://www.jfklibrary.org/Asset-Viewer/ LH8F_0Mzv0e6Ro1yEm74Ng.aspx.

403 **"head-spinning, in...him that night"**: Lewis, *Walking with the Wind*, 198–199.

403 **"I hope that...man are threatened"**: J. F. Kennedy, "Report to the American People on Civil Rights."

404 **"is pre-eminently"**: Burns, *John Kennedy*, 276–277.

404 **"Whether he would bring"**: Ibid., 281.

404 **"His life seems"**: Ibid.

404 **"If an American"**: Kennedy, "Report to the American People on Civil Rights."

405 **"was full of echoes"**: Jonathan Rieder, "The Day President Kennedy Embraced Civil Rights—And the Story Behind It," *Atlantic*, June 11, 2013, http://www.theatlantic.com/

national/archive/2013/06/the-day-president-kennedy-embraced-civil-rights-and-the
-story-behind-it/276749/.

405 **"Twenty million Negro"**: M. L. King, *Why We Can't Wait*, 69.

405 **"Throughout the speech"**: Rieder, "The Day President Kennedy."

405 **"Kennedy now responded"**: Schlesinger, *A Thousand Days*, 966.

405 **"We are confronted...of our daily lives:** Kennedy, "Report to the American People on Civil Rights."

406 **"Just five months earlier"**: Lewis, *Walking with the Wind*, 198–199.

406 **"This is one country"**: Kennedy, "Report to the American People on Civil Rights."

406 **"Walter...over the fence!"**: Sorensen, *Counselor*, 282.

406 **"We couldn't have asked"**: Belafonte, *My Song*, 271.

406 **"Thank you for emerging as the most forthright..."**: Telegram from Jackie Robinson to President Kennedy, June 12, 1963, quoted in Long, *First Class Citizenship*, 171–172.

406 **"As an American citizen...absolute sincerity"**: Ibid., 171.

407 **"one of the most...of American history"**: Telegram from Martin Luther King Jr. to President Kennedy, June 11, 1963, JFKL, https://www.jfklibrary.org/Asset-Viewer/ fXbXxZHwaUmJqbxW_5IrQg.aspx.

407 **"every means and resource...positions of power"**: "Eisenhower Meets Kennedy on Rights," *NYT*, June 13, 1963, 13.

407 **"passing a whole...the right answer"**: Carroll Kilpatrick, "President Calls Others to Talks on Racial Crisis," *WP*, June 13, 1963, A9.

408 **"He exhausts you"**: O'Brien, *John F. Kennedy*, 792.

408 **"A man does"**: Kennedy, *Profiles in Courage*, 246.

408 **"Ten years ago...in the face"**: Wallace Terry, "Negroes' 'Awakened Militancy' Now Centers on Mississippi," *WP*, June 7, 1963, A2.

409 **"storm troopers...Nazi Germany"**: Jack Langguth, "Jackson Police Jail 600 Negro Children," *WP*, May 1, 1963, 8.

409 **"This is for you"**: Emanuel Perlmutter, "Mississippi Victim Lived with Peril in His Job," *NYT*, June 13, 1963, 12.

409 **"This is what you must"**: Wallace Terry, "Evers Was Accustomed to Living with Threats," *WP*, June 13, 1963, A6.

410 **"We're going to kill"**: Ibid.

410 **"We wanted to go home...ever since"**: Ibid.

410 **"If I die"**: Perlmutter, "Mississippi Victim."

410 **"Daddy! Daddy! Daddy!"**: Claude Sitton, "Whites Alarmed," *NYT*, June 13, 1963, 12.

410 **"Turn me loose"**: Ibid.

411 **"Law alone cannot"**: Kennedy, "Report to the American People on Civil Rights."

411 **"Now, people will say...important also"**: King commencement address at Lincoln University, June 6, 1961, in James M. Washington, ed., *A Testament of Hope: The Essential Writings and Speeches of Martin Luther King, Jr.* (San Francisco: Harper, 1986), 213.

411 **"where she sat"**: Wilkins, *Standing Fast*, 291.

412 **"The Negroes are...which touched Kennedy"**: Schlesinger, *A Thousand Days*, 969.

412 **"This is true"**: Ibid., 969–970.

412 **"We want success"**: Ibid., 969.

412 **"There was a good...semi-jocular way"**: Guthman and Shulman, *Robert Kennedy in His Own Words*, 179.

413 **"It may seem"**: Schlesinger, *A Thousand Days*, 970.

413 **"You may be"**: Wilkins, *Standing Fast*, 291.

413 **"I assume you know...the Soviet conspiracy"**: Schlesinger, *Robert Kennedy and His Times*, 357.

414 **"Martin came back…him too":** Raines, *My Soul Is Rested*, 430–431.

414 **"They're Communists…to prove it":** Schlesinger, *Robert Kennedy and His Times*, 358, author interview with Levison.

414 **"You've read about Profumo":** Ibid.

414 **"Kennedy had devoured":** Bradlee, *Conversations with Kennedy*, 230.

415 **"That was an example":** Schlesinger, *Robert Kennedy and His Times*, 358.

415 **"I made it very clear":** "Kennedy Warns Rights Group on Demonstrations," *WP*, June 23, 1963, A1.

416 **"drops kids like":** Andersen, *Jack and Jackie*, 175.

416 **"Mr. Landis, I":** Hill, *Mrs. Kennedy*, 239.

417 **HE'S A KENNEDY:** "He's a Kennedy, He'll Make It," *Boston Globe*, Aug. 8, 1963.

418 **"He put up":** O'Donnell, Powers, and McCarthy, *"Johnny, We Hardly Knew Ye,"* 436.

419 **"copious tears…God is good":** Richard Cardinal Cushing, recorded interview by Edward M. Kennedy, 1966, 18, JFKLOHP.

419 **"The death of the":** Pierre Salinger, *With Kennedy* (Garden City: Doubleday, 1966), 101.

419 **"After the death…out in public,":** Hill, *Mrs. Kennedy*, 248–249.

420 **"Final audio, one, two":** E. W. Kenworthy, "200,000 March for Civil Rights in Orderly Washington Rally," *NYT*, Aug. 29, 1963, 16.

420 **"If we shall suppose":** Ibid.

420 **"stories of the…more kind":** "Reaction to Tragedy Enhanced JFK's Image," *Boston Globe*, Aug. 16, 1963.

420 **"It will be orderly":** Nan Robertson, "Civil Rights Leaders Urge Proud and Orderly March," *NYT*, Aug. 26, 1963, 1.

421 **"Now we cawn't":** Lewis, *Walking with the Wind*, 218.

421 **"It was not just":** Ibid., 210.

421 **"Truck convoys":** "D.C. Resembled Armed Camp as Marchers Arrived in Capital," *Jet*, Sept. 12, 1963, 6.

422 **"It was mind-blowing…and too late":** Lewis, *Walking with the Wind*, 219–221.

422 **"This was a very radical speech":** Marshall, RFK Oral History #7, 593.

422 **"It was a bad speech":** R. F. Kennedy Oral History #7, 593.

423 **"cheap…and too late":** Lewis, *Walking with the Wind*, 227.

423 **"I was stunned":** Ibid., 224.

424 **"Bruce, he runs":** Preston Bruce, recorded interview by Nancy Tuckerman and Pamela Turnure, June 16, 1964, 4, JFKLOHP.

424 **"Oh, Bruce," he:** Simeon Booker, *Jet*, May 26, 1986, p. 26.

424 **"As he moved toward":** Lewis, *Walking with the Wind*, 228.

424 **"Tell 'em about the dream":** Branch, *Parting the Waters*, 882.

425 **"So even though…free at last":** M. L. King, "I Have a Dream," address delivered at the March on Washington for Jobs and Freedom, The Martin Luther King Jr. Research and Education Institute, Stanford University, https://kinginstitute.stanford.edu/king-papers/documents/i-have-dream-address-delivered-march-washington-jobs-and-freedom.

425 **"He's damn good…":** Branch, *Parting the Waters*, 883.

425 **"Boy, he made":** Guthman and Shulman, *Robert Kennedy in His Own Words*, 229.

425 **"At 9 p.m., the":** Kenworthy, "200,000 March."

425 **"There was no violence":** "D.C. Resembled Armed Camp," *Jet*, 7.

425 **"It was an answer":** Marquis Childs, "Triumphal March Silences Scoffers," *WP*, Aug. 30, 1963, A18.

426 **"The only weapon":** "Equality Is Their Right," *NYT*, Aug. 29, 1963, 23.

426 **"Roger Williams…dream come true":** James Reston, "I Have a Dream," *NYT*, Aug. 29, 1963, 1.

426 **"the deep fervor...achieving these objectives"**: John F. Kennedy, "336—Statement by the President on the March on Washington for Jobs and Freedom, August 28, 1963," The American Presidency Project, http://www.presidency.ucsb.edu/ws/?pid=9383.

426 **"relief written all...your case"**: Wilkins, *Standing Fast*, 293.

426 **"He was beside...so well**: Lewis, author interview.

426 **"I have a dream"**: Branch, *Parting the Waters*, 883.

426 **"Mr. President, I"**: William P. Jones, *The March on Washington* (New York: W. W. Norton, 2013), 199.

427 **"I felt that...sort of came together"**: Lewis, author interview.

429 **"The Sixteenth Street"**: McWhorter, *Carry Me Home*, 5.

429 **"Dynamite Bob"**: Ibid., 54.

429 **"They ought to"**: Ibid., 502.

429 **"bandy-legged...on moonshine"**: Ibid., 54.

429 **"tendency to sexually fondle"**: Ibid., 491.

429 **"If you are"**: Ibid., 479.

430 **"Lie on the floor!"**: "Civil Rights: The Sunday School Bombing," *Time*, Sept. 27, 1963, 17.

430 **"Addie? Addie?"**: Rick Bragg, "Survivor of '63 Bomb Recalls Glass Shards and a Sister Lost," *NYT*, May 18, 2002, A1.

430 **"The savage bombing...after today's tragedy"**: Telegram from Martin Luther King Jr. to President Kennedy, September 15, 1963, JFKL, https://www.jfklibrary.org/Asset-Viewer/-crU2bLgN0CcGkys8dkuHg.aspx.

431 **"deep sense of...on the innocent"**: Tom Wicker, "Kennedy Decries Racial Bombings," *NYT*, Sept. 17, 1963, 1.

431 **"The governor said...Governor Wallace"**: Claude Sitton, "Negroes Request Federal Troops," *NYT*, Sept. 17, 1963, 1.

432 **"was at his"**: M. L. King, *Why We Can't Wait*, 134.

432 **"a new stage"**: Ibid., 138.

432 **"No memorial oration"**: Lyndon Johnson, Address, Nov. 27, 1963, Miller Center, http://millercenter.org/president/lbjohnson/speeches/speech-3381.

432 **"turned into a nightmare"**: "King in 1967: My Dream 'Turned into a Nightmare,'" May 8, 1967, at 00:23, NBC Los Angeles, http://www.nbclosangeles.com/news/national-international/NATL-King-in-1967-My-Dream-Turned-into-a-Nightmare-221385251.html.

433 **"I've been to...coming of the Lord"**: King Speech in Memphis, April 3, 1968, *Martin Luther King, Jr. and the Global Freedom Struggle*, Stanford University, http://kingencyclopedia .stanford.edu/encyclopedia/documentsentry/ive_been_to_the_mountaintop/.

433 **"I have some...grace of God"**: "Robert F. Kennedy Speeches: Statement on Assassination of Martin Luther King, Jr., Indianapolis, Indiana, April 4, 1968," JFKL, https://www .jfklibrary.org/Research/Research-Aids/Ready-Reference/RFK-Speeches/ Statement-on-the-Assassination-of-Martin-Luther-King.aspx.

434 **"The murder of"**: R. N. Goodwin, *Remembering America*, 525–526.

434 **"But this murder"**: Ibid., 526.

434 **"Kennedy was white"**: Ibid.

434 **"It was 1968"**: Ibid.

435 **"That could have"**: Thomas, *Robert Kennedy*, 368.

435 **"We are a great"**: June 5, 1968: RFK's California Victory Speech, ABC News Archives, http://abcnews.go.com/Archives/video/rfk-california-victory-speech-assassination -10118429.

435 **"We can do well"**: R. F. Kennedy Speeches, April 4, 1968, JFKL, https://www.jfklibrary .org/Research/Research-Aids/Ready-Reference/RFK-Speeches/Statement-on-the -Assassination-of-Martin-Luther-King.aspx.

436 **proportion of schools:** Emma Brown, "On the Anniversary of Brown v. Board, new evidence that U.S. Schools are Resegregating," *WP*, May 17, 2016, https://www.washingtonpost.com/news/education/wp/2016/05/17/on-the-anniversary-of-brown-v-board-new-evidence-that-u-s-schools-are-resegregating/.

436 **states across the country:** Richard L. Hasen, "Turning the Tide on Voting Rights," *NYT*, Aug. 2, 2016, http://www.nytimes.com/2016/08/02/opinion/campaign-stops/turning-the-tide-on-voting-rights.html?_r=0.

436 **"There is simply…ever could have":** Baldwin, *The Fire Next Time*, 115.

436 **"He had the…to be pushed":** "It's a Difficult Thing," 61.

BIBLIOGRAPHY

Abernathy, Ralph David. *And the Walls Came Tumbling Down: An Autobiography.* New York: Harper & Row, 1989.

Abram, Morris B. *The Day Is Short: An Autobiography.* New York: Harcourt Brace Jovanovich, 1982.

Adler, Bill, ed. *The Eloquent Jacqueline Kennedy Onassis: A Portrait in Her Own Words.* New York: William Morrow, 2004.

Aitken, Jonathan. *Nixon: A Life.* Washington, DC: Regnery, 1993.

Alford, Mimi. *Once Upon a Secret: My Affair with President John F. Kennedy and Its Aftermath.* New York: Random House, 2013.

Andersen, Christopher. *Jack and Jackie: Portrait of an American Marriage.* New York: Avon Books, 1996.

———. *These Few Precious Days: The Final Year of Jack with Jackie.* New York: Gallery Books, 2013.

Arsenault, Raymond. *Freedom Riders: 1961 and the Struggle for Racial Justice.* Oxford, UK: Oxford University Press, 2006.

Axelrod, Alan. *Lost Destiny: Joe Kennedy Jr. and the Doomed WWII Mission to Save London.* New York: Palgrave Macmillan, 2015.

Baldwin, James. *Baldwin: Later Novels.* Edited by Darryl Pinckney. New York: Library of America, 2015.

———. *The Fire Next Time.* New York: Dell, 1963.

Bass, Jack. *Taming the Storm: The Life and Times of Judge Frank M. Johnson, Jr. and the South's Fight over Civil Rights.* New York: Doubleday, 1993.

Belafonte, Harry, with Michael Shnayerson. *My Song: A Memoir.* New York: Alfred A. Knopf, 2011.

Bennett, Lerone, Jr. *What Manner of Man: A Biography of Martin Luther King, Jr.* Chicago: Johnson, 1964.

Berman, Ari. *Give Us the Ballot.* New York: Farrar, Straus and Giroux, 2015.

Blair, Joan, and Clay Blair, Jr. *The Search for JFK.* New York: Berkley, 1976.

Booker, Carol McCabe, ed. *Alone atop the Hill: The Autobiography of Alice Dunnigan.* Athens, GA: University of Georgia Press, 2015.

Booker, Simeon. *Black Man's America.* Englewood Cliffs, NJ: Prentice-Hall, 1964.

Booker, Simeon, and Carol McCabe Booker. *Shocking the Conscience: A Reporter's Account of the Civil Rights Movement.* Jackson, MS: University Press of Mississippi, 2013.

Bowles, Chester. *Promises to Keep: My Years in Public Life, 1941–1969.* New York: Harper & Row, 1971.

Bradlee, Benjamin C. *Conversations with Kennedy.* New York: W. W. Norton, 1975.

Branch, Taylor. *Parting the Waters: America in the King Years, 1954–63*. New York: Simon & Schuster, 1989.

Brauer, Carl M. *John F. Kennedy and the Second Reconstruction*. New York: Columbia University Press, 1977.

Brimner, Larry Dane. *Black & White*. Honesdale, PA: Calkins Creek, 2011.

Brinkley, Douglas. *Rosa Parks*. New York: Penguin, 2000.

Brower, Kate Andersen. *The Residence: Inside the Private World of the White House*. New York: Harper, 2015.

Brugioni, Dino A. *Eyeball to Eyeball: The Inside Story of the Cuban Missile Crisis*. New York: Random House, 1992.

Bryant, Nicholas Andrew. *The Bystander: John F. Kennedy and the Struggle for Black Equality*. New York: Basic Books, 2006.

Burns, James MacGregor. *John Kennedy: A Political Profile*. New York: Harcourt, Brace, 1960.

Califano, Joseph A., Jr. *The Triumph & Tragedy of Lyndon Johnson: The White House Years*. New York: Touchstone, 2015.

Carson, Clayborne, ed. *The Autobiography of Martin Luther King, Jr*. New York: Grand Central, 1998.

———, ed. *The Papers of Martin Luther King, Jr*. Vol. 1. *Called to Serve, January 1929–June 1951*. Berkeley, CA: University of California Press, 1992.

———, ed. *The Papers of Martin Luther King, Jr*. Vol. 2. *Rediscovering Precious Values, July 1951–November 1955*. Berkeley, CA: University of California Press, 1994.

———, ed. *The Papers of Martin Luther King, Jr*. Vol. 3. *Birth of a New Age, December 1955–December 1956*. Berkeley, CA: University of California Press, 1997.

———, ed. *The Papers of Martin Luther King, Jr*. Vol. 4. *Symbol of the Movement, January 1957–December 1958*. Berkeley, CA: University of California Press, 2000.

———, ed. *The Papers of Martin Luther King, Jr*. Vol. 5. *Threshold of a New Decade, January 1959–December 1960*. Berkeley, CA: University of California Press, 2005.

———, ed. *The Papers of Martin Luther King, Jr*. Vol. 7. *To Save the Soul of America, January 1961–August 1962*. Oakland, CA: University of California Press, 2014.

Carter, Dan T. *The Politics of Rage*. New York: Simon & Schuster, 1995.

Cash, W. J. *The Mind of the South*. New York: Vintage Books, 1969.

Chafe, William H., Raymond Gavins, and Robert Korstad, eds. *Remembering Jim Crow*. New York: New Press, 2014.

Clarke, Thurston. *JFK's Last Hundred Days: The Transformation of a Man and the Emergence of a Great President*. New York: Penguin Press, 2013.

Coates, Ta-Nehisi. *Between the World and Me*. New York: Spiegel & Grau, 2015.

Cohen, Andrew. *Two Days in June: John F. Kennedy and the 48 Hours That Changed History*. Toronto: McClelland & Stewart, 2014.

Coleman, David, Timothy Naftali, and Philip Zelikow, eds. *The Presidential Recordings: John F. Kennedy*. Vols. 4–6. *Winds of Change*. New York: W. W. Norton, 2016.

Collier, Peter, and David Horowitz. *The Kennedys: An American Drama*. New York: Summit Books, 1984.

Dallek, Robert. *Camelot's Court: Inside the Kennedy White House*. New York: HarperCollins, 2013.

———. *An Unfinished Life: John F. Kennedy, 1917–1963*. New York: Back Bay, 2013.

Davis, Angela Y. *Freedom Is a Constant Struggle*. Chicago: Haymarket, 2016.

Davis, Tracey, and Nina Bunche Pierce. *Sammy Davis Jr.: A Personal Journey with My Father*. Philadelphia: Running Press, 2014.

DeGroot, Gerard J. *The Sixties Unplugged: A Kaleidoscopic History of a Disorderly Decade.* Cambridge, MA: Harvard University Press, 2008.

Delmont, Matthew F. *Why Busing Failed.* Oakland: University of California Press, 2016.

Dickstein, Morris. *Gates of Eden: American Culture in the Sixties.* New York: Liveright, 2015.

Doyle, William. *An American Insurrection: The Battle of Oxford, Mississippi, 1962.* New York: Doubleday, 2001.

———. *PT 109: An American Epic of War, Survival and the Destiny of John F. Kennedy.* New York: William Morrow, 2015.

Drew, Robert, director. *Crisis: Behind a Presidential Commitment.* Oct. 21, 1963, The Robert Drew Collection.

DuBois, W. E. B. *The Souls of Black Folk.* New York: Signet, 1982.

Emanuel, Anne. *Elbert Parr Tuttle: Chief Jurist of the Civil Rights Revolution.* Athens, GA: University of Georgia Press, 2011.

Eskew, Glenn T. *But for Birmingham: The Local and National Movements in the Civil Rights Struggle.* Chapel Hill, NC: University of North Carolina Press, 1997.

Fairclough, Adam. *Martin Luther King, Jr.* Athens, GA: University of Georgia Press, 1995.

———. *To Redeem the Soul of America: The Southern Christian Leadership Conference and Martin Luther King, Jr.* Athens, GA: University of Georgia Press, 1987.

Farber, David. *The Age of Great Dreams: America in the 1960s.* New York: Hill & Wang, 1994.

Farmer, James. *Lay Bare the Heart: An Autobiography of the Civil Rights Movement.* New York: Arbor House, 1985.

Fay, Paul B., Jr. *The Pleasure of His Company.* New York: Harper & Row, 1966.

Fehrenbacher, Don, and Virginia Fehrenbacher, comps. *Recollected Words of Abraham Lincoln.* Stanford: Stanford University Press, 1996.

Finkelstein, Norman H. *Heeding the Call: Jewish Voices in America's Civil Rights Struggle.* Philadelphia: Jewish Publication Society, 1997.

Gallagher, Henry T. *James Meredith and the Ole Miss Riot: A Soldier's Story.* Jackson, MS: University Press of Mississippi, 2012.

Garrow, David J. *Bearing the Cross: Martin Luther King, Jr., and the Southern Christian Leadership Conference.* New York: William Morrow, 1986.

———. *The FBI and Martin Luther King, Jr.* New York: Penguin Books, 1981.

———, ed. *The Montgomery Bus Boycott and the Women Who Started It: The Memoir of Jo Ann Gibson Robinson.* Knoxville, TN: University of Tennessee Press, 1987.

Golden, Harry. *Mr. Kennedy and the Negroes.* Greenwich, CT: Crest, 1964.

Golway, Terry, and Les Krantz. *JFK Day by Day: A Chronicle of the 1,036 Days of John F. Kennedy's Presidency.* Philadelphia: Running, 2010.

Goodwin, Doris Kearns. *The Fitzgeralds and the Kennedys.* New York: Simon & Schuster, 1987.

Goodwin, Richard N. *Remembering America: A Voice from the Sixties.* Boston: Little, Brown, 1988.

Guthman, Edwin. *We Band of Brothers.* New York: Harper & Row, 1971.

Guthman, Edwin O., and Jeffrey Shulman, eds. *Robert Kennedy: In His Own Words: The Unpublished Recollections of the Kennedy Years.* New York: Bantam Books, 1988.

Halberstam, David. *The Children.* New York: Random House, 1998.

Hamilton, Nigel. *JFK: Reckless Youth.* New York: Random House, 1992.

Harvey, Paul, and Philip Goff, eds. *The Columbia Documentary History of Religion in America Since 1945.* New York: Columbia University Press, 2005.

Haskins, James. *Freedom Rides: Journey for Justice.* New York: Hyperion, 1995.

Hedin, Benjamin. *In Search of the Movement: The Struggle for Civil Rights Then and Now.* San Francisco: City Lights, 2015.

Henderson, Harold Paulk. *Ernest Vandiver: Governor of Georgia.* Athens, GA: University of Georgia Press, 2000.

Herken, Gregg. *The Georgetown Set: Friends and Rivals in Cold War Washington.* New York: Vintage, 2015.

Herndon, Booton, comp. *The Humor of JFK.* Greenwich, CT: Gold Medal, 1964.

Hill, Clint, with Lisa McCubbin. *Mrs. Kennedy and Me.* New York: Gallery, 2012.

Hirschfeld, Burt. *Freedom in Jeopardy: The Story of the McCarthy Years.* New York: Julian Messner, 1969.

Hodgson, Godfrey. *JFK and LBJ: The Last Two Great Presidents.* New Haven: Yale University Press, 2015.

Jakoubek, Robert E. *James Farmer and the Freedom Rides.* Brookfield, CT: Millbrook, 1994.

Johnson, George W., ed. *The Kennedy Presidential Press Conferences.* New York: Earl M. Coleman, 1978.

Jones, William P. *The March on Washington.* New York: W. W. Norton, 2013.

Joseph, Peniel E. *Stokely: A Life.* New York: Basic Civitas, 2016.

Kallina, Edmund F., Jr. *Kennedy v. Nixon: The Presidential Election of 1960.* Gainesville, FL: University Press of Florida, 2010.

Kamin, Ben. *Dangerous Friendship: Stanley Levison, Martin Luther King, Jr., and the Kennedy Brothers.* East Lansing, MI: Michigan State University Press, 2014.

Kelley, Kitty. *Let Freedom Ring: Stanley Tretick's Iconic Images of the March on Washington.* New York: Thomas Dunne, 2013.

Kempton, Murray. *America Comes of Middle Age: Columns, 1950–1962.* New York: Little, Brown, 1963.

Kennedy, John F. *Prelude to Leadership: The European Diary of John F. Kennedy, Summer 1945.* Washington, DC: Regnery, 1995.

———. *Profiles in Courage.* New York: Harper & Row, 1961.

Kennedy, Robert F. *Thirteen Days: A Memoir of the Cuban Missile Crisis.* New York: W. W. Norton, 1999.

Kennedy, Rose Fitzgerald. *Times to Remember.* New York: Doubleday, 1995.

King, Coretta Scott. *My Life with Martin Luther King, Jr.* New York: Holt, Rinehart and Winston, 1969.

King, Martin Luther, Jr. *Strength to Love.* Glasgow: Collins, 1982.

———. *Stride Toward Freedom: The Montgomery Story.* San Francisco: Harper & Row, 1986.

———. *Why We Can't Wait.* New York: Signet Classic / Penguin Group, 2000.

King, Martin Luther, Sr., with Clayton Riley. *Daddy King: An Autobiography.* New York: William Morrow, 1980.

Klarman, Michael J. *From Jim Crow to Civil Rights: The Supreme Court and the Struggle for Racial Equality.* New York: Oxford University Press, 2004.

Koehler-Pentacoff, Elizabeth. *The Missing Kennedy: Rosemary Kennedy and the Secret Bonds of Four Women.* Baltimore: Bancroft, 2015.

Kunstler, William M. *Deep in My Heart.* New York: William Morrow, 1966.

Larson, Kate Clifford. *Rosemary: The Hidden Kennedy Daughter.* Boston: Houghton Mifflin Harcourt, 2015.

Lasky, Victor. *J.F.K.: The Man and the Myth.* New Rochelle, NY: Arlington House, 1966.

Lewis, Andrew B. *The Shadows of Youth: The Remarkable Journey of the Civil Rights Generation.* New York: Hill & Wang, 2009.

Lewis, David Levering. *King: A Biography.* Urbana, IL: University of Illinois Press, 2013.

Lewis, John, with Michael D'Orso. *Walking with the Wind: A Memoir of the Movement*. New York: Simon & Schuster, 1998.

Lincoln, C. Eric, ed. *Martin Luther King, Jr.: A Profile*. New York: Hill & Wang, 1990.

Lincoln, Evelyn. *My Twelve Years with John F. Kennedy*. New York: David McKay, 1965.

Long, Michael G., ed. *Beyond Home Plate: Jackie Robinson on Life After Baseball*. Syracuse, NY: Syracuse University Press, 2013.

———, ed. *First Class Citizenship: The Civil Rights Letters of Jackie Robinson*. New York: Times Books, 2007.

Lord, Walter. *The Past That Would Not Die*. New York: Harper & Row, 1965.

MacMillan, Margaret. *History's People*. Toronto: House of Ananci, 2015.

Martin, Ralph G. *A Hero for Our Time: An Intimate Story of the Kennedy Years*. New York: Macmillan, 1983.

Matthews, Chris. *Kennedy & Nixon: The Rivalry That Shaped Postwar America*. New York: Free Press, 2011.

May, Ernest R., and Philip D. Zelikow, eds. *The Kennedy Tapes: Inside the White House During the Cuban Missile Crisis*. Cambridge, MA: Belknap, 1998.

McCarthy, Joe. *The Remarkable Kennedys*. New York: Popular Library, 1960.

McWhorter, Diane. *Carry Me Home: Birmingham, Alabama, The Climactic Battle of the Civil Rights Movement*. New York: Simon & Schuster, 2012.

Medsger, Betty. *The Burglary: The Discovery of J. Edgar Hoover's Secret FBI*. New York: Vintage Books, 2014.

Meredith, James, and William Doyle. *A Mission from God: A Memoir and Challenge for America*. New York: Atria Books, 2012.

Michaeli, Ethan. *The Defender: How the Legendary Black Newspaper Changed America*. Boston: Houghton Mifflin Harcourt, 2016.

Morris, James McGrath. *Eye on the Struggle: Ethel Payne, the First Lady of the Black Press*. New York: Amistad, 2015.

Morrow, Lance. *The Best Year of Their Lives: Kennedy, Johnson and Nixon in 1948*. New York: Basic, 2005.

Nasaw, David. *The Patriarch: The Remarkable Life and Turbulent Times of Joseph P. Kennedy*. New York: Penguin, 2012.

Neff, James. *Vendetta: Bobby Kennedy Versus Jimmy Hoffa*. New York: Little, Brown, 2015.

Nixon, Richard. *Six Crises*. New York: Simon & Schuster, 1990.

O'Brien, Lawrence F. *No Final Victories*. Garden City, NY: Doubleday, 1974.

O'Brien, Michael. *John F. Kennedy: A Biography*. New York: Thomas Dunne Books, 2005.

O'Donnell, Helen, and Kenneth O'Donnell, Sr. *The Irish Brotherhood: John F. Kennedy, His Inner Circle, and the Improbable Rise to the Presidency*. Berkeley: Counterpoint, 2015.

O'Donnell, Kenneth P., David F. Powers, and Joe McCarthy. *"Johnny, We Hardly Knew Ye": Memories of John Fitzgerald Kennedy*. New York: Pocket Books, 1973.

Paul, Richard, and Steven Moss. *We Could Not Fail: The First African Americans in the Space Program*. Austin: University of Texas Press, 2015.

Pearson, Drew. *Washington Merry-Go-Round: The Drew Pearson Diaries, 1960–1969*. Edited by Peter Hannaford. Lincoln, NE: University of Nebraska Press, 2015.

Peck, Abe. *Uncovering the Sixties: The Life and Times of the Underground Press*. New York: Citadel, 1991.

Peck, James. *Freedom Ride*. New York: Black Cat, 1962.

Perry, Barbara A. *Rose Kennedy: The Life and Times of a Political Matriarch*. New York: W. W. Norton, 2013.

Pinckney, Darryl. *Blackballed: The Black Vote and US Democracy*. New York: New York Review, 2014.

Post, Gunilla von, and Carl Johnes. *Love, Jack.* New York: Crown, 1997.

Powledge, Fred. *Free At Last? The Civil Rights Movement and the People Who Made It.* Boston: Little, Brown, 1991.

Purdum, Todd S. *An Idea Whose Time Has Come.* New York: Picador, 2014.

Raines, Howell. *My Soul Is Rested: Movement Days in the Deep South Remembered.* New York: Penguin, 1983.

Rampersad, Arnold. *Jackie Robinson: A Biography.* New York: Alfred A. Knopf, 1997.

Rampersad, Arnold, and David Roessel, eds. *Selected Letters of Langston Hughes.* New York: Alfred A. Knopf, 2015.

Raymond, Emilie. *Stars for Freedom: Hollywood, Black Celebrities, and the Civil Rights Movement.* Seattle: University of Washington Press, 2015.

Reddick, L. D. *Crusader Without Violence: A Biography of Martin Luther King, Jr.* New York: Harper & Brothers, 1959.

Reeves, Richard, ed. *The Kennedy Years: From the Pages of the New York Times.* New York: Abrams, 2013.

———. *President Kennedy: Profile of Power.* New York: Simon & Schuster, 1993.

Reeves, Thomas C. *A Question of Character: A Life of John F. Kennedy.* New York: Free Press, 1991.

Reich, Scott D. *The Power of Citizenship: Why John F. Kennedy Matters to a New Generation.* Dallas: BenBella, 2013.

Reporting Civil Rights, Part One: American Journalism, 1941–1963. New York: Library of America, 2003.

Reporting Civil Rights, Part Two: American Journalism, 1963–1973. New York: Library of America, 2003.

Rieder, Jonathan. *Gospel of Freedom.* New York: Bloomsbury, 2013.

Risen, Clay. *The Bill of the Century: The Epic Battle for the Civil Rights Act.* New York: Bloomsbury, 2014.

Rosenberg, Jonathan, and Zachary Karabell. *Kennedy, Johnson, and the Quest for Justice: The Civil Rights Tapes.* New York: W. W. Norton, 2003.

Rowan, Carl T. *Breaking Barriers: A Memoir.* Boston: Little, Brown, 1991.

Ryan, Michael S. *Patrick Bouvier Kennedy: A Brief Life That Changed the History of Newborn Care.* Minneapolis, MN: MCP Books, 2015.

Sabato, Larry J. *The Kennedy Half-Century: The Presidency, Assassination, and Lasting Legacy of John F. Kennedy.* New York: Bloomsbury, 2013.

Sachs, Jeffrey D. *To Move the World: JFK's Quest for Peace.* New York: Random House, 2013.

Salinger, Pierre. *With Kennedy.* Garden City, NY: Doubleday, 1966.

Sandford, Christopher. *Harold and Jack: The Remarkable Friendship of Prime Minister Macmillan and President Kennedy.* Amherst, NY: Prometheus, 2014.

Sandler, Martin W., ed. *The Letters of John F. Kennedy.* New York: Bloomsbury, 2013.

Savage, Sean J. *The Senator from New England: The Rise of JFK.* Albany, NY: Excelsior, 2015.

Schlesinger, Andrew, and Stephen Schlesinger, eds. *The Letters of Arthur Schlesinger, Jr.* New York: Random House, 2013.

Schlesinger, Arthur M., Jr. *Robert Kennedy and His Times.* Boston: Houghton Mifflin, 1978.

———. *A Thousand Days: John F. Kennedy in the White House.* Boston: Houghton Mifflin, 1965.

Shaw, John T. *JFK in the Senate: Pathway to the Presidency.* New York: Palgrave Macmillan, 2013.

Shermer, Michael. *The Moral Arc: How Science Makes Us Better People.* New York: St. Martin's Press, 2016.

Shriver, Anthony. "Kennedy's Call to King: Six Perspectives." Georgetown University, Fall 1988.

Sloyan, Patrick J. *The Politics of Deception: JFK's Secret Decisions on Vietnam, Civil Rights, and Cuba.* New York: Thomas Dunne, 2015.

Smiley, Tavis, and David Ritz. *Death of a King: The Real Story of Dr. Martin Luther King Jr.'s Final Year.* New York: Little, Brown, 2014.

Smith, Amanda, ed. *Hostage to Fortune: The Letters of Joseph P. Kennedy.* New York: Viking, 2001.

Smith, Judith E. *Becoming Belafonte: Black Artist, Public Radical.* Austin, TX: University of Texas Press, 2014.

Sorensen, Theodore. *Counselor: A Life at the Edge of History.* New York: Harper, 2009.

———. *Kennedy.* New York: Harper & Row, 1965.

———. *The Kennedy Legacy.* New York: Macmillan, 1969.

Stein, Jean. *American Journey: The Times of Robert Kennedy / Interviews by Jean Stein.* Edited by George Plimpton. New York: Harcourt Brace Jovanovich, 1970.

Stern, Mark. *Calculating Visions: Kennedy, Johnson & Civil Rights.* New Brunswick, NJ: Rutgers University Press, 1992.

Stossel, Scott. *Sarge: The Life and Times of Sargent Shriver.* Washington, DC: Smithsonian Books, 2004.

Sullivan, William C. *The Bureau: My Thirty Years in Hoover's FBI.* New York: Norton, 1979.

Swift, Will. *The Kennedys Amidst the Gathering Storm.* New York: Smithsonian, 2008.

Taraborrelli, J. Randy. *Jackie, Ethel, Joan: Women of Camelot.* New York: Grand Central, 2012.

Thomas, Evan. *Robert Kennedy: His Life.* New York: Touchstone, 2002.

Thompson, Kenneth W., ed. *Portraits of American Presidents.* Vol. 4. *The Kennedy Presidency: Seventeen Intimate Perspectives of John F. Kennedy.* Lanham, MD: University Press of America, 1985.

Waldman, Michael. *The Fight to Vote.* New York: Simon & Schuster, 2016.

Walker, Samuel. *Presidents and Civil Liberties from Wilson to Obama: A Story of Poor Custodians.* New York: Cambridge University Press, 2014.

Walsh, Chris. *Cowardice: A Brief History.* Princeton, NJ: Princeton University Press, 2014.

Warren, Robert Penn. *Who Speaks for the Negro?* New Haven: Yale University Press, 2014.

Washington, James M., ed. *A Testament of Hope: The Essential Writings and Speeches of Martin Luther King, Jr.* San Francisco: Harper, 1986.

Watters, Pat. *Down to Now: Reflections on the Southern Civil Rights Movement.* New York: Random House, 1971.

Weiner, Tim. *Enemies: A History of the FBI.* New York: Random House, 2012.

West, Cornel, ed. *The Radical King: Martin Luther King, Jr.* Boston: Beacon, 2014.

White, Theodore H. *The Making of the President 1960.* New York: Atheneum, 1961.

Widmer, Ted, comp. *Listening In: The Secret White House Recordings of John F. Kennedy.* New York: Hyperion, 2012.

Wilkins, Roy, with Tom Mathews. *Standing Fast: The Autobiography of Roy Wilkins.* New York: Viking, 1982.

Williams, Juan. *Eyes on the Prize: America's Civil Rights Years, 1954–1965.* New York: Penguin, 1988.

Williams, Rhonda Y. *Concrete Demands: The Search for Black Power in the 20th Century.* New York: Routledge, 2015.

Wills, Garry. *The Kennedy Imprisonment: A Meditation on Power.* Boston: Mariner, 2002.

Wilson, Page. *Carnage & Courage: A Memoir of FDR, the Kennedys and World War II.* New York: Yucca, 2015.

Wofford, Harris. *Of Kennedys and Kings: Making Sense of the Sixties.* Pittsburgh, PA: University of Pittsburgh Press, 1980.

Woodward, C. Vann. *The Burden of Southern History.* New York: Mentor, 1968.

Zelizer, Julian E. *The Fierce Urgency of Now.* New York: Penguin, 2015.

INDEX

ABOUT THE AUTHOR

Steven Levingston is the nonfiction book editor of *The Washington Post* and, most recently, the author of *Little Demon in the City of Light*. He has worked for *The Wall Street Journal*, *The International Herald Tribune*, the Associated Press, and *The China Daily*, with stints in Beijing, Hong Kong, and Paris. He grew up in California and graduated from the University of California at Berkeley and Stanford University.